THE SHAKESPEARE BIRTHPLACE TRUST

A PERSONAL MEMOIR

THE SHAKESPEARE BIRTHPLACE TRUST

A PERSONAL MEMOIR

BY

LEVI FOX

O.B.E., M.A., L.H.D., D.Litt., F.S.A., F.R.Hist.S., F.R.S.L., D.L.

Director Emeritus of
the Shakespeare Birthplace Trust

Published by the Shakespeare Birthplace Trust
in association with Jarrold Publishing of Norwich

© *Dr Levi Fox, 1997*

ISBN 0-7117-1001-5

*The author is most grateful to the
following for generous grants towards
the cost of publication.*

*The Trustees of Shakespeare's Birthplace
The John Jarrold Trust
The C.A. Rookes Charitable Trust*

Book design by Mike Fuggle

*Published in Great Britain
by The Shakespeare Birthplace Trust
and printed by Hunter and Foulis Limited*

Contents

Foreword	page VII
Introduction	IX

PART ONE

Beginnings	3
Restoration of Shakespeare's Birthplace	9
Early Progress	17
An Incorporated Trust	24
The Years of Richard Savage, 1884–1910	28
Anne Hathaway's Cottage	41
The Wellstood Era, 1910–1942	46

PART TWO

The Shakespeare Birthplace Trust in 1945	79
The Way Forward	88
The 1950s	106
The Burnside Bequest	135
American Interlude	137
Blueprint for the Future	144
The Shakespeare Centre	151
Quatercentenary Celebrations	181
Progress in the 1960s	199
Sir Fordham Flower, O.B.E., D.L., LL.D.	220
The Garrick Bicentenary Celebrations	224
Anne Hathaway's Cottage Fire	230
The Trust's 125th Anniversary	237
The 1970s	240
The Shakespeare Centre Extension	272
Years of Fufilment	296
The Shakespeare Countryside Museum	329
The Record Ends: My Final Years	341
Sources	346
Index	347

Foreword

by PROFESSOR STANLEY WELLS

Chairman of the Shakespeare Birthplace Trust

By happy chance, publication of this book coincides with the one hundred and fiftieth anniversary of the purchase of Shakespeare's Birthplace as a national memorial. It was following this event in 1847 that the Shakespeare Birthplace Trust came into being. For forty-four years, from 1945 to 1989, the Trust's Director was Dr Levi Fox, who during this time acquired unrivalled knowledge of its early development and himself contributed greatly to its history during a period when its collections, responsibilities, and activities expanded at a dramatic rate attributable largely to his vision and administrative expertise. At its most public level, the Trust, chief custodian of the Shakespeare heritage, is a major contributor to the British tourist industry. Every year the houses for which it is responsible, especially Shakespeare's Birthplace and Anne Hathaway's Cottage, with their beautifully tended gardens, are visited by hundreds of thousands of tourists from all over the world.

But there are other, less public but no less important, aspects of the Trust's activities. Its valuable collections of early printed books and manuscripts, its extensive holdings of local archives cared for and administered by its Records Office, its guardianship of the archives of the Royal Shakespeare Theatre, its Conservation Department, and its Education Department organising courses at all levels from the primary to the postgraduate, render it a potent force for education at a local, a national, and an international level.

In this book Dr Fox offers a detailed, often picturesque chronicle of the Trust's activities throughout its existence with, naturally, especial emphasis on the period of his directorship. A record of notable personal achievement, it also provides unusual insights into the day-to-day workings of a charitable institution with an exceptionally high profile.

STANLEY WELLS

Introduction

I took up my duties as Director of the Shakespeare Birthplace Trust on 1 October 1945, and retired on 30 September 1989, after forty-four years' service. This period has been generally seen as one of significant development in the history of the Trust and, when I relinquished my full-time responsibilities as Director, the Trustees invited me to commit to writing a record of what had happened during those years. At the same time, it was suggested that I should write a history of the Trust from its beginnings in 1847.

I felt honoured to be given opportunity to devote my semi-retirement to a project of this kind. It seemed to me that the two parts of the story should be presented together, and the prospect of examining the Trust's extensive archives for this appealed to me. What I did not realize was the magnitude of the task, or the essentially personal aspect of the period of my Directorship, which in fact constituted my life's work. Part one is a factual record, based on an examination of surviving sources, of the origin and early development of the Shakespeare Birthplace Trust, with particular reference to the restoration of Shakespeare's Birthplace and the subsequent growth of the Trust's activities under Richard Savage and Frederick Wellstood. It is a tribute to the early Trustees who, in the absence of adequate funding, discharged their responsibility in preserving Shakespeare's Birthplace as a national monument with considerable dedication and foresight, and at the same time laid the foundations for its future progress. The story provides a good illustration of the old fashioned, voluntary, British way of doing things.

Part two covers the history of the Trust since 1945. I have found it difficult, in describing the record of these years, not to give the impression of writing my autobiography. Though the Trust's official minutes, accounts and reports form the basis of my narrative, I have drawn on my memory and personal notes for many details not hitherto made public.

In preparing this history I had hoped to have the assistance of the late Miss Shirley Watkins, who had worked as my secretary and personal assistant for almost forty years. She had been involved with all the activities and projects undertaken by the Trust during those years. Sadly, she was stricken with cancer and died before the first chapter was written.

I therefore found myself having to undertake all the necessary research and tracking down of relevant papers. In order to make the book a useful work of reference, I have deliberately included detailed information about the Trust's properties, projects and activities, as well as finance, staff, and management arrangements. Whenever possible, illustrations have been used to add interest to the narrative.

I am grateful to Miss Marjorie Lea and my daughter, Elizabeth Fox, for typing copy, and on many occasions to my wife, who has confirmed my recollection of particular events. I owe a great debt to Miss Paula Haldenby, who has given invaluable help in preparing the final script. My thanks are also due to Jarrold Publications of Norwich for supplying many of the illustrations and for considerable editorial assistance. The Birthplace Trust's photographic collection has also provided illustrations, including photographs presented to the Trust at various times by *The Birmingham Post and Mail*, the *Coventry Evening Telegraph*, the *Stratford-upon-Avon Herald*, the *British Travel Association* and other publishers. Their permission to reproduce particular subjects for illustrations is acknowledged. The Trust's photographer, Malcolm Davies, has taken a few special pictures to fill gaps. The staff of the Trust's records office have always been ready with advice and information. I express my gratitude to the many individuals who have offered encouragement to me and helped in various ways in the preparation of this book.

Last, but by no means least, I am grateful to the Trustees and the Director, Mr Roger Pringle, for giving me facilities to do this work at the Shakespeare Centre and for their sponsorship of the publication of this personal memoir in the year which marks the 150th anniversary of the purchase of Shakespeare's Birthplace for preservation as a national memorial.

The Shakespeare Centre L.F.

PART ONE

The Trust's Origin and Early Development

1847 – 1945

SHAKSPEARE'S HOUSE,

AT STRATFORD-ON-AVON.

THE MOST UNIQUE RELIC AMONGST ENGLAND'S TREASURES

AND INDEED, THE

MOST INTERESTING MONUMENT OF THE POET'S FAME which this Country boasts.

MR. ROBINS

Feels highly flattered at having been selected by the Representatives of the late Mr. THOMAS COURT,

TO SUBMIT TO PUBLIC COMPETITION,

At the Auction Mart, London,

On THURSDAY, the 16th day of SEPTEMBER, 1847,

AT TWELVE O'CLOCK,

THE TRULY HEART-STIRRING RELIC OF A MOST GLORIOUS PERIOD,

AND OF

ENGLAND'S IMMORTAL BARD,

Which, by the course of events, and directions contained in the Will of the late Owner, must be offered to Public Sale; yet with every fervent hope that its appreciation by the Public will secure for it a safeguard and continuance at the Birth and Burial Place of the Poet,

The most honoured Monument of the Greatest Genius that ever lived.

To attempt to panegyrize this interesting and singular Property would be in vain, for (to quote the Poet's beautiful lines)—

> To gild refined gold, to paint the lily,
> To throw a perfume on the violet,
> To smooth the ice, or add another hue
> Unto the rainbow, or with taper light
> To seek the beauteous eye of Heaven to garnish,
> Is wasteful and ridiculous excess.

Mr. ROBINS, therefore, simply invites all who take an interest in this monumental relic (and who is there amongst us does not), to pay a visit to Stratford-on-Avon, in the full assurance that what they will see and feel, now that this remarkable Property may be possessed, will raise a spirit of competition hitherto unknown.

The SWAN and MAIDENHEAD, a thriving Public-house,

Which adjoins, with its Out-buildings, forms part of the Property, extending from Henley Street to the Guildpits,

The whole of which, be it remembered, is FREEHOLD.

THE BOOKS OF AUTOGRAPHS with numerous poetic inspirations, CURIOUS ANTIQUE FURNITURE, and SEVERAL INTERESTING RELICS, will be Sold at the same time.

Visitors may, as usual, inspect this singular domicile; and Printed Particulars, containing a Copy of the Family Pedigree, and much that will interest the reader, with Vignette Views, a Plan of the Property, and a Frontispiece in character with the period, may be had (at 2s. 6d.) Six Weeks prior, at the Swan and Maidenhead, Stratford-on-Avon; the Bedford Hotel, and Mr. ELSTON's Library, Leamington; Dee's Royal Hotel, Birmingham; of WALTER JESSOP, Esq., Solicitor, Cheltenham; at the Auction Mart; and at Mr. ROBINS' Offices, in Covent Garden, London.

Alfred Robins, Printer, 7, Southampton Street, Strand.

Birthplace sale poster

Beginnings

The Shakespeare Birthplace Trust came into existence following the purchase of Shakespeare's Birthplace in 1847 for preservation as a national memorial. The announcement of the sale by public auction of 'Shakespeare's House' at Stratford-upon-Avon, described as 'the truly heart-stirring relic of a most glorious period, and of England's immortal bard ... the most honoured monument of the greatest genius that ever lived', had received considerable publicity by the press and aroused widespread national interest and concern about the future of the building.

The Times found 'something grating to the ear' in the announcement that Shakespeare's house was to be sold, and was justifiably alarmed at the suggestion that it might fall into 'the desecrating grasp of those speculators who are said to be desirous of taking it from its foundations, and trundling it about on wheels like a caravan of wild beasts, giants, or dwarfs, through the United States of America'. Its leading article therefore urged that it should be bought so as to 'secure it against being exposed at any future time to the chances of desecration, destruction or removal'.

The rumour that a plan was on foot to remove the Birthplace to America seems to have produced immediate action. Committees were set up in London and Stratford to raise funds to purchase the property. An appeal for contributions was circulated widely. The immediate object of the purchase was twofold: to rescue the much neglected fabric of the house in Henley Street from its state of disrepair and to provide for its future preservation; and at the same time to place its future management with a responsible body which would administer it as a national memorial to William Shakespeare.

It was common knowledge that visitors to Shakespeare's Birthplace, which had increased in popularity as a shrine of literary pilgrimage since the Garrick Jubilee of 1769, had been shamelessly exploited. Walpole, who visited the house in 1777, describes how he was shown the poet's chair, which he noted had been 'pretty much cut by different visitors', a statement illuminated by another visitor, the Hon. John Byng, in 1785, who recorded that he bought 'a slice of the chair equal to the size of a tobacco stopper'.

Slightly later the celebrated Mrs Hornby, who resided at the Birthplace and acted as a guide from 1793 to 1820, gave it an undesirable notoriety by

Mrs Hornby

imposing on visitors a collection of spurious relics with alleged Shakespearian associations. Washington Irving, who was shown over the house by this lady in 1815, records his impressions in his *Sketch Book*. He instances among the relics she was showing 'the shattered stock of the very matchlock with which Shakespeare shot the deer on his poaching exploits ... his tobacco box ... the sword also with which he played Hamlet ... and the identical lantern with which Friar Lawrence discovered Romeo and Juliet'.

Though profitable for its organizer, this kind of

deception brought credit neither to Stratford nor to Shakespeare, and the ground swell of literary and theatrical opinion was that the time had come to put an end to misrepresentation.

The poster announcing the sale, with its emphatic, bold type, was a masterpiece of publicity. The sale catalogue, the auctioneer's copy of which,

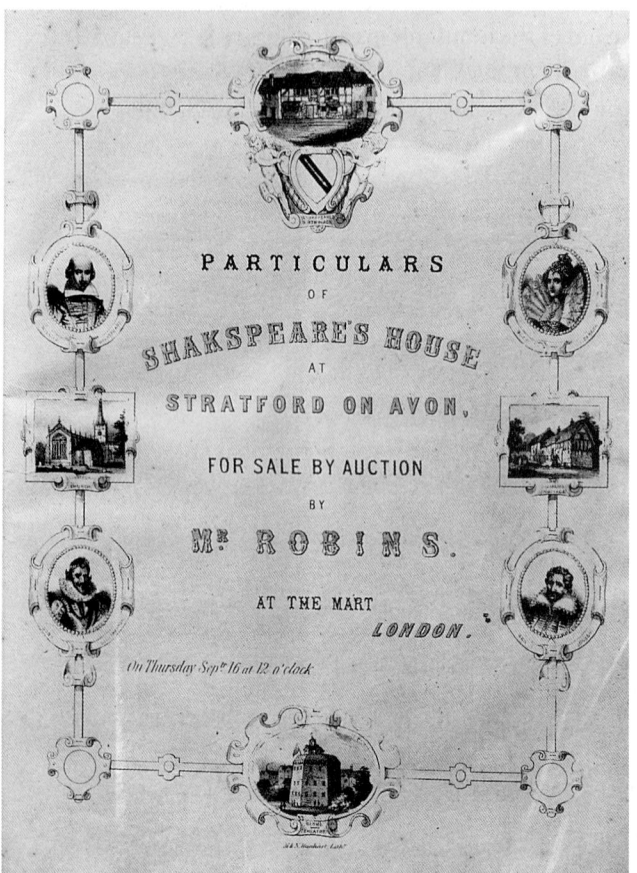

Sale catalogue

containing his notes and record of the bids, is preserved in the collection of the Shakespeare Birthplace Trust, was equally a masterpiece of advertisement. It comprised sixteen quarto pages, with a green cover, embellished with views of the Birthplace, the Church, Anne Hathaway's Cottage, the Globe Theatre and portraits of Shakespeare, Queen Elizabeth I, King James I and Ben Jonson. To supplement the particulars of the sale, which included the Swan and Maidenhead, 'a thriving Public-house' which had been part of the original building, there were included views of the birth-room with figure portraits of Charles Dickens and Widow Court and lengthy extracts from the works of Wheler, Knight, Drake and Irving, together with the Parish Register entries of the Shakespeare and Hart families. The sale was announced to take place at the Mart, London, on Thursday, 16 September 1847, at 12 o'clock.

At a meeting held on 22 July 1847, the Shakespeare Monumental Committee at Stratford-upon-Avon, which had been set up by the Royal Shakespearean Club in 1835 for the purpose of preserving Shakespeare's tomb and of restoring the chancel of Holy Trinity Church, extended its objects to include the preservation of Shakespeare's house. Under the new name of the Shakespeare Birthplace Committee, this body proceeded to purchase for £820 four cottages adjoining the Birthplace offered for sale by Mrs Izod and to appeal for funds 'to purchase and save from further desecration the walls which sheltered the cradle of William Shakespeare'. It was decided 'in consequence of an advertisement for the sale by auction of the property (Shakespeare's House) and also of a public meeting being announced to take place in London, that the time has arrived when the Committee should make known their intention to carry out what was contemplated at the time of the formation of the Committee on the 23 April 1835 for the preservation of the Tomb and Monument of Shakespeare, one object of which was to extend their care to the preservation of the House in which Shakespeare's Father resided in Henley Street, the Birthplace of Shakespeare'. The Shakespeare Club can accordingly claim the credit for having conceived the idea of acquiring Shakespeare's Birthplace for preservation as a national memorial. Mr E. Ashwin, Treasurer of the Borough, was appointed secretary of the Committee.

The surviving minutes of the Committee show that its members, under the chairmanship of Dr Thomas Thomson and the patronage of the High

Steward, the Earl de la Warr, lost no time in enlisting the patronage and support of national personalities and county gentry. Advertisements were inserted in national and local newspapers and copies were sent to booksellers in principal towns requesting them to have subscription lists placed in the various banks. A steady stream of donations provided encouraging evidence of public support. On 20 July 1847 Mr C.H. Bracebridge reported to the Committee that Lord Morpath had agreed on the part of Her Majesty's Government to take charge of the Birthplace, as trustee, if the property were purchased by the Committee. As will be explained later, this arrangement did not in fact prove possible. An appeal notice dated 2 August 1847, signed by Dr Thomas Thomson, chairman of the Committee, announced that His Royal Highness The Prince Albert had donated £250 towards the object.

A similar Committee was set up in London under the chairmanship of Thomas Amyot and an appeal issued on similar lines. Subsequently the efforts of both Committees were co-ordinated. A rival appeal was sponsored by George Jones, an American tragedian who organized the People's Central Committee of the Shakespeare Memorial Fund; but Jones's efforts met with considerable criticism and his project failed.

The response to their appeals was sufficient to justify the Stratford and London Committees to go forward with their plan for purchasing the property. Special performances and entertainments were given in aid of the funds: for instance, *Henry IV* was staged at the Royal Olympic Theatre on 26 August and *Twelfth Night* at the Theatre Royal, Liverpool, on 9 September. How widespread was popular interest may be illustrated by J.S. Coyne's musical extravaganza 'This House To Be Sold (the Property of the Late William Shakespeare); Inquire Within', which was staged at the Theatre Royal Adelphi on 9 September 1847. Another effort to raise money was the publication by Francis Crew of The *Shakspere Newspaper*. The first number was 'planned and brought out within a week'.

At a meeting on 14 September 1847 seven members of the Stratford Committee were appointed to attend the sale with authority to take such steps

Auction Room drawing

for the purchase of the house as might appear necessary; and to use their discretion with regard to the visitors' books which were also to be sold by auction. The sale room scene must have been a memorable occasion. A drawing of it, made by J.W. Archer for the *Illustrated London News* and now in the possession of the Birthplace Trustees, vividly illustrates its quality. A special Shakespeare number of that periodical was published on 18 September 1847, price 6d., containing an account of the proceedings of the sale together with a series of engravings of Stratford, Shottery and Charlecote by W.J. Linton from drawings made specially for the occasion by E. Duncan. Among those present in the sale room were Mr Amyot and Dr Thomson, chairmen of the London and Stratford Committees respectively, Peter Cunningham (treasurer), F.G. Tomlins (honorary secretary), J.P. Collier, F.W. Fairholt, J.O. Halliwell (later Halliwell-Phillipps), Charles Knight and T. Purland. Edmund Robins, the auctioneer, conducted the sale, George Robins having died earlier in the year.

'At one o'clock', says the *Illustrated London News* report, 'Mr Robins ascended the rostrum, amidst loud cheers. He then addressed the company, explaining that the vendor had no interest in the property, he simply acted as the trustee of several minors to whose interest he was bound to look; and in bringing the property before the public for sale, he was merely following a course which the Court of Chancery would have directed if it had been appealed to in the matter. He next stated there was a property attached to the house which yielded a yearly rental of £30. He then read the conditions, and explained that the title to the property would descend to the purchaser or purchasers, from the will of the Great Poet. A person here interposed, and called upon Mr Robins to prove that the house he was about to sell was the identical one in which the poet was born. Mr Robins replied that tradition pointed out this house as that of Shakespeare's birth. His father lived in it, and there could be no doubt that the Great Poet was born in the house and spent the greater part of his life in it. (Cheers.) They must take it as a matter of course. He wished that those who were sceptical on the point would stay away, instead of starting doubts which had no foundation to rest upon. The house was transferred from the hands of Shakespeare's descendants, in 1806, to the present owners.'

The bidding started at 1,500 guineas and continued with bids of £2,000 and £2,100; at that juncture an offer of £3,000 was handed to the auctioneer on behalf of the two Committees. This offer, the original autograph of which is preserved, was accepted and so the property was secured for preservation as a national memorial. When the Stratford Committee met two days later, the Chairman reported the success of the delegation sent to attend the sale: the property had been purchased and a deposit of £600 and contract fee of 10 guineas had been paid by the treasurer. The Committee placed on record its thanks to the gentlemen comprising the delegation 'for the very judicious and satisfactory manner in which their original object had been accomplished'.

The intention was to place the property, once purchased, under the protection of the Government. Negotiations were at once started by the London Committee with the Chief Commissioner of Woods and Forests, with a view to achieving that object. Meanwhile, further efforts were made to raise funds. In December 1847 a sum of £500 was still required to relieve the two Committees from liabilities in connection with the purchase. A 'Shakespeare Night' in aid of the fund was held at the Royal Italian Opera House, Covent Garden, on 7 December 1847, when scenes from Shakespeare's plays were performed. On 20 December 1847 an amateur performance of *Henry IV, Part 1* was given at the Theatre Royal, Manchester, for the same object, and similar amateur performances were given in different parts of the country. Slightly later, Charles Dickens sponsored an appeal for the endowment of a perpetual curatorship of Shakespeare's house. His plan was to make Sheridan Knowles, then in great financial need, the first curator. Dickens organized amateur performances to this end in London, Manchester, Birmingham and elsewhere, in which he and other literary figures of the day took part, these being among the most notable amateur productions of their time, indeed of the whole century. Although he raised a considerable sum of money, the project failed, presumably because it did not eventually prove acceptable to the Stratford Committee.

It is clear from the minutes of its proceedings that the Stratford Birthplace Committee took the initiative and assumed from the beginning that it was to be responsible for the property until such time as it might be taken over by the Government. Thus the Committee arranged for the property to be conveyed by one of its members, Mr Robert Bell Wheler, the well known Stratford solicitor and historian of the town, and for it to be inspected forthwith by Mr Edward Gibbs, a local architect, and a sub-committee.

Although sufficient money was not yet available to complete the purchase, the Committee negotiated arrangements for taking possession of the property on 11 November 1847. Notices were then displayed in the house announcing that moneys left would in future be placed to the credit of the general fund. A lady custodian, Mrs Jarratt, was engaged to be in attendance and she was given a wage of 12 shillings a week. Meanwhile the London bankers were requested to transfer all the funds in their hands to the credit of the Stratford Birthplace Committee at the Old Bank, Stratford-upon-Avon.

Members of the Committee were by this time beginning to be concerned about the financial implications of the responsibility they had undertaken and, in consultation with the London Committee, attempted to raise the balance of funds required.

Visitors to Shakespeare's Birthplace before its restoration

Financial support, however, was disappointingly slow in coming, the initial public enthusiasm having cooled off once the house had been purchased. It was only with the help of a loan of £470 advanced by the Stourbridge and Kidderminster Banking Company (the Old Bank at Stratford) that the purchase was completed in November 1848, and it was not until 1855 that this could be repaid. In the meantime the Stratford Committee did its best to organize further fund raising. In October 1850 it was decided to admit the public to the Birthplace by ticket only, price one shilling, to be obtained from the principal inns and booksellers of the town. An official visitors' book was also instituted, together with a system for recording and accounting for admissions.

Negotiations with the Government for taking over the property proved exceedingly tedious. Although terms for handing over the Birthplace had been agreed by both Committees in February 1851 and representatives appointed to pursue the negotiations, it was reported to the annual meeting of the Royal Shakespearean Club in 1853 that no progress had been made. It appears that a change in administration had taken place at Westminster and that, so far, the approval of the Cabinet had not been secured. The debt to the Stratford bank remained unpaid and the donations of visitors were little more than sufficient to defray the custodian's wages. Indeed, her wages had been reduced from 12 shillings to 6 shillings a week the previous year.

The position still remained unresolved the following year, when at the annual meeting it was reported that efforts to induce the Chief Commissioner of Public Works to implement the promise of his predecessor to arrange for the Birthplace to be taken over by the State had not as yet been successful. As a result, it was felt that the Committee might have to make other plans for providing for the future conservation of the property and for placing it in 'a more satisfactory and creditable condition than that in which it had been kept for some time in consideration of the uncertainty which had prevailed with consideration to the intentions of the Government'.

In the meantime the debt to the bank had been reduced from £90 10s. 11d. to £43 5s. 4d. This was further reduced the following year, and when the Committee met on 12 December 1855 it was reported that the debt at the bank had been cleared and the promissory note of 11 November 1848 had been cancelled. Receipts for the year amounted to £68 12s. 8¾d. and expenses to £32 13s. 10¼d. Visitors' admission fees provided the main source of income, and each year details of visitors coming to the Birthplace were recorded in the minutes.

During the year ended 23 April 1853 an analysis of the signatures of visitors to the Birthplace was recorded, as follows:

England	1,898	East Indies	3
Scotland	41	Hungary	2
United States	306	Isles of South Pacific	1
Ireland	14	Russia	3
Australia / New Zealand	8	Canada	5
South America	4	Silesia	1
France	12	California	1
Egypt	1	Turkey	1
Switzerland	5	China	1
Cape of Good Hope	1	West Indies	2
Germany	8	Spain	3
		Total	2,321

In the next year, 1854, the number increased to 2,878, but decreased to 2,436 in 1855. It is interesting to note that not a single visitor from Japan was recorded. In 1995 no fewer than 5,372 visitors from Japan signed the visitors' album at the Birthplace.

Restoration of Shakespeare's Birthplace

There is ample evidence to show that, at the time of its purchase, the Birthplace property had been grossly neglected from the point of view of maintenance and its original appearance altered in certain respects. The earliest drawing of it, in 1769, shows the building with dormer windows and gable, a deep porch and projecting bay window. In Samuel Ireland's sketch made in 1792, illustrated in his *Picturesque Views on the Upper, or Warwickshire Avon*, ... (1795), the dormer windows and gable had been removed, the bay window altered into an ordinary lattice window, the porch taken away and the front fitted up as a butcher's shop. This use of part of the premises did not improve its appearance; it seems incongruous that the living room of Shakespeare's house should have been used for retailing meat, yet this is what happened. Several early views of the Birthplace show joints of meat hanging in the window. At the same time the adjoining part of the building, traditionally used by John Shakespeare for his trade as a glover and wool dealer, had come to be used as an inn, the Swan and Maidenhead. Into what a poor condition the property had fallen, quite apart from any question of appearance, may be judged from the fact that when its owners put it for sale by private contract in 1804 no purchaser was forthcoming. Three months later, on 7 March 1805, the property was offered for sale by auction, but still it remained unsold. Thomas Court bought it for £210 the following year and took possession in 1808.

It was at this date, or thereabouts, that the Swan and Maidenhead portion of the building was rebuilt at the front in red brick. Some of the old timber framing was removed, but the main cross-beams remained and were hidden behind the new brick frontage. Views of the Birthplace property showing this 'improvement' indicate how drastically it altered the earlier appearance of the building. Fortunately

R. Greene's drawing of the Birthplace, 1769

Eldridge's drawing, 1807

Blight's drawing, 1862

sufficient of the original timber framing remained behind the brick facade to make possible the later reinstatement of the half-timbered frontage on the lines of the earliest drawing. The domestic part of the house stood alongside 'a small mean-looking edifice of wood and plaster', in the words of Washington Irving. Stratford's local historian, R.B. Wheler, describing its appearance in 1824, says: 'The external appearance of these celebrated buildings is not very attractive, nor does the internal arrangement encourage the idea of their having afforded that domestic comfort to a respectable family of which they were nevertheless capable in the reign of Elizabeth'. He attributed the decay of the building to 'the lapse of more than two hundred years' and the want of sufficient repairs whilst in the possession of the Hart family in the eighteenth century, which was burdened with a heavy mortgage and lived in humble circumstances.

The Birthplace Committee accordingly found itself faced with a formidable task of overhauling and reinstating the fabric of the building but lacking the necessary cash to proceed. At first the letting of the Swan and Maidenhead suggested itself as a possible source of income and, with this in mind, the Committee inspected it in the spring of 1855 with a view to placing it in a proper state of repair and demolishing the outbuildings at the rear in order 'not to cause danger or injury to the Birthplace'. For the same reason it was decided that the tenant should not be allowed to carry on business as a beer shopkeeper. Certain modest repairs were put in hand and a tenant chosen.

At the same time the local architect and surveyor, Mr Edward Gibbs, was asked to give an estimate of cost for a number of minor repairs to the Shakespeare house itself. At a cost of £83 4s. 1d. these items were carried out: the space in front of the building was paved with Rowley Regis stone and a sheet of opaque glass was put 'in the room of the heavy shutter now in front of the house'. Meanwhile, the Committee felt the need for regular secretarial support. On 12 December 1855 the secretary, Mr John S. Leaver, who had given his services for the last three years, was offered a gratuity of £15 and a payment of £10 per annum as from 23 April 1855.

At this juncture, towards the end of 1855, a fortuitous circumstance arose which produced far-reaching results. A John Shakespeare of Worthington Fields, near Ashby-de-la-Zouch, and of Langley Priory, Leicestershire, who claimed to be a descendant of the poet, made known his intention to preserve and restore the Birthplace fabric and so ensure 'the rescue of England's most interesting relic from the risk of destruction by fire and from decay'.

Encouraged by this unexpected windfall, the Committee immediately made plans to carry out the necessary work. A separate committee of trustees of the John Shakespeare Fund was appointed to administer the trust and to oversee the programme of restoration in consultation with the donor. After two years it was decided that the John Shakespeare Fund trustees and the Shakespeare's Birthplace Committee should act in concert as one body.

Mr Shakespeare visited the Birthplace and, in consultation with the Committee, agreed that it was important to isolate the property from all adjoining buildings with a view to protecting it from the risk of fire. Steps were taken immediately to purchase the house adjoining the Swan and Maidenhead and to acquire the piece of land next to the White Lion nearby, together with some of the old stabling behind and belonging to it, as being in fact part of the original Shakespeare property. A cottage behind the Birthplace, close to the Guild Pits, was also purchased. A decision was made to get possession of the Swan and Maidenhead, which had been let, and of the cottage adjoining the east end of the Birthplace which the Committee already owned.

At the end of 1856 tenders were invited for taking down the cottages on either side of the Birthplace and for the erection of a temporary fence along the street frontage. Mr William Holtom's bid of £65 for the materials of the premises to be demolished was accepted on 5 March 1857 and the work of demolition, including the cottage behind, facing Guild Street, proceeded forthwith. Thus Shakespeare's

Birthplace was presented as it now appears: an isolated, self-contained building with open space on either side and at the rear, whereas originally it had formed part of a continuous street frontage.

At the Committee's meeting on 5 March 1857, the chairman, Dr Thomas Thomson, and Mr Payne Collier were requested to select 'the most eminent architect conversant with ancient domestic architecture' to give a report on 'the best means of restoring Shakespeare's House to its original state'.

At the suggestion of Mr Payne Collier, a Shakespeare scholar, an approach was made to Mr E.M. Barry, the architect of the House of Commons, who paid a visit to the Birthplace and, in company with Mr Edward Gibbs, the local architect, made a detailed inspection and survey of the building, at a charge of £34. Barry's report, dated 6 July 1857, which is preserved among the Hunt papers in the Trust's records office, recommended a programme of restoration that was accepted by the Committee. In general terms the object was 'to remove at once those portions of the building which are modern and formed no part of the original edifice; to avoid as far as possible touching the existing portion of the old building shown as the Birthplace and to confine the works to restoring that part of the building known as the Swan and Maidenhead in accordance with the old drawing'. In particular, the restoration was to be so designed as 'to remove with a careful hand all those excrescences which are decidedly the result of modern innovation, to uphold with jealous care all that now exists of undoubted antiquity, not to destroy any portion about whose character the slightest doubt does now exist, but to restore any parts needing it in such manner that the restoration can never be mistaken for the old work though harmonizing with it, and lastly to adopt such measures as modern science enables us to bring to our aid for the perfect preservation of the building'. In view of misleading statements which are made from time to time concerning the restoration of the Birthplace, the principles governing the restoration, as quoted, cannot be too strongly emphasized.

Mr Edward Gibbs was commissioned to prepare an estimate of the cost, with proper working plans. The estimate amounted to £692, exclusive of heating and ventilation. Tenders for the 'Works to Shakespeare's House', based on a detailed specification and description of the works to be undertaken prepared by Messrs. Gibbs, Thompson and Colbourne, were then invited from builders in the town, and in August 1857 the Committee entered into a contract with William Holtom. His was the only tender received: £662 for work on the whole building, or £282 10s. 0d. for the front, ends and roof. The Committee gave him instructions to proceed with the work covered by the second estimate, and at the same time authorized minor alterations to a cottage at the rear of Hornby Cottage (the building to the east of Shakespeare's Birthplace), that was to be used as the custodian's residence.

Holtom seems to have proceeded at once, for by April 1858 the major part of the work was completed.

Restoration of Birthplace in progress

On removing the brickwork in front of the Swan and Maidenhead portion of the building, it was found that, although the subsidiary timbers of the framed structure had been removed, the original main beams showing the mortice holes remained. Mr Gibbs, the architect, prepared a plan showing the exact distances apart of the mortice holes. Members of the Committee in company with him then inspected and tested the measurements on site, so as to be able to certify that the timbers would now be put back in exactly the same positions as those in the original structure. This was apparently considered important, as they differed in some respects from the earliest drawing of the building. The work of reinstatement went ahead, the principles laid down by Barry being literally followed. Thus replacement timber members had straight sawn sides; they were not shaped irregularly with the adze as the original timbers would have been.

Some other items were put in hand at this time. A temporary staircase was made in the Swan and Maidenhead to give access to the upper rooms, and downstairs a new oak floor was laid on the old one. A wall was built to separate the Birthplace property from the White Lion, and the Guild Street boundary was marked in readiness for the building of an enclosing wall. In Henley Street a stone plinth was built to define the frontage of the property and a split-larch paling was erected on the stonework on either side of the building as a protection for a yew hedge which was planted behind. The young yew trees were supplied by Mr John Butcher, who had a nursery in Warwick Road, much to the disappointment of Mr Perkins of Leamington Spa, who had apparently been led to believe he would have the order for them. Iron railings, to a design by Mr E.M. Barry, were suggested for erection in front of the Birthplace itself.

Meanwhile, the Committee began to consider plans for the restoration of the penthouse over the front entrance to the Birthplace, the insertion of dormer windows, the warming and ventilation of the building and the laying out of the ground at the rear of the property as a garden and orchard 'with the taste of the olden time'. Contact with Mr John Shakespeare was maintained, the hope being that further financial support from him would be forthcoming to continue the work of restoration, particularly the interior of the house, for which funds were not available.

At the July meeting of the Committee in 1858 the clerk, Mr W.O. Hunt, reported the death of Mr John Shakespeare on 11 June and the news that he had bequeathed £2,500 and an annuity of £60 a year to be paid to the Birthplace Committee from his estate for the maintenance of a custodian. Encouraged by this munificent benefaction, the Committee felt in confident mood and decided to proceed with the restoration of the penthouse, as designed by Mr Barry, and the insertion of a dormer window, together with the laying of a new oak floor in the upper museum and the building of the boundary wall along the Guild Pits.

The bombshell then fell. On 22 February 1859 Mr Hunt reported the news from Mr Shakespeare's solicitors that they were unable to pay any portion of the legacy bequeathed by the late John Shakespeare and that nothing could be done without securing a ruling from the Court of Equity. Not surprisingly, it was decided to challenge this decision in the hope of substantiating the claim of the Birthplace trustees under the will. Meanwhile further planned restoration work was immediately halted.

It was unfortunate that at this critical stage Vice-Chancellor Ward in the Court of Equity ruled against the claim of the Birthplace Committee. In January 1860 it was decided to appeal against this decision, but by the time of the annual meeting on 23 April 1860 news had come that the Chancellor and the Lord Justices had upheld the Vice-Chancellor's decision. In practical terms this meant that the Committee found itself in debt to the sum of £357 12s. 10d., this being the cost of the Chancery law suit and payments owed to local tradesmen for work carried out on the premises.

Again it was decided to appeal to the public to raise funds to liquidate this debt. A sub-committee was appointed and the appeal was advertised. Meanwhile, those to whom the Committee owed money had to be paid and, to meet the situation, a loan of £400 from the bank was negotiated. The weakness of the Committee's financial position is illustrated by the accounts for 1859-60. The total annual income from the Birthplace, with donations, amounted to £141 5s. 6d. Payments, including the custodian's wages of £31 4s. 0d., amounted to £127 6s. 5½d., leaving a balance of £13 19s. 0½d. There was no other money available for further work.

A number of fund raising events produced useful donations, the Masonic Ball held at the Town Hall in April 1860 contributing the handsome sum of £30. The following year the Committee authorized the sale to visitors of small pieces of oak from timber recently taken from the Birthplace, each piece being marked with a steel die to authenticate its association. This particular souvenir proved popular, and in fact one such piece of oak bought by an American visitor at that time was returned to the Trust shortly before my retirement. In a different category was J.O. Halliwell's gift of five hundred copies of his printed *History of the Birthplace*, to be offered for sale to assist the fund.

When the annual meeting of the Committee was held on 23 April 1861, a detailed report was given on what had happened as a result of the 'unfortunate suit'. Mr William Oakes Hunt was thanked warmly for his services in connection with this legal business and also for producing a design for the layout of the ground at the rear of the Birthplace as a garden. With the assistance of Mr Robert W. Hobbes and other members of the Committee, planting of the fruit trees they provided had already started. Other gifts were presented the following year: a cutting from a vine which grew in the garden of Essex House, London; a choice collection of roses given by Evelyn P. Shirley of Ettington; Mr C.F. Loggin's scion of the mulberry tree planted by Shakespeare; and a variety of shrubs from Mr Sole of Banbury.

An unexpected development then occurred. On 12 April 1862 the Committee was informed that Mr C.H. Bracebridge had offered to lend £300 without interest for the purpose of completing the restoration of Shakespeare's house and fitting up the Swan and Maidenhead portion of it as a museum for the reception of Shakespeare relics, together with certain improvements at the custodian's house. This generous offer was accepted with gratitude and the decision made to carry out the work forthwith.

Mr Edward Gibbs was requested to prepare specifications and estimates under the direction of a sub-committee appointed to supervise the restoration.

The Birthplace restoration completed

Of the two tenders received from Stratford builders, that of James and George Calloway of High Street was accepted on 10 May 1862. The restoration of the property proceeded during the following months and the eastern portion of it, the former public house, was fitted up as a library and museum for the reception and display of Shakespeare relics. A heating system, described as 'warm water apparatus' was introduced into the whole building, thereby affording 'comfort to the custodian and visitors'. Framed timbers, together with a porch, were added to the elevation of the custodian's house overlooking the garden, for the purpose of making it harmonize more with the character of the Birthplace itself.

On 31 December 1862 the Committee agreed to make available to the Stratford-upon-Avon Corporation the rooms at the north-western end of the Birthplace to accommodate the Borough collection of historical records, which up till that time had been kept in a small room leading off the Guildhall in Church Street. The Corporation undertook to pay a nominal rent of £1 a year and to be responsible for fitting up the rooms for the storage of these records. At first the Council, through its Clerk, retained day-to-day control of the records, but thereafter an arrangement was made whereby the principal officer of the Committee for the time being was appointed Deputy Record Keeper for the Corporation.

This arrangement owed much to the influence and work of J.O. Halliwell, the Shakespeare scholar who came to play an important part on the Stratford scene. In pursuance of his research for material illustrative of Shakespeare's life and times, he had been allowed to consult the Borough records and subsequently to sort and arrange them as the basis for a catalogue he compiled. This was published in 1863 as his *Descriptive calendar of the ancient manuscripts and records in possession of the Corporation of Stratford-upon-Avon*, described by J.C. Jeaffreson as a 'stately folio', in fact one of the earliest of such compilations. Halliwell was also responsible for binding into volumes the Chamberlains' accounts and vouchers together with the considerable collection of miscellaneous documents and other select items. As a scholar, he appreciated the importance of these records as providing primary source material for the study of Shakespeare's life and times, and it seemed sensible to accommodate them alongside the library and museum the Birthplace Committee was establishing.

How keenly interested Halliwell was in the restoration of the Birthplace and the subsequent fitting up of part of it as a library and museum may be illustrated by the fact that he personally acquired copies of the plans and specifications from Edward Gibbs, the architect. When I first visited the Folger Shakespeare Library, I came across these in the Halliwell-Phillipps collection, together with a series of pencil sketches by an artist named Blight illustrating the appearance of every room in the Birthplace. Halliwell employed this artist to make a record of the restoration work in progress before, during and after completion. Blight's drawings are of special significance, because they provide indisputable evidence about the fabric of the building and the extent to which the timber framing had to be replaced. In each room the drawings show the original timbers, with a different indication of those that had to be replaced. Additionally, sketches were made of individual details as, for example, the fireplace of the lower museum or the stone chimney stack in the attic, which provide evidence of the care taken not to alter or destroy original features of the building. Of special interest is the coloured sketch of the museum as set out in 1863.

Blight's sketches of 'The Room behind the Shop' (the kitchen) and 'The Shop' (the living room)

Halliwell supervised the internal arrangements of the museum's exhibits and received a formal vote of thanks for his services, as well as for his personal gifts of books and other interesting relics for the museum. In the meantime the seal was set to the Committee's efforts to attract support by a number of other presentations which provided the nucleus of the Birthplace collections. The first came from Mr William Oakes Hunt, one of the Committee's most active members, who donated the base of Stratford's ancient market cross and a fragment of stone from the ruins of New Place, to be followed by his gift of a portrait of Shakespeare, the so-called Stratford portrait, which was deposited in the Birthplace in an

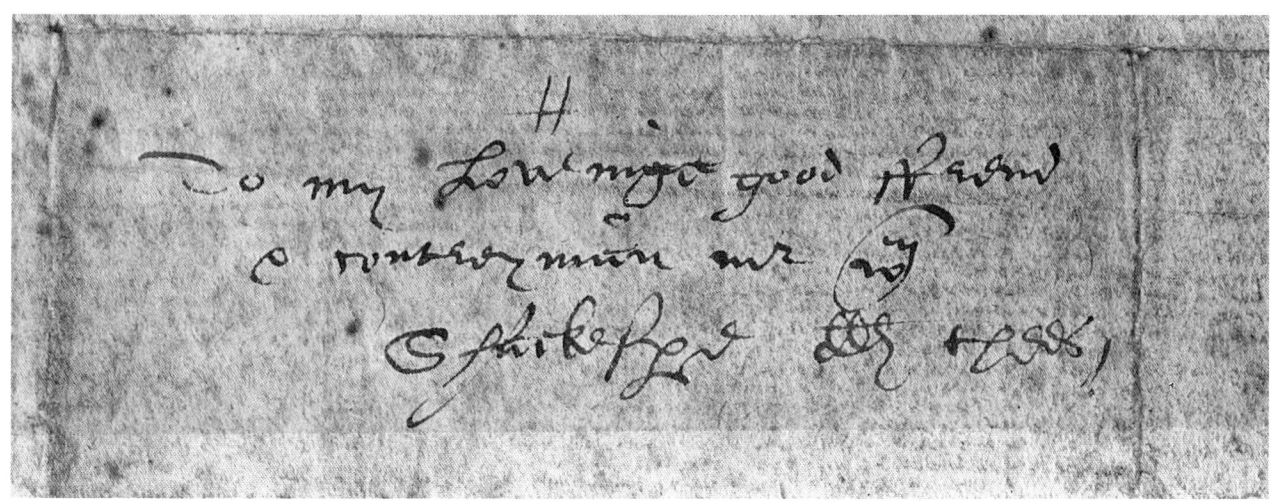

Quyney's letter with accompanying address

iron safe specially made for its security. Later his collection of historical papers was added.

The extensive and valuable collection of records and papers made by the late Mr R.B. Wheler, the Stratford historian, was presented by his sister, Miss Ann Wheler, as well as the collections and drawings made by the late Captain Saunders comprising about fifty volumes. Among other items acquired for the museum was 'Shakespeare's desk', which was transferred from the Grammar School to the custody of the Birthplace Committee.

Shakespeare's desk

The museum portion of the Birthplace thus took shape and, largely due to the energy and enthusiasm of J.O. Halliwell, it was opened to the public by the time the celebrations to commemorate the tercentenary of Shakespeare's birth took place in Stratford and London in 1864. One of the special exhibits the members of the Committee were proud to display in the museum was the celebrated letter from Richard Quyney to Shakespeare, which had been framed and glazed and placed on a stand with a pivot which made it possible easily to see and read the letter and the superscription. Pride of place was also given to the Ely Palace portrait of Shakespeare, so called because it had belonged to Thomas Turton, Bishop of Ely (1780-1864), which was presented to Shakespeare's Birthplace by Henry Graves of Pall Mall, London, on 23 April 1864.

Ely Palace portrait of Shakespeare

Early Progress

The establishment and development of the library and museum marked a turning point in the uncertain fortunes of the Birthplace Committee. The tercentenary festivities gave additional impetus to visitors, and nearly nine thousand people paid for admission to the Birthplace during 1864. According to the accounts there was an average receipt of £4 4s. 7½d. per week, with an average expense of £2 1s. 3d. per week. Though such a performance held little prospect of quickly liquidating the outstanding debt, the steady stream of gifts of books, manuscripts and museum items provided real evidence of serious interest and potential support. A first *Brief guide to the Shakespeare Library and Museum, Stratford-upon-Avon*, price one penny, was produced in 1865. At the annual meeting in 1866 it was reported that Shakespeare's house with the library and museum containing books, pictures and documents illustrative of the poet and his native town had become 'a place of great and increasing attraction'.

It was at this juncture that, being impressed by the extraordinary success of the museum in the short time since its formation, the Committee felt it desirable that the whole operation should be placed on a more permanent basis and with better support, so as to satisfy potential donors that their gifts would be properly appreciated and preserved. Moreover, it was realized that the Birthplace estate, comprising properties purchased at various times and from various parties, had been vested in certain persons, not always the same, really acting as trustees but without any express declaration of trust. Two members of the Committee had now died and, with these considerations in mind, it was proposed that the legal estate should be conveyed to the Corporation of Stratford-upon-Avon and the control and management of the property should be entrusted to a body of trustees consisting of ex officio persons of the town and county, together with a few life members.

The draft of a Deed to accomplish this object was prepared and approved by the Committee and formally executed on 4 July 1866. The parties named were Thomas Thomson, M.D., William Oakes Hunt, gentleman, and Edward Fordham Flower, Esq., of the first part; the said Thomas Thomson and John Payne Collier of the second part; and the Mayor, Aldermen and Burgesses of the Borough of Stratford-upon-Avon of the third part.

After reciting details of the various properties acquired in 1848, 1856 and 1858 with moneys raised by public subscription with the object of preserving Shakespeare's Birthplace as a national memorial, the parties mentioned described the action taken to restore the property and to establish a library and museum and, in order to place the property on a permanent basis, conveyed the legal estate therein to the Mayor, Aldermen and Burgesses of Stratford-upon-Avon in trust for this purpose. The Deed then defined the composition of the body of Trustees who were to have control and management of the properties, and power 'to make rules and regulations for the government, protection and preservation of the said house, library and museum and the grounds and appurtenances thereof'.

The following were appointed to serve as ex officio Trustees: the Lord Lieutenant of the County of Warwick, the High Steward of the Borough of Stratford-upon-Avon, the Justices of the Peace for the Borough, the Aldermen of the Borough, the Town Clerk, the Vicar of the Parish of Stratford-upon-Avon and the Headmaster of the Free Grammar School. The following were named as Life Trustees: Dr Thomas Thomson, John Payne Collier, Charles Holte Bracebridge, James Orchard Halliwell, William Oakes Hunt, Edward Fordham Flower, Robert Hiorne Hobbes and John Atkinson, second master at the Grammar School. Provision was also made for the appointment of any person who might make a donation to the said house, library and museum to the value of £100.

The newly constituted body of Trustees held its first meeting on 4 July 1866. It was resolved that the Mayor for the time being should preside at meetings as chairman. John Shapcote Leaver was re-appointed secretary at his current salary of £10 a year, and the Stourbridge and Kidderminster Banking Company (the 'Old Bank') re-appointed as treasurer. Mrs Ashwin was re-appointed as custodian at her current salary of 12s. a week for the Birthplace plus 2s. a week for the museum, with residence, rent and tax free, and an allowance for coals.

On this occasion it was reported that the western portion of the upper room of the museum, which was dark and inconvenient, had been enlarged and improved by the removal of the modern flooring of the attic. Outside, iron palisades were substituted for the wooden fence on either side of the house in front of the yew hedge. Details of presentations to the museum, which included two ancient maces, long disused, from the Corporation of Stratford, were then recorded and a statement of the year's income and expenditure approved. Although it proved possible to repay £90 of the debt owed to the bank, the sum of £124 13s. 10d. remained outstanding.

From this time onwards the Trustees normally met once a year, usually on or near Shakespeare's birthday, with occasional meetings in between as necessary. A standard pattern of proceedings came to be followed: consideration of any practical matters affecting the property; a review of presentations and purchases for the museum; a report on visitors and accounts, with any matters arising; and the election of new Trustees from time to time.

At the annual meeting held on 3 May 1869 it was reported that the Birthplace and museum - the two were still kept separate - were now 'established on so permanent a basis that there is little or nothing for the Trustees to communicate to the public'. Trustees, however, were informed that a *Catalogue* of articles in the Birthplace and museum had been prepared by the late Charles Hopper and that Trustees should have received copies. This was quite an elaborate publication running to 171 pages, published in 1868 as *Catalogue of the books, manuscripts, works of art, antiquities and relics ... preserved in the Shakespeare Library and Museum*. The following year, 1870, the whole of the debt, £80, remaining to the bank had been discharged and a balance of £9 7s. 5d. was left in the treasurer's hands. This must have been a matter of great satisfaction to the Trustees; for the first time since 1847 the institution was in funds.

Year by year the number of visitors grew, producing a gradual increase in the income available to the Trustees. In 1868 the number of visitors was upwards of 4,500, excluding those who did not sign the visitors' book; by 1873 the number had risen to 9,932. Until 1871 the custodian, Mrs Ashwin, had been solely responsible for the reception and guiding of visitors and for accounting for the money taken. New arrangements were then introduced: an assistant was employed at 18s. 0d. a week to issue tickets and take the admission money, which was then checked by the secretary and taken to the bank. I suspect that the good lady did not like this new procedure. She resigned at Michaelmas 1871, ostensibly on grounds of failing health, and was succeeded by Miss Maria Charlotte Callaway, previously housekeeper at Ragley.

Until this time the library and museum had been arranged and supervised by the Trustees themselves,

Early view of the birthroom

particularly by Mr Hunt and Mr Halliwell, who continued to make considerable gifts from his Shakespeare collection. At the annual meeting in 1872 it was reported that the Trustees had accepted from Mr Halliwell, subject to the condition that they could only be consulted during his lifetime with his permission, his voluminous unpublished annotations on the texts of Shakespeare's plays, illustrated by many thousands of cuttings from early printed books and engravings. A bookcase made of old oak from Shakespeare's house, carved by John Marshall, was acquired to accommodate them in the upper museum.

Following the death in 1873 of Mr Hunt, described in the minutes as 'a most valuable benefactor, friend and adviser', the Trustees took the very wise step of appointing a librarian to supervise and catalogue the books and articles in the museum. Such an appointment was also considered necessary for the purpose of rendering the contents of the growing Shakespeare collections more available to the public. Mr Charles Jackman was appointed librarian on 24 June 1873, at a salary of £15 per annum for the first year plus the free occupation of the new house (later 19, and then renumbered 14, Henley Street) erected by Mr Charles Flower alongside the old White Lion premises, valued as an emolument at £35 per annum. Within less than a year the Trustees were informed that he had made an inventory of books and exhibits, ready for checking by Mr Halliwell.

From the early 1860s, Mr Halliwell's interest and effort had considerably assisted the objects of the Birthplace Committee. In 1861 he had inaugurated a National Shakespeare Fund for the purpose of purchasing and preserving the site of New Place, Shakespeare's last home, and the adjoining gardens, together with the establishment of a museum to accommodate records which illustrated the poet's life and the history and social life of Stratford-upon-Avon in his time.

He had in fact succeeded in acquiring the whole of the New Place property which had belonged to Shakespeare, together with the adjoining Nash's

The Birthplace museum in the 1880's, ground floor

The same, upper floor

House, the residence of Thomas Nash and his wife Elizabeth, the poet's grand-daughter. In 1872 he purchased and demolished the theatre which had been built in 1827 at the lower end of the area occupied by the Great Garden. In the meantime the foundations of New Place were excavated and exposed, to give an impression of the plan and size of the house, and preparations were made for laying out the garden and the establishment of a museum of Shakespeare relics in Nash's House.

In 1875 Mr Halliwell, now styled Halliwell-Phillipps, made known his wish to vest the entire New Place property on a more permanent basis, under the control and management of the Trustees of the Birthplace. With the approval of the

J.O. Halliwell-Phillipps

Birthplace Committee a Deed was accordingly prepared 'to convey and vest the legal estate in the property in the Corporation of Stratford-upon-Avon in trust for such official and other Trustees with all necessary powers, clauses and provisions for the preservation and management thereof by the Trustees'.

The Deed was executed the following year and from that time the Birthplace Trustees assumed responsibility for the management of New Place and the museum in Nash's House associated with it. The Trustees appointed a New Place Committee to deal with matters of detail and to submit reports and recommendations as necessary. At the same time it was decided to form an Executive Committee of three Trustees - the first members were Mr Hobbes, Mr Hunt and Mr Flower - to meet monthly at Shakespeare's Birthplace to conduct the business and general affairs of the Trustees, such Committee to be appointed annually. It was also ordered that the management of the accounts of New Place should be transferred to them.

During 1876 the members of the New Place Committee were very busy dealing with a number of practical matters. The salary of a custodian for the property, Mr T.W. Salmon, was fixed at £20 a year. In consultation with Mr T.T. Allen, a local architect, a plan and design for a new wall to enclose the whole of the area of the New Place property was agreed and tenders for the work were invited from local builders. A poster announcing the details is pasted in the minute book. Ornamental cast iron railings to be fixed on top of the Hornton stone coping on the wall were then designed and tenders invited.

Mr Elisha Court, a local builder, secured the contract for building the wall at a price of £100, plus £3 extra for Hornton stone instead of box stone as quoted, and Messrs. Skidmore of Coventry that for the railings at a cost of £164 10s. 0d. plus £32 10s. 0d. for fixing. The work was carried out under the watchful eye of the Committee, and early the following year the local nurseryman, Mr John Butcher, was employed to stake out the proposed paths in the garden. Subsequently, in view of his involvement with the Birthplace garden, Mr Butcher played an active part in planning and planting the Great Garden of New Place. In May 1877 he was asked by the Executive Committee to quote for keeping in order the gardens at Shakespeare's Birthplace and New Place throughout the year and to ensure that there should always be one man at New Place gardens on Saturdays during the season. Incidentally, he

Early view of New Place garden

quoted a price of £36 2s. 10d. for the work, which was accepted.

There are other references to Mr Butcher, who was well known in the town because of the successful nursery business he ran in Warwick Road. In 1879 he was asked to remove two Wellingtonia trees from the Birthplace garden and to replant them at New Place. If he did so, they cannot have survived, because there are no Wellingtonias at New Place. The following year Mr Butcher's attention was called to the condition of the gardens at the Birthplace and New Place and the Committee's wish to have them better kept.

In May 1877 the following *Regulations for admission to New Place House and Gardens* were approved:

1. Visitors to be admitted through the House to the Gardens every day except Saturdays and Sundays upon payment of 6d. for each person, from 9 a.m. to sunset.
2. The public to be admitted free to the Gardens on Saturdays, at the entrance gate in Chapel Lane.
3. Householders in the town and neighbourhood to be supplied with a key to the Gardens upon payment of 5s. per annum, and on deposit of 2s. 6d. for the key. Subscriptions due on May 5th, payable in advance to the Secretary.
4. Keyholders to be entitled to admission for themselves, their families and friends visiting them.
5. The Trustees to reserve the right of closing the Gardens to keyholders and others on special occasions, not exceeding twenty days a year.
6. The House not to be open on Sundays but the Gardens to be open, to keyholders only, after 1 p.m.
7. Persons damaging the shrubs or otherwise misbehaving themselves to be liable to expulsion from the Gardens; and keyholders to be considered responsible for the good conduct of those admitted with the subscribers' keys.

The minutes of the Executive Committee's monthly meetings from this time onwards record the details of the Trustees' management and development of the properties. Receipts and disbursements of the Birthplace, the museum and New Place were separately reported. During 1877 visitors to the Birthplace numbered 9,750 and to New Place 488, making a total of 10,238. By 1880 this had increased to 11,975. Income now regularly exceeded expenditure and any surplus - such as £200 in 1877 - was invested with the Stratford-upon-Avon Savings Bank to earn 2½ per cent interest. By 1879 the Trustees' capital account had risen to £1,300. With more adequate resources available and recognizing the increased amount of work involved, the Trustees raised the salary of the secretary from £20 to £30 a year.

Housekeeping and practical matters also received attention. Flag poles and flags were provided for Shakespeare's Birthplace and New Place. A bell was hung at the door of the Birthplace so that visitors could summon the custodian on arrival. The mulberry tree in the Birthplace garden was protected by an iron, railed fence put round the trunk. The whole of the timber-work of Shakespeare's Birthplace and of the custodian's house was oiled and varnished 'with a view to the perfect preservation of the Birthplace House'. Appearances mattered: the cast ironwork surrounding New Place was painted and gilded, thus 'adding to the ornamental appearance of the grounds'.

Accessions to the library and Birthplace museum and to the museum at New Place were reported as a matter of regular routine. In October 1877 the Committee considered a memorandum on the use of the library. It expressed concern that, if the books were freely available for use by the curious, the inevitable wear and tear was likely to lead to undesirable damage. Nevertheless, the Trustees felt it their duty, as part of their objects, to allow proper use by serious scholars. A set of rules was accordingly agreed. It was decided that any person wishing to have access to the books must apply to the librarian with a letter from one of the Trustees giving the full name and address of the applicant and the object of his study. Any Trustee giving such a letter was to be considered responsible for the applicant. It was also laid down that no book was to be taken out of the museum on any pretext and that the librarian should be present during the whole time of such consultation and that he should replace the books in the case before leaving the room. Such rules may appear to be unduly strict, but the underlying principles still apply and are followed in connection with the use of the Trust's collections. As with other national libraries, it is usual to check the bona fides of readers, though with a minimum of formality.

The unexpected death of the librarian, Charles Jackman, in June 1879 produced a difficult situation. There was no one immediately available who could take over his duties and, when Mr J.O. Halliwell-Phillipps offered to rearrange the library and museum, the Trustees hesitated to proceed to make an appointment without seeking his advice. Mr Halliwell-Phillipps was critical of some of the exhibits displayed in the Birthplace, which he described as 'absurdly spurious or trivial', and he suggested that certain items should be removed. In particular he recommended that portraits of later Shakespeare actors, pictures and engravings from the plays and irrelevant curios should be transferred to New Place, where they could be stored. His idea was to use the limited space in the Birthplace museum to display and make available for study 'the biographical treasures in our custody'. To this end he advocated that a librarian should be sought who had 'a perfect acquaintance with these, united with palaeographical ability and topographical knowledge'.

Mr Halliwell-Phillipps circulated details of his proposals in printed form to the Trustees and, to finalize matters, the Executive Committee invited him to attend a special meeting on 28 June 1880 to discuss his recommendations. The outcome was that Mr Bruce Tyndall, recommended by him, was appointed librarian as from 5 July 1880 at a salary of £100 per annum, payable quarterly, the engagement to be terminated by either party giving one quarter's notice. He was also allowed six weeks annual leave - a surprisingly liberal stint - subject to the approval of the Committee. He was introduced to the Trustees at their next meeting and entrusted with the keys to the bookcases. After familiarizing himself with the contents of the collection, his first task was to compile a supplement to the catalogue of the museum that had been produced in 1868, which, in the opinion of Mr Halliwell-Phillipps, was not adequate to meet requirements.

Clearly the lay members of the Executive Committee were inclined to take note of the views of this eminent and generous Shakespeare scholar. Thus they decided to exclude from the museum the portraits of all actors of Shakespearian characters with the exception of Garrick, all modern pictures of Shakespearian scenes, books and manuscripts relating to Warwickshire in which there were no notes respecting Stratford-upon-Avon and its neighbourhood, and editions of plays and works on Shakespeare published after the seventeenth century. Mr Halliwell-Phillipps was only interested in the biographical Shakespeare and appears not to have appreciated the dramatist's work and influence as a man of the theatre. In the following year the Committee appointed a sub-committee to select which books, pictures and manuscripts were to be excluded from the Birthplace museum and which were to be sent to New Place. It was the opinion of the Committee that 'New Place should be acceptable for inferior articles and common books not worthy of being at the Birthplace'!

Meanwhile the librarian plodded on, working alongside the custodian as she showed visitors round the Birthplace. He obviously found the rules governing the inspection and use of books in the library inconvenient and irksome and, after discussion and recommendation from Mr Halliwell-Phillipps in 1882, he was authorized to use his discretion as to who should be allowed to see and study books and manuscripts in his custody. He must also have found the regular interference of the Trustees in the running of the library and museum distasteful, and particularly Mr Halliwell-Phillipps's insistence that certain items should be removed. In the spring of 1882 about 650 volumes and pamphlets were transferred, first to New Place and then to the newly established Shakespeare Memorial Library in Waterside.

In August 1882, when the Executive Committee was conducting its routine business, it was reported that Mr Tyndall, the librarian, had been absent for three weeks and that he had not sought permission to be away at the busiest time of the year for visitors. The Committee accordingly decided to withhold payment of his salary instalment due, without waiting for an explanation from him. This action inevitably led to a difference between employee and employers and a detailed exchange of letters, as well as special meetings of the Committee, as recorded in the minute book. In consequence Mr Tyndall tendered his resignation and ceased to be librarian on 5 December 1882. It was unfortunate that Mr Halliwell-Phillipps supported Mr Tyndall in maintaining that the Executive Committee had acted improperly in withholding Mr Tyndall's salary, and for well over a year exchange of correspondence on the issue took place. It was not until the annual meeting of 1884 that the Trustees agreed to let the matter rest.

Meanwhile, the Inspector of the Historical Manuscripts Commission, Mr J.C. Jeaffreson, visited Stratford and reported on his inspection of both the Corporation and Birthplace collections in the Commission's *Ninth Report, Part 1*, 1883. He appreciated the importance of the Shakespearian element in the Borough records: 'To the same bright genius that has made the name of this borough a household word in every civilised region of the earth, the people of Stratford-upon-Avon are indebted for the care bestowed in these later years on the restoration and ordering of their municipal archives'. As for the Birthplace manuscripts, though he referred in some detail to the Gunpowder Plot documents in the Wheler collection, his conclusions were less flattering: 'Though even their most important writings are of no great historic value, the Birthplace Museum manuscripts comprise some interesting letters and memoranda touching the successive Shakespeare Centenary Festivals, that should be perused by future historians of the borough'.

Such observations did not impress the Trustees, who had worked so hard to build up the Birthplace collections, but they added support to J.O. Halliwell-Phillipps's view that the time had come for the compilation of a descriptive calendar of the records in the Trustees' possession. Arrangements to set this in motion were agreed in May 1884. On the recommendation of Mr Halliwell-Phillipps and Mr C. M. Ingleby, an assistant in the Department of Manuscripts, British Museum, Mr G. F. Warner (afterwards Sir George Warner), was offered and accepted the task of calendaring the Birthplace collections, arrangements being made for the work to be done in London.

Warner reported on his work in 1886, pointing out that certain bound volumes of records were badly arranged and that 'the labour expended in arranging the calendar would be far better employed in arranging the papers themselves to begin with'. Consequently he recommended some rearrangement, which was actually undertaken by him in addition to the calendaring of the deeds and documents, an exercise that continued until 1894.

It took two years following Mr Tyndall's departure in 1882 before the Trustees decided to appoint another librarian. In the meantime the Executive Committee concerned itself with the routine management of the properties. Although visitors to the Birthplace totalled 12,400 during 1883, Miss Chattaway, the custodian, felt additional assistance unnecessary. She was clearly an efficient guide and, in the absence of a librarian, the trustees entrusted her with the custody of the keys to the bookcases and drawers.

Meanwhile, the Birthplace garden also received further attention in the spring of 1885, when Mr Butcher was commissioned to plant flowers with Shakespearian associations and to order loads of gravel for the paths. By this time the Trustees had come to appreciate that a well kept garden, planted with association items, added to the interest of a visit to Shakespeare's Birthplace.

An Incorporated Trust

The passing of an Act of Parliament in 1891 which incorporated the Shakespeare Birthplace Trust marked an important landmark in its history.

Although the arrangement whereby a body of Ex Officio Trustees managed the Birthplace and New Place properties vested in the Corporation of Stratford-upon-Avon in 1860 and 1876 worked satisfactorily, it appears that doubts arose as to the legal status and powers of the Trustees, especially with regard to the use of the funds which were being accumulated.

The matter was first raised and discussed at the annual meeting on 5 May 1888, when it was decided to seek the opinion of Counsel. For this purpose a case was prepared by Mr F. Haines, one of the Life Trustees, for the consideration of the Executive Committee. As subsequently approved by the Committee, the case was a recitation of the facts concerning the acquisition of the Birthplace and New Place properties and the Trust's Deeds of the same; that since the acquisition of New Place the Trustees had regarded the two trusts as practically one; that in the interests of both properties, and especially of the Birthplace, a small charge for admission had been made; that the funds arising from these admission charges had been applied indiscriminately by the Trustees to the proper guardianship, preservation and repair of the two properties and to the purchase of objects of interest for the museum and library; and that, after doing all that was necessary, funds amounting to £2,814 2s. 10d. had been accumulated and were likely to increase. The existing Trust Deeds made no provision for the use of such funds and and the Trustees were not certain that they had legal power to apply any of the accumulated money to other objects of Shakespearian or public interest not directly connected with the two properties.

Counsel's opinion was considered by the Trustees at their annual meeting in May 1890 and a sub-committee was appointed to recommend what alterations, if any, were required in the Trust Deeds. The sub-committee comprised Sir Theodore Martin, who had been appointed a Trustee in succession to J.O. Halliwell-Phillipps, Sir Arthur Hodgson, Mr F. Haines, Mr E.E. Baker and Mr C.E. Flower, and it was largely due to their experience and commitment that a solution to the problem was found. They quickly produced a report which met with the approval of the Executive Committee and instructions were given to Sir Theodore Martin to draw up a draft of a Parliamentary Bill embodying the sub-committee's views. No time was lost and in October 1890 special meetings of the Executive Committee and the full governing body were held to consider the prepared draft.

The outcome was that the Trustees formally resolved to promote a Bill in Parliament designed to clarify and define the objects of the Trust. Sir Theodore Martin and Mr Haines were authorized to take the necessary action. Promoting a Parliamentary Bill, as I discovered in 1960, can be a time-consuming business and, judging by the number of consultations and special meetings referred to in the minutes, the procedure in Victorian times was no less demanding.

Reports of the progress of the Bill through its different stages appeared in the press. No difficulty was encountered, but the matter apparently aroused considerable interest in the House of Commons. The Bill received the Royal Assent on 26 March 1891, and became law, as follows:

An Act to incorporate the Trustees and Guardians of Shakespeare's Birthplace, and to vest in them certain lands and other property in Stratford-upon-Avon, including the property known as Shakespeare's

Birthplace; and to provide for the maintenance in connection therewith of a Library and Museum; and for other purposes.

In a long, detailed preamble the Act records the various transactions and arrangements made to date in connection with the Birthplace and New Place properties and the steps taken by the Committee of Trustees for and on behalf of the nation to preserve and maintain them in perpetuity as a national memorial to William Shakespeare, and particularly with reference to the establishment of a library and museum of relics, books, manuscripts, pictures and objects illustrative of the life, times and works of William Shakespeare. To remove doubts as to the validity of this charitable enterprise, Parliamentary authority was accordingly given to vest the estate mentioned in the Trustees and Guardians of Shakespeare's Birthplace to be maintained by them 'in fit and proper order, as a permanent and national memorial of William Shakespeare', together with the library and museum, and with power to enlarge and improve the collections thereby.

The Act also specifically authorized the Trustees 'to acquire, if and as opportunity may arise, any house or lands which are of national interest as being associated with the life of William Shakespeare, or his wife or parents', particular reference being made to 'the cottage of Anne Hathaway, the wife of William Shakespeare; and also the house at Wilmcote, known as the house of Mary Arden, his mother, and any other property known or believed to have belonged to William Shakespeare, or his wife or parents'.

The Act prescribed a constitution for the Trust which remained unchanged until the amending Act of 1930. The Trustees were to be the following Ex Officio persons: the Lord Lieutenant of the County of Warwick, the High Steward of the Borough of Stratford-upon-Avon, the Mayor and Aldermen of the Borough, the Justices of the Peace for the Borough, the Town Clerk of the Borough, the Vicar of the Parish of Stratford-upon-Avon, and the Headmaster of the Free Grammar School of Stratford-upon-Avon; together with the following named Life Trustees: Ernest Edward Baker, the Reverend Charles Evans, Charles Edward Flower, Edgar Flower, Henry Graves, Frederick Haines, Sir Arthur Hodgson, K.C.M.G., Henry Irving, Sir Theodore Martin, K.C.B., and Samuel Timmins. These Ex Officio and Life Trustees were constituted a body corporate, by the name of 'the Trustees and Guardians of Shakespeare's Birthplace', with a common seal and perpetual succession.

The properties previously conveyed to the Corporation of Stratford-upon-Avon, as set out in schedules to the Act, were transferred to the newly constituted Trustees, whose status, responsibilities and powers were defined in detail. The uncertain situation with regard to funds was clarified. The Trustees were authorized to make reasonable charges for admission to the properties and to accumulate or apply any moneys derived therefrom to defray the cost of maintaining the properties and to purchase manuscripts, books, pictures and other items. In this connection they were empowered to receive bequests, donations and subscriptions of land, buildings, money, manuscripts, books, pictures and objects of art and antiquity illustrative of the life, times and works of William Shakespeare. Investment powers were prescribed, together with arrangements for the keeping and annual audit of accounts.

Subject to the provisions of the Act, the Trustees were given power to make, vary or repeal regulations for the management and administration of the Trust estate and Trust moneys and to appoint a secretary, librarian, custodian and other staff as necessary to run the organization. It was laid down that the Trustees themselves were to meet once at least in the course of every year and that they might appoint a committee of their own body of not less than eight members to exercise the delegated responsibility of managing the day-to-day business of the Trust, but with the proviso that the proceedings of such committee should be submitted to the Trustees' general meeting for confirmation or rejection. In this respect statutory confirmation was given to a pattern of management which had existed for many years previously and which then continued basically unchanged until the present time.

When the Trustees met at their Annual Meeting on 18 May 1892, the Chairman, Mr C.E. Flower, spoke enthusiastically of the significance of the Act which, following a great deal of discussion and

Mr C.E. Flower

differences of opinion, had placed the Birthplace Trust on a sound, permanent footing. Mr Flower said there had been general misapprehension that the Trustees were taking away some of the power of the Stratford-upon-Avon Corporation. The Corporation, however, as he explained, never had any power over the management of Shakespeare's Birthplace; it merely held the property in trust. He also said that what the Trustees had done at New Place had now received official approval and that, in his opinion, a certain dignity had been conferred on the Trustees by this statutory recognition.

The members of the Executive Committee lost no time in implementing the provisions of the Act.

They drew up regulations for the management of the Trust and gave Richard Savage, the Secretary and Librarian, supervisory control over the whole organization. In practice he became the chief executive officer of the Trust, being responsible for visitor management, staff, secretarial work and accounts, as well as the library, records and museum collections. At the Annual Meeting of Trustees held on 5 May 1895 it was reported that the byelaws and regulations for the protection and management of the Trust properties had worked 'most satisfactorily'.

A common seal of the Trustees and Guardians of Shakespeare's Birthplace was designed and engraved by Mr Wyon, Her Majesty's Engraver, and deposited in the safe in the records room. It has been a standing procedure from that time to the present that the seal should not be affixed to any document except in the presence of the Chairman and Secretary or, in the absence of the Chairman, of two Trustees and the Secretary. The Trust's seal was altered by Mr Allen Wyon in 1924 so that it could be used for embossing.

The 1891 Act provided a sound basis for the development of the Trust during the next four decades. Apart from the purchase of Anne Hathaway's Cottage, described in a separate chapter, during this period the Trustees acquired additional properties for the purposes of providing accommodation for their staff and preserving the amenities of the Trust's estate: in particular, a piece of land together with two cottages known as the Hornby Cottages in Henley Street, the house and garden at 19 (later 14) Henley Street, acquired for the residence of the Secretary and Librarian, and a cottage and garden ground situated in Emms Court, Sheep Street, to be occupied by the gardener, together with land and cottages immediately adjoining Anne Hathaway's Cottage. With the development of rail and road transport, the number of visitors to Shakespeare's Birthplace and the other properties continued to increase and the library, archives and museum collections were progressively built up and the potential value of them for furthering knowledge of Shakespeare's life, times and works was increasingly appreciated.

By the middle of the 1920s the Trustees felt that steps should be taken to promote an Amending Act of Parliament, to confirm their acquisitions of properties and to confer on them additional powers to further the objects of the Trust. At the same time, experience of the composition of the governing body suggested the desirability of certain alterations to the Trust's constitution.

It took some considerable time for the matter to be discussed and agreed, but on 5 December 1929 the petition for leave to introduce an amending Bill to Parliament was sealed. The Bill passed its readings in both Houses without opposition and the Royal Assent was given to the Shakespeare Birthplace etc. Trust (Amendment) Act on 15 April 1930:

> **An Act to confer further powers on the trustees and guardians of Shakespeare's Birthplace to amend the Shakespeare Birthplace etc. Trust Act 1891 and for other purposes.**

After reciting in the preamble the need for amending legislation, the Act confirmed the acquisition of properties listed in the schedule and conferred on the Trustees further powers to acquire property for the protection of, and in proximity to, or for the better management of the existing property of the Trust. This was a recognition of the need for the Trustees to be able to pursue a more positive policy in the field of conservation. Specific mention was made of Nash's House (in the Act of 1891 referred to as 'New Place' and subsequently known as 'New Place Museum'), which the Trustees were authorized to maintain as a local museum for objects of Shakespearian association or interest or objects illustrating the history of the Borough and neighbourhood.

Finally, the Trustees were given a miscellany of additional powers: to contribute to the preservation and maintenance of property of interest from its association with William Shakespeare or his family or with his period; to accept on loan and maintain any property entrusted to their care; to sell or exchange or lend duplicate articles not required for the proper working of the Trust; to produce and sell publications concerning the Trust's properties or collections; to pay fees to accepted Shakespearian scholars to lecture in the Borough on subjects of Shakespearian interest; to assist (financially or otherwise) any institution, festival occasion or scheme designed to honour William Shakespeare or for the dramatic presentation of his plays or for the general advancement of Shakespearian knowledge; to pay pensions or superannuation allowances to employees of the Trust; and to pay the reasonable travelling expenses of any Trustee in connection with attending meetings of the Trustees.

All these clauses envisaged the progressive widening of the Trust's influence as the guardian of the Shakespeare heritage, and the amendments to the constitution reflected a similar trend. The Act limited the number of Aldermen of the Borough serving as Ex Officio Trustees to seven and the number of Justices of the Peace to eleven. The most significant provision of the Act, however, was the introduction of a new category of Representative Trustees: the Universities of Oxford, Cambridge, London and Birmingham were empowered each to appoint one Trustee 'to act in the execution of the trust', to serve for a period of three years, with eligibility for reappointment. Two meetings of the Trustees each year were to be held with appropriate procedure arrangements, and the established working pattern of delegating the management of the day-to-day business of the Trust to an Executive Committee of not less than five members was confirmed.

In accordance with the provisions of the Act, the first Representative Trustees appointed by the Universities of Oxford, Cambridge, London and Birmingham were respectively Sir Edmund Kerchever Chambers, K.B.E., C.B., M.A., Professor John Dover Wilson, Litt.D., Sir Ernest Henry Pooley, M.A., LL.B., and Professor Ernest de Selincourt, M.A., M.Litt.

Thus was initiated an arrangement which over the years has added valuable expertise and prestige to the governing body of the Trust.

The Years of Richard Savage
1884–1910

The appointment of Richard Savage as Librarian in May 1884 marked a turning point in the Trust's development. The fact that the appointment was made without advertisement or interview suggests that he was already well known to the Trustees, who, after the unpleasant repercussions of Mr Tyndall's resignation, were anxious to avoid further problems. He was in fact a local man. Born at Alcester, he had started work as a pupil teacher at Hanbury, but then joined the clerical staff of Mr M.C. Ashwin, a well known local business man, at Stratford-upon-Avon.

Mr Savage readily agreed to the terms offered: an engagement on a quarterly notice at a salary of £100 a year; three weeks' annual leave to be taken with the permission of the Committee; and daily attendance excluding Sundays from 9 a.m. to 6 p.m., except during the winter months when the hours were to be 9.30 a.m. to dusk. His duties were similarly defined. As Librarian, he was to be responsible for the custody and care of the books and other articles in Shakespeare's Birthplace and New Place, for the preparation and keeping of catalogues and other records, for helping the custodian when necessary in showing the Birthplace Museum to visitors, for assisting the Town Clerk in the custody of the Borough records kept at the Birthplace, and for undertaking such other duties 'as may be reasonably imposed upon him by the Committee'.

Mr Savage took up his post on 1 June 1884 and quickly developed a routine of work: dusting and giving attention to the physical condition of the books and Borough records; listing deeds and preparing them for transmission to Mr Warner at the British Museum; compiling details of presentations; dealing with literary and personal enquiries; indexing the contents of miscellaneous volumes; exploring the Borough records; and generally assisting the custodian, with whom he seems to have established a friendly, working relationship.

When Mr John S. Leaver, who had served as Secretary to the Trustees for many years, died in 1886, Richard Savage was appointed to succeed him as Secretary, at a salary of £30 a year, and the minutes of the Trustees' meetings from this time onwards were written by him. Members of the Committee were impressed by his work and in 1892 he was asked to undertake the overall supervision of the properties vested in the Trustees. The object of his appointment as 'Superintendent', as the minutes described it, was to put an end to the division of responsibilities, which had not worked altogether satisfactorily. Thus he came to discharge the role of general manager as well as Secretary and Librarian, and he held these offices until he retired in 1910.

Savage was a methodical person, and entries in the diaries he kept illustrate his enthusiastic involvement not only with the many practical details of property management but also with the scholarly involvements of his curatorship. As the years passed, he became an authority on local history and Shakespearian subject matter and, although he had had no formal academic training, he acquired palaeographical expertise which enabled him to read and transcribe original documents. He had the instincts of a researcher, and apparently spent his holidays not relaxing at the seaside but investigating record sources at Worcester, London and occasionally Canterbury. 'For many years past', he wrote, 'I have occupied the greater part of my holidays and leisure time in endeavouring to gather together something new - and at the same time authentic - to interest and help the Shakespearean student'. In particular he devoted considerable time and effort in the 1890s visiting neighbouring parishes, and incumbents and officials as far away as Worcester, for the purpose of copying their parish registers and monumental inscriptions. Thus proceedings at the Annual Meeting of the Trust in 1891 included a vote of thanks to no fewer than thirty-nine ladies and gentlemen who had 'during the past year so readily and kindly assisted the Librarian in his researches among parish registers, parish accounts, and papers and private ... manuscripts'. Another worker in this field, J. Harvey Bloom, made during the years 1900-1910 a comprehensive collection of parochial transcripts and notes, now in the Trust's records office, which are constantly in use by students of family history. Harvey Bloom was still active in 1942, and for a short time he was employed as a temporary assistant archivist by the Trust, until he died in 1944.

Shakespeare's Birthplace

The Trustees themselves gave regular attention to the maintenance and housekeeping of the properties. In 1884 a lightning conductor was fixed on the gable end of the Birthplace by Messrs. Berry and Sons of Huddersfield at a cost of £12, and subsequently serviced at regular intervals, an arrangement which was continued whilst I was Director. During 1885 the room over the records office was prepared and furnished for use as a committee room. The Executive Committee held its meetings there, though the Annual Meetings of the Trustees were still held in the Town Hall. The heating system of piped, hot water, as originally installed in the Birthplace, proved inadequate and further apparatus, together with a new boiler, was added in 1885. This early form of central heating served for many years and I believe that the large, ugly, cast-iron pipes and coils in use in the building when I became Director dated back to this time.

In 1887, with the completion of the town's piped water system, a water supply was laid on to the custodian's house, together with a direct main, with hydrant and hose, at Shakespeare's Birthplace 'for the immediate extinction of any fire which might occur'. The hose was sited at the back of the building behind the door leading into the garden. It was there when I became Director in 1945 and I took steps to have it replaced with a modern hose reel.

Occasional references in the minutes point to the Trustees' constant anxiety about the possible risk of fire endangering the Birthplace, and how real this could be was demonstrated on 18 February 1898, when a fire destroyed premises situated six doors to the east of it. At one stage the conflagration assumed such proportions that the Secretary, Mr Savage, and others considered the whole block, including the Birthplace, Hornby cottages and the custodian's house, to be in jeopardy and that it would be impossible for the Stratford Fire Brigade to cope with such a burning mass. A telegram was accordingly sent off to the Warwick Fire Brigade, which very promptly appeared on the scene. Fortunately, owing to the wind dropping and rain falling, the fire did not spread and so the danger to the Birthplace was averted.

There followed an immediate review and overhaul of the appliances in the building, but it was not until 1904 that the Trustees decided to seek the advice of the Chief Officer of the Birmingham Fire Brigade. After an inspection he made a number of recommendations, which also covered New Place and Anne Hathaway's Cottage, and these were acted upon. In particular, a Pearson's Fire Alarm system was installed in the Birthplace; this remained in service until it was superseded by more up-to-date equipment as part of the improvements carried out in the early years of my Directorship.

The Trustees also gave regular attention to the Birthplace garden and continued to use the local nurseryman, John Butcher, to maintain it. In 1882 the beds were redesigned for the planting of flowers and ornamental shrubs mentioned in Shakespeare's works, and a further major programme of improvement was completed five years later. Good flower soil was brought in, plants were replaced, additional flowers introduced and the paths surfaced with gravel.

It was normal practice for individual members of

The Birthplace garden, about 1880

the Committee to make regular inspections of the garden, as well as of the house, with the object of ensuring a high standard of performance by the staff. When, in 1890, it was noticed that the condition of the garden was not as good as it should be, the Trustees instructed the Secretary to call Mr Butcher's attention to the situation. Reading between the lines, I suspect that the Trustees were probably expecting a little too much for what they were paying for part-time labour. In May 1892 they decided to appoint a gardener to the permanent staff, to take charge of the Birthplace and New Place gardens, and necessary tools for him were purchased. This was the beginning of the Trust's garden department.

Visitors

The day-to-day reception and handling of visitors was the responsibility of the resident custodian. When Richard Savage undertook overall management of the properties in 1892, the total number of visitors to the Birthplace for the year was 23,966. Although there was a decrease in attendances during 1893, due partly to the competition of the Chicago Exhibition, which kept some Americans away, each subsequent year saw a steady increase in admissions both to the Birthplace and the museum, which was still offered as a separate attraction. The number of visitors in 1900 was 31,748, and by the time Richard Savage retired in 1910 the annual total had reached 49,177. When this was reported to the Trust's Annual Meeting, it was pointed out that the number exceeded by 4,964 the highest total reached in any preceding year, the record hitherto having stood at 44,218 in 1908.

By this time vouchers according free admission were regularly issued to residents in the Borough of Stratford-upon-Avon, as well as to scholars, schoolchildren and approved learned societies. On an average the number was about a thousand a year. On occasions arrangements were also made for special visits. The British Medical Association, for instance, came in 1882. When the British Association for the Advancement of Science met in Birmingham in 1887, a visit to Shakespeare's Birthplace was included in the programme; and in the same year members of the Pharmaceutical Society were guest visitors. Saturday, 18 May 1895, was a high-light occasion: His Royal Highness The Prince of Wales, accompanied by the Earl and Countess of Warwick and a party from Warwick Castle, visited Shakespeare's Birthplace.

The development of rail and road transport, together with the opening of the Shakespeare Memorial Theatre in 1879, contributed significantly to the growing popularity of Shakespeare's Birthplace. In 1890 admission to the property was included in a tourist ticket to Leamington Spa and neighbourhood issued by the London and North Western Railway Company, and as the years passed railway excursions to Stratford-upon-Avon brought additional patronage. In 1905 a descriptive leaflet was prepared for presentation with the admission ticket to the Birthplace, and a translation in French was also produced.

Throughout the years the international ingredient of patronage was monitored by the Trustees. Each annual report included a table of nations represented, based on signatures and addresses in the visitors' album kept at the Birthplace. The United States always sent the greatest number. In 1887, for instance, out of a total of 16,417 admissions, 9,363 came from the British Isles, 4,482 from the United

States, and the remainder from some thirty-six other nations. It is interesting to note that Americans continued to equal about half the number of British visitors. Out of a total of 42,246 in 1909, for example, 18,541 were from the United Kingdom and 9,790 from the United States.

From 1882 Miss Maria Charlotte Chattaway served as the resident custodian of Shakespeare's Birthplace. She was assisted on occasions by her sister, Miss Caroline, and during the summer months, when most of the visitors arrived, by a seasonal guide, Mr Isaac Edwin Baker, who had previously been master of the Snitterfield school. She received a salary of £100 a year and occupied the custodian's house at the end of the garden, free of rent and rates and with fuel provided. She was expected to be available to receive visitors to the house during the prescribed opening hours and generally to look after the housekeeping of the building. Miss Chattaway apparently discharged her duties in a most courteous and efficient manner, but after seventeen years the mounting pressure of handling the growing number of visitors led her to decide to retire in the spring of 1899. The Trustees placed on record their appreciation of her excellent work and decided to award a joint pension of £50 a year in recognition of the service she and her sister had given. This grant of an annuity to a long-serving member of staff set a precedent which the Trustees followed over the years; it was not until 1946, however, that a pension scheme for all full-time staff was introduced.

The vacant position of custodian at Shakespeare's Birthplace was subsequently advertised and, following interviews of short-listed candidates, Mr and Mrs Joseph Skipsey, formerly custodians of the Durham College of Science at Newcastle upon Tyne, were appointed by the Trustees at a special meeting held on 12 June 1889. Unfortunately this proved to be a short-term arrangement, because the Skipseys resigned on 31 July 1891. The two ladies who succeeded them as joint custodians remained less than two years and were followed by the Misses Hancock, who stayed the course for seven years. Mr and Mrs Alfred Rose of Erdington were appointed joint custodians in 1900, and for the next twenty years the Trustees had no further staffing problems.

When Alfred Rose died in 1910, his widow, Mrs Mary Rose, was appointed chief attendant at the Birthplace and she continued in this capacity until her death in 1921. She discharged her duties with considerable enthusiasm and expertise, and went out of her way to keep in touch with some of the more interesting visitors she showed round the property. These included Mr Henry Clay Folger, the American collector and founder of the Folger Shakespeare Library in Washington, DC; indeed, the Library holds a collection of Mrs Mary Rose's letters and papers, including correspondence concerning the purchase of a carved, mulberry-wood casket.

Mrs Rose was succeeded by Frederick William Tompkins, the assistant custodian at the Parish Church, who was still in charge at the Birthplace when I arrived in 1945. Thus the pattern of long service which has been such a noteworthy feature of the Trust's history started in late Victorian times.

New Place

At the beginning of 1881, Mr T.W. Salmon, who had given valuable service as the custodian of New Place, resigned owing to ill health, and the Trustees gave him £50 in recognition of his service. Out of ten applicants for the post, Mr Bower Bulmer of Loxley was appointed to succeed him as custodian, at a salary of £30 per annum (increased to £3 per month in 1884) plus accommodation, rent and rates free. Mr Bulmer died in 1888 after serving for seven years, and the Trustees appointed his widow to succeed him. Mrs Bulmer died in 1896, and it was at this juncture that Richard Savage, by then Secretary and Librarian of the Trust, was appointed custodian on the same terms, on condition that, with the assistance of his daughters, he undertook to perform the same duties hitherto carried out by Mrs Bulmer. In practice, this turned out to be an excellent arrangement, because the resident Savage family proved to be most satisfactory custodians.

From the beginning, Nash's House (Thomas Nash married Shakespeare's grand-daughter, Elizabeth Hall), situated next door to the foundations of New Place, was styled New Place Museum. Repairs to it were carried out in 1881. The following year a hurricane damaged the mulberry tree, a scion of the one planted by Shakespeare when he lived at New Place, and Mr John Butcher was summoned to render the tree safe and secure by placing iron stays under the heavier branches. In 1883 the Trustees decided to open the garden at New Place free of charge during the summer months, and an assistant custodian was employed to protect the excavations there from damage. The arrangement worked satisfactorily and, although the custodian and Mr Butcher had to be paid more for the extra work of invigilation involved, the free admissions were continued from this time onwards. Evening band concerts were given there by the local Rifle Volunteer Drum and Fife band.

By this time the alto-relievo Shakespeare statue, which had adorned the Boydell Gallery in Pall Mall, London, had been donated by Mr C.H. Bracebridge and erected in the Great Garden, as it became known. Mr Baker of Wellesbourne was employed by the Trustees to overhaul and restore it in 1883, and the statue received further attention in 1892, when it was 'carefully cleaned and a cornice added for its better protection and preservation'. By 1888 the gardens at New Place were reported to have been 'judiciously laid out and planted with the choicest trees and shrubs', many of which had been given by the inhabitants of the town and also visitors.

The Trustees' appointment of a full-time gardener in 1892, as already mentioned, made possible a more regular routine of maintenance, and during

The site of New Place

The alto-relievo statue of Shakespeare

the next few years various improvements and plantings were made. A greenhouse was erected in 1894 and was later replaced by a new one in 1906. Meanwhile, in 1901 the Trustees purchased the

The mulberry tree in New Place garden

cottage adjoining the north-east corner of the garden, access to which was from Emms Court in Sheep Street, to provide a residence for the gardener. In practice it was a highly convenient arrangement to have the gardener and his family living alongside the greenhouse.

Incidentally, on 26 August 1907 a strong gale broke off three great branches from the mulberry tree nearby, and steps had to be taken at once to support the trunk and the remaining branches by 'powerful ironwork'. It is due to the efficacy of the remedial work done at this time that the old mulberry tree still survives and appears to be in a remarkably healthy condition.

At the Annual Meeting of the Trustees in 1907, reference was made to drainage work undertaken at the properties for the purpose of linking the rainwater drains to the town sewer, which by that time had become available. In the course of work at New Place, portions of very early brick walls and the remains of foundations had been excavated which formed the eastern end of the great house built on the site by Sir Hugh Clopton in the late fifteenth century. This discovery was important as giving an idea of the dimensions of the house, which had a considerable frontage to Chapel Lane. A well which supplied water to the house was also found. Three feet in diameter and twenty-four feet deep, it was fed by a spring of water to a level of eight feet. These foundations were accordingly laid out for the inspection of visitors who came to make contact with the physical remains of Shakespeare's retirement home.

Year by year the number of visitors to New Place was recorded in the Trustees' annual report. Compared with Shakespeare's Birthplace, the museum there had a limited appeal. Although 488 people visited it in 1877, during the next ten years the annual number was well below 400. When the remaining foundations were excavated in 1900, the total number was 597, but this was not equalled again until 1910, when attendances reached 611. With income based on a 6d. admission charge, it is not surprising that the upkeep of New Place and the gardens proved a constant anxiety to the Trustees.

Hornby Cottage as today

Hornby Cottage

Mention has already been made of the Trustees' concern about the risk of fire to Shakespeare's Birthplace and the desirability of isolating it further from neighbouring buildings. In particular, it was felt that the two cottages adjoining the Birthplace garden on its eastern boundary, which were, during Shakespeare's lifetime, in the occupation of Hornby the blacksmith, constituted a possible danger to the safety of the house.

It was therefore with considerable satisfaction that the Chairman, Mr Edgar Flower, reported to the Annual Meeting of the Trustees in 1902 that, as the result of his approach to him, Mr Andrew Carnegie, the Scottish business man and philanthropist who was well known for his gifts for libraries, had purchased the property in question and donated it to the Trust. The prospect of demolishing the Hornby cottages thus acquired, as a further precaution against fire, and at the same time enlarging the area of the Birthplace garden, was received with enthusiasm, at least by some of the Trustees. There were others who questioned whether the Trustees were legally empowered under the 1891 Act to demolish the premises in question, the primary objective of the Trust being to preserve and not to destroy. Misleading, erroneous rumours as to the Trust's intentions circulated locally, and the fact that Mr Carnegie had also given money to establish a free library for the town in Henley Street added confusion.

The issue was hotly debated at meetings of the Executive Committee and by the full governing body of the Trustees at the Annual Meeting in 1904, presided over by Sir Sidney Lee, the eminent Shakespeare scholar, who, having been elected a Life Trustee, had taken over as Chairman after the sudden death of Mr Edgar Flower in 1903. Although no decision was reached, Sir Sidney suggested a course of action designed to further the development of the Trust. He stressed the need to provide facilities for students to consult the Trust's library out of range of 'the turmoil of sightseers'; this was not possible as long as the books and manuscripts remained, together with the Librarian's desk, in the upper room of the Birthplace museum. The Trustees themselves also required, and deserved, he suggested, more suitable accommodation for their meetings; they needed 'a habitable and well ventilated room' where they might conduct business without interruption.

It accordingly fell to the Executive Committee to devise a plan to incorporate these ideas and, with the help of Mr Holtom, the local architect, a proposal was prepared with an estimated cost of £1,200 for submission to a special meeting of the Trustees held on 8 October 1904. The original idea of demolishing the Hornby cottages was abandoned, and a decision made to repair and adapt the property for the Trust's own use.

The plan converted the two cottages into one unit, now called Hornby Cottage, together with the adjoining custodian's house, and provided for a new ticket office, board room, Secretary's office, store room, and library where students might have facilities of access to the Trust's collections. The work of repair and adaptation was carried out forthwith and completed by the summer of 1905.

The availability of this additional accommodation made possible certain rearrangements for the Trust's administration and library. As from 1 July 1905, visitors to Shakespeare's Birthplace were required to purchase their admission tickets at the new ticket office situated at the front of Hornby Cottage and then to proceed along the street to enter the Birthplace by the door under the penthouse. This in fact was the procedure followed when I became Director. A descriptive leaflet about the Trust's properties was prepared for presentation with the tickets, together with a translation into French for those needing it. Within a short time it was found that these new admission arrangements worked very satisfactorily; a total of more than 35,000 visitors took advantage of them during that year and from this time numbers progressively increased.

On the first floor of Hornby Cottage the whole of the front part of the building was opened up, with the original sixteenth-century, oak, timber structure exposed, to provide a spacious board room for the Trustees' meetings, together with space for office use. The exterior brickwork of the walls, which had been added during the eighteenth century, remained. Thanks to the generosity of Andrew Carnegie, the headquarters of the Shakespeare Birthplace Trust were accordingly moved from Shakespeare's Birthplace to Hornby Cottage. As will be described later, in 1913 the old custodian's house adjoining at the rear was reconstructed to provide a large, attractive room leading off the board room to serve as the Secretary's office and library.

The Library and Museum

Richard Savage's term of office saw the progressive build-up of the Trust's library, archive and museum collections. Gifts were received and acknowledged in each annual report. They comprised books, deeds and local historical records, copies of documents, coins, pictures and prints, together with Shakespeare relics in considerable variety. Some of the items were displayed in the Birthplace museum, but others, of lesser interest and importance, were transferred to New Place.

A few typical and some significant accessions during this period may be mentioned. In 1886 the Trustees received a gift of 147 deeds and documents relating to Stratford-upon-Avon and neighbourhood, 20 of them concerning the property formerly known as the White Lion inn in Henley Street. In the event the latter turned out to be of special significance, since the Trustees came to own the property and the Shakespeare Centre extension was later built on the site of the White Lion. In the same year the Trustees spent £5 on purchasing deeds of release and purchase of New Place from Sir John Clopton to Hugh Clopton, dated January 1699.

Following the death of James Orchard Halliwell-Phillipps in 1889, his major collection of volumes of notes on Shakespeare's plays, consisting of manuscripts, commentary and original cuttings from early printed books, which had previously been donated subject to conditions in 1872, came into the absolute ownership of the Trustees. Altogether, the collection comprised 186 volumes. Halliwell-Phillipps had been extremely generous to the Trust during his lifetime, frequently presenting copies of rare books - as for example the second complete edition of Ovid's *Metamorphoses*, 1567, and one of the limited editions of his publications, together with prints, pamphlets and miscellaneous Shakespeareana.

In 1896 the Trustees received a valuable bequest. By the will of Mrs Harriet Beisley of Sydenham, Kent, the Trustees were given a library of over a thousand books, pictures and £300 to be invested in support of the museum. Mrs Beisley's husband had been an ardent admirer of Shakespeare and was the author of a work published in 1864 on *Shakespeare's Garden*. He had a particular interest in the history of gardens, plants and herbs but, as reflected in the wide range of subject matter of the books he collected, he was a man of liberal instincts and catholic taste. His library contained some early printed books of great rarity and Shakespearian interest.

Among them was a copy of *Wits Treasury, The Second Part*, 1634, the second impression of a work first issued in 1598 containing the tribute of Francis Meres to Shakespeare's genius. Holinshed's *Chronicles of England, Ireland and Scotland*, 1586, the second and enlarged edition, was the standard book on English history in Shakespeare's age and the source of the plots of almost all the dramatist's history plays. Thomas Wilson's *The Arte of Rhetorike*, in the revised edition of 1567, was a treatise on rhetoric or prose composition from which Shakespeare seems to have drawn many ideas and phrases. Wilson, for instance, appears to have anticipated the character and language of Dogberry, when citing examples of the talk of 'a good fellow of the countery being an officer and mayor of a town, and desirous to speak like a fine learned man, having just occasion to rebuke a runnegate fellow'.

Other important books included in the Beisley bequest were John Lyly's *Euphues and his England*, 1588, containing his famous didactic romance and light comedies, with which Shakespeare seems to have been familiar; *The grete herball*, 1529; the *Herbal* of William Turner, 1568; and *A Hermeticall Banquet, Drest by a Spagiricall Cook*, 1652, a jeu d'esprit on cookery books, good-naturedly ridiculing literary affectations.

The money from the Beisley bequest was invested in two-and-a-half per cent Consols and the interest earned was spent in subsequent years to buy an occasional book for the library. When I became Director, some of the rare books mentioned above were exhibited in Shakespeare's Birthplace; the remainder of the Beisley collection was shelved separately from the general book stock, and it was not until the Shakespeare Centre was built in 1964 that the Beisley books were catalogued and integrated into the main library.

Accessions were varied, and illustrated the range of the Trust's developing collections. In 1891 the Trustees acquired the court rolls of the manor of Henley-in-Arden, together with certain rolls of the manor of Stratford-upon-Avon. The following year accessions included items ranging from an Elizabethan pewter spoon to deeds of local properties, together with Shakespeare prints and copies of a variety of editions of Shakespeare's plays. In 1896 the Trustees purchased the celebrated mulberry wood table from Mr Thomas Hunt for £75, together with the account for making it and its full history. It appears that this impressive piece of furniture, a circular table with top inlaid with mulberry wood, was made in 1825 for Thomas Hunt, son of William Hunt who secured a large portion of the mulberry wood when the tree at New Place was cut down by

Circular mulberry wood table

Francis Gastrell in 1756. For many years it was one of the principal exhibits in the New Place Museum.

With more funds available, the Trustees made a number of important purchases during the next few years. The portraits in oil of David Garrick and Mrs Garrick, at present on display in Stratford's Town Hall, were acquired in 1897. In the following year the Trustees purchased by auction at Sotheby's a very fine copy of the First Folio of Shakespeare's plays, published in 1623, for the sum of £585 plus £30 commission paid to Sotheran and Company for bidding on behalf of the Trust. The Folio was collated with the Grenville Folio in the British Museum and it was certified to be 'quite perfect' and 'the two short leaves' to be genuine. Steps were immediately taken to have an iron, fire-proof safe made to accommodate this new exhibit for display in the Birthplace.

It was also at this time that Sir Theodore Martin, who had been a Life Trustee since 1888, presented to the Trust a fine copy of the *Second Folio*, 1632. This volume had been the property of the late Lady Theodore Martin, neé Helen Faucit, and bears on the front flyleaf her ladyship's inscription to the effect that it was presented to her by Reginald Cholmondeley, Esq., of Condover Hall, Shropshire, in 1878.

Mr. WILLIAM
SHAKESPEARES
COMEDIES,
HISTORIES, &
TRAGEDIES.

Published according to the True Originall Copies.

Gentle Maister Shakespear.

LONDON
Printed by Isaac Iaggard, and Ed. Blount. 1623

First Folio title page

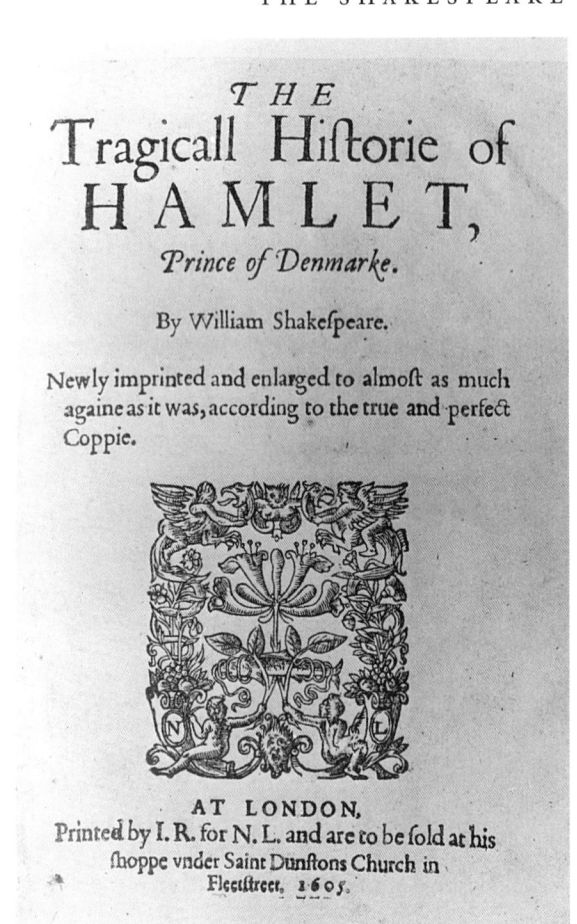

Quarto title page of Hamlet

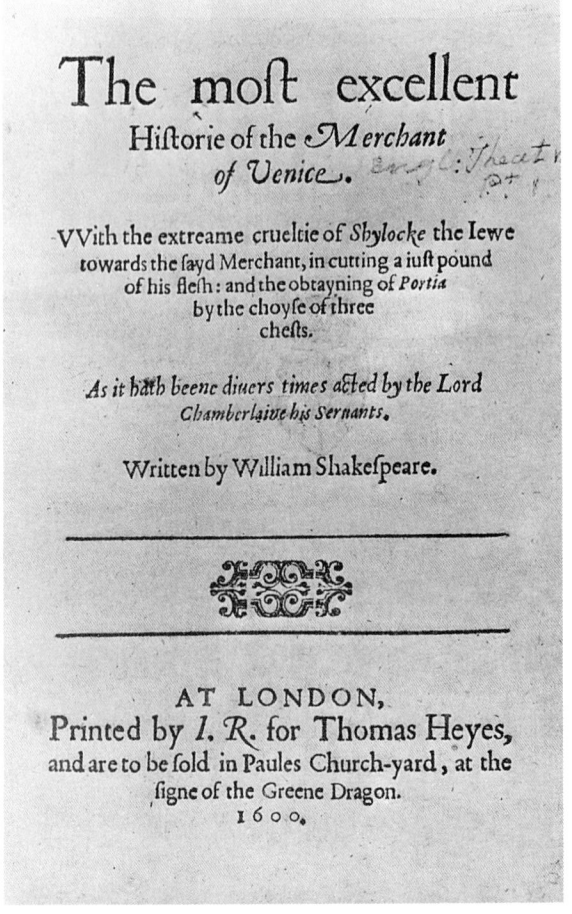

Quarto title page of The Merchant of Venice

In 1899 Mr Ernest E. Baker, another Life Trustee, presented an autograph of 'Jon Hall' on condition that it should have a permanent home in the Birthplace museum and not in the Corporation's archive room. At the same time the Trustees purchased two fine, old, carved coffers, which had been sold out of the birthroom at the sale of the property in 1847. They were secured for the sum of £157 13s. 5d., through the courtesy of Mr Rochelle Thomas, antiquarian and medallist to Queen Victoria and the royal family, who expressed a wish that they should 'be placed in the original position in the room in which Shakespeare was born'. Another associated item, acquired in 1902, was a carved box made from oak of the old market cross in High Street (taken down in 1821) and inlaid with the genuine mulberry wood from the tree at New Place.

The beginnings of the Trust's collection of coins date back to the turn of the century, with the acquisition of some rare items: a silver three-farthings piece dated 1561 and a farthing token of the 'Mearemayd Tavern, Cheapside'; a Stratford halfpenny bearing 'Gulielmus Shakespeare' on the obverse, issued in 1781; and an Elizabethan sixpence dated 1580.

The influence of Sir Sidney Lee soon became apparent after his election as Chairman of the Trust in 1903. Further improvements in the organization of the library and museum were made, and the Trustees embarked on a policy of building up a collection of original books such as Shakespeare may have used and of adding to the pictorial illustrations of the poet's career already held. Copies of the original portraits at Dulwich College were obtained of fellow actors Richard Burbage, Nathan Field and William Sly, and the Warwickshire poet, Michael Drayton. Copies were also made of portraits of the Earl of Southampton and John Fletcher, belonging to the Duke of Portland, of Francis Beaumont and Thomas Sackville at the National Portrait Gallery, and of John Lowin, Shakespeare's fellow actor, in the Ashmolean Museum.

With regard to books acquired, mention may be made of a few of the more important items: a copy of Florio's *World of Wordes*, an Italian-English dictionary published in 1598, which bears the autograph signature of its first owner, George Carew of Clopton, afterward Earl of Totnes, the chief magistrate in Stratford in Shakespeare's time; a fine copy of the rare first edition of Florio's translation of *Montaigne's Essays* from the library of the late Lord Amherst of Hackney; and Roger Ascham's *The Schole Maister*, 1571, a practical treatise on education, which enjoyed great repute in Shakespeare's early life. Copies of the rare Quarto editions of *The Merchant of Venice* and *King Lear* were purchased unbound from Bernard Quaritch and subsequently bound by Messrs. Riviere; also copies of two further Quarto editions of Shakespeare's plays. These were described in detail by the Chairman in a booklet published by the Trustees in 1908: *Four Quarto Editions of Plays by Shakespeare, the Property of the Trustees and Guardians of Shakespeare's Birthplace, described by Sir Sidney Lee*, LL.D., D.Litt., *with Five Illustrations in Facsimile*.

In the meantime, Richard Savage had been busy compiling a complete updated version of a descriptive catalogue of the contents of the library and museum, with critical notes on the history of objects, books and documents exhibited. The resultant *Catalogue of the Books, Manuscripts, Works of Art, Antiquities and Relics exhibited in Shakespeare's Birthplace* was published by the Trustees in 1910. The *Catalogue* was subsequently revised by F.C. Wellstood in 1925 and was reissued at intervals until 1911.

Richard Savage, 1891

Mr Savage's Retirement

At their Annual Meeting on 6 May 1910, the Trustees decided to ask the Executive Committee to consider ways and means of reorganizing the museums at Shakespeare's Birthplace, New Place and Anne Hathaway's Cottage. The Committee accordingly commissioned Mr W.H. St. John Hope, M.A., F.S.A., Assistant Secretary of the Society of Antiquaries, to make a detailed survey and report with recommendations for future arrangements.

In accordance with instructions, Mr St. John Hope visited Stratford-upon-Avon and on various dates between 6 and 18 October 1910 he inspected and checked the whole of the collections in the Birthplace, together with the books in the library and the manuscripts in the records room; at the same time he inspected and made an inventory of the contents of Anne Hathaway's Cottage and New Place Museum. His resultant report, dated 28 October 1910, provided a complete record of the Trust's collections at that time. Copies were printed for private circulation to the Trustees: *A Detailed Report on the Present State of the Collections belonging to the Trust*.

Having considered this report, members of the Executive Committee agreed that its recommendations should be progressively implemented. However, they reached the conclusion that the Trustees would not be justified in entrusting to Mr Savage, who was now sixty-four years old, the new and heavy task of rearranging the collections, since they appreciated that this would need to be the main preoccupation of the Secretary and Librarian for some time.

The Committee therefore invited Mr Savage to retire on 31 March 1911 on a superannuation allowance, a course to which he assented. Having regard to his many years of service and his invaluable work for the Trust, the Trustees awarded Mr Savage a pension of £150 a year. Arrangements were then set in motion for the appointment of a successor. An advertisement attracted 182 applications. Mr Frederick Christian Wellstood, M.A., who had been superintendent of the new reading room at the Bodleian Library and senior assistant there since 1902, was appointed as Secretary and Librarian of the Trust at a salary of £200 a year, with a free residence, rising by annual increments of £10 to £300 per annum.

Savage's retirement marked the end of a chapter of impressive development in the early history of the Trust. In a quiet, unassuming manner, he gave liberally of his time and expertise to his work, and he came to be recognized as an authority on the collections in his care. A tablet recording his years of service is displayed, alongside a similar one for his successor, Frederick Wellstood, in the Trust's records office.

Anne Hathaway's Cottage

The purchase of Anne Hathaway's Cottage for preservation as a national memorial by the Trustees in 1892 marked another milestone in the early history of the Trust.

This property at Shottery, originally a twelve-roomed farmhouse, owned and occupied in Shakespeare's time by the yeoman family of Hathaway, had been recognized as the maiden home of Shakespeare's wife, Anne Hathaway, from the eighteenth century. In his *Picturesque Views on the Upper, or Warwickshire Avon, ...*, published in 1795, Samuel Ireland recorded his visit to the Cottage, which was occupied by descendants of Anne Hathaway's family, and included a drawing of the property. He was shown round the house by an old woman of upwards of seventy, who told him she had slept in the Hathaway bed from her childhood. She absolutely refused to part with the bed, but sold to him as souvenirs a chair called Shakespeare's courting chair and a small purse that had belonged - so she said - to Shakespeare.

With the help of journal entries and guide book descriptions, it is possible to trace the developing attraction of the Cottage to visitors during the nineteenth century. In his journal the Reverend William Harness recorded his visit to Shottery on 20 August 1844 and described in detail the various rooms with their furnishings, which he was shown by Mrs Baker, 'a well behaved most respectable person', who clearly took pride in welcoming visitors and showing them the family heirlooms. When, a few years later in 1847, May's *Illustrated Guide* was published, the Cottage was written up as one of the town's visitor attractions, and the various guide books which followed in later years all contained descriptions of the property.

Although there are no statistics available, the evidence suggests that, with the growing visitor

Ireland's engraving of the Cottage in 1795

Blight's drawing of the Cottage interior

patronage at Shakespeare's Birthplace, the number of those visiting Anne Hathaway's Cottage gradually increased and the resident custodian, Mrs Mary Baker, a lineal descendant of the Hathaway family, proved a popular guide. It also appears that on occasions enthusiastic pilgrims were accorded the privilege of acquiring souvenir items to which associations with Shakespeare or the Hathaway family were attributed. In fact the Cottage was being managed and exploited much in the same way as Shakespeare's Birthplace had been before it was

Anne Hathaway's Cottage

purchased for preservation as a national monument.

This situation was of course known to the local Trustees, who realized that it was highly desirable that the Trust should acquire the property to ensure its preservation and proper management as a national memorial to Shakespeare. However, it was not until the 1891 Act of Parliament conferred power on the Trustees to acquire Anne Hathaway's Cottage that it proved possible for action to be taken.

In June and July 1891 negotiations were entered into with Alderman William Thompson of Evesham Road, Stratford-upon-Avon, for the purchase of Anne Hathaway's Cottage, of which he owned the freehold. Alderman Thompson's asking price of £3,300 was considered too high by the Executive Committee and no further progress was made until March 1892, when the owner advertised the property for sale in two London newspapers, the *London Star* and the *Daily Telegraph*. Fearing that the Cottage might fall into undesirable ownership, negotiations with Alderman Thompson were renewed and a final offer obtained from him to sell the estate to the Trustees for the sum of £3,000.

Special meetings of the Executive Committee were quickly held and the matter was thoroughly considered. The Trust's investments at this time amounted to £2,814 2s. 10d., so the need to raise additional funds had to be carefully weighed. On 31 March 1892 a resolution accepting Alderman Thompson's final offer to sell for £3,000 was unanimously agreed. Although the Committee felt the purchase price was very large, its members could not prudently refuse to accept it, more especially since there was a real prospect of buying from Mrs Baker the furniture and autograph books in the Cottage.

The Committee's decision was reported to the Annual Meeting of the Trustees held on 5 May 1892. Sir Theodore Martin, Mr Frederick Haines and Mr E.E. Baker, Life Trustees who were unable to be present, sent letters of support and, with the exception of one dissentient voice, the purchase was unanimously approved and authority given to negotiate for the furniture. It was the Vicar of Stratford-upon-Avon, the Reverend George Arbuthnot, who made 'a respectful protest', firstly because in his view the price paid was too high, and secondly because he felt that the Executive Committee had exceeded its power in spending such a large sum of money without consulting the full governing body. He did not accept that the time factor and other circumstances justified such action.

The conveyance of the sale was executed on 24 May 1892, and in the meantime negotiations with Mrs Baker concerning the furniture in the Cottage proceeded. In the event the lady turned out to be a very determined person, who demanded a payment of £500 together with a continued custodianship tenure. She remained adamant in refusing to accept a smaller sum suggested by the Trustees and, after special meetings of the Committee, a compromise arrangement was suggested. On 16 July 1893 Mrs Baker agreed to take £500 for the Hathaway furniture and effects, on condition that she should remain in the Cottage, rent free, as custodian at the yearly salary of £75. An important condition, however, was her undertaking to work in accordance with the rules and regulations laid down by the Trustees. Her son, William Baker, who occupied part of the Cottage, was to be allowed to continue to reside there, rent free, for the rest of his life and to assist her with the duties of custodian.

Thus the first steps were taken to put the management of Anne Hathaway's Cottage on a proper basis: opening times and charges for visitors were laid down by the Trustees; Sunday opening was forbidden; printed admission tickets were brought into use and proper accounting procedure adopted. The admission fee was 1s. 0d. for adults and 6d. for children. The acceptance of gratuities by the staff was not allowed. Money taken during the first month, October 1892, when these arrangements operated amounted to £9 16s. 6d.; in March it fell to £3 2s. 0d. and in December £1 5s. 0d. In August of the following year, the peak of the visiting season, takings amounted to £28 8s. 3d.

So far as financial return was concerned, the acquisition of Anne Hathaway's Cottage did not at first appear to be a good investment. However,

Mary Baker on the steps of the Cottage

further expenditure was made to improve the condition of the property and the garden setting. In 1893 a small strip of land on the northern boundary was purchased for the nominal sum of £4 10s. 10d. and the old drain at the back of the house was replaced by a new one, the Cottage wall underpinned and a boundary fence erected. A major item of maintenance, the rethatching of the roof, was put in hand in November 1896. Subsequently a programme of cleaning and repairing the portion of the Cottage open to the public was undertaken. In 1897, during the progress of this work, two ancient lights which had evidently been blocked up for generations in the old sitting room were revealed and were carefully restored. Lightning conductors 'of the most modern and approved kind' were provided at the Cottage by Mr Whincop of Birmingham in 1898.

At the Trust's Annual Meeting held on 5 May 1899 Mr Ernest Baker, one of the Life Trustees present, reported that, in a private capacity, he had that day visited Anne Hathaway's Cottage and he was pleased to say that 'everything was in the best of order' and he was 'charmed with the courteous attention given to visitors'. I suspect he had been welcomed by Mrs Mary Baker, who in spite of her advanced years was still acting as guide. By this time she must have been noticeably frail, since a few months earlier the Executive Committee had decided to provide a fire-guard because of the danger of this elderly lady falling into the fire.

Mrs Mary Baker, described by the Chairman of the Trust as 'the faithful custodian of Anne Hathaway's Cottage who had resided there upwards of 80 years', died on 25 September 1899, aged eighty-seven. Her passing marked the end of an era characterized by a style of visitor guiding which, on occasions, embellished the facts with fanciful story telling. Mrs Baker had become identified with the Cottage because of her friendly welcome to visitors as she stood at the entrance in her Victorian dress and bonnet. Paying tribute to her services, the Vicar of Stratford-upon-Avon said that 'no future custodian would ever hope to present the picturesque appearance which Mrs Baker did as she stood at the door of Anne Hathaway's Cottage to welcome visitors'. Sir Benjamin Stone's photograph of her in this position is a classic recording of her in action.

William Baker succeeded as custodian on the same terms as his mother, assisted by his wife. They were reminded that the Trustees' rules concerning the management of the property must be observed; in particular, gratuities were strictly prohibited and admission of visitors on Sundays was not allowed except by order of the Trustees. Sadly, Mrs Jane Baker died in the autumn of 1901, but her husband continued as custodian, with the help of his two daughters, until he retired in 1910.

With the change of custodianship, the Executive Committee undertook a general review of matters affecting the preservation of the Cottage. The hazard of fire risk continued to be an anxiety. There was as yet no mains water supply for use in the event of an emergency, and open fires were used by the custodian for heating and cooking. How seriously the Trustees took their responsibilities in this matter can be judged from the fact that, at the suggestion of Mr Edgar Flower, Mr Guy Dawber, F.R.I.B.A., a London architect, was called in to inspect the Cottage and to report on the fire risk aspect. In his detailed report he gave his opinion that 'in view of long term use of open fires and the construction of flues and chimneys there seemed little fire risk in the continued use of open fires', but he recommended that a stone kerb should be placed round the fireplace in the sitting room, as in the kitchen, that iron bars should support the kettle ratchet instead of the timber branches across the chimney opening, that the burning of wood in any of the fires be prohibited - only coal or coke allowed - and that the chimneys be regularly swept. With regard to lamps and candles, he saw no reason to anticipate trouble. These recommendations were accepted and acted upon. For the record, open fires were still being used and provided the only source of heating in winter when I became Director, and it was not until the 1950s, when an electricity supply was introduced, making possible alternative heating, that they were discontinued. I was then relieved of the increasingly difficult task of finding a chimney sweep who could tackle the wide, open chimneys in the traditional manner.

The years of Mr Baker's custodianship were comparatively uneventful, apart from the flood of 31 December 1900, when the water from Shottery Brook and the ditch in the field at the rear of the Cottage flooded the roadway and the garden up to the steps leading to the front door of the house. I recall that a similar flood occurred on 11 July 1968, when the approach to the Cottage was completely cut off. I have a photograph of the extraordinary scene showing some young, enthusiastic visitors wading through the water up to their knees as they attempted to reach the entrance to the Cottage.

Flood at the Cottage in 1968

Since that time the Severn-Trent Water Authority has carried out improvements to the brook course and the danger of further flooding has receded.

Between 1895, when statistics became available, and 1910, when Richard Savage retired, the annual number of visitors to Anne Hathaway's Cottage increased by three fold. Actual numbers were as follows:

1895	9,598	1905	18,335
1900	13,652	1907	23,209
1902	15,060	1910	28,368

The Cottage had already become a close runner-up to the Birthplace.

William Baker retired on 31 May 1910 and was succeeded by Frederick Bennett, who had been ticket clerk at Shakespeare's Birthplace since 1905. Mr Baker's departure coincided with the arrival of Frederick Wellstood, the Trust's new Secretary and Librarian. The fortunes of Anne Hathaway's Cottage under his direction will be described in a later chapter.

The Wellstood Era
1910–1942

By the time Frederick C. Wellstood became Secretary and Librarian on 1 November 1910, the Birthplace Trust was firmly established with defined legal and educational responsibilities associated with the conservation of the Shakespearian properties. During the next thirty-two years, until Wellstood's death in 1942, the arrangements which had been evolved to take care of the management of Shakespeare's Birthplace, New Place and Anne Hathaway's Cottage continued to function and develop along lines already established by the early Trustees, and the library, archives and museum collections were steadily increased and used.

Progress, however, was affected by national and international events: the years of the First World War, 1914-18, placed the very existence of the Trust in jeopardy; the general strike of 1926 produced serious recession resulting in a considerable reduction of the Trust's income, as did the economic depression of the early 1930s; and in a similar way the Second World War, of 1939 to 1945, brought a setback to the Trust's normal conduct of activities. The important point is that the Trustees coped with these ups and downs in a characteristically statesmanlike manner.

Having been appointed in 1903, Sir Sidney Lee, the eminent Shakespeare scholar and editor of the *Dictionary of National Biography*, was firmly in control as Chairman and played an active part in formulating policy until his death in 1926. He was succeeded by an equally dedicated Chairman in the person of Mr (later Sir) Archibald Flower, who still held that position when I was appointed Director. I say more about Sir Archibald in a later chapter.

The Executive Committee continued to meet at monthly intervals, and two or three of its members

Sir Sidney Lee

were regularly appointed to serve as a visiting committee responsible for inspecting the properties and reporting their findings and recommendations, if any, at the next meeting. The whole governing body met twice a year, usually in May and October. As from 1924, a third meeting was held for a number of years at the Public Record Office in London. I suspect this was arranged to meet the convenience of the Master of the Rolls, Lord Hanworth of Hanworth, who, having been appointed High Steward of the Borough of Stratford-upon-Avon, had become an Ex-Officio Trustee. He took a very serious interest in the affairs of the Trust, along with the Life Trustees, who at that time included Mr Ernest Edward Baker, Mr Lionel Cust, Sir Francis Robert Benson, Mr Ernest Law and Mr Albert Mansbridge.

The minutes of the Trustees' proceedings were recorded in meticulous detail and the Annual Meetings were reported in the *Stratford-upon-Avon Herald*. Accounting arrangements remained simple but effective, and an audited statement of income and expenditure was published with an annual report on the work of the Trust. For thirty-seven years, until his death in 1924, Mr Francis Ladbury Thompson served as auditor of the Trust's accounts. Messrs. Sharp Parsons and Co, chartered accountants of Birmingham, who acted as auditors for Flowers Brewery and the Shakespeare Memorial Theatre, were appointed auditors to the Trustees in his place and, until the 1960s when this family practice became part of a larger accounting firm (later KPMG Peat Marwick), they served the Trust in an honorary capacity. Throughout, the Trustees used as bankers the Stratford Old Bank, which was taken over by the Midland Bank in 1914. The ex-officio representation on the governing body ensured a close and mutually helpful relationship with the Borough Council, while the active involvement of members of the Flower family provided a link with the Shakespeare Memorial Theatre.

Staffing requirements remained very modest. Apart from the Secretary and Librarian, there were custodians at the three properties, helped by assistant guides as required, mostly part-time, during the summer months when most of the visitors arrived. The winter months, with shorter opening hours to the public, were very quiet; the thought of having a package tour from Japan in the middle of January was something no one could have anticipated at this time!

As yet there was no set pattern for an annual staff review, but at intervals the Trustees considered the circumstances and performance of each member of staff and agreed appropriate revisions in pay. In 1927, for instance, when the total number of employees was still less than twenty, increases in remuneration were given in some instances. The two senior guides at Shakespeare's Birthplace had their wages increased to £3 a week and the ticket clerk to £2 15s. 0d. The head gardener received £4 a week and his assistant £3 3s. 0d. By this time Mr Wellstood had a secretary, whose pay was increased to £2 15s. 0d. a week. Judged by today's standards these levels of pay seem unbelievably small, but in fact they compared favourably with local rates at the time.

All repairs and maintenance work on the properties were carried out by local builders and, when any major item was involved, the Trustees employed an architect to advise and supervise. As already indicated, the Trust now had its own gardener who, as the years passed, came to have the help of one or two assistants.

Judging by the details entered in the minutes of the visiting committee, which were reported to the monthly meetings of the Executive Committee, the Trustees kept a very watchful eye on the management of the properties and the Trust's affairs generally. Although there were occasions when the Secretary and Librarian was able to use his own discretion and initiative, the Trustees normally expected to be consulted on every matter, however small. The income from visitors' fees and sales was watched carefully each month and decisions to spend made according to funds available. There was as yet no regular arrangement for working to an agreed annual budget. Nevertheless, prudent investment of surplus funds was made as they became available and, as opportunity presented, a number of properties were acquired by the Trustees in furtherance of their conservation policy.

Shakespeare's Birthplace

With the development of rail and road transport and the growing popularity of trans-Atlantic sea travel, Shakespeare's Birthplace progressively became a major tourist attraction during Mr Wellstood's time. In 1910 admissions to the property totalled 48,026, and this was roughly the level of visitor patronage

Shakespeare's Birthplace in the 1920s

when the First World War broke out in 1914. For the next four years, however, the impact of war led to a serious reduction in numbers and a decrease in income.

By way of commemorating the tercentenary of Shakespeare's death, in 1916, an exhibition was arranged in Shakespeare's Birthplace of original documents in the Trust's collection illustrative of Shakespeare's life, work and times, together with facsimiles of contemporary Shakespeare documents preserved elsewhere. The exhibition, of which a descriptive catalogue was published, was opened on 22 April and attracted the favourable attention of visitors during the summer. Tercentenary celebrations were also held in the town, but they failed to arrest the decline in the number of visitors to the Birthplace. At the Annual Meeting it was reported that during 1916 receipts from admission charges had dropped by forty-three per cent of the annual takings of the pre-war period. Although expenditure had been reduced as much as possible, the year's accounts showed a deficit of £515, with prospects of nothing better to come in the short term. The Trust's total reserve fund amounted to £3,600.

Confronted with this situation, the Executive Committee decided that urgent action was necessary and submitted recommendations to the Annual Meeting of Trustees in May 1917 which were readily approved and acted upon. New Place Museum was closed and Shakespeare's Birthplace and Anne Hathaway's Cottage were operated on a war-time footing with the help of volunteer ladies. The services of most of the salaried staff - there had been eight full-time and six part-time employees - were dispensed with, only three full-time and two part-time members being retained. A local Ladies Committee, organized by Mrs Scriven, arranged for ladies to give their services to act as guides and to supervise the visitors who came. Mr Wellstood was already undertaking war-time duties in the local recruiting office, but volunteered to exercise general oversight of these arrangements at a reduced salary. The retired Secretary and Librarian, Mr Savage, also gave voluntary help when Mr Wellstood fell ill during the summer.

As Sir Sidney Lee explained to the Trustees, expenditure could only be reduced by taking measures of this kind and, as a possible means of achieving sufficient income, revisions in admission charges were necessary. It was therefore decided to substitute a one shilling admission ticket covering entrance to the Birthplace and the Birthplace Museum conjointly, in place of the two separate sixpenny tickets which had hitherto given visitors the option to purchase one only. At the same time, the admission charge to Anne Hathaway's Cottage was increased from sixpence to one shilling.

These emergency arrangements appear to have worked very satisfactorily. Although the number of visitors continued to decrease as the war continued, as many as 11,526 signed the visitors' album at the Birthplace during 1917-18. Of these, 8,283 came from the United Kingdom, 204 from the United States, 504 from Australia and 233 from Canada, with a few representatives from upwards of thirty other countries. The deficit on the year's working amounted to £218, as compared with £515 in the previous year, and the Trustees were left with a reserve fund of less than a thousand pounds.

Mrs Scriven's volunteer team continued to serve until the Armistice was signed on 11 November 1918, following which the Secretary and Librarian and most of the Trust's previous employees returned to their former duties. Conditions gradually reverted to normal and within a short time visitors started to come back in greater numbers: from 13,381 in 1918, to 31,161 in 1919. The following year the total reached 57,419, and it was because of the problem of handling such a large number that a new staircase was erected at the back of Shakespeare's Birthplace, care being taken not to mutilate or disturb the original timbers. A few years later, in order to assist the flow of visitors, a doorway was opened up in the wall separating the upper floor of the museum from the birthroom.

The decade of the 1920s saw a remarkable increase in the number of visitors, due to the return to peace-time conditions, associated with improved transport and the growing attraction of Stratford's annual Shakespeare Theatre Festival. Announcing a total of 72,840 in 1923, the Chairman observed that this was the second year in succession that the number of visitors to the properties had exceeded any previous record. There was more to come: in 1927, for the first time, with a total of 100,301, admissions exceeded the one hundred thousand mark, and the following year this rose to 118,232. In eight years visitor patronage to Shakespeare's Birthplace had more than doubled. The consequent transformation of the Trust's reserve funds was equally dramatic: in 1921 securities held fell below £500, but by 1927 investments were little short of £15,000.

This high level of visitor patronage was not sustained. The following year saw smaller numbers, and it was not until after the Second World War that totals in excess of one hundred thousand a year were again reached. The early 1930s were a time of world economic recession, and attendances at the Birthplace were seriously reduced. During this decade numbers ranged from 61,777 in 1933, to 74,711 in 1938; and the outbreak of war in 1939 heralded conditions which again placed the Shakespearian properties on an emergency footing. In 1940 there were only ten visitors from the United States who signed the album at the Birthplace, out of a total of 18,496 admissions. Yet in 1944, by which time American servicemen had arrived in this country to take part in the Normandy invasion, no fewer than 22,921 G.I.s, as they were called, visited the Birthplace.

The arrangement for issuing admission tickets at the front of Hornby Cottage worked satisfactorily, and electric light was installed in the ticket office in 1910. Living in the house built by Mr Flower, 19 Henley Street (situated at the side of the Birthplace garden), which the Trustees had purchased in 1910

Victorian house, No. 14 Henley Street

for his official residence, the Secretary and Librarian was able to keep a watchful eye on the property and its management. He was provided with a telephone at home, as well as in his office, and when the burglar alarm was set at night it was connected to his house.

At various times the Trustees considered how display arrangements in the Birthplace and museum could be improved. At intervals Mr Wellstood made changes, putting on display copies of rare books and documents as they were acquired. The exhibition cases on both floors were progressively filled with items of this kind. Occasionally a picture, curio or furnishing item was added. Such was the 'Cupboard of Boxes', belonging to the Corporation of Stratford-upon-Avon, which was transferred in 1914 from the records room, where it had been kept with the Borough archives, for display in the museum. This piece of furniture, with its twelve drawers and double doors, made of oak and banded with iron, complete with its original locks and keys, was made by a Stratford craftsman in 1595 for the safe-keeping of documents and valuables belonging to the town. The cupboard of boxes was displayed in the Birthplace until 1996, when it was transferred to Nash's House. Because it provides an authentic physical link with Shakespeare's time, it has always been an exhibit of special interest to visitors.

By 1923 the catalogue of the contents of the Birthplace, printed in 1910, had sold out. This provided an opportunity to complete the rearrangement and proper classification of the various exhibits in the museum which the Trustees had contemplated for many years. The suggestions made by Mr W.H. (later Sir William) St.John Hope, already referred to, were accordingly acted upon, many objects with little relevance to the history of the Shakespeare family or the Birthplace property being transferred to New Place Museum. A new, illustrated catalogue reflecting these changes was prepared and issued in 1924. A further revised version, produced by the Oxford University Press, was published in 1937.

Nor were amenities for those coming to the Birthplace overlooked. In 1911 the Trustees built a

The cupboard of boxes

small block of lavatories for visitors' use in the Birthplace garden. Necessary maintenance items round the house, mostly of a minor nature, were also regularly undertaken, but no repair work of a major kind took place during the war years.

In the summer of 1922 Mr Guy Pemberton, an architect who had offices at 20a Henley Street, was commissioned by the Trustees to inspect and report on the fabric of Shakespeare's Birthplace; and shortly afterwards Mr Philip M. Johnson, an expert on Tudor architecture from London, also examined the structural condition of the building. The reports of these two architects complemented each other. Although they found that in general terms the fabric of the building was sound, they listed a number of items which needed attention. They also pointed out that, when the restoration of the Birthplace was carried out in 1857-58, some unwise things had been done both to the exterior and the interior of the house, and they suggested a programme designed to remedy the defects.

The Executive Committee decided to act as recommended, and the restoration work was put in hand and completed during the following year. The whole of the main roof, on which many tiles had disintegrated, was thoroughly overhauled and matching replacement tiles used as necessary. The nineteenth-century, iron, rain-water spouting which had perished was replaced by lead-work; the window sills on the Henley Street frontage, which were suffering badly from dry rot, probably due to sappy oak being used in the first instance, were cut away and reinstated with sound material and lead flashings; and the leaded-light glass-work generally was repaired. The stone plinths carrying the framed structure of the building needed attention: sheet lead was inserted between the stonework and the overlying timber in place of the decayed and loose cement filleting previously used, and, where rot had occurred in the timber sills, repair and treatment were applied.

With regard to the timber framed structure, the facing-boards that had been fixed in some places at the time of the original restoration were found to be perished and twisted, with resultant rot and decay caused by water getting behind the old framing. The removal of this exterior veneering involved patient work, making possible the exposure of the original timbers, which were then repaired and treated to arrest further decay.

The porch and penthouse at the front entrance to the building needed particular attention. At the time of the original restoration, Richard Greene's drawing of the Birthplace in 1769 had been used as the basis for work undertaken. Unfortunately, it was not realized that the drawing showed a tiled roof and not a weather-boarded one, such as was then put on, and there were one or two other points of detail that had not been interpreted correctly. Opportunity was therefore taken to remove the perished boarding of the roof and to substitute old, handmade tiles, at the same time remaking the porch gable at a slightly steeper pitch. These alterations, the Trustees were convinced, ensured that the appearance of the front entrance to the Birthplace was in strict keeping with the earliest known representation of the building.

Internally, the chief item which received attention was the ceiling of the birthroom, which was in danger of collapsing in spite of the support given to it by an ugly, iron grid. After many experiments, Mr Guy Pemberton, the architect, hit upon the device of coating the old laths and plaster from above with fibrous plaster, which renewed the ceiling's stability.

The birthroom showing iron grid supporting the ceiling

In reporting this 'ingenious and effective treatment' to the Trustees at their Annual Meeting, the Chairman, Sir Sidney Lee, expressed satisfaction that the work of restoration carried out at the Birthplace had put it in 'that fit and proper condition that our Act of Parliament enjoins the Trustees to maintain it'.

After this comprehensive overhaul, little had to be done to the fabric of the Birthplace, other than occasional maintenance items and the oiling of the timbers, until I came on the scene. However, the Executive Committee kept a careful eye on the situation and arranged for professional inspections at intervals. At the end of 1925 it was decided that a full and detailed historical report on all the properties should be undertaken, together with measured drawings and photographic views, with the idea of publication. Again, Mr Pemberton was commissioned to undertake the work.

In 1937 a further detailed survey of the Birthplace and the other properties was carried out by Mr G.E. Boshier and certain recommended repairs were put in hand. Finally, Mr Edwin F. Reynolds, an architect from Warwick, examined the Birthplace in detail in the spring of 1944 and reported that, apart from a few minor points requiring attention, he considered the state of preservation of the fabric to be very good. He added a suggestion that a complete measured survey of the building would be useful for reference. Action to implement this advice was not taken until after I became Director; I found it very strange that the Trust did not appear to have drawings in connection with the earlier surveys mentioned above.

During the winter of 1927 exploratory excavations were carried out in the Birthplace garden, with a view to establishing whether the foundations of the house adjoining the strip of land which John Shakespeare sold to George Badger in 1597 existed. It was found that all the old foundations had been completely removed, and only brickwork of the eighteenth-century wine vaults of the White Lion inn was discovered.

Five years later, in 1932, the Trustees made an important property acquisition. They purchased for the sum of £3,500 the premises in Henley Street adjoining the residence occupied by the Secretary and Librarian. The property, which was originally part of the White Lion inn, had for a number of years been owned and occupied by the Stratford-upon-Avon Guild, a consortium of local craftsmen producing decorative plaster, leaded-light windows and other specialized work. Sadly, the Guild ran into financial difficulty and had to go into liquidation.

The Trustees' immediate objective was conservation, realizing the importance of being able to control the use of buildings situated in such close proximity to Shakespeare's Birthplace. In the event, the leasing of these premises to the Stratford-upon-Avon Electricity Company (later the Midlands Electricity Board) and to the family firm of builders' merchants, Scott and Co, provided an assured addition to the Trust's income. As will be explained in a later chapter, it was the Trust's possession of this property, lying between Henley Street and Guild Street, that in later years made possible the building of the Shakespeare Centre extension.

New Place and Nash's House

From the beginning, when the Trustees assumed responsibility for its management, New Place had been a loss-making involvement. The main problem in the early years was that it had only a limited local appeal. The gardens were clearly appreciated by regular subscribers and a handful of visitors, and the museum at Nash's House, though small and displaying miscellaneous exhibits, interested a few. Between 1880 and 1910 annual attendances varied generally between 300 and 600; in two years only, 1895 and 1907, did the total rise slightly over 700.

Following the retirement of Richard Savage, the Trustees felt that the time had come to improve the attraction of New Place and so remedy 'their only source of loss'. The matter was discussed in detail, both by the Executive Committee and the whole body of Trustees, at meetings on 11 May and 14 August 1911. Not only was the exterior appearance of

THE WELLSTOOD ERA 1910-1942

Nash's House (New Place), before restoration

The same after restoration

A major scheme of reinstatement and re-presentation was accordingly evolved and implemented over a period of fifteen months, culminating in an official reopening of New Place Museum on 22 April 1912. In the words of Sir Sidney Lee, the object was to adapt Nash's House 'for the first time to serve those public uses for which it was intended when Mr Halliwell-Phillipps purchased it on behalf of the nation fifty years ago'.

The principal exterior change was to the Chapel Street elevation of the building. What the Chairman described as 'the stucco front ... and its barbarous Victorian pillared porch ... a far more modern outrage' was completely removed and replaced by a carefully designed, authentic replica of half-timbered structure, such as the building would originally have had. The work was a fine example of local craftsmanship, carried out under the supervision of the Trust's architect, Mr Guy Pemberton, with whom Mr Guy Dawber, F.R.I.B.A., of London was associated as consultant architect in designing the front.

The Trustees were obviously pleased with the transformation; in the words of the annual report, the renovation 'brought the old house into harmony with its environment' and removed 'a disfigurement of more than half a century's standing'. On the south side of the house, the half-timbered gable end which had been previously hidden by modern brickwork, was also exposed.

The interior of the reconstructed front part of the building was adapted 'for those public uses for which the Trust exists but for which the house was unfitted in its former state'. Modern plaster was stripped from the old beams, and fireplaces which were probably four centuries old were reinstated. The rooms on the first floor were reduced in height to their correct dimensions, as evidenced by the original beams of the walls and ceiling. The cost of all this building work amounted to £497 18s. 2d., with an additional £55 1s. 6d. for architect's charges.

Thus was created space and a suitable environment for the display of exhibits approved by the Trustees, based on the suggestions of Mr St. John Hope. These envisaged a systematic redistribution of

its restored stucco front uninviting, but it was felt that the property did not offer much worth viewing, since only one small room at the front of the house was open to the public the Trust's collections as between Shakespeare's Birthplace and New Place. Whereas at the Birthplace items exhibited were to comprise biographical records and sources relating to the personal history of William Shakespeare and his family, together with early editions of his works and rare books of his period, at New Place the museum display was to be centred on exhibits illustrative of the history of Stratford-upon-Avon both before and after Shakespeare's time, with particular emphasis on local archaeological and historical material, together with pictures and objects of Shakespearian interest and specimens of characteristic furniture of the sixteenth and seventeenth centuries.

New Place Museum was accordingly represented on these lines. Suitable display cases were acquired and an exhibition of local historical, archaeological and Shakespearian objects, labelled and catalogued, was laid out. The collection of coins and tokens which had been in the Trust's possession for over half a century was put on public view for the first time. Many of the pictures were cleaned and revarnished. The famous circular mulberry wood table, Garrick memorabilia and a miscellany of furnishing items and curios added variety to the display.

Within eleven months of its reopening, the number of visitors to New Place totalled 1,746, an attendance more than double that of any previous year. Under the supervision of William Talbot, who had been appointed custodian in 1911, this level of patronage was sustained until the outbreak of the First World War in 1914, when numbers were seriously reduced. However, following the end of the war in 1918 normal conditions returned quickly and during the 1920s New Place experienced a steady build-up in numbers. In 1920 a total of 5,079 people visited the museum and foundations, and by 1929 the number had risen to 26,787.

The economic depression of the early 1930s resulted in a considerable reduction in visitors to New Place, and the attendance of 20,835 in 1936 was the highest annual number for that decade. By the time the Second World War broke out in 1939, the total number of visitors had dropped to 13,993.

War-time conditions brought further reductions, but during 1944 there was a dramatic rise in numbers, when no fewer than 29,753 – almost entirely American servicemen admitted on free vouchers – came to see the museum and the knott garden.

The museum had clearly become an attraction in itself, but the appeal of New Place was greatly enhanced by the remodelling of the gardens there, which was begun in November 1919 and completed during the next two years. The Trustees' basic idea was to redesign and replant the garden area owned and occupied by Shakespeare in his retirement, with a view to restoring its Elizabethan features.

Adjoining the foundations of Shakespeare's last residence a replica of an enclosed Elizabethan 'knott' garden, such as Tudor gentlemen customarily had attached to their homes, was constructed in

The Knott Garden

The Great Garden

New Place

accordance with authentic plans and views in contemporary gardening books. Square in shape and slightly sunken, the garden was divided by paths of Wilmcote stone into four 'knotts' or beds, each of which comprised an intricate, interlaced pattern made with dwarf hedges of box, savory, hyssop, lavender cotton, thyme and other herbs, with the interspaces planted with flowers of many colours. A paved walk, on the top of a dwarf wall of old bricks laid out in Tudor bond and surmounted by a balustrade of Warwickshire elm, was constructed round the sides of the sunken garden and was enclosed by an oak palisade copied from one of the tapestries at Hampton Court. Crab trees were planted to grow up the palisade, and on one side an oak 'tunnell' or shaded 'pleached bower' was made, to reproduce a typical Elizabethan garden feature. The overall result achieved was a 'curious knotted garden' such as was mentioned by Don Armado in *Love's Labour's Lost*: a posy-like mosaic of flowers of varied colours and shapes surrounded by flowering creepers, sweet briar, grape-vine, figs, roses and honeysuckle.

Leading from the knott garden, the Great Garden, which had formed the orchard and kitchen garden belonging to New Place, ran alongside

Chapel Lane and had its own separate gateway entrance for the public. At the upper, knott garden, end a raised, paved terrace was constructed with steps leading down to the central part of the area, which was laid out as a lawn broken only by the ancient mulberry tree, well supported with iron stays, which it was believed had been grown from a cutting of a tree planted by Shakespeare himself. A row of chestnut trees was planted on the furthermost boundary, while alongside Chapel Lane a long border, treated in the formal fashion of Tudor times and planted with summer and autumn flowers, such as hollyhocks, globe thistles, Canterbury bells, lilies, larkspurs and the like, was set against the background of a shaped yew hedge providing the boundary with Chapel Lane and divided into compartments with pillars and buttresses.

Other compartmented beds edged with box were laid out alongside the gravel walk, and these were planted with bulbs and spring flowers and with low-growing summer flowers in common use in Shakespeare's time, such as pansies, primroses, carnations, 'streaked gillyvors', snapdragons, sweet-williams and the like. To complete the plan, at the lower end of the garden a wild bank or heath was mounded on which in 'natural wildness' herbs, wild flowers and other Shakespearian plants were set. The alto-relievo statue of Shakespeare, already mentioned, stood at the end of the wild bank.

The detailed references to this garden project in the minutes of the Trustees' meetings provide evidence of the great care and enthusiasm which went into its design and making. No effort was spared to achieve 'a scholarly historic restoration', as Sir Sidney Lee put it. The work was carried out under the direction of Ernest Law, C.B., F.S.A., a resident at Hampton Court, who became a Life Trustee in 1918 in succession to the Dean of Norwich. Much valuable advice was received from a number of gardening experts, and plants were procured from the gardens at Kew and Hampton Court. Members of the public also offered gifts of plants once the scheme was under way.

Rose trees were given by Their Majesties King George V and Queen Mary, and by Queen Alexandra and the Prince of Wales. When the Trustees received a report on the garden in May 1921, they were informed that these rose trees were flourishing and that the yew hedges were beginning to assume the topiary shapes into which they were being trained. A further red rose tree was presented by the King in 1927, to replace the one given by him in 1920 which was blown down in a gale.

To provide for the convenience of the growing number of visitors, a shelter was built in the north-west corner of the garden, to the design of Guy Pemberton, the architect employed by the Trustees at this time. Price Bros., the local builders who did most of the maintenance repairs to the Trust's properties, were responsible for the work at a cost of £68 10s. 6d. At the same time, in 1927, another local family firm of builders, J.G. Fincher and Co, constructed a new toilet for women at the rear of Nash's House at a cost of £37 10s. 0d. In the following year a sundial, presented by Mr Cass Gilbert, President of the American Academy of Arts, and his wife, was erected on the terrace near to the knott garden.

The Trust's head gardener, Frank Jackson, who was responsible for most of the practical work involved in creating the New Place gardens, was still in the employment of the Trust when I became Director and much of the information recorded above is based on what he told me. He had a vivid recollection of what was done and was able to describe to me details not recorded elsewhere. Viewed from many angles, the New Place garden project was a major undertaking and a considerable achievement. With the attraction of the knott garden and the special character of the Great Garden, the future success of New Place Museum was assured. This was clearly the view of the Trustees, who decided in 1919 to increase the admission charge from sixpence to one shilling.

The history of New Place during the next twenty-five years was comparatively uneventful. Mr and Mrs Alfred Anthony, custodians of Stratford's Town Hall, were appointed joint resident custodians on 29 February 1928. They discharged their duties in an exemplary manner, offering a personal welcome to all who came and conveying in an interesting way the background history of New Place and its foundations and information about the gardens and the museum exhibits of Nash's House.

Members of the visiting committee reported to the Executive Committee on their inspections of the property, and regular attention was given to maintenance requirements. In 1931 an Elizabethan stone fireplace, removed from 35 High Street, was purchased for re-erection in Nash's House, and two years later it proved necessary to rebuild an interior wall which threatened to collapse, and to underpin part of the hall floor. Otherwise no major structural work was required.

From time to time additions were made to the museum's collections and displays and, in particular, Nash's House came to be the repository of important archaeological collections illustrative of the early history of the town and surrounding countryside. In 1922 the Bidford-on-Avon Co-operative Society loaned for exhibition at New Place a collection of Anglo-Saxon grave furniture of pre-Christian date, excavated on the site of a Saxon cemetery at Bidford-on-Avon. The collection was very extensive and of great archaeological value, and included weapons of various kinds, knives, brooches, beads, rings and other personal ornaments, together with a number of fine cinerary urns and other vessels of pottery and bronze.

In the following year another instalment of archaeological finds from the sixth-century burial ground at Bidford was presented to the Trust. It included several objects of special interest, the most important being a unique shield umbo of iron, to which were attached six bronze ornaments heavily plated with gold and decorated with intricate zoomorphic designs. There were also further specimens of varied grave furniture, together with more cinerary urns and a remarkable large bronze bowl beaten from a single sheet of metal. Taken together, the Bidford material formed an outstanding collection of pre-Christian Saxon art and craftsmanship.

By this time Frederick Wellstood had developed a serious interest in archaeology, and he became actively involved in supervising and organizing archaeological investigation which related to the Bidford findings. During 1923-24 he undertook excavations alongside the Tiddington Road at Stratford which established the existence of a Saxon settlement, and material similar to that from Bidford found its way to New Place Museum.

On an adjacent site along the north boundary of the Stratford-upon-Avon golf course, excavations during 1925-26 carried out under Wellstood's direction established the existence of a Romano-British industrial settlement before the period of Saxon occupation. Again, finds of considerable importance as illustrating Stratford's early history were deposited at New Place by the owners of the site, the Corporation of Stratford-upon-Avon. As late as 1938 additions to the collection of late Celtic and Romano-British antiquities at New Place were

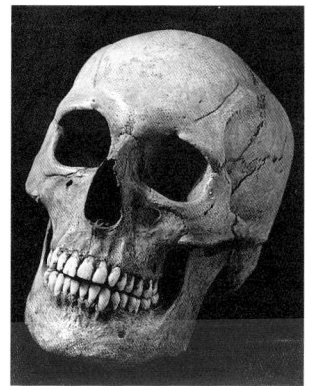

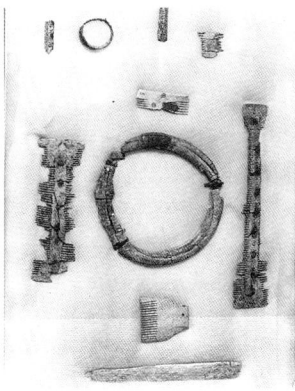

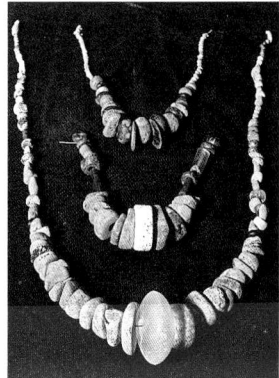

Archaeological specimens at New Place

made from the same site, where Wellstood was still following up his earlier excavations. Full details may be found in a book published jointly by the Corporation of Stratford-upon-Avon and the Trustees and Guardians of Shakespeare's Birthplace: *A Romano-British Industrial Settlement near Tiddington, Stratford-upon-Avon*, by W.J. Fieldhouse, Thomas May and Frederick C. Wellstood (1931).

During 1934-35 the archaeological collections at New Place Museum were further enriched by the accession of a large number of antiquities excavated from the Anglo-Saxon cemetery discovered in April 1934 to the east of Alveston Manor. The items consisted of a number of flint implements of the late neolithic period or early bronze age, and a valuable and varied collection of Anglo-Saxon grave furniture dating from the sixth century A.D. All these finds were formally handed to the Trustees on 24 April 1935 by Alderman John Smith, on whose property the discoveries were made.

At intervals during the year, as Mr Wellstood continued excavations on the site of the Anglo-Saxon cemetery near to Alveston Manor, a large number of archaeological finds dating from the sixth and seventh centuries A.D. were presented to New Place Museum as gifts from Alderman John M. Smith and the Reverend J.M. Knottesford-Fortesque. Selected specimens were put on display.

Apart from the special attraction of its archaeological material, the museum continued to have a general appeal because of the variety of the exhibits displayed. The tercentenary of the death of Dr John Hall was commemorated in the museum by an exhibition of original documents and medical books illustrating his life in the town and by a loan collection of pharmacy jars and surgical instruments of the period. The exhibition was formally opened by the Chairman, Sir Archibald Flower, on 25 March 1935, and Mr Wellstood gave an address on the life of Dr Hall and the relevance of the exhibits. The

Apothecaries' jars

exhibition aroused considerable interest, so much so that the Trustees decided to leave the books and manuscripts owned by the Trust permanently on view. The Trustees were also moved to purchase from Mr J. Whitmore Peek his valuable collection of early apothecaries' jars, many of which had been exhibited in the museum during the past year.

The fact that there were regular additions to the collections and occasional changes in display is evidence that by this time New Place had come to contribute significantly to the Trustees' object of stimulating interest in the historical background of Shakespeare's life and work.

Anne Hathaway's Cottage

During Frederick Wellstood's time Anne Hathaway's Cottage continued to attract an increasing number of visitors. When he took office in 1910, attendances were 28,368 for the year and this level of patronage was generally sustained and increased during the next thirty years, except during the period of the First World War, and the economic depression of the mid 1920s and the early 1930s. In 1920 a total of 20,291 people visited the Cottage, and by 1930 the number had risen to 88,911. When war broke out in 1939, visitors decreased steeply and it was only in 1944, when service personnel were admitted free, that attendances rose again to 49,785.

The Cottage in its garden setting

When William Baker retired as custodian in 1910, he removed certain items of furniture which belonged to him. To fill the gaps, substitute furniture was acquired to supplement the Hathaway pieces which formed the core of the Cottage's furnishings. However, since the custodian continued to live in the house, only part of the property could be shown to visitors and it was not until 1926 that the complete interior was made available for public inspection so far as was practicable.

A staircase and a partition across one of the bedrooms, both modern accretions, were removed and a doorway cut through one of the walls on the first floor, thus making it possible for visitors to pass through the building in a continuous one-way direction. The floor of one of the bedrooms, which was found to be in a shaky condition, was strengthened and supported by an oak beam in the kitchen below. Shortly afterwards the Trustees decided to open up the old chimney and hearth in the kitchen by removing the modern iron canopy and stonework, but the bake oven remained.

It was not until 1910 that a piped water supply was laid on to the Cottage, water for drinking and washing purposes having been taken from the well adjacent to the front entrance. This made possible the installation of a fire hydrant and the improvement of the sanitary arrangements. The thatched

The kitchen with the bake oven

roof of the building was repaired as necessary at various times and was completely re-thatched in 1913 and again in 1943.

The re-presentation of the garden area in front of Anne Hathaway's Cottage in 1923-24 added greatly to the visual attraction of the property. Owing to the laying of the new Shottery sewer in a diagonal line across the garden, the Trustees decided to redesign the area on the lines of an old-world country garden, providing an appropriately colourful setting for the period building: the paths were re-laid with broken Wilmcote stone, and the beds planted informally with an interesting medley of trees, shrubs, herbs and flowers. Not all of them were Shakespearian, but they were essentially English in character, old-fashioned and suggestive of the countryside Shakespeare frequently referred to in his plays. The fences round the property were repaired and, under the guidance of Miss E. Ann Willmott, a well known horticulturalist and author of garden books, footpaths were made to give visitors access to the orchard, which from this time onwards was kept in a tidy condition, attention being given to the aged fruit trees and occasional plantings made. In 1925 a thatched tool shed and new lavatory accommodation were built by the local firm of J.G. Fincher and Co, in accordance with Mr Guy Pemberton's plans, at the lower end of the orchard. In fact, the general layout and character of the garden and orchard which existed when I became Director of the Trust were created at this time.

An interesting discovery was made in 1926 during the course of maintenance work inside the Cottage. Under the floor of the bedroom containing the Hathaway bed a relic of Shakespeare's day was found, namely the oak mount of an original hornbook, on the back of which were the initials of its boy owner, carved with his penknife, variously read as W.S. or W.B. Experts at the British Museum and the Victoria and Albert Museum could not decide which. The latter reading would suggest as the possible owner one of five William Burmans who lived at Shottery in the sixteenth and early seventeenth centuries, but the former, W.S., would give the find an extraordinary interest and value. It is possible that Shakespeare's hornbook found its way to his wife's home and that it was from this specimen that the

The horn book

poet, and perhaps his children afterwards, learned their letters. Unfortunately, the printed sheet containing the alphabet and the horn covering were missing. A full account of this unexpected accession was prepared by the Secretary and Librarian and published in *The Times* on 8 October 1926.

Impressed by the steady development of visitor patronage at Shottery, the Trustees became increasingly aware of the desirability of safeguarding the unspoiled environment of Anne Hathaway's Cottage. The acquisition of neighbouring properties was the only certain way of achieving this and, as opportunity presented itself and with the improved financial resources of the Trust, purchases were made. In 1926 the Trustees bought for £1,600 the garden and two cottages situated on the north side of the Cottage, which were then converted into a residence for the custodian, with a telephone installed for the first time and with its garden levelled and paths made linking it with the Cottage. The work was carried out by J.G. Fincher and Co., at a cost of £425, in accordance with a plan prepared by Mr Pemberton.

The property converted for the custodian's use is now known as Hewlands, which during the 1950s was further adapted to provide a shop on the ground floor to accommodate the Trust's sales activities and a residential flat for a member of staff upstairs. The Trustees also purchased for £416 14s. 0d. a plot of ground measuring 4,060 square yards, with a clump of trees growing on it, adjoining the garden mentioned above.

With the object of safeguarding the rural appearance of the immediate vicinity of Anne Hathaway's Cottage, the Trustees also purchased, for the sum of £175 in 1925, a narrow strip of ground opposite the Cottage between Shottery Brook and the road, which, with its established trees, had the appearance of a small plantation. From this time onwards the Trustees found themselves concerned with the maintenance of this short length of the brook course. From a practical point of view this was important, because in time of heavy rain flooding occasionally occurred. In September 1927, for instance, Shottery Brook overflowed its banks right across Cottage Lane and into the Cottage garden. The operation of the weir on this occasion was apparently not able to prevent the flooding. In 1932 it proved necessary to repair the weir, and the clearance of debris from the brook course was regularly undertaken.

A few years before, in 1927, a water sump fed from the brook was constructed in the plantation immediately opposite the Cottage for use in the event of fire, to supplement water from the town mains. In the following year a belt of trees and shrubs was planted on the north and west sides of the land purchased in 1926 adjacent to the Cottage, a culvert was laid in the roadside ditch and a cartway made over it, oak gates were erected, and a number of fruit trees planted. These details are recorded because they can be related to physical arrangements which still exist.

The purchase of the Shottery Lodge estate, adjoining the garden and orchard of Anne Hathaway's Cottage, in 1931 at a cost of £3,250 represented a further major conservation investment. The acquisition of this property, which included the row of eight brick-built cottages known as New Row, facing Cottage Lane, provided a solid, protective buffer of preserved space on the approach to the Cottage opposite the plantation and brook along Cottage Lane. Standing back in its own grounds and surrounded by a spacious garden and orchard at the rear, the detached residence known as Shottery Lodge, which had belonged to the Bucknall family, was thus saved from undesirable development.

At a time when the the Trustees were involved in capital expenditure in connection with the acquisition of the Welcombe land and the purchase and restoration of Mary Arden's House, the acquisition of Shottery Lodge caused financial anxiety. At first the Trustees considered selling off the house whilst retaining the surrounding ground and the cottages. The opportunity to let the premises to the Youth Hostel Association at the beginning of 1933 saved the situation. This tenancy continued until the house was converted into flats in 1946, as will be related later. In the meantime, the Trustees put the garden and the orchard to their own use; the large greenhouse there was removed and re-erected in New Place gardens. Finally, various improvements were carried out to the eight cottages in New Row and a common drying ground was provided for the tenants at the rear by enclosing a portion of the garden of Shottery Lodge.

In pursuance of the same policy, the Trustees acquired by purchase in 1938 a plot of ground about an acre and a third in extent adjoining the orchard at

Shottery Lodge

the rear of the Cottage. Again, the intention was to preserve the land as a private open space under the provisions of the Town Planning Scheme.

Throughout these years Anne Hathaway's Cottage was presided over by the custodian, Frederick Bennett, who built on the pattern of guiding handed on by Mrs Baker and her son. As time went on Bennett became a kind of celebrity with visitors, to whom he related the history and associations of the Cottage and the Hathaway family with enthusiasm and with an air of authority. He was in fact a very popular guide. He had a special interest in local dialect and could frequently be heard expounding the meaning of words and phrases used by Shakespeare in his plays.

He obviously appreciated the business potential of Anne Hathaway's Cottage, as the number of visitors increased, and in 1924 he incurred the displeasure of the Trustees by selling an unofficial and incorrect guide book which he had written and printed at his own expense without permission, together with postcards and other gift items. The visiting committee discovered these activities, as did also a number of local stationers who complained to the Executive Committee, representing that Bennett's sales constituted unfair competition for shopkeepers in the town.

The upshot was that Bennett was reprimanded for breaking the Trustees' rules and was required to sign an undertaking that in future he would not engage in unauthorized sales or publications. His remuneration was increased to £250 a year, but he had to surrender 428 copies of his booklet guide together with his stock of postcards and other items. Subsequently the Trustees took steps to put the business of selling postcards and gift items on a proper basis. A lady named Mrs Hopkins was employed to sell them in the garden during the summer months, and Bennett was required to supervise and account for these sales activities. As from 1927 the room at the top end of the Cottage came to be equipped and used as 'the postcard shop', an arrangement which continued until the sales operation was transferred to Hewlands in 1993.

Bennett retired on pension in September 1944, and the position of custodian had not been filled when I arrived in the following year. His deputy, Mr John Mitchell, was temporarily in charge.

The Welcombe Estate

The public-spirited action of the Chairman of the Trust, Mr A.D. (later Sir Archibald) Flower, in purchasing the Welcombe estate as a safeguard against undesirable development on the north side of the town will be referred to in a later chapter. Here reference must be made to the decision of the Birthplace Trustees to acquire from Mr Flower a portion of the land which formed part of that estate lying alongside the Stratford to Warwick road.

The sale of the Welcombe estate, which had been in the ownership of the Trevelyan family, took place on 22 November 1929, but prior to the sale Mr Flower had negotiated the purchase of a certain portion of it, including Welcombe House (which later became the Welcombe Hotel) and the land lying between Welcombe House and the Warwick road.

At the Executive Committee meeting on 5 December 1929 Mr Wellstood described in outline Shakespeare's connection with Welcombe and the enclosure of the common lands there, and gave it as his opinion that the land lying between the Warwick road and Welcombe House formed part of the 107 acres of land bought by Shakespeare in 1602 as an investment whilst he was still working in London.

The Trustees unanimously agreed to purchase this land from Mr Flower, at a figure to be fixed by valuation. The two local firms of estate agents, Walker Barnard and Son and Messrs. Hutchings and Deer, were accordingly instructed to prepare a valuation. They inspected the land in question, described in the sale catalogue as lots 3a, 3b, 2a, 2b and 2c on the plan accompanying it, and on 22 January 1930 they submitted a detailed valuation and schedule of the component parts. Together they totalled 63 acres, 2 roods and 14 perches and, taking into account the growing timber thereon, a valuation in the sum of £9,525 was set.

This figure was accepted by the Trustees, who decided to proceed with the purchase, which was subject to a condition in the conveyance that no residential buildings other than a caretaker's house should be erected on the land abutting on to the Warwick road. Thus was achieved another notable acquisition of property by the Trust for preservation as a national memorial to Shakespeare. At the same time, the Trustees' action guaranteed that the unspoiled approach to Stratford along the Warwick road would remain free from the danger of 'ribbon development' which characterized other road approaches to the town at this time.

Subsequently the Trust's Welcombe land was let out for grazing to tenant farmers, the Trust assuming responsibility for fencing, the cutting of thistles and the maintenance of trees. A few years later a row of oak trees was planted in a line parallel to the Warwick road. The annual income from grazing was modest - 30s. 0d. per acre for annual rent - but the conservation gain was beyond price.

Mary Arden's House

The purchase of Mary Arden's House by the Trustees in 1930 represented another important contribution to the preservation of the Shakespearian heritage.

The Shakespeare associations of this historic property at Wilmcote had long been recognized. As the farmstead home of the Arden family of yeoman farmers, it was here that Mary Arden (one of the daughters of Robert Arden), who became the poet's mother, was born and lived before her marriage to John Shakespeare.

John Jordan, the self-educated Stratford antiquarian and self-appointed guide to visitors, who died in 1809, made line drawings of the farmhouse which are preserved in the Birthplace Trust's collection. In the 1860s, at the time of the restoration of Shakespeare's Birthplace, J.O. Halliwell-Phillipps, the Shakespeare scholar and Trustee, commissioned an artist named Blight, who, as already mentioned, recorded the progress of the restoration of Shakespeare's Birthplace, to make sketches of the Arden property, which at that time was occupied by Mr William Neighbour; these are now preserved in the Folger Shakespeare Library. Mary Arden's House was subsequently included in a number of local guide book publications, but it continued to be occupied and used as a working farm.

It is therefore not surprising that the Trustees had in mind the desirability of acquiring the property for preservation as a national memorial to Shakespeare. Indeed, a clause in the 1891 Act of Parliament specifically authorized the Trustees to do so in pursuance of their objects. It was not until September 1929 that Mr Kibler Morgan, the local estate agent, informed the Trustees that Mr Oswald Creed, who had become the owner when Mr G. Smith died in 1921, was desirous of selling Mary Arden's House to the Trust.

The Executive Committee responded immediately and, when the next meeting was held on 28 October, the Secretary reported that, in return for

Mary Arden's House in 1863

The farmyard

£4,000, Mr Creed was prepared to sell Mary Arden's House together with the barns and dovecote and a strip of land adjoining on the west side. At the same time, Mr Wellstood gave particulars to the Trustees of the early ownership of the property and its descent from the year 1561. Being thus satisfied on the authenticity of its Shakespearian association, it was decided unanimously to purchase the property and to enquire whether the vendor would be prepared to sell more land with the house. Negotiations followed, and the owner agreed to include in his offer the front portion of the field adjoining the farmstead, known as the Home Close. Arrangements to purchase were therefore concluded and the common seal of the Trust was affixed to the conveyance of Mary Arden's House from Mr Oswald Creed on 3 May 1930; possession was given on 27 June. The Trustees decided to finance the purchase with a loan from the bank instead of realizing investments, and this was paid off, together with money borrowed for buying the land at Welcombe, over a period of years.

Although the fabric of the property was generally sound, a good deal of tidying-up and certain repairs had to be undertaken before it was ready to be opened to the public, on 4 April 1931. During the summer of 1930 and the following autumn and winter months considerable progress was made. The Trustees were fortunate in securing the professional services of Mr William Weir, the architect of the Society for the Protection of Ancient Buildings, who made detailed inspections of the property and advised on a programme of renovation; and the family firm of Stratford builders, Price Bros., carried out the work. Throughout, the greatest possible care was taken to preserve the ancient fabric, which had been little tampered with over the centuries.

When the Trust acquired the farmhouse, its exterior and interior walls were covered with plaster which had probably been put on towards the end of the eighteenth century. All early views of the building show the stuccoed treatment of the frontage. The stripping of the plaster, recommended by

Mary Arden's House

Mr Weir, revealed the original close-timbered structure, which was in a remarkably good condition. This was left exposed and the timber framing of the inside walls of the great hall and kitchen was similarly revealed. Accretions of recent date, including a small outbuilding at the rear, were also removed from the exterior, but the late-Elizabethan floor which divided the great hall into two storeys was left in place. Within a short time these alterations restored Mary Arden's House to its appearance as a substantial timber framed farmhouse of early sixteenth-century date, with a roof of handmade clay tiles, broken by picturesque dormer windows and a gabled end nearest to the dovecote.

Rear view of Mary Arden's House

The Trustees also received valuable advice and help from Mr Oliver Baker, the well-known local antiquarian and collector, particularly in connection with the acquisition of pieces of furniture and items of domestic equipment of suitable date for display inside the house. The idea was to re-create, so far as possible, the character and atmosphere of the house as suggested by the inventory of Robert Arden's goods, taken after his death in 1556. The main contents and stock of his farmstead comprised tables, forms, benches, coffers and cupboards; bedsteads, bedding and linen; copper pans, brass pots, candlesticks and cooking utensils; a kneading trough, and vessels for milking, cheese making and brewing. As time went on the Trustees were able to purchase representative items of this kind, and on occasion gifts of furniture were offered as, for example, in 1931 when Mr J.H. Every donated an old chair and refectory table.

With the completion of the renovation of the farmhouse, a programme of further work, spread over several years, was undertaken by Price Bros., under the direction of Mr Weir. The area of the farmyard at the rear of the house was tidied up and laid with grass, and borders of herbaceous flowers were planted. Meanwhile, the stone dovecote received attention: the stonework was overhauled, the roof re-tiled and the nesting holes inside cleaned and repaired.

The supply of drinking water proved a problem. In May 1931 samples of the water from the existing

Inside the farmhouse

well were analysed and found to be unfit for drinking. The Trustees accordingly employed Ball Bros. of Stratford to sink a new well, at a cost of 22s. 0d. per foot. This was done, but unfortunately, when water was available for testing from this new source, the analysis proved this, too, unfit for drinking. It was to be several years before Wilmcote had a piped water supply which solved this problem.

In 1933-34, following a hot, dry summer, the Trustees were informed that the walls of the old barn at the rear of the farmyard had tilted considerably and were urgently in need of support. Remedial work was immediately put in hand by Price Bros.; they also took steps to support the archway leading to the rickyard by inserting tie-rods and a steel cable anchored to a concrete bed in the stable. The fact that the leaning archway remained intact until 1996, when rebuilding proved necessary, testifies to the efficiency of the work undertaken at that time.

Little further needed to be done to the farm buildings apart from the re-tiling of the roof of the barn in 1938 and the repair and re-roofing of the

The farming museum in the barn

building next to the cow-shed in 1943. This latter accommodated an old horse-worked cider mill and press, which had been acquired from Wickhamford a few years before.

The Trustees' concern to preserve the property and its environment unspoilt is evidenced by the fact that in 1935 they paid £30 to the S.W.S. Electric Power Co. to lay electric cables, which were being installed to supply the village, underground in front of the house rather than use overhead lines.

Within a short time of Mary Arden's House being opened to the public, the Trustees embarked on a policy for its development which eventually led to the formation of the Shakespeare Countryside Museum, described in a later chapter. It seemed appropriate that the great barn, stable and other farm buildings should be used as a setting for the display of a farming and folk-life collection illustrative of the life of the Warwickshire countryside from Shakespeare's period to modern times.

The concept of a farming museum of this kind met with a favourable response, and during the 1930s the Trustees started to build up, partly by purchase but chiefly by gift, a collection of exhibits, infinitely varied: all kinds of agricultural implements and tools of husbandry; dairy utensils; cooking and household appliances; and furnishings formerly to be found in farms and cottages; together with other items portraying the social and economic aspects of country life, such as crafts, transport, sports and recreations.

The majority of exhibits came from an area roughly within a radius of twenty miles from Wilmcote. In July 1933, for instance, the Trustees accepted gifts of old agricultural implements from Bidford-on-Avon, Aston Cantlow, Exhall and Arden's Grafton. Early in 1936 the Vicar and Churchwardens of Loxley loaned the ancient village stocks, and later in the year the Corporation of Stratford-upon-Avon offered the old, wooden, horse-drawn fire-engine, which had been used for fighting fires in Stratford and the surrounding countryside.

By 1938 the Trustees had acquired a considerable collection of museum exhibits. Some were very old, going back as far as Shakespeare's time, others of more recent date. Nevertheless, they had one characteristic in common in that they provided a physical link with the life of the folk who had peopled the Warwickshire countryside in successive generations. The walls of the great barn and stable provided an admirable back-cloth for the display of the smaller items, while larger exhibits were arranged in groups on the spacious stone-flagged floor.

In July 1939, by invitation of the Warwickshire Agricultural Society, an exhibition of 'Warwickshire Bygones', comprising a selection of exhibits from the Wilmcote collection, was arranged at the Society's annual show. More than 3,000 persons visited the exhibition, and during the months that followed many desirable old farming implements were presented for the agricultural collection at Mary Arden's House.

From the beginning the Trustees were very pleased with this development and with the public interest shown. During the first year Mary Arden's House was opened visitors totalled 1,639. Within two years the number was trebled, and by 1938 it had risen to 6,516. Attendances inevitably slumped during the years of the Second World War, but in 1944, when preparations for the invasion of Normandy were actively under way, no fewer than 10,013 people, mostly members of the Allied services, visited Mary Arden's House, special arrangements for their free admission being offered by the Trustees.

The custodian in charge during these formative years was George Meadows, who had been employed as an attendant at Shakespeare's Birthplace since 1923. The Trustees could not have appointed anyone more suitable. George had the instincts of a countryman and was seriously interested in the history of the Arden family and their farmstead home, as well as in the exhibits in the farming museum. He had the ability to communicate, and few visitors came away without having listened to a fascinating and well-informed commentary, often accompanied by a demonstration of how a particular implement or domestic utensil was used. Many gifts of items for the collection were received as a result of his persuasive presentation. Just as the name of Mary Baker had become vitally associated with Anne Hathaway's Cottage, so the name of George Meadows came to symbolize everything that was characteristic of Mary Arden's House.

Library and Records

The problem of accommodating at Shakespeare's Birthplace the regular intake of books, manuscripts and other items had become quite serious by the time Frederick Wellstood arrived, and his work on the classification and indexing of the library and records emphasized the need for more adequate facilities. The Trustees considered the situation and, at a special meeting held on 11 March 1911, plans were approved for the conversion of the custodian's house, which adjoined Hornby Cottage at the end of the Birthplace garden, into a library, students' room and strong room for records.

Preoccupation with the alterations at Nash's House and New Place, already described, delayed the implementation of the new library scheme, but it proved possible to go forward with the work during 1912-13. Structural alterations on the first floor provided a spacious room to serve as a library and reading room, linked directly with the Secretary's room at the front of Hornby Cottage; while on the ground floor a large strong room was built for the safe-keeping of the Trust's deeds and documents.

The Chairman reported the completion of these alterations at the Annual Meeting in 1914, and the new library and strong room were subsequently equipped with all necessary furniture and fittings. Certain closed bookcases were transferred from the Birthplace, and shelving round the walls of the new library was installed for books, which were then moved from the Birthplace to their new home. The resultant release of space in the Birthplace museum made possible the rearrangement of pictures and other exhibits. The Stratford Corporation records and other manuscripts were also transferred from the old records room in Shakespeare's Birthplace to the new strong room in the reconstructed library building. It was with a feeling of satisfaction that Sir Sidney Lee, the Chairman, reported to the Annual Meeting of Trustees in 1915 that all this had been achieved 'to better advantage' of the Trust's educational work.

With adequate shelving provided in the new library, the Secretary and Librarian was able to introduce an orderly arrangement of the Trust's library, based on a scheme devised to accommodate the special subject matter of the collection. This was a painstaking piece of work, but the classification and reorganization were completed by June 1915. By that time books which had been deposited on loan to the Shakespeare Memorial Library several years before were reclaimed and incorporated with the stock. It is difficult to over-estimate the practical convenience of having all the Trust's printed resources, properly referenced, in one place with facilities for their use by serious students.

The provision of improved storage arrangements for archives was particularly opportune, because on 27 May 1915 the Royal Commission on Public Records, under the chairmanship of Sir Frederick Pollock and of which Sir Sidney Lee was a member, visited Stratford-upon-Avon and inspected the Borough archives and those of the Trust, in the new strong room. Frederick Wellstood, who had been designated Deputy Keeper of the Corporation Records, subsequently prepared for their information lists of both sets of documents. His *Summary Statement of the character of the manuscripts belonging to the Trustees and Guardians of Shakespeare's Birthplace* (1915) describes the collections as consisting at that time of 256 bound volumes and about 5,600 other documents, dealing with the history and antiquities of Stratford-upon-Avon and surrounding country, and with the life and work of Shakespeare, the personal collections being associated with the names of Wheler, Halliwell-Phillipps, Hunt and Saunders. The Commissioners were impressed by the recently provided storage arrangements for the records and by the considerable extent of the Trust's and Borough collections. As Sir Sidney himself reported to the governing body the following year, when referring to the Commission's inspection,

'Stratford-upon-Avon stood high in the scale of merit'.

Until this time it could fairly be said that the principal emphasis in the Trust's collections had been the Shakespearian element, but, with the changing conditions that followed the end of the First World War, the amended property laws and the resultant dispersal of private records, the Birthplace library at Stratford came near to fulfilling the purpose of a general record repository for south-west Warwickshire and parts of adjoining counties. Sizeable accessions of manuscript material accrued at this time, including the first of the larger county family collections deposited, that of Lord Willoughby de Broke of Compton Verney.

The Master of the Rolls, Sir Ernest Pollock (later Lord Hanworth), suggested the Parliamentary Bill in 1930 which, as already described, widened the constitution of the governing body and conferred additional powers permitting the development of the educational side of the Trust's activities.

In 1931 the Master of the Rolls designated the Birthplace library an approved place for the custody of manorial records, thus giving official sanction to its development as a general records office. In speaking about this at the next Annual Meeting of the Trust, Lord Hanworth said he had approved the Birthplace library as a repository, in addition to the already existing one at Birmingham, because 'his policy had been directed with an idea to stimulate local zeal and patriotism. Some people thought these documents should find a home in the larger centres, but this was not his ambition, and he was of the opinion that owners would hand over their records to a centre in their own area ...'

Within a little more than a year the Trustees were able to record the deposit of 402 Warwickshire manorial court rolls by Major Charles Gregory-Hood and 200 court rolls of the manor of Snitterfield by Mr Robert Trevelyan and Mr Thomas Place, besides other documents. The total number of manorial documents received by 1935 was 2,751; and by 1937 this had risen to 5,564. One of the most substantial deposits of manorial records was that made

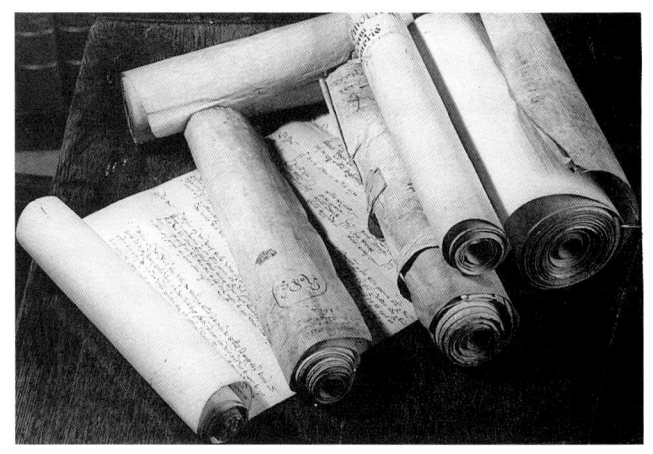

Manorial documents

by Sir Robert Throckmorton, Bt., of Coughton Court, and during the next few years nearly every surviving manorial document in Warwickshire found its way to the Trust's custody. Full details were given in a 'List of Manorial Documents' preserved in the records room of the Birthplace Trust, subsequently prepared by Frederick C. Wellstood and printed in the *Genealogists' Magazine* in September 1942.

Changes affecting accommodation and personnel naturally accompanied these developments. Due to the large intake of manorial material, there was already a serious shortage of storage space for records; the strong room constructed twenty-two years before was full to overflowing. In November 1935 the Committee accordingly asked Mr G.E. Boshier, the architect, to report on the possibility of providing additional fire-proof accommodation for records on the plot of land at the rear of Hornby Cottage. The first proposals prepared had to be amended, but in April 1936 revised plans were approved and tenders invited. Of the six received, that of Messrs. Price Bros. in the sum of £1,570 was accepted.

The old store rooms at the rear of the library were demolished and the new building was erected on the site. It comprised a large strong room and cloakroom facilities on the ground floor, and a second large and a smaller strong room on the first floor, the new extension being linked at both levels with the

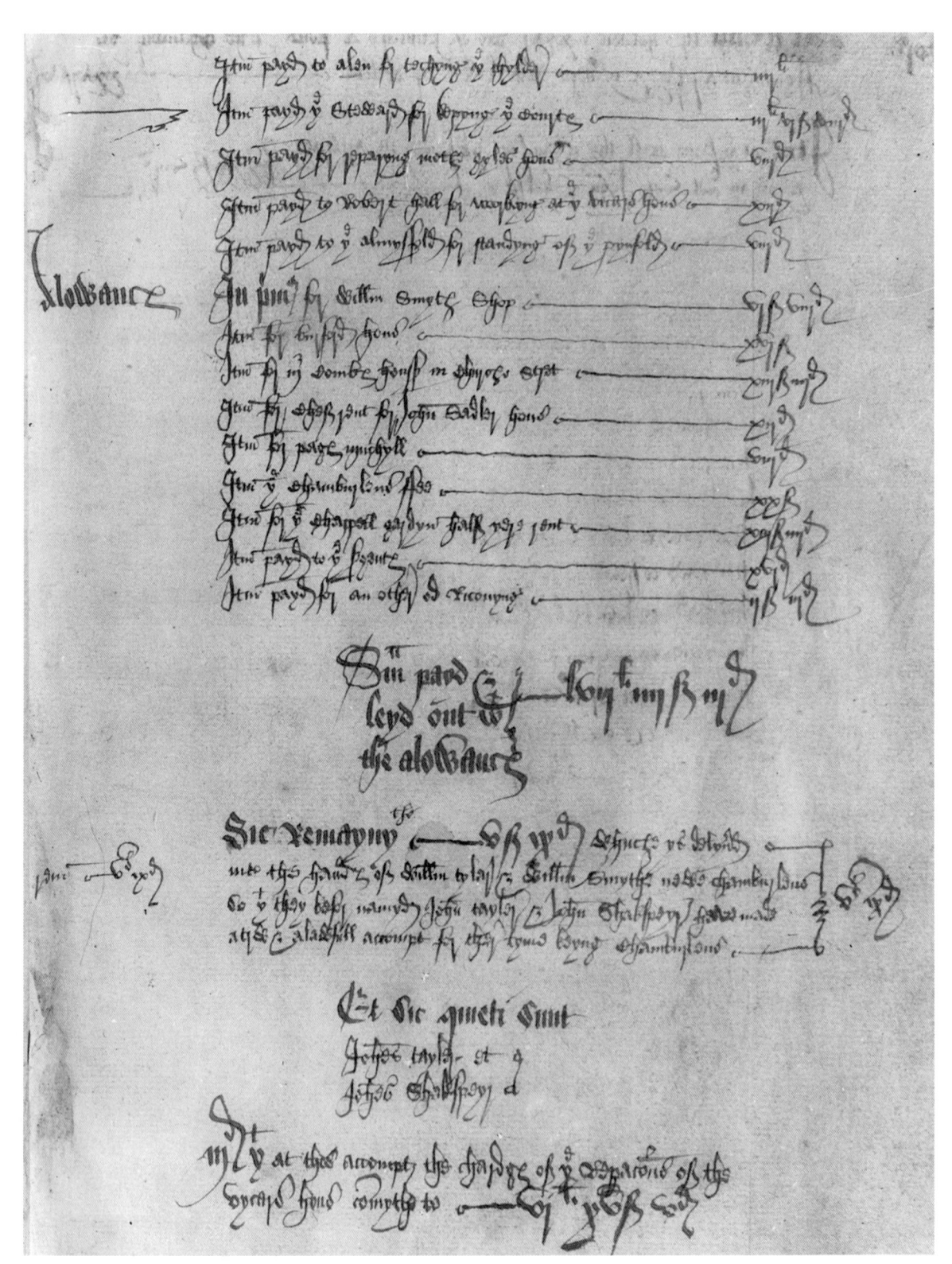

Accounts for 1563-4, when John Shakespeare, the poet's father, was Chamberlain

Borough records

adjoining library. A basement room with exterior access from the rear accommodated the coke-fired central heating boiler which served both the Birthplace and Hornby Cottage. Externally, the new extension had the appearance of a traditional, brick-built, two-storey building, with a tiled roof and leaded-light windows in oak frames; internally, the whole structure had been reinforced with concrete to produce fire-proof strong rooms which were fitted with security doors and steel shutters to the windows. These strong rooms were equipped with steel shelving throughout, to carry specially designed, cloth-covered archive storage boxes of varying sizes.

This accommodation was completed by the beginning of 1937, at which time the Trust's collections, the records of the Corporation of Stratford-upon-Avon and the manorial and other records deposited under the scheme inaugurated by the late Master of the Rolls were moved into the new strong rooms.

The enlarged records repository was formally opened by the Rt. Hon. Lord Wright, Master of the Rolls, on 24 April 1937. He was introduced by Alderman F. Winter, who outlined the origin of the collections of manuscripts in the custody of the Trust and referred to the great number of accessions in recent years which had necessitated the building of the new, fire-proof records rooms. Lord Wright referred to the death of his predecessor, Viscount Hanworth, and the great part he had played in the movement for the preservation of manorial and other records throughout the country. He warmly complimented the Trustees on the design, construction and equipment of the records rooms, which were to prove adequate to meet all requirements until the spacious, modern records office was provided in the Shakespeare Centre extension in 1981.

Up to the early 1930s the Secretary and Librarian had usually worked single-handed on the archive front, but, as the result of a suggestion made by the Master of the Rolls, Lord Hanworth, in 1933, an assistant archivist with legal training, George Tibbits of Warwick, was appointed in 1934. During the next few years useful listing of various categories of documents was undertaken, but the arrangement ended in 1939, with the outbreak of the Second World War, which ushered in a period of some difficulty. Stratford being in a reception area considered safe from enemy air attack, the Birthplace strong rooms

The records room

provided storage space for valuable record and museum items from elsewhere, particularly the City of Coventry. The only damage sustained (and that affecting only two or three volumes of Stratford records) arose from a small intake of water due to a leak in the roof.

Frederick Wellstood's death in 1942 and that of J. Harvey Bloom, who had assisted as temporary archivist, in the following year brought all active work on the records collection to a full stop. Nevertheless, the war years saw continued accessions of records, augmented occasionally by material retrieved from salvage drives. Lord Leigh of Stoneleigh Abbey deposited most of his collection of family and estate documents during this period, including one consignment of eighty-two trunks and storage boxes.

Thus, whereas the Trustees' policy, as envisaged by the terms of their constitution, continued to be devoted primarily to the acquisition of material likely to promote knowledge and appreciation of Shakespeare's life, times and work, it came about by a process of natural growth that the scope of the Trust's records repository was gradually widened to include most aspects of Warwickshire history and topography. The subsequent development of the records office, as also the library, in post-war years could not have happened without the sound basis laid during the 1920s and 1930s.

Notable Accessions

Any record of Frederick Wellstood's time would be incomplete without reference to the growth of the Trust's library, archive and museum collections, for which he was largely responsible. At every meeting of the Executive Committee a list of accessions was submitted and every annual report recorded details of items donated or purchased. The sum total intake was considerable and was infinitely varied in subject matter and value.

Of particular interest were books of the sixteenth and seventeenth centuries, especially those which Shakespeare may have consulted for his source material, or copies with particular associations or Shakespeare references. Funds available for purchases were strictly limited, so the acquisition of a rare title was always pleasing news to the Trustees. A few items may be mentioned by way of illustration.

In 1912 there were two important accessions containing early notices of Shakespeare and his work: Howe's edition of Stow's *Annales, or Generall Chronicle of England*, 1615, in which William Shakespeare, gentleman, is listed by Howe among 'Our moderne, and present excellent Poets which worthely florish in their owne workes, and all of them in my owne knowledge lived togeather in this Queene's raigne'; and *The Scourge of Folly* by John Davies, 1610, consisting of epigrams and sonnets 'in honour of many noble and worthy Persons of our Land' and including an epigram to 'Mr Will. Shake-Speare'.

Three years later copies of other rare books containing Shakespeare references were added. In *Colin Clovts Come home againe*, 1595, Edmund Spenser pays a tribute to Shakespeare as a heroic poet under the Greek proper name of 'Aetion'. Robert Burton's *The Anatomy of Melancholy*, 1624, contains a quotation from *Venus and Adonis* and Shakespeare's name is given in the margin. *Small Poems of Divers sorts*, 1658, written by Sir Aston Cokain, a Warwickshire poet, alludes to the *Induction* of *The Taming of the Shrew*.

Equally important as providing evidence of the popularity of Shakespeare's work was the copy of *Englands Parnassus: or the choysest Flowers of our Moderne Poets ...* edited by Robert Allot and published in 1600. It contains a collection of notable extracts from contemporary poets, no fewer than ninety-five passages from Shakespeare being quoted: evidence that his fame was already established at the date of publication in 1600.

An interesting association item was presented to the Trust in 1920: *A Profitable booke of Maister John Perkins felow of the inner Temple treating of the lawes of Englande* by Richard Tottil, 1567, containing the autograph signature of William Coombe of Warwick, as well as copious notes in his handwriting. It was from this William Coombe, and his

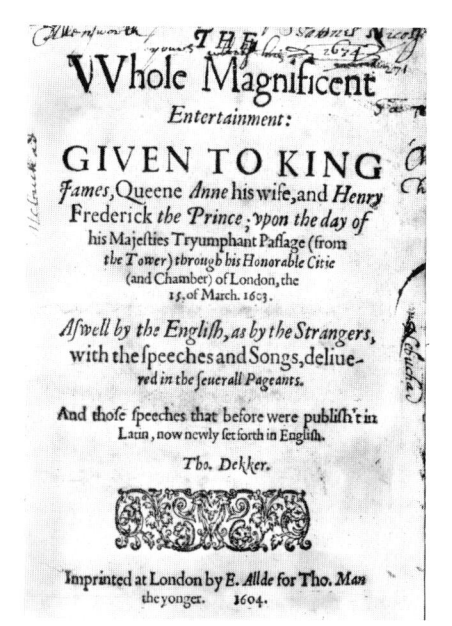

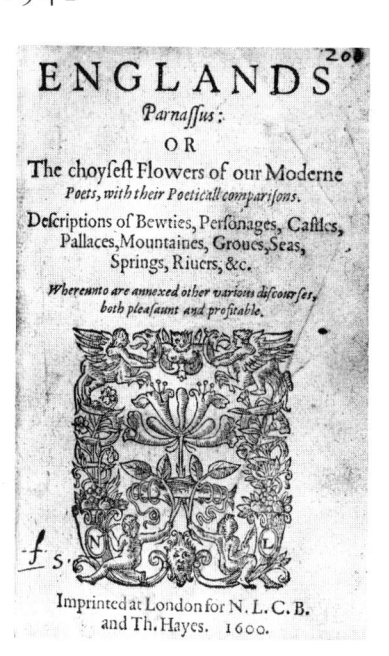

Early printed book accessions

nephew John Coombe, that Shakespeare purchased in 1602 for the sum of £300 the 107 acres of land in 'Old Stratford'. This was the land at Welcombe to which reference has been made.

The Trust's library already contained a representative selection of original books with which Shakespeare's work shows him to have been familiar. Most of them had come from the Beisley bequest of 1896, mentioned earlier, but additions to fill gaps were made at various times. In 1923, for instance, the Trustees received a gift of a fine copy of the 1603 edition of North's translation of *Plutarch's Lives*. This work of reference was first printed and published in London in 1579 by Thomas Vautrollier, whom Richard Field, a native of Stratford and friend of Shakespeare, served as apprentice. Field succeeded to Vautrollier's business in 1597 and he reprinted North's *Plutarch* in 1595 and 1603, and again in 1612. Shakespeare was well read in North's standard version of *Plutarch*, and his Roman tragedies of *Julius Caesar*, *Antony and Cleopatra* and *Coriolanus* were based on it.

Mention should also be made of the acquisition of the collections of books and papers which had belonged to Richard Savage, Sir Sidney Lee and the Reverend Edgar Fripp.

Under the will of Richard Savage, who died in 1924, the Trustees were given the opportunity to acquire, at a mutually agreed price, the whole of his collection of books and papers, manuscript and printed, pictures, busts and relics connected with Shakespeare or pertinent to the objects and aims of the Trust. The whole represented a lifetime's collection and work, and included personal diaries, transcripts of records of local interest and a considerable amount of printed ephemera.

Sir Sidney Lee, who died in 1926, bequeathed to the Trust the copyright of all his published works (except his *Life of Shakespeare*) and of all his literary manuscripts dealing with Shakespeare, Stratford-upon-Avon, or the literature of the sixteenth century; his copy of the original edition of the *Dictionary of National Biography* in sixty-seven volumes; his own copies of all his published writings concerning Shakespeare; one hundred volumes from his general library; some of the silver presented to him on his retirement from the editorship of the *Dictionary*; and £150 upon trust for investment; the income to be applied to the purchase for the library of original publications, manuscripts or prints of the sixteenth or seventeenth century relative to the objects of the Trust. The inscribed silver inkstand presented to Sir Sidney by the contributors of the *Dictionary of National Biography* stood on my desk during the forty-four years of my Directorship and it was used, with a matching pen, on the occasion of each Royal visit. I feel sure Sir Sidney would have approved.

The Reverend Edgar Innes Fripp, who had been a Life Trustee since 1925, died in 1931. Over the years he had acquired an unrivalled knowledge of the life,

David Garrick

The Reverend Edgar Fripp

times and work of Shakespeare. In the course of his research into local and national records for his various publications, which included four little books: *Richard Quyney*, *Shakespeare's Stratford*, *Shakespeare's Haunts near Stratford* and *Shakespeare's Studies*, together with his larger work, *Shakespeare Man and Artist*, published posthumously by the Oxford University Press in 1938, he had amassed a large collection of transcripts, manuscripts, notes and other related material relevant to the study of Shakespeare's life, work and times. The acquisition of this complete personal archive of Shakespeariana of a distinguished Shakespeare scholar was, like that of Richard Savage, a significant addition to the records office.

Accessions, as recorded year by year, were extremely varied. As Shakespeare became more appreciated overseas, the number of translations of

Sir Edward Walker

Sir George Carew

his plays and publications by foreign scholars steadily increased. Typical donations recorded were as follows: in 1923, translations of Shakespeare's plays into Serbian and Armenian, together with a life of Shakespeare in Japanese; and in 1936 ten volumes of all Shakespeare's plays in Russian, Armenian, Turkish-Tartar, Yiddish and Kuwik languages. That Shakespeare's plays were being read and appreciated in unexpected places was illustrated by the fact that, at the Annual Meeting in 1922, the Chairman informed the Trustees that the Siamese Minister had sent to him a donation of one hundred guineas from the King of Siam as a personal contribution to the funds of the Birthplace Trust, explaining that His Majesty was an ardent admirer of Shakespeare and that he himself had translated some of his plays into Siamese.

Other notable accessions acquired during these years were: a contemporary portrait in oils, by or after Van der Gucht, of David Garrick as Steward of the Stratford Jubilee; Henry Chettle's *Englandes Mourning Garment*, an exceedingly rare little volume, printed in London in 1603; a gold medal with a fine portrait bust of Shakespeare, by J.S. and A.B. Wyon, struck in 1880; a mulberry wood writing standish, presented to George Garrick in 1769 by Thomas Sharp; portraits of Sir George Carew by Geldorp, Sir William Walker by William Dobson, and Frances Clopton by Thomas Hudson; a seventeenth-century Commonplace Book of Sir Francis Fane; the manuscript journal of the tour of the Hon. John Byng, afterwards 5th Viscount Torrington, from London to Stratford-upon-Avon in 1785, containing the earliest known account of Shakespeare's Birthplace and its contents; a cup of carved mulberry wood and silver, commemorating Garrick's Jubilee of 1769; a rare black-letter proclamation, dated 7 November 1605, for the apprehension of the chief conspirators concerned in the Gunpowder Plot, among whom was Ambrose Rookwood of Clopton House; a water-colour drawing of the old charnel house which formerly adjoined the north side of Holy Trinity Church, by Thomas Girtin (1775-1802); the Baddesley Clinton collection of records, acquired from Mr C.R. Ferrers; manuscript diaries of Robert Hobbes, a Stratford attorney, for the year 1810, and of Elizabeth Davenport Ashford, who afterwards became his wife, for the years 1797, 1799 and 1824; a fine pen-and-ink-wash drawing of Shakespeare's Birthplace in 1807, by Hugh Elridge; and an eighteenth-century, pewter dinner service of fifty-four pieces, bearing the coat of arms of David Garrick, (acquired jointly with the Governors of the Shakespeare Memorial Theatre).

This selection of notable accessions is recorded to illustrate the variety and scope of subject matter covered by the Trust's collections as they were progressively built up during the Wellstood era. Each item had its own particular relevance and interest. Taken together, and added to similar material acquired from the 1860s onwards, accessions of this kind pro vided a foundation for the continued growth of the library, records and museum collections during the next half century and their developing use for academic and educational work.

Frederick Christian Wellstood

Mr Wellstood died on 7 August 1942. For some time past he had not been a fit man, and his death in the middle of the war produced a difficult situation for the Trustees. Warm tributes were paid to him in many quarters and the Trustees recorded 'the grievous loss' which had befallen the Trust as follows:

> During the thirty-two years of his loyal and indefatigable service, he gained the respect and affection, not only of the Trustees, but of all with whom he came in contact, and by his profound scholarship, the wide range of his antiquarian and archaeological interests, and unfailing charm of personality, immensely increased both the scope and prestige of the office which he so ably filled. To these great gifts he added a capacity for the management of the estates and finances of the Trust, a rare quality in one of his scholarly cast of mind, which was of the utmost value. By constantly striving for the expansion of the activities of the Trust, he added continually to his own burden of work and responsibility, which he shouldered cheerfully and ungrudgingly, and it is no exaggeration to say that his career was one of selfless devotion to duty. The Trust is the poorer by the loss of a brilliant guardian of its interests, and both those for whom he worked and those who worked with him, by the loss of a friend.

Fortunately his widow, Mrs Constance Wellstood, who, as Miss Langley, had worked before her marriage as his secretary, was sufficiently familiar with the Trust's organization and personnel to be able to take temporary charge of the situation. She was appointed Secretary of the Trust and was responsible for the day-to-day management of the organization until I was appointed Director in the autumn of 1945.

F.C. Wellstood, 1935

PART TWO

An Expanding Era
1945 – 1989

The Shakespeare Birthplace Trust in 1945

The period following the death of Frederick C. Wellstood in 1942 had been especially difficult. Apart from all the problems associated with wartime conditions, the Shakespeare Birthplace Trust had been without an experienced chief executive and librarian. Members of the Executive Committee had assumed particular responsibilities, and they were fortunate in being able to call on the services of Mr Wellstood's widow, Constance Wellstood, who had knowledge of the Trust's affairs by reason of her previous employment with the Trust in a secretarial capacity. Mrs Wellstood was appointed Acting Secretary on 7 August 1942, and showed great initiative and competence in managing the Trust's day-to-day affairs during the period of interregnum. She also proved extremely helpful to the new Director and, although she had the responsibility of bringing up a young family, she remained with the Trust until 1952.

The Executive Committee began to think of future arrangements in 1944, when they decided that steps should be taken to appoint a successor to Wellstood, there being no one at that time with experience to deal with the library and archive side of the Trust's activities. In the event, a series of fortuitous circumstances led to my appointment as Frederick Wellstood's successor.

I already had some acquaintance with Stratford-upon-Avon, having visited the Shakespeare Memorial Theatre several times as a boy and, much more frequently, whilst working as the City Archivist of Coventry, an appointment I had taken up in 1938. In fact I had visited Frederick Wellstood concerning Warwickshire records and history, being already involved with the Dugdale Society, of which he was Secretary and General Editor. Soon after the outbreak of the Second World War, I had also sought his help in providing safe storage in the Shakespeare Birthplace Trust's strong rooms for some of the medieval records of the City of Coventry. By that time I had undertaken emergency war duties as assistant to the Town Clerk of Coventry, my particular responsibility being to establish and manage the Food Control Office for organizing the rationing of food and emergency feeding. I was in charge of the Food Office at the time of the German air raid which devastated the city and destroyed the Cathedral, in November 1940. The following year I was called up into the Army and served in the Royal Ordnance Corps.

On my return to civilian life, I resumed my position as City Archivist of Coventry, and in the early part of 1945 I arranged for the return of the city records that had been safely stored at Stratford-upon-Avon during the war years, in readiness for an exhibition I was arranging in St. Mary's Hall to commemorate the 600th anniversary of the incorporation of the City of Coventry. It was at that juncture that I learned that the Birthplace Trustees were considering the appointment of a successor to Mr Wellstood.

The exhibition was visited by three of the Birthplace Trustees, who reported to the Executive Committee that 'they had been favourably impressed by what they saw'. Arising from this visit, I made known my possible interest in applying for the vacancy caused by Wellstood's death, and, upon receiving details of my academic background and experience, the Trustees were 'greatly impressed' and invited me to meet them without delay.

I attended a special meeting of the Executive Committee convened for this purpose on 30 May 1945. The Trustees present were Mr S.C. Kaines Smith (Chairman), Mr G. Baron Ash, Alderman L.T.R. Matthews, the Reverend A.C. Knight, Major C. Gregory-Hood and Alderman R.M. Smith.

By way of introduction, the Chairman outlined the background and nature of the Trust's activities and described the duties and responsibilities of the Secretary and Librarian. The Trustees had already had the advantage of perusing a detailed *curriculum vitae*, accompanied by testimonials, which I had submitted in advance of my visit, but during the course of the long interview that followed I was questioned in detail about my qualifications, experience and interests.

I sensed that the Trustees were impressed by the fact that I had achieved a First Class Honours degree at Oxford University and that I had subsequently held senior research studentships both at Oxford and Manchester Universities. They were interested to hear about my research and work as a professional keeper of records in my capacity as Coventry's first City Archivist, and my varied activities in the spheres of local history, archaeology, museum antiquities and conservation.

Mr Baron Ash, who I knew had been responsible for the restoration and furnishing of Packwood House, questioned me about my knowledge of period buildings, Tudor architecture and furniture, and the fact that I already knew Warwickshire's historic properties and was no stranger to Stratford-upon-Avon was noted and struck the right chord. The Reverend A.C. Knight, who I later discovered was the Headmaster of King Edward VI School, seemed particularly pleased that I was a grammar school product, and Mr Kaines Smith, whom I came to know as the retired Director of the Art Gallery at Birmingham and a formidable authority on pictures, was surprised to hear that I had been involved in a small way with plans for the Herbert Art Gallery at Coventry. One or two members of the Committee questioned me about my experience in organizing food control in wartime Coventry; they were clearly anxious to establish whether I had administrative as well as academic skills, and that I would be capable of managing the Shakespearian properties, supervising the staff and looking after the business side of the Trust. Members of the Committee were interested to hear about my association with Frederick Wellstood, particularly in connection with the Dugdale Society, and my interest in Shakespeare, as evidenced by my visits to Stratford and the Shakespeare Memorial Theatre.

At the end of the interview my hopes rose, when I was asked if I would accept the appointment if it were offered to me. I responded positively and with obvious enthusiasm. I then retired while the Trustees deliberated, and after some time I was recalled, to be told that the Committee had decided to recommend to the governing body my appointment as Custodian and Librarian of the Shakespeare Birthplace Trust with the title of Director, with effect from 1 October 1945. The terms of the appointment were then discussed and agreed between us.

In the simple form of contract subsequently drawn up, it was specified that 'the Director shall carry out all such directions and instructions as the Trustees may from time to time convey to him, but in default he shall control the general management of the Trust and the work of the staff'. So much for my job description! I was offered a salary of £750 per annum, plus the free use of 14 Henley Street, the Victorian house overlooking the Birthplace garden, or an allowance of £100 in lieu. The appointment was to be terminable by six months' notice on either side, and a contributory pension scheme was to be arranged by mutual agreement.

I was invited to attend a special meeting of the full governing body on Wednesday, 27 June 1945, for the purpose of meeting the Trustees and securing their approval of the Committee's recommended appointment. There were fourteen Trustees present, and, after introducing me to each of them, the Chairman, Mr S.C. Kaines Smith, submitted the Committee's report and recommendation and invited me to enlarge further on my qualifications, experience and activities, and to answer questions. At the time I certainly found the experience of being questioned by such a distinguished body of men somewhat daunting. I was delighted that the appointment recommended by the Executive Committee was unanimously approved.

I took up my new post on 1 October 1945. The house offered for my accommodation was at that time occupied by Mr S.C. Kaines Smith, the retired Director of the Art Gallery at Birmingham, who, as a Life Trustee and member of the Executive Committee, had been actively involved in my appointment. I was still living in Coventry, and at first I made the journey each day to Stratford on my rationed petrol. Mr Kaines Smith, however, had decided to leave Stratford, to live on the Stoneleigh estate, and so, on a very wet December day, my wife and infant son moved with me into residence at 14 Henley Street. The house was large and cold, and forbidding in many ways, but it had a dignity and charm of its own, which ensured that we remained there until 1960, when it was ultimately demolished. Indeed, once settled there, the Shakespeare Birthplace Trust became the all-absorbing involvement of my life.

On taking up my duties, I quickly discovered that, as compared with today, the Trust at that time was a small, old-fashioned organization discharging its function in much the same way as it had done for the two or three previous decades. Its activities were centred primarily on the management of the four Shakespearian properties, namely, Shakespeare's Birthplace, New Place, Anne Hathaway's Cottage and Mary Arden's House, together with a few let properties and, to a much lesser extent, with the maintenance of its library, archive and museum collections, which as yet were used only occasionally by visiting scholars.

Stratford-upon-Avon itself at that time was still essentially a small market town, though already well recognized and visited as a place of literary pilgrimage. Its Shakespeare Memorial Theatre, rebuilt and opened in 1932, was already attracting an international patronage. The town had a population of some 15,000, compared with 25,000 today, and had its own self-governing Borough Council and a closely-knit community of family traders. The present high street multiple shops had not yet arrived, and modern problems of traffic and car parking had not arisen. As a countryman not fond of city life, the idea of living and working in a place like this, steeped in history, custom and architectural interest, appealed to me greatly. I quickly realized that the Shakespeare Birthplace Trust was an integral part of this heritage.

The scale of the Trust's operation in 1945 may be illustrated by a few statistics. At that time the total full-time staff employed numbered eighteen, comprising two or three guides at each property, three gardeners, a secretary and an assistant, with part-time cleaners and additional guides in summer. By 1989, when I retired, numbers had increased to 235 regular full-time and part-time staff, with additional seasonal helpers.

The number of visitors to Shakespeare's Birthplace in 1945 was 78,742, with a total of 157,059 to all the four properties. During the next forty years, the number of attendances increased to well over a million each year. The Trust's total income in 1945 was just over £8,000, with a surplus for the year of £424. By 1989 the cost of running the Trust was in excess of a million and a half pounds, with an income of little under two million pounds.

The governing body was appointed in accordance with the provision of the Shakespeare Birthplace Trust Acts of 1891 and 1930. As at present, there were ten Life Trustees; included were national figures, such as the Earl of Clarendon, Mr Anthony Eden and Mr Albert Mansbridge, and, from the county gentry, Sir William Dugdale, Major Charles Gregory-Hood and Mr Graham Baron Ash. Trustees representing the Universities of Oxford, Cambridge, London and Birmingham were, respectively, Mr Edmund Blunden, Professor John Dover Wilson, Sir Ernest Pooley and Mr J.J. Waterhouse. In addition to the High Steward of the Borough, the Headmaster of the Stratford Grammar School and the Vicar of Holy Trinity Church, there was a much larger element of local involvement than at present. By virtue of their offices, the Mayor, the Town Clerk and the seven Aldermen of the Borough were all Trustees, as well as the nine or ten Justices of the Peace serving the Stratford Bench. This latter category of Trustees continued until the office of Justice of the Peace for the Borough of Stratford-upon-Avon ceased to exist, in 1957.

The full body of Trustees met twice a year, and appointed an Executive Committee to assume responsibility for the day-to-day management of the Trust, an arrangement which still continues. A Visiting Committee, appointed by the Executive Committee, dealt with matters affecting the properties, and, similarly, a Finance Committee with staff and business. The Trust's financial year ended on 31 March, and shortly afterwards the audited accounts and a report on the year's work were presented to the Annual Meeting.

The Chairman of the Trust in 1945 was Sir Archibald Flower, who had been appointed a Life Trustee as far back as 1900, and who had served as Chairman of the Executive Committee for the past nineteen years. He continued as Chairman until 1946, when he resigned on grounds of ill health and was succeeded by his son, Lt-Col Fordham Flower.

Sir Archibald was a remarkable gentleman, possessing a profound love of everything connected with Shakespeare, a business capacity of a high order and an unfailing sense of responsibility. As an elected representative on the Borough Council, who held the office of Mayor no fewer than seven times, he rendered priceless service to the town. Head of the successful family brewery business, founded by Edward Fordham Flower in 1831, he will always be remembered for his association with the Shakespeare Memorial Theatre, built by Charles Edward Flower in 1879, and particularly for his efforts in raising money to build the new Theatre after fire had destroyed the old building in 1926.

I shall always remember my first meeting with Sir Archibald, shortly after I took up my duties as Director. Because of his advancing years and failing health, he had invited Mr Ashley Clayton to preside over meetings until his son, Lt-Col Fordham Flower, returned from the army, but he continued to take an active interest in the conduct of Trust business. Thus it was that he invited me to go to see him at The Hill, the Flower family's Victorian residence on the Warwick road. I was received with the utmost courtesy by Miss Margaret Strange, Sir Archibald's secretary and personal assistant, who, as time went on, I got to know very well. Like her master, she had an encyclopaedic knowledge of everything to do with Stratford and the Theatre. I suspected that Sir Archibald wanted to size up the young Director appointed by the Trustees, but any nervousness I may have had quickly disappeared as he put me at my ease; indeed, within a short time we were engaged in friendly conversation, as though we had known each other for a long while. Having questioned me about my career and interests, he told me of his long association with the Trust and his wish that the close links between the Borough Council, the Shakespeare Memorial Theatre and the Trust should continue. I sensed his great pride in Stratford and Shakespeare, and I was particularly interested in what he told me about the part he had played in saving the Welcombe estate at the time it was offered for sale by the Trevelyan family in the late 1920s.

Sir Archibald Flower, 1923

To prevent undesirable development in this sensitive area of unspoiled, typical Warwickshire, part of which had actually belonged to Shakespeare, he told me that he had borrowed money from the bank which had enabled him to purchase Welcombe House and the whole estate. Retaining some of the fields himself and making a gift of some land to the town, he had sold the remainder, subject to safeguards to prevent development. In particular, as already mentioned, he had sold the parkland on either side of the main drive leading to Welcombe House, which was identified with the Welcombe fields owned by Shakespeare, to the Shakespeare Birthplace Trust in 1930, on condition that it should be preserved as open space. This was a major conservation achievement for the Trust, which guaranteed an unspoiled approach to Stratford on the northwest side of the Warwick road. Sir Archibald also told me that he had experienced difficulty at first in disposing of Welcombe House, the large Victorian residence built by the Phillips family. He apparently had tried unsuccessfully to persuade the Warwickshire County Council to buy it for use as a Stratford grammar school for girls, but eventually it had been bought by the Great Western Railway Company and converted for its present use as the Welcombe Hotel.

In addition to the Chairman, the Executive Committee in 1945 had a membership of ten Trustees: Mr Graham Baron Ash, who had restored Packwood House, which he later gave to the National Trust; Mr Ashley E. Clayton, the General Manager of the National Farmers' Union Mutual Insurance Society and a churchwarden of Holy Trinity Church, who presided over the Committee as Acting Chairman; Lt-Col Fordham Flower, who had been elected a Life Trustee in 1940 but who, until the end of the year, was still away on active service; Major Charles Gregory-Hood of Loxley Hall, a descendant of an old county family originally based at Stivichall, on the outskirts of Coventry; the Reverend A. Cecil Knight, the highly respected Headmaster of King Edward VI School, who was succeeded by Mr Leslie Watkins in September 1945; Alderman George A. Lea, a local farmer and butcher

The Director in the library, 1960

possessing an acute business instinct; Alderman Trevor Matthews, a dental surgeon who was a well known public figure and a Governor of the Shakespeare Memorial Theatre; Mr S.C. Kaines Smith, formerly Director of the Birmingham Art Gallery; Alderman Robert M. Smith, principal of the old-established family firm of J.C. Smith, Ltd, in High Street, and the Vicar of Holy Trinity Church, the Reverend Canon Noel Prentice, a Cambridge man who was a keen Shakespearian and an excellent after-dinner speaker.

The Trust's headquarters were in Hornby Cottage, the building situated on the eastern boundary of the Birthplace garden. The front part of the ground floor served as a reception office, where visitors to Shakespeare's Birthplace bought their admission tickets, which they then presented at the front door of the Birthplace, a few yards along the street. The Trustees met in the boardroom on the first floor, an apartment striking for its shining oak floor boards, its exposed original timber beams and the long, early seventeenth-century, shovel-board table in the centre. As Director, I had a desk in the library adjoining, looking out through the leaded-light bay window into the garden of the Birthplace. It was an enchanting position, surrounded, as I was, with bookshelves lining the walls of the library around me.

The minutes of the Executive Committee during 1945 disclose a uniform pattern of proceedings. Month by month the modest receipts from admission fees to the Birthplace and the other properties were reported and necessary payments authorized. Following the end of the war, visitors continued to include a large proportion of service personnel, with occasional special groups, such as a party of Chinese naval officers, guests of the British Council, and Commonwealth representatives taking part in BBC conferences in London.

The number of visitors to the Shakespearian properties during the year showed an overall decrease of nearly five per cent on the previous year, resulting in 78,742 to Shakespeare's Birthplace, 49,640 to Anne Hathaway's Cottage, 23,553 to New Place, and 5,123 to Mary Arden's House. The admission charge to each property was one shilling for an adult and half price for a child. Just over £6,000 had been received from visitors' admission fees, and the surplus, after paying the expenses of the respective properties, was £2,855. Interest on investments of some £15,000 yielded £589, and the sale of publications and postcards achieved £1,345. Garden expenses amounted to £1,045, administrative and library expenses £1,673, and pensions £732. Transfers to the property repairs reserve and the accessions reserve each took £500, leaving a surplus for the year of £424. The total value of the Trust's freehold properties at cost, as shown in the balance sheet, was £35,800.

During the early part of 1945, exhibits which had been removed for safe keeping during the war were restored to Shakespeare's Birthplace and New Place, and there were other indications of a return to more normal conditions. Shottery Lodge, one of the Trust's properties adjacent to Anne Hathaway's Cottage, which had been requisitioned for war use, reverted to the Youth Hostels Association, which

Shottery Lodge

had previously occupied it, though later in the year the Trustees decided to terminate the tenancy, in order to convert the building into residential flats for Trust staff. Similarly, the Old Malt House in Guild Street, which had been used by the emergency fire service during the war, was vacated and let to the Stratford-on-Avon District Ambulance Association. The Committee also concerned itself with minor maintenance items around the properties, such as the cutting of thistles at Welcombe by land girls, and the repair of greenhouses at New Place and the construction of frames there.

So far as Shakespeare's Birthplace was concerned, the Trustees had felt for some time that it presented a rather dreary and uninteresting appearance. Mr Edwin F. Reynolds of Warwick, an architect who was well known for his experience in dealing with period buildings, had accordingly been asked in 1944 to prepare a report and to advise what could be done to improve the situation. Arising from this, a first step, taken at once, was to have flower boxes made and positioned in front of the Birthplace in Henley Street, but further proposals concerning possible improvements to the interior were deferred until the new Director could submit his ideas.

Practical matters of this kind were the concern of the small Visiting Committee, whilst the Finance Committee met more frequently, to deal with staff and money matters. The Trustees had already agreed to undertake a comprehensive review of staff before

I arrived on the scene, and one of my first tasks as Director was to make a preliminary survey of all aspects of the Trust's work, with particular reference to staff.

It was a strange and rather forbidding experience for me, as a young man of thirty, to find myself responsible for the management of a group of staff most of whom were old enough to be my parents or grandparents. Owing to war conditions and natural causes, the total full-time establishment numbered eighteen, plus part-time and seasonal help, as compared with twenty-two in 1939. The staff were mostly aged and long-serving. Five of them were over sixty-five (two being turned seventy); four were between sixty and sixty-five; and three between fifty-five and sixty. Only three employees were below forty.

Mr W.F. Tompkins, aged seventy, had been the senior guide at Shakespeare's Birthplace since 1922; he was a kindly, gentle man with a great sense of duty, well informed and with a formidable repertoire of Shakespearian anecdotes acquired over the years. Mr H. Bean, who acted as the doorkeeper and collector of tickets when visitors entered the Birthplace, had been there since 1925; though competent, he did not strike me as an inspiring character, and he regularly read his newspaper in between discharging his other duties. Mr W.G. Gadsby, who sold the admission tickets for the Birthplace from his small enclosed room in the office building, had also been appointed in 1925; he was a smart, military-type of man, well suited to dealing with the many, varied types of visitors. Miss Dorothea Sheppard, a friendly, willing lady who was very proud of her association with the Trust, had been selling postcards and helping as an attendant since 1927. At New Place, Mr and Mrs A. Anthony, who had been resident custodians since 1928, offered a homely welcome to all who came, and at Anne Hathaway's Cottage Mr J. Mitchell, who had served as an attendant during the same period, had recently been appointed deputy custodian following the retirement of Mr F.W. Bennett after thirty-four years' service as custodian there. As already mentioned, George Meadows, appointed in 1923, had been in sole charge of Mary Arden's House from the time of its purchase by the Trust in 1930.

The longest-serving member of staff was Frank Jackson, the head gardener, who, when I arrived, had completed forty-eight years' service, having joined the Trust in 1897, and who did not retire until he had added another four years to this record. During that period I got to know him very well, my country and gardening interests providing a common link between us.

Jackson was a remarkable character. He was a well-built man of medium height with a fresh complexion and a moustache; he was always smart in appearance, with his white, hard collar, polished boots and cloth cap. A local man, living in the gardener's cottage alongside the greenhouses at New Place, he had only been away from Stratford on a few occasions during his lifetime. He had apparently volunteered for service during the First World War, but had been promptly sent back as being unsuitable, for what reason I never discovered. At the time when the knott garden was being laid out at New Place in the 1920s, he was sent to Lincolnshire to buy tulips, and occasionally he took his wife and son on a Sunday train excursion from Stratford station to Weston-Super-Mare. At other times he just worked, getting up to tend the greenhouses at 5.30 a.m. and, with the help of his assistant, Charles Trueman, who had worked alongside him for twenty-six years, taking all the other tasks involved in the maintenance of the Trust's gardens and estate in his stride.

Frank was the very epitome of all the qualities of a born gardener: loyal, respectful, hardworking, modest and kind. His experience was based on practical knowledge of his traditional craft, and what he did not know about trees, plants, flowers and the processes of propagating and grafting was not worth knowing. Somehow, he symbolized all that the Trust had stood for since Victorian times: dignity, good manners, and pride in being entrusted with the heritage of Shakespeare and Stratford. He told me how strict the Trustees had been in his early days, and recalled how the head gardener under whom he worked as a young man had been instantly dismissed when, early one afternoon, one of the Trustees inspecting New Place garden noticed that he had been drinking a little too freely during his lunch break.

One thing I particularly remember: Jackson had a profound distrust of any form of mechanisation. At that time all the grass at the properties was cut by hand mowers, and the orchards at Anne Hathaway's Cottage by scythe and sickle, in the same way as in Shakespeare's time. When I suggested to Jackson that the Trustees might be willing to provide a motor mower to lessen his labour of hand-scything the grass in the orchard, he implored me not to spend money on such a machine; mechanisation of that kind he saw as an instrument of the devil, which would make men idle. Garden transport in those days was a handcart, which could frequently be seen conveying plants from one property to another.

Speaking of Frank Jackson, I have one regret, namely, that I did not record his speech. Every now and again in conversation he would use words and phrases spoken in a Warwickshire accent which Shakespeare himself would have instantly recognized. The same also applied to George Meadows at Mary Arden's House, who was as much a part of Warwickshire history as the old agricultural implements and tools he took such pride in collecting and explaining. He was a bachelor, who lived with his sister at Alveston, and he rode every day on his bicycle to Wilmcote and back. I discovered that, in the absence of a money safe at Mary Arden's House, he took the cash collected from visitors' admission fees home with him every night for safe keeping, but I never remember finding a penny discrepancy in his accounting. George was a kindly man and a first class guide, who thoroughly enjoyed his work and was fond of children.

All these employees with whom I found myself working were loyal, dedicated, friendly people, who took great pride in belonging to an organization which had very much a family feeling about it. All remembered Frederick Wellstood and spoke of him in appreciative terms; equally, they knew his widow and supported her in carrying on after his death. Everyone knew each other and all appeared to be content with their working conditions and remuneration. The level of wages, as compared with the present day, seems almost unbelievable. The long-serving chief guide at Shakespeare's Birthplace, responsible for supervising the property and the staff, received £4 5s. 0d. a week, and the wages of other attendant staff ranged between £2 0s. 0d. and £3 5s. 0d. a week. The experienced head gardener was paid £4 5s. 0d. a week plus the free use of his cottage with lighting and fuel, and his assistant £3 10s. 0d. a week. Charles Trueman, who held the latter post, somehow managed to build himself a bungalow on the Luddington Lane and to keep a pig on that wage. I remember how one morning, before he started work, Charles knocked on the back door of 14 Henley Street, where we lived, and handed over to Mrs Fox a carefully wrapped package containing a joint of pork, explaining that he had killed his pig a few days before. Food rationing, a legacy of the war years, was still in force, so the offering was more than acceptable. The gesture was typical of his generous nature, and it was a sad occurrence when Charles later met with a fatal accident, as he was riding home on his bicycle one dark night along the Evesham road.

Although I was a stranger, as it were, and a young one at that, it did not take me long to feel part of this type of organization. One of the first things I did was to talk to each member of staff, asking questions about his or her work and what was involved in it. When I enquired why something was being done in a particular way, or the reason for a certain procedure, I invariably received the same reply, namely, that this was how it had always been done. Everyone seemed to be happy with the existing arrangements, and I sensed that change was not likely to be considered necessary or even desirable.

It was therefore particularly fortunate that at this juncture another newcomer, in the person of Lt-Col Fordham Flower, appeared on the scene and became involved with the new Director in the management of the Trust. Sir Archibald Flower had been waiting for the return of his son, Fordham, from war service

Shakespeare's Birthplace in the 1920s and 30s

to take over his many responsibilities, including the chairmanship of the Birthplace Trust, as well as of the Shakespeare Memorial Theatre. I can well remember my first meeting with Colonel Flower, on the eve of his return to civilian life. Though I do not have a record of the exact date, it was within a few weeks after I became Director. What stands out in my memory is that, although we had never met before, I instinctively felt that he was a man of vision, with whom I could share ideas and work in harmony.

After a general discussion, we embarked on a tour of inspection of the Trust's properties, and we talked as he drove me in his car from one to another. At each property I introduced the staff to him and a detailed inspection followed. Colonel Flower felt that Shakespeare's Birthplace presented a dull and old-fashioned appearance, and that changes needed to be considered to make it more interesting and appealing to visitors. The garden was well kept, but he noted, with an indication of disapproval, the presence of ivy, which covered the end of the building and the adjacent offices. At New Place ivy climbing up the railings on top of the wall which enclosed the site of the foundations suggested a Victorian policy of excluding the public from view, while the museum-type of display in Nash's House, next door, was very miscellaneous in its subject matter and did not excite much enthusiasm. Anne Hathaway's Cottage he found much as he had expected: picturesque and sentimental, with its well kept garden and orchard, but possessing little in the way of amenity for visitors. Mary Arden's House, with its display of old Warwickshire agricultural implements in the barns, scored full marks under the care of George Meadows, the custodian, with his fascinating repertoire of country reminiscences and folklore.

We returned from Wilmcote along the Ridgeway, which at that time had the appearance of a little-used country track, rather than a widened secondary road, as at present. As we drove along, we compared notes about our impressions and ideas as to what needed to be done to improve the attraction of the properties. I remember telling Colonel Flower that I thought it would take five years to carry through a programme of comprehensive overhaul and re-presentation, realizing that staff and finance would play a decisive part in any proposals I might put forward. In actual fact, it took nearly ten years for the seeds sown at that first meeting to come to full fruition; but I was assured from that time that in Colonel Flower, shortly to be elected Chairman of the Shakespeare Birthplace Trust, I had someone with whom I could share a vision of re-defining the role of the Trust to take advantage of the changed conditions of the post-war period.

The Way Forward

At the Annual Meeting of the Trustees held on 11 May 1946 Lt-Col Fordham Flower was elected Chairman of the Shakespeare Birthplace Trust, in succession to his father, Sir Archibald, to whose long and valuable service warm tribute was paid by the Reverend A. Cecil Knight. Disclaiming that he possessed the outstanding ability of his father, Colonel Flower accepted the office with 'diffidence and trepidation'. Being conscious of the immensely increased responsibility of being Chairman of the Trust, as well as of the Shakespeare Memorial Theatre, 'the vista of this Trust', he said, 'seems to open out into a long avenue of expanding work and responsibility. Every Shakespearian interest has a most enormous national and international significance. I believe Stratford is on the threshold of a new and widely expanding era, and all our policies have to shape along these lines ... I hope you will support me in preparing a policy of expansion, and of welcome to everybody from all over the world'.

This pronouncement struck the keynote to what, in fact, happened during the next five or six years, and subsequently during the continuing period of my Directorship. As indicated in the previous chapter, the most important task confronting the Trustees after the cessation of hostilities in 1945 was to undertake a comprehensive review of the Trust's administration in all its aspects, to re-interpret its role in the changed conditions of the post-war period, making changes as necessary, and at the same time to plan for future possible requirements.

Acting on recommendations contained in my first report, the Trustees proceeded without delay to make a number of important decisions which provided the foundation for the future expansion and development of the Trust's work. At the top of the list was the problem of staff: the desire to be generous to those who had given long and loyal service, and the need to replace them with younger, suitable people. The establishment was accordingly reviewed in a realistic manner, the particular needs of each property being assessed, and provision made for improvement and anticipated expansion. Higher rates of pay in accord with post-war expectations were agreed, staff regulations revised and a superannuation scheme introduced. Prior to this time there had been no fund to provide pensions for the Trust's employees on retirement, though the Trustees had always granted ex gratia pensions. The aggregate cost of this arrangement had by now become a major charge on the Trust's slender resources and, clearly, a new policy had to be formulated.

Before the end of 1946, new chief guides for Shakespeare's Birthplace and Anne Hathaway's Cottage were appointed, and additional assistant staff and gardeners recruited. The Director was given secretarial help, and an experienced assistant librarian archivist, Mr John Ellis, joined the staff. Thus it proved possible to transfer much of the Trust's work to a younger team of employees and, as the years passed, new staff were recruited to meet developing needs. By 1951 the pay roll numbered twenty-seven full-time and ten part-time regular staff, plus additional summer helpers. Within five years, salaries and wages had increased from £2,500 a year to four times that amount.

Arrangements for managing the properties were also reviewed, and revised regulations for the admission of visitors approved. Publicity received attention: an attractive leaflet describing the Shakespearian properties, the first of a long series over the years, was produced; and new notice boards and direction signs, designed in a distinctive style with green background and gold lettering, which came to be associated with the Trust, were provided for the properties.

In the office, new procedures were adopted to meet the Trust's developing needs. Prior to my appointment the majority of letters had been written by hand, but, with the increased volume of correspondence, the use of the typewriter became indispensable. Perhaps the biggest change was in connection with the Trust's book-keeping and accounting arrangements. Up to the time of my appointment a cash book and single ledger, linked with day books kept by the properties, served all requirements; but as from April 1946 a more detailed, revised system of book-keeping was introduced. This, with a few modifications and additions, continued to meet all the Trust's accounting requirements for the next forty years. At the same time, a new format for the published annual report and statement of accounts was adopted.

I remember very clearly the arrangement for paying wages in my early days. Every Friday each employee in turn came in person to the office to collect his or her wages in cash, the details of which were entered in a large ledger which had been in use since 1921. Each recipient signed on the appropriate line. Petty cash payments, such as house expenses, sundries bought for the gardens, or gardeners' train fares to Wilmcote, were also entered on the same page and paid. There was no question of confidentiality, the book lying open for all to see; only when a different accounting system was adopted did it prove possible to introduce personal pay packets.

Looking back, I can see that the pay-day arrangement I have described typified the old-world, almost feudal, character of the Trust: but it had merit, in that it was personal, and every week it provided me with an opportunity to enquire about the state of health of each member of staff, to hear about visitor patronage and any other news, and to deal immediately with house-keeping requirements, problems or grievances, if any. This personal relationship between management and staff became a corner stone of my policy during the whole period of my Directorship. Throughout the years, I personally interviewed and appointed every employee, whether full- or part-time; progressively my family, as it were, grew to a considerable size, but to the end it proved possible to retain the informal, close relationship of Director and staff which characterised my early days.

The annual audit, which now takes several weeks to complete, was likewise a simple procedure. In my first year, Mr Parsons, the principal of Sharp, Parsons and Company of Birmingham, a well known firm which audited the accounts of Flower and Sons, Ltd, at the brewery, came in person, in an honorary capacity, to conduct the Trust's audit. He completed the checking of the books and vouchers during the morning and, after we had had lunch together, he spent a little time preparing a summary statement of accounts for inclusion in the annual report. For years afterwards the audit rarely took more than three days, but during that time a thorough scrutiny and checking of the many facets of the Trust's business was completed. I recall that invariably the auditors demanded to see the original title deeds of the Trust's freehold properties, which were listed on the balance sheet. Any unused admission tickets from the previous year were always destroyed as part of the audit procedure.

The minutes of the monthly meetings of the Executive Committee of the Trustees disclose a uniform pattern of proceedings. Details of the numbers of visitors to the Birthplace and the other Shakespearian properties, and the resultant income, were carefully monitored, and care was taken to ensure that expenditure was kept within the budget, which by this time had become an essential part of the Director's management scheme. Once a quarter I produced an estimated statement of accounts, so it was always possible to see how the year's income and spending were shaping.

For the first few years, the number of visitors showed little increase, since petrol rationing restricted home patronage and there were as yet few tourists from abroad. Nevertheless, as conditions after the war gradually returned to normal, admissions to the four properties started to increase. It was during the financial year ended March 1948 that, for the first time since 1927, visitors to Shakespeare's Birthplace exceeded one hundred thousand, a record which seemed particularly appropriate for the year which marked the centenary of the purchase of the Birthplace and, in effect, the one-hundredth anniversary of the beginning of the Shakespeare Birthplace Trust. Patronage, however, was still uncertain, the following year's admissions showing a slight decrease. In 1949 the total number of visitors rose to 135,000, with Anne Hathaway's Cottage exceeding 100,000 for the first time. By 1951, the Festival of Britain year, admissions reached 185,000 at the Birthplace and 142,000 at the Cottage, the increases being largely due to the greater numbers of overseas tourists, particularly from the United States.

Throughout the immediate post-war period, the Trust's economy was precariously poised, and the Trustees had to take great care to operate within a very modest budget. Rental and investment income was quite small and, in the absence of an endowment fund, it was the proceeds of visitors' fees which had to sustain the whole basis of the Trust's operation. Faced with the prospect of inadequate income to meet increased overhead costs and wages, and particularly the backlog of maintenance on all their properties, the Trustees decided to increase visitors' admission fees for the 1948 season: the 1s. 0d. charge to each property was raised to 1s. 3d., with an inclusive ticket admitting to the four properties increased from 2s. 6d. to 3s. 0d. I recall that the decision to do this was taken not without considerable hesitation and misgiving.

The plain fact was that, with a surplus of only £224 for the year 1947, additional resources were needed. There was so much that needed to be done. At Mary Arden's House, for instance, there were no public toilets (indeed, the village had as yet no mains water supply), so one of the first building projects I was involved in was the planning and erection of a small toilet block alongside the great barn on the rickyard side. Mr Edwin F. Reynolds was the architect, and the Stratford family firm of Fincher and Company were the builders. Their estimate for the job was £237. At first the Trustees were refused a building licence to proceed, but, after pressure, the building was eventually allowed and was completed in 1948, the final bill being £467.

The greenhouses at New Place, which served as the base of the Trust's garden activities, were urgently in need of overhaul, and new cold frames had to be built. The interior of New Place Museum, which had received no attention for years, was redecorated, and repairs were carried out at Mary Arden's House, together with a miscellany of minor maintenance items and improvements, too numerous to mention, at the other properties.

Shottery Lodge and Brooklands

A major improvement project which the Trustees undertook at this time was the conversion of Shottery Lodge, the Victorian detached house standing in its own grounds near to Anne Hathaway's Cottage, into four self-contained residences. The idea behind this was to improve a dilapidated property which was situated in a sensitive position near to the Cottage, and at the same time to provide accommodation for new members of staff who might be recruited from outside the town. In fact two of the units, when they became available in 1947, were occupied by newly-appointed guides working at Shakespeare's Birthplace and Anne Hathaway's Cottage.

The original house had been enlarged, and it was a rambling place with little amenity. For a number of years it had been occupied by the Youth Hostels Association, which had also converted the detached stable block for use with the house. The building was urgently in need of attention, and the garden and orchard area belonging to it, which must have been a most attractive feature of the property when it had belonged to the Bucknall family, had been neglected and allowed to run wild.

I remember Mr Edwin Reynolds, the Trust's architect, telling me how difficult he had found it to plan the division of the building into four convenient living units, more especially since the permissible expenditure was limited by building licence requirements, as well as by the Trustees' resources.

He apparently thought of the solution to the problem very early one morning when in his bathroom at home – he lived in a Georgian house at Northgate, Warwick – and he immediately went into his study next door and committed his idea to the drawing board. Reynolds was a friendly, elderly gentleman, who typified the best qualities of the Edwardian period, when he had trained as a young architect. He possessed amazingly wide experience and expertise, and I learned a great deal from him when we made site inspections.

The building work at Shottery Lodge was carried out by the Stratford family firm of Smith and Unitt, at a cost of slightly less than £3,000. As a corollary to the conversion, the grounds attached to the Lodge were re-allocated: a garden plot was given to each of the flats, as well as to the adjoining New Row cottages, the frontages of which were also improved. The planting of shrubs and the recovery of the garden and orchard area around Shottery Lodge provided an attractive setting for the house, and represented a major contribution to the improvement of the immediate environment of Anne Hathaway's Cottage.

Quite fortuitously, another opportunity presented itself to the Trustees the following year, to safeguard the approach to the Cottage. In September 1948 they purchased the property known as Brooklands, comprising a large detached residence standing on the corner of the road leading to Anne Hathaway's Cottage, which had nearly two acres of land attached to it, running alongside the road down to Shottery Brook. Brooklands had been the home of the family of Fincher, a well known firm of builders. Occupying the site of an earlier farmhouse, of which portions were probably incorporated, it was a substantially built, spacious residence, which had been altered from time to time. At the rear it looked out onto a well kept garden and orchard, which sloped down to the brook and beyond which the car park for visitors to Anne Hathaway's Cottage was constructed in later years. The Trustees rightly felt it important to ensure that this property should be preserved against possible undesirable development and, at a time when their cash reserve was very small, they had the courage and foresight to spend £9,500 on its purchase.

Edwin Reynolds, who by this time had established himself as the Trust's architect by reason of his successful conversion of Shottery Lodge, was asked to prepare a plan to divide Brooklands into two self-contained residences, each with a small enclosed garden at the rear, the remainder of the garden and orchard ground being retained by the Trust as a reserve garden for the growing of herbs and bedding plants. Smith and Unitt, the Stratford builders who had already done excellent work for the Trust, undertook the conversion, which was finished in January 1950. The two units were then rented to tenants, Brooklands and its grounds being thus safeguarded as an important contribution to the environmental amenity of Anne Hathaway's Cottage. Sadly, Edwin Reynolds did not live to see this happen, and it fell to his partner, Mr T. Spencer Wood, to complete the project. Subsequently, Spencer Wood took over all the architectural work of the Trust, until his partner, Mr Laurence Williams, succeeded him in 1960.

Shakespeare's Birthplace

More important and far reaching in its implications for the visiting public was the programme of improvements to Shakespeare's Birthplace, which was one of the main concerns of the Trustees between 1945 and 1950. After the neglect of the war years, necessary repair work on the exterior fabric of the Birthplace was undertaken in 1946 as a priority, and various improvements made to the layout and presentation of the garden, particularly the planting of more herbaceous flowers alongside those mentioned in Shakespeare's plays. The ivy, which had hitherto covered the chimney stack of the building at the east end and the gable and walls on the west side of the office and library building, was removed. Sir Fordham had a particular dislike of ivy, and it was not long before it disappeared from the other properties also.

Another significant change was made in connection with arrangements for the admission of visitors to the Birthplace. The practice of issuing admission tickets at the Trust's office building, now known as Hornby Cottage, was discontinued, and a counter for reception and sale of tickets was provided in the room at the west end of the Birthplace which had originally been used for the storage of records. From this time onwards, visitors entered the Birthplace directly from Henley Street, through a door under the portico which had hitherto remained closed; this arrangement of direct access continued to operate until the Visitors' Centre was built nearby, in 1981.

The space originally occupied by the ticket office in Hornby Cottage was adapted and fitted for use as a sales area, where postcards and related items could be sold. From very small beginnings, centred on the sale of a few dozen postcards and a catalogue of the Birthplace exhibits, the Trust progressively developed its role during the next few years as a bookseller of Shakespearian publications and commemorative gifts, providing a service which satisfied the needs of the visitors and at the same time contributed useful supplementary income to the Trust's budget.

Shakespeare's Birthplace Centenary Celebrations

The year 1947 was a special one in another way; it marked the centenary of the purchase of Shakespeare's Birthplace in 1847 for preservation as a national memorial. The anniversary provided an opportunity to remove many of the early printed books and other items which had formed the core of the museum display and which showed signs of deterioration due to over exposure, and to substitute a select commemorative exhibition on the anniversary theme. The original poster of the auction in 1847, together with playbills and other contemporary items, portrayed the extraordinary public interest and enthusiasm aroused by the sale itself; and a sequence of original drawings illustrated the history of the fabric of the building both before and after its purchase, with particular reference to the restoration undertaken by the Trustees during the years 1857-62.

The centenary exhibition attracted considerable attention during the visiting season, and emphasis was focussed on the anniversary when the second Shakespeare Conference, organized by the University of Birmingham and the British Council, met at Mason Croft in August 1947. On 19 August I gave a paper to the Conference on 'Shakespeare's Birthplace: a retrospect on the occasion of the centenary of its purchase'. I then used this as the basis of an illustrated article entitled 'The Heritage of Shakespeare's Birthplace', published in 1948 in the first volume of *Shakespeare Survey*, the new annual survey of Shakespearian study and production, issued under the joint sponsorship of the University of Birmingham, the Shakespeare Memorial Theatre and the Shakespeare Birthplace Trust.

On Wednesday, 20 August, a unique commemorative event took place. The Trustees gave a garden party, to which the Shakespeare scholars attending the Conference, members of the Stratford-upon-Avon Corporation and other representative guests

Centenary garden party group

were invited. Those attending were able to inspect books, prints and records in the Trust's collections, displayed in the Trustees' room, the library and the records room, as well as the exhibition in the Birthplace. The Mayor of Stratford-upon-Avon, Councillor Eric Baildham, and the Chairman of the Trust, Lt-Col Fordham Flower, welcomed the guests, who were addressed by Dr John Dover Wilson, Emeritus Professor of English at the University of Edinburgh, who represented the University of Cambridge on the governing body of the Trust, Professor Pieter Harting, Professor of English and Rector Magnificus at the University of Amsterdam, and Dr S.G. Dunn, a Professor of English who had worked in India before retiring to live in Stratford. The international appeal of Shakespeare was symbolized by the presence of so many distinguished scholars from overseas countries.

On the actual centenary date, 16 September 1947, the Chairman gave a broadcast talk on the BBC, on the subject of 'Buying Shakespeare's Birthplace', and on 28 November an oak tree was planted in the Birthplace garden as a permanent reminder of the centenary celebrations. The ceremony was performed by the Mayor of Stratford-upon-Avon, who was, most appropriately, Councillor Lt-Col Fordham Flower, Chairman of the Trust, in the presence of Trustees and representative guests, including Sir Archibald Flower, High Steward of the Borough of Stratford-upon-Avon and formerly Chairman of the Trust, together with his grandchildren, Caroline and Charles Flower.

Re-presentation of Shakespeare's Birthplace

In the meantime, the Executive Committee of the Trustees had devoted considerable time and thought to the problem of improving the attraction and interest of Shakespeare's Birthplace. Soon after my appointment as Director, Edwin Reynolds, the architect, had been asked to survey the interior of the building and to advise what could be done, but it fell to his successor, T. Spencer Wood, and myself to prepare detailed recommendations. These were contained in a report, considered and approved by the Trustees at a special meeting in August 1949. During the following autumn and winter, a programme of work which completely transformed the interior appearance of the Birthplace was carried out with the help of a local builder, D.J. Dyer, who had in his employment a small team of craftsmen experienced in exercising the traditional skills required to tackle an unusually demanding job of this kind.

As a preliminary to a comprehensive overhaul of the interior fabric of the building, two major installations were undertaken: the renewal of antiquated central heating, and the introduction of electrical power and concealed lighting. First, the ugly iron

Planting of centenary oak tree

pipes and coils which comprised the original ineffective central heating, installed in Victorian times, were dismantled and replaced by a less obtrusive, up-to-date heating system, based on the use of smaller pipework and radiators, fed by an underground main which ran across the garden from a new boiler housed in a basement at the rear of Hornby Cottage. To undertake an installation of this kind without impairing the visual appearance of the various rooms of this sixteenth-century, half-timbered building required considerable care and ingenuity, and a number of devices to camouflage pipes and radiators had to be contrived.

In a similar manner, the wiring of the Birthplace for electricity had to be planned and executed most carefully. As a precaution against possible fire risk associated with the introduction of electrical current, a type of copper-covered cable known as pyrotenax was used. Apart from its safety aspect, it also had the advantage of being pliable and almost indestructible, so that it proved possible to conceal it under floors, behind beams and above ceilings, with the result that, when completed, there was no visible evidence of electrical wiring or fittings. Power points were put in hidden places, and lighting sources concealed in fireplaces and behind specially made, oak pelmets above windows and doors. The overall effect achieved was a subdued level of general illumination appropriate to the character of the period rooms, with provision for the lighting of exhibition cases in the museum part of the building.

There followed a comprehensive making-good of all the floors, walls, ceilings, plasterwork and woodwork, accompanied by a detailed inspection and treatment of all the timberwork structure against worm. All superfluous fitments and wires, with the exception of a few 'historic' nails, were removed; and it was decided, after careful investigation, to dispense with the antiquated, obtrusive fire alarm installation, which was activated by batteries needing constant attention and which would occasionally misbehave and give false alarms at the Director's house, to which it was linked.

The Trustees themselves showed a keen interest in what was going on, and gave instructions as to the detailed work to be undertaken in various parts of the building. In particular, they decided that the time had come to introduce colour into the interior of the Birthplace. Up till then, the wall panels between the timber framing had remained in the dark colour of the concrete material that was used to replace the wattle and daub plaster and brick infilling when the building was restored in the 1860s. The decision to decorate the rooms in an off-white shade of a special kind of matt paint produced a complete new look, which emphasized the character of the half-timbered structure. At the same time, the bare, oak floor boards, which had hitherto been mopped with water and which often looked drab and dirty, were cleaned and polished with bees-wax, the natural grain of the old oak being revealed in the process.

As a young man, I found the responsibility of supervising this far-reaching transformation of the interior of one of Britain's most famous historic buildings a somewhat daunting, but nevertheless exciting and satisfying, experience. I still remember very clearly what was done in the various rooms before the interior was painted, and, for the purposes of record, some details should be mentioned.

Starting at the bottom, as it were, attention was first given to the cellar, under the kitchen. Basically the Wilmcote stone of which it had been constructed was in a remarkably good condition, but it needed cleaning down and re-pointing, and defects in the steps leading down to it, the evidence of wear over the years, had to be repaired. Concealed lighting was introduced at the cellar head, to make it possible for visitors to look down the cellar steps, through a slatted panel inserted in the old oak door controlling access at the top.

In the kitchen, the stonework over and around the fireplace was cleaned and pointed, and the massive oak beam spanning the wide, open hearth was exposed. The removal of cracked plaster at the back of the fireplace revealed evidence that a bake oven had originally existed on the left-hand side, but had been filled in with brickwork at a later date, when no longer required. In Shakespeare's time bread would have been baked here for the household, and ale brewed for drinking in an adjoining outhouse at the rear. The existing recess, or small room, leading from the kitchen was fitted with a door of old oak, into which the original front door of the Birthplace was incorporated.

In the adjoining living room, the broken, stone-flagged floor, believed to be original, was carefully overhauled; and the stone plinth supporting the timber framing was stripped of its coating of whitewash and cleaned down, and a number of bricks which had been inserted were removed and substituted with stone. The main feature of the room, namely the fireplace, was cleaned of its peeling plaster and whitewash, to reveal an impressive, open hearth, constructed with a mixture of Wilmcote stone and early handmade bricks; and with a worn, sooted fireback and fireplace hearth, which provided tangible evidence of its regular use for heating the room in Shakespeare's time and later years.

Fireplaces in other rooms also received attention. In the room which had been adapted for use as the ticket office, replacement brickwork restored the wide, open hearth, and in the inner room of the museum downstairs – the old Swan and Maidenhead portion of the building – the stone and brick surround of the fireplace was cleaned down and re-pointed, as necessary. In the process, a small recess on the right-hand side of the fireback, which had been filled in and plastered over, was opened up to reveal a place where kindling and a tinder box had originally been stored. Inside the recess was found an early key (probably seventeenth-century), part of a quill pen, a broken, old, clay pipe, some coins of George III dated 1771, 1773 and 1799, a fragment of an old comb, and the lid of a tinder box, together with fragments of tinder and flint. These finds, though mostly of a later date than Shakespeare's day, throw interesting light on the domestic history of building, particularly since part of the premises was occupied by descendants of Shakespeare and his sister for nearly two hundred years.

In the museum on the first floor, the fireplace at the top of the stairs received similar treatment, the exposed stonework up to the ceiling level thus becoming an impressive feature. A small fireplace recess at the far end of the museum was filled in and the wall plastered over to provide a flat space for exhibition display. A number of ventilators inserted in the walls at the time of the original restoration, which were thought to be ugly and unnecessary, were removed.

The room leading from the museum, the traditional birthroom, received what amounted to a complete face-lift. Before work started, all the timbers, ceiling and walls were coated with flaking plaster and faded whitewash, on which names and tributes to Shakespeare had been written by visitors from the eighteenth century onwards. The leaded-light panes of glass in the window also bore autographs scratched on by celebrities who had been allowed the privilege of recording their visit, in the days before the Birthplace came under the care of the Trust. They included the names of Walter Scott, Izaak Walton, Robert Browning, Thomas Carlyle, Isaac Watts and Edmund Keen. The room presented an extraordinary sight, almost every inch of wall and ceiling space being covered with writing of this kind. The majority of the tributes were sincere and even touching, but, with the passage of time, many had become indecipherable; some, also, had been obliterated by the rude remarks of vulgar scrawlers. To some, the birthroom in this condition presented an unusual fascination, but the reaction of others was one of disapproval and disgust. As the author of one guide book, who came in the middle 1930s, wrote: 'the room should be as Shakespeare saw it, not with its walls scrawled on by every loon and lout who comes this way'. In other respects, also, the room was not inspiring. With its scanty furniture and monumental bust of the poet, it looked dull and bare, lacking the warmth and character which the principal bedroom of the Shakespeare family home would undoubtedly have had.

It was a courageous decision on the part of the Trustees to obliterate this unique evidence of international homage to Shakespeare, and I myself am

Wattle and daub

certain that it was necessary, both on aesthetic and hygienic grounds. Moreover, the record was not lost, because a complete photographic copy of the autographed walls and ceiling had already been made for the Trust's archives. In the event, the removal of the whitewash revealed the original oak timber framing and wattle and daub panels, which were found to be in good condition. The plaster coating of a small

Gates in Birthplace garden

section of one of the panels on the left of the window was scraped away, to illustrate how a wattle of interlaced osier sticks covered with a coarse mixture of clay, straw and pebbles ('daub') was used to fill the spaces between the timber members. It was whilst this exhibit was being prepared that a small hand-wrought dress pin of sixteenth- or early seventeenth-century date was found embedded in the plaster; inevitably the thought occurred as to whether it could possibly have belonged to the poet's father.

Another interesting discovery was made in the birthroom. The removal of peeling plaster which had covered the chimney stack revealed the original, small fireplace which had been bricked in, and above it a stone mantelpiece. Behind the brick infill was found a quantity of pieces of handmade, window glass, of an age much older than any other glass in the building. The reinstatement of the fireplace, with its quaint mixture of stone and brick, added a feature which seemed particularly appropriate in a bedroom which must have been comfortable and warm, when used by the poet's parents.

The original narrow staircase which led from the kitchen below was preserved intact and, in the interests of safety, was cordoned off to prevent its being used by visitors, who, having been encouraged to follow a one-way route through the building, now passed directly from the birthroom into the two adjoining bedrooms at the rear of the house, over the kitchen and lobby. Little needed to be done, except to remove the unsightly ventilators and refurbish the exposed timber structure and raftered roof. Below, at the foot of the stairs, a fire hydrant and hose reel were installed in a concealed position, behind the door leading into the garden.

It was also at this time that a number of improvements were carried out in the garden of Shakespeare's Birthplace. Outside the back door of the house, a paved path of York stone was laid along the whole length of the garden, from east to west, and stone steps were provided down to the wide, gravelled path which ran to the Guild Street entrance in the northern boundary wall of the garden. The base of Stratford's medieval stone cross, which had originally stood underneath the old market house in High Street, remained in the centre of the path as an interesting reminder of the town's history; and, in order to commemorate the long association of Sir Archibald Flower with the Trust, a new pair of wrought-iron gates were presented by the Flower family to replace the old gates at the Guild Street entrance to the garden. Dwarf stone walls were also built to protect the exterior base of the new yew hedge on either side of the frontage of the house in Henley Street.

Whilst these improvements were proceeding inside and outside the Birthplace, I prepared a report containing suggestions for re-presenting the interior of the building, the Trustees having indicated that they would like everything possible to be done to achieve a more attractive and interesting display. My suggestions were far reaching in their practical and visual implications, but they received the enthusiastic approval of the Trustees. The proposed changes were made during the autumn of 1949 and the early months of 1950.

Hitherto, the main emphasis in Shakespeare's Birthplace had been on the museum, accommodated in the part of the building which had been used originally by the poet's father for his business as a glover and wool dealer, and in later times converted to the Swan and Maidenhead inn. The museum rooms on both floors were equipped with old-fashioned, oak exhibition cases, in which were displayed copies of Shakespeare Quartos and Folios and books with which Shakespeare's works show him to have been familiar. There was also a selection of Shakespeare medals, together with coins mentioned by the poet or in use during his period. The walls were almost completely covered with framed, early views of Stratford-upon-Avon and the Birthplace, portraits of William Shakespeare and his friends and contemporaries, facsimiles of documents relating to the poet's parents, relatives and friends, and a considerable miscellany of related subject matter. There were some curious items, such as twelve pieces of wood from the tree in Windsor Park known as Herne's oak, referred to in *The Merry Wives of Windsor*, which fell down in 1863; an eighteenth-century hunting-sword, with narrow curved blade, which had belonged to Alderman John Payton, a former Mayor of the town; a piece of oak cut from the corner of another exhibit, known as Shakespeare's desk, at about the beginning of the nineteenth-century; a brass, seventeenth-century finger-ring, thought to have belonged to Dr John Hall; and a fragment of stone from Shakespeare's monument in Holy Trinity Church.

The rooms at the west end of the building, which had comprised the Shakespeare family's home, were sparsely furnished and conveyed little of the atmosphere of the homely domestic setting in which John and Mary Shakespeare would have lived and brought up their children. In the living room, the only items of furniture were a chair, two joint-stools and a striking clock in a mahogany case, made by Thomas Sharp of Stratford-upon-Avon in about 1790; and in the fireplace were displayed a bell-metal cooking pot with hanger, pot-hook and chain, and a wooden rack for spits above. In the kitchen, the fireplace was well equipped, with an iron fire-back, a pair of iron cobbolds, a bell-metal cooking pot and an iron fat-melting pan; but the only items of furniture were an oak bench, a joint-stool and the original half-hatch door from the entrance to the Birthplace. Other smaller exhibits were an Elizabethan leather bottle, a wooden mousetrap of early date, two rush-light holders and the wooden door of a bacon cupboard.

The birthroom had changed little in appearance over the years and, as already mentioned, was sparsely furnished, as shown in the early published views of it and as depicted in the small, framed, Fenton-ware pot lid, produced in the early nineteenth century, which was displayed on one of the walls. A plaster cast of Shakespeare stood on a small table at the far side, opposite to the window, the inscribed signatures on which constituted the chief feature of interest in the room. There were no furnishings to suggest that the room had been used as a bed chamber, apart from a linen chest of early seventeenth-century date, which had apparently been in the Birthplace before the property was sold in 1847. There was also a carved, oak chest of the period of Henry VIII and an Elizabethan oak desk which had formerly belonged to the College at Stratford, whose priests had served Holy Trinity Church nearby during the medieval period.

In the upstairs rooms at the rear, there were an old, oak, trestle-type table, such as was used in the sixteenth century, an oak chest made from parts of a seventeenth-century bedstead, and another joint-stool. There was also a painted plaster cast of Shakespeare, moulded in 1814 from the original bust in Holy Trinity Church, together with two old, painted signboards, each with the inscription 'The Immortal Shakespeare was born in this House', which had been originally fixed below the birthroom window, to attract visitors as they came along Henley Street.

Taken as a whole, the Shakespeare family's home portion of the Birthplace, just described, gave the impression of being bare and lacking warmth and comfort. To improve its presentation in a meaningful and practical way inevitably involved change and the introduction of a number of pieces of furniture and accessories more directly related to the kind of home John Shakespeare and his family would have enjoyed. There were two factors which influenced my recommendations to the Trustees as to what could be done. The first was the need not to over-furnish the rooms, in view of the increasing number of visitors, already in excess of a hundred thousand a year, passing through them. Sufficient space to move and view conveniently was vitally important. Secondly, the information contained in a number of original inventories preserved in the Borough records, detailing the effects of middle-class Stratford tradesmen, provided authentic evidence of the furnishings and utensils commonly in use in homes of this kind in Shakespeare's time.

The problem of locating and acquiring suitable authentic items to make possible the proposed re-presentation of the various rooms was not easy. I found myself visiting shops dealing in antiques over a wide area, an exercise which, in spite of many disappointments, produced some very good finds. I kept a record of items purchased for the Trust and, if only for the prices paid as compared with present-day values, one or two illustrations may be of interest. From Silvesters of Solihull, a family firm of antique dealers, I bought a Jacobean child's cradle, of the type Mary Shakespeare would have used for her family, for £16 10s. 0d., an early copper warming- or plague-pan with an iron handle for £9 15s. 0d., and a large, seventeenth-century, brass alms dish, engraved with the figures of Adam and Eve, for a similar sum. A panel of Jacobean needlework from Grainger-Brown of Warwick cost £30 0s. 0d., and a fine Staffordshire porcelain figure of Shakespeare, made about 1800, was bought at Oxford for £15 0s. 0d. Several items of furniture, including the single half-headed bed for the birthroom at a cost of £32 10s. 0d., a seventeenth-century, oak arm-chair at the same price, and a pair of single chairs, came from S.W. Wolsey, the specialist collector of early oak furniture in London. At that time, J.H. Newstead had an excellent antiques shop in Sheep Street, Stratford-upon-Avon, and he was able to find for me a variety of very good, early kitchen utensils, stoneware jars, samplers and smaller furnishing items. Mr Newstead was also an excellent photographer, and I often used his services, together with those of Ernest Daniels of Bridge Street.

Turning, then, to what was done. The small room through which visitors entered Shakespeare's Birthplace from Henley Street was equipped with a fixed reception counter just inside the front door. In other respects, it was a typical furnished room, with a seventeenth-century, oak chest of drawers and a mural cupboard of similar date, together with an oak side-table and chairs which, though of later period, were of simple, country style, the product of local craftsmen, used from Elizabethan times onwards. The open hearth was suitably equipped with pewter, brass and copper items, which, together with early stoneware, added a touch of colour.

In the living room, an early seventeenth-century arm-chair with oak-panel back, which had traditional Shakespeare associations linked with the Falcon Inn at Bidford-on-Avon, was given pride of place next to the fireplace. Early specimens of stoneware jars, rushlight holders, wine bottles and similar items were displayed on a shelf above the massive oak lintel across the open hearth. A seventeenth-century,

Staffordshire figure of Shakespeare

The Birthplace living room

The Birthplace kitchen

small, boarded chest, a joint-stool and an early, oak, low dresser lined the walls, and a warming- or plague-pan with an iron handle provided an interesting domestic utensil which would be found in every home of the period.

A similar treatment was given to the kitchen, where the baby-minder in the centre of the stone floor continued to attract interest as a curious device for protecting young children from the perils of an open fire. An early, oak food cupboard with a pot shelf underneath, an oak bench, a joint-stool and a circular cricket table completed the furnishings. A small tapestry panel, an original, slipware baking dish and several platters and kitchen utensils were added, to supplement the ancient cooking equipment and utensils arranged in the open hearth.

Upstairs, furnishings were introduced into the birthroom, to suggest its original use as the principal bed chamber of John Shakespeare's home. In particular, a simple, oak, half-headed bedstead became the focal point of interest in the room. Though of late seventeenth-century date, it was typical of the beds used by middle-class traders in Shakespeare's Stratford. Its planked head and stump foot gave the impression of solidarity, and the heavy rails at the sides of the bed were drilled to carry ropes that supported a rush, platted mattress and coarse woven sheets. A coverlet of Jacobean needlework added colour, and alongside the bed was placed a baby's oak cradle, the panelled body of which was carved with rosettes and diamonds and raised on shaped rockers. Joint-stools, back stools covered with old, floral needlework, and a carved oak chest of Henry VIII's period completed the furnishings; and the addition

The birthroom before restoration

The birthroom as re-presented, 1950

of samplers and a few smaller decorative items gave a feeling of intimacy and comfort to this principal apartment.

Limited space precluded the introduction of a bed in the upstairs rooms at the rear. The old, oak trestle table was kept under the window looking into the garden; other items included an early seventeenth-century, oak chest, back stools and jointstools. A mid seventeenth-century, walnut, cane arm-chair filled a corner over the stairhead, and an early nineteenth-century spinning wheel, basically of the same type as those found in the homes of Stratford families in Shakespeare's time, was introduced to suggest an important aspect of domestic activity.

Simultaneously with the changes described above, the museum portion of Shakespeare's Birthplace was completely re-presented. Suitable pieces of period furniture were introduced into the small rooms leading into the museum, on both floors. Downstairs the wide, open hearth, with its iron fireback and array of early fireplace equipment, suggested a setting for an oak arm-chair, a box stool and a low-back settle with a linenfold chest and side-table nearby. Rush matting on the floor and curtains fitted to the window here, as also to all the windows throughout the building, added a feeling of warmth and comfort. This area also seemed to be an appropriate place to display, on the walls, maps and early views depicting the Warwickshire and Stratford which Shakespeare knew, as a background to the exhibits in the adjoining, larger museum room.

All the old, free-standing showcases were removed from the ground floor museum area, leaving the middle of the room clear for the free movement of visitors. The framed exhibits and other items which covered the walls were also removed. This made possible the introduction, on three sides of the room, of a series of specially designed display cases, fixed to the walls at eye level. A great deal of thought had gone into the problem of providing a suitable display arrangement which, whilst being practical, would not be intrusive in this setting.

I should like to record that Mr Ewart Edmonds, the Managing Director of the family firm of museum fitters in Birmingham which designed and supplied the cases, offered extremely valuable advice to the Trustees and myself in this matter. The fitments which were installed proved to be excellent for the display of books or documentation, and the concealed interior lighting was so contrived as to provide hidden illumination for the room. A system of numbering the cases encouraged visitors to view the display in a logical order, thus fitting in to the one-way route of inspection through the Birthplace, which became established from this time onwards.

The whole of the exhibition space downstairs was accordingly used to present a series of exhibits which traced the history and associations of the Birthplace. These included documents which substantiated the ownership and occupation of the property by the Shakespeare family, a pedigree of the family, records illustrating the history of the physical fabric of the building, and the original auction sale poster and other contemporary material relating to the movement which led to the purchase of Shakespeare's Birthplace for preservation as a national memorial in 1847.

At the top of the stairs leading to the upper part of the museum, the small ante-room provided an opportunity to call attention to the unusual fireplace of brick and stone, and to use it as a setting for the display of a number of domestic artefacts of Shakespeare's period. There was also space for a seventeenth-century side-table and desk box, together with two different types of arm-chairs and jointstools. Pride of place, however, was given to the ancient school desk, traditionally known as Shakespeare's desk, which came originally from King Edward VI School, Stratford's free grammar school, and had been displayed in the Birthplace since 1863.

The upper museum room was fitted on three walls with the same specially designed exhibition cases as downstairs, the floor area thus being left free. The ancient, oak floor boards were polished and handmade rush mats introduced, to give a feeling of warmth and colour, and the removal of hanging exhibits from the walls emphasized the character of the timber framing and the open, raftered ceiling. The Ely Palace portrait of Shakespeare was placed at a high level at the far end of the room to provide a focal point of interest, and other portraits were displayed in a flat, panelled case below.

The main sequence of cases was then used to present an ordered display of items illustrating the parentage, career, works, sources and growing appreciation of the poet. A selection of documents and rare books of Shakespeare's period, including some Quartos and a copy of the First Folio, were shown, with descriptive captions, together with a collection of medallic representations of Shakespeare and various translations of his plays into foreign languages. Taken together, the sequence of exhibits provided the visitor with a tabloid view of the essential facts of Shakespeare's life, works and reputation.

The basic idea was to make the museum as informative, lively, interesting and self-explanatory for the visitor as possible. At the same time, I was extremely keen that the Birthplace should offer a guide service of high quality, and that interested visitors should be offered helpful information and not be left to pass through the building without receiving attention. To this end, I started a policy of recruiting and training staff to act, not merely as attendants supervising the flow of visitors, but as well-informed, knowledgeable guides, capable of welcoming and talking to individual visitors and groups about the history of the Birthplace and its associations and, more generally, about Shakespeare's life and work. To be a successful guide, able to arouse and sustain the interest of the many types of visitors, young and old, who come from all over the world, demands a combination of qualifications. It requires more than a sound knowledge of the subject matter in question and a keenness to develop an increasing involvement with it; patience and courtesy, and a genuine interest in people, are essential, as well as the ability to remain natural and spontaneous, and not to become a repetitive, parrot-like, talking machine. Nor must it be forgotten that there are occasionally visitors who question the authenticity of the Birthplace, or even the authorship of the plays; considerable tact and expertise in dealing with such are needed, and a good guide must develop a technique to counter, in a convincing manner, the assertions of the anti-Shakespearians.

I have always held the view that the guides who work for the Shakespeare Birthplace Trust occupy a position of great responsibility and privilege, and that the good name and prestige of the institution relies greatly on the standard of their performance and the impression they give to the visiting public. Because of this, throughout the whole period of my Directorship I personally interviewed and appointed all the guides, at the same time advising and instructing them on how to discharge their duties. Right from the beginning, I developed the concept of a team effort, recognizing that every member of staff was involved and made a contribution to the successful running of the Trust.

A Busy Life

What surprises me, in looking back on those early years, is the extraordinary range and variety of work I undertook alongside the projects described above. The concept of delegation by the Director did not exist, because there was no one to whom one could delegate. Indeed, until a few years before I retired I did not have a deputy. Staff management was very personal. On occasions I prepared and paid the wages; similarly, I received, checked and banked money collected from admissions and sales. I selected and ordered every postcard, publication and commemorative item sold, and I planned sales arrangements at the properties. At busy times, as, for example, at bank holidays, it was not unusual to find me behind a publications counter, acting as a sales assistant. I also did a lot of unobtrusive observation inside and outside the properties, an invaluable method of understanding the behaviour and expectations of the visitors who came. The accounting and business side of the Trust's activities was my everyday concern, as also the practical running of the gardens and maintenance of the properties; these were responsibilities for which my country upbringing and knowledge of crafts proved of great assistance. The Trust had no transport as yet for garden or general use; consequently, I found myself on occasions using my car to provide transport between the properties. I recall that several times I took the only motor mower the gardens possessed to Redditch for maintenance attention. I also arranged the sale of surplus fruit from the orchards at Shottery and the distribution of quinces to local Trustees, in accordance with a tradition which the head gardener told me had been followed for many years. There were also occasional visits to nurseries to buy trees and shrubs, and the planting of replacement oaks on the Trust's land at Welcombe gave me particular pleasure. Tree planting has always been one of my enthusiasms.

On the subject of gardens, it was at the beginning of 1947 that the Trust's garden staff took over the maintenance of the Shakespeare Memorial Theatre's garden alongside the river, and the provision of flower boxes and baskets around the Theatre itself. It fell to me to negotiate the details of this arrangement with the Theatre management, and for the next twenty-five years I took pride in ensuring that the Theatre garden and the flower boxes and hanging baskets around the Theatre were kept up to the highest standard.

The Shakespeare Memorial Theatre Library

Another involvement with the Shakespeare Memorial Theatre dates from the same time, namely my assumption of responsibility for supervising the Theatre's library, which had been built up over the years alongside the library of the Shakespeare Birthplace Trust. A step towards securing co-ordination between these two collections of dramatic and Shakespearian material had been taken in 1938, when my predecessor was appointed honorary librarian of the Shakespeare Memorial Theatre and was given an assistant to work there under his direction. Unfortunately, the plans he had made to classify and catalogue the Theatre's library on the same system as the Trust's library had to be abandoned at the outbreak of war. A fresh beginning had to be made, and shortly after Sir Barry Jackson became Director of the Theatre in 1946 he invited me to examine and report on the library, at the same time as I was making a detailed survey of the contents and condition of the Trust's library with a view to getting the Trustees to establish a policy for its future development and use. I was therefore able to take a look at the two collections together, and to assess their potential value for the Shakespeare student and scholar.

I submitted detailed reports both to the Governors of the Theatre and to my Trustees, and made recommendations for the future development of both libraries on the basis of a common classification and cataloguing system, with the long-term objective of amalgamating the two libraries. Such an arrangement, I suggested, would eliminate duplication and enable the limited resources that both institutions had available for book purchases to be used to advantage, at the same time greatly adding to the convenience of readers wishing to use the libraries. These recommendations were readily approved, and I became the Theatre's honorary librarian and was given an assistant to work on the reorganization of the Theatre library, which was housed in the portion of the original Shakespeare Memorial building in Waterside which had escaped the fire in 1926. I then initiated a programme of work to deal with the back-log of accessions in the Trust's library and to start the re-cataloguing system agreed. In the course of years, this co-operation between the Theatre and the Trust in the matter of library provision proved highly satisfactory, culminating in the fusion of the two libraries, when suitable accommodation became available to house them in the new Shakespeare Centre in 1964.

Educational Activities

Apart from appreciating the unique character of these library collections, I quickly realized the potential importance of the contribution that the Shakespeare Birthplace Trust could make in the educational and academic spheres. On my appointment as Director in 1945, I inherited a close association with the British Council, which had been particularly active in looking after the interests of overseas service personnel in Stratford during and immediately after the Second World War. Its representative, Ernest Burbridge, was a very capable lecturer, and one of his ideas was to link together the British Council, the University of Birmingham, the Shakespeare Memorial Theatre and the Shakespeare Birthplace Trust, to form a Stratford Board of Studies, for the purpose of arranging lectures and courses to supplement the production of the plays. This was the basis of a policy of co-operation which was adopted by the bodies concerned, and which was continued and developed over the years.

The Trust also had a close link with the Borough Council of Stratford-upon-Avon, whose Aldermen and Town Clerk were Ex Officio Trustees. Shortly after my arrival, the Council appointed me as Deputy Keeper of the Borough Records, an office I still hold. The Borough collection of historical archives for which I assumed responsibility was remarkably complete, and provided original source material for the history of every facet of local community life from the twelfth century to modern times. I quickly found myself devoting as much time as possible to exploring the collection, and it was not long before I undertook the compilation of the official Stratford-upon-Avon Town Guide, and started to assemble material for a history of the Borough Town; all this alongside as much concentrated reading on Shakespeare's life, work and times as I could possibly manage.

In addition, I gave occasional lectures and was also able to complete personal historical work on Leicestershire – my subject as a university research student had been the Earldom of Leicester – and Coventry history, on which I had been engaged before I came to Stratford. In 1947 *Coventry's Heritage*, a short, general history of Coventry, based on my research into the City archives there, was published, followed by *Leicester Forest* in 1948. For a few years I continued to play an active part in the Coventry branch of the Historical Association, and in 1947 I became the Secretary and General Editor of the Dugdale Society, a role which my predecessor, F.C. Wellstood, had filled. My consequent involvement with scholars engaged in the editing of a wide range of Warwickshire historical records was to prove an invaluable experience, though little did I realize at the time that I was taking on a life-time commitment to the Dugdale Society. Much of this work was done in my own time, but it could not have happened without the secretarial assistance provided by the Trustees.

There was never a dull moment in my working day. I enjoyed dealing personally with a steady, growing stream of postal enquiries concerning a variety of antiquarian, historical, literary and theatrical subject-matter, and giving service to the occasional scholar who came to use the Trust's library and records. The Trustees were interested and supportive, and often one of them would call to have a little talk: Mr S.C. Kaines Smith, to tell me about his work on the pictures at Stoneleigh Abbey; Mr Graham Baron Ash, to report his latest purchase of a tapestry or piece of furniture for Packwood House, or to make comment about the Trust's gardens; the Vicar, the Reverend Canon Noel Prentice, to compare notes about the new Shakespeare production he had just seen at the Theatre; Alderman R.M. Smith, always the purveyor of the latest local news; Alderman Trevor Matthews, concerned about the town's publicity and the need for a better Stratford guide book; Alderman E.P. Ray, publisher of a monthly magazine, *The Shakespeare Pictorial*, who was already formulating plans for Stratford's part in the forthcoming Festival of Britain, in 1951; and, more frequently, the Chairman, and Mr Ashley Clayton, who presided over the Executive Committee when Colonel Flower was not available.

Among others who came to see me, I remember one or two for special reasons. One morning a lady called and said she had a present to hand over. Imagine my surprise and delight when, unwrapping the package she gave me, I found it contained a fine copy of a Quarto edition of *Love's Labour's Lost*.

The donor was Mrs S.B. Davies, daughter of Ernest E. Baker, a former Trustee. Less satisfactory was the outcome of the visit of a gentleman who announced that he had a valuable Shakespeare possession which he thought the Trustees would like to acquire. The item in question was packed in a carrier bag, and turned out to be no less than Shakespeare's walking stick – or so I was assured – which had been cut into a number of short lengths. Put together, they had clearly been a cane walking stick. When I enquired about the provenance of the stick and asked why the owner believed that it had belonged to Shakespeare, he pointed confidently to a polished metal plate attached to the top piece of the stick, on which the words 'William Shakespeare' were engraved. I then had to explain, as tactfully as possible, that the stick was a good example of the expertise of a certain Birmingham souvenir manufacturer, and that it fell outside the scope of the Trust's collecting policy.

One regular visitor was Dr R.V. Westwood, who was the librarian in charge of the Stratford-upon-Avon Public Library, nearby in Henley Street. He had a special interest in early printed books, and he would often call to recommend the acquisition of an item for sale which he thought the Trust's library should possess. Sadly, there was very limited money available at the time for this kind of accession, but occasionally I could not resist acting on his advice. I remember, in particular, buying at a bargain price a remarkably good copy of *The generall historie of the Turkes*, by Richard Knolles, the fourth edition, printed by Adam Islip, 1631.

Harvard House

Another regular visitor was the well known Stratford doctor, Dr Donald Sutherland Murray, whose surgery was in Trinity College, in Church Street. Dr Murray was a keen collector of a wide range of antiques, and was interested in Stratford's history. Because he discovered I had similar interests, he often called at my office to compare notes with me. Sometimes he would tell me about the latest addition to his collection of pharmacy jars, or would bring a parchment document for me to decipher for him. He might describe a piece of furniture or a picture he had seen in the house of one of his patients, and on one occasion he appeared bringing a section of a handmade, clay drainage pipe of unusual design, which he had come across near Shipston-on-Stour.

Dr Murray was a fascinating character. I discovered that he had been Marie Corelli's doctor, and I learned a great deal about her and her home, Mason Croft, from him. Because of his association with Miss Corelli, Dr Murray had come to be involved with Harvard House, the maiden home of Katherine Rogers, mother of John Harvard, the founder of the Harvard University. Marie Corelli had purchased and restored the house, which was situated in High Street, Stratford-upon-Avon, subsequently persuading Edward Morris of Chicago to buy it and present it to Harvard University, as a memorial to John Harvard. Dr Murray had, in fact, for a few years

Harvard House

been one of the five Trustees of the Harvard House Memorial Trust, appointed by the President and Fellows of Harvard College, and, as the local man on the spot, he had supervised and managed the property. One morning when he called, he announced that Sir Alfred Brumwell Thomas had died. In my ignorance, I am afraid I did not know who he was, but Dr Murray explained that Sir Alfred was one of the Trustees of Harvard House, a body that included the Earl of Athlone, the American Ambassador and the Master of Emmanuel College, Cambridge. He then took me by surprise, by saying that he thought I would be a suitable person to succeed Sir Alfred as a Trustee. I protested that I was not of the status of the distinguished, elderly gentlemen who were Trustees, but he pointed out that I had personal knowledge of the house, which the others had never visited, and insisted that he needed a young, experienced person to share the responsibility of managing Harvard House with him. Several months later I realized the seriousness of Dr Murray's suggestion, because I received a certificate recording a resolution of the President and Fellows of Harvard College, dated 20 September 1949, appointing me as a Trustee of the Harvard House Memorial Trust, in place of Sir Alfred Brumwell Thomas. This was the beginning of a personal involvement with the management of Harvard House which continued during the whole period of my Directorship, and culminated in an arrangement, made at the beginning of 1991, whereby the Trustees of Shakespeare's Birthplace assumed responsibility for the future conservation and use of the property. This is not the place for it, but the story of my trusteeship of Harvard House is worth telling. A copy of the resolution of the President and Fellows of Harvard College in 1991, recording appreciation of my involvement with Harvard House, is reproduced opposite.

Amid all these preoccupations, I somehow found time to keep personal diaries during these years. The entries I made were usually brief, but sufficient to convey an impression of the pattern of my day's work and duties. They recall the people I met, the meetings I attended, the visits I made, the lectures

Certificate from Harvard College

I gave, the routine of jobs undertaken, and the infinite variety of my activities. Clearly, I then had boundless energy, and I worked all hours, as evidenced by entries such as 'a busy day dashing about' or 'worked all day into the evening', Saturdays and Sundays being regarded as normal working days. Occasionally an entry recalls a special or pleasant occasion, such as, for example, on 8 January 1951, when one reads 'purchased a nice, old frying pan at Ashby for £3'. On that particular day I had gone to propose the toast to my old school at Ashby-de-la-Zouch, at the Old Ashbeians' dinner. Having arrived in the afternoon, I had visited the antiques shop at the bottom of Market Street, and had come across a good specimen of an old domestic utensil, which I thought would fill a gap in the kitchen display at one of the poroperties. At the price offered, it was a bargain buy: evidence that the interests of the Shakespeare Birthplace Trust were never out of my mind!

The 1950s

The decade of the 1950s saw a number of significant events and developments.

Shakespeare's Birthplace received two royal visits, one in 1950 and the second in 1957, and there were a number of other special occasions when scholars and official representatives from overseas visited the properties. At the same time, general visitor patronage continued to increase almost year by year, as conditions gradually returned to normality after the war. Considerable progress was made in dealing with the back-log of deferred maintenance at the Trust's properties, and a number of improvements were carried out. In particular, a complete re-presentation of New Place was undertaken. In 1958 the Trust received the Burnside bequest. The educational side of the Trust's work also began to develop, and regular additions were made to the library, archives and museums collections.

The Trust played an active part in the Festival of Britain programme in 1951, and Hall's Croft, recently acquired and restored, was opened to the public and also used as the local centre for the Festival. The Hall's Croft Festival Club came into existence at that time, and the first poetry readings, which led to the inauguration of the Stratford-upon-Avon Poetry Festival, took place there.

King George VI and Queen Elizabeth leaving the Birthplace, 1950

The Trust's staff and administrative arrangements gradually expanded during these years, and the need for additional accommodation to house the Trust's growing office and library was increasingly felt. To meet the situation, the Trustees began in 1958 to consider plans for a new headquarters building which would incorporate provision for the library and associated study facilities. The Shakespeare Centre, opened in 1964 to mark the quater-centenary of the poet's birth, resulted from these early deliberations. At the same time, it was felt that the statutory powers of the Trust needed revision, in order to consolidate the Trust's progress to date and to give the Trustees authority to take care of future development. The outcome was the Shakespeare Birthplace, etc., Trust Act of 1961, which re-defined the objects and constitution of the Trust in a comprehensive way.

The Royal Visit of 1950

The visit of Their Majesties King George VI and Queen Elizabeth, accompanied by Her Royal Highness The Princess Margaret, on Thursday, 20 April 1950, was a red-letter event for Stratford-upon-Avon. The announcement of their programme for the day, which included visits to the Town Hall, Shakespeare's Birthplace, Holy Trinity Church, the Shakespeare Memorial Theatre and a special matinée performance of *King Henry VIII*, had been received with considerable enthusiasm, and preparations by all concerned were soon actively in hand. The railway station received a speedy face-lift, and the streets along the route the royal party was to follow were tidied up, buildings re-furbished and flower decorations arranged.

The Stratford-upon-Avon Borough Council co-ordinated arrangements, but it fell to me, as a young man with no previous experience of royal visits, to plan the part of the programme involving Shakespeare's Birthplace. Appreciating the role played by the Lord Lieutenant of the County on these occasions, I resolved to telephone Lord Willoughby de Broke, who was the Lord Lieutenant at the time and also one of my Trustees, to seek his advice. 'Come over to see me at Kineton, Fox,' he said; 'we'll sort things out in five minutes.' So off I went to his house at Kineton, where I was most cordially received; literally within a few minutes he outlined to me the drill to be followed. 'No need to get fussed up like they do at the Town Hall' he said, and I quickly realized he was a man of great experience who knew all the answers. In the event, the procedure he suggested proved flawless, and I was able to use it as a guide on the occasion of subsequent royal visits with Lord Willoughby as the key figure. I also came to have a friendly association with him in connection with his family history and records. Lord Willoughby deposited his estate and family papers in the records office of the Birthplace Trust and, whenever he received an enquiry about them, he always referred to me. Lord Willoughby was also a highly respected figure in the world of horse racing, and I often encountered him at the Stratford Race Course during the period when, from 1969 until I retired, I was invited annually to present the Garrick Trophy.

The morning of 20 April started with mist, which had cleared into bright sunshine by the time the train bearing the royal party arrived at Stratford station. A civic group, headed by the Mayor of the Borough, Councillor B.S. Cooper, and the Town Clerk, Mr T.E. Lowth, welcomed the royal visitors, who then proceeded by car to the Town Hall. The streets along the route were lined with crowds, who cheered and waved flags as an expression of their welcome.

In the ballroom of the Town Hall the Aldermen, Councillors, chief officers and other dignitaries were presented, and Their Majesties mingled with the assembled guests. They were particularly interested to inspect the ancient charters of the Borough and the list of Mayors from 1553 onwards in the Council Chamber.

Leaving the Town Hall and proceeding along High Street and Henley Street to Shakespeare's Birthplace, the royal party received a rapturous welcome. The branches of cherry blossom decorating the immediate approach to the Birthplace looked especially beautiful in the clear morning sunshine.

On arrival at the gate leading into the Birthplace garden, the Lord Lieutenant presented Lt-Col Fordham Flower, Chairman of the Trust, with Mrs Flower, who in turn presented Mr Ashley Clayton, Mr and Mrs Leslie Watkins, and myself as Director, with Mrs Fox. It was a colourful scene. The Queen wore a powder blue, two-piece outfit and a close-fitting hat trimmed with osprey feathers, and Princess Margaret looked particularly attractive in an ensemble of grey and black checked taffeta with a Dutch-bonnet hat. All the other ladies had dressed in colourful spring-like attire with matching hats, and the gentlemen wore morning suits.

Although it was a formal occasion, there was no hurry and the royal visitors quickly made all of us feel at ease. When the King was told that Mr Watkins was Headmaster of Shakespeare's old school, he asked about the age of the school and the number of boys there. 'You were not there while he was there, I hope' he said. I also remember that when the Chairman mentioned my name to introduce me, the King turned to the Queen and whispered 'He wrote the book, you know', an indication that a certain amount of homework had been done in advance of the visit. A posy of flowers gathered from the gardens of the Shakespearian properties was presented to the Queen by Caroline Flower, daughter of the Chairman, and another by her younger brother, Charles, to the Princess.

Escorted by the Chairman and myself, the royal visitors clearly enjoyed their leisurely inspection of the garden, before entering the Birthplace by the back door. The King chatted to the head gardener, Frank Jackson, who, with his staff of gardeners, had worked hard to ensure that the paths, flower beds and shrubs were presented to advantage. We stood talking for a little time beside the quince tree, before going into the house, where the members of the press were not allowed.

As Director, I had the privilege, accompanied by Colonel Flower, of acting as guide to the royal party as we made an inspection of the various rooms. The King was particularly impressed by the solidarity of the half-timbered structure – the centuries-old, hardened beams of oak – and the historical evidence substantiating the ownership and occupation of the premises by John Shakespeare, the poet's father. In the kitchen, where I demonstrated the baby-minder, a vertical pole with horizontal bar and metal holding strap attached, to safeguard a toddling child from the open fire, the King was clearly fascinated. He turned to the Queen and said 'They ought to make them today; we could have one for Charles'.

The programme had allowed only twenty minutes for the visit to Shakespeare's Birthplace, but, even before we had finished inspecting the rooms on the ground floor, I realized that we were overstaying the allotted time. The King and Queen and the Princess were clearly enjoying themselves away from the public gaze, and the questions they asked left me in no doubt that they were genuinely interested. Indeed, it was an experience I shall never forget; they were relaxed and natural, and they might well have been my best friends, visiting the Birthplace for the first time.

It was difficult to move the royal visitors away from the exhibits in the upper museum, and each of them attempted to read signatures cut on the panes of the leaded-light window in the birthroom. Their tour upstairs ended with the signing of a special visitors' book on a table in the room overlooking the garden at the back of the building. Whilst doing so, the King joked about the special pen provided, which proved difficult to use, and at that moment Sir Alan Lascelles, the Private Secretary in attendance, who was waiting at the top of the stairs, held up his arm and pointed to his wrist watch, clearly indicating that time was running out. 'It's always like this', King George remarked. He then got up from the stool on which he was sitting, and the Queen and the Princess tidied themselves, as the party prepared to leave the seclusion of the house. They left through the front door, to encounter the cheers of the crowd waiting outside, but not before they had thanked the Chairman and me for the arrangements made for their visit. 'What a pity we cannot stay longer', said the Queen. As for the Princess, she had already told me that she had been looking forward to seeing what Shakespeare's Birthplace was actually like, and in reply to my question as she left 'Has it been as interesting as you expected?' she said 'Infinitely better'.

The royal party then proceeded to the Collegiate Church of the Holy Trinity, passing along High Street, Chapel Street and Church Street into Old Town. They were received by the Vicar, the Reverend Canon Noel Prentice, who showed them round the Church. They were particularly interested to see the Parish Register, containing the entries of Shakespeare's baptism and burial, the ancient font in which he was christened, and the poet's grave and monument in the chancel.

Leaving the Church, the royal visitors then drove down Bridge Street and Waterside to the Shakespeare Memorial Theatre, where they were greeted by Lord Iliffe, President of the Governors, Sir Archibald Flower and the Director, Mr Anthony Quayle. They made a tour of the Theatre, and the King was very interested to hear how the stage operated and to see work in progress in the workshops and wardrobe.

Lunch followed, after which the royal party saw a special matinée performance of *King Henry VIII*. The prologue to the play was spoken by John Gielgud and the epilogue by Harry Andrews. Anthony Quayle took the part of Henry VIII and Gwen Ffrangcon-Davies played Katherine. The King and Queen and the Princess greatly enjoyed the performance, as did the audience of special guests. In the last scene Rosanna Quayle, the baby daughter of Anthony Quayle, was brought on the stage as the infant Princess Elizabeth, by her nanny, Rosalind Atkinson, much to the delight of everyone. After speaking to members of the Company, the royal visitors then left the Theatre, to rejoin the royal train at the station. Their stay in Stratford had lasted seven and a half hours and, from every point of view, was adjudged to be an outstanding success. So far as Shakespeare's Birthplace was concerned, the resultant publicity and prestige gave impetus to an increase in visitor patronage, while the royal visit to the Memorial Theatre, of which the King was the Patron, conferred official encouragement, resulting in enhanced prestige which was reflected in increased box office business for the production in question.

Hall's Croft

Less than a year after the royal visit, the official opening of Hall's Croft, on Wednesday, 4 April 1951, was another event of considerable importance. Hall's Croft, the home of William Shakespeare's daughter Susanna and her husband, Dr John Hall, who was one of the leading medical practitioners of his day, was the only remaining property with Shakespeare associations which was not in the possession of the Birthplace Trust. Its acquisition and restoration must be regarded as a significant milestone in the history of the Trust.

The opening ceremony was performed by Sir Ernest Pooley, K.C.V.O., M.A., LL.D., a Life Trustee who

Official opening of Hall's Croft

Hall's Croft about 1860

was Chairman of the Arts Council of Great Britain, in the presence of Lt-Col Fordham Flower, Chairman of the Trustees, Alderman Trevor Matthews, then Mayor of Stratford-upon-Avon, Mr T. Spencer Wood, the Trust's architect, and myself as Director, with a supporting company of Trustees and representative guests. Sir Ernest used a pair of scissors presented by Mr Spencer Wood to cut a tape giving access to the front door of the house, and the guests were then invited to accompany the official party to inspect the interior and the garden. Tea was served in the Festival Club portion of the building and speeches followed. The Committee responsible for organizing Stratford's programme of events to celebrate the Festival of Britain during 1951 had already decided that Hall's Croft was to serve as the town's festival centre, so that the official opening of the building also inaugurated the local festival programme.

It was almost two years earlier, in June 1949, when local rumour reported that Hall's Croft was to be offered for sale by the owner, Lady Elizabeth Montagu, that the Executive Committee authorized me to investigate the possibility of acquiring it. My first step was to seek an opportunity to inspect the house, which up till that time I had viewed only from outside its frontage in Old Town. It had the appearance of a building of historical and architectural interest, though my impression was that it looked neglected and in need of overhaul.

I discovered that John Slater, an actor in the Company at the Memorial Theatre, was living there, and when I knocked at the front door he greeted me to the accompaniment of the ferocious barking of a very large and menacing dog, which he restrained as I entered the hall. He then led me on a detailed inspection tour of the house and the garden and, for the first time, I was able to see the rear elevation of the building, partly disguised by a liberal growth of ivy.

I was greatly fascinated, because I realized at once that here was a Tudor building of unusual character, with many interesting architectural features. What struck me forcibly was that internally the house had been given a Victorian appearance, the timber framed walls of the rooms having been plastered over and painted in various colours. Although the kitchen and domestic facilities were very basic and appeared to have little in the way of modern amenity, the house clearly had the feeling of being lived in. I was surprised at its size and the number of rooms, particularly on the first floor, where I later found there were no fewer than nine bedrooms. I was shown what must have been the earliest type of water closet in Stratford, approached from the landing, and a bathroom in the rear wing, which in itself was a museum piece. I came away very excited, realizing that, if the Trustees succeeded in acquiring the property, I might find myself involved in a challenging exercise of restoration and conservation.

I was told that agents, the firm of Jackson, Stops and Staff, had already been instructed to offer Hall's Croft for sale by public auction at the Town Hall on 16 September 1949, unless previously sold privately. I immediately obtained a copy of the sale particulars from the agents: it described Hall's Croft as 'one of the most interesting houses in the town, with many old-world features', adding 'there is every reason to believe that Hall's Croft was the residence of Shakespeare's favourite daughter, Susanna, who married the well known Stratford physician, Dr John Hall, in 1607'. The property was freehold, with a rateable value of £97 0s. 0d., and producing a rent of £44 9s. 2d. for the half-year. Vacant possession was offered on completion. The particulars included a brief description of each room, with dimensions, and a note about the domestic offices at the rear, which were said to include a butler's pantry, a servants' hall and a scullery. In the kitchen there was an iron range for cooking, a stone sink with a force-pump for water alongside it, and fittings which comprised a large cupboard and dresser.

I subsequently reported my impressions to the Trustees, and strongly recommended that, in the interests of conservation, the Trust should attempt to purchase the property. I represented that this was an opportunity not to be missed, stressing how important I thought it was that the Trust should become the owner of the home of Susanna

Shakespeare and Dr John Hall, the only historic building with Shakespeare associations outside its care. I was naturally delighted that the Trustees were unanimously in agreement and that they authorized me to negotiate the purchase of the property in advance of the auction.

Once the agents and owner were informed of the Trust's serious interest, the advertised auction was cancelled and there followed exchanges of letters which eventually led to the purchase of Hall's Croft by the Trust on 3 November 1949 for the sum of £11,000, which at that time represented a realistic market price for a property of this kind.

The financial implications of this transaction presented the Trustees with an immediate problem. The Trust's total available cash reserve, as represented by investments, amounted to some £7,000, the interest from which contributed towards general running costs. The possibility of selling Brooklands, which had been recently purchased, in order to raise money was seriously considered, but it was decided instead to seek an overdraft from the Midland Bank, Ltd.

I well remember visiting the Manager of the Midland Bank, Mr Ted Lovett, to negotiate an overdraft on the most favourable terms possible. Mr Lovett was one of the old style of bank managers, a character ideally suited to running a branch in a market town, where farmers were the major customers. He himself was rather like a farmer, friendly and practical, with a natural sense of business. A well known local personality, he exercised considerable authority and was able to take decisions without reference to remote superiors. Knowing Mr Lovett only by reputation before my visit, I first of all introduced myself as a countryman, and somehow managed to talk about stock sales, pheasant shooting and farming matters generally, before coming to the real purpose of my visit. He then listened most carefully to the case I outlined on behalf of the Trust for financial help to meet the cost of purchasing Hall's Croft, and eventually I left his office with the promise of an overdraft facility on very generous terms. Subsequently the Midland Bank extended and increased the overdraft, to assist the Trust to meet the cost of restoring and preparing the property for opening to the public.

Having acquired Hall's Croft, the Trustees proceeded at once to plan its restoration and future use. Mr T. Spencer Wood, the Trust's architect, who had considerable experience in dealing with historic, timber framed buildings, was asked to survey the property and report on its condition. His report was considered and important decisions were taken at a special meeting of the Executive Committee held on 15 November 1949.

In Mr Wood's view, Hall's Croft was a building of outstanding character, quite apart from its Shakespeare associations. The oldest part of the

Hall's Croft in 1949

house was of early sixteenth-century date. Originally it comprised a small, double-fronted dwelling with a barn or outbuildings at the rear, and had been enlarged in the time of Dr John Hall to form a more imposing residence. The frontage had been extended, and the outbuildings at the rear enlarged and linked to the original house by a new hall and staircase. Further alterations had been made during the eighteenth and nineteenth centuries.

Though the structure was basically sound, Mr Wood advised that the house needed a comprehensive overhaul, and that attention should be given to a number of major items, to ensure its future stability and conservation. The absence of piped drainage around the building and the lack of a damp course had resulted in rot and decay, which had spread into some of the rooms inside, an example being in the parlour, where the floor boards had been laid directly on to the soil and were found to be completely rotten, with ivy sprouting between the joints. In addition, various ill-advised improvements which had been carried out at different times had seriously weakened the structure. In the end wall of the parlour, for instance, a French window had been inserted to give access to the terrace and garden outside. To do this, the main horizontal sill had been cut away, with the result that the timber framing had started to lean outwards towards the street, and had consequently been supported by a brick pillar propping the jettied overhang at the front of the house. Larger windows, replacing the small original ones, had been inserted on all elevations. At the front, facing Old Town, an inappropriate bay window had been added at both floor levels, the timber framed structure having been mutilated to make this possible. Over the main front entrance another bay window, supported by timber posts, had been added. In the attic area, where most of the timber was original, some still bearing the bark when it was cut, the main cross trusses had been sawn away in the middle to open up the floor space, probably to make possible the attic's use as a dormitory when Hall's Croft became, for a time, a boarding school, called Cambridge House.

Having considered the architect's report, the Trustees readily agreed that their primary responsibility was to re-instate and restore the original sixteenth-century house, and that immediate steps should be taken to do so as accurately as possible. They also decided that, as a second part of the operation, the more modern rooms on the south side of the building should be adapted and extended for use as a Shakespeare centre, where activities allied to Stratford's annual Shakespeare festival and linked with the rapidly expanding cultural work of the Trust and of Stratford-upon-Avon generally could be accommodated. It was felt that, during the Festival of Britain year, a Festival Club should be provided there. At the same time, the garden was to be rescued from its neglected state, and completely re-designed and replanted on the lines of an old English garden.

As Director, I was given authority to implement these plans, and during the autumn and winter months of 1949 to 1950 all necessary preparations were put in hand. Mr Wood, the architect, undertook a comprehensive survey and submitted detailed recommendations, which were considered and approved by the Trustees on 26 April 1950. He then prepared measured drawings, drew up a specification and formulated a plan of action. Planning permission was sought, and a licence to proceed was obtained from the Ministry of Works, which at that time controlled the use of labour and materials for building purposes. A beginning on the clearance of the garden was made and a plan for its replanting agreed. I must confess that I personally was responsible for suggesting the general design and content of the garden, and in Harold Goodyear, who had succeeded Frank Jackson as the Trust's head gardener, I had an enthusiastic supporter who was able, with his assistant gardeners, to translate my ideas into practice.

By the spring of 1950 preparations were sufficiently advanced for the restoration work to proceed. The architect recommended that William Sapcote and Sons, Ltd, of Birmingham, a family firm of builders responsible for some excellent examples of half-timbered restoration work in the Midlands, should be appointed as general contractors. At a meeting on 8 May 1950 the Executive Committee discussed and agreed with a representative of this firm and the architect detailed arrangements for the work, including labour, materials, payment, time schedule and the like. The Trustees received an assurance that the work would be completed in nine months, and the contract was entrusted to Sapcotes, who started work on 3 June. On both sides there was a sense of urgency and excitement, all concerned knowing that the finished product, as it were, needed to be completed in readiness for the start of the Festival of Britain in the following spring, and that it must be of show-quality standard.

For me, the experience of exercising general

supervision during the months that followed proved invaluable; indeed, much of what I know about half-timbered construction, building methods and materials I owe to the regular site meetings when I joined Mr Spencer Wood and Mr William Sapcote and his foreman, to inspect progress and make decisions about what next was to be done.

One of the first tasks undertaken was the construction of a new cradle of oak in the attic, to carry the weight of the roof and to stabilize the structure. This proved to be a particularly tricky operation, in view of the great size and weight of the large oak beams that had to be used. Each elevation of the building then received detailed attention: missing and decayed timber members were replaced with old, seasoned oak; new window frames of appropriate size and design were constructed, to replace the larger windows that had been inserted later.

Fortunately, one or two original window frames – one complete with glass – were found hidden behind lath and plaster in the walls of the house, and these provided details of size and moulding which were faithfully copied. Original mortice holes found in the studding also gave clues as to the dimensions and positions of the original fenestration.

Extremely skilful work was involved, and the result was achieved only because Sapcotes still had in their employment a small team of very experienced craftsmen, capable of using traditional materials with traditional skills. All the timber used, for example, was worked by hand using the adze, a tool which all carpenters in Shakespeare's time would have known and used. The foreman on the site was a Stratford man, Will Burton, who led his men and planned and supervised the day-to-day work in a most competent manner; and the firm gave him

Hall's Croft after completion of restoration, 1951

impressive back up. I have a vivid recollection of a deaf and dumb carpenter who worked on the restoration: he was a superb craftsman, with whom Mr Sapcote and his foreman had an uncanny way of communicating and giving instructions; and, because he could not converse with his mates, his output was quite outstanding.

I followed the progress of the work at Hall's Croft on most days, and I found it very satisfying to see the various craftsmen using their tools. It gave me quite a thrill to watch a carpenter using the adze to shape a replacement piece of oak, or a mason re-installing the Wilmcote stone plinth which supported the timber framing, while the casting of lead to make a rainwater downpipe or gutter was something I had not seen before. Great care and skill were needed in knowing how to support the heavy timber structure while replacement beams or studs were inserted.

At the same time as the exterior fabric of the house was thus being conserved, work proceeded inside. In turn, each room was overhauled and restored as near as possible to its original condition. This applied also to the cellar and the roof space. An entirely new central heating system was installed, and electric lighting provided in an unobtrusive manner. Lath and plaster which had covered the timber framing and wall panels were removed in the various rooms, occasionally revealing important features of the original structure. On the landing on the first floor, for instance, the removal of the lath and plaster revealed the timber framed external wall of the original sixteenth-century house, with its jettied overhang, as well as a small original window intact. This wall had been covered over, to serve as an interior wall, when the new hall and staircase were added. Also upstairs, the partitions that had been put up to form small bedrooms at the front of the house on the first floor were removed, opening up the present large room, which came to be used for exhibitions. There were occasional surprises as, for example, when a Victorian iron grate was removed from the end bedroom, revealing behind it an original brick fireplace and a stone surround which had one jamb hacked away. With care, it proved possible to fashion a replacement stone jamb to match the other side, thus restoring the sixteenth-century fireplace.

Considerable effort had to be expended in undoing the embellishments of later times, such as the thick, dark varnish which concealed the natural quality of the oak staircase, and the panelling on the walls of the lounge. Finishing details were also important: the metal casements for the windows were made to an original pattern by Bert Edge, the local blacksmith, and handmade glass was used for the glazing, by the Stratford firm of Nelder and Southam.

Severe frost at the beginning of 1951 slowed down the completion of work on the rear elevation, and the re-laying of the terrace slabs was finished only just in time for the official opening in April. In the meantime, and simultaneously with the restoration of the house, the garden was re-designed and replanted by the Trust's own garden staff, most of the work being done during the late summer and autumn of 1950. The plan adopted envisaged a treatment that would portray something of the fashionable formality of sizeable gardens of Shakespeare's day, and at the same time create the natural atmosphere of a domestic garden, full of familiar trees, flowers and shrubs. Much of the area was turfed with grass to give a lawn, graced by a picturesque, old mulberry tree which had been rescued from its collapsed state on the ground, and flanked on the far side by a stately row of poplars, with a raised terrace

The garden elevation, Hall's Croft, 1951

at the top end. A long, paved path, leading from the terrace at the back of the house to a sundial by the north wall, was planted on either side with borders of roses and herbaceous flowers, with a beech hedge and screen of trees to hide a block of toilets and a new greenhouse in the yard behind. A long border on the north side of the garden was planted with a variety of shrubs, and a small plot was devoted to herbs used by Dr John Hall in his medical work.

Whilst this programme of restoration work was proceeding, plans for the use of Hall's Croft were being formulated. The Trustees felt that, quite apart from its associations, this fine Tudor house and its walled garden would have a general appeal and should therefore be open to the public along with the other Shakespearian properties. They were keen, however, that Hall's Croft should not be presented merely as a preserved historic building or museum, but that it should also serve as a centre of live activities, allied with the Shakespeare festival at the Memorial Theatre and linked with the rapidly expanding cultural work of the Trust. Hence, it was envisaged that Hall's Croft and its garden should figure prominently in the local programme for the Festival of Britain.

To give effect to these ideas, it was decided to furnish the house in the style of a middle-class Tudor home, such as Susanna Shakespeare and her husband, Dr Hall, would have known, and to extend and equip the more modern part of the building, on the south side, to provide the amenities and facilities of a Shakespeare centre, where exhibitions, recitals and a variety of social and literary activities could take place, together with the establishment of a Festival Club.

I counted myself fortunate in being given the responsibility to translate these ideas into effect. To furnish a Tudor house of such outstanding character in an authentic and meaningful manner presented a challenge, and offered a unique opportunity to try to re-create the atmosphere of a successful, professional man's home, such as Dr John Hall's must have been. I could not have done this without drawing on the experience and advice of Mr S.W. Wolsey, an acknowledged authority of international repute on sixteenth- and seventeenth-century oak furniture. Wolsey had an unrivalled knowledge of existing furniture of that period, both in public and private collections, and, having been in the antique furniture business all his life, he knew where and when it was possible to negotiate the purchase of particular items. Numbered among the institutions he served were the Victoria and Albert Museum, Colonial Williamsburg in Virginia and many others in this country and abroad.

It was with Wolsey's help that I was able to acquire, on behalf of the Trust, for the furnishing of Hall's Croft a collection of original, representative,

The entrance hall, Hall's Croft, 1951

The parlour, Hall's Croft, 1951

fine pieces of oak furniture. Thus, the parlour was furnished with an extending refectory table dated about 1600, joint-stools, several chairs, a settle, a side-table, a coffer and smaller pieces. Each of the rooms was individually treated: an early bookbinder's press sat comfortably in the raised, long apartment traditionally known as the library, near to a table on which a copy of Dr Hall's *Select Observations on English Bodies* was displayed. An alcove there also seemed an appropriate place to put a late eighteenth-century, pine, carved figure of Shakespeare, based on the statue in Westminster Abbey, which came from a country house in Wiltshire. The adjoining dispensary was furnished in the style of a consulting room, such as Dr Hall would have had, complete with an aumbry and chest, apothecary jars for medicines, herbs and pills, herbals, pestles and mortars, and the like. Susanna's kitchen, with its open hearth and medley of country-made pieces of furniture and cooking equipment, added a homely touch, re-creating the busy atmosphere of domestic and cooking activity.

Upstairs, the exhibition room provided an ideal setting for a long, fine, seventeenth-century refectory table, and specially designed wall cases were fitted to the walls, to accommodate an exhibition on the Garrick Jubilee and the Stratford Festivals, followed later by one depicting the theme of medicine in Shakespeare's time, with particular reference to the life and work of Dr John Hall. In the small bedroom nearby, an exquisitely carved, small, four-poster, Tudor bedstead formed the centre piece of a furnished setting suggesting the atmosphere of a cosy bedroom regularly in use. Colour and warmth throughout the house were added by the hand-made curtains for the lattice windows, which had been made from material that had previously served as the hangings on an early four-poster bed. The iron rods and brackets on which they hung were made by the local blacksmith, who also produced the wrought-iron lighting brackets in the parlour and entrance hall. It was attention to every detail of this kind that characterised the work undertaken, and the Trustees made frequent visits to inspect progress.

The other rooms of the house, on the south side, were furnished to meet the anticipated needs of the Festival Club which the Trustees had decided to operate there. The panelled room on the ground floor, with its striking stone fireplace, was furnished

Dr Hall's Select Observations

with chairs and tables as a comfortable lounge, and the room above it, with its unusual domed ceiling, made an attractive reading and writing room, which was subsequently often used by student groups. The large, modern room, which had been added to serve as a music room at the beginning of the twentieth entrance lobby. However, the Hall's Croft Festival Club rooms were completed and officially opened on 5 May 1951.

Whilst the programme of restoration, as described above, was proceeding, the financial implications of the Hall's Croft project continued to be a source

Pine statue of Shakespeare

The dispensary, Hall's Croft

century, became the main Club room, with an adjoining annexe which had been the kitchen when Hall's Croft was bought by the Trust. Building restrictions at the time, due to the shortage of labour and materials following the war, only allowed the building of a small, modern kitchen at the rear to service the Club's refreshment requirements, and several years passed before a larger and better equipped kitchen could be built. For the same reason, visitors and Club members in 1951 and for some time afterwards had to accept the restricted toilet facilities in the garden, until it was possible to provide the new toilets, leading off an improved

The kitchen, Hall's Croft

of anxiety to the Trustees. At an early stage the architect had warned them that the cost of re-instating and restoring the old part of the house could be between £8,000 and £10,000, apart from the cost of furnishings and fittings and excluding the provision of the new building envisaged in the ultimate plan. The total cost of the complete project, including the purchase, was estimated at £45,000, towards which the most the Trust could contribute was £12,000.

With some hesitation the Trustees decided, at a special meeting held on 19 July 1950, to launch an appeal, on as wide a basis as possible, with the object of raising the remainder of the money required, a sum of £33,000, 'to make possible the preservation of this unique Shakespearian building for use as an international centre of culture', this being the objective set out in an illustrated appeal brochure. The Mayor of Stratford-upon-Avon, Alderman Trevor Matthews, who was a member of the Executive Committee of the Trustees, lent his active support to the appeal, and invitations to contribute, signed by him, were sent out on the widest possible scale.

As Director, I found myself assuming the role of fund raiser, an exercise of which I had had no previous experience. I tried to think of all those who might conceivably support a conservation project of this kind, but, although there was a steady response from a wide circle of Shakespeare lovers, the result was disappointing. The fact that war broke out in Korea the week after the appeal was launched did not help, and there were no major donations from business or foundation sources. Meanwhile, an extension of the Bank's overdraft facilities enabled the contractors' accounts to be met.

The appeal continued during 1951, but with diminishing response, and, when the Annual Meeting of the Trustees was held on 14 May 1952, the Chairman reported that the total sum raised by the appeal so far was only £4,817 17s. 9d., which included a grant of £2,000 from the Arts Council of Great Britain. At that date the balance sheet disclosed that the Trust was in debt to the extent of £18,494 7s. 10d., a formidable figure at a borrowing rate of five per cent. Contributions to the appeal during the next two years continued to be disappointing, and amounted only to £183 18s. 7d., making a total of £5,001 16s. 4d. when the appeal was closed. Borrowing from the bank therefore continued, until the debt incurred was liquidated.

The total cost of the Hall's Croft project, covering the purchase, restoration and furnishing, amounted to £41,617 19s. 9d. When reporting this to the Trustees, the Chairman summed up their feelings as follows: 'General appreciation of what has been done at Hall's Croft leaves no doubt that, in spite of financial embarrassment caused, this has been money well spent. As a building, it is the finest possession of the Trust, whilst its furnishings and amenities are quite exceptional.' During its first season, Hall's Croft attracted over 33,000 visitors, and the Festival Club there enrolled more than five hundred members. As Stratford's festival centre, its exhibitions, poetry readings, concerts and lectures contributed significantly to the local Festival of Britain programme and pointed the way to much that followed in later years.

The British Council

By the middle of the 1950s, certain other important developments had occurred. Shortly after Hall's Croft became available, the British Council had to vacate Mason Croft, in Church Street, and found itself looking for alternative accommodation. As it so happened, a suite of rooms on the upper floor at

British Council party, 1954

the rear of Hall's Croft was at that time unoccupied, and the Trustees decided to offer this accommodation for use as the Council's Stratford office, together with facilities for British Council staff and visiting students to use the Club.

This was the beginning of a closer working arrangement between the Trust and the Council. As Director, I developed a most friendly and mutually helpful arrangement with Miss Phyllis Mann, who had succeeded Ernest Burbridge as the Council's representative in charge of the Stratford centre. Regular courses for overseas British Council students were held at Hall's Croft, and Miss Mann acted as a gracious hostess for a regular stream of distinguished scholars and visitors from overseas. Invariably I was invited to meet them, and to act as their guide when they visited Shakespeare's Birthplace and the Trust's library. The public relations aspect of this involvement with the British Council was very rewarding, and on many occasions copies of foreign translations of Shakespeare's works were presented to the Trust's library. Hall's Croft in fact proved to be an ideal centre for these activities.

The Shakespeare Institute

It was also in 1951 that the University of Birmingham took possession of Mason Croft, once the home of Marie Corelli, and Professor Allardyce Nicoll, with the help of private benefaction, founded the Shakespeare Institute there. Himself an acknowledged authority on the history of the drama, Nicoll's idea was to establish an academic base in Stratford-upon-Avon which would have access to the Shakespeare Memorial Theatre and the library resources of the Birthplace Trust, and to develop there a post-graduate school of research centred on Shakespeare and the drama. He appointed Professor Charles Sisson as his deputy and a few Fellows to assist with the teaching. I myself was invited to be an Associate Honorary Fellow, and I contributed by instructing small groups of Institute students who came to explore the Trust's archives.

The publication of *Shakespeare Survey*, by the Cambridge University Press, dates to this time. Professor Allardyce Nicoll conceived the idea of publishing an annual survey of Shakespearian study and production, to be planned by an advisory board of international scholars. Sponsorship for the project was secured from the University of Birmingham, the Shakespeare Memorial Theatre and the Shakespeare Birthplace Trust. I myself contributed a paper on 'The Heritage of Shakespeare's Birthplace' to the first volume, which was issued in 1948. Subsequently the annual publication of *Shakespeare Survey* has become firmly established as the leading Shakespeare survey, appealing to the scholar, the student of theatre and the archivist, while at the same time presenting material likely to be of interest to a wider public.

The close co-operation between the Trust and the Institute in those early days developed over the years under Professor Nicholl and the Directors who followed: Professor Terence Spencer, Professor Philip Brockbank and, currently, Professor Stanley Wells. All these have served in turn as Trustees, by representing the University of Birmingham on the governing body of the Shakespeare Birthplace Trust.

Stratford's Charter Celebrations

At that time there was also a close association with the Stratford-upon-Avon Borough Council, whose Aldermen and Town Clerk served as Trustees and provided regular contact with town affairs. The year 1953 marked the four-hundredth anniversary of the granting of the charter of incorporation to Stratford-upon-Avon in 1553, and, in support of celebrations organized by the Borough Council, the Trust arranged an exhibition of Borough records at Hall's Croft, illustrating town government over the centuries. As Deputy Keeper of the Borough Records, I had already written the official guide to the town two years earlier, and I was now invited to write a short history of Stratford, to mark the quater-centenary charter celebrations. The time factor for this was worrying, because considerable research with the Borough records was involved. Most of this and

The Guild Chapel from the school quadrangle, about 1900

the writing had to be done in my own spare time, but the effort was well worth while and I enjoyed the task. The resultant volume, *The Borough Town of Stratford-upon-Avon*, published by the Borough Council, was well received and quickly came to be regarded as the official history of Stratford; unlike most other books on Stratford, the emphasis of its treatment was not on Shakespeare, but on town government and the physical, economic and social aspects of local community life.

The charter celebrations clearly stimulated an interest in the history and traditions of the town. Lectures I had given on the subject during the two previous years had been well attended, and there was a ready demand for a more serious course of study on Stratford's history and records, which the Extramural Department of the University of Birmingham invited me to conduct in the autumn of 1953. I have repeated this course every year since then, the responsibility for organizing it having been taken over more recently by the University of Warwick from the University of Birmingham. I have always regarded close-working co-operation with our neighbouring universities as of the utmost importance.

The Friends of the Guild Chapel

It was also as a result of the interest generated by the charter celebrations that in 1954 the Friends of the Guild Chapel of Stratford-upon-Avon came into existence. The ancient Guild Chapel at that time needed urgent attention: its exterior fabric was in an advanced state of decay and the Chapel itself was little used. The Friends planned and raised money to undertake a phased programme of restoring the exterior stonework and completely re-furnishing the interior. The movement to preserve this important part of Stratford's heritage owed its birth to a small group of local enthusiasts, led by Councillor Miss Gwendoline Phillips, who had recently served as Mayor of the Borough, and myself. Miss Phillips became the Founder President of the Friends, and I suppose it was inevitable that I should be appointed Chairman, a position I have held to the present day. This is not the place to tell the story of the work of the Friends in restoring and caring for the Guild Chapel, but it should be placed on record that throughout the years the Trustees of Shakespeare's Birthplace have given support to the Friends of the Guild Chapel in many practical ways.

The Coronation

The year 1953 also marked the coronation of Her Majesty Queen Elizabeth II. King George VI was already a sick man when he visited the Birthplace in 1950, and in less than two years the Trustees found themselves offering their profound sympathy to the Royal Family and their homage to the young Queen Elizabeth II. To commemorate her coronation, the Trustees decided that their primary contribution should consist of a number of desirable improvements to the properties and gardens. They also

Planting of coronation rose tree, 1953

arranged a garden party at Hall's Croft and, as a more permanent reminder, planted in the garden of Shakespeare's Birthplace a standard rose tree, of the variety named Ena Harkness, which had been graciously presented to the Trust by the Queen. The official 'handing-over' ceremony of the rose tree was performed by the Lord Lieutenant of Warwickshire, Lord Willoughby de Broke, assisted by Lady Willoughby de Broke, in the presence of a company of Trustees and representative guests on the day of the Queen's coronation, 2 June 1953. To mark the coronation year a beech tree, also, was planted at the lower end of the Great Garden of New Place. It was at this time, too, that the Trustees contributed a gift of plants for a Shakespeare garden being laid out in Paris and a flag for the Shakespeare Festival in Toronto.

General Progress

These, of course, were high-light occasions, but meanwhile the work of managing the day-to-day business of the Trust kept the Executive Committee and the Director very busy. Each month's attendance figures for the Birthplace and the other Shakespeare properties were eagerly noted, because the admission fees paid by visitors constituted almost the entire income then available to the Trust. It was never very easy to decide when admission charges should be increased, but as from 1 April 1951 the payment for admission to each property was again raised, to 1s. 6d. for adults and 6d. for children, with an inclusive ticket to the five houses at 4s. 6d. In pursuance of their policy of encouraging educational visits, school parties visiting all the properties were offered a concessionary price of 1s. 3d. per head.

The Chairman, Colonel Flower, always supported me in pricing the Trust's end product, as it were, in a realistic way and, after a few years' experience, accurate budgeting proved the corner stone of the Trust's success. Although visitor patronage did not come up to expectations during the Festival of Britain, within a few years visitors to all five properties had increased in an impressive way. By 1955 the attendances for the year, the highest so far, were as follows:

Shakespeare's Birthplace	204,818
Anne Hathaway's Cottage	168,333
New Place	33,288
Mary Arden's House	25,885
Hall's Croft	29,993

To these totals should be added the number of Stratford residents who took advantage of the free admission concession which operated at that time and until the Borough became part of the Stratford-on-Avon District, as a result of local government reorganization in 1976. The numbers admitted free of charge in 1955 were: Shakespeare's Birthplace, 360; Anne Hathaway's Cottage, 242; New Place, 334; Mary Arden's House, 240; and Hall's Croft, 350. During the next few years, the upward trend continued and new attendance records were reached. On bank holiday Monday, 5 August 1957, no fewer than 3,348 visitors were admitted to Shakespeare's Birthplace.

In order to meet the increased overheads and the cost of the Trust's developing activities, admission charges to the properties were increased again as from the beginning of the 1958 season. The cost of a single adult admission to the properties was raised from 1s. 6d. to 2s. 0d., and the price of an inclusive ticket from 4s. 6d. to 5s. 0d. In accordance with established policy, the charges for children were kept as low as possible, the increase being from 6d. to 9d. and, for school party inclusive tickets, from 1s. 3d. to 2s. 0d.

In practice these charges were seen by the visiting public as reasonable, and by 1960 the total annual attendances at the properties were as follows:

Shakespeare's Birthplace	225,575
Anne Hathaway's Cottage	177,379
New Place	33,882
Mary Arden's House	31,097
Hall's Croft	31,846

An analysis of the addresses given by those who signed the visitors' book at the Birthplace during the year established that more than half of them came from abroad, and that roughly half of those were from the United States. Over a hundred and fifty nationalities were represented and, as had always been the case, Germany headed the list among the non-English-speaking countries. It is interesting to note that in 1992 Japan overtook Germany's lead, and by 1995 Japanese visitors were nearly twice as many as those from Germany.

It was increased revenue from the visitors' fees and the greatly developed sales of publications that made it possible within a very few years for the Trustees to pay off the bank overdraft incurred by the purchase and restoration of Hall's Croft, and to spend money on improvements and the provision of amenities designed to enhance the appeal of the properties. The minutes of the Executive Committee meetings record the sequence of items undertaken.

Anne Hathaway's Cottage

Particular attention was focussed on Anne Hathaway's Cottage, where amenities for the increasing number of visitors were surprisingly rudimentary. New toilets for the use of visitors were a priority. The old single toilet and the coal-shed near the orchard end of the Cottage were accordingly demolished, and replaced by a new toilet block, more accessible but discreetly tucked away in a corner of the garden. Another problem was the parking of visitors' cars and coaches, which frequently caused obstruction in front of the Cottage and along the road to Hathaway Hamlet. Hence I found myself discussing with the Borough Engineer, Mr Philip Smart, a plan for providing a car park on a plot of neglected land belonging to the Stratford-upon-Avon Borough Council alongside Shottery Brook and off the approach road to the Cottage. By this time I had established friendly working arrangements with Mr Smart and the other town officials and, on their recommendation, a lease of the site was offered on favourable terms by the Council to the Trust. A visitors' car park was constructed, and brought into use at the beginning of the 1953 season. Particular care was given to the landscaping aspect, and I greatly enjoyed designing the layout of the parking area and the planting of trees and shrubs by the Trust's garden staff. Almost immediately the park proved its usefulness, as the road outside the Cottage was relieved of standing vehicles.

I have always been conscious of the need to safeguard the natural environment of Anne Hathaway's Cottage, and I was particularly pleased when, in the same year, the Trustees purchased the field known as Briar Furlong, adjacent to the orchard at the Cottage, as an additional protection to the amenities of this area. Even more satisfying was the opportunity which occurred in 1958, when the land adjoining the car park known as the Pound Ground, which the Trust had also acquired, was planted with forest trees, in accordance with a scheme approved by the Forestry Commission. Oak trees were interplanted with spruce, which for years afterwards provided a supply of Christmas trees for use at the properties. The Chairman of the Trust, Colonel Flower, shared my enthusiasm for this scheme; we both liked the idea of growing oak timber which, at some distant date, might well be used to repair the Shakespearian properties.

Anne Hathaway's Cottage itself also received attention. The thatched roof had been repaired in 1951, but by 1954 a complete rethatching was needed. The chimney stacks were first overhauled, and arrangements made to secure an adequate supply of combed wheat straw, which was the traditional material used for thatching in Warwickshire. The work was carried out by an Irish thatcher, Peter Slevin, who used some twenty tons of straw on the roof. Visitors were fascinated to see him at work, and the Cottage received a good deal of useful publicity. Incidentally, Peter Slevin himself benefitted, because shortly afterwards he was invited to go to Canada to thatch the replica of Anne Hathaway's Cottage which was built as a tourist attraction in British Columbia.

A careful overhaul of the interior of the Cottage was also undertaken, accompanied by alterations in

Rethatching the roof of Anne Hathaway's Cottage, 1954

presentation designed to enhance the interest of the various rooms. The emphasis continued to be on the furnishings and belongings of the Hathaways and their descendants, ranging from the original Hathaway bed, dining table and built-in dresser, to a medley collection of furniture and domestic possessions of later date. Opportunity was taken to equip the stone-flagged buttery, or dairy, with a number of dairy and farming utensils similar to those mentioned in an inventory taken on Bartholomew Hathaway's death in 1624. At the same time, the chamber upstairs nearest to the orchard (called the 'broad solar' in 1624), which had hitherto been kept closed, as an empty room, was now furnished with representative pieces of furniture of the period of Anne Hathaway or earlier, in order to give the impression of an Elizabethan interior such as might have been found in a good, middle-class yeoman's farmhouse comparable with that of the Hathaways.

Maintenance Work

Away from Shottery, a considerable amount of building and maintenance work was undertaken at the other properties. A new greenhouse and range of garden frames were built at Hall's Croft in 1951. All the stone-paved paths in the knott garden at New Place were re-laid and renewed, as necessary, in 1954 and, by arrangement with the Governors of the Shakespeare Memorial Theatre, the use of a much-needed reserve garden in the paddock immediately adjoining Hall's Croft was secured. The Trust continued to use this for growing plants and flowers to cut for display in the properties until 1983, when the Theatre required the land for its own development plans; in consequence the Trust moved its garden base to The Hill, as will be described in a later chapter.

In 1954 the restoration of the stone chimney stacks at Shakespeare's Birthplace presented a problem. The stone used at the time the building was restored, in the 1860s, was the blue-grey limestone from Wilmcote, a material which had weathered badly, and the slab cappings needed urgent replacement. The problem was to find suitable stone of the same kind, because the quarry at Wilmcote from which this type of stone was originally obtained had ceased to operate at the beginning of the century. Fortunately the contractors, William Sapcote and Sons, Ltd, had masons in their employment who could deal with a situation of this kind; they secured permission from the farmer in whose field the old quarry working at Wilmcote was situated, and proceeded to hew slabs of stone suitable for capping the chimney stacks. I learned much about the mason's craft by watching them reducing the slabs to their final size and shape, in the covered enclosure they erected as a temporary workshop on the lower path of the Birthplace garden.

During the years which followed and right down to the 1980s, I developed a close association with Sapcotes' masons, not only as they worked for the Trust, but also as they carried through successive stages of restoring the stonework of the ancient Guild Chapel. Like the builders of our magnificent old cathedrals and parish churches, they were superb craftsmen who loved their work.

Nash's House and New Place

It was at this time also, during the autumn and winter of 1954 to 1955, that the Trustees undertook a long-overdue programme of repairs and improvements at Nash's House, adjacent to New Place. At their meeting on 3 October 1954, the Executive Committee considered and approved my proposals for a comprehensive overhaul of the fabric of the building and for far-reaching changes in its interior presentation.

Chimney stacks, roofs, brickwork and the timber framed structure were all carefully repaired, as necessary; and inside, improvements to the central heating system and the installation of concealed electrical lighting were followed by a detailed re-furbishment of each individual room and redecoration throughout. The somewhat primitive amenities of the custodian's living quarters at the rear were upgraded, and at that time it occurred to me that, when opportunity presented itself, the rooms on the first floor and the small kitchen below, which at that time were used as living accommodation, would lend themselves to adaptation as an extension to the museum part of the building. However, it was not until the resident custodian moved out in 1972 that this proved possible.

Supplementary to this work, the changes approved by the Trustees for the re-presentation of the interior of Nash's House were made. The basic idea was to emphasize the architectural features and character of the house and, at the same time, to present a more appealing and interesting interior display. To this end, the miscellaneous collection of furniture, showcases and museum exhibits were removed from the ground floor, and in their place a representative collection of authentic period furnishings and exhibits were arranged, to give an impression of the background of domestic life in Shakespeare's time. As in the case of Hall's Croft, I had the rare opportunity of planning the detail of this transformation and of acquiring for the Trust fine specimens of furniture, pictures, tapestry panels and the like, such as might have been found in William Shakespeare's comfortable retirement home, New Place, situated next door. As before, I received considerable help from Mr S.W. Wolsey in tracking down suitable items. The Trustees themselves were supportive throughout, and Mr Graham Baron Ash, in particular, gave me the benefit of his considerable

Nash's House, as re-presented, 1955

knowledge of Tudor furnishings and indeed donated an attractive tapestry panel for display over the fireplace in the front room.

The ground floor of Nash's House thus assumed an entirely new look, warmth and colour being added by curtains and rush mats and by flower arrangements, which from this time became a feature in all the Trust's properties. The more formal display of museum exhibits, illustrating aspects of Stratford's history, was restricted to the two small front rooms on the first-floor, which were equipped for the purpose with specially designed wall cases supplied by A. Edmonds and Company, Ltd, of Birmingham.

These changes provided an opportunity for an appraisal and sorting of the various museum collections in the Trust's possession. The Trustees decided to dispose of a few items, such as a collection of archaeological material relating to Mancetter, which they offered to the Birmingham City Museum and Art Gallery, and a painting of St. Mary's Church, Warwick, which was presented to the Vicar and Churchwardens there. Inevitably, a considerable amount of local and Shakespearian museum material had to be put in reserve and, in order to provide storage facilities, the attic rooms of Nash's House were fitted with suitable racks and cupboards. In addition, a room on the second floor was equipped for the occasional use of students wishing to study particular archaeological or museum items. It was at this time, also, that Mr H. Vernon Spreadbury, a distinguished stained-glass artist who had made Stratford his retirement home, undertook the glazing of the window on the main staircase with sixteenth-century glass.

This comprehensive programme of work at Nash's House was completed in time for its re-opening to the public, at the beginning of April 1955; an official ceremony to mark this event, to which representative guests were invited, took place on Thursday, 12 May, the day of the Trust's Annual Meeting.

Other improvements designed to attract more visitors to Nash's House and the foundations of New Place were made within the next two years. Until that time, the closed front door of Nash's House, which led straight into one of the main rooms, had tended to deter visitors from entering; to overcome

Trustees at re-opening of Nash's House

this problem, a small vestibule was constructed with an inner door, which enabled the outer front door to stand open, thus providing a more inviting entrance. Immediately inside, to the left of the entrance vestibule, a small reception and sales counter was also added.

Even more important, from a visual point of view, were the removal of the ivy-covered, tall, cast-iron railings – a physical link with Victorian times – and the lowering of the wall which enclosed the Chapel Lane corner of the site of the foundations of New Place. Suitable old bricks were found for necessary repairs to the wall, which was finished off with a coping of Clipsham stone, and a new wrought-iron gate made by the Birmingham Guild was provided in the wall, near to Nash's House, to give access from Chapel Street. This 'opening-up to view' policy particularly appealed to the Chairman and, as subsequent experience showed, what was done at New Place contributed greatly to an increase in visitors to this property during the following years.

The Role of Craftsmen

My experience of these various projects had by this time taught me the importance of being able to employ experienced craftsmen versed in traditional skills, and I sensed that in due course the Trust would benefit by employing its own team of maintenance men. I first appointed Eric Bartlett as a painter and handyman, followed by Percy Davis, a carpenter, in 1955; but for some time to come the Trust was fortunate in being able to use the services of local builders, and particularly of D.J. Dyer, who was responsible for the work at Nash's House and New Place. He had in his employment a number of experienced country craftsmen, and for some years they did much of the maintenance work around the Trust's properties. When Mr Dyer's firm ceased to operate at a later date, the Trust was able to offer full-time employment to several of them, to form the nucleus of its own maintenance department. They were a good set of men and made an excellent team: Percy Basson of Welford-on-Avon, bricklayer and mason; George Nason of Preston-on-Stour, painter and decorator; and Les Mansell, plumber, the bachelor son of the former blacksmith of Pebworth. They all rode to work on their bicycles; they were excellent timekeepers, loyal and conscientious, and took great pride in their work.

Mary Arden's House

How fortunate the Trust was in having help of this kind was illustrated further by the work of carpenters, bricklayers and painters, when William Sapcote and Sons, Ltd, were employed to undertake a comprehensive overhaul of Mary Arden's House during 1956 and 1957. The farmhouse, barns, dovecote and other farm buildings had been put in good shape following the purchase of the property by the Trust in 1930, but very little attention had been given to them since. A detailed examination and overhaul of the fabric of the farmhouse was accordingly undertaken, followed by interior re-decoration and treatment of the exterior. I still remember the discussion which took place between the architect and the builder, as to whether the exterior timberwork of the house should be darkened with stain or not; the decision reached was that the application of any form of stain or dark preservation applied to the oak would destroy the attraction of its natural, bleached condition. The timberwork was therefore left untreated, and great care was taken to obtain a paint of suitable texture and shade for the plaster panels, both inside and outside the house. Mr T. Spencer Wood, the Trust's architect responsible for supervising all this work, was always prepared to give attention to the minutest detail. There followed a comprehensive programme of repairs to the barns, which by now were providing accommodation for the Trust's growing collection of old farming implements and other reminders of Warwickshire rural life.

A Variety of Projects

Several miscellaneous minor projects were undertaken during these years. The plot of ground at the rear of Anne Hathaway's Cottage was laid out with grass and shrubs, and other improvements in that vicinity, including the cleaning out of the brook flowing through the spinney opposite to the Cottage, were carried through. On the Trust's land at Welcombe mature trees were felled and replacements planted. The roof of Hall's Croft was re-tiled in the autumn of 1957 and additions made to the greenhouse and cold frames there. At Hornby Cottage, the building near to Shakespeare's Birthplace which continued to serve as the Trust's headquarters, considerable improvements were completed by the spring of 1959. At the front of the building, a new counter and display fitments were provided in the sales department and the stock room was re-arranged; at the rear, the conversion of an outside store into a strong room provided additional space for archives and made possible the use of the small, first-floor record room as a working area for students. Improved cloakrooms for staff were provided, and at the rear of the building a new block of visitors' toilets for ladies was constructed, incorporating a boiler house in a basement room underneath to serve the Birthplace and Hornby Cottage.

Development on all Fronts

Altogether, it was a time of considerable development, which made possible much that happened later. Hall's Croft progressively established itself as one of the Shakespeare property attractions; the Festival Club there quickly proved its usefulness, and grew in popularity as a base for the annual Poetry Festival, exhibitions and a variety of cultural activities. Relations with the Shakespeare Memorial Theatre, the British Council and the University of Birmingham became closer, and a pattern of co-operative planning of lectures and courses for the season was followed.

As already mentioned, at the beginning of 1952 the Governors of the Theatre agreed in principle to amalgamate the Theatre's library with the Birthplace Trust's library, when opportunity presented itself, and from that time I assumed the role of honorary librarian to the Theatre. With the help of an assistant librarian, who undertook the day-to-day work in the library in Waterside, I was responsible for overall supervision and general planning. Considerable progress was made with the re-classification and cataloguing of the Theatre collection alongside the Trust's library, and the foundations laid for the ultimate union of the two libraries.

Although resources were strictly limited, some important accessions of early printed books were made, as well as of current Shakespearian publications. To mention a few items only, I was particularly pleased to acquire in 1954 a fine copy of the 1587 edition of Holinshed's *Chronicles of England, Ireland and Scotland*; Swinburne's *A briefe treatise of testaments and last wills*, 1590-91; George Bishop's *A catalogue of the bishops of England ...*, 1601; Cotgrave's *Dictionarie of the French and English tongues*, 1611; and Worlidge's *Systema agriculturae*, 1675. During the next five years I managed to purchase copies of a

Piano recital at Hall's Croft

number of other sixteenth- and seventeenth-century books covering a wide range of subject matter, to fill gaps in the collection. Notable items were: *All the workes of J. Taylor the water poet*, 1630; George Wither's *A collection of emblems, ancient and modern*, 1635; *Ovid's Metamorphoses*, translated by Sandys, 1632; *The Whole woorkes of George Gascoigne, Esquyre*, 1587; John Manwood's *A Treatise and Discourse of the Lawes of the Forrest*, 1598; and William Burton's (Leicestershire's first historian) copy of Fynes Moryson's *Itinerary containing his ten yeeres travell*, 1617. Important additions were also made to the Trust's record collections: apart from the family and estate records of the Leigh family of Stoneleigh Abbey, major accessions were the Archer collection deposited by the Earl of Plymouth, and the Gregory-Hood collection relating to the family and its estates in Warwickshire and elsewhere; also a collection of eighteenth-century letters (1733-1789) written by the Reverend Joseph Greene, the Master of Stratford's Grammar School, to his brother Richard, apothecary and surgeon at Lichfield.

In view of my earlier training and experience as an archivist, I was naturally pleased with the development of the Trust's record collections. The appointment of Miss Elizabeth Gillan as a records assistant in 1953 enabled the work of sorting and cataloguing to go forward, and each year saw a greater use being made of the records by students and scholars. A number of useful reference works were acquired for their use, including a copy of Dugdale's monumental *Monasticon Anglicanum* and *The Complete Peerage*. I was equally fortunate in being able to recruit excellent staff to help with the business and secretarial work of the Trust. Following Mrs Wellstood, I had a succession of assistants who dealt with book-keeping, wages and accounts: Mrs Joan Busby, Miss Jane Easton and Miss Patricia Brown, who remained with the Trust until 1981. Miss Shirley Watkins, who came as my private secretary on 10 December 1951, quickly became an indispensable helper; she held that position for forty years, until she retired in 1991.

By 1960 I had been able to build up the staff generally to deal with the expanding work of the Trust. In addition to my personal secretary and accounts assistant, two assistant secretaries completed the headquarters office staff, alongside the library and records assistants. Each of the Shakespearian properties was separately organized, with a chief guide and deputy; at Shakespeare's Birthplace there were, in addition, two full-time assistant guides. At each property part-time guides were employed as required, particularly during the summer months, to help with the influx of visitors. Caretaking and cleaning were done by part-timers, and as yet the only maintenance men were a painter and handyman, a carpenter and handyman, and a junior assistant. By this time Harold Goodyear had established himself as head gardener, and no fewer than ten assistant gardeners had been recruited to cope with the Trust's garden and estate work, as well as that of the Shakespeare Memorial Theatre.

An assistant gardener at that time was paid £9 15s. 0d. a week; a carpenter and handyman, £10 10s. 0d.; and guides, according to experience and responsibility, from £7 0s. 0d. to £15 0s. 0d. a week. The records assistant with graduate qualifications had a salary of £750 a year, slightly more than the senior secretarial and accounts staff. The Director's salary was £2,250 a year, an amount roughly comparable to what was being paid to heads of departments in universities at that time. These details of remuneration are given for the purpose of record; they must be seen as illustrating the prevailing market value of different types of labour in Stratford-upon-Avon. The Trust's budget of £24,250 for staff for the whole of 1960 represented a major item in the total annual of £36,250, and as set against a budgetted income of £39,000. In the event, business proved better than was forecast, resulting in a balance of £4,188 surplus on the year's working.

The Trustees

Major Charles Gregory-Hood was one of the Trustees responsible for appointing me as Director, and it was not long before I established a friendly association with him, by reason of our mutual interest in the history of Coventry and the Gregory family. As a member of the Executive Committee, he regularly attended meetings and showed a particular concern for the development of the Trust's archive collections. I well remember visiting him on several occasions at his home at Loxley Hall to view his family pictures and records, which included some exceedingly rare documents of early medieval date. He was very proud of his family's history and possessions, and I felt it was extremely public-spirited of him to deposit some of his family records with the Trust; his son, Colonel Alexander Gregory-Hood, added the remainder of the collection some years later. The Trust was fortunate at that time in having gentlemen of this kind as members of the governing body, as well as scholars who were always willing to offer advice and support.

Sir William Dugdale, a descendant of the herald and antiquary of the same name who produced the classic county history of Warwickshire in 1656, was another Trustee with whom I had regular contact. Sir William was President of the Dugdale Society, of which I was the Secretary and General Editor, and he played an active part in county affairs, providing a useful link with the Shire Hall at Warwick. In 1956 the Trustees assisted the Dugdale Society in making arrangements for a conference on English Historical Scholarship in the Sixteenth and Seventeenth Centuries, held at Warwick, to commemorate the tercentenary of the publication of Dugdale's *Antiquities of Warwickshire*. I subsequently prepared a record of the papers delivered at this conference, which was published in a volume, *English Historical Scholarship in the Sixteenth and Seventeenth Centuries* (Oxford University Press, 1956).

Another good friend and supporter of the Trust in those years was Dr T.S.R. Boase, President of Magdalen College, Oxford, who had been appointed a Life Trustee in 1949. I have a vivid recollection of accompanying Mr Ashley Clayton, our Deputy Chairman, to Oxford on a very cold, frosty morning to invite him to allow his name to go forward for election as a member of the governing body. A kind, friendly, unassuming man, Dr Boase was a scholar of considerable eminence. I first met him when, as an undergraduate at Oxford, I attended his lectures at Hertford College. Later, as the Director of the Courtauld Institute of Art, he became an acknowledged authority on pictures, with a specialized knowledge of Shakespeare in art, and *The Oxford History of Art* was subsequently published under his general editorship. He was also a theatre man and, as a Governor of the Shakespeare Memorial Theatre, he took a particular interest in the picture gallery there. He visited Stratford frequently, and invariably called on me to discuss and advise on Trust business, or indeed any matter of local interest. It was at his suggestion that the newly established Friends of the Guild Chapel invited Mr S.E. Dykes Bower, Surveyor of the Fabric of Westminster Abbey, to act as their architect for the restoration of the Guild Chapel. Dr Boase later gave strong support to the Trustees' proposal to build a new Shakespeare Centre as the Trust's headquarters, and was particularly helpful with suggestions for its artistic embellishments.

In a similar manner, I received considerable encouragement and support from the well-known Shakespearian scholar, Professor John Dover Wilson. He had been appointed in 1949 to represent the University of Cambridge on the Trust's governing

Professor John Dover Wilson taking to students

body, and he became a Life Trustee in 1951; Mr S.C. (later Sir Sydney) Roberts succeeded him as Cambridge's representative, and at the same time London University appointed Dr (later Sir) Ifor Evans to succeed Sir Ernest Pooley. The following year, Professor Nevill Coghill became the representative of Oxford University. There can be no doubt that an academic ingredient of this quality not only conferred prestige on the Trust; it provided also a wealth of experience and specialized knowledge, which frequently proved invaluable to the Executive Committee and the Director. The attendance of these 'outside' Trustees at the Annual and Half Annual Meetings was always a great source of encouragement to the local members and myself, in carrying the burden of running the day-to-day affairs of the Trust.

Distinguished Visitors

One aspect of my work which I greatly enjoyed was that of receiving and acting as guide to the distinguished visitors who came to Shakespeare's Birthplace. It would be tedious to record a list of these, because every year brought along one or more of them. I particularly remember, however, the visits of certain individuals, such as that of Mr Malenkov, Vice-Chairman of the Soviet Council of Ministers and Minister of Power Stations, who came in 1956. Closely surrounded by his entourage, he listened intently as I described, with the help of his interpreter, the features of the Birthplace and some of its more important exhibits. Throughout, his face remained expressionless, displaying a stolid look which I later discovered characterised his compatriots from the political sphere. He was clearly more interested in power stations than Shakespeare! Quite different were the reactions of the members of the Bolshoi Theatre Ballet Company, led by Madame Ulanova, who came in the autumn of 1956; they clearly enjoyed their visit and showed a keen interest in everything I said.

It was in the same year that Dr Louis B. Wright, Director of the Folger Shakespeare Library, in Washington, DC, a distinguished Shakespearian scholar and American historian, came to see me. This was the first of many visits and the beginning of a life-long friendship between us, in the course of which Dr Wright developed a warm affection for Stratford-upon-Avon and the Trust. In 1964 he was elected a Life Trustee, and maintained this connection until his death, in 1984.

Hardly a year passed without the Foreign Office or the British Council bringing distinguished politicians or scholars from overseas to Shakespeare's Birthplace. I have a vivid recollection of the visit of the first Indian Professor of English brought by the British Council. After conducting him over the Birthplace, I showed him a few of the Trust's treasures in the records room, including a copy of the First Folio, which he had never seen before. He was visibly moved and asked my permission to touch it. Of course I agreed, and when he had placed his finger on the title page he fell on his knees, lifted his hands above his head and said a prayer I could not understand. The look of ecstasy on his face was unbelievable: it was clearly the greatest moment in his life.

Madame Ulanova of the Bolshoi Ballet Company

By this time I had come to appreciate the unique drawing power of Shakespeare and the respect in which he is held by people of all nationalities. The distinguished guests who came in 1958 provided an excellent illustration. They included the Director of the Folger Shakespeare Library, the Director of the Moscow Arts Theatre, the Ruler of Sharjah, the Minister of Education and the Speaker of the Parliament of Pakistan, the Rector of Leningrad University (Professor A.D. Alexandrov, a distinguished mathematician and translator of Shakespeare), members of the French National Theatre and a party of top government officials from Bahrain and Dubai. In the following year official representatives from abroad included the chief directors of the museum services in Sweden and Denmark, groups of Russian museum directors and librarians, and the Polish Minister of Education. In 1960, special arrangements were made for the visit of the King and Queen of Nepal, and other distinguished guests received during the year were the Rector of Ankara University, the Director of the New York State Historical Association, Lady Eden, wife of the former Prime Minister, Sir Anthony Eden, the Deputy Governor of Jerusalem, the Minister of Culture for the Ukraine, and several parties of Soviet delegates, writers and actors.

Even more impressive, as symbolising the universal recognition of the genius of Shakespeare, were the annual birthday celebrations organized in the poet's honour by the Shakespeare Birthday Celebrations Committee, whose members included representatives of the Borough Council, the Shakespeare Memorial Theatre, the Shakespeare Birthplace Trust and a number of other interested bodies in the town. From 1947, as Chairman of the Committee, I was responsible for organizing the event, and the Birthplace Trust came to provide the necessary office and secretarial facilities. In pursuance of the Committee's policy of inviting all the countries with diplomatic representation at the Court of St. James to take part, by the end of the 1950s the celebrations has assumed the character of an international occasion absolutely unique in its purpose and attraction.

The Shakespeare birthday celebrations in the 1950s

Official diplomatic representatives of sixty or seventy countries attended, together with distinguished personalities of literature, art and the theatre, sharing with local people in a corporate act of homage to our national poet. The birthday luncheon, with its traditional toasts, the ceremonial unfurling of the flags of the nations in the central streets of the town, the floral procession from Shakespeare's Birthplace to the poet's tomb in Holy Trinity Church, and the birthday performance of a Shakespeare play at the Theatre attended by these distinguished guests, all provided evidence of the world-wide recognition of Shakespeare and Stratford-upon-Avon, and of the importance of the role of the Birthplace Trust in preserving the Shakespearian heritage.

The Royal Visit of 1957

For the second time in seven years, Shakespeare's Birthplace was honoured by a visit from Britain's monarch. On Friday, 14 June 1957, Her Majesty Queen Elizabeth II, accompanied by her husband, HRH The Prince Philip, Duke of Edinburgh, spent nearly six hours in the town, visiting the Town Hall, Shakespeare's Birthplace and Holy Trinity Church, before going on to the Shakespeare Memorial Theatre.

Preparations for the visit over a period of weeks had ensured that the town had never looked more attractive. Bathed in brilliant sunshine, it was gay

The Royal party in the Birthplace garden

Reception of the Royal visitors

cheering crowds, local school groups in particular offering an excited welcome.

After being received at the Town Hall by the Mayor, Councillor P.R. Worth, the royal visitors met civic representatives and were then shown the Council Chamber and some reminders of the Borough's history and traditions. Prince Philip was reported as showing a particular interest in the civic regalia.

The arrangements for the reception of the royal visitors at Shakespeare's Birthplace followed closely the pattern of the 1950 visit. The Queen and Prince Philip entered the garden from Henley Street, and the Mayor asked leave to present the Chairman of the Trust, Sir Fordham Flower, who in turn presented Lady Flower, Mr Leslie Watkins, the Deputy Chairman of the Executive Committee of the Trust, and Mrs Watkins, and myself, as Director, and Mrs Fox. Members of staff watched from a distance in the garden, and only accredited press were allowed to accompany the party.

Just inside the garden Elizabeth and Patricia Fox, the five-year-old twin daughters of the Director, dressed in tussore silk dresses and pretty straw bonnets, were shyly waiting to present to the Queen a basket of flowers and herbs gathered from the Shakespeare gardens. As they stepped forward with their gift, the Queen gave them a warm smile, and as they were making their curtsies there was a sudden gust of wind. Closely observant of what was happening, Prince Philip leaned over and warned 'Mind your hats'. Like lightning, two little pairs of hands whipped up to hold on to the two straw bonnets, in obedience to the royal command. They were just in time and, as the breeze died away, neither was left hatless; needless to say, parents were much relieved.

It was a colourful occasion. A slender figure, the Queen wore a green gros grain coat over a matching frock, patterned in yellow to tone with her vivid yellow, swathed chiffon hat. She wore a pearl necklace, a diamond brooch on her lapel and tiny ear-rings. The Duke, tall and immaculately dressed, bronzed and smiling, made an impressive figure.

The royal party proceeded slowly along the paved path towards the back entrance to Shakespeare's

with flowers, nearly all the buildings along the royal route being decorated with colourful hanging baskets and window boxes. The flags of the nations were flown in Bridge Street and the route was lined with

Birthplace, admiring the green expanse of lawn and the stately cedar tree beyond. The Queen questioned Sir Fordham about the mulberry tree and the quince, and paused to admire the rosemary and rue, the thyme and mint, and the other herbs, all of which were mentioned by Shakespeare. Closely following behind, Prince Philip engaged me in lively conversation. The garden was looking at its best; the only disappointment was that the Ena Harkness standard rose that the Queen had given to the Trust to mark her coronation was not yet in bloom.

Escorted by the Chairman and myself, the Queen and the Duke entered the Birthplace, where W.H. Dyke, the chief guide, and Dorothea Sheppard, the longest serving member of the guide staff, were presented. The press and other accompanying dignitaries were excluded at that point, as a result of which the royal visitors were able to enjoy a relaxed inspection of the building and its exhibits. It was a tremendous pleasure and honour for me to act as their guide. They were interested in the structure and furnishings of the house, and repeatedly asked questions about particular items. The Queen showed interest in the various pictures of old Stratford on display, and was anxious to know to what extent the town's old buildings had been preserved. Upstairs the royal visitors commented on the records relating to the parentage of Shakespeare and his career; these included the Quyney letter, the only surviving letter written to Shakespeare, the earliest extant copy of Shakespeare's will, and the First Folio and several Quarto editions of the plays. The Queen was visibly touched when she came to the case containing photographs of her mother and father, taken when they visited the Birthplace in 1950.

What impressed me most was the friendly, natural manner of the royal visitors and their genuine interest, as evidenced by our general conversation and the questions they asked. The fact that they overstayed the time allotted for their inspection did not seem to concern them, and they could not have been more gracious in expressing their thanks and appreciation.

After signing the visitors' book upstairs at the end

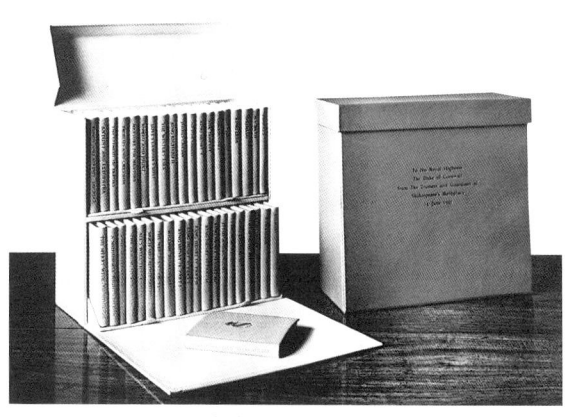

Presentation sets of Shakespeare's plays

of their tour, the Queen and Prince Philip came down the stairs at the back of the Birthplace, passing through the kitchen into the living room. At this point Edward and Elizabeth Flower, children of the Chairman, presented to the Queen sets of the New Temple edition of Shakespeare's plays for Their Royal Highnesses Prince Charles, Duke of

HM Queen Elizabeth II leaves the Birthplace, accompanied by the Chairman, Sir Fordham Flower

Cornwall, and Princess Anne. These small-sized volumes had been specially bound in leather – cherry red colour for Prince Charles and light buff for Princess Anne – and were contained in leather cases, bearing inscriptions recording the presentation from the Trustees and Guardians of Shakespeare's Birthplace. The Queen was clearly delighted, exclaiming 'Oh, how lovely!' as she picked up one of the volumes for inspection, adding, as she acknowledged Edward and Elizabeth Flower, 'I hope you have read them all'.

The royal visitors left the Birthplace by the front entrance into Henley Street, to the cheers of a large crowd which had assembled there. They then drove along High Street, past the almshouses, gay with flowers, to Holy Trinity Church, where the Vicar, the Reverend Canon Noel Prentice, acted as their guide. Afterwards he was reported as saying 'The Queen thought our church was very wonderful and very beautiful'.

The royal visit continued with an inspection of the Shakespeare Memorial Theatre, followed by lunch and a special performance of *As You Like It*, a play the Queen said she had not seen before. In the event, with Dame Peggy Ashcroft playing Rosalind, the production could not have proved a more enjoyable finale to a most memorable day for Stratford and the Shakespeare Birthplace Trust.

The Burnside Bequest

One of Stratford's well known public figures during my early years as Director was Mrs J.L.T. (Emily) Evans, of Burnside, Shottery, where she had taken up residence in the late 1920s. A lady of outstanding personality and remarkable energy, she played an active part in a number of local organizations. She had been instrumental in forming the Stratford branch of the British Legion, and throughout her life had a special regard for the welfare of ex-service men. Having been appointed a Justice of the Peace in 1942, she became an Ex-Officio Trustee of Shakespeare's Birthplace and continued as such until 1949, when Stratford lost its own magisterial bench. She was elected a Life Trustee of the Birthplace in 1956; she died in 1958.

The range of Mrs Evans's interests took in many facets of Stratford life. She was a Governor of the Shakespeare Memorial Theatre and, as a member of its Executive Council, was actively involved with its management; she also served on the Shakespeare Birthday Celebrations Committee. A keen churchwoman and supporter of St. Andrew's Church, Shottery, she was also a Governor of Shottery School. Mrs Evans identified herself with the Women's Institute movement, and was the key figure running the Stratford branch of the English Speaking Union. She took great delight in entertaining overseas visitors at her home, and the grounds of Burnside were regularly made available for tea parties and charitable functions.

I feel that these personal details about Mrs Evans should be recorded, not only because I developed a friendly personal association with her, but because she can claim to be the Birthplace Trust's most generous benefactor. I well remember being invited to tea at Burnside with my wife and young son, soon after I took up my duties as Director. At that time Burnside, a detached Victorian house with later additions, standing in its own well maintained grounds alongside Church Road, Shottery, made a most attractive setting for an afternoon tea party, complete with a summer-house and shady trees; the kitchen garden was well planted, and John Evans, Emily's husband, who was the history master at King Edward VI School, took a particular interest in growing mushrooms and grapes.

Mrs Evans owned the fields around Burnside, including the Home Field, which ran down to the brook alongside Cottage Lane, opposite to Anne Hathaway's Cottage. She had an acute sense of the need to protect this unspoiled environment from undesirable development, and during her lifetime she strongly supported the cause of conservation. She took great delight, for example, in having the period cottages she owned re-thatched in the traditional style. She also successfully opposed a plan to build on the small plot of land in Tavern Lane adjacent to the picturesque thatched cottages, known as Tapestry Cottage and Wild Thyme, which she owned.

Looking ahead to the future, and having no family of her own, as early as 1938 Mrs Evans had offered to convey to the Birthplace Trustees on certain conditions her residence, Burnside, and land of

Burnside, Shottery

some seventeen acres at Shottery, in order to safeguard as much as possible the neighbourhood of Anne Hathaway's Cottage. The offer was accepted with appreciation but, so far as I can establish, no formal arrangement to implement this intention was made at that time. Subsequently, after I got to know her, Mrs Evans talked to me on several occasions about this proposal, but it was not until she made her will, shortly before her death, that the details of what she had in mind were made known.

In her will Mrs Evans devised to the Shakespeare Birthplace Trust the freehold property known as Burnside and all her other freehold property situated within one mile of Burnside, subject to certain conditions. The most important of these was that, in the event of her death before that of her husband, John Evans should enjoy a life interest in all the property, which would be administered by Mrs Evans's own trustees until the time of his death. In practical terms the consequence of this was that the Birthplace Trust would have no voice in the management of Burnside and the estate, and would derive no financial benefit from it, until after Mr Evans's death.

The second condition was that the Birthplace Trustees should assume responsibility for paying the estate duty which would arise. Although the Trust was a recognized charity, there was at that time no provision in law for exemption from the payment of duty on a bequest of this nature.

Finally, Mrs Evans made clear her wishes by stipulating that the Birthplace Trustees should not erect any new building upon any part of the property bequeathed. In other words, this was a complete conservation provision designed to ensure the permanent maintenance of a green buffer, safe from development, linked with the land the Trust already owned, in the neighbourhood of Anne Hathaway's Cottage.

The Burnside bequest, as it came to be known, comprised Burnside itself and the Home Field immediately behind it, together with adjoining land in Church Lane and Cottage Lane; two recently-built houses in Cottage Lane, known as Montgomery and Alamein, and a timber bungalow nearby occupied by the gardener (later demolished because of its condition); the half-timbered, thatched cottage known as Brookside, opposite to Shottery Church in Church Road; a row of brick-built cottages, nos. 6, 8, 10 and 12 in Church Road; and the picturesque, period, thatched cottages known as Tapestry Cottage and Wild Thyme in Tavern Lane.

The Trustees accepted this bequest with its conditions, with warm appreciation, and made an immediate payment of £6,105 in respect of the estate duty. However, it was not until after the death of John Evans in 1975, nearly twenty years later, that the Trust took possession of Burnside and the properties that went with it. In the meantime, Burnside had been leased to one or two tenants and, unfortunately, the house and its grounds had not been maintained to the standard set by Mrs Evans; the other properties had also deteriorated through lack of adequate maintenance. The consequence of this was that, whilst finding themselves in possession of real estate of greatly enhanced market value, the Trustees were faced with the need to undertake a comprehensive programme of repairs and improvements which took several years to complete. A major project, which will be referred to in a later chapter, was the conversion of Burnside into five self-contained flats.

The importance of Mrs Evans's generous bequest cannot be over emphasized. Linked with the land and houses already owned by the Trust in the immediate vicinity of Anne Hathaway's Cottage, the Burnside estate provided a solid flank of preserved land which guaranteed an unspoiled approach to this rapidly developing tourist attraction. It also provided an incentive in later years for the Trustees to acquire a few other properties to complete the preservation of this area of Shottery.

American Interlude

The year 1957 was also notable for another pleasant interlude, namely my first visit to the United States, which was made possible by the generosity of the Trustees of the Folger Shakespeare Library in Washington, DC.

The primary purpose of my visit, as Director of the Trust, was to represent Shakespeare and Stratford as an ambassador from Shakespeare's Birthplace. To this end I had planned a programme to make contact with various institutions concerned with libraries, records, museums and pictures, with a view to inspecting their collections and seeing something of their methods; to meet and compare notes with scholars and research workers in the Shakespearian field; to visit historic buildings preserved as national memorials and to observe their management arrangements; to give a few lectures; to discharge one or two specific duties; and lastly, and certainly not least important, to spend some time at the Folger Shakespeare Library, where I was accorded the status of a Visiting Fellow, examining the Library's collections and the technical aspects of its working, as well as doing some research in my own field of interests. In addition, I was anxious to get to know more about the way of life, the character and the outlook of the Americans, who, up to that time, I had only encountered as tourists visiting the Shakespearian properties. Thanks to advance planning and a great deal of help which I received from the Birthplace Trust's Chairman, who had already established useful contacts in the United States, and from Dr Louis B. Wright, the Director of the Folger, and other scholar friends, I was able to carry through a programme which, in retrospect, was incredibly ambitious.

My stay lasted six weeks, from 18 September to 29 October. Travel by sea was still very popular at that time and I made the journey, lasting five days each way, in the liner, *Queen Elizabeth*, and greatly enjoyed the experience. Going out, the passengers were mostly Americans and Canadians returning home, with some Continentals and a handful of English people; on the return journey the first-class passenger section was barely one-third full. The *Queen Elizabeth* was noted for her smooth running and, apart from one rough day when the sea came over the deck, the outward and return voyages were very comfortable and relaxing. I was greatly impressed by the standard of service, and pleased to see that Stratford-upon-Avon and Shakespeare were featured on the table menus. As a Rotarian, I attended and presided over a meeting of Rotarians on board, arranged by the purser. There were other memorable occasions, such as when we were summoned on deck in mid-Atlantic to view the liner's sister ship, the *Queen Mary*, passing within a short distance in the opposite direction, and when, a day or two later, we sailed past the Statue of Liberty on the approach to New York.

My travels in the United States were confined to the eastern seaboard. I stayed for different periods in New York, Washington, DC, and Virginia. I was particularly fortunate in that, quite by accident, my visit coincided with that of HM Queen Elizabeth II and HRH Prince Philip. Thus I found myself staying at the Williamsburg Inn at Williamsburg just before the royal visitors arrived, and there was great excitement in anticipation of their visit. I was also in Washington when they came, and then I moved to New York and was there when they arrived. Everywhere I was impressed by the warm enthusiasm with which the Queen and Prince Philip were received. The ticker-tape welcome in New York had to be seen to be believed.

New York is a city unto itself, and it struck me as being fantastic from every point of view. Its vast size, the physical impact of its skyscraper buildings, the rush and turmoil of its traffic, and the busy activity of its incredibly immense, diverse population left me almost stunned at first. Fortunately I had friends who were able to take me in hand and, with their guidance, I saw a good deal of the city and its environs. I sailed round Manhattan Island, which gave me a good impression of the physical aspect of New York and its role as a busy port for shipping. I explored several of the famous buildings, including the Empire State Building and the Rockefeller Center, and took some photographs from the top of one of the tallest skyscrapers. This particular building was one of the largest financial office blocks at the lower end of Wall Street, and I was told that the number of people working in it exceeded the population of Stratford-upon-Avon. I was also taken to see one of the latest music hall shows, *West Side Story*, at the Winter Garden theatre in Broadway. I found the theatre very uncomfortable; the show was highly acclaimed and for me was quite a new experience.

New York possesses a number of fine galleries and libraries, some of which I visited. I was entertained at the Harvard Club, my involvement with Harvard House providing a useful contact. I spent a day at Queen's College, Flushing, a little distance outside the city, where I lectured. I found it an interesting experience to meet American students at close quarters in their own setting and to confer with members of the staff of the English department. It was on this occasion that I was taken on a tour round Long Island and shown the famous pleasure beach known as Jones' Beach.

I also had various excursions into the surrounding country, which gave me an impression of the American highway arrangements for handling traffic. The open countryside in the early autumn was particularly lovely, especially the contrasting colours of the foliage of the trees which lined the routes. It was on one of these excursions that I was taken to see the new Shakespeare Festival Theatre at Stratford, Connecticut. Unfortunately the Shakespeare season there had finished, so I was not able to attend a play, but I was interested to see the somewhat unusual design of this wholly timber-built theatre. As the years passed, I followed the fortunes of the Stratford Festival at Connecticut, and on a return visit in 1964 I was able to see Shakespeare performed there.

From New York I travelled by railroad via Philadelphia to Washington, DC, a city different in every way. From a physical point of view I found it an imposing city, some ten miles square, with streets well laid out and with plenty of open spaces and trees. As the seat of central government, Washington possesses many striking public buildings and government departments, mostly built of light coloured stone or pure white marble in the classical style.

To attempt to describe all the buildings I visited would take too much space, but mention must be made of a few which I found especially interesting: the domed Capitol, the equivalent of our Houses of Parliament, with its amazing collection of statuary inside; the Smithsonian Institution, comparable to our Victoria and Albert Museum, with its five buildings containing exhibits illustrative of every facet of American history and life, ranging from early steam engines to the dresses worn by the First Ladies of the United States; the National Gallery of Art, with its superb collection of pictures representative of all schools and including masterpieces such as Constable's painting of Salisbury Cathedral; the National Archives building, similar in function to our Public Record Office, where members of the public could see the Bill of Rights, the Declaration of Independence and other records relating to the States which comprise the Union; the Supreme Court of Justice, a massive building of pure white marble, with incredibly hot central heating and excellent cafeteria facilities which I used whilst working at the Folger Library nearby; and the Library of Congress, with its maze of corridors and thirty-six million books (the figure at that time, so I was told), where I met the Librarian and several assistants and was shown something of the working of the Library. I was surprised by the wealth of early English printed books and manuscripts in the Department of Rare Books. How completely different from our modest library collections at Stratford-upon-Avon!

I must also mention my visit to Washington Cathedral. Started fifty years before, it was still not completed, and I was there on the occasion of the fiftieth anniversary of the laying of the foundation stone. There was a special service of celebration, and I was surprised to find that the Bishop of Coventry, the Rt Reverend Cuthbert Bardsley, who was a Trustee of Shakespeare's Birthplace and well known to me, was there to represent the Church of England and to give the anniversary address. After the service Bishop Bardsley introduced me to the Bishop of Washington, and also described to him the restoration of the Guild Chapel at Stratford-upon-Avon and the development of the Chapel of Unity at Coventry Cathedral. It was a happy coincidence that I was present at these impressive celebrations.

I have left the Folger Shakespeare Library till last. I naturally found it the most fascinating and important of all Washington's institutions, because of my own interests and the purpose of my visit. Its founder was Henry Clay Folger, the President of the Standard Oil Company, who, during the early years of this century, collected a vast treasure house of books and manuscripts, and towards the end of his life provided a magnificent building to accommodate them, at the same time endowing the Library and entrusting its administration to the Trustees of Amherst College. The Library was opened on 23 April 1932.

As a building, the Folger is comparatively small compared with some of the large public buildings nearby. Constructed of pure white marble, it stands on a garden site in close proximity to the Library of Congress and the Supreme Court of Justice and not far from the Capitol. I was told that Mr Folger did a series of deals in the property market over a period of years, with the idea of acquiring a suitable site in the right place. He certainly succeeded.

Architecturally, the exterior of the building is striking, by reason of the dignity and simplicity of its modern design. The exterior elevations are relieved by very attractively carved friezes and panels depicting scenes from Shakespeare's plays, together with various Shakespearian and other quotations. What surprised me was the contrasting interior of the building, which is Elizabethan in character. Inside what appears to be a simple, almost functional type of building, you find yourself in a setting which has a Tudor atmosphere.

Leading off the entrance lobby, where publications were on display and sale, an exhibition gallery of impressive size and proportions provided an excellent setting for pictures, books, manuscripts and related material from the Folger's collections. Members of the public had free access to this area, beyond which was a full-sized replica of an Elizabethan theatre, complete with projecting stage, galleries and all the features of the playhouse in which Shakespeare's plays were performed. At the time of my visit this replica theatre, based on a design by the Folger's first Director, John Quincy Adams, had not been used for acting purposes because of licensing requirements, but it provided an excellent study piece and occasionally it was used for special lectures. I myself was invited to give a lecture in this theatre on 'Shakespeare and Stratford-upon-Avon'. It was an interesting experience, speaking from the stage to a capacity audience which filled the pit and the surrounding galleries. I was surprised to find out afterwards what long distances some of those present had travelled, and I was kept for a considerable time answering questions and meeting people with whom I had corresponded but had not previously met. Altogether, it was a rewarding experience.

Equally impressive was the Library itself, comprising a large reading room, almost like one of the college halls at Oxford, with timbered roof and bookshelves lining its walls; bookstacks below ground, providing secure and monitored atmospheric conditions for the storage of rare books; accommodation for staff; and all the facilities that should go with a special library, such as reference apparatus, cataloguing, bookbinding and conservation, and research. Thanks to the friendly co-operation of the Director, Dr Louis B. Wright, and his staff, I was not merely able to visit the Folger as a spectator and to use its resources as a reader, but was also given the opportunity to study the physical and technical aspects of the Library's work, an experience I knew would be useful when I came to plan the Birthplace Trust's library development.

The Folger can rightly claim to be one of the world's great libraries. It possesses a uniquely rich and comprehensive collection, not only of Shakespeariana but of general sixteenth- and seventeenth-century source material. Of the two hundred and odd copies of the First Folio edition of Shakespeare's works known to exist, at the time of my visit the Folger possessed no fewer than seventy-nine copies, together with the greatest number of other Folio and Quarto editions gathered together in one place. Incidentally, the British Museum has five copies of the First Folio and three copies are preserved at the Shakespeare Centre, two belonging to the Birthplace Trustees and one to the Royal Shakespeare Theatre.

I was astonished by the breadth and depth of the Folger's acquisitions, and I made it my business to examine material of special relevance to the library and records collections of the Birthplace Trust. I found the Halliwell-Phillipps collection a particularly rewarding hunting ground, and in a number of instances discovered that the Folger possessed items which filled gaps in the Trust's collections. To give an example, I was surprised to find copies of the plans of Shakespeare's Birthplace drawn up at the time of the restoration of the property following its purchase in 1847, together with a series of original sketches by an artist named Blight, who had been commissioned by Halliwell-Phillipps to record every detail of the restoration of the building, room by room. None of these records is preserved at Stratford. I also came across a number of the earliest extant albums recording the names of visitors to Shakespeare's Birthplace at the beginning of the nineteenth century. Dr Wright was clearly impressed by the interest I showed in them, and must have noticed the envious look in my eyes; thanks to his recommendation, the Trustees of the Folger Library generously presented these visitors' albums to the Birthplace Trustees in 1964.

Another important item I was able to examine was the original diary – comprising seventeen small volumes – of the Reverend John Ward, Vicar of Stratford-upon-Avon from 1648 to 1679, which contains several references to Shakespeare and local subject matter. Slightly later in date, but of equal importance, were the letters and papers of the Reverend Joseph Greene, master of the grammar school at Stratford from 1735 to 1772, who was a keen Shakespeare scholar and antiquary. I found that these letters actually completed a collection of Greene's correspondence with his brother Richard, founder of the Lichfield Museum, and the Honourable James West of Alscot Park, which had been given to the Birthplace Trust three years before my visit. Greene's memoranda covered a variety of topics: the history of the King Edward VI School; the first recorded production of a Shakespeare play in Stratford, in 1746, together with a unique copy of the *Othello* play bill used to publicize the occasion; a description of the restoration of Shakespeare's monumental bust in Holy Trinity Church in 1748; items relating to the Garrick Jubilee of 1769; and a deal of material throwing light on social conditions in eighteenth-century Stratford.

Born of my contact with him at the Folger, Joseph Greene became one of my favourite characters. During the next few years I researched him further, tracing more of his letters and memoranda, and in 1965 the Dugdale Society published my edition of the *Correspondence of the Reverend Joseph Greene*.

The scope and value of the Halliwell-Phillipps collection was further illustrated by the series of volumes labelled *Shakespeare Rarities and Artistic Miscellanies*, in which I found a considerable number of original prints, paintings and drawings of Stratford buildings and local scenes and of Shakespearian subject matter. Joseph Greene and his brother Richard had both been interested in drawing and in perspective recording. The south-east prospect of Stratford-upon-Avon published in 1746, the earliest-known view of the town, was the work of Richard Greene, as was the earliest-known drawing of Shakespeare's Birthplace. The collection also included the earliest measured plan of Holy Trinity Church and the original design of the present spire of the Church by Timothy Lightholler, which replaced the earlier small wooden steeple in 1764. I not only recorded items like this, but took steps to have either photographic or microfilm copies made for the Shakespeare Birthplace Trust.

Apart from my research at the Folger Library, I was fortunate to enjoy the hospitality of several friends in their homes and also to see how Americans looked after their heritage. I saw excellent examples of well kept, colonial-type houses in Alexandria, together with its attractive little church. I also visited Mount Vernon, the late eighteenth-century home of George Washington, overlooking the Potomac River, which is preserved as one of America's principal historic properties. I was struck by the careful presentation of its rooms and by its beautiful natural setting. Numerous tourists were passing through the house at the time of my visit, under the watchful eyes of attendants strategically positioned. All the arrangements seemed to be working smoothly, but I could not help feeling that the personal guide service offered to visitors at Shakespeare's Birthplace was lacking.

Another rewarding experience was the short visit I was able to pay to Williamsburg, Virginia. Travelling from Washington by Greyhound Coach, I was able to get a good impression of the unspoiled, wooded countryside, with small residential settlements scattered along the route, and of Richmond, through which we passed, with its striking Georgian and Victorian buildings. I found that Colonial Williamsburg had been restored and presented as a cultural and educational centre portraying an important chapter of eighteenth-century American history.

Williamsburg had in fact been the capital of Virginia from 1699 to 1780, and it was here that America's civil and spiritual freedom blossomed. The preservation and restoration of the town to its original appearance and purpose was started in 1926 by Mr John D. Rockefeller, and by the time of my visit the whole project had been completed and was proving to be a major tourist attraction. I quickly discovered that its appeal centred on its history and heritage, its gardens, the architecture of its eighteenth-century buildings with their collections of furniture and furnishings, its shops and handicrafts, and preservation research of all kinds, including archaeology.

I found that the whole concept had been well planned and executed. Excellent arrangements for the reception and handling of visitors were provided at an information centre built just outside the preserved area of the town. Here lodging could be arranged and information about the historical background of Williamsburg and its principal exhibition buildings was presented in an imaginative manner; I thought that the continuous showing of a film in the theatre which formed part of the information centre provided an excellent introduction to the experience. Armed with an admission ticket bought here, I joined with other tourists to explore this historic town, choosing to walk rather than to take advantage of the free bus service to the various buildings open to visitors.

There was much to see. Most magnificent of the restored buildings was the Governor's Palace, standing at the end of a green vista planted with catalpa trees and surrounded by landscaped gardens and ornamental canal. It is a faithful replica of the early eighteenth-century palace which served as the official residence of seven royal governors. It was a most lavishly appointed mansion, and one could not fail to be impressed by the meticulous manner in which the various rooms had been furnished, exactly as they would have been originally. Here the atmosphere of the period was re-created by the presence of attendant staff attired in the kind of clothes they would have worn when the governors were in residence. This arrangement of presenting staff in period costume in all the public buildings certainly added colour and life to what otherwise would have been a static display. The thought naturally occurred to me as to whether the Trustees should be following this example at the Shakespearian properties; my reaction, both spontaneous and considered, was that a superior guide service such as the Trust offered, with its emphasis on the educational aspect of heritage, was much more in keeping with our British tradition and temperament.

Surpassed only by the Governor's Palace as the centre of colonial social life, was the Raleigh Tavern, built in 1705, which had apparently played host to George Washington and other leading public figures. The Capitol, which accommodated the House of Burgesses, the colonial Parliament, had also been rebuilt to is original plan and design. The Wythe House, restored and refurnished, gave an excellent impression of a typical town house of a colonial man of means, while the Brush Everard House portrayed the domestic setting of a moderately well-to-do Williamsburg merchant. Also of historic interest was Bruton Parish Church, where I attended a service and afterwards met the vicar.

Among the other exhibition buildings I visited were the Public Gaol, where debtors and criminals had been confined; the Public Magazine, originally a storehouse of arms for the protection of Virginia and now housing a collection of period military equipment; the Old Court House, a museum of archaeological material excavated in the restored area; Robertson's Mill, a reconstructed working mill grinding corn for sale to visitors; one of the several reconstructed taverns – I think it was the King's Arms Tavern – where I had a meal in the colonial style, with costumed waiters serving dishes prepared from colonial recipes; and a number of the working craft shops situated along the central street, presided over by costumed staff who had been trained to demonstrate the use of traditional materials and methods, using original-style equipment. I found it fascinating to see a printer using an eighteenth-century hand-press to produce broadsheets – which visitors could then buy – in the manner he would have done in the days of colonial government; a wig-maker dressing a wig in his shop; a silversmith fashioning his ware; a baker putting his oven to good use; a chandler making candles; a blacksmith at his forge; as well as other craftsmen, such as a cabinet-maker, milliner, shoemaker and apothecary, displaying and explaining their trades.

By good fortune, my guide and host at Williamsburg was Edward M. Riley, Director of Research, who had been responsible for the investigations which had made possible the restoration of the colonial capital. I was greatly impressed by the scholarly concept of the whole enterprise, and I learned much about the archaeological exploration undertaken and the research, both in the United States and in our own public records, into contemporary record evidence concerning this early chapter of colonial history.

As it so happened, the 350th anniversary of the first permanent settlement at Jamestown in 1607 was also being celebrated at the time of my visit to America. I was taken to see the reconstructed settlement, together with the replicas of the three ships that had brought the colonists, moored in the James River at the place where they had originally landed, and the Yorktown battlefield. Everywhere I sensed a great pride in what had been done to preserve and bring to life this early chapter of American history.

I had two new experiences whilst staying in Williamsburg. The first happened early on the Sunday morning, when a sudden downpour of rain and wind of hurricane force swept through the town, with a driving torrent of water literally cutting down young trees in its path. Fortunately the storm passed over as quickly as it came. Secondly, I was taken to see a game of American football between the College of William and Mary and a team from the south. I must confess I found it difficult to follow the game, but I enjoyed and shared the excitement of the spectators and was amazed at the antics of the players, who were equipped like space-men; also the part played by the cheering bands at each end of the pitch was something new to me. The excitement when William and Mary won the match was quite infectious and I was whisked away for a celebration at the Golden Horseshoe Club, where I observed that each member had a private locker from which he produced liquid refreshment. I learned that strict licensing regulations necessitated this method of provision.

My treatment in Williamsburg was typical of the

friendship and hospitality I received everywhere during my American visit. At the Folger Library I encountered several Shakespeare scholars engaged in research, and the conversations we had over lunch or afternoon tea shared with the library staff were extremely useful. As it so happened, Dr William Beattie, the Librarian of the National Library of Scotland, was one of the visiting Fellows, and I remember we shared a visit to the Rare Books Department of the Library of Congress.

Apart from these contacts, which in some cases developed into close associations in later years, I learned a great deal about the character of Americans, their outlook and their way of life, and I took note of a few practical items which helped me when planning improved facilities for American visitors coming to Stratford. In a general way, I also found it interesting to encounter at first-hand American reactions to certain matters which were currently in the news at that time. Among them were the problem of integrating black and white pupils in schools; the serious epidemic of Asian 'flu, which appeared to have crossed the Atlantic from Britain to Washington; and the startling news that Russia had successfully launched the first satelite into space. How was it that a nation other than the United States could possibly have achieved this?

I came away feeling that the more our two peoples could see of each other, the better. Observing the Americans in their home environment was an experience which greatly assisted me later, when planning for their reception as tourists coming to the Shakespearian properties, or as students or scholars attending courses or conferences. In the area of library and academic work, especially in the sphere of Shakespeare studies, I concluded that we had much to offer each other; and, as the years progressed, my association with the Folger Shakespeare Library enabled more effective arrangements for co-operation with the Birthplace Trust to develop. The combination of pleasure and business had made my American visit a most rewarding interlude.

Blueprint for the Future

Returning from the United States on the Queen Elizabeth gave me opportunity to think. What lessons had I learned from my American visit and how could they be applied to the Shakespeare Birthplace Trust? Were there any ideas for future development that I could recommend to the Trustees? What of my own future career? Clearly, I was enjoying my work as Director and I could see the possibilities of significant progress ahead. Already, working and living in Stratford was proving very congenial and the attraction of the surrounding area appealed strongly to my instincts as a countryman. Would it not therefore be sensible for me to throw my whole energy into developing the role and work of the Trust and no longer entertain thoughts of possibly moving away to a university academic post, which would almost certainly have involved working in a city environment? For better or worse, I decided on the Stratford option and, though I was tempted in later years by offers of alternative employment, my attachment to the Birthplace Trust was too strong for me to entertain the idea of ceasing to work for Shakespeare and Stratford.

What ideas, then, had I at that time for enhancing the status and role of the Trust? First, a revision of the Trust's objects and constitution as a charitable organization existing for the unique purpose of doing honour to our national poet, William Shakespeare, was urgently necessary. The suggestion had been made at an early Annual Meeting of the Trustees that steps should be taken to revise the constitution and terms of reference of the Trust, as defined in the existing Acts. Secondly, a bold, imaginative scheme for a new building to serve as the Trust's future headquarters and to accommodate its library and study facilities needed to be planned and provided as a priority. Thirdly, whereas the Trustees had hitherto concerned themselves primarily with the management of the Shakespearian properties, much more emphasis should be placed on conservation and the development of the Trust's educational and academic work. Finally, in 1964 the 400th anniversary of Shakespeare's birth would provide a suitable opportunity for the Trust to play a premier role in organizing celebrations, enlisting the interest and support of Shakespeare lovers throughout the world, focussing international attention on Shakespeare and Stratford-upon-Avon, and at the same time conferring prestige and benefit on the Birthplace Trust.

As already described, the Trust's objects and constitution were defined in the Shakespeare Birthplace Trust Act of 1891, as amended by the Act of 1930. A close scrutiny of the statutory provisions of these Acts led me to feel that they needed to be updated in a number of ways. Arrangements which were designed to apply in 1891 and in 1930 were no longer appropriate to the changed conditions of 1960. The post-war years had seen far-reaching developments and expansion in the activities of the Trust and, looking ahead to the possibility of a new building project in 1964 which would make possible a further extension of the Trust's sphere of influence, revisions to the statutory basis of the Trust seemed desirable.

The Trustees gave preliminary consideration to these ideas on 7 March 1960, when it was decided that the matter should be investigated as soon as possible. The Director was asked to prepare a report and recommendations for the Committee's perusal in advance of the next meeting. The memorandum I prepared summarized the provisions of the Trust Acts of 1891 and 1930, and indicated against each section suggestions for possible revision. It was considered in detail by members of the Executive Committee of Trustees on 1 April 1960 and received general approval. The Committee decided to submit a recommendation to the Annual Meeting of the Trustees, that steps should be taken forthwith to promote an amending Act on the basis of the revisions proposed. The Director was asked to circulate full details to all members of the governing body, and at the same time to seek the advice and help of one of the Life Trustees, Lord Radcliffe, in connection with this matter.

It was highly fortuitous that a legal gentleman of such wide experience and eminence should have been associated with the Trust at this juncture. Lord Radcliffe, who was created a Viscount in 1961, was probably the country's best known legal figure, having been a Lord of Appeal in Ordinary and the chairman of a number of Royal Commissions and Committees of Inquiry. He was also a highly respected academic, actively associated with a number of national institutions. He had a particular interest in Shakespeare, and at the local level was the first Chancellor of the University of Warwick and President of the Stratford-upon-Avon Society. He had been elected a Life Trustee of Shakespeare's Birthplace in 1958, and had already shown a keen interest in the Trust's activities. My approach to him met with an immediate, favourable response, and on 19 April I visited him at his country residence at Hampton Lucy. We discussed the memorandum the Trustees had considered and he explained the procedure that would be involved in promoting a new Bill. He recommended that the Trustees should use the firm of Dyson, Bell and Company of 15 College Street, London, to act as Parliamentary draftsmen and London agents in this matter; and it was agreed that the Trust's local solicitor, Mr T.E. Lowth of Robert Lunn and Lowth, Stratford-upon-Avon, should be asked to act for the Trustees at the local level.

These suggested arrangements received the ready approval of the Executive Committee and the subsequent endorsement of all the Trustees. On 31 May Lord Radcliffe arranged for me to meet Mr M.A. Liddell of Dyson, Bell and Company, and he invited both of us to have lunch with him at the House of Lords. The circumstances and ideas for the revision of the Trust Acts were discussed and, with Lord Radcliffe's guidance, a suggested plan of action was formulated. It was a friendly, informal occasion and extremely useful in its outcome. Lord Radcliffe stressed how important it was to ensure that the objects of the Trust, as redefined, should be wholly charitable in law, and he suggested a possible form of wording for them. Mr Liddell emphasized the importance of eliminating all possible opposition whilst the Bill was in its draft stage.

All this was a new and interesting experience for me, and during the months that followed there were frequent discussions with Mr Lowth and Mr Liddell, involving a number of visits to London. On one or two occasions we found ourselves conferring with Counsel in Chambers in one of the Inns of Court. There was much work to be done. In particular, the proposals had to be submitted to the Charity Commission, the Inland Revenue and the Attorney General, and necessary adjustments made to ensure their approval. In this connection the advice and help of a leading Tax Counsel was sought, a precaution taken to confirm that the Trust's extended powers as envisaged in the Bill were in complete conformity with its basic charitable objects and, as such, eligible for tax exemption by the Inland Revenue.

In the event, as drafting proceeded it was decided that an entirely new Bill, as opposed to one containing several amendments, was necessary. It fell to the Executive Committee to consider the draft Bill, when prepared, and a few adjustments were made. It was at this stage that the Stratford-upon-Avon Borough Council made known its disapproval of the proposal in the Bill to reduce the number of Council representatives on the governing body of the Trust. Hitherto, the Mayor, High Steward and all the Aldermen of the Borough, together with the Town Clerk, had served as Ex Officio Trustees, but in the revised constitution the town's representatives were reduced to the Mayor, the High Steward and three Aldermen. The Council's views were carefully considered, but the Trustees were unanimously of the opinion that a reduction on the lines proposed would be appropriate in the new constitution.

A draft of the new Bill, embodying the various amendments made during the period of consultation mentioned above and having been considered by the Executive Committee, was approved by the full body of Trustees at their Half Annual Meeting held on 22 October 1960, and the following resolution was unanimously approved:

That the Trustees and Guardians of Shakespeare's Birthplace promote a Bill in Parliament in the Session 1960-61 to redefine and extend the objects of the Shakespeare Birthplace Trust; to vary the constitution of the Trustees of the said Trust and to extend the powers of the Trustees; to repeal the provisions of the Shakespeare Birthplace, etc., Trust Act, 1891, and the Shakespeare Birthplace, etc., Trust (Amendment) Act, 1930, and to re-enact subject to variations certain of the provisions of those Acts, and for other purposes.

A second resolution authorized the common seal of the Trust to be affixed to the necessary Petition to support the Bill; and the Executive Committee was empowered to agree such alterations in the Bill as might prove necessary as it progressed.

After the terms of the draft Bill had been approved by the Trustees, certain statutory procedures had to be followed in order to comply with Standing Orders of the House of Commons relating to Parliamentary Bills. The Bill was deposited by the Trust's agents on 26 November 1960 and statutory advertisements containing a brief statement of its contents were published in *The London Gazette*, *The Times* and the *Stratford-upon-Avon Herald* on 2 and 9 December. Copies of the Bill were made available for public inspection at this time and copies were also served on all parties likely to be affected by its provisions.

The charitable status and tax position of the Trust were cleared and a few other adjustments made to satisfy the observations of interested Government departments, during the early months of 1961. On 16 May the Bill reached the point of going before the Lord Chairman's Committee, which I attended as representing the Trustees, accompanied by Mr Lowth. A few questions were asked, as members of the Committee went through the terms of the Bill, to ensure that all the necessary procedures had been completed. One question asked I particularly remember: Why was it proposed to include the Bishop of the Diocese as one of the Ex Officio Trustees, but not the equivalent representative of the Free Churches? I cannot now recall what explanation or justification I gave, but fortunately their Lordships were satisfied and the Bill was passed to go forward through the necessary stages in the House of Lords and before the House of Commons. A Petition from the Institute of Municipal Treasurers and Accountants, asking for the inclusion of their members with those of other accountancy bodies eligible for appointment as auditors of the Trust's accounts, was satisfactorily resolved, and a few amendments made by the Commons were agreed by the House of Lords. All this happened during June and July, thus enabling the concluding stages in the passing of the Bill to be completed before the House rose for the summer recess.

The Bill received the Royal Assent on 27 July 1961, as the Shakespeare Birthplace, etc., Trust Act, 1961, and its provisions became operative as from 1 November 1961.

The purpose of the legislation was stated in the preamble to the Act. The powers conferred on the Trustees by the Acts of 1891 and 1930 were 'insufficient to permit the full development of the purposes for which the trust was originally formed' and 'with a view to providing for the nation a perpetual memorial to William Shakespeare' it was deemed expedient 'to redefine and extend the objects of the trust', to vary the constitution of the Trustees and to extend their powers.

As redefined, the objects of the Trust were set out as follows: 'to promote in every part of the world the appreciation and study of the plays and other works of William Shakespeare and the general advancement of Shakespearian knowledge'; 'to maintain and preserve the Shakespeare Birthplace properties for the benefit of the nation' (consisting of property which is of historic interest as being associated with William Shakespeare or members of his family and any other property of historic interest which may be acquired by the Trustees for the purposes of the Trust); 'to provide and maintain for the benefit of

Shakespeare Birthplace, etc., Trust Act, 1961

the nation a museum and library of books, manuscripts, records of historic interest, pictures, photographs and objects of antiquity with particular but not exclusive reference to William Shakespeare, his life, works and times'.

For the furtherance of these objects, the Act conferred very considerably extended powers on the Trustees, particularly in connection with the acquisition of property for conservation purposes, the maintenance of the Trust's museum, library and archive collections, and the development of educational and academic activities associated therewith. The Trustees were given powers to take care of the practical aspects of the management of their properties, and separate clauses envisaged a developing role for the Trust, providing facilities for Shakespearian research and study and the extension of its influence overseas. The Trustees' financial arrangements, the keeping of accounts and annual audit, as well as investment powers, were also defined in detail.

A section of the Act dealt specifically with the appointment, constitution and functions of the Trustees. As from the appointed date, the governing body was to comprise thirty-five Trustees, including the existing Trustees with the exception of the Town Clerk and the Aldermen of the Borough. There were to be five different categories of Trustees: nine Ex Officio Trustees, being the Lord Lieutenant of the County of Warwick, the High Steward of the Borough, the Mayor of the Borough, three Aldermen appointed by the Council of the Borough, the Bishop of the Diocese of Coventry, the Vicar of the Collegiate Church of Holy Trinity and the Headmaster of King Edward VI School; twelve (instead of ten) Life Trustees, appointed by the governing body; nine Representative Trustees, one each to be appointed by the Arts Council of Great Britain, the British Museum, the Warwickshire County Council, the National Trust, the Shakespeare Memorial Theatre and the Universities of Birmingham, Cambridge, London and Oxford, the newly founded University of Warwick being added in 1966 under a permissive clause; and five Local Trustees appointed by the main body.

The Act required the Trustees to hold an Annual Meeting each year and at least one other meeting, and they were given power to make, alter and revoke regulations with respect to the management and administration of the Trust's property, the holding of meetings and the conduct of proceedings. Provision was also made for the appointment of an Executive Committee and any other committees that might be necessary and the delegation of any functions of the Trustees to them. This confirmed an arrangement whereby the day-to-day management of the Trust's affairs was exercised by a small Executive Committee, with the proviso that its proceedings were subject to confirmation or otherwise by the Trustees in general meeting. This arrangement continues, the Executive Committee meeting each month and for special purposes as required.

At a special meeting held on 25 November 1961, the Chairman, Sir Fordham Flower, made particular reference to the passing of the Act, describing it as 'marking one of the most important milestones in the history of the institution' and expressing the

Trustees' indebtedness to Lord Radcliffe for his advice and help at all stages in connection with its promotion. At the Annual Meeting of Trustees held the following spring, Sir Fordham again emphasized the significance of the new Act. 'On the one hand', he said, 'the passing of the Act is a formal recognition of the century or more of distinguished service rendered by this institution in honour of Shakespeare; on the other, it is in effect a blueprint for future development and increasing usefulness'. He continued, 'Our planning must inevitably benefit from the wider experience and contacts of an enlarged governing body. As a charity recognized in law, the Trust can now address itself to the task of attracting resources and support which will enable its influence increasingly to be spread all over the world'. Sir Fordham then went on to ask the press to make it known that the Birthplace Trustees were anxious to receive gifts and bequests, not merely of books and Shakespearian material, but of money and property that could be used to further the objects of the Trust.

Immediate action was initiated to take advantage of the provisions of the Act to enlarge and widen the representation of the governing body. The following new Trustees were appointed: Sir William Emrys Williams (Arts Council of Great Britain), Sir Frank Francis (British Museum), Alderman W.S. Howard (Warwickshire County Council), Mr C.R.N. Routh (National Trust), Mr Dennis L. Flower (Royal Shakespeare Theatre), Mr Peter Boddington, Mrs T.N. Waldron and Mr T. Spencer Wood (Local Trustees), Aldermen Leigh Dingley, G.A. Lea and D.E. Woodman (representatives of Stratford-upon-Avon Borough Council).

In addition, the following existing Trustees continued to serve, making up the full complement of the governing body: Lord Willoughby de Broke (Lord Lieutenant of the County), Sir Denys Lowson (the High Steward of the Borough), Councillor S.C. Rosser (the Mayor of the Borough), the Rt Reverend C.K.N. Bardsley (Bishop of the Diocese of Coventry), the Reverend T. Bland (Vicar of Holy Trinity Church), Mr Leslie Watkins (the Headmaster of King Edward VI School); Life Trustees: the Earl of Avon, Sir William Dugdale, Bt, Sir Fordham Flower, Mr G. Baron Ash, Mr T.S.R. Boase, Sir Ernest Pooley, Bt., Professor J. Dover Wilson, Mr Trevor Matthews, Lord Radcliffe, Professor J.R. Allardyce Nicoll; Professor T.J.B. Spencer, Sir Sydney C. Roberts, Sir Ifor Evans and Professor Nevill H.K.A. Coghill, appointed respectively by the Universities of Birmingham, Cambridge, London and Oxford.

It was at this meeting that Sir Fordham suggested that, since several of the Trustees were attending for the first time, it might be useful for the Director to sketch in a little of the background of the work of the Trust and to give his observations on the future of the Trust as he saw it.

By chance I kept a copy of what I said to the Trustees on that occasion. Following a summary sketch of the origin and development of the Trust, I described the current activities and organization of the institution, as already recorded in earlier chapters. This then led to what on the agenda was called the future role of the Trust. My report continued as follows:

The future role of the Trust will be basically a development of the Trust's present role, with new departures and fresh emphasis, perhaps in a number of directions. My own feeling is that in future our responsibilities will become wider and more important as they become more international in their contacts and their implications. What we are doing now is already of considerable interest and importance outside Stratford-upon-Avon and this country, and this process, as I see it, is likely to continue. The Trust in the future must clearly continue its work of preservation, and it must continue to develop the appeal of this side of its work. The attractive presentation of the Shakespearian properties provides an admirable, direct means of stimulating the popular appreciation of Shakespeare and, indirectly, of many facets of the heritage of this country. You will know what considerable changes and improvements have been carried into effect at the properties during the past fifteen years. I am certain that in one or two directions things still need to be done. We must continue to build up our collections of material of all kinds, and I think that we have got to be sufficiently sensitive to the rapidly changing conditions of our day to be willing to adapt our sight-seeing arrangements and other amenities to keep in touch with the requirements of our time. I think that opportunity will come along for the Trustees to embark on particular individual projects, such as, perhaps, the expansion of the farming and folklore museum at Mary Arden's House, and possibly one or two other things of that kind as well.

I also feel that in the future, and in the not very distant future, the Trust must extend its sphere of influence in the matter of preservation. There are no more Shakespearian properties to acquire, to the best of my knowledge, but there are still in and around Stratford-upon-Avon some very good specimens of sixteenth- and seventeenth-century architecture, the future of which should be protected. At a time when our own town is likely to see many physical changes, it must be a matter of concern to the Trustees to ensure that all possible steps are taken to safeguard the essential character of Stratford-upon-Avon as the town of Shakespeare's birth and death. I think we have a duty to the world in this matter. The new Act makes possible the acquisition by gift to the Trust of property of all kinds, and I think that this aspect of our work and of our powers should be made known and implemented when suitable offers are received.

The most exciting possibilities of development in the future, however, are on the educational and academic front, and these are symbolized by the new building project on which the Trustees have embarked in readiness for the 400th anniversary in 1964 of Shakespeare's birth. As you know, what we have chosen to call the new Shakespeare Centre will provide not merely a new administrative headquarters for the Trust, long overdue, but also a library, a reading room, study facilities and all the things we have lacked and felt we needed up to the moment. For the first time it will be possible to bring together the resources of the Birthplace and the Theatre collections, and to make them available to students and scholars under the right conditions. In fact, we must go forward with a policy of expansion and, if I may use the word, exploitation. I envisage an appreciable development of the library and study side of the Trust's activities. I think that this must go hand in hand with the cultivation of what I may call the popular appeal and, apart from being, as it were, in its own right a modest memorial to the poet, the new Centre must, above everything else, establish itself in the shortest possible time as an effective workshop for the Shakespearian student.

We must envisage the need to employ experienced staff to make available to students the resources of the library and to develop the study side of our work. We must have funds to add regularly to the collections of books and research material and, as I see it, to be able to offer research grants to scholars and students in the same way as the Folger Shakespeare Library does. We obviously cannot ever aspire to have its wealth, but there are occasions when it would be very proper indeed to be able to offer a grant in aid to a student or a scholar wanting to come here to work on our material. Money will also be needed for lectures, courses, publications and educational activities which it will be the object of the Centre to encourage, over and above what the Birthplace Trust is at present able to arrange and finance. As I see things, there should be no overlapping with the Shakespeare Institute or with anything which the University of Birmingham and other universities are doing or sponsoring. Indeed, all we want to do is to be able to provide the kind of facilities which will make Stratford more attractive and effective as a centre of Shakespearian research and study, in co-operation with and with the support of these established academic bodies. And I think we must bear in mind always the desirability of relating our research plans and activity to the supreme opportunity and obligation we have of stimulating Shakespearian appreciation and of promoting Shakespearian knowledge at all levels. Given the resources, I am sure that it will prove possible to do this. There are many things we could do for schools. We could provide interesting exhibitions and lectures. We have never had any money really to devote seriously to publication projects, and, most important of course, we can and must in the future have a much more effective liaison with Shakespearian institutions and bodies overseas.

This vision of the future role of the Trust is bound up, as you all know too well, with the problem of finance, and the Trustees have been facing up to this in connection with the appeal which is in process of being organized in connection with the 1964 project. The fact is that, although the Birthplace Trust has far-reaching international opportunities and responsibilities, it has never possessed an endowment fund and it receives no financial support from outside, its main income being derived from admission fees paid by visitors to the properties. The income in post-war years has been sufficient to meet normal expenditure, but has not left any margin for reserves. So one is brought to the conclusion that, if the future policy which I have, perhaps inadequately, sketched is to go forward, a point has been reached in the history of the institution when the need to provide an assured financial basis in the future is imperative. It is fairly clear to me that the admission income from our historic properties cannot really be expected to provide for all the ideas put forward and, because of this, an element of endowment has been included in the appeal objective. I am sure that the Trustees have taken a very proper and wise step in deciding to offer Shakespeare lovers all over the world the opportunity to mark the 400th anniversary of Shakespeare's birth by contributing, not merely towards the cost of a new building, but towards the cost of endowing it and making possible its future development on the lines indicated.

To what extent my vision of the Trust's future role proved to be correct may be judged from the chapters which follow.

The Shakespeare Centre

By the middle of the 1950s the need for additional accommodation for the Trust's office, library and records collections was becoming increasingly felt, and from time to time I discussed the problem with the Chairman. Sir Fordham Flower fully appreciated that we were already working under difficult conditions and that the Trust's future progress could well be impeded unless something were done to alleviate the situation.

Following informal soundings with several of the Trustees, the members of the Executive Committee decided to hold a special meeting on 20 November 1957, to give preliminary consideration to the matter. It was an extremely useful meeting, the outcome of which was that the Chairman took advantage of the Half Annual Meeting of Trustees, which followed on 4 December 1957, to report on the discussions in detail. Sir Fordham explained that Hornby Cottage, the building originally presented to the Trust by Andrew Carnegie in 1903 and subsequently enlarged in 1913 and 1936, was hopelessly inadequate from almost every point of view. The Trust's activities, he said, had increased at least threefold since the end of the war and a point had been reached when there was not sufficient room for office requirements alone, quite apart from additional accommodation required for the expanding library and records collections and the academic work associated with them. Sir Fordham went on to report that the Committee felt that the provision of a new headquarters for the Trust alongside the present building was the only satisfactory long-term solution, and that, quite fortuitously, 14 Henley Street, the house occupied by the Director, would be shortly vacated, and this could be adapted to provide short-term office accommodation. Following a general discussion, the Trustees approved in principle the ideas suggested and authorized the Executive Committee to proceed to prepare a plan.

Evolution of the Plan

The basic preliminary planning for the new building took place during the next two years. By the spring of 1958 the members of the Committee had considered and approved my suggestions as to the kind of accommodation required, and they decided to seek the professional advice of their architects, Wood and Kendrick and Williams. By this time the senior partner, T. Spencer Wood, who had been responsible for the restoration of Hall's Croft, was being assisted by another partner, Laurence Williams, F.R.I.B.A., and, whilst they were both involved in the early stages of planning, it fell to Laurence Williams to assume responsibility for the project, as failing eyesight was limiting Mr Wood's involvement.

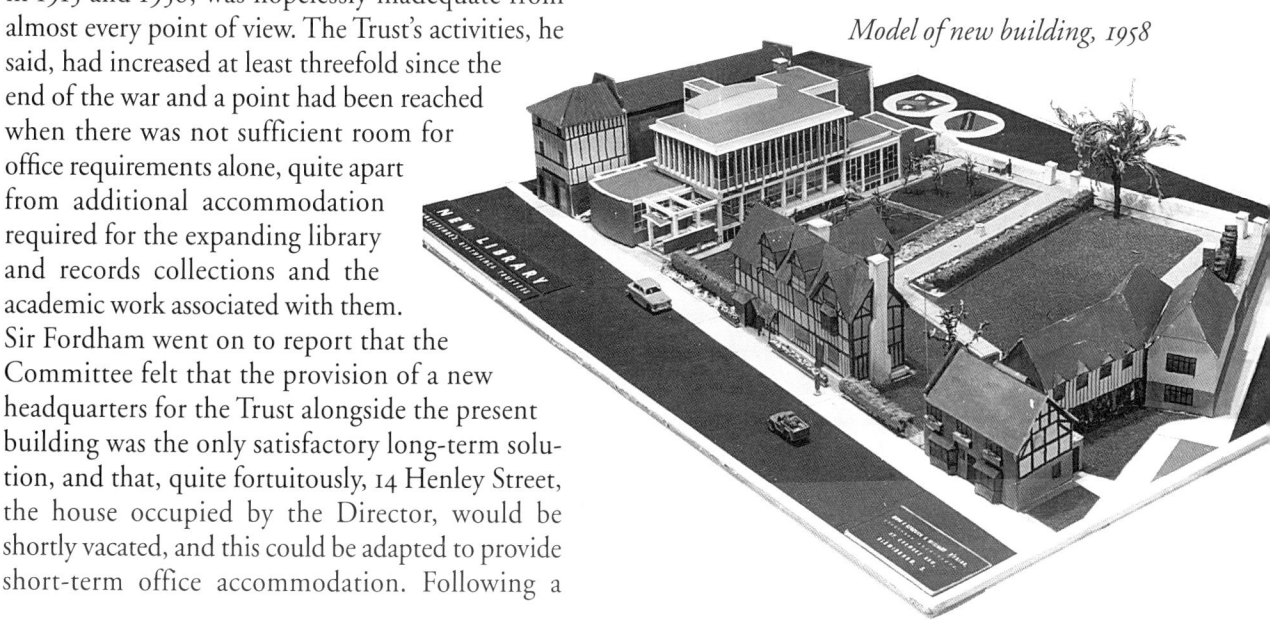

Model of new building, 1958

The architects were first asked to consider whether the requisite accommodation could be provided on the site of 14 Henley Street and, having satisfied themselves that this was possible, to prepare sketch plans and tentative designs. Preparations proceeded on these lines during the year, and at the same time a considerable programme of alterations and improvements was carried out in Hornby Cottage during the following autumn and winter, providing more adequate arrangements for the library and records departments, as well as enlarged facilities for the storage and sale of publications. At the rear, a new boiler house was built, together with new toilets for lady visitors to the Birthplace. In the meantime, the Trust's office had been moved temporarily to 14 Henley Street.

In March 1959 the Executive Committee was able to consider sketch plans and tentative alternative designs for the new building. By this time it had been established that the site could accommodate a building with a very attractive garden elevation, adequate in size for the purposes envisaged and providing possibilities for extension in future years. Detailed discussions with the architects took place and, following a process of elimination and adjustment, a proposition was agreed for submission to the Annual Meeting of Trustees in May 1959. A scale model was made to illustrate the visual impact of a building of modern design on such a sensitive site.

At this stage opportunity was taken to seek the views of certain other members of the governing body. I made journeys to Oxford to confer with Dr Tom Boase of Magdalen College and Professor Nevill Coghill of Merton, both of whom spent considerable time going over the plan of the proposed building in detail and commenting on the suggested elevational treatment. In general, both thought the plan was an excellent one, and they made a number of useful suggestions about possible internal re-arrangements and some details of the exterior design. I kept a copy of my notes recording the points raised in these discussions, and it is interesting to see how many of them were taken care of in the architects' final drawings.

One did not, of course, expect to receive unqualified approval from all the Trustees for what was in fact an extremely bold and somewhat uncompromising modern treatment. Professor Allardyce Nicoll of Birmingham University was not happy about the modernistic exterior treatment proposed, though he thought the interior arrangements for library and study facilities were skilfully planned. He favoured a more traditional approach and, whilst conceding that a building of the half-timbered style of the Birthplace was out of the question, he felt that an adaptation of a Georgian design, 'something which was dignified and suggested tradition', would harmonize well in this setting. This view was not shared by other Trustees, such as Lord Radcliffe, who made the point that the building would be judged on the quality of its design and workmanship as a product of our time.

I found discussions of this kind were at once encouraging and helpful to the architect, Laurence Williams, and myself. In general they established that, except for one or two Trustees who had reservations about a modern, contemporary style, there was a consensus view that the new building should not attempt to reproduce or imitate an older architectural idiom; that it should be an outstanding example of the use of basic building materials and should reflect contemporary architectural taste. All agreed that, in view of its siting alongside Shakespeare's Birthplace, the height and scale of the building were crucial, and it was suggested that as much accommodation as possible for library storage should be provided below ground. On a point of detail, it was generally agreed that the roof level of the new building should be at the same height as the ridge of the roof of the Birthplace. Sir Fordham Flower, who was at that time heavily involved as Chairman of the Coventry Cathedral Reconstruction Committee, was enthusiastically in favour of a bold approach, envisaging a building of contemporary design, notable for the quality of its architectural detail and craftsmanship and embodying the work of living artists and craftsmen.

The Trustees discussed the project in detail at

their Annual Meeting on 9 May 1959 and, with the help of plans, elevational drawings and a scale model, the architects added support to my recommendation that a development of this kind and scale was both possible and desirable. The conjectural cost at this stage was given as £100,000 (the ultimate figure was about £200,000) and a provisional timetable outlined which was geared to completion and an official opening on 23 April 1964. There was ready agreement that the project should be linked with the celebrations on this date to mark the 400th anniversary of Shakespeare's birth, but, in view of the meagre liquid cash reserve, it was appreciated that only with a large measure of financial support from outside could the project go ahead. It was at this juncture that it became evident that, as Director, I would need to assume the role of fund-raiser, and the Trustees asked me to prepare a memorandum suggesting how the necessary money could be raised.

The Trustees were unanimous in their approval in principle of the plan put forward, but there was uncertainty and doubt in the minds of a few about the proposed elevational treatment of the building and, particularly, the large element of glass on the Birthplace side. The cost aspect was also a matter for concern. It was accordingly very fortunate that, so far as the design was concerned, the Trustees decided to act on the suggestion of Dr Boase to seek the advice of the Royal Fine Art Commission and to defer a decision until the Commission's opinion was known.

Representatives of the Fine Art Commission, led by Mr Frederick Gibberd, paid a visit on 25 June 1959 and studied the proposals on the site, in consultation with the Trust's architects and myself. Mr Gibberd was himself a distinguished architect, who, a few years later, designed the Roman Catholic Cathedral at Liverpool; he was also responsible for the modern building on the corner of High Street and Sheep Street in Stratford. Subsequently, the Commission considered the matter at a meeting on 8 July, and a few days later the Secretary reported that the Commission recommended the Trustees to accept the design proposed, in its general lines. At the same time, it was suggested that the design could be improved by some simplification of the architectural treatment. The Secretary also indicated that the Commission was in no way frightened by the modernity of the scheme submitted, and indeed did not share the view that the building should be designed in an older style. On the subject of siting, the Commission saw no objection to the proposed slight encroachment on the Birthplace garden and the erection of a building of the size and height proposed on the site of 14 Henley Street.

The architects had a further opportunity to confer with the Commission's representatives, and discussed with the Trustees certain points of architectural detail in the proposed design. They also suggested a different treatment of the end wall of the reading room. Revisions were then made with a view to taking care of the suggestions put forward by members of the Commission, and revised drawings were re-submitted for consideration at the Commission's meeting held on 14 October 1959. On the following day the Secretary reported that the revised design submitted by the Trust was acceptable to the Royal Fine Art Commission.

The Plan approved

The timing of this approval was particularly helpful, because it enabled the Executive Committee to prepare a detailed report and recommendations for consideration by the Trustees at their Half Annual Meeting held on 14 November 1959.

In retrospect, this particular meeting must be regarded as one of the most important in the whole history of the Trust. The Trustees present engaged in a lively questioning of all aspects of the proposed new building project as detailed in the report. I kept notes of what was said and, as an illustration of the kind of discussion that went into the making of this ambitious scheme, the following details should perhaps be recorded. Mr T.E. Lowth, Stratford's Town Clerk and a real Stratfordian, saw it as of immense importance for the town and as a vote of confidence in the future development of the Trust. Sir Sydney

Roberts of Cambridge University, who earlier had not been happy about the proposed treatment of the upper storey of the building, now gave it his warm support and suggested that the rounded end of the reading room should be relieved by some kind of textured treatment of the exterior brickwork. All were agreed that the choice of a hand-made brick, both for colour and texture, was all-important, and the idea of using basic materials, and particularly wood inside, was favoured. Dr Boase of Oxford, a Life Trustee, spoke in favour of the contemporary design and expressed the view that the panelled treatment of the elevation overlooking the garden was particularly imaginative and that the fenestration would harmonize with the Birthplace. Sir Barry Jackson, another Life Trustee, expressed concern about the problem of heat likely to be generated by such a large amount of glass. Indeed, every Trustee present had something to say: Alderman Trevor Matthews spoke about the possible embellishment of the brickwork apse end of the reading room, a point which was taken up by the Vicar, the Reverend Canon Noel Prentice, who suggested that it might be carved in relief in the same style as that used in the rebuilding of the Shakespeare Memorial Theatre; Mr Leslie Watkins, the Headmaster of King Edward VI School, was anxious that the building should harmonize with the Henley Street scene and not call undue attention to itself; the Mayor considered the design first class. There were questions about the size of rooms, the choice of materials and the likely cost of maintenance. Letters containing the observations of Trustees unable to be present were also considered, and the architect, Laurence Williams, was given adequate opportunity to answer questions and to elaborate further his architectural concept for a building which he realized must in a manner be unique.

At the conclusion of the discussion, the Trustees unanimously approved the design suggested for the new building to serve as the future headquarters of the Trust on the site of 14 Henley Street, and in accordance with a time schedule which envisaged that it should be finished and ready for an official opening on 23 April 1964, as the Trust's major contribution to the 400th Shakespeare anniversary celebrations. This was a bold and confident decision, bearing in mind that the Trust's liquid cash reserves totalled slightly less than £50,000. Of this, it was decided to allocate £25,000 to initiate a fund for the new building. The Executive Committee was authorized to proceed with all necessary action to implement this decision and to launch an appeal inviting contributions to this anniversary project.

The decision to go forward having been taken, quick action followed. Before the end of 1959 an application for planning permission was made and a press conference announcing the project was held. By that time I had also produced suggestions as to possible sources of financial help. In the following New Year it was decided to exhibit a model of the proposed new building in the town and, taking advantage of my association with the Printer to the Oxford University Press, an illustrated brochure describing the building and inviting contributions to an appeal for it was produced.

When the Trustees held their Annual Meeting on 14 May 1960, the Chairman, Sir Fordham Flower, was able to report that considerable progress had been made with the detailing of the building within the general plan and design agreed, and that consultants had been appointed to advise on structural matters, heating, lighting and similar services. Adjustments to the plan and elevational treatment had been agreed and decisions made concerning floor finishes, wall treatments and internal fittings generally. The keynote throughout was to be simplicity, dignity and suitability for the purpose to be served by the particular part of the building in question. On the subject of finance, Sir Fordham announced that the time had come for the appeal to be made public; and the spirits of all those present were raised when he announced that Mr G. Baron Ash, a Life Trustee, had initiated the fund by sending a donation of £1,000.

During the following months, the architects continued discussions with the Executive Committee and the Director concerning detailed requirements in the building; samples of materials to be used were examined and approved; and in September 1960 the Trustees agreed bills of quantities which were submitted to selected contractors. Tentative plans were considered for laying a foundation stone in April 1961.

The Problem of Finance

The problem of finance then produced a temporary set-back. At a special meeting of the Executive Committee on 19 October it was reported that, tenders having been received, the complete building with furnishings and equipment would cost £150,000, against the £100,000 originally estimated. The general feeling of members of the Committee was that it would not be expedient to embark on such a considerable financial undertaking until the response to the appeal was known. It was accordingly decided to defer the beginning of the building for a year, a decision which was endorsed by the full meeting of Trustees on 22 October.

The delay had certain advantages. It gave the architects time to finalize outstanding details and to negotiate a contract price with a firm selected from those who had put in tenders. It also provided an incentive for the Director and the Committee to address themselves seriously to the problem of raising money. Very quickly I became a salesman for the scheme, and found myself soliciting support from business and personal sources and exploring the possibility of getting grants from educational foundations and trusts. The first results of my labours were not particularly encouraging, but I was absolutely convinced that, once the project was known and appreciated, support would be forthcoming. The idea of using the services of a professional firm of fund-raisers was also pursued, and this eventually led the Trustees to appoint John F. Rich and Company in July of the following year to advise and assist with an appeal, an arrangement which continued until the beginning of 1964.

Meanwhile, the Shakespeare Anniversary Council had been set up in the town to plan Stratford's 1964 celebrations. Right from the beginning, the completion of the new Shakespeare Centre, with its official opening by a royal personage, was envisaged as the focal event of the anniversary programme. Each meeting of the Council provided a useful opportunity to report progress and to solicit further support for the appeal.

The 1964 Pavilion

On 18 May 1961 a '1964 Pavilion', erected in the garden of Shakespeare's Birthplace, was officially opened by the Mayor of Stratford-upon-Avon. Its purpose was to inform visitors about the significance of the 1964 anniversary and at the same time to publicize the Trust's project and to invite contributions towards its cost. Designed by Laurence Williams, the Pavilion quickly attracted attention by reason of

Opening of the 1964 Pavilion

its novel design and presentation, and it proved an outstanding success from a public relations point of view. Octagonal in shape, with a pointed roof and glazed panels facing the garden path along which visitors walked after leaving the Birthplace, the Pavilion provided an ideal setting for a scale model of the proposed building, together with a display of plans, elevational drawings and a description of what was proposed. A model globe feature attached to a column in the centre of the floor symbolized the universality of Shakespeare's appeal, and collecting slots labelled with the names of the major countries of the world were incorporated in a circular table fixture below. This proved an admirable device for attracting casual donations from visitors coming from the named countries. In addition, or as an alternative, visitors were invited to contribute the cost of a small item for the building.

The list displayed was as follows:

1 brick	2s. 6d.	(3 for $1.00)
1 floor tile	2s. 6d.	(3 for $1.00)
1 unit wood panel	10s. 0d.	($1.50)
1 book shelf	£1 1s. 0d.	($3.00)
1 piece of marble	£3 10s. 0d.	($10.00)
1 unit of stone	£5 5s. 0d.	($15.00)

Each donor received a small printed certificate bearing my signature. This idea of gift opportunities was extended to major items of furnishing and equipment, and even to particular component parts of the building when the appeal really got under way during the following year. By the end of the summer of 1962, a total of 11,500 items had been purchased for the building.

Preparations on all fronts continued during 1961. At the Annual Meeting on 27 May an impressive progress report was given. The Trustees were obviously pleased with both the mood of optimism and evidence of the growing appreciation of the international significance of the 1964 anniversary, and also the favourable prospects of support for the Trust's project. A revised time-table of operation which envisaged starting the building in the autumn was approved, and tentative plans were made for the

The 1964 Pavilion

laying of a foundation stone in the spring of 1962. On the subject of the appeal, agreement was given for the employment of professional fund-raisers. At the same time, the target of the appeal fund was raised to £250,000, the sum estimated to meet the cost of the building and of a modest fund to provide an assured income for its upkeep when erected and to make possible the development of the Centre as a study centre.

The Contract approved

The following months saw intensive work by the architects in finalizing plans and getting tenders based on revised bills of quantities. By September the Executive Committee was able to reach a decision to recommend the governing body to go forward. Thus, at their Half Annual Meeting on 7 October 1961 the Trustees accepted the tender of the firm of general contractors, Higgs and Hill, Ltd, in the sum of £124,460, and authorized work to go forward in accordance with the time-table agreed, which planned completion of the building in time for an official opening on 23 April 1964. Bearing in mind that less than a quarter of the money required had as yet been raised, this must be regarded as a momentous decision, reflecting the confidence and foresight of the Trustees and their Director.

An official contract-signing ceremony was held in the 1964 Pavilion in the Birthplace garden on 16 November 1961, in the presence of the Deputy Mayor of the Borough (Alderman Leigh Dingley, J.P.), Trustees, the architects and representative guests. I explained the contract documents, which were then sealed and signed by Sir Fordham Flower, as Chairman, and myself on behalf of the Trust, and by Mr Ronald Hill, Chairman of Higgs and Hill, Ltd, the general contractors to whom the work had been entrusted. Sir Fordham then addressed the meeting, as follows:

In years to come today's little ceremony will be looked back upon as a landmark in the history of the Shakespeare Birthplace Trust. As far back as 1950 the Director, Mr Levi Fox, began to persuade the governing body that more adequate accommodation was required to provide for the rapidly expanding activities of the Trust, and at his suggestion some four years ago the Trustees decided to erect a new building for this purpose and to associate it with the forthcoming 400th anniversary of Shakespeare's birth.

Much has happened since then. As you know, we have evolved a project to build and endow a new Shakespeare Centre, occupying a site on the far side of the garden of Shakespeare's Birthplace, and have invited Shakespeare lovers all over the world to contribute to it, as an international birthday present to Shakespeare on 23 April 1964. The signing of the contract just completed indicates that the phase of preliminaries is now over and that the decks are being cleared for action. Building operations will in fact commence on 4 December and the new Centre should be ready for an official opening on the 400th anniversary occasion in 1964.

The Trustees are particularly pleased to have Higgs and Hill, Ltd, as general contractors for the scheme. They are a firm of considerable prestige and have been associated with a number of buildings of national importance. Because of its special nature, you will understand that to the Trustees the new building is something more than a structure in the modern medium. Itself a symbol of the genius of Shakespeare, the new Centre must in every respect be an epitome of all that is best in technical and artistic achievement, a building that in its class will evoke the interest and, we hope, the admiration of people from all over the world.

Mr Hill, we believe that we can count on you and your co-Directors, your staff and workmen, to co-operate with our architects, quantity surveyors, professional advisers and sub-contractors, to produce within the time-table we have agreed a building of which you yourselves will be proud and which will be a fitting memorial of this unique anniversary occasion. Of one thing you may be certain. You will get the greatest possible support from the governing body and Director of the Trust. We shall watch the progress of your operations with enthusiastic attention and we shall look forward to sharing one or two other important ceremonies with you as this new product of our age rises on the site of its Victorian predecessor.

By this time the Trust's office organization, which had temporarily occupied 14 Henley Street for the two previous years, had been moved back into its original accommodation in Hornby Cottage. The boardroom and the library on the first floor were partitioned to provide small working offices which, in spite of being cramped and far from ideal, proved acceptable as a temporary arrangement until the new building was finished. Inevitably, the activities of the library and records department had to be somewhat curtailed.

The Start of Building

Work on the demolition of 14 Henley Street and the clearance of the site started on 4 December 1961, and behind the protective hoardings erected in Henley Street amazingly good progress was made. By the beginning of February 1962 the demolition was completed and excavation had started for the basement area of the new building. Having lived for fifteen years in the house that was pulled down, I followed this initial phase of operations with very great interest. As I expected, portions of the cellars of the White Lion, the eighteenth-century coaching inn that had occupied part of the site, were unearthed and remains of walls which linked up with a plan of the inn in the Trust's collection were disclosed. A deep well, full of water, which had served the brewhouse, was found to have been covered by a massive slab of Wilmcote stone, presumably when no longer required. The only object found during the digging was a breastplate from a suit of armour, probably of seventeenth-century date. Could this possibly have provided a link with the troubled period of the Civil War, when soldiers were billeted in the town?

By the early spring of 1962 the contractors had completed excavation and were preparing the foundations of the basement. The first columns for the frame of the structure arrived shortly afterwards, and during the summer months work proceeded according to plan. Incidentally, I arranged, for the purposes of record, for photographs to be taken from the start and at each successive stage to the end of building operations. By December preparations for the casting of concrete for the roof were in hand, and the shell of the building had taken shape.

Laying of the Foundation Stone by HRH The Princess Alexandra of Kent

The official laying of a foundation stone for the building was performed by Her Royal Highness Princess Alexandra of Kent, on the afternoon of Thursday, 28 June 1962. A good deal of thought had gone into the arrangements for this ceremony, which the Trustees saw as a significant launch of their scheme. The foundation stone itself was conceived as a special feature of the new building. Instead of being a traditional, inscribed panel laid as part of a wall just above ground level, the stone was designed to be a distinctive, free-standing marker, occupying a prominent position at the extreme corner of the front of the building, a few yards from Shakespeare's Birthplace and facing Henley Street.

The material chosen was Hornton stone, supplied by Hornton Quarries, Ltd, situated just off the main Stratford to Banbury road, not far from the top of Sunrising Hill. The stone itself was in three sections, mounted on a plinth. A large, single slab, weighing some twelve to fourteen hundredweights, formed the front half of the stone, and a similar slab the back. Both these sections had been fixed in position in advance of the ceremony. The third section was a large, flat coping-stone, which held the other two together, and it was this that was laid when the ceremony took place. Inside the stone a cavity had been provided, and into this a sealed, lead casket had been placed containing the following items:

A sixpence and a shilling issued in 1564, the year of Shakespeare's birth, and coins minted in 1962: a half-crown, florin, shilling of English design, shilling of Scottish design, sixpence, threepenny piece, penny and two halfpennies.

A bound copy of the Shakespeare Birthplace, etc., Trust Act, 1961, autographed by all the Trustees of Shakespeare's Birthplace.

A copy of the annual report and statement of accounts of the Trust for the year ended 31 March 1962.

Copies of the three parts of the 1962 programme of the 103rd season of plays by William Shakespeare at the Royal Shakespeare Theatre.

Copies of programmes of the 1962 productions at the Royal Shakespeare Theatre: *Measure for Measure, A Midsummer Night's Dream, The Taming of the Shrew* and *Macbeth*, each autographed by the actors and actresses taking part.

The visit of HRH Princess Alexandra of Kent – her first to the town – was a special occasion for Stratford. After a morning of public engagements in Birmingham, the royal visitor was greeted by enthusiastic, friendly crowds as her car approached Shakespeare's Birthplace from Bridge Street, where units of the Royal Air Force from Wellesbourne Mountford and of the Royal Engineers and Royal Pioneer Corps from Long Marston assisted the police in lining the route. On her arrival at the garden entrance to the Birthplace, the Princess was greeted by the Mayor of the Borough (Councillor

W.H. Huxley), accompanied by the Mayoress, the High Steward (Sir Denys Lowson) and Lady Lowson, the Lord Lieutenant of Warwickshire (Lord Willoughby de Broke) and Lady Willoughby de Broke, the High Sheriff of Warwickshire (Lt-Col J.B. Challen) and Mrs Challen, the Chairman of the Shakespeare Birthplace Trust (Sir Fordham Flower) and Lady Flower, the Town Clerk of Stratford-upon-Avon (Mr D.M. Balmford) and Mrs Balmford, who were all waiting on the pavement.

The official party entered the Birthplace garden, where Sir Fordham presented the following Trustees and their ladies: Mr Leslie Watkins and Mrs Watkins, Mr Trevor Matthews and Mrs Matthews, Alderman G.A. Lea and Mrs Lea, Alderman Leigh Dingley and Mrs Dingley. I was then presented, as Director, together with my wife, and we soon found ourselves chatting in a friendly, informal manner. We were all struck by the charm and attractive personality of the Princess. She wore a bright, shocking pink, duster coat with three-quarter-length sleeves, and a white, petalled hat. Following these presentations, a posy of flowers, gathered from the Shakespearian gardens and arranged in a wickerwork basket, was presented to Her Royal Highness by Elizabeth and Patricia Fox, the Director's ten-year-old twin daughters. They were dressed alike, in pretty pink and white summer dresses, and wore wide-brimmed straw hats decorated with flowers. The Princess was clearly delighted, and spent a few moments chatting to the little girls, asking them where they lived and where they went to school. Proceeding along the paved path, the royal visitor passed the rose tree presented to Shakespeare's Birthplace by Her Majesty the Queen to mark her coronation year, and was then invited by Sir Fordham to inspect the plans and drawings of the Shakespeare Centre in the 1964 Pavilion in the garden. It was at this point that Laurence Williams, the architect, was presented. The Princess showed considerable interest in the plans and spent a little time discussing particular points with Mr Williams. In the meantime, the Trustees and their ladies and other representative guests had taken up their positions in a covered stand erected in the street for viewing the stone-laying ceremony. Special places had also been provided for children from local schools, boy scouts, girl guides and junior members of the Red Cross. Music was provided by the Royal Air Force Band from RAF Locking, seated in the garden of the Birthplace near to the foundation stone.

Passing through the Birthplace into Henley Street, escorted by the Chairman and myself, Princess Alexandra walked to the site of the stone, where Mr Ronald Hill, Chairman of Higgs and Hill, Ltd, the general contractors responsible for the building, was presented. In introducing and welcoming Her Royal Highness, Sir Fordham referred to the forthcoming 400th anniversary of Shakespeare's birth on St George's Day, 1964, 'perhaps the most significant

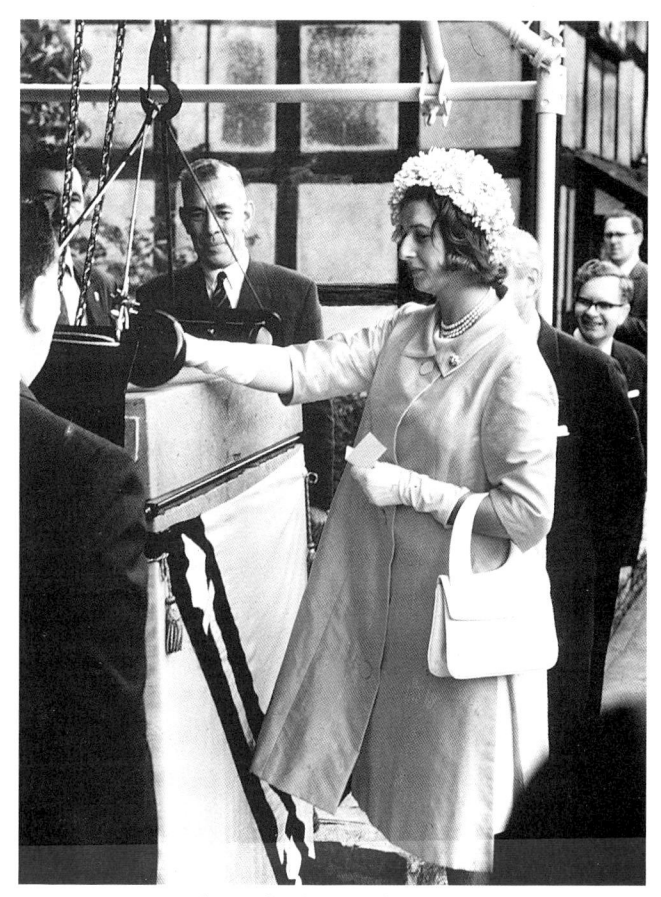

HRH Princess Alexandra laying the foundation stone

anniversary of its kind', he said, 'so far celebrated in this country'. He then described the Trust's building project and announced that 'lovers of Shakespeare throughout the world' were being invited 'to join in this tribute to him', adding 'we hope it will be an international birthday present to him, this new and excellent building'.

The Princess was then invited to lay the stone. Mr Ronald Hill passed a silver trowel (first used by Queen Victoria in 1886 and subsequently by several royal personages for stone-laying ceremonies) to Mr Williams, the architect, who handed it to the Princess to spread the mortar to bed the stone. The stone was then lowered into position and Mr Hill handed a maul to the architect, who passed it to Her Royal Highness to tap the stone in position. Having satisfied herself that she had finished what she was expected to do, the Princess declared the stone well and truly laid, and she then pulled a cord releasing the Shakespeare flag which had covered the lettering at the base of the stone. The inscription, carved by Ronald Robbins, a master mason of Hornton Quarries, read:

> TO THE LIVING MEMORY OF
> **WILLIAM SHAKESPEARE**
> THIS FOUNDATION STONE
> FOR THE SHAKESPEARE CENTRE
> WAS LAID ON 28 JUNE 1962
> BY
> HER ROYAL HIGHNESS
> PRINCESS ALEXANDRA OF KENT

The ceremony having been completed, the official party returned to Shakespeare's Birthplace and, as Director, I then had the privilege of acting as guide to Her Royal Highness as she made an inspection of the property. Away from the crowd and the public view, I found her a relaxed and charming person. We made a room-to-room tour of the house and she showed particular interest in the display of items in the upstairs museum, illustrative of the parentage, life, work and reputation of Shakespeare. Having signed the distinguished visitors' book, the royal visitor left the Birthplace by the front door and, to the accompaniment of the cheers of the waiting crowd, proceeded by car to Hall's Croft, where arrangements for an informal garden party had been made.

Invited representative guests had already assembled to greet the Princess on her arrival. The weather was kind and the garden made a perfect setting for a colourful occasion of this kind. Her Royal Highness took up her position at the head of a table on the terrace, as tea was served to the Trustees and their ladies, civic dignitaries and other invited representative guests. After tea, the Princess walked round the garden, admiring the herbaceous border and the raised terrace at the end of the expanse of lawn. Before she left, the Chairman presented to her a water-colour painting, nearly 150 years old, taken from a scene in *The Taming of the Shrew*, entitled 'Launce and His Dog', by Richard Westall. Altogether, a happy and successful chapter in the Trust's history.

Progress of Building

Following the laying of the foundation stone, building operations went forward according to plan, apart from a period of eleven weeks at the beginning of 1963 when work had to be suspended because of the unusually severe weather. By the spring the main structure was well on its way to completion, and the general contractors arranged for a traditional 'topping out' ceremony, performed by Sir Fordham Flower as Chairman of the Trust, on 11 April 1963. It was a very wet day. Six months later the main structure was completed, and when the Trustees, as well as the press, were invited to view the progress of the building on 4 October, they encountered a small army of technicians and craftsmen busy making detailed contributions to the various finishing processes. The new book-stacks in the basement were completed and equipped, and the transfer of the library and theatre collections of the Royal Shakespeare Theatre into this new accommodation, alongside the Birthplace library, started before the end of the year. Outside, the part of the Birthplace

THE SHAKESPEARE CENTRE

Topping out ceremony

The Shakepeare Centre on completion

garden adjacent to the new building was re-designed and re-planted at this time.

It was fortunate that in their architect, Laurence Williams, the Trustees had a man of liberal instincts and of very good taste and artistic perception. I myself had a most enjoyable and rewarding experience in working with him. We both shared a love of craftsmanship and, within the limits of financial constraints, set out to achieve the highest possible standard of finishings and decor. We were always prepared to go to endless trouble to get the detail right. Being of a very practical bent, I was able to visualize the actual working and use of each part of the building, and invariably Laurence Williams was able to accommodate my ideas.

Interior Decor and Furnishings

We both agreed that the interior of the building should have a distinctive character, and we had long discussions as to how this could be achieved. Because we both shared a love of timber, we decided to suggest that this typically English material should be used for wall cladding and fittings throughout the

Laurence Williams, architect of the Shakespeare Centre

principal parts of the building. Samples of different woods were accordingly considered by the Trustees in August 1962, and the choice fell on cherry for wall panelling and veneered surfaces.

The well known firm of timber merchants, Henry Venables, Ltd, of Stafford, was entrusted with the responsibility of finding the timber required, a task made particularly difficult by the quantity of cherry wood needed and the architect's stipulation that the wall cladding should be supplied in through lengths of eight and nine feet. The wild woodland trees of *prumus avium* were the only source available, and the suppliers had to search the countryside to find exceptional specimens of this species which could be purchased and prepared for this purpose. Over a hundred suitable trees were located and brought from the midland counties, and even from Yorkshire, Norfolk and south Wales. Some 2,896 pieces, sawn from over a hundred logs, were required for the job. The selection, matching and kiln-drying of the timber were entrusted to Henry Venables, Ltd, while Venesta (Veneers), Ltd, worked closely with the timber suppliers, going to very great trouble to find matching cherry-wood veneers.

The work of using these prepared materials to create the superb interior of the new building was undertaken by Joinery Products, Ltd, whose craftsmen created the beautiful panelling and fitments which brought character and a subtlety of colour all of its own. The outstanding feature of this work, as I well recollect, was the element of personal interest and involvement on the part of the suppliers and craftsmen and their close liaison with the Trust's architect. All were extremely proud of their contribution to an unusually fine building, conceived as an international birthday present to our national poet.

Laurence Williams and I were equally agreed that, for an attractive setting of this kind, furniture and fittings of dignified modern design and craftsmanship were essential, and that care should be taken to ensure that carpets and curtains harmonized in tone and texture. Members of the Executive Committee of Trustees were most generous in their endorsement of these ideas, and we were virtually given a free hand to settle all details of furnishing within the overall budget allowed.

For general furnishings, an extremely rewarding association with Gordon Russell Furnishings, Ltd, of Broadway, Worcestershire, was established. With the advice and help of Sir Gordon Russell – the country's leading designer and maker of quality furniture – and his experienced staff, the furnishings of each room were chosen to relate to use and to harmonize with the decor. For the conference room on the first floor, for example, a specially designed board-room table with a figured rosewood top and walnut base and with green leather-upholstered chairs, provided an ideal centre piece for a room striking by reason of its cherry-wood panelling, with woven curtains and carpet designed and supplied by Tibor Reich, the clever, Stratford-based, Hungarian-born textile designer whose fabrics had won him international acclaim. Gordon Russell, Ltd, were also responsible for the joinery and the furnishings of the library reading room, with its central circular table and separate working spaces for readers, together with the large card index cabinets in the catalogue area. The Director's room and adjoining working offices on the first floor were each furnished with specially made desks and chairs, matching cabinets, tables and other pieces. Taken as a complete suite, they presented a pleasing example of good quality modern design and craftsmanship.

For the book-stacks and strong room, protected by Chubb security doors, specially designed stove-

Library book-stack

enamelled steel shelving, storage drawers and cabinets were supplied by Sankey Sheldon, Ltd. The combined library resources of the Trust and the Theatre contained a vast miscellany of material, apart from books, and so required special accommodation. Every fitment was designed to meet a particular requirement. The lighting of library bookshelves was also a problem, and special care was taken to install tungsten lighting, appropriately sited, to provide for satisfactory book-stack illumination.

Furnishings and equipment of this standard, designed as an integral part of the decor, gave the building a special character; but its attraction was enhanced by a number of artistic embellishments contributed by living artists and craftsmen.

Artistic Embellishments

Laurence Williams and I considered the treatment of the approach to the building to be all-important. From the beginning, we had shared with the Trustees the feeling that the exterior brickwork of the curved end of the reading room facing Henley Street needed some kind of relief. Various suggestions were made and explored, and the solution was eventually found when the sculptor, Douglas Wain-Hobson, an Associate of the Royal College of Art, was commissioned to produce a sculptured relief in bronze, abstract in design, to be fixed on the upper part of the curved, brickwork wall immediately to the left of the portico entrance. It is a striking piece of architectural modelling, depicting the influence of Shakespeare emanating from his plays and encircling the world.

Bronze sculptured relief

More readily intelligible, and intended to catch the eye of everyone entering the building, was the large, carved panel planned to flank the right-hand side of the entrance portico, announcing the name of the building and recording its official opening as

Shakespeare Centre entrance panel

the Birthplace Trust's commemorative project for the 1964 Shakespeare anniversary.

This lettered panel was designed and carved by John Skelton, a sculptor and lettering artist well known for commissions undertaken in a number of cathedrals, including the newly built Coventry Cathedral. The material chosen for the panel was black Bon Accord Aberdeen polished granite. It measured 23 ft. by 4 ft. 6 ins., and the letters inscribed were 7 inches high. They were carved by pneumatic chisel and finished by hand, using tungsten-tipped tools. All the setting out and the work of carving was done in situ, and I well remember how, for several weeks before the official opening date, John Skelton and his assistant, Paul Wherle, sat underneath a temporary awning shelter, exchanging good humoured chat with passers by as they fashioned the letters on this very hard material. Absolutely precise cutting and finishing of the carving were essential. Throughout the whole of the operation there was obvious enjoyment and pride on the part of the sculptor and his assistant.

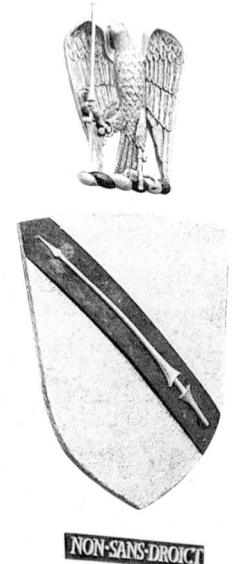

John Skelton was extremely versatile, and was equally happy drawing or working in wood, metal and fibreglass. He was responsible for the large, modelled Shakespeare coat of arms, made of fibreglass, which was fixed on the gable-end of the adjoining building, the former Midlands Electricity Board showrooms which were later demolished when the Centre was extended. Its purpose was to serve as a kind of advance directional alert to the Centre for visitors coming along Henley Street.

Arms of Stratford town and Shakespeare

Shakespeare coat of arms

Inside, in the Stratford room, leading from the entrance hall, he also designed and made an artistic plaque in hand-hammered copper incorporating the arms of Shakespeare and Stratford-upon-Avon, to indicate the close association between Shakespeare and the town. Skelton's skill as a lettering artist was also repeated on a panel in the conference room on the first floor, recording the names and dates of the chairmen and chief officers of the Trust from its inception, while a cedar-wood, carved rendering of Shakespeare's coat of arms and a walnut statuette of Lady Macbeth sleep-walking showed his skill as a carver in wood.

Handmade bricks and tiles, stone, marble, metal and wood were the basic materials used in the building, but it was the skilful treatment they received at the hands of gifted artists and craftsmen that added special interest. This was well illustrated by the engravings of Shakespeare characters, the work of John Hutton, on the glass panels which enclosed the small vestibule leading into the main entrance foyer. The architect and I felt it desirable to relieve the bareness of this large expanse of glass by engraving, and we suggested to John Hutton, whose engravings of prophets, saints and angels on the large screen of the new cathedral at Coventry had received much publicity and commendation, that here was an opportunity to illustrate the theme of Shakespeare's understanding of humanity by portraying on the glass panels some of his principal characters.

Hutton was excited by the suggestion and quickly produced ideas, which were accepted by the Trustees on 2 January 1963, and for the next fifteen months he devoted himself whole-heartedly to the commission. The artist himself furnished me with the following description of his work:

I was asked to design and engrave on glass some figures from Shakespeare's plays, and the first problem lay in deciding which characters could, without a detailed background, be instantly recognizable by people who were not deeply versed in Shakespearian scholarship. In the end, it was decided that I should show only those characters from Shakespeare's tragedies, comedies and historical plays who could stand by themselves without distracting background detail. Those selected are:

Tragedies:	Macbeth and Lady Macbeth
	Hamlet and Ophelia
	King Lear and Cordelia
	Romeo and Juliet
	Othello and Desdemona
Histories:	Antony and Cleopatra
	Julius Caesar
	King Richard III
Comedies:	Falstaff
	Titania and Bottom
	Portia and Shylock

As the emotional scope of engraved glass is limited, I have concentrated on the heads and hands, without any particular accent on dress or period. Where two figures are shown on the same panel, I have chosen those which are strongly related by emotional tension. For instance, Othello is gripping Desdemona's arm, accusing her over the finding of the fatal handkerchief. In portraying Macbeth and Lady Macbeth, I have shown the hallucinations that their imaginations conjured up – in Macbeth's case the dagger, and in Lady Macbeth's the blood on her hands, which was, of course, real enough in the scene where she smeared the grooms' faces so cold-bloodedly. The technique is a fairly realistic one, as I do not find it possible to see these figures as mere abstract patterns – they have for me too much humanity and passion.

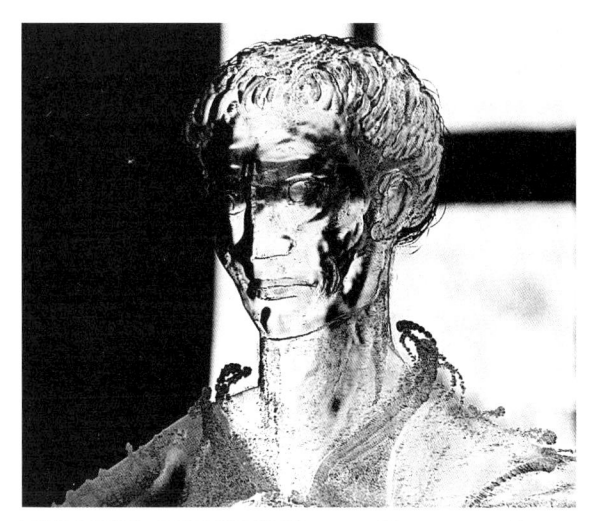

John Hutton's glass engravings. From the top: Hamlet, Richard III and Titania

The engraving is done with a series of grindstones attached to a flexible drive, and the glass is ordinary plate glass. The outstanding quality of engraved glass of this kind is the way it can change as one sees it in different lights and as the spectator moves to different parts of the room. It should be evanescent and not wholly visible from all points of view.

Seen against different backgrounds, the faces change and reveal the different aspects of their expressions. I have used this particular quality of changeability of expression to try and pay tribute to the extraordinary variety of interpretation offered by Shakespeare's characters.

I greatly enjoyed the experience of working closely with such a talented artist engraver. Initially we discussed the characters selected, and he himself took great pains to familiarize himself with the characteristics of the chosen subjects. He produced a small outline sketch as the basis of a larger, more finished drawing of the character concerned, and, when this satisfied his interpretation, he used it to portray a life-size drawing in chalk, to be used as his blueprint for engraving. The work was undertaken in Hutton's Studio in the basement of his flat in Maida Vale, London, and I visited him there to see how things were proceeding on a number of occasions. It was fascinating to see the glass panels mounted on frames round the studio in various stages of completion, but more particularly to see the engraver in action, donned in smock and mask, assaulting the plain glass with his drilling devices. Towards the end he was working on Antony and Cleopatra, and he confessed to me that he had found this particular character pair difficult; 'I had to revise them twice,' he said. Seeing him at work, I realized what tremendous concentration was required to produce the engraved image on a panel, and I asked him what happened if he made a mistake. 'That would blue the whole thing', he said, 'you cannot rub out'.

Although a sample panel, of Lady Macbeth, had been brought to the Centre for inspection by the Trustees on 2 October 1963, it was not until a few weeks before the official opening date that the complete series was finished. The responsibility for transporting such valuable artistic items from London to Stratford was considerable, more especially since it proved impossible to find an insurance company willing to cover the risk. In the event, the panels arrived safely and were installed a week or two in advance of the other major artistic embellishment for the entrance hall, the statue of Shakespeare.

Statue of William Shakespeare by Douglas Wain-Hobson

In June 1963 Douglas Wain-Hobson, who was already working on the abstract plaque for the exterior of the Centre, was commissioned to produce a statue of William Shakespeare in bronze as a centre piece for the entrance hall, to be set against the background of an off-white marble screen. Raised on a plinth, this full-size standing representation of Shakespeare is a striking focal point for the entrance hall and looks straight across the garden of his birthplace. The dramatist is depicted as a powerful, almost dominating, figure: a big character, portraying the all-embracing and everlasting genius of a unique personality and symbolizing the vitality of the first Elizabethan age.

It was a fascinating experience for me to follow the progress of this sculptured figure, starting with an outline sketch illustrating the sculptor's idea, followed by a moquette designed to give a three-dimensional impression and leading to a full-scale plaster model used for casting the bronze statue. When finished, it was a very considerable weight, and I well remember how it was transported from the foundry in London to the Shakespeare Centre, lying on a wooden cradle on a low-loading vehicle. It arrived late at night, when Henley Street was free from traffic, and great skill was required to off-load it and to ease it gradually on rollers through the front doors of the building into the entrance hall. To erect it into a standing position on the plinth provided was, to say the least of it, a precarious and nerve-racking experience, but the task was successfully accomplished. As always, there were willing hands to help, and the feeling of excitement and achievement was more than an adequate reward for all the effort involved.

Another major embellishment was the carved, lettered wood panel in the reading room of the library. Having worked as a young research student in a number of uncomfortable places, it was my idea that the reading room should be treated in a manner that would give it the atmosphere of a well appointed study, a concept which also appealed to the architect. Cherry wood was accordingly again chosen for the wall cladding, and specially designed individual readers' desks fitted under the bronze-framed windows on either side of the carpeted room. A circular display table provided a centre piece, with lighting from a dome in the roof. At the service end, the librarian's desk was finished with walnut veneers, and at the opposite end, a range of shelves was provided at low level round the curved wall. Gordon Russell, Ltd, were responsible for the skilful joinery and chairs.

The reading room

Nicolete Gray's carved panel

Laurence Williams and I felt that the upper part of the curved end wall needed to have some kind of artistic treatment, possibly a feature suggesting the presence and influence of William Shakespeare among his contemporary writers. We explored a number of ideas and then, by chance, a press report about an exhibition of architectural lettering by a lady named Nicolete Gray suggested the answer. I compiled a list of Shakespeare's fellow writers and sought her advice, explaining the character of the reading room and our general idea. We received an immediate, enthusiastic indication of interest. She suggested that the whole of the area of the curved wall above the book shelves should be treated as an unusual panel constructed of different woods, the name of William Shakespeare being carved in large letters across the centre and the names of the other contemporary writers displayed in different sizes and styles of lettering in the background. A small model illustrating the attraction of a novel treatment of this kind was submitted to the Trustees on 3 April 1963. It was unanimously approved, and Nicolete Gray was commissioned to proceed.

To provide the basic panel for her work, a skilful piece of joinery had to be prepared. While the main body of the panel was in solid cherry, a number of other species of wood were inlaid to an agreed design related to lettering positions. The woods chosen were a bluish-grey sycamore, dark red rosewood, light red camwood and ebony shot with black. The prepared panel, which extended the whole length of the curved wall, was transported in sections to the artist's studio in the basement of the British Museum. There she worked on the lettering, carving it out of the solid timber, some raised and some recessed, using different shapes and sizes related to the various timbers.

It was not until a few weeks before the official opening that the panel was ready to be transported and installed in the reading room. Nicolete Gray then came down, and for a number of days gave finishing touches to her carving on the site. It was fascinating to see her at work with her chisel, but more so to listen to her interpretation: William Shakespeare, a giant of a man, a genius, holding the stage, as it were, with a company of poets and dramatists occupying positions of varying prominence in the background. To her, the size and shape of every name had a subtle significance. It was only then that I discovered the source of Mrs Gray's knowledge and enthusiasm: she was the daughter of the poet Laurence Binyon, the former keeper of prints and drawings at the British Museum. The beauty and dignity of her carved lettering, symbolizing the status and influence of Shakespeare among his contemporaries, had given the finishing touch to the reading room.

The Appeal

As already indicated, right from the beginning the Trustees had appreciated the considerable problem of financing the Shakespeare Centre project, the cost of which increased as details were finalized. The original target of £100,000 had to be revised to £250,000, the Trustees deciding that it would be provident to add to the cost of the actual building a small element of endowment to meet the expense of maintaining and developing the work of the Centre when completed.

During 1961 and 1962 I made a number of selective fund raising approaches and learned some useful lessons in the process. My efforts met with only limited success, and hopes that major contributions might be forthcoming from educational foundations and charitable trusts proved disappointing. It was

The appeal prospectus illustration

accordingly agreed to use the services of a professional firm of fund-raisers, John F. Rich Company, Ltd, with whom preliminary discussions had already taken place, to organize a general appeal and, if possible, to extend it to the United States and Canada. In the event, the American campaign proved impossible, though throughout these years there was confidence that the Birthplace Trust's commemorative project would attract support from countries overseas as well as from Britain. I remember making the point that, unlike a school or university or church appeal, there was no set or known constituency in the case of William Shakespeare, who belonged to the world. On more than one occasion I also voiced a personal view that it seemed almost incredible that Shakespeare, the world's greatest dramatist, who was clearly such a priceless asset to Britain with unique international prestige, should have to be subjected to the need to beg.

Begging, however, proved necessary. By the time building operations were under way, the need for cash to meet the contractors' accounts had become urgent. A satisfactory overdraft arrangement to meet immediate requirements was operated with the Midland Bank, and the fund-raising consultants completed their preliminary survey and moved into action by the autumn of 1962. On their recommendation, a number of well known public and business personalities were persuaded to lend their sponsorship to the appeal, and the Trustees as individuals were asked to make approaches to possible sources of support with which they had contact. At the same time, a number of national and local firms were invited to give their financial backing, the level of contribution at this stage being considered to be important as the basis for a much wider, extended appeal to be made during 1963.

Reactions were encouraging, but I soon learned that, although we had produced and distributed another attractive appeal brochure, success could only be achieved by keen personal effort and salesmanship. In practice, it proved difficult to involve the Trustees, with one or two exceptions, and it fell to me to approach and visit heads of companies and organizations likely to assist. There were some disappointments, but gradually contributions started to arrive. My greatest success was with the Nuffield Foundation. Hitherto, its trustees had used most of their charitable funds to support medical and allied projects, and it was only after a long period of discussion and negotiation that they were persuaded to interest themselves in such a cause as the Shakespeare Centre. Eventually I succeeded in getting them to agree to be responsible for an identifiable part of the building and its equipment; this ultimately led to a decision that the Nuffield Foundation would offer a grant of £77,000 to provide the entrance exhibition hall and library facilities for the new Centre.

In reporting this gift to the Trustees at their Annual Meeting on 16 May 1963, the Chairman described it as 'extremely handsome and generous', and said that the approaches and negotiations which had led to the final outcome had all been undertaken by the Director, and that the Trustees were very much indebted to him for the way in which he had handled the matter. In recognition of the gift, the Trustees were happy to acknowledge the association of Lord Nuffield's name with the part of the building in question by calling the library reading room the Nuffield Library.

Two further initiatives were also agreed at this time: one local and one international.

Realizing that the Shakespeare Centre project was Stratford's major commemorative contribution for the quatercentenary year, it was decided to invite the local community to assume responsibility for providing a Stratford room in the Centre, at an estimated cost of £25,000. The room leading directly from the entrance exhibition hall, with windows overlooking the Birthplace garden, was accordingly so named and equipped for lectures, meetings and exhibitions and with facilities for serving refreshments provided alongside.

This idea of local involvement, carrying with it the prospect of an attractive meeting place for organizations in the town, appealed strongly. The Stratford-upon-Avon Borough Council generously gave £2,500, and local firms, shops, professional and business interests, schools, societies and clubs, as well as individual residents, all contributed. Before the end of the year more than two-thirds of the target had been raised, and donations continued right up to the anniversary date. Apart from money, certain items of furnishing for the Stratford Room were donated: the plaque of the Shakespeare and Stratford coats of arms, already referred to, given by Mr and Mrs Fred Stock; furnishings for the rostrum paid for by the Shakespeare Club of Stratford-upon-Avon; a lectern designed and made by the Royal Engineers of Long Marston; and a clock presented by Messrs Archer and Coote of Greenhill Street. Perhaps this is also the place to record that the local firm of Saville Tractors, Ltd, met the cost of the carved panel in the library reading room, already described; that a Stratford tradesman, Mr Harold Green, had a silver inkstand designed and made for the board-room table in the conference room; and that Mr George Pragnell, a jeweller of Wood Street, gave a set of leather-bound writing pads for the same table, which are still in use.

The second initiative was to involve the world. It was decided to invite all the Ambassadors and High Commissioners in London to associate themselves as sponsors with the project and to ask the governments of their countries to identify themselves with it, either by making a money contribution to the appeal fund or by providing something in kind for the new building.

The timing of this move was opportune, because, by the middle of 1963, growing publicity had firmly established the concept of the Shakespeare Centre as an international birthday present to the memory of Shakespeare in 1964, and preparations for celebrations in many other countries were already being planned.

The approach to the diplomatic corps was also helped by the excellent relations over the years with Ambassadors and High Commissioners who had attended the annual Shakespeare birthday celebrations at Stratford and had taken part in the ceremony of unfurling the flags of the nations.

The response was generally very satisfactory. By the time the Trustees held their Half Annual Meeting on 4 October 1963, I was able to report that fifty-one Ambassadors and High Commissioners had already agreed to act as sponsors of the appeal, and that contributions from a number of countries already received had helped to raise the appeal total to nearly £170,000. The number of diplomatic sponsors subsequently increased to sixty-seven.

The effort expended on this diplomatic exercise was considerable, involving the circulation of a special brochure, followed by personal contact with each representative and, when possible, by a visit or visits, either by the resident appeal campaign organizer or by myself. Some visits were immediately successful, or sufficiently promising to warrant further contact; some were disappointing or completely negative. Clearly, there were instances when diplomats had difficulty in persuading their governments to support the cause of another country's national poet; but the exercise was at least worth while from a public relations point of view, and helped to publicize the forthcoming 400th anniversary of Shakespeare's birth.

How difficult the task could be was illustrated by my own experience when I visited the Soviet Embassy. Although I had an appointment, I was kept waiting in silence under the eye of a watchful guard attendant, who appeared to view me with suspicion. Clearance by him having been obtained, I was eventually ushered into a large, oblong-shaped room, completely bare of furnishings except for bench seating in the centre. On the wall at the far end a large mural painting, which I guessed depicted a scene from the Siberian steppes, seemed to unfold a vista of a bleak and uninviting country. Again I was left in solitary waiting for some time, and the silence and bareness of the setting gave me an uncomfortable, eerie feeling. The Cultural Attaché then arrived and, after we had exchanged civil greetings, I explained the object of my mission. I referred particularly to the contacts I had already had with scholars, actors and distinguished public figures from the Soviet Union when they had visited Shakespeare's Birthplace, and to the regular attendance of Soviet diplomatic representatives at the annual birthday celebrations at Stratford. We then found ourselves talking about the Russian theatre and the popularity of Shakespeare there, both on stage and in translation. All seemed to be going well, until I enquired whether the Soviet Union might like to join with other nations in associating itself with the international tribute to Shakespeare on his 400th birthday, as symbolized by the Shakespeare Centre project, and to make a contribution to the appeal. There was silence. Surely, the Attaché then enquired, was it not the responsibility of the British Government to provide funds to make possible a memorial of this kind in honour of its national poet? In the Soviet Union this would certainly have happened, so I was told. Regrettably, the response was negative. I immediately sensed there was little point in pursuing the matter further; my enthusiasm and salesmanship were no match for politics. I took my leave and was greatly relieved when I heard the heavy doors locked behind me as I left. On reflection, it was somewhat embarrassing to have to accept the fact that, whilst the Trustees were soliciting contributions from countries overseas, no financial help had been offered by Her Majesty's Government, apart from a modest grant from the Arts Council of Great Britain.

In contrast, my visit to the Embassy of the Federal Republic of Germany (popularly known as West Germany) met with a warm reception and immediate success. Germany, of course, was the first European country to recognize the genius of Shakespeare, and over the years its scholars had made, and continue to make, a significant contribution to Shakespeare study and writing. Moreover, Germany had always sent more of its people to visit Shakespeare's Birthplace than any other non-English-speaking country; and the Trustees of Shakespeare's Birthplace and the Trustees of the Goethehaus in Frankfurt had exchanged annual greetings and laurel wreaths on the birthdays of Shakespeare and Goethe. The Ambassador handed over to me a donation for £5,000, together with an expression of pleasure at being allowed to participate in the 1964 anniversary appeal. In a similar way, the Japanese regarded it as a privilege to be invited to contribute to the appeal. On the morning of the birthday itself, 23 April 1964, the Ambassador came from London to the Shakespeare Centre for the express purpose of offering congratulations and presenting a handsome donation to the appeal on behalf of the Japanese people.

The idea of suggesting 'gift opportunities' to potential donors also paid dividends. Arising from a friendly association with the Deputy High Commissioner in London and following his inspection of the new building as it neared completion, the Government of Jamaica sent a small consignment of blue mahoe, the national timber of Jamaica, which was fashioned into a curved panel at the end of the conference room. Bermuda decided to underwrite the cost of the Shakespeare coat of arms, carved from Cedar of Lebanon, which subsequently adorned this panel. The Government of India sponsored the fine board-room table made by Gordon Russell for the conference room; Ethiopia met the cost of the furnishings of the Director's office; and perpetual motion clocks for all the principal rooms in the building were given by Switzerland. Denmark commissioned the Royal Porcelain Factory at Copenhagen to design and produce a wall plaque of Elsinore Castle and a large porcelain figure of Titania and Bottom, as special exhibits for the building; and

The Director's office

the Shah of Persia (now Iran) sent an exquisite, hand-woven carpet panel, out of his 'personal regard for Shakespeare'.

Another special gift which should be recorded was the engraved glass rose bowl for the board-room table, designed by Professor Godden and presented by the Royal Society of the Arts. In a similar category, a tall circular vase, embellished by John Hutton's engraving of the dance of the reapers in *The Winter's Tale*, was given by the association of the wives of the staff of the American Embassy to serve as a centre piece on the table in the middle of the library reading room. This latter gift came about as the result of a friendly association I had with the late Dr Myers, the then Cultural Attaché at the United States Embassy in London. When the new building was nearing completion, I showed Dr Myers and his wife round and referred to the appeal and the response the Trustees were getting; whereupon Mrs Myers announced that she was sure her 'women', namely the wives of the Embassy staff, would like to present something, and she asked for my suggestions. The outcome was a specially commissioned vase, made by the Whitefriars glass company, which John Hutton engraved in his distinctive style. On Wednesday morning, 15 April 1964, exactly a week before the official opening of the Centre, I attended a reception at the American Embassy and, in the presence of a company of ladies who had contributed to its cost, the wife of the Ambassador handed over the vase to me. It was a happy occasion for all concerned.

The appeal by this time was reaching its final phase. By 1 January 1964 the total raised was £176,000, with promises of further contributions to come, and a subscription list was published in *The Times*. By 9 March, when the members of the Executive Committee inspected the completed building, the total had risen to £180,000. During the remainder of 1964 the appeal remained open and gifts continued to be received. Although the Trust found itself left with little cash reserve, by the end of the year all commitments in connection with the Shakespeare Centre project had been met. According to the audited accounts, the cost of the new Shakespeare Centre, including fixtures and fittings, was £200,827 7s. 4d.

A report detailing the progress of the appeal, prepared by the consultants, is preserved in the Trust's archives, together with the names of all donors, as well as those who 'bought' bricks, floor tiles, wood panels, book shelves, pieces of marble, bags of cement and other sundry items, when visiting the 1964 Pavilion in the Birthplace garden. By 4 October 1963 no fewer than 22,763 people from all over the world had received certificates for their small 'purchases', a number which exceeded 30,000 during the anniversary year.

We were all delighted with this practical evidence of international involvement; the Centre project had always been conceived as a birthday present with which anyone who wished could be associated. In a more tangible way, evidence of international participation is available in the Shakespeare Centre for all to see. The Trustees decided that one of the fifty-two windows on the first floor of the building should be allotted, by way of acknowledgement, to each overseas country which responded to the appeal. Each window sill was therefore labelled with a small, simple plaque recording the name of the donor nation: a constant reminder of the universal regard in which Shakespeare is held, and that the Shakespeare Centre was made possible by the generosity of Shakespeare lovers all over the world.

The Official Opening

Arrangements for the official opening of the Shakespeare Centre were considered in the early part of 1963. There was general agreement among the Trustees that Her Majesty Queen Elizabeth II should be invited to perform the opening ceremony on St George's Day, Thursday, 23 April 1964, the 400th anniversary date of Shakespeare's birth, and that this event should be linked with Her Majesty's participation in the programme of birthday celebrations and the opening of the 1964 Shakespeare Exhibition, planned by the 1964 Shakespeare Anniversary Council.

An invitation was accordingly conveyed to Her Majesty, and all concerned with preparations in Stratford were delighted when an indication of acceptance was received from Buckingham Palace. What was not appreciated at that juncture was that the Queen would be giving birth to her fourth child, Prince Edward, in March 1964, and that on medical advice she would not be undertaking any public engagements until after the end of April. When these circumstances became known, the Trustees hoped that His Royal Highness Prince Philip, Duke of Edinburgh, would take Her Majesty's place. He readily agreed to visit the Shakespeare Centre and to attend the celebrations on 23 April, but indicated that he would prefer the new building to be opened by someone who might be seen to represent the international significance of the project.

The choice fell upon the Hon. Eugene R. Black, the Chairman of the American 1964 Shakespeare Committee. As President of the World Bank, Mr Black was a well known international figure and, by reason of his personal interest in Shakespeare, he was no stranger to Stratford-upon-Avon. He had in fact attended several of the International Shakespeare Conferences held at Mason Croft, and I myself had established a very friendly relationship with him. Right from the beginning, he had been particularly interested in our plans at Stratford for celebrating the quatercentenary year, and he had persuaded President John F. Kennedy to set up a State Committee to organize a programme of events in the United States. Apart from being Chairman of that Committee, he was also President of the festival organization which had built and operated the Shakespeare Theatre at Stratford, Connecticut.

Mr Black was a great traveller, who in his professional capacity made frequent visits to third-world countries, advising and arranging financial aid from the World Bank. He frequently found himself in London, and often he would telephone me to ask if I could get him a ticket for the play at the Royal Shakespeare Theatre. He always stayed at the Welcombe Hotel and he invariably met me to compare notes about the progress of the Centre project and the planning of Stratford's celebrations programme. I remember the occasion in the late summer of 1963 when he telephoned me from London to say that the First Lady of the United States, Mrs Jacqueline Kennedy, who was the President of the American 1964 Shakespeare Committee, would like to attend the celebrations in Stratford on 23 April 1964, and to ask if this would be possible. He told me that the President had agreed that she should come. Imagine my surprise and excitement at the prospect! However, since Her Majesty the Queen had already promised to come, I wondered what she would feel about this. I explained to Mr Black the situation and said that I would need to get clearance from Buckingham Palace. In actual fact a favourable reaction was received and, as Director of the anniversary celebrations, I began to address my thoughts to the detailed arrangements which would be appropriate to take care of the visits both of our own Queen and America's First Lady.

Then the blow fell. President Kennedy was assassinated; America and the whole world were severely shocked. Plans for American participation and celebrations fell into abeyance. Then, not long afterwards, came the disappointing decision that, as already mentioned, the Queen would not be able to attend the celebrations in person. A fresh start had to be made.

In the changed circumstances and having regard to the programme of celebrations on the anniversary date, and with Mr Black's agreement, the Trustees decided that the official opening of the Centre should be on the afternoon of Wednesday, 22 April. As Director, it fell to me to make all necessary arrangements.

My immediate concern was to ensure that the new building, with its furnishings and embellishments, was absolutely complete and in a condition fit to be inspected by a distinguished opener and a royal personage, as well as by other invited guests. For three months previously the library collection of the Royal Shakespeare Theatre, as well as that of the Birthplace Trust, had been in the process of being moved into the book-stacks of the new building. This process completed, the administrative offices were equipped and prepared for occupation, as indeed were all the other parts of the building. In the Birthplace garden the new flower beds were planted and flower boxes prepared at the entrance to the Centre. A day for press and media inspection was arranged, and filming of the building made for inclusion in a television programme planned to cover the anniversary day's celebrations.

An impressive number of guests, including donors and representatives of overseas countries and organizations, were invited to watch the opening ceremony. For their convenience a covered stand was erected in the street opposite to the entrance to the Centre where the ceremony was to take place; and during the period of waiting before the ceremony music was played by the Band of the Corps of the Royal Engineers.

The Hon. Eugene Black arrived at the entrance to the garden of Shakespeare's Birthplace, where he was received by the Chairman of the Trust, Sir Fordham Flower, and Lady Flower. Sir Fordham presented His Worship the Mayor of Stratford-upon-Avon, Councillor C.G. Kemp, and the Mayoress, Lord and Lady Avon, and myself as Director. This official party then passed along the garden path and entered the Birthplace from the rear; subsequently we left the building by the front door and proceeded along Henley Street to the front entrance of the Centre, where a small group of special guests was awaiting. These included the High Sheriff of Warwickshire (Mr W.M. Maddocks) and Mrs Maddocks, the High Steward of the Borough (Sir Denys Lowson, Bt.) and the Hon. Lady Lowson, Mrs Levi Fox, Mr Laurence Williams, the architect of the new building, and Mrs Williams.

In his introduction, the Chairman of the Birthplace Trust described the new Shakespeare Centre as 'an international birthday present', and said that it was the intention of the Trust that it should be used by people from all over the world; indeed, it was particularly appropriate that a distinguished gathering of representatives from many nations should be present at its inauguration. Sir Fordham welcomed Mr Black, referring to his personal interest in Shakespeare and his role as Chairman of the American 1964 Shakespeare Committee, and then invited him to perform the opening ceremony.

Mr Black first addressed the company, describing the Centre as 'a splendid memorial to the great Elizabethan and a workshop of the highest order in which all may explore Shakespeare's literature and endow themselves with new learning'. By accepting the assistance of other nations to construct the Centre, Mr Black said that Great Britain was only reclaiming a small share of what she had so generously given. 'If Englishmen were able to collect royalties on their literary legacy', he continued, 'the United Kingdom would never need fear a deficit in the balance of payments'. Shakespeare, Mr Black said, had exercised an inestimable influence on the thoughts and, indeed, on the entire culture of all peoples and ages which had come after him. It therefore seemed fitting that at the site of his birth the world should signify, in some small measure, 'a recognition of our immense indebtedness'.

Following Mr Black's address, Mr Laurence Williams presented him with a pair of silver scissors with which he cut the ribbon across the entrance. Mr Black declared the Centre open and released the Shakespeare flags which covered the inscription shown below, on the black granite marker panel flanking the entrance.

THE SHAKESPEARE CENTRE

BUILT BY THE SHAKESPEARE BIRTHPLACE TRUST TO COMMEMORATE THE 400TH ANNIVERSARY OF THE BIRTH OF WILLIAM SHAKESPEARE 1564 - 1616 WITH THE HELP OF CONTRIBUTIONS FROM SHAKESPEARE LOVERS OF MANY NATIONS. OPENED ON 22 APRIL 1964 BY THE HON. EUGENE R. BLACK CHAIRMAN OF THE AMERICAN 1964 SHAKESPEARE COMMITTEE. VISITED BY HIS ROYAL HIGHNESS THE PRINCE PHILIP DUKE OF EDINBURGH K.G., K.T. ON THE POET'S BIRTHDAY 23 APRIL 1964

Sir Fordham Flower Chairman   Levi Fox Director   Laurence Williams Architect

The ceremony having been completed, the official party made an inspection of the Centre, during which Mr Black met Mr Ronald Hill, representing the main contractors, Mr Michael Forbes, assistant architect, and some of the artists and craftsmen who had contributed to the building. At the end of the inspection a case containing specimens of the official medal designed by Paul Vincze to commemorate the 400th anniversary of Shakespeare's birth was presented to Mr Black. The official party then left by the garden and proceeded to Hall's Croft, where they were joined for tea by other invited guests following their inspection of the building.

On the following morning, 23 April, His Royal Highness Prince Philip, Duke of Edinburgh, visited the Centre. Arriving by helicopter at Ham Meadow on the Warwick road, the Duke drove by car to the Shakespeare Centre along streets lined with cheering crowds. He was welcomed by a guard of honour formed by men of the Queen's Own Warwickshire and Worcestershire Yeomanry, of which the Queen was Honorary Colonel. At the entrance to the Centre he met the High Steward of the Borough, Sir Denys Lowson, and Lady Lowson, Sir Fordham and Lady Flower, the Director of the Trust and Mrs Fox, and the architect, Mr Laurence Williams, and Mrs Williams.

Sir Fordham and I then had the privilege of taking His Royal Highness on a tour of the building. Throughout the visit he displayed a lively interest in everything he saw, and kept me busy answering his questions. 'What was the abstract bronze on the wall near the entrance?' he asked; I explained that this was a symbol of Shakespeare's global influence. The next items to attract his attention were the engraved glass panels depicting Shakespeare characters, the work of John Hutton, and he was fascinated to hear how the engraving was done. Inside the entrance hall the eye-catching sculptured statue of Shakespeare seemed to hold his attention as we proceeded to view the library reading room. He was clearly impressed by the character of this room and, when I pointed out the wood carved panel on the end wall recording the names of Shakespeare's contemporaries, he joked

Official opening of the Shakespeare Centre

Mr Eugene Black unveils the Shakespeare Centre panel

about the absence of Francis Bacon. He then inspected the book-stacks and strong room in the basement, where the Trust's most valuable treasures were kept. He showed particular interest in the First Folio of Shakespeare's plays, published in 1623.

At various points during his tour of the Centre the Duke asked questions of the architect, Laurence Williams. Before leaving, he signed the distinguished visitors' book in the conference room and

Presentation of Shakespeare medals to HRH Prince Philip, Duke of Edinburgh

HRH Prince Philip leaving the Birthplace

the Chairman presented him with a set of the official 1964 Shakespeare medals, designed by Paul Vincze. On leaving the Centre, he walked along the garden path and into the Birthplace, which he left by the front door in order to attend the 400th birthday anniversary luncheon in the pavilion that had been erected on the bank of the Avon, alongside the temporary building which accommodated the Shakespeare Exhibition.

Anniversary Occasion

The new Shakespeare Centre provided within one building the accommodation and facilities which the Birthplace Trust needed at that time to discharge its function, and offered scope for short-term expansion. Thought had also been given to possible future needs, and the plan had been so devised that an extension could be added to the building in years ahead, on the site of adjoining properties already owned by the Trust.

The Centre was intended to serve both as the administrative headquarters of the Trust and as a study centre based on the Trust's library and archive collections. Its basement book-stacks, with their specially designed shelving and storage equipment, provided excellent accommodation for the combined libraries of the Birthplace Trust and the Royal Shakespeare Theatre, with space for expansion. The reading room operated on a system which enabled readers to requisition any items they needed from the reserve stacks below, and was an integral part of the Centre's study facilities, while the Stratford room provided a convenient setting for lectures and exhibitions, when used in conjunction with the entrance hall. On the first floor a compact suite of offices for the Director and staff provided adequate accommodation for the Trust's administration and included a conference room for meetings of the governing body and other special uses. Amenities for staff had not been overlooked, and for security purposes a resident caretaker's flat had been incorporated in the building at the rear.

This was the finished product which the Trustees

First meeting of the Trustees in the conference room

inspected when they held a special meeting on Saturday, 25 April 1964, to mark the 400th anniversary of Shakespeare's birth. In welcoming the Trustees to their first meeting in the conference room at the Centre, the Chairman, Sir Fordham Flower, said that this was a unique occasion which would go down as a landmark in the history of the Trust. He reviewed the circumstances which had induced the Trustees to embark upon the Shakespeare Centre project, and said that the reactions of the distinguished guests who had visited the new building during the period of the birthday celebrations were unanimously favourable. He felt that the Trustees, with their Director and architect, had every good reason to be proud of the birthday present which had been created to commemorate the 400th anniversary of Shakespeare's birth. There was 'a great feeling of achievement,' said Sir Fordham, but also 'a feeling of great humility'.

Sir Fordham then called upon the Vicar of Stratford-upon-Avon, the Reverend Thomas Bland, who was present as an Ex Officio Trustee, to bless the new building.

The Chairman explained that the Trustees had decided to mark the anniversary year by appointing, to fill existing vacancies in the category of Life Trustees, three distinguished gentlemen who had taken part in the anniversary celebrations and who had been invited to attend the meeting. They were the Hon. Eugene R. Black, Lord Langton Iliffe and Dr Louis B. Wright. Mr Black and Dr Wright, Sir Fordham described as 'leaders of the Shakespearian

The new Life Trustees

cause in the United States', and referred at some length to the contacts between them and the Trust over the years. Mr Black, he said, was known as 'a world figure' and as 'a great lover of Shakespeare', who was keenly interested in the work of the Trust and the Royal Shakespeare Theatre. Dr Wright, as Director of the Folger Shakespeare Library in Washington, DC, he described as 'the keeper of the most valuable deposit of Shakespeariana in the world' and as an eminent Shakespeare scholar and historian. Speaking of Lord Iliffe, Sir Fordham referred to his business associations with Warwickshire and his close connections with Stratford, at the same time recalling that his father had been President of the Governors of the Royal Shakespeare Theatre for twenty-five years and that his wise guidance and influence had helped to shape the Theatre's future. He acknowledged Lord Iliffe's generous support of the Shakespeare Centre project.

These three gentlemen were unanimously elected Life Trustees, and each expressed his appreciation of the honour conferred on him.

The Chairman also took opportunity to refer to the success of the programme of celebrations which had been carried through by the Shakespeare Anniversary Council, and he paid a special tribute to the Director and his staff, who had carried the burden of preparations and the organization of the events. The occasion was a particularly happy one, and at the conclusion of the meeting the Trustees adjourned to the Welcombe Hotel for lunch with their ladies.

Another Royal Visit

Many of the diplomatic representatives who attended the celebrations inspected the new building during their stay in Stratford, and several returned later in the summer. At the same time there was a regular stream of distinguished visitors keen to see the anniversary project, and there were several occasions when presentations were made. There was general approval and compliment for the dignified character and decor of the building, and many admired the detail and quality of its design and craftsmanship. The skilful use of wood frequently evoked comment.

The highlight of the summer of 1964 was another royal visit. On Saturday morning, 11 July, the Trustees were honoured by a visit of Her Majesty Queen Elizabeth the Queen Mother, when she came to Stratford to perform the opening ceremony of the Stratford-upon-Avon Canal. For a whole week the banks of the Avon from Clopton Bridge to Holy Trinity Church were lined with decorated canal and river craft from many parts of the country, and against this background of boating activity a festival programme of exhibitions, competitions, music and fireworks was staged.

The re-opening of the canal was in itself an event of considerable significance. Originally constructed between 1793 and 1816, the Stratford Canal was linked to the Grand Union Canal at Lapworth and, until the middle of the nineteenth century, was a prosperous commercial waterway. Then successive railway owners discouraged traffic and neglected maintenance, and by the early 1930s the canal had become derelict and impassable. An attempt to bring about an official closure of the canal in 1958 provoked widespread opposition, and a successful campaign to save the waterway was launched and led by the Inland Waterways Association. In 1960 the National Trust undertook responsibility for the canal. Under its direction and with the help of voluntary contributions and services, the prodigious feat of dredging and rendering navigable again the thirteen-and-a-half miles of derelict waterway was accomplished.

Arriving by train at the railway station, Her Majesty was welcomed by the Lord Lieutenant, Lord Willoughby de Broke, and the Mayor of the Borough, Alderman Percy Wheeler, with other dignitaries and their ladies. She first visited the Town Hall, where the Aldermen of the Borough, chief officials, and their wives were introduced to her. The flags of the nations made a colourful spectacle in the centre of the town as the Queen Mother proceeded along High Street and Henley Street, which were decorated with flowers and lined with cheering spectators.

Her Majesty looked especially charming as she paused and looked round at the entrance to the Centre, at the same time acknowledging the crowd across the street and the groups of children waving their flags and posies. The usual presentations took place: the Chairman, Sir Fordham Flower, and Lady Flower, and myself as Director and Mrs Fox. Reading the inscription on the black granite panel as she climbed the steps, she was immediately impressed by John Hutton's engraved panels of Shakespeare characters. By this time Mr Laurence Williams, the architect, had been introduced, and together we explained to her, as she fingered the raised polished surfaces of the panels, the technique which John Hutton had used to produce them.

Waiting to be presented to her in the entrance hall were the Trustee members of the Executive Committee and their wives. Her Majesty chatted first to one and then another in a friendly, natural manner, and then, accompanied by the Chairman, the architect and myself, she made a leisurely tour of the building. She was intrigued by the fact that Douglas Wain-Hobson's bronze statue of Shakespeare was eyeless, but appreciated the sculptor's representation of the dramatist as a robust, commanding figure. She liked the atmosphere of the Stratford room and said what a good idea it was to provide accommodation of that kind for local community use.

The association of the library reading room with the name of Nuffield was explained to her and, once inside, she asked questions about its use and the role of the Birthplace Trust in the academic sphere. Opportunity had been taken to display for her inspection specimens of prompt copies of Shakespeare's plays, with illustrations of theatrical productions at the Royal Shakespeare Theatre. She admired the engraved circular bowl on the table and the carved lettering of the panel on the end wall.

Downstairs in the basement she expressed surprise to find such well equipped book-stacks, and even more so in the strong room when she saw the shelves bearing the Trust's collection of early printed books. As always happened on these occasions, the question of the survival of the manuscripts of Shakespeare's plays was raised. This inevitably led to

HM the Queen Mother examining the First Folio

the production of specimens of the Trust's Quarto copies of the plays and of the First Folio. The latter never fails to interest, and, exactly in the manner I had used when the Duke of Edinburgh came in April, I found myself turning over the pages and explaining them to Her Majesty. As always on these occasions, the time allowed was too short to browse further, but before Her Majesty moved on to the conference room on the first floor I was able to show her the original Parish Register of Stratford-upon-Avon and to point out the baptism and burial entries of William Shakespeare. I again found myself saying that I thought this was the most precious record in existence.

Her Majesty leaving the Shakespeare Centre

Re-opening the Stratford Canal

Climbing the stairs and glancing at the Persian carpet displayed as a wall hanging, Her Majesty stood on the landing to admire the Royal Copenhagen porcelain figure of Titania and Bottom, and the Shakespeare tapestry designed and made by Tibor Reich. Advancing through the open door into the conference room, she paused, carefully surveyed the whole scene, and exclaimed 'What a most beautiful room!' With the morning sun streaming through the tall, bronze-framed windows, the long, polished, rosewood table with its round, glass bowl filled with roses made a striking centre piece to the room, while the cherry-wood panelling of its walls and the blue mahoe screen provided a background which harmonized with the carpet and curtains designed by Tibor Reich. The eye was drawn to the tall, slim statuette of Lady Macbeth sleep-walking, which stood in the glazed corner at the far end of the room, and the flower arrangement of mixed summer blooms at its base. Her Majesty fingered appreciatively the fine, English timber of the wall cladding, and she was quick to notice the small, metal plates on each window sill that recorded the names of the countries which had made contributions to the building.

After signing the distinguished visitors' book – the same book she had signed when she came as Queen in 1950 – Her Majesty left the Centre, acknowledging with her winning smile the applause of the waiting crowd. She proceeded to inspect the Shakespeare Exhibition on the banks of the Avon, and during the afternoon embarked on a narrow boat to sail down the newly restored canal. After performing the official opening ceremony, she inspected the Festival of Boats assembled on the river, leaving by the garden of Avonside, hard by Holy Trinity Church. In the evening she attended a gala performance of *Henry V* at the Royal Shakespeare Theatre.

It is impossible to describe the pleasure this visit gave to all concerned, and in a message sent afterwards by her Private Secretary to the Mayor of Stratford, her visit was described as 'a memorable day, one on which Her Majesty will look back with real pleasure'.

Quatercentenary Celebrations

The full story of this splendid chapter in the history of Stratford-upon-Avon and the nation has still to be written, but, since the Trustees of Shakespeare's Birthplace and their Director played a key role in the arrangements right from the beginning to the end, mention of their involvement must be included in this record.

The 1964 Shakespeare Anniversary Council

The Trust was responsible for initiating the whole business. Following informal discussion I had with the Chairman and the Trustees, steps were taken at the beginning of 1961 to set up a body known as the 1964 Shakespeare Anniversary Council, comprising representatives of local and outside organizations likely to be interested in taking part in planning a programme of commemorative events and activities for the anniversary year. Sir Fordham Flower was appointed its Chairman, and I myself Deputy Chairman and Director, with Shakespeare's Birthplace serving as the Council's headquarters.

The Director addressing members of the tenth International Shakespeare Conference at Hall's Croft, 1961

The function of this *ad hoc* body was to plan and organize suitable celebrations in Stratford-upon-Avon and to co-ordinate the contributions of the various institutions and bodies willing to take part; to be responsible for publicity and generally to exercise oversight of all aspects of the 1964 anniversary arrangements; and to undertake liaison with organizations overseas concerned with the planning of similar celebrations.

By the early summer of 1961 the Anniversary Council had already considered and agreed in general terms a provisional pattern of celebrations for 1964. At a tea party held at Hall's Croft on 29 August 1961 for delegates of the University of Birmingham's tenth International Shakespeare Conference I was accordingly able to outline to those present Stratford's tentative proposals, and to solicit their interest and support in encouraging the planning of commemorative events in their respective countries.

The next two years were spent in finalizing the programme, and, when 1964 came, Stratford-upon-Avon was able to present to the world a unique Shakespeare Anniversary Festival, beginning with a week's festivities centred on the traditional birthday celebrations and lasting until the end of the summer. The Festival programme, concentrated into six weekly periods spread through the summer, included choral and orchestral concerts with chamber music and specially commissioned music; a star-studded Poetry Festival with special commemorative recitals; a series of exhibitions; folk dance and song with an international folk dance festival, lectures and conferences; film versions of Shakespeare's plays; a variety of exhibitions, recitals, commemorative productions and events arranged by local schools and societies; all set against the attraction of a cycle of Shakespeare's history plays at the Royal Shakespeare Theatre and a major Shakespeare Exhibition accommodated in a temporary building on the banks of the River Avon, illustrating the life and career of William Shakespeare in the setting of Elizabethan and Jacobean England.

Exhibitions at the Shakespeare Centre

The Trustees' major contribution was the new Shakespeare Centre, already described, a commemorative birthday present which, with its modern design and artistic embellishments, focussed attention on the present and future, as well as on the past. During the summer months a constant stream of visitors took advantage of the Trustees' decision to 'open to view' the new building, and they themselves played host to a number of visiting organizations and conference groups.

An additional attraction was an exhibition of Shakespearian rarities presented in the Centre. The entrance hall, with the built-in exhibition cases in the Stratford room, made an appropriate setting for the Centre's first exhibition of rare Shakespeare books and manuscripts, most of which had been generously loaned by their owners as a gesture of compliment and homage to Shakespeare.

Alongside exhibits from the Trust's collection, the following special items were displayed:

The Bishop of Worcester's Register, which records the issue of a marriage licence on 27 November 1582 between 'Wm Shaxpere et Anna Whateley de Temple Grafton'.
Worcestershire Record Office

Shakespeare's Marriage Bond, 28 November 1582.
Worcestershire Record Office

King Charles I's own copy of *Mr William Shakespeares comedies, histories, and tragedies ... 1632.* HM The Queen

The History of Henry the fourth ... With the humorous Conceites of Sir John Falstaffe. Newly corrected by W. Shake-speare 1608. *The Bodleian Library*

Foot of Fine for New Place, 1597, recording the conveyance of New Place to Shakespeare.
The Public Record Office

The Register of the Stationers' Company, showing the transfer of copyright of four of Shakespeare's plays: '6 a booke called Hamlett' '9 The taming of A Shrewe', '10 Romeo and Julett' '11 Loves Labour Lost'.
The Stationers' Company of London

The 'Diary' of Philip Henslowe (d.1616), the theatre manager, which records the companies that played at his theatre (presumably the Rose), the names of the plays, and the takings.
The Governors of Dulwich College

Queen Elizabeth I's polyglot *New Testament* (Greek, Latin and Synac), published by John Immanuel Tremellurs at Geneva in 1569. It was dedicated to Queen Elizabeth. This is the Queen's own copy.
Lord Leigh of Stoneleigh

Pleasure reconcild to Vertue, by Ben Jonson, 1617-18, together with MS copy of this masque and two drawings by Inigo Jones. *The Duke of Devonshire*

The following items from the collections at the Shakespeare Centre were also included:

Original letter from Richard Quyney addressed to his 'Loveinge good Frend and contreyman mr. Wm. Shackespere', 1598.

Articles of agreement made by Willm. Shackespeare of Stretford in the County of Warwicke, gent. concerning his Welcombe estates, 1614.

'The Accompte of m^r Robert Salusburye and John Sadler, Chamberlens, for the year 1568-69.' This covers the period during which John Shakespeare served as Bailiff of Stratford-upon-Avon, and records payments made by the Corporation for the first time to actors visiting the town and performing in the Guildhall.

'The noate of corne and malte', an inventory of stocks of corn and malt in the borough early in 1598. It shows Shakespeare to have owned the substantial quantity of ten quarters or eighty bushels of corn and malt.

Nicholas Rowe's edition of Shakespeare's plays, the first critical and illustrated one to appear, published in six octavo volumes in 1709.

During the second half of the summer an exhibition on the theme of 'Shakespeare in Translation' was presented at the Shakespeare Centre. The purpose of this was to illustrate the international interest in Shakespeare and at the same time to call attention to the collection of translations in the Centre library built up by the Trust over the years. Out of a total of some seventy languages, space available made possible the display of only about half that number, in each case the earliest translation being shown.

It is interesting to note that many of the versions of Shakespeare's plays in oriental languages – particularly the early ones – were adaptations rather than translations, especially when intended for representation on the stage. Characters and settings were occasionally changed to suit the countries concerned, passages were omitted, and new scenes and songs introduced.

The Shakespearian Properties

With regard to the Shakespearian properties, all necessary repairs and outstanding items of maintenance were completed in time for the anniversary year, in order that visitors might see the houses, and their gardens, to the best possible advantage. The timber framing of Shakespeare's Birthplace had been carefully overhauled and treated, and its dark, dust-coated panels cleaned to give them a softer appearance. The layout of the Birthplace garden alongside the new building had been redesigned and flower beds planted. Anne Hathaway's Cottage had received similar attention, and its thatched roof repaired. Paths in the garden had been relaid and fencing renewed, and other improvements had been made in the vicinity of the Cottage, including the re-surfacing of the car park. All the properties had been redecorated inside and generally refurbished.

The Trustees had decided that emphasis should be placed on the ever-increasing appreciation of Shakespeare, and that every opportunity should be taken to promote interest in Shakespeare's plays and the background of his life, work and times, at all levels. At the Birthplace an improved display of pictorial and documentary exhibits on the ground floor illustrated the background of Shakespeare's Warwickshire and Stratford and, in particular, the evidence concerning the history and associations of the property itself; and on the upper floor a tabloid exhibition introduced the visitor to the main facets of Shakespeare's life, career, work and influence.

Festival Events

Hall's Croft was also used as the setting for special Festival activities. Between April and June the exhibition room on the first floor was used to display an exhibition of nineteenth-century theatrical designs by members of the Grieves family, selected and arranged by John Carroll. There followed an exhibition of 'Shakespeare and his Contemporaries', comprising rare books illustrating the works of Elizabethan and Jacobean writers, which was planned to run concurrently with the Poetry Festival. Directed by Patrick Garland with the assistance of Richard Marquand, the 1964 Stratford-upon-Avon Poetry Festival was the most ambitious staged by the Trust since this annual event started in 1954. Readings were given on Sunday evenings in the Town Hall, Hall's Croft and the Royal Shakespeare Theatre during July and August. Roy Fuller was the 'Poet of the Year' and those taking part included Judi Dench, Fenella Fielding, Barbara Kelly, Diana Rigg, Bernard Braden, Paul Hardwick, Alec McCowen, Clive Swift and Patrick Wymark. The Arts Council of Great Britain lent support to the Poetry Festival and, with its help, poems were specially commissioned to commemorate the Shakespeare anniversary. These were included in the opening recital, and subsequently published as *Fifteen Poems for Shakespeare*.

Closely linked with the Poetry Festival, music played a prominent part in the anniversary year's commemorative events. Against the background of the Theatre's productions of the Shakespeare history plays, the Shakespeare Exhibition, lectures and academic activities, leading musicians came to

Chamber music concert in the library at Charlecote Park

Stratford-upon-Avon to render their tribute to Shakespeare in a series of concerts and recitals. Although the responsibility for organizing these lay with the Shakespeare Anniversary Council, the Birthplace Trust played an active part in providing practical support, and it was due to the success of these musical events that the Trustees subsequently embarked on a policy of arranging a programme of music, including chamber music concerts at Charlecote Park, each summer.

Publications

The Trustees also supported a number of publication projects. In association with the publishing firm of Jarrold and Sons, Ltd, of Norwich, concise illustrated booklet guides, for which I was responsible, were produced for each Shakespearian property, together with a general guide to the town. The Trustees also sponsored *The 1964 Shakespeare Anniversary Book*, an illustrated account of Shakespeare's life and work, together with the background history of Stratford's festivals. A copy of this publication was distributed as a free commemorative souvenir to all children attending schools in the town.

Another publication sponsored by the Trust was *Celebrating Shakespeare*, produced the following year as a comprehensive, illustrated record of the part played by Stratford-upon-Avon in commemorating Shakespeare's 400th anniversary. Unfortunately, it took much longer to complete a larger commemorative book, that I had planned for issue in 1964; it was not until 1972 that *In Honour of Shakespeare: the History and Collections of the Shakespeare Birthplace Trust* was published. One reason for the delay was the fact that I was devoting much of my leisure at this time to the writing of a history of my old grammar school at Ashby-de-la-Zouch, which was planning to celebrate on 10 August 1967 the 400th anniversary of its foundation. Right back to my undergraduate days I had been collecting material for a history of the school, and the Governors' invitation to me to finalize the work for publication on the anniversary date was too tempting for me not to accept. The result was *A Country Grammar School: A History of Ashby-de-la-Zouch Grammar School through Four Centuries: 1567 to 1967*, produced by the Oxford University Press.

Commemorative Items

Apart from its Festival activities, the Shakespeare Anniversary year will be recalled by the great variety of commemorative souvenir items produced to mark the occasion. As Director, I was much involved in offering advice and help as specially bound editions of the plays, books both scholarly and popular, commemorative issues of periodical literature, first day covers and press features appeared in profusion. Following the tradition of previous Stratford festivals, the Birthplace Trust struck a Shakespeare

The 1964 Shakespeare commemorative medal

The 1964 Shakespeare Commemorative items

medal, designed by the eminent medallic artist, Paul Vincze, which was produced in platinum, gold, silver and bronze; there was also a silk woven bookmark, made by the Coventry firm of J. and J. Cash, Ltd, which had produced similar items for the tercentenary celebrations in 1864. New fabrics inspired by Shakespeare and the Warwickshire countryside and designed by Tibor Reich, some for use in the new Centre, were sponsored by the Trust, which also undertook the sale and distribution of the official gift items approved by the Shakespeare Anniversary Council. For this purpose a Festival shop was equipped and opened in the former Coach and Horses Inn, situated opposite to the Birthplace, which the Directors of Flower and Son, Ltd, the local brewery, had made available for use as the Festival Office. The china and glass decorative pieces manufactured by the firms of Wedgwood, Royal Doulton and Webb's English Crystal in limited issues quickly sold and established themselves as collectors' items.

Shakespeare Postage Stamps

It was, however, the special issue of Shakespeare postage stamps by the British Post Office that received the widest publicity and commendation all over the world, together with the production of an official first day cover for use with them and franked with Stratford's own postmark for the anniversary year. The Birthplace Trust can claim credit for the Shakespeare stamps, and the story of how they were achieved is worth telling.

I first wrote to the Postmaster General on 14 September 1961, asking him to consider the issue of special postage stamps during the Shakespeare anniversary year, but I quickly received a negative, uninterested response. The reply, dated 2 October, stated that the Post Office had 'never issued stamps to commemorate the birth, death or achievements of individuals, however distinguished or admired'; and because of this traditional policy it would not be possible to show on postage stamps the picture of any other person, however illustrious, alongside that of the Queen. Another reason stated was that if a precedent were set, it would be impossible for the Post Office to turn down similar requests.

The Trustees and the Anniversary Council felt with me that this was not an acceptable decision, so during December 1961 I began to enlist help from many sources to reinforce the request for re-consideration, which I sent this time to the Director-General of the Post Office. I pointed out that in our opinion Shakespeare was in a class by himself; he was our national poet and dramatist, a unique institution, admired and respected all over the world; and that, with other countries already planning special stamp issues in Shakespeare's honour, it was a matter of national prestige that the British Post Office should depart from its traditional policy in this instance. These representations produced an acknowledgment to the effect that the matter would be looked into, so I realized that the door was at least open.

During the weeks that followed, I organized a campaign of support with the object of convincing the Postmaster General that Shakespeare really was a special case. Approaches were made to bodies such as the British Council, the Arts Council of Great Britain and the Royal Society of St George; to Commonwealth High Commissioners and to the Colonial Office; to national bodies such as the British Philatelic Society, the Philatelic Traders Society and the British Centre of the International Theatre Institute; and to the Stratford Chamber of Trade and other local groups. All sent in their representations urging the issue of special stamps. Additionally, the support of distinguished public figures such as Lord Avon, Viscount Radcliffe and the Member of Parliament for Stratford-upon-Avon, John Profumo, gave their support; Mr Profumo in fact took the trouble to see the Postmaster General personally, to advocate serious favourable consideration of the matter. The result was that, as Director of the Shakespeare Anniversary Council, I was asked by the Post Office to supply further information and reports on the progress of preparations for the 1964 celebrations.

Official first day cover with Shakespeare postage stamps, 23 April 1964

It was a long, hard battle, but in retrospect I think the turning point came when I persuaded a senior officer of the Postal Services Department to visit Stratford on 4 December 1962, to discuss the matter on the spot. Not only was I able to describe to him the provisional programme for the Festival and to emphasize its international significance; I was able to show him the structure of the new Shakespeare Centre rising from its foundations. Nevertheless, more than a further year passed without any indication of likely success. During the early part of 1963 I made repeated enquiries of the Post Office and fed in more evidence to support our request. Finally, and as a last throw, as it were, I arranged for the matter to be raised at question time in the House of Commons, in April 1963. This elicited the news that a favourable decision had in fact just been made and, already briefed, the Postmaster General announced in reply to the House that 'a wide variety of commemorative festivals and exhibitions in this country' were being arranged to mark the 400th anniversary of the birth of Shakespeare and that, taken together, they would constitute 'an outstanding event fully warranting a special stamp issue'. This decision was communicated to me, as Director of the Festival, on 26 April 1963.

It took the rest of the year for the Post Office to make the necessary detailed decisions and preparations, and in choosing the designs submitted by invited artists the Postmaster General had the assistance of an Advisory Committee set up by the Council of Industrial Design. A press and broadcast notice giving full information on the special issue of 'Dramatic Stamps on a Theatrical Theme' was released on 10 February 1964. For the first time in the history of the British postage stamp, another head (that of Shakespeare) was to appear alongside that of the monarch.

The stamps were designed by David Gentleman, a free lance artist who had already done work for the Post Office. Using a technique of wood engravings for the figures, the stamps were produced by a photogravure process. With their vivid colours on sombre backgrounds, the artist portrayed the velvety darkness of a stage set against the white background of an envelope with the Shakespearian characters spotlighted. The 3d. stamp, with its violet background and grey characters, featured Puck and Bottom in his ass's head; the 6d. stamp, in olive green and with character in orange and yellow, portrayed Feste the clown; on the 1s. 3d. stamp, grey-brown with characters in turquoise and deep pink, the star-crossed lovers Romeo and Juliet appeared in the famous balcony scene; Henry V, praying in his tent on the eve of the Battle of Agincourt, was featured in pale purple against a deep blue background. A 2s. 6d. stamp, in light brown colour, incorporating a vignette of Hamlet contemplating the skull of Yorick, was designed by two brothers, Robin and Christopher Ironside. David Gentleman also designed a Post Office first day cover envelope. These postage stamps, accompanied by new facilities for servicing first day covers and special philatelic posting arrangements in the principal towns of the country, proved to be a prodigious success, attracting a world-wide demand and earning the Post Office extremely rewarding business. At the beginning of December 1964 it was reported that, to date, about 195 million single stamps of the Festival issue had been sold; that only residual stocks were left; and that these would be completely cleared shortly. A successful precedent having thus been set, the issue of special stamps to commemorate national figures and events subsequently became a regular feature of Post Office activity.

World Homage

Meanwhile, the whole world prepared to rise up in homage to Britain's national poet and, by the time the anniversary came, Shakespeare was celebrated in a great variety of ways in many countries. Commemorative medals, stamps, translations, learned and popular publications, together with many kinds of souvenir items, were produced in considerable quantity. Specimens of many of these were sent as presents to the Birthplace Trust and a constant stream of messages of greetings and tributes were received, some addressed to William Shakespeare himself. Taken together, they constituted a unique testimony to the universal esteem in which the dramatist of Stratford-upon-Avon was held throughout the world.

From the Soviet Union there came tributes from scholars and actors, but particularly interesting were those from a number of schools in different states where English was being taught and Shakespeare studied. It was illuminating to hear that exhibitions and recitals were being arranged and scenes from Shakespeare's plays performed by Russian children. One school in the Ukraine forwarded a verse composition, accompanied by a translation, in honour of Shakespeare, and described plans to produce excerpts from *Hamlet* and *Romeo and Juliet*. At one of these schools the teacher was clearly a Shakespeare enthusiast, as well as an accomplished linguist, and she had organized an international friendship group amongst her pupils. Beginning with the exchange of greetings initiated in 1964, I subsequently kept in touch with her, and continued right down to the present time to exchange letters and literature with her. By name Ellena Romanchuk, she worked hard over the years, through her teaching of English and her love of Shakespeare, to foster friendship and understanding between our two countries. Her burning ambition was to visit Stratford, and for a long time she tried to get permission to travel, but without success. It was only after the break-up of the Soviet Union in 1990 that she obtained a visa to come to visit Shakespeare's Birthplace and the Royal Shakespeare Theatre. When she came to see me, the meeting was very emotional; had she been given the crown jewels she could not have been more appreciative and excited!

Many greetings and tributes came in the form of verse, and one or two were set to music. Shakespeare lovers in India, Pakistan, Brazil and South Africa, to mention only four countries, sent verse compositions, in some instances with requests that they should be published. Shakespeare medals were sent from Argentina, Canada, Czechoslovakia, India, Italy, Portugal and the United States. Not surprisingly, American Shakespeare societies, festivals, schools and individual Shakespeare lovers were well represented, but equally so the European countries, particularly Germany, France and Spain. Letters were also received from Japan, China, Israel, Cyprus, Poland, Bulgaria, Belgium, Australia and New Zealand, taken as a random selection from a very big collection.

There were, of course, some oddities. One writer from Rhode Island in the United States ventured to 'put the cream on his greatest play' by sending an article on the subject of the missing scene in *King Lear*. An Indian admirer excelled himself by producing an extraordinary, illuminated scroll containing a verse tribute written on cartridge paper, covered with blue silk, 'as a wrapper of his coffin', so ran his accompanying description, 'and appearance of glittering stars with two white bright planets marked in one of them 1564 and on the other 1964 and a monogram of the poet's name thereon'; a present to Shakespeare which until the time it was posted had been kept 'sacred and secret, untouched'. Another self-styled poet, an English visitor who had spent three days in Stratford over the period of the birthday celebrations, was so moved that she went into the Public Library near to the Birthplace and in the space of forty minutes penned an amazing verse composition on the interpretation of Shakespeare.

Invariably those who sent greetings were keen to receive information about Shakespeare and Stratford's Festival programme, so that in every case a two-way channel of communication was established, resulting in a kind of international network of Shakespeare lovers, societies and institutions, the fore-runner of the International Shakespeare Association, formed some years later. The following letter, addressed to the Chairman of the Shakespeare Birthplace Trust from the Head of the English Department at the Malayan Teachers College in Penang, may be given as an illustration of the kind of contact that was established:

The cast of *Julius Caesar* and the English Department of this College, through which the play was performed on the 14th and 15th April thank the Birthplace Trust most warmly for the honour which it has done them. The Shakespeare medallion, which we have received, has given us great pleasure. It is being mounted on perspex in a case with a mirror behind it to reflect the obverse and will be fixed on its own support against a wall in the Library of the College.

The performance of the play meant a great deal to the students, children and adults of Penang. It was done in our open-air theatre and as a spectacle was lovely. The actors were Chinese, Malay and Indian and they made the play their own. Cassius was excellent and Antony very good; the crowd was magnificent, better our producer said than an English crowd could have been, because so uninhibited. On behalf of the students and all who helped, I am most grateful for your recognition of their big effort.

As Director of the Festival, I personally found the whole experience extremely exhilarating and rewarding, though I must confess the pressure of organizing and supervising all the arrangements weighed heavily on me. Fortunately I had excellent secretarial assistants in the persons of Shirley Watkins and Jennifer Gibbs, and enthusiastic service from the temporary staff recruited for various duties in the Festival Office. At all times Laurence Williams, the Trust's architect, with whom I had almost daily contact, was a great pillar of strength with regard to practical requirements. Throughout, the Trustees were most supportive, as were all the members of the Trust's staff, working in their different capacities. I must also place on record the encouragement and support I received from my wife and family. My young son Roger, in particular, gave invaluable practical help in many ways and was frequently involved in the detailed arrangements for events. There was a wonderful team spirit and pride in what was being achieved, and every day brought fresh evidence of goodwill and keenness to be associated with the celebrations.

Presentation by delegates of the Calcutta Arts Society

Special Presentations

There were other memorable happenings. The first was a magnificent gesture of goodwill by the Trustees and Director of the Folger Shakespeare Library in Washington, DC, when they presented to the Birthplace Trustees the earliest visitors' books of Shakespeare's Birthplace and Holy Trinity Church, which had been bought by the founder of the Library, Henry Clay Folger, in the early years of this century. I happen to know that it was Dr Louis B. Wright, the Director with whom I had formed a close friendship, who was responsible for arranging the donation of these valuable and interesting records. I think this came about because, as already mentioned, on the occasion of my visit to the Folger some years before I had cast envious eyes on these visitors' books and made meaningful remarks about them, when I had been shown them in the bookstack vault of the Library.

The Trustees had always regretted the absence from their collection of the early visitors' books, covering the period 1821-47, which had passed into other hands at the sale of Shakespeare's Birthplace in 1847. When they came into the market again, nearly fifty years later, the Trustees were unsuccessful in obtaining them. There were, of course, visitors' books at the Birthplace long before these, but little was known of their whereabouts in succeeding years. The earliest-known surviving register of this kind is one dated 1812-19, which also formed part of the Folger Trustees' munificent gift. It was appropriate that the first two visitors signing the register in 1812 were Americans, from Baltimore and Boston.

Still other volumes included in the gift from the Folger Trustees were two inscribed 'Tribute of respect to the Bard of Avon, the immortal Shakespeare', covering the period 1819-89, and two inscribed 'Names of the Visitors to the Tomb of Shakespeare', dated 1844-60. These are rather more mysterious, as they overlap other series, but the keeping of visitors' books was evidently an established practice in nineteenth-century Stratford and in some cases, it seems, more than one series was kept, perhaps intermittently, in one building. The last-named series was, as vouched by a note at the end, 'collected at the tomb of Shakespeare by Mr Thomas Kite, parish clerk of Stratford-upon-Avon', and linked up with a series of Church Albums already in the Trust's possession.

Many famous and well-known names find a place in the various visitors' books which made up this remarkable gift. In the first, for 1812-19, is a record (but not the autograph) of an earlier visit by the Prince Regent on 6 September 1806. Visitors who signed the book included Dr Arnold, the future Headmaster of Rugby, Washington Irving, the Duke of Clarence (later King William IV) and the Duke of Wellington (the last two on 26 August 1815). A considerable amount of verse was added, some of which was reproduced in Mary Hornby's pamphlet, *Extemporary verses written at the Birth Place of Shakespeare by persons of genius ...*, which seems to have run through five editions between 1817 and 1820. Prominent visitors who signed in the 1821-47 book included Sir Walter Scott, Charles Dickens, Edmund Kean and Richard Cobden. The intermediate volumes, of 1819-89, carry the signatures of Mrs David Garrick, Charles Kean and H.W. Longfellow; while those who paid their tribute at Shakespeare's tomb during the period 1844-60 included Wilkie Collins, Herbert Spencer, J.R. Lowell, Delia Bacon, Helen Faucit Martin, Nathaniel Hawthorne and Victor Hugo.

Another presentation of a different kind took place on 11 October 1964, when a delegation from the Calcutta Arts Society, accompanied by diplomatic representatives from the Indian High Commission, made a special visit to the Shakespeare Centre. With impressive ceremony and the recitation of speeches, songs and prayers, the leader made a presentation to the Chairman of the Trust of an ivory plaque on which was carved the text of a poem in praise of Shakespeare composed by the great Indian poet, Rabindranath Tagore. During the course of the proceedings the leader swung a censer, presumably containing sacred oil, to the accompaniment of his recitation, and by mischance spots of the oil fell on Sir Fordham Flower's suit. Nothing daunted, he made a most appropriate response to this unusual tribute to Shakespeare.

American Celebrations

An outstanding event of the anniversary year was the visit of representatives of the Trust to the United States, to take part in the celebrations arranged by the American 1964 Shakespeare Committee. During 1962 and 1963 I had regular contact with Mr Eugene Black, the Chairman of the Committee set up to organize official celebrations in America, and, as already mentioned, plans were well advanced when President Kennedy was assassinated. A temporary postponement of the celebrations understandably resulted, and it was not until the weekend of 20 to 22 June 1964 that the programme of events took place. Sir Fordham and Lady Flower, Mrs T.N. Waldron (a former Alderman and Mayor of Stratford), Mr Laurence Williams, the Trust's architect, with Mrs Williams, and myself as Director were invited as guests to represent Stratford at the celebrations, together with certain literary and theatrical personalities.

A special circumstance, however, made it necessary for me to travel to the United States on 6 June, in advance of the others, the reason being that I had been invited by the President and Trustees of the George Washington University in Washington, DC, to attend their annual Commencement to receive an honorary degree. This took place on Sunday evening, 7 June, when the President conferred on me the degree of Doctor of Humane Letters, in recognition of my services to Shakespeare.

It was a memorable day. Starting with a lunch reception where I met other distinguished guests, including General and Mrs Dwight D. Eisenhower, we then attended the Baccalaureate service in Washington Cathedral, walking in ceremonial procession, clad in cap and gown, and occupying preferential seats in the choir stalls. I was much impressed by the Cathedral, a magnificent modern Gothic building, erected in stages over a period of some fifty years. The Gloria in Excelsis Tower had just been completed. The Cathedral was filled to capacity with friends of the University, parents and students, and the service, with its ceremony and music, was conducted with dignity and to the obvious enjoyment of the congregation. It was a very moving experience.

After a short rest during the afternoon, I was then taken to a reception and supper given by the President of the University at his residence. There were a number of distinguished persons present, in addition to the honorary graduands, and it was at this point that I found myself talking to General Eisenhower and his wife, both of whom were friendly and unassuming. It transpired that the General himself and three eminent academics were to receive honorary degrees, in addition to myself.

The Commencement ceremony which followed took place out of doors in the University Yard in the presence of a very large company, which included all the young people waiting to receive their degrees. Following the entry of the academic procession, in which we all appeared in caps and gowns, the University Marshall formally announced the Commencement, the National Anthem was sung, and an Invocation spoken by the Director of University Chapel. Alumni Achievement Awards were presented by the President of the Alumni Association, and the President of the University conferred Emeritus status on four recently retired Professors.

Each of the five candidates for honorary degrees was then presented in turn and a citation given about him. I was seated next to General Eisenhower and came fourth; Philip Henry Highfill, Jr., Professor of English Literature, was responsible for submitting my credentials. The wording of his submission had a typically American flavour about it. After summarizing my career, he referred to the 'strategic role' I was playing 'in the restoration and preservation of his (Shakespeare's) birthplace and the monuments, both literary and physical', which enabled 'coming generations continually to appreciate his greatness'. He then described the various offices I held and assured the company that in the performance of them I had 'combined energetic, executive talent with the professional abilities of archivist, archaeologist, palaeographer, horticulturalist, and historian, both literary and social'. All this and more, about 'devoted achievements in the preservation of historical facts and artifacts', and 'productive assistance to scholars and to the public in attaining a profounder understanding of Shakespeare and the Shakespeare period'.

The President of the University conferred the appropriate honorary degree by placing on the candidate a hood, the colour of which denoted the academic field of the institution granting the degree, and then by presenting to him a diploma bearing the seal of the University and recording the citation. Each of the recipient honorary graduates acknowledged the honour and addressed the company. In my case this provided a unique opportunity for me to talk briefly about the significance of the Shakespeare quatercentenary. Then followed the conferment of degrees in course by the President to the very large number of students in the various categories. The whole proceedings lasted nearly three hours. Afterwards we enjoyed American hospitality at its best.

The few days that followed provided some welcome relaxation and interesting activity. I was able to renew my acquaintance with Dr Louis B. Wright, the Director, and the staff of the Folger Shakespeare Library, and to do a little investigation and research there. I recall it was on this occasion, when I consulted the library catalogue there, that I came across the original account book for Compton Verney for 1562-64, complete with the Verney family bookplate. The quiet, relaxed atmosphere of the Library, the friendly helpfulness of the staff and the opportunity to meet other scholars working there made my short stay most enjoyable. There was an excellent exhibition of Folger rarities on display to mark the quatercentenary, and I myself gave a lecture in the Elizabethan theatre to a capacity audience. I was also able to visit the Shakespeare exhibition in the Library of Congress, to talk to the University Womens Club, to attend a meeting of the Washington Rotary Club, and to spend a little time visiting the National Gallery of Art and the Smithsonian Museum of History and Technology.

I was also invited to attend the 400th Shakespeare anniversary celebrations arranged for members of the United Nations at the Shakespeare Festival Theatre at Stratford, Connecticut, on Saturday, 13 June. Diplomatic representatives of overseas countries belonging to the United Nations, together with a company of other distinguished guests, attended a special performance of *Much Ado About Nothing*, preceded by a reception and buffet supper which took place in the open air, outside the Theatre, in a temperature a little below 100 degrees Fahrenheit. I remember the occasion very well, because I was told by one of those present, who had already seen the Queen's Birthday Honours list, that I had been awarded the O.B.E. Sir Fordham Flower, who was also present with Lady Flower, congratulated me, but expressed disappointment that my work for the quatercentenary celebrations had not been recognized by a higher award. The same sentiment was echoed in many of the letters of congratulations I found waiting for me on my return home.

The Shakespeare Festival Theatre at Stratford, Connecticut, was also the setting for the opening events of the official programme of Shakespeare anniversary celebrations arranged by the American 1964 Shakespeare Committee, presided over by Mr Eugene Black. On Saturday morning, 20 June, a large, distinguished company of guests, including myself and the representatives of the Birthplace Trust, arrived at the Stratford Motor Inn, a pleasant motel-type of hotel situated a few miles away from the Festival Theatre. This was a timber-built structure, modelled to some extent on the old Globe Playhouse, which had been erected in 1955, largely due to the enthusiasm of Lawrence Langner, who was well known for his pioneering theatrical work with the Washington Square Players, and with the support of Eugene Black and Joseph Verner Reed. In the early afternoon we attended a gala performance of *Hamlet*, given by the Festival Theatre's own company.

Returning to the Stratford Motor Inn, we were then entertained to cocktails, followed by an anniversary dinner in the Mermaid Tavern. The setting and the arrangements were admirable, and the company of nearly two hundred guests enjoyed an ample, traditional menu, the main course of which was 'the heart of the prime rib of beef' and Yorkshire pudding, with fresh asparagus and salad. Suitably chosen 'Shakespeare' wines and claret enlivened the proceedings and, for those who wished to smoke, 'Shakespeare' cigars were offered with the coffee. After the briefest respite, we returned to the Festival Theatre for the anniversary performance of *Much Ado About Nothing*. There was then an opportunity for us to meet the actors and to inspect the Theatre generally, and, particularly, to view the collection of works of art relating to Shakespeare's plays and their performance, displayed in the corridors, lounge and lobby of the Theatre. These comprised original paintings, water-colours, drawings, sculpture, playbills and books acquired by purchase, gift or loan, representing a selection of Shakespearian memorabilia which, it was hoped, would eventually be displayed in a gallery to be built as an annexe to the Theatre. Among the exhibits, I admired the Chesterfield portrait of Shakespeare, so called because it had formed the centre piece of paintings of literary figures in the library of the Earl of Chesterfield in the eighteenth century. Whether consciously or not, I obviously gave the impression that I was sorry that a portrait of such interest had not found its way to Stratford-upon-Avon. Imagine my surprise and delight, therefore, when at a later

The Chesterfield portrait of Shakespeare

date this picture was sent back across the Atlantic as a present to the Shakespeare Birthplace Trust, thanks to the generosity of Lincoln Kirstein, the owner. I made sure that it was hung in a position of honour in the upstairs foyer of the Shakespeare Centre, just outside the conference room.

Early next morning, Sunday, 21 June, we were conveyed by coach and then by air from La Guardia Airport in New York to Washington, DC, for the next event of the programme. This took place at the Folger Shakespeare Library, where, in the early evening, upwards of 250 guests were invited to 'A Midsomer Nightes Feaste holden at the Manor of

Henrie Folger', to 'do honour to the Poet of Stratford, William Shakespere, he beynge in his foure hundreth yeare and muche Spoken of in all landes so that Halfe the Worlde do quote his Wordes to his Honour and Everywhere Men do marvel at His Grete Fame'. Guests were received by the Trustees and Director of the Folger Library 'where one maye lerne and yet withal be merie', each receiving a printed welcome, as follows:

It beinge a Custome of old to name a Lorde of Misrule to be of Use and Helpe in Feastes, we have this daie appointed Giles E. Dawson to this Offyce that He maye give suche Directions as may be of Comfort and Help to Oure Guests.

Because of the grete Presse of Numbers and the Scarcitie of Comely and Able Serving Men and Maids, It hath beene Necessarie to Have Each Guest Serve himself for the Maine Course as the Lorde of Misrule will Signifie. It Hath ever been a Mark of Honour to have Noble Guests choose for themselves that Which they woulde Eate.

The reading room of the Library, hitherto used only for study and research, made a perfect setting for this historic event. The room itself had the appearance of a Tudor hall, with timber-clad walls and shelves, and with a replica of the Shakespeare bust in Holy Trinity Church looking down from above the entrance, flanked with classical columns; and the furnishings had been rearranged to make possible table-settings for a very special feast. Table ware, drinking vessels and cutlery reproduced Elizabethan patterns, and serving men and maids in period costume added a realistic touch, as course after course, accompanied by appropriate beverages, was served.

Because of the historic nature of the event, the menu of the feast is reproduced as follows:

Man shal not live by books alone nor spende all his houres in studie lest he growe peevish and sour of countenance. It is not fitte nor mete that lernynge shoulde beget dumpishnesse nor spleene nor unkinde thoughtes nor solemn faces. The acquaintance of bookes of ancient authores, full of good lernynge shoulde make us of a cherful disposition and tolerant spirit and lead us to believe that man is not as Grass which springeth up Today and soon Withereth awaye, but the rather to knowe that we are here to Make the most of this Worlde wherin we Finde Ourselves and not to Repine nor find Faulte with Godes handiwork. It seemeth good from tyme to tyme to be merie and to feaste, to remember our friendes, and to honour such great ones as be a credit to humankinde, which God knoweth needeth examples of greatness set before it. Wherfore, this being Midsomers Night, and a season given to mirthe since heathen tymes, We do think it wel to call to minds the spirit of good cheer bequeathed to us by that great poet and player William Shakespere, who was ever mindful that feasting and laughter purgeth melancholike humours to the behoof bothe of us and our fellows that must endure us. Let us therefore eat and be merie and thinke upon the gude things that life doth offer.

An atmosphere of festival and celebration pervaded the whole proceedings, as guests were served cocktails in the Elizabethan style by costumed waiters. Each then received instructions as follows:

FIRST, FOR THE TEMPTING OF THE APPETITE

There be pickled mushrooms, black olives soaked in oil, eggs boiled and pickled, cowcumbers-in-little, red beets, and other mishmash stuff which the skimble-skamble French do call *hors d'oeuves*.

SECOND, THE MAINE COURSE

Guests Maie Take Their Trenchers to the Serving Board to Pick out that whiche they would Eate. Being of Charitable mindes, they will scrape any broken Meates and trifling stuff into the Great Dishe kept for the Poore and Those that be in the Manor Gaol. Let Our Guests helpe themselves bountifully and be Mindful not to Stumble in the Carrying of their Trenchers. We beg that Ye throw no bones under the Table. Forks being newfangled and unhandy things, ye must not stick thy eye nor thy neighbor therewith.

The Victuals for this Course:

Salmon boiled gently and served with dressing of Cowcumbers in Canary wine

Roaste of Beef
Capon roasted after ye Parson's receipt
Young Pigg roasted on the fire
Some stuffe called after the new manner, Spinashe
Midsumers Sallet, made with God knowes what
odd stuff found hereabouts
Pye of Artichoke
Lobster dressed in a pye
Sallet of Green Leaves dressed with oil
Manchets, being the best white bread and Brown Meal Bread

THIRD, SWEETMEATES AND SUCH TRIFLES

The serving Men and Maides will take away the Guests trenchers and bring on such Sweetmeates as May be had.

Syllabubs in Rastons, they being a sort of cake, not so big as to fatten a mouse
Marche panes   Comfits   Suckets

That ye maie Not be Athirst, there be Wine of France and good English Ale as ye maie wish, served unto you as ye eate.

A newe drinke in fashion amongst the heathen Turkes, called after their manner, *coffee*, maie be had after the feaste, on the battlements of the Manor House.

Tobacco pipes and snuff, good to clear the head of rheums, are at hand upon the tables. The pipe stem dipped in wine helpeth the taste and maketh it easie on the lip.

I have a vivid recollection that the meal did more than justice to the occasion. For months afterwards, Mrs Waldron, who was one of the Birthplace Trust guests, could not cease talking about the size of the steak laid on the platter before her! Speeches were naturally an integral part of the proceedings. Dr Louis B. Wright, the Director of the Folger Library, spoke of the significance of the anniversary and the contribution Shakespeare had made to world civilization, to the unique attraction of Stratford-upon-Avon as a place of literary pilgrimage, and to the work of the Birthplace Trust and the Royal Shakespeare Theatre in furthering appreciation of Shakespeare. In very complimentary terms he voiced the gratitude of Shakespeare lovers all over the world to those responsible for planning the Shakespeare Anniversary Festival at Stratford-upon-Avon and to myself, as Director, for overseeing the whole operation. Sir Fordham Flower responded, mentioning the close ties which Shakespeare had forged between the New World and the mother country and complimenting America on its programme of celebrations. Altogether, it was a memorable occasion. Falstaff would certainly have approved!

On the next morning, Monday, 22 June, we were collected from our hotels and conveyed to the pier, where we embarked on a boat, the 'Diplomat', which took us down the Potomac River to Mount Vernon. In view of the hot weather, guests had been advised to wear sports clothes and to prepare themselves with sunglasses, shade hats and tan lotion. It was a leisurely, comfortable cruise, and a buffet luncheon was served as the boat proceeded slowly down the river. Having debarked at Mount Vernon, we were escorted on a guided tour of the famed house of George Washington and we had ample opportunity to view the surrounding grounds. Because of my responsibilities as custodian of Shakespeare's Birthplace, I was particularly interested to see how the Americans preserved and presented their national memorial.

After a relaxing return cruise to Washington, DC, guests prepared for the final event on the official programme of celebrations, namely, a reception at the White House at the invitation of President and Mrs Lyndon B. Johnson. This turned out to be a historic occasion, because Shakespeare was performed in the White House for the first time. As a preliminary to guests being received by the President and Mrs Johnson, a group of actors from the Festival Company at Stratford, Connecticut, gave a performance of scenes from Shakespeare's plays in the East Room, much to the delight of all present. The President and the First Lady visibly enjoyed the performance, and afterwards received the members of the Shakespeare Anniversary Committee and their guests. There was an atmosphere of informality and friendship, and those present were able to move freely and to enjoy the hospitality provided. It was at

Presentation of Shakespeare medals to President Johnson

this juncture that Sir Fordham Flower, accompanied by Lady Flower and myself, engaged the President and Mrs Johnson in conversation and made a presentation to them of a case containing a numbered set of the official 1964 Shakespeare Anniversary medals, by Paul Vincze, in platinum, gold, fine silver and bronze. This gesture came as a surprise to them, and attracted much interest and attention from the photographers present. After our return home the President wrote to Sir Fordham, sending coloured photographs of the presentation autographed with his best wishes and a message of appreciation from his wife, Ladybird Johnson, 'for the commemorative coins that will happily recall our 'Shakespeare Day'. Sir Fordham kindly passed on one of these photographs to me, a souvenir of a unique event which I treasure.

The White House reception over, the official celebrations were finished, but for a few special guests Eugene Black had another surprise in store. We were invited to dinner at the Alibi Club, situated quite near to the White House, which we were led to believe was America's most exclusive club, with a very small membership restricted to a handful of the country's leading business and public men. The club room was comfortably furnished and adorned with works of art and other embellishments which past members had presented, and the attraction of the setting was equalled only by the hospitality to which we were entertained and the friendship of all those present. A very special meal had been prepared in our honour, and Eugene Black, clearly pleased with the success of the programme of celebrations, was the perfect host.

There remained for me, personally, one further special occasion before I returned home. Leaving Washington, DC, I proceeded to New York, where, after a day or two spent visiting the sights and museums, I was the guest of honour at a luncheon arranged by the University of New York on Thursday, 25 June, followed by a ceremony at which President James M. Hester of the University conferred on me the New York University Medal, an award reserved for especially distinguished visitors. A circular bronze medallion, it was suspended from a chain and bore on its face the New York University's seal; on the reverse side was a reproduction of the Hall of Fame for Great Americans, situated on the Bronx campus, and my name as the recipient. I was told that among those who had previously received the University Medal award were Robert Frost, the poet, Sir Ifor Evans, the Provost of University College, London, Sir Julian Huxley, Francis Poulenc, the composer, Lord Beveridge, Jacqueline Bouvier Kennedy and Sir Kenneth Clark.

The medal was presented to me at the conclusion of the lunch by President Hester, who also handed over a leather-bound case containing a citation in the form of a letter, the text of which was as follows:

For more than a quarter of a century you have been working in an unusually effective way as archivist, librarian, author, and administrator to make the past of your country and its greatest writer presently real to the English-speaking world.

Since 1945 you have been Director of The Shakespeare Birthplace Trust. Under your leadership, the house in which Shakespeare was born and homes and gardens related to his residence in Stratford-upon-Avon have been restored and maintained with the result that millions of visitors to Shakespeare's birthplace have had an opportunity not only to read and see his plays but also to live in historical imagination in the England of his Tudor community.

From time to time New York University confers upon an unusually distinguished visitor its University Medal. On this four-hundredth anniversary of the birth of William Shakespeare, it is my privilege, by the authority vested in me, to welcome you to our academic fellowship and to confer upon you our University Medal.

It fell to me to respond and, in addressing the company, I emphasized the bond between our two peoples forged by Shakespeare and referred to the dramatist's unique contribution to the civilized world. As with the George Washington University award, I expressed appreciation of the generous action of the New York University in conferring the Medal which, though a personal honour for me, was conceived as a significant tribute to Shakespeare in his anniversary year.

On the return journey home by sea on the liner 'SS America', I had time to relax, to reflect on the magic of Shakespeare, and to appreciate how much the world looked to Stratford-upon-Avon as its source and focal centre. I realized more than ever before that, alongside the Royal Shakespeare Theatre, the Birthplace Trust held a position of tremendous privilege and responsibility in preserving the Shakespearian heritage, and, with its new headquarters, the Shakespeare Centre, now completed, thoughts of possible development were uppermost in my mind. Some useful ideas, which unfolded as the years passed, came to me in the middle of the Atlantic.

A Royal Garden Party

Arriving in Stratford on 4 July, I hardly had time to get back to a normal routine before the final grand event of the anniversary year occurred. Her Majesty Queen Elizabeth II arranged a garden party at Buckingham Palace on Tuesday, 7 July, as her contribution to the Shakespeare anniversary year. Personalities of theatre, literature and the arts, together with representative public figures, both national and local, were invited, also several Trustees and their ladies, and myself as Director and Mrs Fox. It was a relaxed and happy occasion, and Sir Fordham Flower, as Chairman of the 1964 Shakespeare Anniversary Council, had arranged for those of us who had been involved in organizing the celebrations to be presented to Her Majesty. When I found myself speaking to her, she recalled her visit to the Birthplace a few years before and enquired about the Shakespeare Centre, which she had not as yet seen. She asked about plans for developing its activities and wished the Trust all success. Other members of the royal family intermingled informally with the guests, and the allotted time for the party seemed to pass all too quickly. As with the White House reception, this was an occasion which seemed to put an official seal on all our efforts to do honour to our national poet.

A Year to Remember

This royal occasion was followed by the Annual Meeting of the Trustees, on 18 July, which provided an opportunity for a review and assessment of the anniversary celebrations. Proceedings followed the usual lines, with a report on the year's work and adoption of the annual audited accounts. The Chairman, Sir Fordham Flower, pointed out that the normal activities of the year had been overshadowed by the preparations for the celebrations of the 400th anniversary of Shakespeare's birth. He referred in detail to some aspects of the many-sided and complex operation which I had carried through in my capacity as Director of the Shakespeare Anniversary Council, and he expressed the Trustees' gratitude to me and my staff for our excellent services. I was then invited to give a resumé of the planning and execution of the anniversary programme and to report particularly on the Shakespeare Centre. The Trustees were much impressed by my account of reactions overseas and the links forged with Shakespeare lovers in many countries. I concluded by saying that I felt that the 1964 anniversary should be regarded as one of the most significant chapters in the history of Stratford-upon-Avon, and that its success presented a challenge and incentive for the further development of the Trust's activities. The Trustees unanimously endorsed these sentiments, and at the luncheon which followed they presented to me, as a token of their appreciation, a water-colour painting of a harvest scene by Peter de Wint.

On New Year's Eve, Thursday, 31 December 1964, the Chairman, Trustees and Director of Shakespeare's Birthplace invited all those who had been actively involved in the year's celebrations to a cocktail party at the Shakespeare Centre, which was followed by the showing of a full-length film, produced by Anglia Television, recording the events of the 1964 birthday celebrations. A most fitting, enjoyable finale!

Progress in the 1960s

The building of the Shakespeare Centre and the 1964 Shakespeare anniversary celebrations tend to overshadow the 'business as usual' record in the 1960s. Indeed, the decade witnessed the consolidation of the Trust's progress to date and saw a considerable development of its work in several directions.

Visitor Patronage

The following statistics provide evidence of the growth in popularity of the Shakespearian properties during these years:

	Total for 1960	Total for 1964	Total for 1970
Shakespeare's Birthplace	225,575	321,760	390,704
Anne Hathaway's Cottage	177,379	223,760	305,114
New Place	33,882	59,106	64,203
Mary Arden's House	31,606	51,854	52,323
Hall's Croft	32,484	49,387	47,816
	500,926	705,867	860,160

With the return of more normal conditions after the war years, the numbers of visitors to the Shakespearian properties had gradually increased during the 1950s; but it was the world-wide publicity and growth of interest in Shakespeare generated by the 400th anniversary in 1964 that produced attendances hitherto thought unattainable. During July and August of that year the daily number of visitors to Shakespeare's Birthplace frequently exceeded 3,000, but the busiest day of the season was Whit Monday, 18 May, when 3,434 visitors were admitted. Attendances at the other properties similarly increased and an analysis of the nationalities of those who signed the visitors' book at the Birthplace suggests that at least sixty per cent of them came from abroad.

During 1965 and 1966 attendances did not reach the record levels of 1964, although on Wednesday, 27 July 1966, the highest number of visitors to the Birthplace in a single day so far, 3,444, was achieved. From 1967 the trend turned upwards again. The number of visitors to Anne Hathaway's Cottage during the year reached more than a quarter of a million for the first time, and on Wednesday, 26 July 1967, 2,400 people were admitted, a record for a single day. From this time onwards every year saw an increase in admissions to all the properties. Daily records were again achieved: on Sunday, 27 July 1969, 2,919 people visited Anne Hathaway's Cottage, and on Thursday, 7 August, 3,755 visited the Birthplace. In the same year the numbers of visitors to New Place and Mary Arden's House exceeded for the first time the records set up in 1964.

The practical implications of coping with this increase in visitor patronage were considerable, and improved arrangements for handling and guiding of visitors were introduced. By this time a one-way system of inspection at Shakespeare's Birthplace, with guides stationed in each room, had become well established, but, since everyone had to enter the building through the front door from Henley Street, the process of reception, which involved the purchase of an admission ticket, was difficult at peak times. Queues of visitors waiting to be admitted, and inevitably causing congestion on the pavement outside, were quite common; while the arrival and waiting in Henley Street of the growing number of coaches bringing tourists from London aggravated the situation. Although the town's economy clearly benefitted from this increased business, there were frequent complaints about the nuisance caused, particularly from some local residents who had little sympathy for tourists. As a temporary expedient, a length of kerbside waiting for coaches on the Birthplace side of the street was provided, but in practice this often proved inadequate. It became increasingly clear that the problem could only be solved by the provision of a reserved waiting place for coaches as near as possible to the Birthplace but clear of the street. Unfortunately, there appeared to be no possible site available at that time, and it was not until 1970 that the necessity of providing a coach terminal for Shakespeare's Birthplace came to be considered by the Trustees.

At Anne Hathaway's Cottage it proved easier to provide improved facilities for reception and guiding. Hitherto visitors had used the gateway entrance and path situated immediately alongside the Cottage, buying their admission tickets at the main door; now a small wooden kiosk was built at the lower end of the garden, to provide a new entrance reception point, where visitors could purchase their tickets before proceeding along a path through the middle of the garden, leading to the steps in front of the Cottage entrance. If waiting for admission became necessary, as often happened at peak times, visitors were able to stand along the footpath inside the grounds, viewing the garden on either side of them, instead of forming a queue on the pavement outside the entrance gate. Linked with a one-way circuit of inspection inside the Cottage and finishing with an exit through a newly equipped publications room at the orchard end of the house, this new arrangement proved convenient for both visitors and staff, and greatly assisted the handling of larger numbers.

Again, the problem of dealing with the nuisance caused by the waiting of the growing numbers of cars and coaches in Cottage Lane had to be tackled. Fortunately the existing car park had been planned with a view to possible extension, and in 1965 the parking area here was almost doubled. At the same time an entirely new park for the exclusive use of coaches was constructed on land the Trust owned a few yards past Anne Hathaway's Cottage, along Cottage Lane. Particular care was taken to design and site this so that, with landscaped planting on all sides, the environmental quality of the Cottage's surrounding was not impaired. The Trustees were always appreciative of the sensitive nature of this locality and, at the same time as these changes were taking place, they were pleased to be able to purchase a small plot of land between Shottery Grange, further along Cottage Lane, and land they already owned near the coach park.

Distinguished Guests

Apart from fee-paying visitors and educational groups which were frequently accorded free admission, a regular stream of distinguished personages came to the Birthplace and Anne Hathaway's Cottage during these years. As well as scholars and professional heads of institutions overseas, there were diplomatic representatives of foreign countries and ministers of their governments, together with well known personalities of the theatre and the arts. Indeed, the Foreign Office and the British Council frequently asked for special arrangements to be made for distinguished foreign visitors who had made known their wish to come to see Shakespeare's Birthplace. It fell to me personally to receive them and to act as their guide: one of the unusual facets of the Director's job which gave me considerable pleasure.

The list of distinguished visitors during these years is too long to record, but a few should be

Anne Hathaway's Cottage car park

Visit of Soviet space woman, 9 July 1964

mentioned, as illustrative of the world-wide interest in Shakespeare shared by many different types of people.

The highlight of 1960 was the visit of the King and Queen of Nepal; others who came during the same summer were the Rector of Ankara University, Turkey, the Director of the Folger Shakespeare Library in the USA, the Minister for Culture of the Ukraine, and the Deputy Governor of Jerusalem. In 1964 the Russian authorities arranged for Valentina Nikholayeva-Tereshkova, the first Soviet spacewoman, to include Stratford in her world tour. I well recall her visit to the Birthplace, which seemed to give her great pleasure. She was a quiet, unassuming lady and, with the help of the interpreter who accompanied her, we talked quite freely as I sat alongside her in the official car as we went to Anne Hathaway's Cottage and Mary Arden's House. She clearly enjoyed the experience of visiting these, and she presented me with a small pin-type badge before she left. Members of the Bolshoi Ballet company came in 1965; it was a particularly happy occasion. They were a lively group of attractive young artists, who seemed to be enjoying the break from their ardous dance programme. The following year there was a visit from members of the Polish Popular Theatre, the Gorki Theatre of Leningrad, USSR, and the Leningrad State Kirov Ballet company. In 1968 Professor Akira Okada brought a group of Japanese dancers from Tamagawa University, Tokyo.

Distinguished literary pilgrims who came were Yukio Mishima, the Japanese novelist, Gobal Sharman, a leading Indian writer, and Dr Amado M. Yuxon, poet laureate of the Philippines, who, on the occasion of his visit to the Birthplace, presented a posthumous award to William Shakespeare on behalf of the President of the Philippines. This was an unusual gesture; most gifts to the Trust were translations, Shakespearian publications or material relating to Shakespeare productions or festivals.

It was a pleasing and informative experience to be able to meet and compare notes with the steady stream of professional heads of institutions from overseas, who were always keen to know more about the objects and activities of the Birthplace Trust. Among those who came at this time, I recall the Director of the New York States Historical Association, the Director of the School of Librarianship at the Vatican, the Director General of the Museum of Literature at Budapest, and the Director General for Cultural Affairs from the Netherlands.

Since 1951 there had been a special bonus in alternate years, when the Shakespeare scholars attending the International Shakespeare Conference organized by the University of Birmingham at Mason Croft were also among the visitors. The opening of the Shakespeare Centre enabled the Trust to develop a more active association with them, more especially as the importance of the library collections at the Centre became more widely known. The garden party at Hall's Croft arranged for the Conference delegates by the Trustees became an established and popular event.

An Expanding Organization

The growth of visitor patronage, just described, produced increased income for the Trust, but, at the same time, expenditure rose to meet the cost of the needs of an expanding organization. Year by year the budget I prepared had to be extended to take care of the additional work load.

In 1960-61 the budget for the year was based on

an estimated income of £39,500 and an expenditure of £37,500; by 1970 the corresponding figures were £100,575 and £90,320. The Trustees realized that the Trust's economy was precariously poised, but there was always hesitation about increasing admission charges. However, the price of a single admission ticket to the Birthplace or the Cottage was increased to 2s. 6d. as from the beginning of the 1964 season, and this, together with the income from sales, which during the decade rose from £8,491 to £28,365, held the situation. In 1960-61 there was a surplus of £3,975 on the year's working; in 1969-70 the surplus was £8,330. Although the cost of maintaining and staffing the Shakespearian properties increased gradually each year, the surplus from admission charges, resulting from the larger numbers of visitors, grew to an even greater extent, thereby providing the funds necessary to sustain the expanding organization. In 1960-61 the surplus from Shakespeare's Birthplace and the other properties was £26,016; by 1969-70 it was £30,328.

Three major heads of expenditure showed very large increases during this period. In 1960 the cost of maintaining the Trust's gardens amounted to £6,572; ten years later the figure was £12,689. One additional gardener, making a total of twelve, had been added, but the main factor was the sharp increase in the level of wages. In 1960 an experienced assistant gardener was paid £9 15s. 0d. a week; ten years later the same man earned £17 10s. 0d. Similarly, expenditure on maintenance staff had risen sharply, due not only to higher wages paid, but also to the fact that the team of craftsmen/handymen had been increased from three to six. Opportunity had occurred, when Flowers Brewery in Stratford closed in 1968, to take on two experienced painters and a bricklayer formerly employed by the Brewery. As an illustration of the impact of the cost of wages, in 1960 the Trust's carpenter and handyman was paid £10 10s. 0d. a week; by 1970 his wages had risen to £20 15s. 0d.

The largest increase, however, was in respect of administrative and library expenses, the total cost rising from £10,316, in 1960, to £39,834 in 1970.

Until 1960 my headquarters staff comprised a private secretary (Shirley Watkins), two secretarial assistants, a cashier/book-keeper, and John Ellis, who was responsible for library and records with the help of an assistant. By 1970 the office staff had expanded to include one other assistant secretary and a part-time accounts person. When the Shakespeare Centre was opened in 1964, a full-time caretaker, a receptionist and several part-time domestic staff had been appointed, together with a full-time, qualified librarian and an assistant, responsible for the day-to-day working of the new library arrangements. Dr Dobb, the first Senior Librarian appointed, left after two years and was succeeded by Mrs M. Darvill, who remained in charge of the library until 1974. Miss Eileen Robinson, who had previously acted as assistant librarian at the Theatre library in Waterside, joined the Shakespeare Centre library staff in 1964 and remained until she retired in 1979. In 1967, following the end of the 'wage freeze' rendered necessary by the state of the national economy, three young graduates were added to the establishment, to implement and develop the academic and educational work of the Trust. These were Robert Bearman, who still remains in the Trust's employment as its Senior Archivist; Christine Penney, an assistant librarian who left within a few years; and Roger Pringle as an educational assistant. As the years passed, Mr Pringle became progressively involved in the development of the Trust's educational work and with its annual Poetry Festival. He became Deputy Director in 1985 and was appointed to succeed me as Director in 1989. From a total of thirty-three full-time staff in 1960, the team had grown to fifty, with additional part-time helpers, by 1970. Together they formed a firm basis for further expansion, which characterized the 1970s and 1980s.

Maintenance Routine

The maintenance of the Shakespearian properties and of the Trust's growing estate was rather like that of the Forth Bridge, requiring a regular, recurring programme of attention. A routine treatment of the timber structure and re-painting of the interior of the Shakespearian properties was established, most of the work being undertaken by the Trust's own maintenance men during the winter months. The greenhouses and garden frames at New Place and Hall's Croft had to be regularly painted and repaired, and attention given to garden paths, fences and hedges. The tenants of the Trust's let properties also needed occasional help with plumbing, leaking roofs or other emergencies. The services of outside craftsmen were used as necessary to undertake work beyond the Trust's labour resources, and at this time we had very satisfactory arrangements with one or two Stratford firms of family builders, particularly D.J. Dyer, Ltd. The Trust was also fortunate in being able to employ an experienced thatcher to take care of the thatched roof at Anne Hathaway's Cottage. Repairs to this roof were carried out in 1959, and a new ridge extending its whole length was put on in 1962.

It was at this time that improvements to provide more modern amenities were carried out at three of the eight let properties known as New Row Cottages, situated in Cottage Lane, next to Anne Hathaway's Cottage. Work of this kind attracted the support of improvement grants from the local authority, and during the next few years each of the remaining cottages in the row received similar treatment as opportunity presented itself. The frontage approach to these cottages was also improved, each tenant being given a small front garden for shrubs and flowers, as well as a useful garden plot at the rear.

Also at Shottery, a project of special interest was undertaken when the Trustees decided to plant the Pound Ground, a field of some ten acres abutting on to the car park, with oak and Norwegian spruce trees, in accordance with a scheme approved by the Forestry Commission. Sir Fordham Flower, the Chairman, was just as keen on tree planting as I was, and he readily supported my suggestion that the Trust should be growing oak timber for possible use in repairing the Trust's Tudor buildings at a distant date. I enjoyed discussing the scheme with the Forestry Commission's representative, who suggested that for each row of oak trees planted we should plant a double row of spruce, so that in the short term the Trust might benefit by thinning out the plantation and so having small trees to sell at Christmas. In fact this is exactly what we did; the Trust sold Christmas trees for several years, beginning in 1964, and only decided to discontinue the practice when a local nurseryman to whom a quantity of trees had been supplied went into liquidation and was not able to pay for them. Nevertheless, the forest at Shottery, as it came to be called, continued to provide Christmas trees for seasonal display in the Trust's own properties right through the years to the present time. Securely fenced round, this woodland area has developed into a nature reserve providing sanctuary for a variety of wild life and birds.

A few other items which illustrate the considerable range of work undertaken should perhaps be mentioned. In 1960 the stable block at Shottery Lodge was converted to provide four garages, and the following year a new wagon shed was erected at the rear of Mary Arden's House and the visitors' lavatory at New Place was rebuilt. In 1962 the fence along the whole length of the Warwick road frontage of Welcombe Park was renewed with a traditional cattle-proof fence of cleft oak. In 1963 a thorough overhaul of the roofs and gables of Mary Arden's House and Hornby Cottage was undertaken and, following the unusually heavy wear and tear of the 1964 anniversary year's visitor patronage, the stone floors at Shakespeare's Birthplace and Anne Hathaway's Cottage were carefully repaired in readiness for the 1965 season. At the same time, long overdue improvements at the Hall's Croft Festival Club were completed. The kitchen was enlarged and re-equipped and indoor cloakrooms provided. The outbuildings at Hall's Croft were also converted, to include a staff mews flat and toilet facilities for those working outside. Finally, additional hovels, or open-fronted sheds, were built for the display of agricultural exhibits at Mary Arden's House.

In 1966 electricity was introduced into Anne Hathaway's Cottage for the first time. Prior to this the only heating provided in winter was the open log fire in the parlour, and there was no artificial lighting. Because of potential fire risk, it was decided that the use of open fires should be discontinued, and a limited amount of electric heating and lighting was installed. It was a particularly difficult exercise, to achieve an installation that was both completely concealed and safe, so that nothing appeared out of keeping with the character of the rooms. In 1968 a self-contained flat for staff caretaker use was provided at 22 Cottage Lane, the detached cottage known as Hewlands, adjacent to the Cottage, and the ground floor rooms were converted for use as a 'craft house', where the products of local craftsmen could be displayed and sold. In 1968 improved reception facilities for visitors and for the sale of publications were provided at Shakespeare's Birthplace and New Place, and during 1969 and 1970 smoke detection systems were installed in all the Shakespearian properties.

Some of the repairs and improvements mentioned above required the use of second-hand, matching materials, which sometimes were not easy to obtain. Because of this, it seemed a sensible idea for the Trust to build up a small reserve stock of the items most frequently needed: Wilmcote stone, bricks, hand-made clay roofing tiles and oak. Blue-grey lias stone had been used in all the properties for foundation walls and flooring slabs, but, since the quarries at Wilmcote and Grafton which supplied it had ceased to be worked at the beginning of the present century, I occasionally found myself bargaining with the owners of farm buildings in neighbouring villages who were prepared to see them pulled down and so release the stone for sale. Another source of supply was available when older houses in Stratford had their paved floors of Wilmcote stone replaced by modern materials. I was always on the look-out for the re-roofing of local buildings, which often provided sound, hand-made tiles no longer required, while the demolition of old outbuildings and garden walls yielded bricks of varying sizes. The very early, thin bricks were particularly difficult to find. Occasionally redundant oak beams from demolished buildings became available; although very awkward to re-use, they could often be cut into smaller pieces of sound, seasoned timber which were very useful for minor repairs. The fact that the Trust had its own craftsmen experienced in handling and working traditional materials of this kind made the acquisition and storage of them an excellent conservation investment.

Property Acquisitions

From this summary of practical matters, it is evident that the Trustees were pursuing a consistent policy of improving the amenities of the Shakespearian properties; at the same time, they were constantly aware of the risk of undesirable physical changes in the town and the need for them to use their influence to help to preserve its character. They realized that the only certain way of preventing the damaging effects of unsympathetic commercial development was for the Trust to become owners of properties which they could then control, in a manner similar to the National Trust. Unfortunately, the Trustees did not have capital available for this purpose and, although under the provisions of the Birthplace Trust Acts they were authorized to buy or lease property, it was only when they had saved a reserve of funds from their normal activities that they were able to make purchases of property with the object of conservation in mind.

Henley Street was a particularly sensitive area, and the need to preserve the immediate surroundings of Shakespeare's Birthplace was strongly felt. The Trust already owned several buildings nearby, including numbers 14, a Victorian house next to the Birthplace, and 15 and 16, which were let as business premises. In 1960 the Trustees purchased, with vacant possession, the adjoining premises, 17, 18 and 19 Henley Street, which had been used for many years as a sub post office and retail shop. Originally these buildings, considerably altered in later times, had formed part of the eighteenth-century White Lion inn. They had access and outbuildings to the rear from Guild Street and, together with the adjoining properties already owned by the Trust, provided a possible site for the new Shakespeare Centre. Their purchase was an important strategic acquisition. With very minor adaptation, the properties then purchased were let to tenants on a short-term basis for approved business use. They were subsequently demolished when the Shakespeare Centre extension was built.

There were other property acquisitions in Henley Street. At its junction with Guild Street, a corner building comprised several small shops, facing the Birmingham road. The Trustees were able to buy one of these shops, number 25, in 1965. It was felt important to be able to control the future possible development of this property at the apex of the street, and ownership of one of its units by the Trust offered the appropriate safeguard. The shop was then leased out for business use, the Trust's rental income being appropriately increased.

On the opposite side of Henley Street to Shakespeare's Birthplace there were two purchases in 1969: the shop with living accommodation above, number 39, for a number of years owned and run as the Puppet Centre by Waldo and Muriel Lanchester, the well-known puppeteers; and 45, a large antiques shop owned by Grainger-Brown, situated immediately in front of the Birthplace alongside the former Coach and Horses inn, which, after serving as the Festival Office in 1964, had been used for a time by Flowers Brewery as temporary office accommodation and then let for the sale of craft products. The acquisition of the Puppet Centre provided the opportunity for the Trustees to establish their own bookshop, which was named the Centre Bookshop, to provide for the growing demand for Shakespearian publications, and to rent the rooms on the first floor as office accommodation. In the case of number 45, in view of its commanding position the Trustees went to considerable trouble to find a tenant willing to accept conditions as to the type of business carried out there. It was felt that Henley Street already had too many general souvenir shops, and that a high class jewellers selling quality products would enhance the attraction of the street. As normally happened when the Trust bought a property, the building was completely overhauled and any necessary improvement made.

At the opposite end of the town, two Victorian properties were bought by the Trustees in 1966, to safeguard the approach to Hall's Croft. These were numbers 17 and 19 Old Town, being the two end

The Centre Bookshop, 39 Henley Street

The ornate barge-boards of 19 Old Town

units of a block of three dwellings built in 1841-42, standing on the corner of Church Street and Old Town. Number 19 occupied a site adjacent to the end of the garden of Hall's Croft. As buildings, they illustrate a style of architecture not well represented in Stratford and, with their gables decorated with carved barge-boards and with hood moulds over the windows, they contribute significantly to the character of the street leading to Hall's Croft and Holy Trinity Church. Number 17 was subsequently divided into two residential flats and, following their usual policy, the Trustees selected tenants who appreciated living in a period environment of this kind.

Perhaps even more important as a positive contribution to the preservation of Shakespeare's Stratford-upon-Avon and countryside was the purchase, in 1967, of the property known as The Hill, with its surrounding fields and spinneys totalling some forty-two acres, situated less than a mile to the north-east of the centre of the town. Standing some two hundred yards back from the main Stratford to Warwick road, The Hill was a residence of Victorian date, occupying an elevated position amidst matured trees, formal gardens and woodland, and enjoying commanding views across the Avon. Until his death in 1966, it had been owned and occupied by Sir Fordham Flower, Chairman of the Trust, and by his family for three generations before him.

The circumstances leading to the purchase of The Hill are worth recording. After Sir Fordham's death, his widow, Lady Flower, continued to live there for a time with her growing family, but she soon felt she did not wish to maintain such a large house and estate. The family trustees accordingly decided to offer the property for sale, and for many months it was advertised and offers invited. It did not occur to any of the Trustees at that juncture that the Trust should consider its possible purchase for conservation reasons and, in any event, available funds were very meagre. Information then reached me that an interested party had given instructions for a plan to be prepared for the residential development of the lower field belonging to The Hill alongside the Warwick road. To me this was a danger signal and, since I could not bear the thought of seeing possible 'ribbon' housing development along the Warwick road, I decided to take some action.

The situation was delicate, because Mr Dennis Flower, the cousin of the late Sir Fordham, who succeeded him as Chairman of the Trust, was one of the Flower family trustees, and had therefore an interest in selling the property. I decided not to involve him, but consulted informally the senior members of the Trust's Executive Committee, suggesting how important I felt it was that the Trust should attempt to buy The Hill and seeking their authority to negotiate with the agents. I am glad to say my proposition received ready approval. It did not then take me long to agree with the agents a purchase price, of £65,650, for the freehold of the house and the estate, thus forestalling the spoliation of this attractive, rural approach to Stratford-upon-Avon.

The fields on the north side of The Hill link with the area of parkland on the Welcombe estate which once belonged to William Shakespeare as part of his investment in property. As already described, the Birthplace Trust had purchased the Welcombe land situated on either side of the main entrance to the Welcombe Hotel as far back as 1930, with the object of keeping it as open space, providing a rural scene of green parkland, scattered trees and woodland, and letting the fields to tenant farmers for grazing sheep and cattle. The acquisition of The Hill fields by the Trust made possible this area of conservation, thereby helping to secure on that side of the road the unspoiled character of one of the main approaches to the town.

In these matters the Trustees appreciated the co-operative attitude of the County Planning Authority, which on a number of occasions sought their opinion in connection with proposals affecting possible development. In particular, the Trustees felt it their duty in 1968 to oppose the application of the South Warwickshire Sports Trust for planning permission to build a sports centre on riverside land alongside the Warwick road. Apart from the fact that the proposal conflicted with the Trust's recent conservation acquisition of The Hill estate on the opposite side of the road, the Trustees felt strongly that this area of green meadowland by the river should be preserved as open space, and that a building of the scale and design proposed would be seriously out of keeping with the background and general character of Stratford.

In view of the far-reaching implications raised by the sports centre project, the Trustees suggested that a Public Inquiry should be held to examine all aspects of it. An Inquiry, which lasted three weeks, was accordingly held in the Town Hall in January 1969. The Trustees' case was ably presented by Mr Stephen Brown, QC, and the hearing aroused considerable interest, focussing attention on the issue of conservation with particular reference to riverside meadowland on the Warwick road. The outcome was that the Minister decided to refuse the application to build the projected sports centre. The Trustees were particularly pleased, because in his official report he endorsed the Trust's point of view that 'to develop on this Warwick Road frontage so far beyond the urban fringe would destroy the open and rural approach to this historic town, which is so much a part of our national heritage and held in world-wide esteem as a cultural and tourist centre'. Encouraged by this decision, the Executive Committee continued to watch closely the situation regarding planning and conservation matters in the town, and on occasions made known its views to the Minister concerned, the County Planning Officer and other interested bodies.

At Shottery and Wilmcote useful additions were made to the Trust's estate. In 1965 a pair of small semi-detached dwellings, situated on the same side of Cottage Lane as Anne Hathaway's Cottage and a few yards away, were purchased. They were simple, brick-built houses, each possessing a small garden at the front and at the rear, probably built in the 1920s. Though of no special architectural character, their proximity to the Cottage made it desirable for the Trust to control them; at the same time, the Trustees were able to use them to provide accommodation for members of staff. Again, and for the purpose of extending the protected area around Anne Hathaway's Cottage, the opportunity occurred the following year for the Trustees to acquire some seven-and-a-half acres of land which formed part of the Manor Fruit Farm at Shottery, adjoining land already owned by the Trust.

In 1965 the Trustees were also able to buy the picturesque property known as the White Cottage, situated in Church Lane within a few yards of the Burnside properties they already owned. Originally a small, half-timbered, thatched building of late sixteenth- or early seventeenth-century date, with an extension at the rear, the cottage sits comfortably in its own small, self-contained garden, surrounded on three sides by the open field which the Trust had received from the Burnside bequest. In its category, this was an important conservation acquisition; as with Brookside, opposite Shottery Church, and the thatched cottages in Tavern Lane already owned by the Trust, it provided another typical specimen of the smaller type of dwelling common in Shottery in Shakespeare's time.

At Wilmcote, at the same time in 1968 as the Trustees were supporting the Warwickshire Planning Authority in refusing permission for houses to be built on the field opposite to Mary Arden's House, they seized the opportunity to purchase the Glebe Farm, the farmstead adjoining Mary Arden's House, situated on the corner overlooking the village green, together with a small field at the back which went with it. The object of the purchase was to thwart a plan to build houses on the site, and was the outcome of a friendly discussion I had with the owner, Mr Bob Ansell, the brewer, who, when I represented to him the damaging environmental effects of the development proposed, readily agreed to abandon the idea in the interests of preserving the character of the village.

At that time the Glebe Farm was in an extremely neglected condition, and was occupied by an elderly tenant farmer, Mr George Holmes, who appeared to live happily there with his sister in conditions which were more in keeping with Shakespeare's period than the twentieth century. Although the farmhouse and farmyard buildings were similar in age and type to those of the Arden farmstead nearby, they had suffered considerable alteration and adaptation over the years and, due to lack of maintenance, the condition of the property as a whole was in an unbelievable state of disrepair and squalor.

When members of the Executive Committee made an inspection of their newly acquired property, they could hardly believe what they saw: living conditions in the farmhouse of a most rudimentary kind; a kitchen with an old, stone sink and a pump for water alongside it, complete with a copper for washing clothes and open fire, the room crammed with utensils, an ancient bicycle and an untidy array of effects of all kinds; a cool dairy, with its original stone slabs and floor still being used as it would have been in Tudor times; an exceedingly muddy farmyard at the back of the house, surrounded by farm buildings of crumbling stone with doors which were either broken or non-existent; an ancient cart standing in a puddle and an abandoned old tractor a few yards away; a stable being used to fatten calves, with trodden dung inside, piled to a depth of two or more feet, which had been allowed to accumulate during the winter months; leaking roofs, and a sinister hole near the ridge of the barn; several small outbuildings in varying states of disrepair; broken stone steps leading to the granary; a disused pigsty with a self-set elder tree sprouting in its yard; an odd miscellany of tools and implements lying around, both inside and outside, including horse collars that were mouldy and nibbled by vermin, and harness pieces hanging on nails where they had been left when last used, decades before; and, in the adjoining small paddock, several old, rusty implements, barely visible because of the nettles growing round and through them; a dilapidated hovel filled with discarded farm stuff, a corrugated metal shed, timber, fencing materials and heaven knows what lying around in glorious disorder; and, to complete the scene, ducks and an old English breed of cockerel and hens enjoying their free-range environment; finally, what had once been a typical country garden at the front of the farmhouse, but was now a wilderness of weeds and overgrown shrubs.

George Holmes, the tenant farmer, acted as our guide as we surveyed this scene. To him it was home, a very dear place, and no amount of persuasion or inducement by the Trustees during the next year or two could entice him to vacate the premises. Because of the risk of undesirable publicity which would almost certainly have arisen had they taken legal action to secure occupation, the Trustees decided to wait until George died. This did not happen until the end of 1978, and it was not until nearly a year later that the Trust secured possession of the Glebe Farm. In the meantime, however, a detailed programme of restoration of the property was prepared,

The Glebe Farm in 1975

and the concept of linking it with Mary Arden's House to form a Shakespeare Countryside Museum was approved by the Trustees. This will be described in a later chapter.

My one personal regret is that I did not record the various conversations I had with George Holmes, with whom I established a friendly rapport. In appearance and speech he was a typical country farming type, who might well have been around in Shakespeare's time. Of medium height and fresh complexion, George always wore a coat flowing open, loosely fitting trousers, a cloth cap well pulled down, and heavy, dirty, hobnail boots. Speaking with a Warwickshire accent, he used colloquial words and phrases which reflected his rural background; he lived in the past and did not accept kindly the changed conditions of the post-war years. Being of country origin myself, I always enjoyed my contacts with characters of this kind, and I must confess that, although I was keenly anxious to take the Glebe Farm in hand, I had every sympathy with George's wish to stay there for the rest of his life. In the event, the period of waiting proved helpful, in that it gave opportunity for a reserve of funds to be built up for use when circumstances allowed.

Another small property acquisition should be mentioned. In 1969 the Trustees were able to purchase one of the stone-built cottages, number 7, in the row on the opposite side of Aston Cantlow Road, facing the Glebe Farm. By becoming the owner of one unit in the block, with a spacious garden frontage, the Trustees ensured that there could be no undesirable development in Aston Cantlow Road immediately opposite to the Glebe Farm.

The Trust's Collections and Educational Work

Apart from conservation and property matters, the 1960s saw some considerable progress in building up the Trust's library, archive and museum collections, and their growing use by students and scholars. Each year the number of visits by readers increased: in 1969 a total of 1,266 reader-visits to the library was recorded, with 522 to the records office. When the extended accommodation and facilities of the Shakespeare Centre became available, a number of educational activities were initiated. In particular, a service of introductory talks and displays at the Centre was offered to school and student parties, as a preparation for visits to the historic properties or to a theatre performance. This new service soon proved popular with teachers and pupils, as also the small exhibitions which were held two or three times a year in the entrance hall and the Stratford room at the Centre. These covered a variety of subject matter, ranging from local history topics and special events to Shakespearian bibliography, theatrical material and current productions at the Royal Shakespeare Theatre. From another point of view, these exhibitions provided an opportunity to illustrate and publicize the variety and wealth of source material in the Trust's collections.

Meanwhile, the annual Poetry Festival at Hall's Croft, with its supporting exhibition displayed there, continued to develop under the direction of Douglas Cleverdon, who had succeeded John Carroll, and subsequently under Patrick Garland; indeed, by this time the exhibition room on the first floor, where the poetry readings were held, proved too small to accommodate the growing audience. For several years the readings were relayed to those sitting below in the Club room, but continued increasing pressure of demand eventually led to the re-locating of most of the readings in the music room at the Shakespeare Institute, by kind permission of the University of Birmingham.

In this and in other matters, especially the arrangements of talks and lectures, there was ready co-operation between the Trust, the University of Birmingham, the British Council and the Royal Shakespeare Theatre. The Trustees were also able to count on the interest of the Stratford-upon-Avon Borough Council in allowing the occasional use of the Town Hall for recitals. Following the success of the musical events of the 1964 anniversary year, the Trust also undertook, with the encouragement and support of the Arts Council, the arrangement of a short series of music concerts each summer, as a contribution to Stratford's overall cultural programme. A madrigal concert at Hall's Croft, held outside on the terrace at the rear of the house when weather permitted, became an established fixture and, with the co-operation of the National Trust and the Borough Council, concerts were held at Charlecote Park and the Town Hall, and on occasions in the Royal Shakespeare Theatre and Holy Trinity Church.

The provision of the new bookstacks with related facilities at the Shakespeare Centre marked the beginning of a new chapter in the history of the Trust's library and made possible the expansion of the records department in the old office building, which was reorganized with more spacious accommodation for staff and readers. In the Centre library good progress was made with the arrangement and consolidation of the combined collections of the

Trust and the Royal Shakespeare Theatre. A revised accessions recording system was introduced; old catalogue cards were revised and uniform classification and cataloguing imposed on the library as a whole; theatre programmes, playbills, prompt copies and production records were specially stored; and useful reference aids prepared. A working procedure for the transfer of material relating to the current plays was agreed and operated with the Royal Shakespeare Theatre from this time.

With space now available, accessions to the library and records office began to increase at a steady rate. Arising from the 1964 celebrations, a vast amount of material generated by the anniversary was received from all parts of the world. This took the form of festival brochures, exhibition catalogues, press cuttings, programmes of events, together with translations of Shakespeare's plays, publications about Shakespeare and miscellaneous printed matter in many languages. Subsequently copies of new translations and Shakespeare studies were presented to the library most years, thus swelling the number of normal accessions purchased.

Apart from the regular addition of Theatre records, a policy was pursued of obtaining copies of new books dealing with every aspect of Shakespeare study and related subject matter, and of acquiring essential reference publications to fill gaps in the library's holding. Money available for book purchases was still limited because of the Trust's other commitments, but the Trustees never lost sight of the need to build up a reserve of funds to make possible the acquisition of any special item which might become available. During my first year as Director, the Trustees had agreed to my suggestion that an Accessions Reserve should be established, by transferring £500 from the revenue account. This reserve was regularly used for making purchases for the Trust's collections; at the end of each year the reserve was made up to its original amount, and gradually increased when the year's accounts allowed. By 1964 the Accessions Reserve stood at £5,000.

I was very proud of the impressive collection of sixteenth-century and seventeenth-century books already in the library alongside the early Shakespeare editions and other rarities, and my ambition was always to acquire additional titles as resources and opportunity allowed. Among the few items falling into this category added during these years were Lambard's *Eirenarcha: of the office of the Justices of the Peace in foure bookes*, 1592; Ruggle's *Ignoramus*, 1630; Hopton's *Concordancy of Yeares*, 1616; Barrough's *Method of physick*, 1617; Fulke Greville's *Certaine learned and elegant workes*, 1633; Sarpi's *Historie of the Council of Trent* trans. Nathaniel Brent, 1629; and Meriton's *A Guide for Constables ...*, 1685. I also felt that the library should possess copies of the finely printed editions of Shakespeare's plays and other texts of interest, and particularly publications of the Shakespeare Head Press, originally based in Stratford in the house in Chapel Street which had been occupied by Shakespeare's friend, Julius Shaw. During these years I was very happy to acquire copies of the Shakespeare Head Press editions of Plutarch's *Lives*, 1928, and of Spenser's *Works*, 1930-32; the Doves Press edition of *Hamlet*, 1909; the Nonesuch edition of Shakespeare's *Works*, 1929-33; the Cranach Press edition of *Hamlet*, edited by J. Dover Wilson; and the Shakespeare Head Press edition of Froissart's *English Chronicles* in a limited edition of eight volumes, illuminated by Miss M.G.M. Scriven of Stratford, who had included these in a bequest to the Trustees.

On the archive side, there was a steady intake of record material relating to many facets of the history of Stratford-upon-Avon and Warwickshire. Considerable deposits of deeds and documents were received from the offices of local solicitors, as well as personal and estate records from the families of Leigh of Stoneleigh, Throckmorton of Coughton Court, Gregory-Hood of Loxley, and Willoughby de Broke of Kineton. The owners of local businesses were also encouraged to deposit unwanted records; in 1969, for instance, the Trustees accepted a deposit of a large collection of business books and records belonging to the brewery of Flower and Sons, Ltd.

Regular additions were also made to the local history reference collections used by record searchers, and a few items of special interest were acquired: Robert Bell Wheler's annotated copy of the first edition of Dugdale's *Antiquities of Warwickshire*, 1656; a manuscript Dictionary of Arts and Sciences compiled by John Hughes (1714-96), the antiquary of Admington and Stretton-on-the-Fosse; and a copy of Richard Lily's *Poems and translations on several occasions*, 1727, which had belonged to the Reverend Joseph Greene, with manuscript notes in his hand. Joseph Greene (1712-90) was master of Stratford's Grammar School and vicar of Weston and Welford-on-Avon. An outstanding classical scholar, he was well known as a bibliophile and antiquary, and he had a life-long friendship with his brother, Richard Greene, who founded the celebrated Lichfield Museum, and with the Honourable James West of Alscot Park, politician and antiquary, whose zeal for collecting books, manuscripts and curiosities made him a leading figure in scientific and antiquarian circles. Joseph kept up a regular exchange of letters both with his brother and Mr West. Apart from their value as a source of local history, they disclose a lively interest in Shakespeare and contain new evidence on the beginnings of Shakespearian appreciation and production in Stratford-upon-Avon. The Trust already owned a collection of Joseph's letters to Richard, and over a period of years I was able to link these with other letters and papers in the possession of the West family and with material in the Folger Shakespeare Library and elsewhere. The results of my research into this interesting character were published by the Dugdale Society in 1965 in a volume, *Correspondence of the Reverend Joseph Greene: parson, schoolmaster and antiquary (1712-1790)*.

Special mention should also be made of the arrangement whereby, on 28 September 1966, the Trustees accepted on deposit for safe keeping the original Parish Register of Holy Trinity Church, which records the baptism and burial entries of William Shakespeare. Up till that time the Register had for many years been displayed in a case in the Church, opened to show the baptism and burial entries. Although every care had been taken of this priceless exhibit, I noticed that the parchment of the

Deposit of Parish Register of Stratford-upon-Avon, 1966

folios displayed had already faded slightly and that exposure to light over a long period had inflicted a degree of deterioration. I therefore suggested to the Vicar, the Reverend Thomas Bland, and the Churchwardens that a facsimile copy should be substituted for display in the Church and that the unique original Register should be kept in honourable retirement, as it were, under ideal conditions for its future well-being alongside the Birthplace Trust's rare books in the new Shakespeare Centre, and that it should be produced for inspection only on very special occasions. These terms were readily agreed, and the Trustees were happy to present a complete facsimile copy of the Parish Register to the Vicar and Churchwardens for display in the Church.

The 1960s also saw the beginning of the Trust's audio and visual collection of tapes and films concerned with Shakespeare and Stratford-upon-Avon. As Director, I was frequently interviewed by radio, press and film representatives, and, whenever I made a recording, I ensured that a copy was presented for the Trust's archives. Examples which spring to mind were the film of the Shakespeare birthday celebrations programme for the 400th anniversary and the opening of the Shakespeare Centre in 1964, made by Independent Television, and a BBC feature programme on Stratford-upon-Avon and the Shakespeare Country, for which I provided the introduction and commentary, shown on the BBC Channel 2 on 21 December 1967. In a sense these were historical records, but in the course of time copies of Shakespeare films and recordings of individual productions and programmes were added. During the next twenty-five years the Trust's audio-visual collection developed into a significant ingredient of the library's resources, and came to be increasingly used for study and teaching purposes.

Some notable additions were also made to the Trust's picture and museum collections at this time. In 1960 Professor John Dover Wilson, one of our distinguished Life Trustees, presented a crayon portrait of himself, drawn by Robert Lyon, with whom he had a friendly association. In spite of his acknowledged eminence as a Shakespeare scholar, Professor Wilson was a modest, unassuming man, and I recall his hesitation and diffidence when he asked me whether I thought the Trustees would be willing to accept a gift of this kind. I assured him that an honoured place would be found for it in the conference room, and I am only sorry that the Trust does not possess portraits of other distinguished Trustees.

In 1961 a fortuitous circumstance resulted in the Trust's purchase of the portrait of William Shakespeare by Gerard Soest (d. 1681). For some time previously I had been in friendly contact with Mr Kingsley Adams, the Director of the National Portrait Gallery, and his deputy, Mr David Piper. One day I received a telephone call from the Director, enquiring whether the Trust had funds available to buy a Shakespeare portrait which he felt should be in the ownership of an institution in this country, and preferably in Stratford, and which, for lack of money at that time, he was not able to purchase for the National Portrait Gallery. He proceeded to describe the picture, painted probably somewhere between 1660 and 1680, which had been engraved early in the eighteenth century. The portrait was just about life-size and the subject was represented in a three-quarter view. The expression of the face was delicate, the beard and moustache slight, and the hair curly and thick. The costume, he added, represented what the artist presumably thought Shakespeare would have been wearing in his lifetime, and the collar suggested some possible relation to the Chandos portrait in the Gallery's collection. The picture came from the collections of Sir J.F. Grey and the Earl of Stamford, and had been sold in the auction room at Christie's in 1954; it subsequently went abroad and passed into the hands of a firm of art dealers in Lisbon, Portugal, from whom Kingsley Adams was anxious to rescue it.

Realizing the significance of this picture, I contrived to find the necessary money to enable Mr Kingsley Adams to negotiate its purchase for the Trust. The deal was completed, and the Soest portrait was brought back from Lisbon for the Trust in the diplomatic bag. Very little attention was needed to put the picture into good order, and it was rehoused in an early seventeenth-century frame of carved wood with gold-leaf moulding. When the Shakespeare Centre was opened, the Soest portrait was hung on the panelled wall immediately behind my desk in the Director's office. It is not surprising that I came to have a special affection for this portrait of Shakespeare; I always felt that the great man, 'my boss', was looking down on me over my shoulder.

Another Shakespeare portrait, which, as already mentioned, had been on display at the American Shakespeare Festival Theatre at Stratford, Connecticut, in 1964, was donated to the Trust by Lincoln Kirstein of New York in 1967. It was the so-called 'Chesterfield' portrait, which is probably the first known variation on the Chandos portrait. According to the National Portrait Gallery, the most likely attribution of authorship is to Peter Borseler, a Dutch painter working in England in the 1660s and 1670s. Vertue, who saw it about 1740, thought the head to be a recent alteration to an older picture, but closer examination has not confirmed this. According to Mr David Piper, who described the picture in *O sweet Mr Shakespeare I'll have his picture*, a pamphlet published by the National Portrait Gallery in 1964, 'this is a re-creation of the poet in terms of the

The Soest portrait of Shakespeare

eloquent baroque style of Van Dyck, and consorts admirably with the re-creations of some of Shakespeare's plays, also in very baroque, if French-inspired, terms of music, decor and rhetoric, staged in London by Davenant after the restoration of the live theatre following the Puritan closing-down'.

Two years later, in 1969, a picture of considerable literary interest, depicting Sir Walter Scott at Shakespeare's tomb, was purchased by the Trust with money contributed by the Friends of Shakespeare's Birthplace. This was an association which the Trustees had inaugurated in 1965, at my suggestion, to give Shakespeare lovers all over the world an opportunity to support the objects and work of the Birthplace Trust by contributing a modest annual subscription. The Trustees' idea was to extend the Trust's influence in the international sphere and, at the same time, to produce supplementary funds which could be devoted to the development of the Centre's academic work and the enrichment of its library and other collections. Initially about three hundred Friends, including some thirty Shakespeare societies, had been enrolled, but year by year the number gradually increased. The Scott painting was the first of a succession of acquisitions made possible by the funds of the Friends.

According to signatures in the surviving visitors' book, Sir Walter Scott, an enthusiastic admirer of Shakespeare, visited the Birthplace with his sister on 8 April 1828; and the following entry in his Journal records the visit: 'We visited the tomb of the mighty wizarrd. It is in the bad taste of James Ist's reign; but what a magic does the locality possess! There are stately monuments of forgotten families; but when you have seen Shakespeare's, what care we for the rest?' Although Scott was a life-long devotee of Shakespeare, this seems to have been his only visit to Stratford, four years before his death at the age of sixty-two.

The oil painting, by Sir William Allan, R.A., a friend of the family and a President of the Royal Scottish Academy, depicts Scott standing in the chancel of Holy Trinity Church in reverential posture, paying homage to the genius he so much admired. The purchase of this picture came about as the result of a telephone call I had received from a friend in London. From his description of it, I realized that the Trust was not aware of its existence and, when I heard that the National Gallery of Scotland was showing interest in its possible acquisition, I decided that quick action to secure it for Stratford was essential. I accordingly bought it and, when the Trustees saw it, they readily endorsed my action: a place for the picture was immediately found in the conference room.

Another accession of special literary interest was the original medallion of Shakespeare worn by the celebrated actor, David Garrick, when, as Steward,

The Garrick medallion

he presided over the Jubilee celebrations in Stratford-upon-Avon in 1769, on the occasion of the first festival held in honour of the bard. The medallion was one of several personal items belonging to David and Mrs Garrick which had been preserved by the descendants of Garrick's executor; they

Sir Walter Scott's visit to Shakespeare's tomb, 1828

included two exquisitely embroidered dresses and shoes worn by Mrs Garrick at the Jubilee, one of her diaries, a presentation silver service engraved with Garrick's arms, and various theatrical records. I made a journey to inspect them where they were kept at a house in Wimborne Minster and I persuaded the owner to loan the dresses and silver with other items for temporary display at New Place Museum. When, in 1961, the question of their possible purchase by the Trust arose, the Trustees had only available at that time sufficient funds to buy the medallion, the diary and a few small items, the dresses and silver being returned to the owner. The prize exhibit, however, was secured: the carved mulberry-wood medallion representation of Shakespeare, enclosed in a neat gilt frame, complete with its original silk ribbon, exactly as recorded in the well known engraving of Garrick by T. Saunders, from the painting by B. Van der Gucht, in which he is depicted holding the insignia of the office of Steward, which he discharged at the Jubilee.

There were also some notable additions to the Trust's general museum collections, particularly at Mary Arden's House. In 1960, following a visit I made, Mr C.H. Whitehead of Boddingtons Farm, Luddington, donated an old Warwickshire farm wagon, made over 130 years before to the order of his grandfather by Thomas Fleming of Gaydon. The latter was a well known wheelwright and wagon-builder, and the specimen given to the Trust exemplified his high degree of skill and craftsmanship. As with other items acquired, the need to provide suitable storage and display accommodation was appreciated; within a short time the Trustees decided to erect a hovel-type of outbuilding at Mary Arden's House, to accommodate the wagon and similar vehicles. The area of the former rickyard there provided a suitable siting, and further instalments of hovel units were added as the number of farming exhibits increased. A specially designed, tall shed was completed in 1966, to provide for the display of two gypsy caravans bought during the previous year.

The circumstances leading to the acquisition of these Romany caravans are worth recording. As the Trust's farming collection increased, it occurred to me that an attempt should be made to add specimen caravans illustrative of the life of the gypsy folk who had frequented the surrounding countryside from Shakespeare's time to the present day. The problem was how to secure authentic examples of these horse-drawn wagons, but an element of good fortune provided the answer. Arising from a press report, I made contact with a man who had studied Romany lore and had contacts with the gypsy community. Having made known my possible interest in acquiring exhibits for historical preservation and display, I commissioned him to 'spy out' in Warwickshire in the hope that he might locate any suitable wagons that would be available for purchase. Nothing happened for some time, but then he reported that he had seen two unoccupied caravans in a field in the northern part of the county and that, after enquiring, he had found the owner, with whom he felt he could do business. I asked him to find out more about the caravans and, under the pretence of recording them for the purpose of his study, he came back with photographs and detailed descriptions.

They were of two types: one a ledge wagon, and the other a barrel-top version. Both appeared to be basically sound, but in a neglected condition and in need of overhaul. It transpired that the owner of them had two wives and that he had accommodated his two families in these separate quarters. Assessing a possible purchase price was not easy, and a deal clearly could only be done in cash by someone like

Warwickshire farm wagon

Gypsy caravans

my agent, who had ingratiated himself into the gypsy community. Bargaining then took place on my behalf, and it was agreed that, if a certain sum of money was paid to the owner in the field where the caravans were situated on a certain morning the following week, the wagons would be handed over. Quick action was necessary; I arranged for a low-loading transporter vehicle to be sent, with the Trust's head gardener carrying the money, to meet the agent at an agreed rendezvous at the appointed time. The deal was completed in the field, as arranged, and later that afternoon two gypsy caravans were delivered to Mary Arden's House, the latest accessions to the rural collection.

The next problem was how to get the caravans overhauled and re-painted in traditional Romany style, and it took some time before this happened. I realized that special craftsmanship and artistry, based on a knowledge and experience of Romany tradition, were necessary. Jim Berry provided the answer.

Knowing that a ledge caravan of similar type was in the museum at York, I contacted the curator there and sought his advice as to a possible Romany restorer. He immediately told me that the man I wanted was Jim Berry, a master gypsy artist craftsman, well known in the north of England, and he gave me an accommodation address at which he thought I might make contact with him. I wrote a letter to Jim, explaining in simple terms what I wanted and asking whether he would be interested in helping me. I waited anxiously for a reply: nothing came. Several weeks afterwards, I wrote again: again silence. Finally, and as a last bid, I sent a third letter, hoping he might have returned to his base. Weeks passed and there was still no response. Then one morning, when I arrived at the entrance to the

Shakespeare Centre just before 9 a.m., there, standing on the steps, was an unmistakable gypsy character: a well built man of medium height with a swarthy complexion and dishevelled hair, wearing a red handkerchief round his neck and with coat flowing open. Who could it be, but Jim Berry? We quickly identified ourselves. Standing at the side of the street was an old motor van, in which his son-in-law had driven him from Yorkshire during the night. He announced that he thought he had better come to see the job and, almost before I knew what had happened, he produced a loose passenger seat from inside the van, put it alongside the driver for me to sit on, while he crouched on the floor behind, and off we went to Wilmcote. The vehicle appeared to be just about roadworthy, but that was all.

On arrival, Jim viewed the two caravans, which looked rather forlorn, standing near the plum trees in what, at that time, was the open field behind the cow-shed and now forms part of the coach park area. I stood in silence and watched with fascination as he inspected the wagons from top to bottom, inside and out, weighing up every detail, rather as did the old dealer in the village where I was born when he vetted a horse. I then asked him what he thought of them. 'You've got two good 'uns, gaffa', pronounced Jim, to my great delight, and he then proceeded to tell me they were the work of Bill Wright, the famous maker of gypsy caravans. He could show me his mark, he said, inside the brass caps on the wheel hubs. In a short time I learned that Bill Wright's caravans had certain structural features, as well as traditional decorative treatment. He then described what needed to be done to restore the caravans to a first class condition, and I sensed that he fancied the prospect of being asked to do the work. If I could wait a little time, he said, he would come and take them in hand. The next question was, What would it cost? Here my upbringing as a countryman came in useful, because I knew I would have to bargain. This is exactly what I did and, after some discussion, Jim and I agreed an arrangement of payment by cash as the work proceeded, and we shook hands to clinch the deal.

I waited anxiously for a message when Jim could come to start on the agreed commission, but none came. Then on Saturday morning, 8 May 1965, when I arrived at the front of the Centre, there stood Jim, complete with living-van, wife, grand-daughter and dog, ready to take up temporary residence at Wilmcote, to restore the caravans. And there he installed himself, near the plum trees, setting up his tripod for an open air fire, a clothes line for drying washing, and other outside sundries, and for the next few weeks he tackled the job with enthusiasm and expertise.

I paid regular visits to see what was going on and, in the process, learned a good deal about the caravans and the Romany way of life they illustrated. The bodywork of the wagons had to be stripped of peeling paint, a new canvas top provided for the barrel-roofed wagon, and various pieces of carving renewed, before final painting and decoration could take place. But these operations were not all done in sequence; I was intrigued to find that Jim had several of them under way at the same time. It was an experience to see such a master craftsman and artist at work. I remember seeing him, one bank holiday morning, putting the finishing touches to one of the axles and wheel of the big caravan. He sat on the grass in his shirt sleeves, one leg on either side of the wheel which was jacked up; the maroon painting of the axle and wheel had been finished, and he was in the process of applying the yellow decorative patterns. Alongside him he had a tin lid containing paint and, using a fitch brush, he painted a pattern in free style on the axle; then, slowly revolving the wheel, he added lines to the spokes and a thin line perfectly positioned round the rim. His was the gift of a natural artist, able to work without effort or blueprint.

On my visits I usually found myself talking to Jim's wife, a gentle lady, short in height, with long, black hair in plaits and bright blue eyes, wearing a colourful dress of gypsy design, complete with apron, and curious, pointed, laced boots. Having in mind that I would attempt to furnish the interior of the caravans as their gypsy occupants would have had them, I took opportunity to learn from her what items there would have been, ranging from the small iron stove, cooking utensils and coverings for the bunk bed, to the oil lamps, soft furnishings and ornaments.

The work of restoration proceeded according to plan, except that, about half-way through, Jim presented himself at my office one morning, obviously very perturbed. He had come to explain that he had received a message that his daughter's caravan in Yorkshire had been damaged by fire, and he felt obliged to go and put things right. So off he went, but he returned within a short time to finish his work on the caravans. He packed up and went home on 6 July, but came back in September to satisfy himself that all was well.

It is not surprising that this episode generated a good deal of interest. The caravans made a good subject for the photographer, and features appeared in the British Tourist Association's periodical *In Britain* and in the *Warwickshire and Worcestershire Magazine*, as well as in film reports made by the BBC and ATV. This publicity also assisted the building up of the farming collection at Mary Arden's House. Among other items presented to the Trust at this time were an old corn-kibbling machine, an early Bomford and Evershed threshing machine, a splendid set of cooper's tools and a variety of utensils. The caravans were moved into their newly constructed shed on the side of the rickyard in 1966.

Speaking for myself, I became increasingly aware of the potential educational value of developing the presentation of this kind of historical exhibit and, with the thought of possibly linking the newly acquired Glebe Farm with Mary Arden's House in due course, a plan for a future Shakespeare Countryside Museum began to crystallize. In 1969 the Trustees accepted an offer of the Sunday Times to commission a feasibility study to investigate the possibilities of such a project. In consultation with the Trust's architect, Laurence Williams, and myself, a survey was made by Robin Wade and a tentative blueprint was prepared. The Trustees readily gave their blessing in principle to the idea, but, since heavy expenditure would be involved and possession of the Glebe Farm was still awaited, they decided that the suggested Shakespeare Countryside Museum project must be kept in abeyance until considerably larger financial resources became available to the Trust. In one respect this enforced delay had an advantage: it gave adequate time for me, in occasional consultation with Laurence Williams, the Trust's architect, gradually to evolve a mental vision of what the prospective Shakespeare Countryside Museum might ultimately become. This will be described in a later chapter.

Sir Fordham Flower, O.B.E., D.L., LL.D.

The untimely death of Sir Fordham Flower at the age of sixty-two, on 9 July 1966, cast a shadow over the Trust at a time when everything seemed to be going well.

For twenty years, alongside his chairmanship of the Royal Shakespeare Theatre, Sir Fordham had

Sir Fordham Flower, O.B.E., D.L., LL.D.

presided over the governing body of the Trust with dignity and skill, enthusiastic commitment and adventurous foresight. During this period I had established a close, friendly rapport with him; together we shared the same ideals and carried through plans which had set the Birthplace Trust on a course of development for the future. He had played a prominent part in the 1964 Shakespeare anniversary celebrations, and without his persuasive support the Shakespeare Centre would not have happened.

His health had given cause for anxiety for a little time, and it was for this reason that he decided to resign the chairmanship of the Trust at the Annual Meeting in May 1966, the presumption being that the office would be assumed by his cousin, Mr Dennis L. Flower, who was in fact then elected Chairman.

A few days after the Annual Meeting Sir Fordham sent me the following letter:

> The Hill
> Stratford-upon-Avon
>
> 24 May 66
>
> Dear Dr Fox,
>
> I thought that the A.G.M. went off very smoothly and happily last Saturday, and the modified agenda served its purpose admirably.
>
> I don't intend to be sentimental in this letter, but I do find it hard to express how satisfying and rewarding it has been to me to have worked closely with you over the last twenty years. A Chairman, retiring under these circumstances, is bound to garner a large measure of praise and kudos. But in effect, and no one realizes this more than me, what we were really reviewing last Saturday was *your* life's work, and I for one will be eternally grateful for all you have done for Stratford.
>
> I'm not being falsely modest myself, because I know what I have been able to achieve as your Chairman – holding fast on certain lines when others would incline to give way – striking out for a 20th century building for the new centre when the majority would really prefer to play for safety with some kind of compromise repro. – having of course from time to time to decide definitely one or other of two equally meritable courses of policy – and things like that.
>
> Anyway for me it's been a very happy partnership, and its worked well, and it has undoubtedly been both fruitful and successful. So all I can say is Thank you.
>
> Yours ever
> Fordham Flower

My first duty on hearing the news of Sir Fordham's death was to arrange for the Shakespeare flag at the Birthplace to be flown at half-mast, and so it remained until his funeral on 14 July. I had inherited this traditional observance of paying tribute to Trustees when they died, and over the years I ensured that the practice was continued.

Sir Fordham was born in 1904, elder son of Sir Archibald Dennis Flower of The Hill, Stratford-upon-Avon, and was educated at Winchester and Sandhurst. As an officer in the Ninth Queen's Royal Lancers, he served from 1924 to 1932 overseas, mostly in Egypt, Palestine and India, then returning to Stratford to enter the family's brewing company. In 1939 he re-joined his regiment, being promoted Major in 1940 and Lieutenant-Colonel in 1944. He had a distinguished career during the Second World War: he landed in Normandy on D-Day with an assault corps; he was twice mentioned in dispatches, created an O.B.E. in 1945, and made an Officer of the Order of Orange-Nassau in the same year.

Back at the brewery after the war, he was appointed Chairman of Flower and Sons, Ltd, in 1953 and of Flowers Breweries in 1958, and when the firm was taken over by Whitbread and Co., Ltd, he became a director of Whitbread. He was appointed a Deputy Lieutenant of Warwickshire in 1952 and was knighted in 1956. Sir Fordham was a considerable traveller and also a devotee of winter sports. He married in 1934 Hersey Catherine Balfour, and they had two sons and two daughters. He lived at Shottery Manor until Sir Archibald's death, when he moved to the family home at The Hill.

Sir Fordham, whose father had been seven times Mayor of Stratford-upon-Avon, followed in a great family tradition of public service, and became one of Warwickshire's most eminent figures. He was elected to the Stratford-upon-Avon Borough Council in 1933 and was Mayor of the Borough in 1947 and 1948, resigning his seat in 1949. He served as a member of the Warwickshire County Council from 1939 to 1947, and had also been chairman of the local Conservative Association. His most notable public service, however, alongside his chairmanship of the Birthplace Trust, was to the Royal Shakespeare Theatre, which had been founded by his great uncle, Charles Edward Flower, in 1879. He followed Sir Archibald as Chairman of the Governors, becoming the fourth member of his family to hold that position. Sir Fordham also served as chairman of the committee set up after the war to plan the re-construction of Coventry Cathedral, which had been destroyed by enemy air attack in 1940. In 1964 the University of Birmingham conferred on him an honorary doctorate in recognition of his work for Shakespeare.

Upon his death warm tributes were paid to him from many quarters. The Bishop of Coventry, Dr Cuthbert Bardsley, referred to his passing as 'a grievous loss to the Cathedral and to the Diocese', making the point that 'he did more than almost anybody else to bring into existence a magnificent new Cathedral, which has captured the attention of the world'. The Provost of Coventry, the Very Reverend H.C.N. Williams, echoed similar sentiments, describing him as 'the most courteous negotiator, who was able, by his courtesy, to reconcile conflicting passions, particularly on the subject of art, in which he was of more than average ability'.

The Artistic Director of the Royal Shakespeare Theatre, Peter Hall, spoke of the great transformation of the Theatre that had taken place under his guidance, including the establishment of a London base at the Aldwych Theatre and the formation of a permanent Royal Shakespeare Company. Describing him as 'wise and adventurous', Peter Hall said Sir Fordham's imaginative work in public life was 'completely selfless'; he managed the remarkable feat of successfully blending a career in business and in the arts. 'He believed in, and helped to create, a forward-looking policy', said Mr Hall, and paid tribute to the inspiration and support he had given to successive directors at the Stratford theatre: Sir Barry Jackson, Anthony Quayle, Glen Byam Shaw and, of course, to Peter Hall himself.

My feelings as Director of the Trust were very similar. I felt that Stratford had lost one of its most distinguished townsmen and the Shakespeare cause one of its most enthusiastic advocates. I referred particularly to his enlightened versatility and friendly leadership, and said he would be especially remembered for the skill and verve with which he helped to mould institutions with which he was closely associated to the changed conditions of the post-war world. Several of the Trustees echoed these sentiments, and the following tribute of Professor John Dover Wilson, who had formed a friendship with the Flower family after his election as a Life Trustee in 1931, admirably expressed their assessment of him:

'His triumphs as Chairman both of the Birthplace and of the Theatre are well known to all the Trustees. Let me only say that they were the fruits of statesmanship – of a statesman who was prepared to take great risks, as he did in the matter of the building of the new Centre at the Birthplace, and considered it his function to encourage and support the Director and company of the Theatre and if necessary to defend them. And what a man he was! How wise, how understanding, how kindly as a host, when he delighted to welcome scholars and actors together at The Hill. We shall not look upon his like again.'

A memorial service held in Holy Trinity Church, Stratford-upon-Avon, attended by a capacity congregation of people who came to take part in a public tribute to Sir Fordham, was conducted by the Bishop of Coventry, Dr Cuthbert Bardsley, on Monday, 25 July, 1966. Leading members of the Royal Shakespeare Company, together with the Theatre Wind Band, took part in a special programme of readings and music; and Anthony Quayle, a former director and actor who had worked closely with Sir Fordham, gave a moving address. 'All of us here', he said, 'are diminished by his death, as if a promontory were washed away by the sea'... 'He would have been the last to see himself as a promontory. But that was what he was. And now that that promontory is washed away, we can begin to discern its strength and size'... 'in a shifting, uncertain world, he was a man – a man ready and prepared to shoulder responsibilities, standing well founded amongst all the demands of a complex life. Perceptive, amused, magnanimous, with an endless zest for each succeeding day, always giving more than he received. He loved life, and he served it well.'

Less theatrical, but equally personal and sincere,

Unveiling the tablet alongside memorial gates at New Place

were the informal remembrances and tributes paid to their late Chairman by the Trustees at their Half Annual Meeting on Saturday, 29 October 1966. Having had the privilege of knowing and working closely with Sir Fordham for over twenty years, I also paid a tribute to his memory, both personally and on behalf of the staff of the Shakespeare Birthplace Trust, as follows:

'Following an equally remarkable father, Sir Fordham will be remembered for his enlightened leadership and wise judgment in all matters affecting the good name of Stratford and Shakespeare. Always alive to his family's tradition of public service, he succeeded in combining business ability with artistic appreciation to an unusual degree, and he displayed qualities of integrity, versatility, firmness of purpose and liberal outlook in his approach to the many tasks for which he so willingly worked.

My association with Sir Fordham in his capacity of Chairman of the Shakespeare Birthplace Trust, an office he held for twenty years, was a most happy experience. He was a man with whom one could share a vision, and I shall always be grateful to him for his consistent encouragement and support in helping to re-shape the Shakespeare Birthplace Trust to the changed conditions of post-war years, and subsequently in carrying through a series of projects culminating in the building of the Shakespeare Centre and the celebrations of the 1964 Shakespeare anniversary year.

Sir Fordham had the ability to look at Stratford from the outside as well as the inside, and no-one had a greater appreciation of our special responsibilities to the world. Always aware of tradition and the achievements of the past, fully alive to the problems and opportunities of the present, he possessed a quality of adventurous far-sightedness which made him a leader of authority and influence. In this role, and as a chairman, the Trustees found Sir Fordham to be an outstanding personality, persuasive, considerate and courageous. As he himself often said, he believed in delegation and was always willing to leave the technicalities and details to others. But it was he who supplied the inspiration, and herein lay the secret of his success.

The Trustees and staff, as also his many friends throughout the world, treasure the memory of a man who made an important contribution to the life of Stratford-upon-Avon and Warwickshire, and indeed to the prestige of this country. Men of his calibre these days are scarce, and our loss is a heavy one.'

It was on this occasion that, following the business meeting, the Trustees proceeded to the Great Garden of New Place, where a short ceremony took place. Mr Dennis Flower, the Chairman, unveiled a tablet built into the wall alongside new wrought-iron gates recently placed at the top entrance to the garden in Chapel Lane. The Trustees had in fact decided to provide these gates as a permanent reminder of Sir Fordham's service to the Trust, when he announced his retirement from the chairmanship earlier in the year. The wording of the tablet, carved by John Skelton on a panel of black granite, recorded the Trustees' permanent tribute.

> The Great Garden of New Place
> These Entrance Gates were provided by the Trustees of Shakespeare's Birthplace as a token of appreciation to Sir Fordham Flower O·B·E Chairman of the Trust 1946-1966

Whenever I walk through these gates into the garden at New Place, my mind goes back to the many occasions when I used to pick up my papers in advance of a Trustees' meeting and make my way to Sir Fordham's room in the Brewery Street offices. It was there that discussions and decisions were made that vitally influenced the development of the Trust.

The Garrick Bicentenary Celebrations

The year 1969 will be remembered for the Garrick bicentenary celebrations, in the organization of which the Shakespeare Birthplace Trust played a prominent role.

The immediate occasion for the unique events of 1769 was the dedication of Stratford's new Town Hall by the famous actor, David Garrick; and during the Festival, or Jubilee, as it came to be called, presided over by Garrick himself, a programme of banquets, balls, processions, concerts, firework displays and horse-racing, was staged over a period of three days, from 5 to 8 September. An impressive temporary amphitheatre was built on the banks of the River Avon, and the celebrations were attended by a large company of literary and theatrical personages who had come down from London especially for the occasion. The events thus received nation-wide publicity, and captured the public imagination.

The Garrick Jubilee, the first Shakespeare Festival to be organized in the town, was a landmark in Stratford's history. Garrick himself, the greatest theatrical figure of his day, became the town's first honorary freeman, and presented a statue of Shakespeare to adorn the exterior of the Town Hall which he had been invited to dedicate. The Jubilee marked the beginning of Stratford as a literary and tourist attraction, and had considerable influence in popularising Shakespeare and stimulating interest in his plays.

Realizing that, in the Jubilee, Shakespearian appreciation and Borough history were uniquely blended, it seemed appropriate that suitable commemorative events should be staged to mark the bicentenary in 1969. With the agreement of the Trust's Chairman, Mr Dennis Flower, I accordingly arranged for an informal meeting in November 1967 of representatives of bodies likely to be interested in promoting a programme of celebrations. The outcome was the formation of the Garrick Celebrations Committee, which had its inaugural meeting at the Shakespeare Centre on 21 February 1968. The Committee consisted of representatives of the Stratford-upon-Avon Borough Council, the Shakespeare Birthplace Trust, the Royal Shakespeare Theatre and the Shakespeare Institute of the University of Birmingham. Mr Dennis Flower was elected Chairman, Dr Stanley Wells Deputy Chairman, and I became the Director responsible for organizing the celebrations, the headquarters of which, it was decided, should be the Shakespeare Centre.

The Committee agreed that its function should essentially be concerned with planning and co-ordination, and that its task should be to encourage, advise and guide contributions to a programme of festival activities likely to be made by local organizations, at the same time maintaining liaison with national and other bodies, such as the Garrick Club, that might wish to participate. A general pattern for the celebrations was approved. It was agreed that throughout the summer season the normal activities of the various bodies should be slanted towards the Garrick celebrations, which would help to educate public opinion on the significance of the Jubilee. These activities would then culminate in three days of concentrated celebrations, coinciding with the original Jubilee dates of 6, 7 and 8 September, which in 1969 would fall on a Saturday, Sunday and Monday.

During the following months the various bodies represented on the Committee considered what they could offer towards a festival programme, and by August 1968 good progress had been made. At that juncture, however, the Borough Council had not yet indicated the degree of its involvement, and it was not until the beginning of 1969 that various uncertainties were resolved and the general pattern of the programme was finally approved. In the meantime, the assistance of the local Chamber of Trade had been sought, to encourage shopkeepers to re-furbish and decorate their premises with flowers so that the town might look at its best during the summer, and, in order to achieve wider publicity, a special Stratford-upon-Avon postmark had been designed, to be introduced by the Post Office on 1 January 1969.

The Shakespeare birthday celebrations held on St George's day, 23 April, marked the beginning of the programme of special events arranged to commemorate the bicentenary year. As Chairman of the Birthday Celebrations Committee, it fell to me to be responsible for all practical arrangements, with the help of my staff at the Shakespeare Centre. On Sunday, 20 April, the traditional Shakespeare Service was held at Holy Trinity Church, and in the evening the first of the Birthplace Trust's concerts for the season took place in the Town Hall. A recital entitled 'If Music be the Food of Love', consisting of music in the English theatre from 1500 to 1750, was given by the Early Music Consort, a talented group of young artists directed by David Munrow. On the eve of the birthday, 22 April, the Mayor of Stratford-upon-Avon held a civic reception and cocktail party at the Town Hall for diplomatic, civic and other guests. The birthday programme itself, on 23 April, was on a more elaborate scale than usual and, in order to provide more adequate accommodation for the luncheon than in previous years, when the event had been held in the conference hall of the Theatre, a special pavilion was erected in the garden of the Royal Shakespeare Theatre, beside the river. The toast of 'The Immortal Memory of William Shakespeare' was proposed by the Earl of Harewood and that of 'The Theatre' by the Director-General of the British Council, Sir John Henniker-Major. Ambassadors, High Commissioners and other diplomatic representatives of the countries of the world were present in good numbers, subsequently taking part during the afternoon in the ceremony of unfurling the flags of the nations, followed by the floral procession to Shakespeare's Birthplace and on to the poet's tomb in Holy Trinity Church. A birthday performance of *The Merry Wives of Windsor* rounded off the proceedings in the evening.

As a back-cloth to events which followed, the Trust presented an exhibition at the Shakespeare Centre from May to October on 'The Great Stratford Jubilee'. Its purpose was to illustrate the background, origins and preparations for Garrick's Jubilee, and some of the events which took place in Stratford. It was the most ambitious exhibition staged at the Centre since 1964, and contained a number of loaned items of special interest, which supplemented the material from the Trust's own collections. There were several paintings of Garrick, depicted in different character roles, loaned by the Garrick Club, together with a variety of personal items, such as Garrick's signet ring and dress sword and the mulberry wood box, and scales used for weighing his medicines. The Trust's own collections provided most of the documentary and visual exhibits, with a full selection of Garrick memorabilia ranging from the original mulberry wood medallion worn by Garrick as Steward of the Jubilee to medals, ribbons and silk favours produced in 1769. The British Museum loaned the original letter to Garrick from the Mayor and Corporation of Stratford-upon-Avon, 3 May 1769, announcing that the Freedom of the Borough was to be bestowed on him, and also the richly carved mulberry wood casket in which the Freedom scroll was presented. Particularly colourful and exquisitely made were Mrs Garrick's embroidered silk dress and the velvet suit worn by Garrick as Steward of the Jubilee. The exhibition also contained silver and silver gilt medallions commissioned by the Birthplace Trust and designed by Paul Vincze to commemorate the Jubilee bicentenary, and printed tapestry panels by Tibor Reich, depicting the heads of Shakespeare and Garrick in mosaic and the scene at Stratford's market cross during the original celebrations.

In July another exhibition, on the theatre of 'David Garrick and his Contemporaries', was opened at Hall's Croft by Dr Roy Strong, to coincide with the Stratford-upon-Avon Poetry Festival held there. Most of the exhibits had been loaned by the University of London Library, the National Portrait Gallery, the Victoria and Albert Museum, the Duke of Devonshire and the Trustees of the Chatsworth Settlement, and John Carroll, who chose and arranged them. The exhibition presented a number of manuscripts, books and pictures relating to the actor David Garrick and some of the famous men of letters of his time. Nearly all the books displayed were published during Garrick's lifetime (1717-1779), and included items from his personal library, notably a unique, finely-bound presentation copy of John Stow's *A Survey of London*, 1598, with Garrick's bookplate and autograph signature on the title page.

The Poetry Festival took the form of poetry readings by theatre and literary artists on nine Sunday evenings, culminating in a special programme, 'Shakespeare in the Eighteenth Century', devised and directed by Douglas Cleverdon, held on 24 August in the Royal Shakespeare Theatre. Members of the Theatre company, Barbara Jefford, Rosalind Shanks, Julian Glover, William Squire and Gary Watson, declaimed scenes from Shakespeare in the version that playgoers saw in the eighteenth century, as revised and re-written by Dryden and Davenant, Nahum Tate, Colley Cibber and David Garrick himself.

This was a natural build-up to the concentrated period of festivities. which started on Friday evening, 5 September, when the Mayor, Councillor Malcolm Ray, and the Corporation of Stratford-upon-Avon sponsored the Garrick Jubilee Ball, held in the elegant upper room at the Town Hall in which Garrick had stood to dedicate the building to the memory of William Shakespeare, on the opening day of the Jubilee. Steps were taken to make the civic ball a very special occasion: at midnight there was a surprise for the dancers, when the scene in which David Garrick was presented with the insignia of the office of Steward of the Jubilee by the Mayor was re-enacted. Royal Shakespeare Company actors Jeffery Dench and Geoffrey Hutchings, attired in appropriate eighteenth-century costumes, played the parts of the Mayor of Stratford and David Garrick. The re-enactment was excellently stage-managed, with due ceremony and the recital of words as originally used, and the band played 'The Warwickshire Lad', a song which was heard for the first time at the Garrick Jubilee.

The colour and gaiety of this event characterised the festivities of the days that followed. During the weekend, the Shakespeare Morris Men of Stratford-upon-Avon, assisted by visiting folk dance teams, gave displays of dancing on the Bancroft Gardens and in the town. During the afternoon of Saturday, 6 September, a Garrick Jubilee Race Meeting was organized by the Stratford-upon-Avon Racecourse Company on the same meadow in Shottery on which the original Jubilee race had been run two hundred years before. To commemorate the race for the Jubilee Cup in 1769, a handicap two-mile hurdle race was run for a new Garrick Jubilee Cup, a fine silver cup designed and supplied by George Pragnell, jeweller of Stratford-upon-Avon. Jockey Willie Robinson won the Garrick race on Mugatpura, in a thrilling, close finish with co-favourite Henry the Fifth, and the cup was presented to the trainer by Dame Peggy Ashcroft. Six other races, named after Shakespearian characters, were run, the winners receiving a silver dish in which was set one of the Garrick medallions designed by Paul Vincze. All the races had good entries and attracted a large concourse of race-goers and considerable publicity. A souvenir publication, *Racing at Stratford*, described the historical background of the commemorative occasion, giving details of the race which took place in 1769, when torrential rain had flooded the low-lying meadow.

On Saturday evening a Jubilee Banquet, organized by the Shakespeare Club of Stratford-upon-Avon in association with the Shakespeare Birthplace Trust, took place in the eighteenth-century ballroom of the Town Hall. In the presence of a capacity audience of representative guests and Shakespeare devotees, Dame Veronica Wedgwood, the distinguished historian and writer, who was currently the President of the Shakespeare Club, described the banquet as 'commemorating history in the presence of history'.

In proposing the toast to David Garrick, Dr Thomas Boase, the President of Magdalen College, Oxford, who was on the governing bodies of the Royal Shakespeare Theatre and the Shakespeare Birthplace Trust, recreated in words the scene re-enacted the night before. He described Garrick as having been in the centre of 'a Shakespeare boom', performing some of the plays more or less as they had been originally written. Stratford's choice of Garrick stemmed from 'a very reasonable commercial sense', recalling that little had been done locally to recognize Shakespeare's dramatic achievement, since Sarah Siddons's grandfather performed *Othello* in the old Town Hall in 1746. Indeed, that was the first occasion on which any of Shakespeare's plays were known to have been performed in the town; when the King's Players visited Stratford in the 1620s, they were paid six shillings *not* to perform! It was Garrick who suddenly gave a great impetus to the recognition of our national poet by organizing a festival in Stratford. Those who came through the rain in 1769 were the fore-runners of the multitude of visitors who, since that time, have made Stratford 'the greatest secular place of pilgrimage in the world'.

On Sunday morning, 7 September, a commemorative service of the arts, directed by Canon Joseph Poole of Coventry Cathedral, was held in Holy Trinity Church. This was particularly appropriate, because in 1769 the Jubilee had opened with a performance in this church of Dr Thomas Arne's oratorio *Judith*, conducted by the composer. James Boswell praised the oratorio as 'an adorable performance', but wished that 'Prayers had been offered, and a short sermon preached', adding that 'it would have consecrated our Jubilee, to begin it with Devotion, with gratefully adoring the Supreme Father of all spirits from whom cometh every good and perfect gift'. The commemorative service, under the title of 'Garrick's Folly Remembered', remedied this omission. The Bishop of Coventry, the Right Reverend Cuthbert Bardsley, took part, together with members of the Royal Shakespeare Company, musicians, trumpeters and singers. The Mayor and Corporation of Stratford, in traditional civic procession, attended with other representative guests and the church was filled to overflowing.

Mr John Strickson, the organist at Holy Trinity Church, played the organ and harpsichord; fanfares were sounded by the Heralds of the Coventry School of Music; musical selections were played by the principal strings of the Orchestra da Camera; the singers of Holy Trinity Church Choir were augmented by the Stratford Madrigal Choir; and the readers were Judi Dench and Donald Sinden of the Royal Shakespeare Company. The service was a joyful and moving tribute, the combination of music, song and spoken word aptly giving praise and thanks for the artists in every age. As was reported in the local press the following week: 'Madrigals floated their ethereal mystery down the church from the chancel, hymns were lustily chorused, choristers released their pure treble notes on the more profound sounding-board of male voice, delicate warp and weft were woven by harpsichord and strings, strident fanfares rewakened echoes of the past – and sensitively spoken words made a magical blend with music, to bring a crowded church to deep understanding that it is many benefactors, known and unknown, remembered and forgotten, whose harvest is reaped by successive generations'.

During the Sunday afternoon an even larger crowd of spectators watched a Garrick Jubilee Cricket Match, arranged by Dame Peggy Ashcroft in association with the Stratford-upon-Avon Cricket Club, when a Stratford Club side played against past and present members of the Royal Shakespeare Theatre and the Garrick Club. Apart from providing considerable amusement, the match raised a useful sum of money for the Shakespeare Theatre Trust. Meanwhile, in the Bancroft Gardens the band of the Royal Regiment of Fusiliers played a programme of music which included pieces specially composed in 1769 for the Garrick Jubilee.

There was a further accent on theatre and music when the Garrick Jubilee Concert, arranged by the Birthplace Trust, was presented in the Royal Shakespeare Theatre on the Sunday evening. It took the form of a programme of eighteenth-century music, given by the London Mozart Players and directed from the harpsichord by Raymond Leppard. Pieces included the Overture from *The Padlock*, by Charles Dibdin, as first produced at Drury Lane in 1768; Symphony No. 4 by William Boyce, originally played at Drury Lane in 1751; Duets by François André Philidor and Niccola Piccinni; and Symphony No. 29 in A Major, written by the eighteen-year-old Mozart in 1774. The soloists were April Cantelo (soprano) and Alexander Young (tenor). The programme concluded with a light-hearted performance of Garrick's *Ode to Shakespeare*, with musical accompaniment by Thomas Arne and including the well known arias first sung at the Jubilee. Garrick's performance of his *Ode* in the Jubilee amphitheatre, on 7 September 1769, was the most memorable event of the Jubilee. It was also the event which best exhibited Garrick's many talents: his flair for organization, his gifts of showmanship, his aptitude for writing, and his supreme ability for acting. The revival of the *Ode* was therefore a natural ingredient of this celebratory occasion, and its rendering by Paul Rogers, the singers and the orchestra, enjoyed a rapturous reception. There was, in fact, an atmosphere of magic and elegance about the evening's concert difficult to describe.

The two remaining events of the celebrations programme took place on Monday, 8 September. At noon a young mulberry tree, grown from a cutting of the original tree believed to have been set by Shakespeare in the Great Garden of New Place, was planted in the garden by the Trust as a continuing reminder of the Garrick celebrations. The ceremony of planting was performed by Dame Peggy Ashcroft in the presence of a company of Shakespeare enthusiasts, and the plaque shown below was placed alongside it.

> THIS MULBERRY TREE, OFFSPRING OF THE
> PARENT TREE NEARBY, WAS PLANTED BY
> DAME PEGGY ASHCROFT
> ON 8 SEPTEMBER 1969 TO COMMEMORATE
> THE 200TH ANNIVERSARY
> OF THE FIRST SHAKESPEARE FESTIVAL
> AT STRATFORD-UPON-AVON
> ORGANIZED BY DAVID GARRICK IN 1769

In thanking Dame Peggy for thus perpetuating the mulberry tree association in what he described as 'this hallowed spot', the Chairman, Mr Dennis Flower, presented to her two of the Garrick bicentenary medals – one of gold and one of silver – which had been designed by Paul Vincze and sponsored by the Trust. The medal bore both a Shakespeare and a Garrick design. The obverse depicted a new representation of Shakespeare, based on the artist's interpretation of the Soest portrait, with standing figures of a young man and a young woman paying homage to Shakespeare, symbolizing the growing appreciation of the genius of the poet by succeeding generations and particularly by the young people of our own time. On the reverse, against a theatrical background suggested by curtains and the masks of comedy and tragedy, the medal portrayed the actor David Garrick in his role as Steward of the Stratford Jubilee, carrying his wand of office and looking at the carved mulberry-wood medallion he wore throughout the festival. The words from the *Ode* recited by Garrick at the Jubilee were incorporated in the composition.

The concluding event of the bicentenary programme, arranged by the Trust, was 'A Bicentenary Celebration', devised and directed by Richard Digby Day, which took place in the Town Hall on Monday

Dame Peggy Ashcroft planting the mulberry tree

The Garrick bicentenary medal

evening, 8 September. A group of young artists – Dorothy Reynolds, Jane Wenham, Angus Mackay and John Quentin, with Chuck Mallett on the piano – presented a lively, amusing entertainment based on contemporary records and press reports of the original Jubilee. The personality of the master performer, David Garrick, was vividly portrayed, providing a clue to the understanding of his concept of the Jubilee and giving added interest to the eye-witnesses' accounts of the events of the three-day Festival.

Further details of these historic events are given in my paper, *A Splendid Occasion: the Stratford Jubilee of 1769*, published by the Dugdale Society in 1973 and also by the Trust in a separate presentation edition.

The efforts made by the Shakespeare Birthplace Trust to keep Garrick's memory alive were amply justified by the appreciative response of all who took part. The great actor himself would not have been displeased!

Anne Hathaway's Cottage Fire

News of a fire that had seriously damaged Anne Hathaway's Cottage during the night was announced in the BBC's early morning radio bulletin at 6 a.m. on Saturday, 22 November 1969. For the next twenty-four hours my telephone rang incessantly, the press and the media seeking details of the occurrence and friends and well wishers expressing dismay and sympathy. Within hours news was flashed round the world and calls came in asking for information from the United States, Australia and European countries. The disaster made headline international news.

The fire, which involved the top third, or orchard end, of the Cottage (furthest from the road), was discovered at about 12.45 a.m., less than two hours after the customary late-night routine safety inspection had been made by the member of the Trust's staff who lived in Hewlands Cottage nearby. The alarm was given by Mr Robert Pickin, one of the Trust's tenants, who was returning to his flat at nearby Shottery Lodge. When he saw flames leaping into the darkened sky, he thought it was a bonfire but then, as he approached Cottage Lane, he realized that the thatched roof of Anne Hathaway's Cottage was engulfed in a furious blaze. He summoned the fire brigade, which was on the scene in four minutes, and further assistance was called from Alcester, Bidford-on-Avon and Leamington Spa.

Anne Hathaway's Cottage fire

Damage following the fire at Anne Hathaway's Cottage; on the right, the Hathaway bed

Divisional Officer John Paul was initially in charge of the operation, until the arrival of Warwickshire's Fire Chief, Frederick Capron, with his deputy. I was told that, when the brigade arrived, flames were spreading through the roof and leaping from the windows. The fire had started in the end ground-floor room, which was used for display and sale of publications and gifts, and it had spread rapidly through the boarded ceiling into the furnished bedroom above, and then to the raftered, thatched roof which covered it. The speed at which the fire had spread and the intensity of the blaze were commented upon by the fire-fighters, who had to use breathing apparatus to enable them to enter what by that time was a raging inferno emitting clouds of suffocating smoke. Almost one third of the long roof was well alight, but, due to the skilful work of the fire crew, it was held at the point where there was a break in the roof level. It was a dark, wet night, and in pouring rain the firemen played their hoses both on the fire and on the lower part of the building not yet involved, at the same time pulling off the blazing thatch.

Meanwhile, a courageous attempt was made to save the contents of the building. Wearing breathing masks, the firemen entered the burning upper rooms and brought out all the movable pieces of furniture and accessories, some already burned and charred. These were piled and protected under sheets at the lower end of the garden. There was a problem with the Hathaway bed, which stood in the bedroom adjoining the room on fire. It could not be dismantled and carried downstairs to safety, like the smaller movable pieces of furniture, so it was pushed to the far end of the room, a tarpaulin sheet was put over the top of it and water constantly played on it.

Because of this initiative, the most precious heirloom of the Hathaway family, though blackened and damaged by water, was saved. The training and experience of the fire crews in salvage operations proved invaluable, and what might have been an unmitigated disaster for the furniture and contents proved less serious than could have been expected.

I was summoned to the scene shortly after the fire was discovered, and it was fortuitous that I was at home in Stratford at that time. On the evening of 21 November I had been in Leicester giving a lecture to the Leicestershire Historical and Archaeological Society, with which I had a close association, and arrangements had been made for me to stay the night. The meeting having finished, for reasons I cannot possibly explain, I declined the offer of accommodation for the night and returned to Stratford shortly before midnight. It was not long before I found myself witnessing a scene at the fire which made me feel sick with sadness and dismay.

Shortly before 5 a.m., being anxious to see the extent of the damage for myself, the Chief Fire Officer escorted me up the back staircase, which had miraculously escaped major damage, into the bedroom where the Hathaway bed had been pushed to safety. Part of the ceiling had already gone, and through the charred timbers of the wall on the left I saw the gutted room below, in which the fire had started. By this time, much of the smoking thatch had been stripped off and lay in smouldering piles inside and outside the damaged part of the building. The charred timbers and scorched rafters made an eerie spectacle against the darkness, as firemen continued to damp down the debris.

The firemen did a remarkable job, and in fact saved two thirds of the Cottage from being destroyed. Nevertheless, all the rooms were soaked with water, and the walls and ceilings blackened with smoke. For months afterwards, even when the whole Cottage had been redecorated, the acrid smell of fire lingered.

It was at this juncture that I made a quick return home, to inform the BBC and to break the news to the Chairman and the local Trustees. At the same time, I contacted the Trust's architect, Laurence Williams, who set out immediately from his home in Church Stretton to come to the scene. By the time I returned to Shottery, a group of people who had heard the news had assembled to witness the spectacle. The Chief Guide of the Cottage, Mr Harold Abraham, with his deputy, Mrs Grace Collins, had been there all night together with one or two other members of staff who lived nearby. Gardeners and other helpers then arrived, followed by journalists and press photographers who had been alerted, all anxious to get a full story. Dealing with the media, in fact, subsequently took a good deal of my time.

The fire having been extinguished, tarpaulin sheets were spread over what was left of the exposed part of the building, to provide a degree of protection from the rain which continued to fall. Firemen concentrated on damping down the smouldering piles of thatch lying on the ground. Meanwhile, the salvaged furniture and contents which had been covered over with sheets at the bottom of the garden were moved for safety, and later assessment, to the outbuildings of Shottery Lodge, nearby.

During the morning, members of the Trust's Executive Committee met in emergency session and were joined by Laurence Williams, who had already inspected the fire damage. I described what had happened, and gave an eye-witness account of the sequence of events and the action I had already taken on the site during the night and early morning. The loss to the Trust, I said, would be considerable, but, although the situation was serious, I felt confident that the Cottage could be restored to its original appearance and character. The process of reinstatement, however, would be difficult and costly. I expressed the opinion that the fire could not possibly have been caused by an accident, and gave the reasons which led me to form this conclusion.

The Trustees took speedy action to deal with the emergency situation. They authorized me, as Director, in consultation with Laurence Williams, to take all necessary action to safeguard the damaged structure of the Cottage and to proceed with all possible speed to organize its restoration to its former condition. I was also given full authority to take such action as I might think necessary in respect of all other aspects of the situation. The Committee decided to invite William Sapcote and Sons, Ltd, of Birmingham to assume the responsibilities of main contractors for the restoration of the property and to ask the Police to investigate the circumstances leading to the fire.

Following their meeting, the Trustees made an inspection of the fire damage for themselves. They all felt a great sense of shock and sadness, but were impressed to see the efforts of staff and other volunteers already busy mopping up and helping to clear the debris, a process which continued over the weekend. Pressmen who had converged were anxious for comment, and the question on everybody's lips was how the fire could possibly have happened. Asked if arson was suspected, I said I was not in a position to make any suggestion yet, but it could not be ruled out as a possibility. Whilst adopting this cautious attitude, right from the first I had a firm instinct that somehow the fire had been started deliberately, and that the only other possible cause, namely an electrical fault, was highly unlikely.

Very speedy action followed. Within a few days of the fire, scaffolding was erected and a temporary roof put over the damaged structure; and even before the tasks of survey – greatly helped by measured drawings the Trust already had – and assessment were completed, plans were made to proceed with the reinstating of the Cottage. Site meetings were held and various sub-contractors consulted; in general, it was proposed to use the services of firms with which the Trust had long-standing associations. The necessary permissions for the work to go ahead were readily forthcoming from the County Planning Officer and the Borough Engineer.

Meanwhile, investigations into the cause of the fire proceeded. The Police called in a forensic expert, who examined the charred woodwork, sifted through the debris and took away items for examination. It was established that the electrical installation was not at fault. Watching all this, I became more convinced than ever that the fire was not an accident, but had been deliberately started. Then, as the Trust's workmen cleared away the sodden pile of straw and charred timber inside and outside the burnt-out room, I noticed two clues which supported my theory. The opening casement of the leaded-light window, which had been buried in the pile, had a missing opening catch, and as clearance proceeded the detached piece was found. This suggested forcible entry through the window. Then, when the floor of the room was cleared, I saw brown scorch marks on the stone-paved floor alongside the charred woodwork of the sales counter. This suggested that here was the point of ignition which started the fire.

This information was passed on to the Police, who by this time were appealing for information about anyone seen in the vicinity of the Cottage before or after the alarm had been received. On 26 November, four days after the occurrence, they arrested a twenty-one-year-old young man, Alan Charles Jacques, a builders' labourer who lived in the town. He was charged with arson, remanded on bail by the local magistrates and, after a second hearing, was sent for trial at Warwick Assizes. When I gave evidence at the Assizes on 14 January 1970, I said that £25,000 worth of damage had been caused to the building and between £5,000 and £7,500 to the contents. Jacques pleaded guilty. It was said that he set fire to the Cottage after a quarrel with his girl friend, whom he had met during the evening. A witness who gave evidence said that Jacques had been drinking heavily, and that later he had accompanied him to a restaurant where Jacques asked the waiter for a box of matches. He had then proceeded just before midnight to the Blue Star Garage, where he bought petrol in a can, explaining that a friend's car had run out of petrol. In the event, a patrol police officer had witnessed the sale but had no grounds for suspicion. Jacques had then walked to Shottery, forced the opening light of the window in the publications room, climbed in and spent some time pouring the petrol over the counter and on goods on display. Having climbed back out of the building, he threw a lighted match through the window into the petrol-soaked area, resulting in an instant blaze of intense ferocity. In defence, Jacques pleaded that at the time he was 'rather upset and mixed up' in his mind and admitted he was 'a bit scared'. He left the scene and quickly made his way home, running along the path by Hathaway Hamlet. In passing sentence, the Judge told Jacques that 'the target for your vengeance on this night was to set fire to one of the most precious buildings left in the country'. 'It's no thanks to you that this building is not today a completely gutted shell', he added, sentencing the offender to prison for four years.

As already mentioned, the fire attracted considerable publicity. For weeks afterwards I received a steady stream of letters and messages from well wishers expressing concern and sympathy, some accompanied by small donations of money to assist the restoration. Firms and individuals also offered their services, together with timber, pieces of furniture, paintings and other items for possible use in replacing what had been lost. A few offers to buy pieces of charred timber were received, but politely declined. Several of those who came to view the property at that time recounted their visits to the Cottage, and I recall one, in particular, who described the interior of the Cottage as it was when she was shown round under the guidance of Mrs Baker, who died in 1894.

The Trustees were fortunate in securing as main contractors the services of William Sapcote and Sons, Ltd, the firm which had undertaken the restoration of Hall's Croft. They still had in their employment a number of experienced craftsmen able to use traditional materials with traditional tools and expertise. The Trustees were also extremely fortunate in being offered, as a gift by Flower and Sons, Ltd, a large quantity of superb, seasoned English oak, which had come from Clifford Manor when alterations were carried out there. This, together with timber from the Trust's own stock, provided most of the necessary replacement material.

The task of reinstatement was one of considerable complexity, and difficult to cost on a fixed price estimate; for this reason, the Trustees agreed with their architect's recommendation that the work should be paid for on the basis of a fixed-fee form of prime cost contract, and a quantity surveyor was employed to monitor the cost of the operation at every stage. The middle of March 1970 was set as a completion date, so all involved had a target to which to work. Regular site meetings were held to discuss and agree every detail of the restoration programme, and surviving notes of these meetings provide evidence of the extreme care taken to plan, execute and supervise the work. As much of the original timber framed structure as possible was kept, and replacement members to complete the reconstruction were fashioned by experienced carpenters, using the adze and other traditional hand-tools. This attention to age-old construction methods was repeated at every stage of the project. Wooden pegs were hammered through the beams to hold the

Craftsmen at work on the reinstatement of the Cottage

framework securely; cleft-oak lathing was used to fill the panels between the studding, and a plaster coating added that consisted of lime mortar and cow hair, mixed to a specification as near the original as possible. Lighting was installed under the temporary roof, to enable work to go forward during the dark, cold, wintry days.

The rethatching of the roof – the whole Cottage had to be done – was entrusted to David J. Rimell of Binton, whose family had produced several generations of thatchers, and the material used was Warwickshire grown, combed wheat straw. Incidentally, one of the offers received after the fire was from a firm willing to cover the roof with plastic thatch! Mr Norman Dixon, the Stratford electrical contractor who had already worked on the Cottage, renewed the electrical wiring, and Nelder and Southam, another local firm which had served the Trust for many years, remade the leaded-light windows with antique glass specially obtained on the advice of Mr Vernon Spreadbury, the stained glass artist who lived in retirement in Stratford and who was responsible for the windows in the chancel of the Guild Chapel. The counter and fitments in the shop were replaced by A. Edmonds and Co., Ltd, museum contractors of Birmingham who had provided the original fittings. Mr W.R. Clarke, the local signwriter, produced an impressive, large notice board recording all these details, which was erected inside the entrance to the garden for the information of visitors.

While work on the building was proceeding, the problem of dealing with the salvaged furniture had to be tackled. A sixteenth-century, oak, linenfold chest and a fine, early seventeenth-century, oak, upholstered arm chair had been burnt to charred skeletons, but in the majority of cases the furniture had been damaged, to a greater or lesser extent, by fire and water. The need was for careful cleaning and overhaul by a professional antique furniture restorer. Again, the Trust's association with Mr S.W. Wolsey, the authority on Tudor and Jacobean oak furniture, produced the answer. He arranged for a cabinet maker who had previously worked for him, R.A. Windley of Westcott, Surrey, to take away to his

Re-instatement of Anne Hathaway's Cottage after the fire: notice board

workshop all the items needing attention and to do what was necessary. Included was the Hathaway bed, with its hangings, which was dismantled, together with the bed from the adjoining chamber with its linsey-woolsey curtains. Everything was completed and returned by the middle of March; the transformation of the blackened, charred pieces had to be seen to be believed. At the same time, new curtains, made of a simple, hand-woven material, were provided for all the windows in the Cottage by Gordon Russell, Ltd, of Broadway.

Whilst all this was going on, I found myself engaged in negotiations with the Trust's insurers, the General Accident Fire and Life Assurance Corporation. The Trustees had Anne Hathaway's Cottage and its contents included in a general fire insurance policy, but, because it had always been their practice to carry most of the risk themselves in order to avoid an impossibly heavy burden of charges, the sums insured were only nominal amounts. The building itself, for instance, was only covered for £20,000, and the furniture, fittings and general contents for £4,185. Individual pieces were covered, but only for nominal amounts, as for example, the early seventeenth-century arm chair which was destroyed. This was itemised at £40, but when I made enquiries about a possible replacement, the price quoted was £665. There was also barely any cover for the stock of publications and gift items in the room that had been destroyed. It therefore appeared that the Trust would be faced with a considerable loss, more especially since the temporary closing of the Cottage, and its subsequent operation for four months on a restricted basis, resulted in a reduction in income from visitors and sales.

The insurance company appointed an assessor, and the Trustees also decided to use professional services to assist with the negotiations. Because an inventory existed, I was able to itemise every piece of furniture and other contents affected, and from stock records to provide a full list of sales items destroyed. I also produced figures to substantiate a claim for 'loss of profits'. All this took considerable time, and

Anne Hathaway's Cottage as restored after the fire, 1970

it was not until towards the end of 1970, when the total cost of restoration including labour, materials, architect's and surveyor's fees was known, that a final settlement was reached. The Directors of the General Accident Insurance Corporation were extremely generous: they decided not to apply the principle of average, because of their special relationship with the Trust and their desire to assist. The Trust received £19,000 in respect of damage to the building, £1,500 for the furniture and contents, and £2,200 in connection with loss of profits. My own estimate was that the whole episode had cost the Trust a total expenditure of some £30,000, so, all things considered, the Trustees came out of it very well.

The work of restoration was completed on schedule. It was achieved by intensive, enthusiastic team work, motivated by skilful direction, craftsmanship of the highest order in many directions, and a determination to get the task completed in time for the beginning of the visiting season. The builders having departed by mid-March, the furniture and other effects were restored to their customary places and the publications room re-stocked in readiness for the anticipated influx of visitors keen to see the property in its restored condition.

Anne Hathaway's Cottage re-opened to the public on Good Friday afternoon, 27 March 1970. A long queue quickly formed in the garden, and although rain, frost and snow marred the four-day Easter holiday period, upwards of 7,000 people were admitted. Easter Monday's visitors alone totalled 2,671, a figure which was equalled and exceeded on a number of occasions during the summer. The Chief Guide, Harold Abraham, reported that many were surprised that the interior showed such little evidence of the damage inflicted by the fire, and that everything looked 'almost as before'. Such favourable reactions were a well deserved encouragement and reward to the staff for all the effort they had expended since the disaster occurred.

The members of the Trust's Executive Committee were equally relieved and pleased that this unfortunate chapter in the history of Anne Hathaway's Cottage had come to such a satisfactory conclusion. On Friday evening, 10 April 1970, they gave an informal party in the Cottage to all those who had been involved in the work of restoration, as a token of their appreciation and thanks. A fitting end to a nightmare experience.

The Trust's 125th Anniversary

Saturday, 16 September 1972, marked the 125th anniversary of the purchase of Shakespeare's Birthplace in 1847 for preservation as a national memorial and, to commemorate this milestone in the history of the Trust, special events were arranged at the Shakespeare Centre on three successive evenings. Members of the Stratford-upon-Avon Borough Council, with their ladies, and Friends of Shakespeare's Birthplace living locally were invited on 14 September, members of the Birthplace Trust's staff on 15 September, and Trustees and other representative guests on 16 September.

Guests were invited to inspect Shakespeare's Birthplace, where exhibits illustrating the history and associations of the property and the life and work of Shakespeare were on view. Displays of items from the Trust's records, archaeological and local history collections had been prepared in the records office in Hornby Cottage; and in the Shakespeare Centre itself a selection of theatrical material was displayed in the reading room, and in the conference room on the first floor some of the more important, rare, early printed books from the library were put on exhibition. A buffet supper was served in the Stratford room.

A specially printed, illustrated programme had been produced for the reception on 16 September. The Trustees and their guests were received by the Chairman of the Trust, Dennis Flower, and myself as Director, and they were introduced to Dr Louis B. Wright, Emeritus Director of the Folger Shakespeare Library and a Life Trustee of the Birthplace, who had come over from the United States with Mrs Wright, to be guest of honour. In welcoming the company present, the Chairman briefly recalled the history of the Birthplace and the growth of the Trustees' responsibilities and activities in honour of Shakespeare during the past 125 years. He referred to the cultural links between the United States and our country and, in particular, to the great contribution of Americans to Shakespearian scholarship. In introducing Dr Wright, Mr Flower described him as a staunch friend of Stratford-upon-Avon and the Trust, whose erudition and publications placed him in the fore-front of American scholars. The Trustees were highly appreciative of his presence on such a special anniversary occasion.

Addressing the company, Dr Wright expressed his deep appreciation to the Director and Trustees for inviting him to come as a special guest on this occasion. 'For more than 125 years', he said, 'my countrymen have been attracted to Stratford. During the Middle Ages men and women thought they had to make a pilgrimage to Santiago de Compostela for the salvation of their souls. In later times millions of Americans, with almost the devotion of medieval pilgrims, have come to Stratford for their cultural salvation. They have even bought bushels of holy relics to take back to the United States. One great collector, Henry Clay Folger, acquired enough of Shakespeare's mulberry tree to make a fair reconstruction of that miraculous growth. When I became Director of the Folger Shakespeare Library, I discovered in the attic a bundle of sticks carefully tied up in red tape and labelled: "Splinters from a pew in Holy Trinity Church". These had been bought at a price from an American dealer. How much kindling wood has been thus translated into pure gold I do not know.'

He continued, 'For more than forty years I, too, have been a pilgrim constantly returning to Stratford. It is a matter of satisfaction to see the enormous improvement in that time in the way Shakespeare has been made vivid and significant to the throngs who regard Stratford as their Mecca. The present Director and his staff have worked wonders in recent years and deserve the world's gratitude. They have made a visit to Stratford an occasion of both delight and instruction.'

'Dr Fox, the distinguished administrator of the Birthplace Trust, has a great reputation on both sides of the Atlantic, and I would like at this point to express my admiration for the phenomenal accomplishments that have taken place during his term of office. The combination of historical learning and extraordinary administrative ability in the same personality is rare. The Birthplace Trust has been fortunate in finding such a personality as Dr Fox. The wise policy of property acquisition in recent years has done much to preserve the ancient heritage of Stratford. Dr Fox has also been able to organize the physical assets of the Birthplace Trust into an institution of paramount importance for the cultural and intellectual benefit of the thousands who come to Stratford. Only those who have seen the transformation that has taken place in recent years can realize the full significance of this change. At this time, it is a pleasure for me to pay a tribute to Dr Fox for what he has done.'

Dr Wright then briefly sketched the story of events leading to the purchase of Shakespeare's Birthplace in 1847, as already recorded in part one of this book. He recounted Washington Irving's well known description of his visit to the Birthplace in 1815 and the story that the American showman and circus magnate, Phineas T. Barnum, had made an unsuccessful attempt to buy the Birthplace in order to cart it off, stick and stone, to exhibit in his museum in New York.

'For many reasons', Dr Wright commented, 'I am glad that America does not have to bear the onus of robbing Britain of this national treasure. We have enough sins to answer for as it is. But Barnum's instinct for what his countrymen would pay to see was correct. Any place even named Stratford can now set up in the theatrical business and do well. We have Shakespeare festivals at Stratford, Connecticut, and Stratford, Ontario, that attract visitors from the whole North American continent. Three weeks ago I visited Ashland, Oregon, a country town of 13,000 inhabitants in the north-west part of the United States. There for the past thirty-seven years a Shakespeare theatre has flourished without foundation support or subsidy of any kind. Ashland has also become a place of pilgrimage for thousands of Americans because it has played Shakespeare straight, without distracting gimmicks and without reading into his words meanings that the poet never intended. As a result Shakespeare has become Ashland's most lucrative industry.'

'Oddly enough, however, it took some time for Stratford to realize the treasure that it possessed. Even yet, I gather, there are those in the town who only dimly realize that Shakespeare is one of Britain's most profitable attractions for tourists who bring millions of pounds to this country each year ... Shakespeare has become an industry of national, as well as local, profit ... Never in history has a poet managed to create such a far-reaching industry.'

'The story of the further vicissitudes of the Birthplace are not my concern at the moment,' he continued, 'and will be better told by others, but I would like to mention a performance in London on 7 December 1847, at the Royal Italian Opera House in Covent Garden to raise money in aid of the fund to purchase the Birthplace. The best actors and actresses joined in giving scenes from nine of Shakespeare's plays. Charles Knight, the editor and publisher, wrote a prologue spoken by Mr Phelps in which these lines occur:

> But Shakespeare's home, his boyhood's home is ours.
> Ye, who this night kind greetings bring to cheer
> The histrionic groups assembled here, –
> Cherish the task, with reverent love to hold
> One relic of our drama's age of gold.
>
> The Pilgrims come: Ohio and the Rhine
> Send forth their worshippers to Stratford's shrine –
> And still they come to hail, from every clime,
> The Poet of all countries and 'all time'.
> Is the work finish'd – or but yet begun?
> Complete! Maintain! Do all that needs be done!
> Yes! England's heart now beats at Shakespeare's call –
> The Muses' bower is saved – yours is the pledge for All.

In conclusion, Dr Wright commented, 'The task of completing, preserving, and maintaining, pledged in 1847, still requires the kind of effort and vigilance that the present Director and Trustees so ably demonstrate. The task is endless but infinitely worth while. Meanwhile the pilgrims continue to come, not only from Ohio and the Rhine, but from all the world. And they now go away with something better than fake relics. Thanks to instructive exhibitions, carefully planned lectures and a variety of other educational offerings by the Birthplace Trust, the pilgrims return more learned and more inspired than when they came. That day in 1847 when the Shakespeare Association acquired the Birthplace was fortunate for Stratford and the world.'

The Trustees could not have wished for a more appreciative commendation of their efforts, and for the remainder of the evening they shared with their guests the opportunity to see some of the treasures from the Trust's collections laid out for their inspection. There was an element of local pride among the Stratfordians present, and the production of a large birthday cake in the shape of Shakespeare's Birthplace, given by six local traders and made by Tom Pargeter, baker of Bridge Street, was a particularly happy gesture.

The publication of *In Honour of Shakespeare*, a copiously illustrated book describing the history and collections of the Trust, on which I had been working for some time past, was planned to coincide with this anniversary occasion.

The 1970s

The decade of the 1970s saw continued growth and development of the Trust's activities at a rate unprecedented. The Garrick bicentenary celebrations and the fire at Anne Hathaway's Cottage had both, in different ways, provided publicity which stimulated visitor patronage and interest in the work of the Trust. During the year ended 31 March 1970 the total of 860,160 visitors to the Shakespearian properties represented an increase of 110,000 on the previous year. Daily admission records were achieved: 2,919 people visited Anne Hathaway's Cottage on 27 July 1969, and on Thursday, 7 August, 3,755 were admitted to Shakespeare's Birthplace. Once started, this upward trend continued. There were other contributory factors: a general increase in tourists visiting the country, assisted by better marketing promotion, improved and competitive air transportation, and favourable exchange rates; and the continued growth of interest in Shakespeare abroad, as evidenced by the steady stream of translations, foreign publications and programmes of Shakespeare productions received at the Shakespeare Centre.

In 1971 there was a further increase of nearly 105,000 visitors during the year, and another record day attendance of 3,131 visitors to the Birthplace was achieved. The following year the number of visitors to the properties exceeded a million for the first time, the increased numbers at the Birthplace and the Cottage being almost entirely due to the growing volume of overseas package tours. It was at this time that the tourist agencies were beginning to bring organized tours from Japan, some of them during the winter months, which had always been previously the quiet time when maintenance inside the properties could be undertaken. During 1973 admissions to Shakespeare's Birthplace – a total of 507,293 – exceeded half a million for the first time, with Anne Hathaway's Cottage not far behind with 419,330. On Easter Day, 22 April 1973, 4,044 people were admitted to the Birthplace, exceeding the previous record total of 4,003 on 13 August 1972. During 1975 attendances at the properties exceeded the previous record total of 1973, and during the following year there was an increase of nearly a further 100,000. The increase in organized party visits from European countries and the Far East was particularly noticeable.

This surge of record-breaking statistics reached its climax in 1977, the Silver Jubilee year of Her Majesty Queen Elizabeth II, when the total number of visitors to the properties reached nearly one and a half million. The actual figures were:

Shakespeare's Birthplace	661,429
Anne Hathaway's Cottage	522,526
New Place	114,696
Mary Arden's House	96,738
Hall's Croft	90,821
making a total of	1,486,210

The proportion of visitors from abroad reached the highest level so far, and amounted to approximately three quarters of the total. A considerably

Loggia at Anne Hathaway's Cottage

greater number of organized tours came from Scandinavia, the European countries and the Far East, in addition to the Commonwealth countries and the United States. The Trust was fortunate to enjoy the benefit of the unique attraction of the Queen's Jubilee festivities, and it was not to be expected that this peak patronage would continue. In fact, the years that followed into the 1980s saw a downward trend, due partly to a world-wide economic recession and particularly to the unfavourable exchange rate for American visitors.

Visitor Management

The satisfactory handling of visitors on the scale described presented a challenge to the Trustees, Director and staff. At Shakespeare's Birthplace all those wishing to view the property had to enter the house through the front door, direct from the street, an arrangement which often led to queues forming on the pavement outside and to the discomfort of the waiting entrants in time of rain. The arrival and waiting of coaches in the street also caused conjestion, with accompanying noise and fumes, resulting in complaints from residents and concern on the part of the Town Council. The police had a difficult situation to control, but the Trust was always able to count on their co-operation in organizing the unloading and waiting of vehicles. What emerged from this experience was a realization by the Trustees that a priority need was to provide better facilities for visitors coming to the Birthplace, and at the same time to solve the problem of coaches in Henley Street. From 1971 onwards the members of the Executive Committee addressed themselves to this problem. How the solution was found will be told in the chapter on the Shakespeare Centre extension.

The situation at Anne Hathaway's Cottage was also difficult, but in a different way. Queues often formed at the doorway entrance, but the long, paved garden path, bordered with colourful flowers, provided a pleasant waiting space, and those on the footpath outside had the benefit of a picturesque view of the Cottage. The car and coach parks already provided worked extremely well, but proved inadequate for the increased numbers of visitors, and extensions to both were constructed in 1976. In the case of the coach park, particular care was taken to lower the level of the extended parking area at the rear of the existing park, so as to conceal the presence of waiting vehicles there. Amenities for visitors were also improved by the building of new toilets. The ground floor rooms of Hewlands, the cottage previously occupied by the custodian, had already been opened up for use as a craft house; and an adjoining loggia connecting with an amenity building for visitors was added in 1977. This particular development, together with the Jubilee Walk, described later in this chapter, received a commendation in the Stratford-on-Avon District Council's Design Award Scheme.

Apart from the practical implications of wear and tear resulting from the sheer volume of the visitors who came, there was also the problem of 'throughput' at the Birthplace and the Cottage. It was fortunate that at this time two very experienced chief guides were in immediate control at these properties. Harry Dyke, at Shakespeare's Birthplace, was a dedicated, well informed Shakespeare enthusiast, who had a remarkable facility of being able to communicate with all who came and of leading a team of guides who ensured that all the visitors received value for money. Harold Abraham, at Anne Hathaway's Cottage, was cast in a similar mould; he was able to organize his staff to operate a guiding sequence which ensured that all the visitors passed through the rooms of the Cottage and came away with an impression of the interest of its architecture, furnishings and associations.

An Expanding Organization

The Trust's staff had to be increased considerably to deal with this additional workload. New guides were recruited and trained to work in the properties and, with the growth of the Trust's sale of publications and gift items, additional part-time sales assistants were employed. The number of gardeners under the head gardener, Harold Goodyear, was increased to nine, and, with Leslie Page as head of maintenance, the team of craftsmen experienced in different trades was built up to five. During these same years several new members of staff were enlisted to help with the administrative and academic work. They included two additional secretaries, one being Miss Paula Haldenby, who is still in the Trust's employment as senior assistant secretary and who has helped me in the preparation of the text of this book. Five part-time helpers in the office and accounts departments and an administrative assistant, Geoffrey Randall, the former Clerk to the Stratford-on-Avon Rural District Council, who had become available following local government reorganization, were recruited. Two additional assistant librarians, an assistant archivist and a museums assistant completed the headquarters staff. By 1980 I was responsible for an establishment of fifty-two full-time and ninety-eight regular part-time staff, every one of whom I had appointed and knew personally.

This enlarged organization was made possible by the very considerable increase in the Trust's income which characterised these years. This resulted not merely from the greater number of visitors, but from the increases in admission charges to the properties which the Trustees agreed from time to time. A careful consideration of ticket prices was an integral element of the annual budgetary exercise undertaken by the Executive Committee on the basis of forecasts I prepared. In 1974 the price of an adult admission ticket to Shakespeare's Birthplace was increased from 25p to 30p, the 10p charge for children remaining unchanged. In 1976 the ticket price rose to 35p, and to 40p the following year. In 1978 admission to the Birthplace and the Cottage cost 45p for adults and 20p for children, and at the other three houses the prices were 30p for adults and 15p for children. An inclusive ticket giving admission to all the properties continued to be offered at a discount rate, with modest charges for organized school and student groups.

In 1970 the income from admissions to the properties was £86,803 (net surplus £30,238); by 1980 this had risen to £508,527 (net surplus £329,592). With the addition of income from rents, interest on investments, surplus on the sale of publications and miscellaneous receipts, the Trust's total net income rose similarly, from £68,635 in 1970 to £705,734 in 1980. On the expenditure side, there were proportionate corresponding increases. Apart from the overheads and running costs of the Shakespearian properties, the Trust's total expenditure in 1970 amounted to £59,306, as compared with £273,163 in 1980. Over the same period garden expenses increased from £12,689 to £59,771, and administrative and library expenses from £39,834 to £160,236. The surplus on the year's working in 1970 was £9,329; in 1980 the surplus was £432,571. It followed that, after allowing for the considerable cost of improvements and property purchases during this period, the Trust's finances had come to be in a surprisingly satisfactory condition. Year by year surplus funds were transferred to a reserve built up for accessions, and particularly to a fund intended for future property acquisitions and development. As at 31 December 1980, this reserve stood at £1,816,000.

It is interesting to recall the salaries and wages paid to different categories of staff at this time. In 1970 my private secretary and accounts assistant each received a salary of just under £2,000 per annum; ten years later they were paid £6,000 and £7,000. Part-time accounts staff in 1970 were paid at the rate of 56p per hour; by 1981 this had been increased to slightly above £2.00 an hour. The salaries of qualified academics working in the library and records office in 1970 ranged between £1,250 and £1,750 per annum; in 1981 the equivalent rates were between £5,000 and £7,000. The pay of assistant guides and sales staff in the properties in 1970 averaged £13 a week; in 1980 this had risen to between £65 and £80 a week. Assistant gardeners in 1970 were paid £20 a week; ten years later the rate varied between £65 and £80 a week. Craftsmen in the maintenance department received between £22 and £25 a week in 1970; by 1980 the comparable figures were between £90 and £100 per week.

By comparison with present day levels of remuneration, the salaries and wages detailed above appear to be very small, but, in relation to the value of money at the dates stated, they represented fair terms of employment. The pay policy of the Trustees was to be as generous as possible to their staff, and great care was taken each autumn, when the establishment review took place, to appraise the circumstances and performance of each employee and to upgrade remuneration accordingly. Unlike local authorities, the Trustees did not tie themselves to particular scales of pay; they preferred to set their own levels, an arrangement which in practice tended to be more beneficial both to the employer and the employee. They also recognised long service, and offered generous sickness leave and pension provision. Although the staff often found themselves working under great pressure during these busy years, I cannot remember receiving a single complaint about working conditions or pay.

Security and Maintenance

Following the fire at Anne Hathaway's Cottage, the Trustees decided to install fire detection systems in all the Shakespearian properties. In addition to

Shakespeare's Birthplace in the 1970s

being costly, this proved to be quite a major operation. Considerable care and ingenuity were required to conceal the necessary cables and to position the smoke detectors in the various rooms without calling attention to them. Each property was dealt with

Craftsmen at work in the Birthplace, 1971

in turn, and by the end of 1971 the task was completed. At Mary Arden's House electrical wiring was introduced into the building for the first time. This made possible the use of electrical heating during the winter months, in lieu of the open, log fires in the kitchen and hall.

Remembering what had happened at the Cottage, it was a great relief to me, and indeed to all the Trustees, to know that all these precious buildings were protected in this way and linked by automatic, direct telephone line with the fire service. Within minutes of an alarm, a fire engine would arrive in front of Shakespeare's Birthplace. However, as any one who has had experience of these devices knows, alarm installations of this kind can in practice prove very troublesome. Whenever there was thunder and lightning, one or other of the installations was invariably activated. From time to time I would also be summoned by the fire brigade, usually at night, which had been called out on a false alarm. The smoke detectors were very sensitive and could be easily set off by slight movement, such as when dust was blown across one of them in the barn at Mary Arden's House on a very windy night, or when an insect flew in front of one of them at Shakespeare's Birthplace.

A number of major maintenance works and improvements were also undertaken at this time. During the early spring and autumn of 1971 the exterior fabric of Shakespeare's Birthplace underwent a comprehensive examination and overhaul. Each member of the timber framed structure was inspected, repaired if necessary, and treated as a protection against beetle and worm attack. The infilling plaster panels were cleaned down and any defects made good, and the stone plinths and chimney stacks were brushed down, decayed portions being renewed and re-pointed. It was at this time that one of the original wattle and daub panels on the front elevation of the house was exposed to view and suitably protected, and the fragile, old window-glazing of the birth-room, which bore the signatures of early visitors, was encased with a transparent covering on both sides. In the interests of safety the Wilmcote stone cappings on the tops of the chimneys of the Birthplace were replaced with York stone. Experienced craftsmen of the same firm which had restored Hall's Croft and Anne Hathaway's Cottage after the fire were

Sundial in the Birthplace garden

employed to do the work, their use of traditional tools and skills as they shaped a piece of timber or stone proving an additional attraction to visitors coming to Shakespeare's Birthplace. Extensions and improvements were also carried out to the lavatories at the Birthplace, as well as at the Cottage. Flood lighting was installed in the garden of the Birthplace in 1972, primarily as an additional safeguard against vandalism during the hours of darkness, but also as a means of calling attention to the interest of its architecture.

During the previous year an ornament of pleasing modern design was placed in the Birthplace garden alongside the Shakespeare Centre: a sundial, designed by John Skelton, which Mrs S. Marshall presented in memory of her late father, Alderman Leigh Dingley, who had been a Trustee for many years and served as a member of the Executive Committee.

Extension of New Place Museum at Nash's House

In 1972 the vacation of the rooms at the rear of Nash's House, adjacent to New Place, which had been used as accommodation by a resident custodian, provided the opportunity for the Trustees to implement a plan they had contemplated for some time. In the absence of a town museum, they felt it desirable to make certain adaptations within the framework of the existing building so as to provide further public rooms for the display of archaeological and local history exhibits. On the ground floor, the small kitchen at the rear, with its brick-built fireplace and former bake-oven opening, was furnished to give an impression of the physical background of domestic life in Shakespeare's time. Upstairs, by removing a staircase, passage and bathroom of later date, it proved possible to open a spacious room which could be approached from the top of the main staircase and which, when equipped with modern showcase equipment, provided an admirable gallery for the display of archaeological and local history material illustrating the history of Stratford-upon-Avon before Shakespeare's time. The small rooms at the front of the house were then fitted with fixed wall exhibition cases, incorporating concealed top lighting for the rooms, which were used to display items illustrative of later chapters in

THE 1970S

The new gallery, New Place Museum

The old kitchen, Nash's House

the town's history. Opportunity was also taken to improve facilities for the storage of the Trust's reserve museum collections in the attic rooms. This project was completed in readiness for an official opening of the new museum extension by Mrs J.B. Priestley (Mrs Jacquetta Hawkes, the well known archaeologist and author) in November 1973. It was also at this time that, with a view to providing greater security, the wrought-iron railings enclosing the site of New Place, adjoining, were strengthened and augmented.

Mary Arden's House

For the next two or three years attention was focussed on Mary Arden's House. The need to provide parking facilities for cars and coaches visiting this property was being increasingly felt, and the Executive Committee decided to use part of the area of the Trust's own land in the paddock facing Station Road for this purpose. Planning permission for the construction of a car park, accompanied by careful landscaping and linked with the erection of a new reception building for visitors, was obtained. Its construction went ahead in 1974, and the new reception arrangements for visitors and the car and coach park were brought into use at the beginning of the 1975 season. This scheme met with warm general approval and the Trust's architect, Laurence Williams, received

Mary Arden's House, new reception building

the top award, a wall plaque, for it, out of forty entries judged by an outside panel of assessors in the Stratford-on-Avon District Council's Award Scheme, set up to stimulate and recognize building projects of good design throughout its area.

The members of the Committee also reconsidered and approved a tentative plan for linking the Glebe Farm premises (when, in due course, occupation was obtained) with Mary Arden's House itself, to make possible improved storage and display arrangements for the rapidly growing farming and folk collections. They authorized the submission of an overall scheme for outline planning approval, so that a blueprint for a Shakespeare Countryside Museum could be to hand for progressive implementation when opportunity arose.

In the autumn of 1973 the Trustees were pleased to have the opportunity of purchasing Albany House, together with its large garden, with the object of preventing undesirable development on the opposite side of the road approaching Mary Arden's House. The property was subsequently converted into two self-contained flats, with garages and patio area, and the large garden was left undisturbed.

It was at this time also that, after a period of negotiations that had taken some seventeen years, the purchase of part of the field opposite Mary Arden's House was completed, thus protecting the open, rural view in front of this property. It had been a hard fight to achieve this conservation objective.

The Trustees had repeatedly opposed successive planning applications for permission to build bungalows on the field and, throughout, had refused to pay full development price for this piece of agricultural land. I recall giving evidence at a Public Inquiry held at Alcester, when the owners appealed against the County Planning Committee's refusal to allow residential development on the site. At the conclusion of the hearing I accompanied the Inspector who conducted the Inquiry to Wilmcote, to inspect the site. After viewing the field, I described to him the historical and architectural interest of Mary Arden's House, and somehow persuaded him to go inside the farmhouse, where I guided him upstairs to look through one of the small dormer windows facing the field under threat. He stood and gazed, without a single word being spoken, but I sensed that our plea for conservation had succeeded. With the verdict against development, the owners eventually agreed to sell the land to the Trust. One of the first things I then did was to plant a row of trees and shrubs on the boundary of the land acquired. I regard the Trustees' success in preventing development on this site as a vital contribution to preserving the character of the village. It gave me great pleasure, in later years, to see the two donkeys which Mr Peter Boddington had given to the Trust grazing in this field.

In the autumn of 1975 a serious attack of deathwatch and furniture beetle was discovered in the interior timberwork of the end portion of Mary Arden's House nearest the dovecote, and plans were immediately agreed for a start to be made in the new year on an extensive repair and preservation treatment. Having some years before had experience of dealing with a similar problem at Harvard House, I instantly recognized the nature of the trouble when my attention was called by the chief guide to the holes, large and small, which had recently appeared in the oak members of the structure, following the unusually dry summer. The beetle had suddenly burst into live activity, and had already reduced certain parts of the timbers to a hollow, sponge-like condition. A major repair and treatment operation,

Mary Arden's House, restoration of gable end, 1976

involving almost the complete restoration of the gable end, was necessary. The work, carried out by experienced carpenters of Sapcote and Sons, Ltd, was done in two stages: the first at the beginning of 1976, and the second during the following autumn and winter, completed for the beginning of the 1977 visiting season.

It was at this time also that, after prolonged negotiations, the Trustees succeeded in purchasing the former Congregational Chapel adjacent to Mary Arden's House and the Glebe Farm, in Aston Cantlow Road. It was subsequently converted into two flats. The purchase included the small graveyard attached to the chapel, in which a few burials had taken place within living memory, and an embarrassing situation arose a year or two later, when the Trustees were asked to allow the interment of a person whose relative had been buried there. However, I had taken the precaution of ensuring that the churchyard was legally closed, and the Trust's reponsibility was merely to keep it in a tidy condition. Again, this property acquisition was made in order to prevent undesirable development or user alongside the Glebe Farm.

Welcombe and The Hill Estate

Back in Stratford, the Trustees continued to be concerned with the future conservation of the Welcombe and Hill estates. During his lifetime Sir Archibald Flower had presented to the town, as a site for a future new hospital, a small area of land near the top of The Hill fields. With the nationalization of the health service, this was no longer required for its original purpose and, in order to round off The Hill estate, the Trustees succeeded in buying it back in 1972, at a price negotiated with the District Valuer.

In 1977 the Trustees opposed on amenity grounds a plan for a provisional northern by-pass for Stratford-upon-Avon proposed by Warwickshire County Council, which would have necessitated the construction of a road starting from the Warwick road and cutting The Hill estate into two parts. In the event this scheme was dropped, and superseded in 1979 by an alternative route skirting Snitterfield, which the Trustees supported and which was eventually implemented. The Hill estate and the Welcombe hills were accordingly preserved unspoiled.

At the same time, the Trustees were approached to lease the area of parkland adjacent to the Welcombe Hotel, which had hitherto been let to tenant farmers for grazing, to make possible the construction of a golf course by British Transport Hotels, Ltd, the owners of the Welcombe Hotel. The Trustees saw in this the prospect of an attractive conservation arrangement with a good business return attached to it. The terms of a lease, which provided for a considerable amount of tree planting, were agreed in 1978; the layout of the golf course was approved; and work on its construction began. I found it a very interesting experience to confer with

The Welcombe golf course

the architect, an Irishman with a number of golf courses to his credit, who was responsible for designing the Welcombe course. A considerable programme of tree planting was included in the project. As the years have passed, the landscaping has matured and the golf course now presents a rural scene of well-cared-for green parkland alongside the main Warwick road approach to the town.

Henley Street Conservation

Equally important from the point of view of providing a safeguard against undesirable development and use, were the further acquisitions of properties in the immediate vicinity of Shakespeare's Birthplace.

Henley Street cottages

Following the closing of the Stratford Brewery, Whitbread Flowers, Ltd, began to off-load the various properties they owned in the town but no longer required. Among them was the row of five brick-built cottages, 32-36 Henley Street, standing on the opposite side of the street to the Shakespeare Centre.

Modest and unpretentious in size and appearance, and incorporating portions of earlier, timbered structure, they formed a characteristic part of the street scene and there was a useful area of garden at the rear. The Trustees bought them in 1971, with the idea of keeping them as occupied cottages. Although they lacked modern amenities and represented a financial liability from the point of view of rental return, their condition was fair, and called for the kind of careful maintenance and improvement which had become a regular part of the Trust's conservation policy. In succeeding years attention was given to each cottage, and in 1975 nos. 32 and 33 Henley Street were converted and extended to provide two small business units and a first-floor flat.

In 1972 the Trustees also bought the former Coach and Horses inn, which was situated immediately opposite to Shakespeare's Birthplace. A few years before, Whitbread Flowers, Ltd, had transferred the inn's licence to a new public house on the Alcester road and, except for the short time when the building was used as the 1964 Festival office, little had been done to maintain and keep it in repair. The range of outbuildings at the rear, clustered round the inn yard, were dilapidated, and the general appearance of the property from the Birthplace across the road left much to be desired.

In view of its prominent position, it was felt that conservation considerations were of paramount importance in this instance. Laurence Williams, the Trust's architect, produced a comprehensive scheme, designed at once to improve the appearance and condition of the property and its yard, and to adapt it for practical, economic use. When completed in 1976, the ground-floor rooms provided a well equipped refreshment facility, which it was decided to name the Centre Coffee House, and three self-contained flats were created on the two upper floors.

Additions were made at the rear to replace the unsightly, sub-standard outbuildings, and the former inn yard was finally completed in 1978, when two single-storey, brick-built, craft studio/shops were erected at the top end. This development subsequently became known as the Centre Craft Yard. The Trustees and their architect were particularly pleased that the Coach and Horses improvement project, incorporating the craft studio concept, was selected as a prize winning entry in an architectural competition for re-furbished property, entitled 'A New Lease of Life'.

Another former brewery property, the Brewery Club in Guild Street (re-named the Embassy Club), was acquired by the Trust in 1971. Built as a club house for the recreational needs of employees of Flowers' brewery in late Victorian times, the building was of solid construction, containing spacious rooms and caretaker's quarters. It was its position, however, near to the rear of the Shakespeare Centre, which made its acquisition most desirable, thoughts of a possible extension to the Shakespeare Centre being already very much in my mind. In the event, this building was later incorporated into the extension plan for the Shakespeare Centre, to accommodate the Trust's records office.

Property Maintenance

As the Trust's properties increased in number, a regular round of maintenance attention was established. At any given time a variety of work was in hand: considerable repairs and improvements were carried out to the recently acquired shop premises, 45 Henley Street, opposite to the Birthplace; defective chimney stacks at Brooklands, 57 Shottery, were rebuilt, and the slated roof of Shottery Lodge relaid; the semi-detached houses, 26 and 28 Cottage Lane, Shottery, were extensively upgraded. The gardener's cottage at New Place was improved in 1973, and in the following year eight garages were built behind the New Row Cottages at Shottery. To provide for the growing needs of the gardens, a new Dutch-type glasshouse was erected at Hall's Croft and the large greenhouse at New Place renewed. Another operation of a different kind was the cutting-back of the overhanging yew hedge alongside the Chapel Lane boundary of the Great Garden of New Place, and the subsequent fixing of protective railings along the boundary wall.

The Trust took possession of the Burnside estate at Shottery in 1975, in accordance with the terms of the bequest of the late Mrs Emily Evans, as already described. For several years previously the properties had received the minimum of maintenance attention, and some were in urgent need of repair and modernization. The Trustees were particularly concerned about the neglected condition of Burnside and its grounds, which had been leased by the Burnside trustees to a tenant who had proved very unsatisfactory. By the time the Trustees succeeded in

Re-thatching of cottages in Tavern Lane

getting possession, the house had deteriorated further and the question of its future use raised a difficult problem. In the event, during 1979 the Trust's architect produced an imaginative scheme for converting the house into six residential units. Meanwhile, a programme of improvements to Wild Thyme Cottage and Tapestry Cottage in Tavern Lane, which included the rethatching of the roofs, was completed in 1977; and in the following year major restoration work was carried out at the White Cottage in Church Lane.

The extremely violent gale experienced nationwide at the beginning of 1976 inflicted an unprecedented trail of damage around the Trust's properties, and resulted in much additional work for the garden and maintenance staff. Two major limbs were torn from the cedar tree in the Birthplace garden, which in turn brought down a length of the garden wall, and the tip of the large beech tree in the Great Garden of New Place was snapped off. In addition to the dozens of trees blown down in the gale, the prevalent scourge known as Dutch elm disease, which had already necessitated fellings at The Hill and Welcombe during the two previous years, claimed further casualties. Instead of disposing of the elm timber or allowing it to be burned, I arranged for all the sound trunks to be taken away and cut into planks or boards, and brought back to The Hill to be stored; in consequence, for years afterwards the Trust had a supply of seasoned elm for maintenance and repair projects immediately available, when timber on the market was commanding a very high price. Elm boards, for example, were required at intervals to renew the wooden rain water gutters and down pipes at Mary Arden's House.

Anything to do with trees was always taken seriously by the members of the Executive Committee, and in the autumn of 1979 they had an unwelcome decision to make in connection with the large beech tree which had for so long been a particular feature of the Great Garden of New Place. Following two hot, dry summers, the tree was dying and had become unsafe and, in the interests of public safety, felling was the only course of action possible.

Because of the restricted access to the garden, the felling and clearance operation proved exceedingly difficult, but all was completed without mishap and a new, young beech tree was planted nearby at the beginning of 1980.

Being of a practical bent, I found it a rewarding experience working with the Trust's architect, Laurence Williams, in the planning of the many projects mentioned above. Moreover, in practice I acted as clerk of works, paying regular visits to see the progress of jobs in hand, and I frequently found myself discussing particular problems or suggestions with the bricklayers, carpenters and tradesmen at work. In the process, I constantly added to my knowledge of building and craft techniques, and shared the men's pride in workmanship and a job well done.

Educational and Academic Activities

I was equally fortunate during these years in being able to plan and develop a number of significant educational and academic activities of the Trust. Within a few years of its opening, the Shakespeare Centre proved its usefulness in a variety of ways. In particular, each year saw the development of the service of introductory talks and lectures offered to visiting parties of school children and students, and the short-term use of the Centre's facilities for lectures and seminars for overseas student groups. Meetings of local societies and allied activities also took place in the Stratford room. From 1970 onwards arrangements were made for the six weeks' Shakespeare Summer School, organized by the Extra-Mural Department of the University of Birmingham, to be based on the Centre and to provide the accommodation required. The upper floors of the building adjoining the Centre, which had been let to the Midlands Electricity Board, were re-occupied by the Trust and adapted for use as an annexe, with a large assembly room for lectures and smaller rooms for seminars. This association with the Extra-Mural Department also resulted in the Centre being used during the winter months for classes on several evenings each week, as well as courses involving the use of archive material in the records office. Starting in 1973, Shakespeare courses for overseas teachers of English were arranged in association with the Department of Education and Science, and these became a regular fixture each year. Among other special uses were the week-end seminars on English history, organized between 1975 and 1978 by British Airways for overseas travel agents. The existence of the Centre and the services it could offer were by this time more widely known. This was also evidenced by the considerable number of postal enquiries received concerning literary, historical, theatrical and museum matters, and by the Trust's increased sales of publications and educational aids.

The preparation and mounting of exhibitions also became a regular feature of this developing educational policy. Two or three exhibitions were presented each year at the Shakespeare Centre and at Hall's Croft. In 1971 an exhibition illustrating the work of Paul Vincze, F.R.B.S., the medallic sculptor and creator of the Trust's special Shakespeare medals, was arranged at the Centre to coincide with the issue of the first of his series of *Shakespeare Commemorative Medallions*, the one depicting *Hamlet*. At Hall's Croft there were exhibitions on the subjects of 'Money and Wealth in Shakespeare's England' and 'The Elizabethans at School'. In the following year exhibitions there featured 'The Elizabethans in Paradise', illustrating the Elizabethans' interest in gardens and flowers, and 'Shakespeare and his Contemporaries'; and at the Centre: 'Law and Order in Stratford', 'O Rare Ben Jonson' and 'A Warwickshire Family through the Ages'.

Frequently opportunity was taken to stage an exhibition of theatrical material linked with the season's plays at the Royal Shakespeare Theatre or with some special commemorative event. Such an occasion was the exhibition in 1974, 'In Honour of J.B. Priestley', consisting of books, manuscripts and pictures celebrating the life and work of the eminent novelist and playwright, who was also a Life Trustee of Shakespeare's Birthplace and was eighty in that year. In 1975 attention was focussed on the 400th anniversary of the birth of Shakespeare's son-in-law,

Paul Vincze and his first Shakespeare medal

Dr John Hall, by presenting a new exhibition, intended to be semi-permanent, at Hall's Croft on 'Dr John Hall and the Medicine of his Time'. The United States Bicentennial in 1976 was marked by an exhibition at the Shakespeare Centre on 'The Elizabethans and America', and this was followed by 'Victorian Stratford', based on material from the records office, which proved to be of particular interest to Stratford residents and schools. Occasionally, as in 1977, rare and fine books from the Trust's library were put on view and, as a contribution to the events arranged to mark the Silver Jubilee of Her Majesty Queen Elizabeth II, the summer exhibition was devoted to a celebration of her illustrious predecessor, Queen Elizabeth I, entitled 'Gloriana'. In 1978 'Shakespeare the Countryman', followed by 'Pillars of the Community: Notable Stratfordians, 1300-1900', proved extremely popular, only to be surpassed by 'The Elizabethan Woman' the following year.

These examples are given to illustrate the variety and range of subject matter covered by these exhibitions, and as an indication of the wealth of material in the Trust's library, archive and museum collections. During the 1970s work in the library and records office proceeded along lines now well established. Good progress was made with sorting, accessions, classification, cataloguing and the preparation of reference aids. Regular instalments of bookbinding and repairs to records were undertaken, together with conservation treatment of archaeological material. The advantage of the amalgamation of the Theatre and Birthplace collections became increasingly apparent, and the regular intake of production records from the Royal Shakespeare Company contributed to the growing recognition of the library as a special centre for theatre and library research. The number of students and scholars using the reading room in the library all the year round gradually increased and, at times when courses or the Summer School were in session, readers often filled all available places. To me this was a most pleasing and rewarding development, and the Trust was fortunate in having a dedicated, experienced staff of assistant librarians working under the senior librarian, Miss Marian Horn, who married my educational assistant, Roger Pringle, in 1977. The library staff comprised Miss Eileen Robinson, who had been responsible for the Theatre library prior to its transference to the Shakespeare Centre in 1964; Miss Mary White, who stayed until 1993, when she left to marry Professor Reg Foakes, a Shakespeare scholar who frequently used the library; and Miss Sylvia Tompkins, who, having married Mr Richard Morris, the present chief guide of Mary Arden's House, in 1982, still remains and is now the deputy librarian. As in other departments, the team spirit and pride in the work generated good public relations and complimentary comment from those who appreciated the quality of the individual service they received.

Accessions

With increased income, it proved possible to spend more on the library, though still considerably less than I would have wished. In addition to the regular purchase of new publications and the steady stream of gifts of translations and foreign publications, some notable accessions were made during these years. Tape recordings made by the late Professor John Dover Wilson were acquired from the BBC, and from this time onwards copies of films about Shakespeare were added whenever possible. In 1973 seven books from the Phillipps Library were purchased at Sotheby's. Two were of special interest. The first was *Polimanteia*, a tract by William Covell on true and false astrology, published in 1595. The work includes a marginal reference to *The Rape of Lucrece* with the words 'All praiseworthy Lucrecia (of) Sweet Shakespeare', which appears alongside a passage discussing the work of several contemporary poets. Shakespeare's *Lucrece* had been published in 1594, and this allusion (the second reference to Shakespeare in a printed book) indicates the popularity that the poem had achieved as soon as it appeared.

The second was Estienne's *A Mervaylovs Discourse vpon the Lyfe of Katherine de Medicis*, 1575, the title-page of which bears an inscription recording the gift of the book by Susanna Hall to R. Grace. This political pamphlet on the life of Katherine de Medicis, attributed to the scholar Henri Estienne, was first printed in 1574 and soon became available in English translation. The inscription makes this copy of unique interest: 'Liber R. Grace: ex dono amice D. Susanne Hall'. Colonel Richard Grace was chamberlain to the Duke of York, later James II, and was probably among the retinue of Queen Henrietta Maria when she came to Stratford-upon-Avon and stayed at New Place, in 1643. If Shakespeare's daughter Susanna gave this little book to Colonel Grace at this time, it is likely that it had come to her among the contents of the poet's home, when she inherited New Place in 1616. This volume may therefore be the only book surviving from those owned by William Shakespeare.

The Trustees were assisted in the purchase of these books by a contribution from the Purchase Grant Fund administered by the Victoria and Albert Museum, and also by money from the funds of the Friends of Shakespeare's Birthplace, who by this time had become firmly established as an international body of Shakespeare lovers keen to support the work of the Trust. Further gifts from these two sources also made possible the purchase in 1974 of

Title page of A Mervaylovs discourse, *1575*

Machiavelli's *The Arte of Warre* (1588), Withals's *A Dictionarie in English and Latine for Children* (1608), Valentinus's *Enchiridion Medicum* (1609) and Estienne's *Maison Rustique* (1616).

The foreign content of the library continued to grow, mainly by reason of the Trust's association with scholars who had either worked at the Shakespeare Centre or visited it, and the fact that from 1974 onwards the Centre was recognized as the headquarters of the International Shakespeare Association also attracted gifts. During 1979, for instance, publications were received from France, Turkey, Japan, Norway, Cyprus, Romania, Georgia, Bulgaria, Canada and the United States. Copies of the new bi-lingual translations in German and English of *Othello* and *Measure for Measure* came from West Germany, whilst various theatre items were presented by the National Theatre of East Berlin, whose Director had visited the Centre. The library's accessions continued to reflect the developing emphasis of interest on Shakespeare as a man of the theatre and the production of his plays. In this context the Royal Shakespeare Theatre's collection of prompt copies, incidental music, costume designs, photographs and production records, as also of press cuttings, continued to multiply in proportion to the increased amount of work undertaken by the Company in its four theatres and whilst on tour.

A major addition to the library in 1979 was the collection of books and literary papers of Alan Dent, author, journalist and critic of the theatre and films. The materials he left related to all aspects of his career, and included documents and correspondence with many theatrical personalities over a period of fifty years, as well as some four thousand books on drama, the theatre, English and French literature, music and biography.

Each year saw useful additions to the Trust's records and museum collections. Arising from local government re-organization in 1976, considerable deposits of nineteenth-century and twentieth-century municipal records from various departments of the former Stratford-upon-Avon Borough Council were added to the Borough collection, while deposits of minute books and papers by local societies, together with the business records of several Stratford firms, provided valuable source material for the study of many facets of local community life.

In 1974 the Trustees accepted a bequest of original drawings, paintings and transparencies relating to the frescos in the Guild Chapel, made by the late Wilfred Puddephat, art master at the King Edward VI Grammar School at Stratford. There were also a number of valuable and interesting individual record accessions, an example being a notebook by an ex-pupil of 'The Old House', Stratford-upon-Avon. This school, like many other private establishments of its type, is otherwise virtually unrecorded. These notes, based on contemporary drawings of the outside and inside of the school, constitute an invaluable source of local history. In a different category were the tape recordings of audio and television programmes about Shakespeare and Stratford. Particularly interesting were the recording of the BBC's live 'Nationwide' television programme on Stratford in 1977, centred on the Great Garden of New Place, and the video recording of the BBC television film featuring the 1979 Shakespeare birthday celebrations.

Considerable publicity was focussed on the work of the Trust's records office at this time. During the period 5 to 10 November 1979 International Archives Week was celebrated across the world, the idea being to increase public awareness of archives and the need to preserve them adequately. In common with similar bodies around the country, the records office organized several events as part of this important exercise. A major exhibition was mounted in the Shakespeare Centre containing some of the Trust's choicest manuscript items, which ranged from a charter of King Stephen to scurrilous posters issued when King George IV's morganatic wife returned from abroad in an attempt to be crowned Queen in 1820. Particularly gratifying was the number of groups from local schools and societies which visited the exhibition. A light-hearted entertainment, entitled 'Yours, Disgusted', was also given at the Shakespeare Institute. It demonstrated, by readings from the local Victorian press, that the minor irritations and difficulties which beset us today are nothing new. The readings were given by drama students from the South Warwickshire College of Further Education. The records office also arranged an open day and invited members of the public to visit the reading room and to see a small display of the work of the office. Attendance surpassed all expectations, with some five hundred people taking advantage of the occasion. Press coverage of these activities was very good, and a number of small accessions, mostly photographs of local events or personalities, were received as a result, and several members of the public visited the records office to study.

There was also a steady intake of museum items during these years. In 1978 the Executive Committee was pleased to have the opportunity to purchase, again from the funds of the Friends of Shakespeare's Birthplace, two original water-colours of Shakespeare scenes by Henry William Bunbury (1750-1811): 'Romeo and Juliet with Friar Laurence' and 'The supposed death of Imogen and the two sons of Cymbeline'. The following year Mrs Joyce Pugh of Brighton presented a gold brooch with an inset picture of Shakespeare's Birthplace, painted according to the details of the building between 1862 and 1867. Very different were the farm wagons and carts deposited by the Hodges family of Long Marston, the collection of blacksmith's and plumber's tools purchased when the contents of the Forge at Pebworth were sold, the mason's hammer used by a Mr Osborne on the construction of the

Bunbury's watercolour of 'Romeo and Juliet with Friar Laurence'

Welcombe monument, a thatcher's needle, and an ancient drug press from a local pharmacy, together with a miscellany of old dairy and butcher's utensils. These details are given to illustrate the variety and range of the Trust's collections policy.

An unusual gift was a small, wooden stool, presented by the grand-daughter of the Reverend Charles Hutchins, who had purchased it when he visited Anne Hathaway's Cottage in 1872. At that time the Cottage had not yet been acquired by the Trustees, and the resident custodian, Mrs Mary Baker, clearly managed the sight-seeing with an eye to profitable business. At any rate, it was a fine gesture to return the stool to its original home.

I can recall a few other occasions when objects which had been removed from the properties by visitors, as souvenirs, were returned. One morning, for instance, I received a long package in the post bearing an American postmark but with no indication of the sender. Carefully wrapped up inside it was an iron rushlight holder and a note which bore the words 'from one who is repenting'. The artifact had been stolen from New Place Museum years before, but conscience had at last stirred. There was also the occasion when I heard from a friend at the British Embassy in Washington, D.C., that a small tapestry panel had been sent to the Embassy anonymously. For some reason or other he had a feeling that the panel might well have come from Stratford, so he sent me a photograph of it. I instantly recognized the tapestry as the panel which had been removed from its wall fixing in the bedroom at the lower end of Anne Hathaway's Cottage a year or two before, and the loss of which had been accepted as irretrievable. The tapestry was immediately returned, and restored to its original place in the Cottage.

All available space for storage in the records office at the rear of Hornby Cottage had by this time been taken up by the greatly increased volume of archive material received, and both staff and readers wishing to use the records worked under difficult conditions. As the 1970s progressed, the need for more adequate accommodation and updated facilities, such as were eventually provided in the Shakespeare Centre extension, became increasingly urgent. Nevertheless, the numbers of students and scholars using the records gradually increased, and the value of the Trust's collections for the study of local and social history became more widely known. Their importance from the point of view of Shakespearian subject matter was illustrated by the research of Professor S. Schoenbaum, a distinguished American Shakespeare scholar, who spent some time in 1975 locating and examining every document of Shakespearian interest. These were then specially photographed and included as facsimile reproductions in his *William Shakespeare: A Documentary Life*, published by the Oxford University Press in 1976. Another publication, *Stratford, Past and Present*, for which I personally was responsible, included illustrations of Stratford scenes and buildings based on early photographs in the Trust's collections.

The Festival Club, Music and Poetry

Equally satisfying to me was the progressive development of activities which originally had been regarded as peripheral to the Trust's main objects. The Festival Club at Hall's Croft, which started as an experimental, modest facility, had by this time become firmly established as a social amenity, with a membership of local and country people as well as of visitors. During the summer months the garden was particularly appreciated by members, and good use was made of the catering service, which was improved. In 1974 the magistrates granted a licence to me, as Director, to enable licensed drinks to be served with meals and, in accordance with the requirements of the licence, the Hall's Croft Advisory Committee, which had been set up in 1952 after the Club was inaugurated, came to an end and was replaced by a General Committee; a new set of rules for managing the Club also had to be devised and approved. The economics of running the Club continued to be a cause of anxiety to the Trustees, but the presence of the British Council Office in the building underpinned its usefulness as an amenity for the reception and use of student groups and visiting scholars; and, throughout the period of this association, the Trust, and myself in particular, enjoyed a very friendly relationship with its officers. The Club also continued to provide facilities for the meetings of a number of local organizations.

The Stratford-upon-Avon Poetry Festival, organized by the Trust and still associated with Hall's Croft, where it had originated, had by this time become an established annual event, as also the programme of summer music concerts, which had continued since 1964. Until he left Stratford in 1978, Mr John Strickson, organist of Holy Trinity Church, acted as the Trust's music adviser and, with his help and with the assistance of funding from the Arts Council of Great Britain, a short series of concerts was arranged during the summer months. These were held at the Shakespeare Institute, the Town Hall, Holy Trinity Church and the Royal Shakespeare Theatre. Until 1978 the National Trust made available the library at Charlecote Park for a chamber music concert each summer, and madrigal concerts at Hall's Croft proved a popular regular fixture. On a fine summer evening the terrace at the rear of the house made an ideal setting for the outdoor rendering of madrigals of Tudor and later date; when the weather was not suitable, the concert took place in the music room at Mason Croft.

The Poetry Festival had a regular following of patrons and, as it outgrew the accommodation at Hall's Croft, most of the readings were held in other places in the town, as mentioned above. The practice of entrusting the direction of the Festival to an outside director continued until 1972, when it was decided to invite a number of guest contributors to be responsible for particular programmes. This arrangement proved to be very satisfactory, and it provided an opportunity to involve Roger Pringle, the Trust's educational assistant. Within a short time he proved himself to be a very skilful deviser and director of readings, and from 1978 he assumed responsibility for arranging the complete Festival. Nine readings were held, on successive Sunday evenings during July and August, each programme being built around a particular theme. The work of living poets, who, whenever possible, were invited to take part, was represented in the selection of topics. Two, and occasionally three, readers normally took part, frequently members of the Royal Shakespeare Company.

A number of highlight occasions spring to mind, as in 1975, when the Festival was opened with a personal anthology chosen by J.B. Priestley and Mrs Priestley, with Judi Dench and Michael Williams as readers. In 1977 the opening recital, devised by John Carroll, who had succeeded Christopher Hassall as director of the Festival, took the form of a special programme in Holy Trinity Church, 'A Remembrance for Shakespeare', in which Princess Grace of Monaco, Richard Pasco, John Westbrook, Peter Pears and John Strickson took part. It was on this occasion that I found myself acting as escort and guide to Princess Grace, then at the height of her popularity. She was a most charming lady, highly intelligent and with a genuine interest in Shakespeare. At this time it was also customary to arrange a short-term exhibition at Hall's Croft associated with the Poetry Festival. In 1978, for example, 'Poets of our Time', celebrating the work of ten contemporary poets, was mounted there. The following year Dame Peggy Ashcroft took part in the opening recital of the Festival.

The activities just described were, of course, recurrent, each year tending to see an improvement

Princess Grace of Monaco and readers

or embellishment on the previous year's performance. During the 1970s there were, however, a number of non-recurrent special events which called attention to the work of the Trust in different ways and added generally to the prestige of the institution.

An American Lecture Tour

My visit to Virginia in the United States in 1971 to give lectures fell into this category. On several occasions following 1964 I had received invitations to visit universities and Shakespeare organizations overseas, particularly in the United States of America, but my preoccupation with so many important projects in Stratford left me with little opportunity for travel. Whenever I was away from the office, even for a few days, an accumulation of matters to be dealt with always awaited my return. However, my visit to Virginia at the invitation of the Virginia Commonwealth University proved to be a rewarding, though arduous, experience. Travelling by air, I arrived at Richmond, where I was accommodated at the Jefferson Hotel. The hotel was built on the grand scale, with furnishings reminiscent of Victorian and Edwardian splendour and comfort. It had a spacious entrance area, with massive marble columns carrying a balcony running round its sides and approached by an impressive central staircase. The quality of the hotel's service left nothing to be desired; I received from everyone I met a friendly, pro-British welcome.

Using the hotel as a base, my hosts had arranged for me an intensive programme of lectures spread over four days. Each day I lectured two or three times, to university groups and teachers in Richmond and to several colleges and schools in neighbouring towns to which I was taken. My lectures, some illustrated, covered a wide variety of topics centred on Shakespeare's life, times and work, Stratford-upon-Avon and its development as a place of literary and theatrical pilgrimage, and the Shakespearian properties and the work of the Trust, with particular reference to its value for visiting students. I also lectured on the Elizabethan playhouse, Shakespeare as a man of the theatre, and the history of Shakespeare productions – linked with the work of the Royal Shakespeare Company. Everywhere I encountered a lively interest, and I formed the impression that at the senior level their students were very good. A few had already visited Stratford, and others were planning to come. I had opportunity to confer with members of staff, including my hosts, Dr Walter R. Coppedge, the Assistant Vice-President, Dr Arnold Fleshood, Dean of the School of Education, and Marion Nesbett, Professor of Education, whom I had met several times before when she visited Stratford, all of the Virginia Commonwealth University.

My hosts had also planned for me a programme of social activities and visits, which were enjoyable and instructive. On my first evening there I found myself the guest of honour at the annual dinner of the English Speaking Union, held in the splendid ballroom of the Jefferson Hotel. I learned that membership of this organization was rated highly in Richmond and the surrounding area, and the large company present made no secret of their affection for England, the mother country. It fell to me to make the principal speech and to propose the toast of the President of the United States. All seemed to go extremely well, and my presentation of a pair of Shakespeare medals to the Union President proved to be an excellent public relations gesture.

On the second day I found that the University had arranged a tea reception in my honour at Windsor House, an elegant eighteenth-century building standing in a lovely garden setting. Here I met academics, teachers, public figures and a host of friendly people. Nor was private hospitality on the part of my hosts lacking, and it was extremely relaxing and pleasant to find myself being entertained in the informal setting of family homes. Apart from its buildings of modern construction, Richmond was notable for its wealth of traditional colonial houses and shops, and there was generally much to see. One of the buildings which fascinated me most was the one occupied by the Virginia Historical Society. It was no other than the reconstructed house known as the Priory, from Warwick, which had originally belonged to the Puckering family. In the 1920s this building had been sold to an American, who had arranged for it to be taken down, stone by stone, then transported across the Atlantic and re-erected as part of England on a site in Richmond, Virginia. My judgment was that the task had been faithfully and competently carried out, and the landscaped garden provided a perfect setting for this period building.

It had been arranged that I should spend the weekend at Williamsburg, as guest of the Director of the Jamestown Foundation, Mr Clive Rouse, and his wife. The eighty miles' journey there was through open country, with plantations and scattered colonial farms and houses in natural settings on the way. The weather was fine and warm, and the foliage of the trees was particularly beautiful. Along the route we called to see what I was told was one of the finest surviving colonial plantation houses, timber-built, standing in a wooded setting alongside the Potomac river. It was a comfortable dwelling with a good deal of character. Standing nearby in the grounds was an ice house, a circular building constructed partly below ground, in which blocks of ice cut from the river were stored during the winter.

At Williamsburg I found that a small reception had been arranged for me, followed by dinner in colonial style at one of the restored inns. On the Sunday morning I attended service at Bruton Parish Church, where I met the Rector. Two years before I had found accommodation for him and his wife when they visited Stratford. I also met the visiting preacher, who turned out to be a former chaplain of my old college, Oriel, at Oxford. In the afternoon I was taken to see the battlefield at Yorktown, where Cornwallis fought the English in 1781, and in the evening to Newport News, where I was entertained by the Hon. Lewis McMurran and his wife. He was a leading member of the House of Delegates of the Commonwealth of Virginia and, as Chairman of the Jamestown Foundation, he had played an active role in arranging the celebrations in 1957 to mark the establishment of legislative government in the New World, at Jamestown in 1619. Sir Fordham and Lady Flower had been among the representatives from this country who attended these observances to commemorate the establishment of English civilization overseas, and I had had the pleasure of meeting the McMurrans on one or two occasions when they had visited Stratford.

It was a busy schedule and, before returning to Richmond for further lectures, I was taken to Jamestown, where the Director of the Foundation gave me a conducted tour. I found it very interesting and useful to see the arrangements for handling the visitors who came, and I was impressed by their methods of display and presentation of information. Those responsible had certainly been successful in re-creating the visual impact and atmosphere of this early chapter of colonial history. Public relations were also well managed, and whilst I was there I was interviewed by the press, with a consequent full-page write-up in the Richmond newspaper.

I left Richmond on 5 May for Washington, DC, where I was able to spend two days before returning home. Apart from meeting the Trust's Life Trustee, Dr Louis B. Wright, who, following his retirement as Director of the Folger Shakespeare Library, had become Historical Consultant to the National Geographic Society, I spent most of the time at the Folger Shakespeare Library. There I met the new Director, Dr O.B. Hardison, Jr., and discussed with him possible ways of developing closer co-operation between our two institutions. He was keen for the Folger to be associated with the Trust in the marketing of various publications, together with Paul Vincze's Shakespeare medallions and visual material illustrative of Stratford and the Shakespearian properties. Equally valuable to me was the opportunity afforded by my brief visit to renew acquaintances with the Folger Library staff and to be brought up to date about their academic programmes.

Reverting to Dr Wright, it was at this time that he first tested my reactions about a suggestion that the Birthplace Trust might be associated with him in the planning of a short series of educational films about Shakespeare which the National Geographic Society might possibly sponsor. When I was able to discuss this idea with the Executive Committee of Trustees, it met with the ready approval of the members and, as will be mentioned later, a project for filming was eventually agreed.

By this time, Mr Dennis Flower had become firmly in control as Chairman of the Trust, with Peter Boddington as Deputy. It had not taken long for me to establish with Mr Flower the same friendly and constructive relationship I had enjoyed with his predecessor, Sir Fordham Flower. He had a keen sense of the special character and role of the Trust, and invariably supported the proposals I put forward for extending the Trustees' influence in the sphere of conservation. He favoured the acquisition of further properties for this purpose. With his relaxed manner and genial personality, he made an excellent chairman, and I was fortunate in that, in practice, he gave me a free hand to manage the Trust's affairs, being content to offer advice when requested. Mr Peter Boddington was equally supportive. He took a great interest in everything to do with the Shakespearian properties and, with his experience as a local magistrate, he brought a balanced judgment to matters affecting the Trust's business and staff. As in Sir Fordham's day, the Committee still remained small, its other members being Mr T.E. Lowth, the local solicitor who had also been Stratford's last part-time Town Clerk, Mr N.S. Pratt, who had succeeded Mr Leslie Watkins as Headmaster of King Edward VI School, and Mrs Trevor Matthews, the American widow of Alderman Trevor Matthews, who had died in 1964. Together they had an unrivalled knowledge of local affairs, but they were also able to appreciate the importance of the Trust's role in the wider national and international spheres. Thus they received the report of my visit to Virginia with considerable enthusiasm. As Director, I was indeed fortunate to enjoy such a friendly and rewarding relationship with Trustees who were always willing to listen to my suggestions for future developments and activities.

The International Shakespeare Association

The establishment and early development of the International Shakespeare Association, leading to the International Shakespeare Congress of 1976, was another significant involvement of the Trust at this time. The idea of inaugurating a world-wide Shakespeare association was first put forward at an international gathering of Shakespeare scholars held at Vancouver in 1971, and in 1973 the Birthplace Trustees agreed to undertake the necessary preparatory action to put it into effect. It accordingly fell to me to write letters inviting individual scholars and institutions around the world to support the creation of an association of this kind. Reactions from abroad, especially from Germany, Japan and the United States, were most encouraging, and an *ad hoc* Committee of international scholars was set up for the purpose of drafting a constitution and making preparations for a permanent organization.

Much of this preliminary work had to be done by post, but, at a meeting of the Committee held at the Shakespeare Centre in September 1974, a final version of a constitution for the Association was discussed and agreed. The first officers were elected at this meeting. I suppose it was logical that, as the person who had undertaken much of the initial preparatory work, I was appointed Secretary of the Association, with my assistant, Roger Pringle, as Honorary Treasurer. I also became the Deputy Chairman, with Professor Kenneth Muir of the University of Liverpool as Chairman. The Committee decided that the headquarters of the Association should be at the Shakespeare Centre, and the Birthplace Trustees agreed to the request that they should continue to provide the necessary office accommodation and facilities.

In all this preliminary work the Trust played a major role. The International Shakespeare Association accordingly came into existence to further the development of Shakespeare interests throughout the world, by linking together the various separate Shakespeare associations and societies, planning international Shakespeare congresses, and establishing an information service concerning research in progress, Shakespeare productions, publications and translations, international societies, and other matters of interest. Membership of the Association, linked with the payment of an annual subscription, was open to any person of any country wishing to support its objects, as well as corporate membership for academic, theatrical and library oganizations or institutions having interests in common with the work of the Association.

The progressive growth of the Association gave me considerable satisfaction, extending, as it did, the influence of the Birthplace Trust to many new contacts overseas. Within a short time several hundred members enrolled, and the steady stream of correspondence and enquiries which ensued provided evidence of the usefulness of the service offered by the newly founded Association.

The first newsletter issued to members, in April 1975, contained the important announcement that the Committee had accepted a proposal of the Shakespeare Association of America and the Folger Shakespeare Library that the Association should arrange a World Shakespeare Congress, to take place in Washington, DC, in April 1976 as part of the American Bicentennial celebrations, together with an offer of funding to make this possible. The prospect of such a significant send-off for the Association was too good to be missed.

Time for the necessary detailed planning was all too short, but, with its experience of organizing an annual conference for its members, the Shakespeare Association of America was able to offer considerable advice and help concerning possible arrangements. In May 1975 I went over to Washington, DC, to confer with the American programme committee that had already been set up to liaise with the International Shakespeare Association in planning the programme and practical arrangements for the Congress. Over a period of three days of intensive consultation, a blueprint for the week's activities was agreed.

It was decided to hold the Congress at the Statler Hilton Hotel in Washington, DC, from 19 to 25 April 1976 and, with the help of generous funding already secured from the National Endowment for the Humanities and other sources, to invite the participation of scholars from as many countries overseas as possible. The Congress was to be officially designated as part of the American Bicentennial celebrations and was seen as a major cultural event for the United States. It was appropriate that 'Shakespeare in America' was chosen as the overall theme for the Congress, and a programme for the week, comprising lectures, general sessions, seminars, exhibitions and related activities was planned around the following themes: 'Shakespeare in America'; 'Shakespeare in our Time'; Contemporary Approaches to Shakespeare'; 'Shakespeare on Film'; 'Shakespeare on the Stage'; and 'Shakespeare as an International Presence'. The chairmen, lecturers and participants were chosen to represent the widest possible international spectrum.

This programme, embellished with numerous receptions, visits, musical recitals, performances and a variety of social occasions, came to fruition as planned in April 1976, and attracted the attendance of nearly a thousand delegates, representative of the whole world of Shakespeare scholarship. The British Ambassador, Sir Peter Ramsbottom, and several distinguished Americans graced the opening ceremonies, when the address 'Shakespeare in America' was given by Alistair Cooke, the well known broadcaster. Shakespeare scholars spoke on specific topics on succeeding days, and at the plenary meeting Anthony Burgess gave a lecture on 'Shakespeare as Culture Hero'. Other memorable contributions were the annual Shakespeare birthday lecture of the Folger Shakespeare Library, given by Jorge Luis Borges on 'The Riddle of Shakespeare', and the English Speaking Union's lecture by Lord Hailsham of St Marylebone, former Lord Chancellor of England, on 'America's Heritage of English Common Law'. Scores of Shakespeare scholars participated in the daily seminars, which covered a wide range of subjects related to the principal themes.

During the Congress a general meeting of members of the Association was held. The work and recommendations of the Committee received unanimous endorsement, and useful discussion about future possible activities took place. Sir John

Gielgud was elected President of the Association, and Professor Maynard Mack of Yale University, the Vice-President. There was evident satisfaction with the Congress arrangements as a whole, and it was decided that a further international Congress should be held in five years' time. The re-elected Committee was given full authority to manage the Association's affairs and to plan the next Congress.

In practice, meetings of the Committee were subsequently held at the Shakespeare Centre in alternate years, when members found themselves in Stratford attending the International Shakespeare Conference organized by the Shakespeare Institute of the University of Birmingham at Mason Croft. On the occasion of the meeting in 1978 Professor Maynard Mack, Vice-President, gave the first of a series of International Shakespeare Association lectures, on the subject *Rescuing Shakespeare*, which was published the following year as the Association's Occasional Paper No. 1. Proposals for the future development of the Association were discussed at this time, and a decision made to investigate the possibility of holding a second World Shakespeare Congress in 1981.

Apart from memories of a most friendly and meaningful international Shakespeare gathering, which gave impetus to the newly-formed International Shakespeare Association and focussed attention on Stratford-upon-Avon as the headquarters of it, mention should be made of two permanent reminders of the Congress: the volume of proceedings of the Congress, entitled *Shakespeare: Pattern of Excelling Nature*, published by the Delaware University Press in 1979; and a commemorative medal, in bronze and silver, sponsored by the Association and the Birthplace Trust, and designed by Paul Vincze. The Congress medal depicted a representation of Shakespeare, with the masks of tragedy and comedy symbolizing his dramatic genius, superimposed on shelves of books suggestive of the influence of his works. The striking design of the obverse, evoking the spirit and achievement of national independence, linked the cultural theme of the Congress with the American Bicentennial celebrations.

Shakespeare Films

When I was in Washington in 1975, discussing plans for the projected World Congress, the opportunity occurred for me to pursue further with Dr Louis Wright his idea, as already mentioned, of making short educational films on the life and plays of Shakespeare for classroom use. The matter had been reported to members of my Executive Committee, who had given their approval in principle, and Dr Wright had by this time recommended a project of this kind to the National Geographic Society, one of whose regular activities was the production and distribution of educational films. The head of the Society's Television Division had also paid a visit to Stratford-upon-Avon for informal discussions with me, and he had been much impressed by the possible locations for filming I had shown him.

In company with Dr Wright, I was accordingly invited to take part in detailed discussions at the Society's headquarters in Washington with members of staff likely to be involved with the suggested filming project. It appeared that a series of educational films, 'Decades of Decision', dealing with episodes of American history, for which Dr Wright had acted as historical consultant, had recently been produced

The International Shakespeare Association's 1976 Congress medal

in preparation for the American Bicentennial, and had met with a very favourable reception in schools and colleges, as well as with television companies. It was felt that a similar series on 'The World of William Shakespeare' would be equally of value for classes in literature, history and dramatic production.

With this experience and object in mind, over a period of a few days we considered and agreed a tentative blueprint for a short series of sound and colour films for classroom use, starting with an introduction on 'Shakespeare of Stratford and London', together with three of the most widely taught Shakespeare plays, *Hamlet*, *Macbeth* and *Romeo and Juliet*, presented in condensed, thirty-five-minute productions.

It was suggested that these Shakespeare films should be jointly sponsored by the National Geographic Society and the Shakespeare Birthplace Trust. All production costs were to be met by the Society; in return for this association and the facilities provided for filming in the Trust's properties, the Trustees were to be offered the exclusive distribution rights of the films in Great Britain. As Director, I was invited to be associated with Dr Wright as historical consultant. A tentative programme for the production of the films was agreed.

On my return to Stratford, I submitted details of the suggested arrangements for the film project to the Trust's Executive Committee, whose members gave it their enthusiastic approval. Meanwhile, work on the scripts had already started and during the summer Dr Wright, accompanied by his personal assistant, Mrs Elaine Fowler, together with the producer and other representatives of the National Geographic Society, visited Stratford-upon-Avon for further discussions and exploration of suitable locations for filming. My visit to Washington for the World Congress in April 1976 enabled me to continue these discussions and to agree final plans for filming and production.

At that time the plan of action was for the film crew to take all the outside shots in Stratford and the surrounding countryside during the summer months, but in the event, due to a prolonged drought which resulted in the gardens and countryside being dried up and lacking their customary beauty, filming was postponed until the spring of 1977. I then found myself giving advice and help to the producer and his film crew. Each of the Shakespearian properties was filmed, together with scenes in Stratford and the surrounding countryside. I particularly recall the beauty of Baddesley Clinton on the sunny spring morning we visited it, and of shots taken at places like Aston Cantlow, Temple Grafton, Welford, Bidford-on-Avon and the Fleece Inn at Bretforton.

The World of William Shakespeare series of documentary films was completed during 1978. It comprised 'Shakespeare of Stratford and London', portrayed by surviving scenes which Shakespeare himself would have recognized and with graphic material from his own time; 'Hamlet: the Time is out of Joint'; 'Romeo and Juliet: Star-crossed Love'; and 'Macbeth: Fair is Foul and Foul is Fair'. In each case the abbreviated film version was based on the essential story of the play, retaining Shakespeare's language and including the best known poetic and philosophical passages. Settings and costumes for the plays were designed to resemble those that might have appeared in a performance on Shakespeare's own stage. Each film was accompanied by an illustrated teacher's guide containing a synopsis of the play, background information about it, a chronology high-lighting the events and personalities of the world of Shakespeare, a description of the Elizabethan playhouse, sources of quotations and a bibliography.

The Visit of Her Majesty Queen Elizabeth II to Hall's Croft

In 1975 the Royal Shakespeare Theatre celebrated the centenary of its inauguration, and an appeal was launched to ensure the future maintenance of the fabric and amenities of the Theatre building. The Trustees of Shakespeare's Birthplace made a donation of £10,000 to the appeal fund. As a means of publicizing their need and attracting support, the Theatre Governors decided to create a Centenary Garden at Avonbank and to organize a week-end of celebrations.

When it became known that Her Majesty Queen Elizabeth II was expected to associate herself with this event, the Chairman of the Trust, Mr Dennis Flower, wrote to offer a warm welcome to the Queen and to invite her to include in the programme of her visit an inspection of Hall's Croft. He explained that 1975 marked the 400th anniversary of the birth of Dr John Hall, and that the Trustees were presenting a commemorative exhibition at Hall's Croft. He also explained that as a contribution to European Heritage Year, which would be receiving national recognition, the Trustees felt it would be appropriate to call attention to the various conservation projects undertaken by the Shakespeare Birthplace Trust, of which Hall's Croft was an outstanding example.

The invitation was graciously accepted. On the afternoon of Friday, 27 June 1975, Her Majesty Queen Elizabeth came to Stratford-upon-Avon to perform the opening ceremony of the Centenary Garden and subsequently to visit Hall's Croft. Arriving in the Bancroft, in front of the Royal Shakespeare Theatre, Her Majesty was received and official presentations made. She then walked to the banks of the Avon and embarked on a gaily decorated boat, *Jubilee II*, on which she sailed down the river to the Centenary Garden. She disembarked to a peal of bells from Holy Trinity Church, sirens from barges moored along the river bank, and the applause of crowds of admirers, and as she stepped ashore into the garden she was greeted with Handel's Water Music and the National Anthem. Presentations followed and, in the presence of a large assembly of guests, she performed the official opening ceremony of the Centenary Garden and inaugurated a week-end of centenary celebrations.

It was a warm, pleasant, summer afternoon, ideal for this special garden party occasion. The Queen walked from the Centenary Garden into Old Town and then on to Hall's Croft, in front of which representatives of the Trust stood in readiness to welcome her. On her arrival, the Lord Lieutenant of Warwickshire, Mr Charles Smith-Ryland, a Trustee of Shakespeare's Birthplace by virtue of his office, introduced the Chairman of the Trust, Mr Dennis Flower, who presented his mother, Mrs Spenser Flower, Mr Peter Boddington, the Deputy Chairman, and Mrs Boddington, and myself, the Director. Proceeding inside, the Chairman invited Her Majesty to make an inspection of the house under my guidance. With the sunshine gleaming through the leaded-light windows on to the carefully polished pieces of period furniture and tastefully arranged flower displays, Hall's Croft could not have looked more inviting.

In the parlour the Chairman presented Mr Laurence Williams, the Trust's architect whose firm had been responsible for the restoration of Hall's Croft, and Mrs Williams. The Queen questioned him about the structure and type of building and the practical aspects of maintenance. The royal guest was clearly impressed by the quality of individual pieces of furniture in the parlour, the library and the dispensary, where the display of early, colourful pharmacy jars caught her eye. In Susanna's kitchen she chatted with Mrs Winifred Parsons, the deputy chief guide, about the kind of cooking arrangements and utensils used in Shakespeare's time. Upstairs in the exhibition room the Chairman presented members of the Executive Committee of Trustees: Mr T.E. Lowth, Mrs Trevor Matthews and Mr N.S. Pratt with Mrs Pratt. Here an exhibition on the life and work of Dr John Hall, with special reference to the theory and practice of medicine in his time, had been arranged. After viewing the exhibits and noting the remedies prescribed, the Queen exclaimed 'I don't think I should like to have been ill at that time'. It was at this point that she signed the distinguished visitors' book and the Chairman presented to her, as a reminder of her visit, a water-colour painting of Hall's Croft by its chief guide, Arthur Keene, F.R.S.A.

Leaving by the back door, Her Majesty then crossed over the paved terrace at the rear of the house, around which members of staff were standing, and, escorted by the Chairman and the

HM the Queen in the garden at Hall's Croft

Director, together with the Trust's head gardener, Harold Goodyear, she proceeded slowly along the paved path with its wide, herbaceous borders on either side, towards the sundial and arbour at the top end. As she walked along she occasionally paused to look at particular flowers, making comment or asking questions about them. I noticed that she had the same detailed knowledge of plants as her late father, King George VI, had displayed when he visited Shakespeare's Birthplace. Retracing her steps across the expanse of lawn, she remarked, when she saw the ancient mulberry tree, part of the reclining trunk of which was supported on a brick pier and had new growth shooting from its base, that she had a similar tree on one of her estates which had fallen down and then started to sprout a young tree to take the place of the old one. Guesses were made about the age of the mulberry tree, which the Queen thought was at least three hundred years old.

The occasion was a particularly happy one. Away from the attention of the press, Her Majesty was relaxed and appeared to be enjoying the friendly informality of the visit. She looked particularly charming in her summer attire: a soft green and white flecked, silk dress and jacket with a white border, and with a matching white turban hat, trimmed with the same material as her dress, and white accessories. It seemed to blend comfortably with the natural beauty and colour of the garden setting.

From Hall's Croft the Queen proceeded by car to the Guild Chapel and then on foot, to the applause of a flag-waving and cheering crowd, to the Town Hall, where she sealed a document establishing the Centenary Garden. She was later joined by HRH The Duke of Edinburgh for a gala performance of *King Henry V* at the Royal Shakespeare Theatre.

For all concerned the royal visit had been a great success, and the following letter from the Queen's

Private Secretary received by the Chairman amply rewarded all the effort of organization involved.

Buckingham Palace
28 June 1975

Dear Mr Flower,

I am commanded by the Queen to write to tell you how much she enjoyed her visit yesterday to Hall's Croft. Her Majesty was delighted you had suggested this addition to her programme at Stratford-upon-Avon and was most interested in the fascinating house itself.

The Queen has particularly asked me to thank you for the charming watercolour which was given her on behalf of the Trustees and which will make such a pleasant souvenir of a pleasant occasion.

Yours sincerely,
Bill Heseltine

Dennis Flower, Esq.,
Chairman of the Shakespeare Birthplace Trust

Mrs Lindon B. Johnson in the knott garden at New Place

Distinguished Visitors

During the 1970s the established practice of receiving distinguished visitors to Shakespeare's Birthplace and the other properties continued, and I have very pleasant recollections of several special occasions.

A few weeks after the celebrated ballet dancers, Valerie and Galina Panov, had been allowed to leave the Soviet Union in 1974 after a long period of well-publicized representation on their behalf, I received a telephone call from London to the effect that they would like to pay a private visit to Shakespeare's Birthplace, without the attentions of the media. I therefore agreed to an arrangement whereby on a Sunday afternoon, when the building was closed, I would meet them at the back of the Shakespeare Centre. Accompanied by an interpreter, the young couple arrived and we entered the Shakespeare Centre through the back door without being seen.

For more than a full hour I was then able to give them a private view of the building and particularly the library and its collections, from which I had produced for their inspection some early ballet material. It was an amazing experience to observe

Princess Chichibu at Anne Hathaway's Cottage

the reactions of these two attractive young people. They could hardly realize they were experiencing freedom; they seemed almost to be floating on air, like a pair of birds suddenly released from a cage. They left as they came, appreciative and delighted that they had made contact with the greatest of all artists, William Shakespeare, and their visit remained a secret.

In 1976 visitors to the properties and the Shakespeare Centre included delegates to the International Shakespeare Conference, for whom the traditional garden party was held at Hall's Croft, together with a number of official guests from overseas. Mrs Lyndon B. Johnson, the widow of America's former President, with her daughter, made a private visit in July. She spent some time viewing the exhibits in the Shakespeare Centre and Shakespeare's Birthplace, and I then escorted her on a tour of the other properties. She showed particular interest in the gardens, and asked questions about the plants and herbs of one of the gardeners working in the knott garden at New Place. During the course of our conversation as we went round the properties, Mrs Johnson recalled the American quatercentenary celebrations in 1964 and said that right from that time she had hoped she might be able to visit Stratford-upon-Avon. To mark the occasion, I presented to her on behalf of the Trustees an American Bicentennial medal designed by Paul Vincze.

Later in the year there was another interesting link with America. Members of the Natick Shakespeare Club, which was celebrating the centenary of its foundation and claimed to be the oldest club of its kind in the United States, paid a special visit to the Shakespeare Centre. As Director, I welcomed them on behalf of the Trust and there followed a friendly exchange of news and views. The goodwill generated by the visit was evident, and to mark the occasion the delegates presented an engraved plaque on behalf of the Club, together with a donation to the Trust's funds.

Another special visit I remember was that of Her Imperial Highness Princess Chichibu of Japan, in the summer of 1979, to whom I devoted nearly a day, escorting her on visits to the Shakespeare Centre, the Birthplace and the other properties. She was a most gracious lady, with an excellent command of English and with a surprising knowledge of English gardens and flowers. It seemed particularly appropriate that an eminent Japanese personage of this kind should come, in view of the steadily increasing numbers of Japanese visitors to Stratford-upon-Avon and the growth of serious interest in Shakespeare among Japanese students and scholars. I was able to tell her about the Trust's developing association with Japanese scholars and how impressed we were by the activities of the Shakespeare Society of Japan. I was also able to speak of my own personal experiences with Japanese students, particularly those who had come to do research in the Centre library or who, as members of the Shakespeare Summer School, had attended the seminar on Elizabethan handwriting that I had conducted over many years.

The Princess was also interested to hear of the arrangement whereby a finely-bound copy of Shakespeare's *Complete Works* was sent each year to the University of Mie in Tokyo, for presentation to the best student of English. I explained that this annual gift was made possible by the generosity of an American Shakespeare-lover, who conceived it as a means of fostering international friendship. I myself had received great pleasure from organizing it, because invariably the prize was awarded to a promising young student whose later progress in the academic sphere I was able to follow, and with whom I had enjoyed a continuing, ever-widening correspondence.

The Visit of Her Royal Highness The Princess Anne

Earlier in the year the Trustees were honoured by another royal visitor. On Tuesday, 29 May 1979, Her Royal Highness The Princess Anne, Mrs Mark Phillips, came to Stratford-upon-Avon to open formally the new Heritage Theatre, which had been established in Waterside as a novel audio-visual experience for tourists and which depicted the visit of Queen Elizabeth I to Kenilworth Castle in 1575. Following this, Princess Anne was to pay her first visit to Shakespeare's Birthplace, the Shakespeare Centre and Anne Hathaway's Cottage.

At the Heritage Theatre civic and other official presentations were made, before the Princess performed the opening ceremony and subsequently witnessed the presentation of the audio-visual programme. She then left for Shakespeare's Birthplace, travelling along Waterside, up Bridge Street, into Henley Street. A pattern of procedure for the reception of the royal visitor which experience had shown to work satisfactorily, was followed. Immediately inside the garden entrance to the Birthplace the Vice-Lord Lieutenant of Warwickshire, Captain F.H.M. Fitzroy-Newdegate, presented the Chairman of the Trust, Mr Dennis Flower, who in turn presented the Deputy Chairman, Mr Peter Boddington, and Mrs Boddington, and myself as Director. A few members of the Trust's staff had been invited to view from a selected position in the garden.

The Chairman and the Director escorted Her Royal Highness along the garden path and entered Shakespeare's Birthplace from the rear. I then had the honour for some twenty minutes of escorting her, and as we went through the building the chief guide, Mr George Rooke, and one or two regular members of staff who worked in the property were presented. Away from the press, the Princess, in relaxed mood, proved herself to be an unassuming, friendly person who was enjoying the experience of being able to inspect a national monument she had read about and had always wanted to visit. She commented on the condition of the rooms and the effective display of exhibits. Many questions were asked and answered, but, as always on these occasions, the time allowed in the programme for the visit was all too short.

Leaving the Birthplace by the same rear entrance, Princess Anne was interested to see the quince tree, with other trees, herbs and flowers mentioned by Shakespeare, as she walked along the path to enter the Shakespeare Centre, situated alongside the garden. In the entrance hall the Chairman presented the Trustee members of the Executive Committee and their wives: Dr Gareth Lloyd Evans and Mrs Lloyd Evans; Mr T.E. Lowth and Mrs Lowth; Mrs Trevor Matthews; and Mr N.S. Pratt and Mrs Pratt. These formalities over, the function of the Centre as the Birthplace Trust's headquarters and as a library and study centre was explained and features of interest in the entrance hall were pointed out and described.

Her Royal Highness then inspected the reading room, the book-stacks downstairs and the conference room on the first floor, and opportunity was taken to present the senior librarian, Mrs Marian Pringle, and a few members of staff as she toured the building. A selection of rare books from the library's collection, the subject matter of which I thought would interest the Princess, was laid out for the occasion. In fact she was particularly interested in the publications dealing with country life and rural pursuits, especially *The Grete Herball*, 1529, *The Booke of Falconrie* and *The Noble Art of Venerie or Hunting*, by George Turberville, 1611, and Thomas De Grey's *The Compleat Horse-man and expert ferrier*, 1670. As always on these special visits, the prize item shown was the Trust's copy of the First Folio of Shakespeare's works, 1623; and, anticipating the production of *The Merry Wives of Windsor* which the Princess was to attend in the evening at the Royal Shakespeare Theatre, her attention was also drawn to the Trust's copy of the Quarto edition of that play, published in 1619. In the entrance hall before she left, the Chairman invited Her Royal Highness to sign the visitors' book and to accept a small, framed Wedgwood plaque of Shakespeare to commemorate her visit.

Leaving the Shakespeare Centre by the front entrance, the Princess, looking cool and elegant in a striking black and gold ensemble with a wide-brimmed, matching hat – Shakespeare's colours – received an enthusiastic welcome from the waiting crowd as she entered her car to proceed to Anne Hathaway's Cottage. The route taken was along Henley Street, High Street, Chapel Street, Church Street, Chestnut Walk, Evesham Place and Shottery

HRH Princess Anne in the Birthplace garden

Princess Anne at Anne Hathaway's Cottage

Road, chosen to give Her Royal Highness a view of the central streets of Stratford, passing the Guild Chapel, the old Grammar School and the Almshouses in Church Street.

Upon her arrival at the garden gate leading to Anne Hathaway's Cottage in Cottage Lane, it fell to me to receive the Princess and to escort her on a tour of the garden, the Cottage and the orchard. Opportunity was taken to present the chief guide, Mr Harold Abraham, and members of staff who were on duty. The weather could not have been kinder, and in the bright, warm, summer sunshine we moved leisurely along the paths, viewing the informal plantings of flowers and herbs which gave a characteristic flavour to this old garden, while the green expanse of the orchard with its irregularly spaced, mixed fruit trees completed the rural setting. The Cottage itself likewise fascinated the royal visitor, who asked questions about its associations and history as she went from room to room, pausing particularly to examine the Hathaway bed at the top of the stairs in the parents' room. Passing the pair of cruck timbers on the way to the kitchen below, she commented on the solidarity and strength of this early form of house structure, and then asked questions about the arrangements for cooking and baking bread. It was at this point that Her Royal Highness was invited to sign the visitors' book.

As we walked slowly to the gate before she left, I was able to point across the road to the entrance to Jubilee Walk, alongside the brook, and to mention that it was the Trustees' most recent conservation project. She then paid a brief visit to the Town Hall, and completed her first visit to Stratford-upon-Avon by attending a performance of *The Merry Wives of Windsor* at the Royal Shakespeare Theatre. In the letter subsequently received by the Chairman of the Trust, Her Royal Highness said that she 'thoroughly enjoyed her visit' and, having never visited Stratford before, 'found many things to interest her'. She sent a special 'thank you' to me for my 'very informative guided tours', and expressed the hope that 'the extension to the Shakespeare Centre will prove to be a great success'.

The Queen's Silver Jubilee

On Tuesday, 7 June 1977, there were national celebrations to mark the Silver Jubilee of Her Majesty Queen Elizabeth II's accession to the throne. On the occasion of their Annual Meeting the Trustees and the Director felt that it would be appropriate to send a message of loyal greetings to the Queen, and the following telegram was accordingly sent:

> On the occasion of their Annual Meeting the Trustees of Shakespeare's Birthplace beg to tender to Your Majesty Queen Elizabeth II their cordial greetings and congratulations in your Silver Jubilee Year. They are deeply appreciative of the interest which Your Majesty and members of the Royal Family have always shown in the work of the Birthplace Trust and they recall with pleasure your visits to Stratford-upon-Avon. May it please Your Majesty to accept a message of loyalty and good wishes from the Trustees, Director and staff in Shakespeare's own words: 'Health, and glad tidings, to Your Majesty.'

In reply, the following telegram was received:

> Levi Fox Director, Trustees of Shakespeare's Birthplace, Henley Street, Stratford-upon-Avon. The Queen sincerely thanks you and the Trustees and staff of Shakespeare's Birthplace Trust for your kind and loyal message on the occasion of Her Majesty's Silver Jubilee which she very much appreciated.
>
> PRIVATE SECRETARY

The anniversary day was declared a special bank holiday. The Trustees decided to open the Shakespearian properties to the public on that day, and the number of visitors exceeded expectations.

Consideration had been given by the Executive Committee some time in advance as to possible ways of commemorating the Silver Jubilee in a permanent form. Apart from a number of minor improvements which it was decided to undertake around the Shakespearian properties, two new projects were considered and agreed: the construction of a new pedestrian approach to Anne Hathaway's Cottage, and the creation of a Jubilee Educational Fund.

At a meeting of the Executive Committee on 13 October 1976, I outlined a proposal I had been planning in my mind for some time. I indicated that at present visitors on foot to Anne Hathaway's Cottage found themselves intermingling with coaches and cars down the narrow approach along Cottage Lane from Brooklands corner in Shottery village, and I suggested that a field-path approach for pedestrians would be much safer and more attractive. My idea was that a path should be provided for pedestrians, starting from an area of green on the corner opposite Brooklands, going across the field owned by the Trust and following Shottery Brook for a short distance, before passing over a rustic bridge, to be constructed to span the brook in the spinney, and emerging on to the lane at a point opposite to the existing reception kiosk. Suitable tree and shrub planting alongside the path, which would remain private and under the control of the Trust, would be undertaken, while the area of green at the entrance would be landscaped in the manner of a small village green. I suggested that this scheme would add to the amenities of Shottery and could possibly be undertaken as a project to mark the Queen's Silver Jubilee.

The Committee's approval having been received, it gave me great pleasure to organize the practical implementation of the scheme. I first sought the co-operation of the tenant farmer to whom the field was let for grazing, and he agreed to surrender a portion of it, to be fenced off to make the path possible. A detailed plan was then produced for the layout and the necessary construction work, including the timber footbridge and the programme of tree and shrub planting to be carried out by the Trust's own garden staff. At the same time the assistance of the Severn Trent Water Authority, which was responsible for Shottery Brook, was sought, to clear and improve the course of the brook in the vicinity of the footpath.

By the spring of 1977 the plot of ground through which the path was to run was already fenced, and during the summer the path was laid down, the timber footbridge constructed, and entrance gates provided. The clearance of the brook took a little longer than was expected, but all was finished and the planting of trees alongside the walk completed during November. By this time the Trustees had decided to name the project Jubilee Walk, and to organize an official opening occasion on Thursday, 1 December 1977.

The opening ceremony was performed by the Lord Lieutenant of Warwickshire, Mr C.M.T. Smith-Ryland, who unveiled a plaque sited just inside the entrance at Brooklands corner, in the presence of Trustees, civic representatives and invited guests. The assembled company then walked along the path, turning alongside the brook and crossing the footbridge to the exit gate, before going into Anne Hathaway's Cottage. A reception there, which followed, provided an opportunity to propose a toast to Her Majesty the Queen and to thank all those who had contributed in various ways to commemorate the Jubilee year. In this connection reference was made to the planting of various trees to mark the Queen's anniversary, including an oak tree planted at Mary Arden's House by the Stratford-upon-Avon Young Farmers' Club, on 12 November 1977.

The Chairman also announced that the Trustees had decided to establish a Silver Jubilee Educational Fund, with the object of encouraging research and publication based on the Trust's library, records and museum collections. The idea was to build up a fund from which occasional awards could be offered to students and scholars wishing to work at the Shakespeare Centre, and to assist the publication of approved works of Shakespearian scholarship. With only limited resources available, the Trustees initiated the Fund with the sum of £5,000, but from this modest beginning additions were made in subsequent years, as the Trust's general financial situation allowed and as opportunities to use the Fund increased.

It has always been my hope that, like the Folger Shakespeare Library, the Birthplace Trust might one day find itself in possession of an endowment fund, and have sufficient resources to be able to offer fellowships and other research awards to develop the use of its library and archive collections. Hopefully, a benefactor may at some future date provide the

Jubilee Walk. From the top: the footbridge, the opening ceremony and alongside the brook

necessary money to make possible the development of the Silver Jubilee Educational Fund along these lines. There could be no more appropriate way of extending the influence of the Trust in the educational and academic sphere.

The Shakespeare Centre Extension

It took nine years to plan and build the Shakespeare Centre extension, which was completed in 1981. The story of the evolution of the project and its ultimate acceptance by the appropriate authorities is somewhat tedious and complex but, in the interests of historical record, a summary of it must be included in this account.

Being concerned about the growing adverse publicity the Trust was receiving as the result of the problems caused by the greatly increased number of coaches in Henley Street bringing visitors to Shakespeare's Birthplace, I first made a tentative proposal as to a possible solution to the Executive Committee in June 1971, and suggested the advisability of long-term planning with regard to future requirements of the Trust. Basically my suggestion was to build an extension to the existing Shakespeare Centre which would complete the original concept and provide facilities to meet a variety of needs. The members of the Committee decided to invite their architect, Laurence Williams, to confer with me to investigate the ideas I propounded, as a preliminary to submitting a report and recommendations for further consideration.

We both got very busy and, at a special meeting of the Committee held on 15 September 1971, submitted a tentative proposal, at that time called the Birthplace terminal project, designed not only to provide unloading and reception facilities for coaches visiting the Birthplace, but also envisaging an entirely new system for handling visitors to the property. The scheme suggested also provided for additional accommodation and facilities at the Shakespeare Centre, which it was felt would be needed to take care of the Trust's expanding educational, academic, cultural and administrative needs during the next twenty-five years or more.

Members of the Executive Committee were excited by the ideas put forward, and decided to submit them to the full body of Trustees at the Half Annual Meeting in October 1971. On that occasion the Chairman explained in some detail the difficulties being experienced in the handling of coaches in Henley Street, and emphasized the urgency of finding a solution in order to guarantee the future patronage of the package tours, which accounted for nearly forty per cent of the Birthplace's admission income.

The Trustees gave their approval in principle of the scheme suggested and, with the object of countering the suggestion put forward at a recent meeting of the Borough Council that coaches should be banned entirely from Henley Street, a press statement was issued letting it be known that the Trustees were aware of, and concerned about, the situation and that they were actively working on a plan to provide a solution. This decision enabled consultations to take place with the County Planning Officer and representatives of the Stratford-upon-Avon Borough Council, the Planning Committee of the Warwickshire County Council, the Department of the Environment and the police. Reactions were encouraging, and the Trustees decided to ask their architect to prepare a revised version of the original plan which would take care of the various points put forward during these discussions, and at the same time to submit suggestions as to possible elevational treatment of the extension block.

The Chairman reported generally on the situation at the Annual Meeting in May 1972 and suggested that, because of mounting pressure from the Borough Council concerning the coach problem, plans should be ready for submission to the Planning Authority by the autumn. Laurence Williams and I accordingly set out to meet this deadline, and a special meeting of the Executive Committee was arranged for 20 September 1972, to consider revised plans and sketches showing possible elevational treatment of the proposed new building. The members of the Committee were impressed by this revised scheme and decided they would recommend the Trustees, at their Half Annual Meeting on 28 October 1972, to approve the proposals for submission to the planning authority.

At this meeting finished drawings, with prospective sketches and a block model, were submitted by the architect and the background of the need for an extension to the Shakespeare Centre was explained in detail. The scheme proposed was designed as a logical enlargement of the original building, for the dual purpose of providing reception facilities for coaches and visitors, linked with a new arrangement for viewing the Birthplace, and at the same time providing accommodation the Trust was likely to need for its educational, academic and administrative requirements in the foreseeable future. The Trustees unanimously approved these proposals for the Shakespeare Centre extension, as it came to be called, and a formal planning application, supported by a detailed explanatory memorandum and model, was submitted on 20 February 1973.

By the time of the Trust's Annual Meeting in May 1973, no decision had been reached by the planning authority. Local reactions, as reported in the press, were unfavourable and unconstructive, but outside Stratford the proposals appeared to be regarded as enlightened and far-sighted. At the beginning of July representatives of the Trust were invited to meet members of the Borough Council and the Warwickshire County Council, and at this meeting it became apparent that the scheme as submitted was not likely to receive unqualified planning approval. The Trustees were not able to secure from the Borough Council any assurance that it would co-operate by making available premises adjoining the Centre which belonged to the Council, for use as part of the required site. Having weighed all the observations and the factors involved, the Executive Committee therefore decided to ask that the application should be held in abeyance in order that alternative possibilities could be investigated.

Subsequently, in consultation with the Committee, an alternative suggestion was produced by the architect for an extension building involving only the site of the Trust's own properties adjacent to the Centre. The main difference between the original scheme, which provided complete parking and terminal facilities for coaches, and the revised proposal was that off-loading facilities only, as opposed to a waiting area for coaches, would be provided in Guild Street and that, with the co-operation of the Borough Council, coaches after unloading would proceed to an area of the Windsor Street car park to wait until their passengers re-embarked. The smaller building it would be possible to erect on the site would include a reception concourse for the use of visitors, basement provision for library and records storage, an additional reading room linked with lecture room and assembly facilities on the first floor, and additional rooms above.

The Trustees approved the alternative scheme at their Half Annual Meeting on 27 October 1973, and authorized the Executive Committee to finalize the details for submission to the planning authority. The Trust's second application for planning permission was submitted on 15 February 1974, together with the necessary plans, drawings and perspective sketches. In a supporting memorandum, the Trustees confirmed their willingness to co-operate with the Borough authority by supplementing their provision of a terminal off-loading bay in Guild Street and offering to provide a waiting and re-loading facility in the Windsor Street car park. The Trustees were prepared to lease a suitable area, and to undertake the necessary site works to enable such an arrangement to function satisfactorily.

Although the Borough Council's Planning Committee recommended approval of the extension scheme in principle, their recommendation was turned down by the Borough Council in full session, at its last meeting before the re-organization of local government; and the application was then referred to the newly created Stratford-on-Avon District Council. On 6 May 1974 informal discussions concerning the project took place with representatives and officers of the District Council and an inspection of the site was made. The Trust's second application was considered on 8 May 1974 and refused. According to press reports of the proceedings of the Council, the Trust's proposals were very severely criticized by some members, chiefly on non-planning grounds and with little recognition of the purpose of the project or the process of consultation leading up to the final plans.

This adverse verdict inevitably produced a feeling of great frustration and irritation, and it was only with persuasion and encouragement that I assured Laurence Williams, the architect, that we must not be too discouraged, but must work together to overcome opposition. The Executive Committee held a special meeting on 16 May 1974 to discuss the situation. Having studied reports of the statements of the Council's representatives and officers concerning the Trust's proposals, I gave it as my opinion that it would be a waste of time and resources to pursue the matter further at the local level, and I therefore recommended that the Trustees should give notice of appeal against the decision forthwith. Before deciding to take such action, however, the Trustees felt that Mr Laurence Williams, who had received the formal notification of refusal, should seek an opportunity to confer with the Council's officers concerning the reasons for the adverse decision.

On the occasion of the Annual Meeting of Trustees held two days later, on 18 May 1974, a detailed discussion of the situation took place. Several members of the governing body expressed their concern and disappointment at the apparent hostile attitude of the local authority and of the local press to the Trust's plans, which were of such vital significance to Stratford-upon-Avon. In particular, Lord Radcliffe, who with other Trustees had taken a great personal interest in the formulation of these plans, felt that, although the Trust's status was recognized outside the town, there was a complete lack of appreciation on the part of the Stratford authority of the importance of the function of the Trustees on behalf of the nation and the world, and especially of the urgent need for them to plan boldly and imaginatively in order to meet their responsibilities in the future. 'If the scheme were resolutely and arrogantly opposed by those in charge of the development of Stratford-upon-Avon,' he said, 'Trustees must bring the matter to a head ... the Trust cannot go on planning if plans are not considered seriously'.

The Trustees accordingly decided to hold a Special Meeting to consider the whole matter further. This took place on 10 August 1974. The architect reported that he had now had discussions with representatives of the Department of the Environment, the County Planning Office, the County Surveyor's Department and the Stratford-on-Avon District Council concerning the rejection of the Trust's second application. He concluded by saying that in his view, as the architect responsible for the scheme, it would be impossible to reconcile the divergent views he encountered with the requirements the Trustees had laid down in his brief. He was not convinced that all the relevant facts as detailed in the supporting memorandum had been fully and fairly considered, and was disappointed to find such an unwillingness to recognize that a carefully conceived work of modern architecture could be fitted into traditional surroundings. He added that he had formed the impression that no reasonable, or possible, modification of the plans would meet with approval at the local level.

The Trustees unanimously decided to lodge an appeal; the services of Mr Stephen Brown, Q.C., were retained and, acting on his recommendation made in the light of his considerable knowledge of the background of the whole project and of all the circumstances involved, notice of appeal was lodged. Mr Stephen Brown subsequently acted successfully for the Trust in connection with an appeal concerning a long-term improvement proposal for the five cottages situated opposite the Shakespeare Centre (32-36 Henley Street), which was also the subject of a Public Inquiry.

When the Trustees held their meeting in May 1975, they inspected and approved a model illustrating the Shakespeare Centre extension proposal. Apart from this, no further progress with the scheme was possible, since no date had yet been fixed for the

Public Inquiry which had been promised in connection with the Trustees' appeal against the refusal of planning permission. It was not until October that the Committee learned that the Inquiry had been scheduled for 25 February 1976. Mr Richard Tucker, Q.C., was engaged to appear on behalf of the Trust but, because the Department of the Environment had only allocated two days for the hearing, it proved impossible for it to proceed and it was adjourned until 11 May. The Inquiry lasted ten days. In the meantime, the possibility of using a portion of the existing Windsor Street car park to provide a terminal for Birthplace coaches and cars was investigated, and a scheme designed to meet the requirements of the various authorities concerned was prepared in readiness for an outline planning application.

On top of my normal activities and duties as Director, all this unwelcome but unavoidable work constituted a considerable, time-consuming burden. Fortunately I was able to share this with Laurence Williams, with whom I continued to work in increasing harmony, since we both shared the same vision of the unique role of the Birthplace Trust and of the responsibilities of the Trustees to the world. Because of this, we were convinced that the Shakespeare Centre extension project was absolutely essential and reasonable, and that in due time we would overcome all obstacles. I also had the support and encouragement of my wife and family who, over the years, had followed and shared the various projects and fortunes of the Trust. By now the Fox family had become an integral part of this Shakespeare enterprise.

On 5 November 1976, the eve of the Trustees' Half Annual Meeting, the decision of the Secretary of State for the Environment was announced. He had dismissed the Trust's appeal, the primary cause of refusal arising from the highway objection to the coach off-loading arrangements incorporated in the proposed extension.

The Final Plan

The Executive Committee accordingly found itself having to carry out a complete re-appraisal of the situation, and it took a further year for the solution to be found. The Trustees were quite clear by this time that the only possible arrangement to solve the coach problem lay in the Windsor Street car park. Further discussions therefore took place both with the Town and District authorities, as well as with the planning officers, in the hope of agreeing a fresh scheme. Attention was now focussed on the possibility of the erection of a multi-storey car park at the rear of the existing car park area, and the construction of a terminal for the reception and waiting of coaches bringing visitors to the Birthplace at the front. The District Council was by now anxious that the coach and car parking problem should be settled, but held the view that the Trust should provide the maximum number of car spaces in the proposed multi-storey car park, to compensate for the kerbside places being lost in Henley Street and Windsor Street. There were also a number of technical and practical requirements that had to be met, and it took a number of months before the Trust's architect was able to satisfy them. At the same time, revisions to the plans and elevational treatment of the extension building which was to form part two of the Shakespeare Centre project had to be considered and approved by the Executive Committee.

At their meeting on 11 May 1977, the members of the Committee felt that at last there was light to be seen at the end of the dark tunnel. The architect submitted his final proposals for the scheme, which fell into two parts: the construction of a Birthplace coach terminal and multi-storey car park in Windsor Street; and an extension to the Shakespeare Centre, designed to provide for the Trust's immediate requirements and particularly incorporating a reception concourse for visitors to the Birthplace. The arrangements in Windsor Street were to be based on an agreement whereby the site for the terminal and multi-storey park was leased to the Trust for ninety-nine years at a peppercorn rent; in return, the Trustees were to bear the cost of constructing the terminal and the multi-storey car park, and on completion the latter was to be handed over by the Trustees as a gift to the District Council.

The Committee decided to recommend the approval of these proposals to the Annual Meeting of Trustees on 20 May 1977, and to seek authority to finalize details with a view to submitting a formal planning application. The Trustees unanimously approved the recommendation and, following further refinement of details, authorized the submission of the plans to the District Council on 14 July 1977. The Trustees asked that the Council should be informed that the two proposals complemented each other and that the project could not go forward until approval for both parts had been given.

The delay which followed was frustrating. The application was considered by the Development Services Committee of the District Council on 16 November 1977 after its members had inspected the listed buildings in Henley Street which it was proposed to demolish in order to make the development possible. The brick-built, eighteenth-century cellars, which had belonged to the White Lion inn that had occupied the site, fell into the grade two listed buildings category, and this conferred on them an element of protection which was difficult to remove. I well remember showing the cellars, as well as the sub-standard building above, to members of the District Council's Planning Committee, and explaining to them that the cellars were unsuitable for use as book-stack storage; that they were not unique from an architectural point of view; and that, in fact, the whole project depended on their demolition. I think I went so far as to say that the cellars should never have been included in the listed category. In the event, the Committee deferred making a decision on the planning application until 25 January 1978 in order that further discussion on certain points of detail could take place with the Trustees. The year 1977 therefore did not end as happily as we had hoped.

It was consequently a great relief to the Executive Committee that the Development Services Committee of the Stratford-on-Avon District Council decided to recommend approval of the Trust's Shakespeare Centre extension proposals, including the coach terminal and multi-storey car park in Windsor Street, when the application was considered further on 25 January 1978. Since the demolition of listed buildings was involved, the Committee's new recommendation had to be approved by the Secretary of State for the Environment. A further anxious waiting period followed, and it was not until 8 May 1978 that clearance of the Trust's plans was received, thus enabling the District Council to issue the necessary planning permission. It had been a long and hard battle; it now remained to satisfy the governing body as a whole that, in view of the very considerable increase in estimated cost, the project must go forward as soon as possible.

Decision to Proceed

Members of the Executive Committee were fully committed to recommending the 'go ahead', though they realized that another fund-raising appeal would be necessary to supplement the reserve already built up for this project. When the Trustees held their Annual Meeting on 20 May 1978, the Committee had already formulated a plan of action and timetable of operations. The target suggested was to complete the coach terminal and multi-storey car park by the end of 1979 and to have it fully in use for 1980. The Shakespeare Centre extension building would take two years, but should be completed by the autumn of 1980 and be available for use by the beginning of the 1981 season. I was also able to outline a programme of investigations, negotiations and preparations which would need to be followed to enable the Committee to have a firm recommendation to proceed ready for submission to the Half Annual Meeting of Trustees in the autumn. The proposals as submitted received the unanimous approval of all the Trustees. In consultation with the Director, the architect was authorized to proceed with all necessary preparations.

The six months that followed were a time of intense activity, involving frequent consultations with the Executive Committee and regular working sessions between the architect and myself. A detailed re-examination of the internal planning of the extension building was undertaken and certain interior adjustments and practical improvements were incorporated in revised drawings. The instructions of the Trustees were sought on a considerable number of matters relating to the design, materials, treatment and services for each part of the building. Messrs. Silk and Frazier were appointed as quantity surveyors, and Messrs. K. Chmiel and Partners as consultant engineers. At the same time, discussions took place with officers of the Stratford-on-Avon District Council concerning aspects of the design and construction of the multi-storey car park. In this connection the Trustees decided to offer to bear the additional cost of providing foundations to the multi-storey car park adequate to take two additional half-decks at the top, which the Council decided should be added at its own expense.

The necessary legal agreement, under Section 52 of the Town and Country Planning Act, 1971, confirming arrangements between the District Council and the Trust for the use of the Windsor Street site was also completed: the Council granted to the Trustees a lease of the coach park area for a term of ninety-nine years in consideration of the construction of the multi-storey car park and a peppercorn rent.

Consultations also took place with occupiers and owners of adjacent properties concerning the practical implications of building operations once a start was made on the extension project, and with the County Engineer with regard to traffic and parking arrangements in Windsor Street and Henley Street. The Trustees made it known that they were opposed to the re-introduction of car parking in front of the Birthplace Trust properties in Henley Street, and suggested that consideration should be given to the possibility of rendering completely traffic-free the short length of Henley Street between Meer Street and Windsor Street. The Trustees can in fact claim credit for having advocated the concept of pedestrianization which, though at first not favoured by some traders in the street, was implemented several years later.

Bills of quantities, an essential preliminary to the next step, were completed and sent to twelve firms of national standing which were invited to tender for the contract by 27 October 1978, and a special meeting of the Executive Committee was held on that day to consider a report I submitted on the tenders received. A perusal of them established that they were extremely competitive and, although all of them proved to be a little higher than forecasts had suggested, it was felt that they reflected current building costs fairly accurately. The figures submitted also made it clear that it would be advantageous to use the same contractor for both the extension building and the terminal and multi-storey car park.

The lowest tender for the complete project was that of Miller Buckley Construction, Ltd, of Rugby in the sum of £1,471,045, and this was some £75,000 lower than the second offer. An intensive exercise, carried out by the architect, the quantity surveyors and the consultant engineers, had established that savings in the region of £150,000 could be achieved without reducing the size or seriously impairing the quality of the final product. Thus the tender figure of Miller Buckley could be reduced to approximately £1,320,000. Bearing in mind, however, that building operations would take two years, it was established that allowance for fluctuations due to rising building costs – running at a rate of approximately one-and-a-quarter per cent per month – together with professional fees and furnishing could bring the total cost of the whole scheme when finished in early 1981 to approximately £1,635,000. The original forecast of total cost on completion had been one-and-a-half million pounds. For record purposes, the ultimate cost was some two million pounds.

By the time the Trustees met at their Half Annual Meeting on 4 November 1978, all preparations for a decision by the full governing body had been made. I submitted a comprehensive report embodying the recommendations of the Executive Committee. On reflection, I feel it marked another milestone in the history of the Trust. After summarizing the history of the project and the vicissitudes of its evolution over a period of six years, I recommended that, in the interests of the future development of the institution, it was vital that the scheme as now agreed should go forward without delay. The final plans were displayed and carefully examined and the Trustees made observations and asked questions on many aspects of the proposals. Not surprisingly, the question of the Trust's ability to meet the cost was raised and members of the Executive Committee were able to assure their colleagues that the project was not, in their opinion, beyond the resources of the Trust. Careful house-keeping had already built up a cash reserve which, with the anticipated surplus of income during the next few years, would meet the major part of the outlay. They felt that, for a number of reasons, this was an opportune time to proceed, but they were anxious that the Trust should not spend all its accumulated reserve, and would have liked to see a bigger balance of funds left on completion than was forecast. With this end in view they felt that the project should be used as an opportunity for the Trust to seek support in money and in kind. They suggested that approaches should be made to foundations and trusts, to selected companies, and possibly a few interested individuals, organizations and the Friends of Shakespeare's Birthplace, and recommended that an appeal for £250,000 would be appropriate.

The general reaction was strongly favourable and the Trustees decided unanimously to accept the tender of Miller Buckley and to proceed with the scheme forthwith. The Executive Committee was empowered to conclude all necessary contractual arrangements and to complete all legal formalities with the Stratford-on-Avon District Council, with the object of ensuring that an active start on the project could be made in January 1979 and completion achieved by the end of 1980. The Committee was also authorized to organize a selective appeal on the lines indicated. The Chairman congratulated the Director, the architect and the other professional agents who had been involved, for having completed all necessary investigations and preparations in time for the Half Annual Meeting.

Following the meeting, a press statement announced the Trustees' decision to go forward with what was described as 'the most important development in the whole history of the Birthplace Trust'. The construction of the coach terminal and car park, it continued, 'should greatly assist the town's traffic problem and eliminate the waiting of coaches in Henley Street'; the reception centre, when completed, 'should make a visit to Shakespeare's Birthplace more convenient and enjoyable'; while the facilities of the new building would make possible 'the continued expansion of the Trust's educational and academic work, as well as providing assembly accommodation for general needs in Stratford'.

Subsequently, the final stages of negotiations and preparations having been completed, the building contract with Miller Buckley Construction, Ltd, was signed at the Shakespeare Centre on 14 December 1978.

The Extension Building

As already explained, the purpose of the extension building was to meet a dual need: to provide an entirely new arrangement for handling the increasing number of visitors to Shakespeare's Birthplace; and to provide for the growing educational, academic and administrative requirements of the Trust, and at the same time indirectly to make available for the town improved facilities for cultural, conference and assembly activities.

The extension site adjoined the existing Shakespeare Centre on the north-west side and was formerly occupied by the premises numbered 15, 16 and 17 Henley Street, which had to be demolished to make possible the development. When the Shakespeare Centre was planned and built, it had been envisaged that an extension to it on this site might be necessary at a future date. The new building was accordingly linked with the Shakespeare Centre at all levels, so that, from a practical as well as from a design point of view, the two parts formed a complete whole.

The area of the site between Henley Street and

Guild Street was excavated to provide special basement accommodation to serve as an extension to the library book-stacks, strong room and work rooms in the existing Centre. To meet the growing needs of the library two further book-stacks, together with a sound-studio suite and ancillary work rooms, were provided. At the Guild Street end of the basement, two archive strong rooms of special design, approved by the Public Record Office, were provided to accommodate the Trust's record collections, including the Stratford-upon-Avon Borough records, which were transferred from the inadequate records department in the Trust's old headquarters building, Hornby Cottage. Plant rooms and stores were included in the complex.

Apart from providing improved facilities for the library, the whole of the ground floor, with entrance from Henley Street, was designed as an attractive foyer or concourse to serve as the reception and arrival point for all visitors to Shakespeare's Birthplace, superseding the arrangement whereby visitors entered the house through the front door. The idea was to provide a Visitors' Centre, as it was decided to call it, equipped with all the facilities a visitor might expect to find: a convenient arrangement for the purchase of admission tickets; adequate toilets; waiting and lounge seating; information and display illustrating the attractions of the town, the productions of the Royal Shakespeare Theatre and the Shakespearian properties; a sales counter; a first aid room and facilities for disabled persons; and, finally, a display of theatrical costumes worn by the actors taking part in the BBC's current series of Shakespeare productions. An exit at the rear of the concourse opened on to a path skirting the back of the Shakespeare Centre and linked with a paved walk through the garden, which guided visitors along a one-way route to enter the Birthplace by a new entrance door at the side of the house.

The first floor of the extension provided a self-contained suite of accommodation, linked with the Centre but with a separate entrance from Henley Street, thus enabling it to be used at times when the remainder of the building was closed. It comprised a multi-purpose assembly hall with a seating capacity of two hundred and fifty, a lecture room to accommodate one hundred, a foyer, seminar rooms and offices, together with cloakroom and refreshment facilities. The Trust needed accommodation of this kind for lectures, poetry readings and concerts, as well as for the courses of students, summer schools and university activities it sponsored. It was also envisaged that at certain times accommodation of this kind might be used for conference purposes and as a meeting place for local organizations. Upstairs at second floor level, a lounge or sitting-out area, with a kitchen adjoining equipped for the service of light refreshments, was provided for use with the facilities on the first floor, together with a small, compact group of seminar or office rooms, staff room and toilets for staff. There was access at this point to a self-contained flat for a resident caretaker.

At the rear of the extension and approached from Guild Street, the adaptation of the former Embassy Club building (previously the Brewery Club) made possible the provision of an enlarged records office on two floors, linked with new, spacious, strong-room storage for the Trust's records collections in the basement. Because the Club building adjoined and in effect formed part of the site, it proved possible to integrate it conveniently into the new complex with an independent access on ground level and

The Shakespeare Centre extension

connections with the assembly suite on both floors. This development was planned to provide improved facilities for the Trust's records and museum staff, as well as for readers and seminar groups using the local history library for which accommodation was provided alongside the main reading room.

Designing a building to meet the special requirements described above, sited within a few yards of the Birthplace itself, presented an unusual challenge and opportunity. The Trustees' aim was to produce a building which would discharge its various functions conveniently and efficiently, but which, at the same time, would repeat the quality of the Shakespeare Centre of which it would form an integral part, thereby adding to, and not detracting from, the views of Henley Street and Guild Street, of which the building would form part.

In producing this design, the architect had a number of particular considerations in mind. His primary concern was to design an extension of domestic scale, suitably modelled to link the existing Shakespeare Centre with the half-timbered building standing adjacent to the north-west in Henley Street, so as to produce a natural linking unit in the street scene, rather than a dominant block. Similarly, in Guild Street the design attempted to avoid the appearance of a large frontage, and in fact it was broken down into reasonably sized elements which contribute to the scale and environmental character of the street. Of vital importance was the use of materials sympathetic to the existing Centre and adjoining properties, particularly red, handmade facing bricks and roofing tiles, anodised aluminium window frames, and natural stone and wood finishings. The architect's brief also envisaged the possibility of including in parts of the building a number of appropriate artistic features and embellishments contributed by living artists and craftsmen. The Trustees, Director and architect were all agreed that, whilst everything possible should be done to preserve and enhance the appeal of Shakespeare's Birthplace as one of Britain's best known national memorials, it was essential that the Trust should equip itself with a building of quality, both pleasing aesthetically and useful from a practical point of view, to provide for its current and future requirements.

The Progress of Building

In accordance with a working programme and timetable agreed, both the Windsor Street and Henley Street sites were handed over to the contractors on 8 January 1979. Photographs of the Henley Street properties which had to be demolished were taken as a record, and any furnishings, fittings and materials that might possibly be re-used in connection with the Trust's normal maintenance work were removed.

An active start was made on both sites and in spite of adverse weather conditions good progress was made. Excavations for the foundations of the multi-storey car park in Windsor Street got under way and behind a screen of hoardings demolition of buildings and the clearance of the Henley Street site began. Acting on the suggestion of the architect and myself, the Trustees decided that, instead of arranging for foundation stones to be laid in connection with the extension building and the coach and car park, it would be more appropriate to provide plaques or marker stones which would record the completion of each part of the Shakespeare Centre extension project. It was decided that in the case of the coach terminal and car park an official opening should be planned for the middle of December 1979, while in the case of the extension to the Centre a distinguished person should be invited to perform an opening ceremony on Shakespeare's birthday in 1981.

These targets having been set, all concerned went to work with a will. By March all the main drainage and foundation work in Windsor Street was well advanced, and the first columns for the multi-storey car park were in position. In Henley Street, a giant overhead crane had appeared; demolition of the buildings on the site having been completed, excavation for the basement of the extension was proceeding. A careful look-out for possible archaeological finds was kept on both sites, but nothing was found; in Henley Street, however, an underground stream coming from the Guild Street direction was encountered.

There were frequent consultations at this stage with the Executive Committee, concerning the choice of materials and the kind of services required in the building. The Trustees approved a sample of a handmade facing brick, from Ibstock Building Products, Ltd, of Leicestershire, that was almost identical to the bricks used in the original Shakespeare Centre. Each brick was made by hand in the old fashioned way, and over 90,000 bricks were needed for the extension, 2,000 of them being of unconventional shapes, high-lighting the unique design. It was also decided to use handmade, sand-faced, dark, antique clay roofing tiles made by Keymer Brick and Tile Company, Ltd, of Sussex. Pearce and Cutler, Ltd, of Birmingham, the firm responsible for the bronze and aluminium window frames and doors in the original Centre, were chosen to fabricate, supply and fix the entrance doors, screening and window frames in Georgian bronze colour and natural anodised finish. The services of the How Group, a specialist firm in the field of heating and ventilation, were enlisted to advise on the most appropriate types of installations for the different parts of the building. Preliminary consideration was also given to possible artistic features and embellishments, and I was asked to submit suggestions.

By the early spring of 1979, excavations in Henley Street had been completed and attention was concentrated on the construction of reinforced supporting walls round the perimeter of the basement area. In Windsor Street the concrete framing of the multi-storey car park was gradually taking shape. Weather conditions, though, continued to slow down operations and, when I reported on progress to the Executive Committee in June 1979, I informed the Trustees that since the beginning of the contract in January forty-five working days had been lost as a result of consistently unfavourable weather. Due to the efforts made, however, it was estimated that the programme of construction was running approximately only two weeks behind schedule. In July members of the Committee inspected the progress of work on both sites. They were impressed by the multi-storey car park, which had already reached the top-tier level, while the construction of the basement walls and floor in the extension building was proceeding rapidly.

I must confess that I found the whole operation fascinating and exciting, and there were few days when I did not make a personal inspection. I had regular sessions with Laurence Williams, the architect, and together we frequently sought the instructions of the Executive Committee on suggestions we put forward relating to the finishing and furnishing of various parts of the extension building. There were many problems, cost and suitability of materials often having to be weighed. A case in point concerned the treatment of the floor of the Visitors' Centre. In view of the anticipated heavy wear to which the floor area would be subjected, it was felt that a tile of light beige colour with a textured, hard surface would be both pleasing and practical; but, as it so happened, no English manufacturer appeared to be able to supply what was wanted. The Trustees accordingly chose a particular type of tile made in West Germany.

By the autumn work on both sites was proceeding satisfactorily. An attendant's kiosk controlling the entrance to the coach terminal area was nearing completion, and the multi-storey car park was well on the way to being finished. By this time it was possible to appreciate its overall size and capacity to

Birthplace coach terminal and multi-storey car park

accommodate a total of two hundred and fifty cars on four floors, as well as the main features of its design. Being of a plate-slab construction only a minimum number of supporting columns were required, and the brick cladding round the concrete structure harmonized with the setting. It had the usual staircase and ramps and provision for a passenger lift, delivery of which was awaited.

On Thursday, 1 November 1979, a traditional topping-out ceremony for the multi-storey car park was held in the presence of all who were involved in the project together with Trustees and local guests. Completion followed quickly and the Trust took over the finished coach terminal and multi-storey car park on 30 January 1980.

The new arrangements for the management of coaches and cars were brought into use on 4 February 1980, the date on which revised traffic orders applicable to Windsor Street and Henley Street came into effect. At last, after many years of

Birthplace coach terminal

effort on the part of the Trustees, the waiting of coaches and cars in front of the Trust's properties in Henley Street, always an unsightly and intrusive arrangement, was no longer allowed. The convenience of the new terminal facility was quickly appreciated by the coach operators, whose continued business bringing visitors to Shakespeare's Birthplace was also ensured.

An official opening ceremony for the coach terminal and multi-storey car park was held on Thursday, 21 February 1980, at 12 noon in the presence of Trustees, representatives of the Stratford District and Town authorities, the contractors and other guests. After the Chairman of the Trust, Mr Dennis Flower, had briefly addressed the assembled company, he unveiled a black granite marker plaque, built into the front of the kiosk at the entrance to the terminal, bearing the following inscription:

THE SHAKESPEARE BIRTHPLACE TRUST
THIS TERMINAL FOR COACHES BRINGING VISITORS TO SHAKESPEARES BIRTHPLACE WAS CONSTRUCTED BY THE BIRTHPLACE TRUST

THE MULTI-STOREY CAR PARK WAS ALSO BUILT BY THE TRUST AND PRESENTED TO THE STRATFORD-ON-AVON DISTRICT COUNCIL WHICH MADE AVAILABLE THE SITE & PROVIDED AN ADDITIONAL STOREY

OPENED FEBRUARY 1980

The company then proceeded to the Shakespeare Centre, where Mr Flower spoke with some pleasure of the significance of the occasion. The construction of the terminal and multi-storey car park in just over a year, following six years of planning negotiations, represented what he described as 'a notable achievement' and he paid a warm tribute to the team of contractors whose work had made it possible. The project, Mr Flower explained, also provided evidence of a real union of purpose and willingness to work together on the part of the local authorities and the Birthplace Trust, and he expressed appreciation to the District Council and the Town Council for having made available the site in Windsor Street.

The car park, Mr Flower added, had cost a great deal of money which had been earned by very hard work. It could not have happened without Shakespeare. Although the facility was intended to assist the institution which exists to do honour to Shakespeare, at the same time the Trustees hoped that it would serve the convenience and best interests of Stratford people and that it would be welcomed as an improvement to the environment. For this reason the Trustees were happy to make a present of the multi-storey car park to the town.

Mr Flower accordingly asked Councillor R.A.C. Lucas, the Chairman of the Stratford-on-Avon District Council, to accept the car park as a gift from the Trust and to assume responsibility on behalf of the Council for its future management. He then handed to him a signed document recording the gift and the arrangements agreed between the Trust and the District Council, and Councillor Lucas made an appropriate reply.

Strange as it may seem, and in spite of protracted negotiations, the Trustees did not succeed in acquiring the use of any free parking places in the multi-storey car park for their own staff. However, they were able to secure the agreement of the Council to a commercial lease of twelve parking spaces on the ground-floor deck of the car park.

Meanwhile, satisfactory progress on the extension building continued. Mild weather early in the year allowed the roof and brickwork to be completed, thus enabling interior structural work and the installation of services to go forward. A detailed scheme to take care of heating, ventilation and air conditioning in various parts of the building was suggested by the How Group and was accepted, and the electrical installation was undertaken by the Stratford firm of N.W. Dixon, Ltd, one of whose senior electricians, Mr Bill Adams, had undertaken most of the electrical work carried out in the Trust's properties over a period of years and, incidentally, continued to look after the Trust's electrical requirements until he retired in 1993. Bill typified the English craftsman at his best: behind his quiet, unassuming manner, he was a man of great experience and technical skill, able and willing to use his patience and ingenuity to overcome any problem he might encounter. Security for the basement bookstacks and archive strong rooms was entrusted to Chubb Alarms, Ltd.

By March 1980 the giant crane that had greatly facilitated the constructional work had been removed from the site and during the summer months the installation of services and finishing processes inside the building went ahead. For me personally this was perhaps the most interesting and satisfying stage of the building programme. I often watched the plasterers at work and, in particular, I remember the occasion when I stood and watched a plasterer putting the final finishing coat on one of the circular piers in the Visitors' Centre. It all seemed so simple as, with great ease and skill, he smoothed the surface of the plaster to make a perfectly round pillar. Talking to the man who was doing this work, he told me that this was a rare opportunity for him to exercise the skills he had been trained to use. He invited me to see him the following day making a replica length of plaster skirting to match the existing Victorian pattern in the room which was being prepared as the reading room of the records office. Again he displayed an almost magical skill which, whilst clearly giving him immense satisfaction, produced a matching piece of plaster skirting that was perfect. I think I should record a sad sequel to this episode. After the extension building was finished and in use, the same man asked my permission to bring his son to see the plasterwork he had done. When I met him I realized how proud he was to have contributed to what he called a wonderful building, but I was very sorry when he told me that since he finished work on the Centre extension he had been unemployed. 'There is no demand for high quality work of this kind,' he explained, 'but at least you've got something here worth looking at'.

My other favourite craftsmen were the carpenters, particularly those employed by Gordon Russell, Ltd, who were responsible for the design, manufacture and fitting of the wall and ceiling panelling in the assembly hall, including the doorways and other woodwork. European cherry was the timber used for this area, the carefully chosen grain and colour of the cladding giving the same pleasing appearance as the cherry-wood panelling in the conference room of the original Centre. The same carpenters were responsible for the vertical oak screen in the visitors' concourse on the ground floor, designed to accommodate the display of Paul Vincze's Shakespeare medallions, and this screen was continued to first-floor level to form a glazed wall to the area in front of the bar. In contrast, English beech was chosen for the timber boarding in the lecture room, later named the Wolfson Hall. This was supplied and fixed, with associated joinery, by Henry Venables, Ltd, the well known firm of timber merchants of Stafford, which had provided the English cherry panelling used in the original Centre, as well as structural timbers used for repairs in the Shakespearian properties. Equally impressive were the contributions made by A. Edmonds and Company, Ltd, of Birmingham, the firm which over the years had designed and supplied showcases and counters for the Shakespearian properties. In the extension building they were responsible for the construction of the metal display windows on Henley Street, as well as recessed showcases in the lecture room and the main visitors' concourse. Here they also designed and supplied the reception counter, canopy and plant trough, together with the sales counter and back-fitting; and on the first floor the bar, with its counter front and canopy finished in bronzed metal and fitted with oak veneer and formica. These details are given to illustrate the individual character of the widely varied requirements which had to be met.

All these finishing items had to be fitted into a programme designed to bring the building to completion by the end of 1980, so that movable furniture and equipment could then be installed. Orders were placed for book-stack and records storage shelving, but specially selected items of furnishings for the assembly hall, the lecture room and the other rooms in the extension were individually designed and made by Gordon Russell, Ltd, of Broadway, to whose designers and craftsmen the Trust owes a considerable debt. I personally had enjoyed a friendly relationship with Sir Gordon Russell himself, and still worked closely with his staff at Broadway, particularly Mr Ray Leigh, the Managing Director, and Mr Martin Hall, whose advice on carpets and curtains was invaluable. Evidence of our friendly association was provided by the presentation made by the firm of an oak table and lectern for the assembly hall in memory of the late Sir Gordon Russell.

During the summer months the Trustees approved a plan for re-designing the layout of the end portion of the Birthplace garden, alongside the Centre. This provided a paved walk from the exit at the rear of the visitors' concourse, which passed a fountain and led through the garden to a new doorway entrance which it had been decided to insert in the end of the Birthplace. The cost of the fountain was met by the trustees of the late C.A. Rookes. The work was carried out during the autumn, in readiness for the introduction of the new visitors' approach to the Birthplace linked with the use of the new Visitors' Centre.

So far as the building was concerned, the concluding months of 1980 were a period of considerable activity. Inevitably, there were some unforeseeable problems. The plaster in the basement rooms, for example, took much longer to dry out than was expected, with a resultant hold-up in decoration and a short delay in transferring the records collection to its new accommodation. Another unfortunate incident occurred: a fire destroyed the premises of the local model-making firm of Severn-Lamb, Ltd, which was actively producing a globe model for the Visitors' Centre, thus necessitating a fresh start to be made. By December 1980 the hoarding enclosing the Henley Street elevation had been removed and the paving of the forecourt was under way. By the end of January 1981 the main contractors had completed their work, and all was ready for the installation of a number of specialized features and the introduction of furnishings and equipment.

At the April meeting of the Executive Committee, I reported that the Visitors' Centre had been brought into public use on 23 March 1981, and that the exhibition of costumes from the BBC Television series of Shakespeare plays set up at the lower end of the concourse had aroused considerable interest. First impressions were that the new arrangements for handling visitors to Shakespeare's Birthplace were working very satisfactorily. Special admission tickets were printed and issued to commemorate the opening of the Visitors' Centre.

The assembly hall, which it had been decided

should be called the Queen Elizabeth Hall, was used for the first time on Sunday, 5 April, for a concert given by the Stratford-upon-Avon Wind Bands Association, and the acoustics and sound-proofing of the building were found to be excellent. On Tuesday, 7 April, an open day for representatives of the press, individuals and firms involved in the construction of the building was well attended. Arising from this, part of a 'Blue Peter' programme on BBC Television was filmed at the Shakespeare Centre. Particular interest in the new assembly facilities was shown by conference organizers and, as a public relations exercise, an evening reception was held on 28 April for local people who were interested to see the new building. Reactions about it were universally favourable, comments being made by many about the imaginative design and the quality of the finishings and furnishings.

The transference of the records office from the rear of Hornby Cottage into its commanding new quarters in the adapted Embassy Club building at the rear of the extension was completed by the early summer. This enabled a start to be made on a programme of renovation in the old records office building, designed to improve the accommodation and facilities of the Trust's growing publications department and associated stock room area. Before the end of the year, the rooms on the first floor of Hornby Cottage, including the original boardroom, which had for several years been partitioned to provide temporary office accommodation, were restored to their former condition. Thus the year 1981 saw the completion of the Shakespeare Centre project, the need for which was first recognised in the late 1950s.

Artistic Features

Right from the early stages of planning, the Trustees readily endorsed the recommendations of the architect and myself that opportunity should be taken, as in the case of the original Centre, to use the services of living artists and craftsmen to produce artistic features relevant to the purpose of the building. Various suggestions were considered, and the ones which were adopted eventually produced a number of artistic embellishments which gave a distinctive character to the extension.

All of us were agreed that emphasis should be placed on features which, whilst appealing artistically, would convey information of interest to visitors. It was therefore decided to provide plaques fixed to the wall on either side of the main entrance portico, above which was the centrally placed VISITORS' CENTRE panel. One of these was to be used to record the official opening of the extension; the other to call attention to the interesting historical association of the site, on which had originally stood the White Lion inn, one of Stratford's best known coaching hostelries.

The White Lion Inn plaque

The sculptor commissioned for this work was Paul Wehrle, who, as an apprentice to John Skelton, had assisted with the carving of the lettering on the large granite panel at the entrance to the Shakespeare

Centre in 1964. Incidentally, it was whilst he was working in the Centre that he met his future wife, Sarah Nation, who at that time was a member of my staff, a library assistant. The material chosen for the plaques was black Belfast granite, and a lower-case type of lettering of a dignified Roman character was used for legibility and informality. Although the inscriptions on each panel were completely different, they were designed to balance and complement each other, and the letters themselves were entirely hand-cut. The same sculptor also produced three smaller plaques in Welsh slate which were put up in different places: an inscription concerning a brick bearing the date 1746, removed from one of the cellars which had been demolished; a direction notice pointing the way for visitors to the Birthplace garden; and a small commemorative plaque bearing the name of Chris Rookes, the local wine merchant with whom the Trust had had a long and friendly association, placed alongside the fountain to commemorate his generous support of the Trust.

Immediately inside the entrance to the Visitors' Centre the large expanse of handmade brickwork on the left provided a suitable position for a panel of information explaining the role and activities of the Shakespeare Birthplace Trust. Richard Kindersley, sculptor and letterer, was commissioned to design and provide an artistic layout of lettering to fill this space. The type used consisted of specially designed characters of varying sizes made from cold-cast bronze, polished and sprayed with lacquer, which were superimposed on the brickwork surface. This was an original concept of architectural lettering embellishment: because of its layout and the size and shape of its individual characters, it immediately registered as a special artistic feature, at the same time conveying to visitors who read it the following information:

THE SHAKESPEARE BIRTHPLACE TRUST

THE BIRTHPLACE TRUST IS A SPECIAL KIND OF EDUCATIONAL INSTITUTION OF CHARITABLE STATUS WHICH EXISTS TO DO HONOUR TO

WILLIAM SHAKESPEARE

IT CAME INTO EXISIENCE IN 1847 WITH THE PURCHASE OF SHAKESPEARE'S BIRTHPLACE
BY PUBLIC SUBSCRIPTION FOR PRESERVATION AS A NATIONAL MEMORIAL

THE TRUST MAINTAINS THE FOLLOWING PROPERTIES WHICH ARE OPEN TO THE PUBLIC:

SHAKESPEARE'S BIRTHPLACE THE HOUSE WHERE SHAKESPEARE WAS BORN
ANNE HATHAWAY'S COTTAGE HOME OF SHAKESPEARE'S WIFE BEFORE HER MARRIAGE
NEW PLACE THE FOUNDATIONS OF SHAKESPEARE'S LAST HOME WITH NASH'S HOUSE ADJOINING
MARY ARDEN'S HOUSE THE TUDOR FARMSTEAD WHERE SHAKESPEARE'S MOTHER LIVED
HALL'S CROFT HOME OF SHAKESPEARE'S DAUGHTER SUSANNA, AND DR. JOHN HALL

ALONGSIDE ITS CONSERVATION RESPONSIBILITIES THE TRUST UNDERTAKES EDUCATIONAL, CULTURAL & ACADEMIC ACTIVITIES
WITH THE OBJECT OF FURTHERING KNOWLEDGE AND APPRECIATION OF SHAKESPEARE'S LIFE, WORK AND TIMES
IN EVERY PART OF THE WORLD. TO THIS END IT HAS BUILT UP SPECIALISED LIBRARY, ARCHIVE AND MUSEUM COLLECTIONS
FOR THE USE OF STUDENTS AND SCHOLARS OF ALL NATIONALITIES
THE SHAKESPEARE CENTRE ACCOMMODATES THE TRUST'S ADMINISTRATION, LIBRARY, RECORDS OFFICE & STUDY FACILITIES

THE PANEL WAS PRESENTED BY MR PAT BARRETT

The cost of this lettered panel was donated to the Trust by the late Mr Pat Barrett, the proprietor of a local firm called Motorways Plant, Ltd. He was a generous man and on several occasions assisted the Trust in various ways as, for example, by providing a low-loading transporter vehicle to convey the gipsy caravans I have described in an earlier chapter, and by transporting farm wagons from Long Marston to Mary Arden's House.

Richard Kindersley was also responsible for designing and executing the large, oblong-shaped tablet of Welsh slate positioned on a projecting wall facing visitors at the right-hand side of the entrance area of the main concourse. This was given to the Trust by the Welcombe Hotel, with which, by reason of our interest in the Welcombe estate, I had enjoyed friendly association through its successive managers over the years. Under the heading of 'Shakespeare and his Times', the idea was to use a simple list of dates and events to put Shakespeare in the context of the Elizabethan age. No fewer than 1,288 letters had to be carved and painted to produce this unusual chronological feature shown opposite.

The overall appearance of the tablet immediately arrests attention, and I have been interested to observe the reactions of visitors looking at it. To those from our own country, the dates of national events like the Spanish Armada or the Gunpowder Plot recall history lessons and textbooks; for overseas visitors, and particularly Americans, the dates recording the discovery of the New World and the evidence that Shakespeare was alive at the time the first English settlement was made in Jamestown, Virginia, are particularly significant.

Alongside 'Shakespeare and his Times', a mural of colourful ceramic tiles was produced, to occupy almost the full width of the wall on the right-hand side of the foyer entrance. Appreciating that an understanding of Shakespeare requires not merely a knowledge of the history of the period in which he lived but also of the physical environment and character of the town in which he was born and died, Christina Sheppard, a specialist designer in pottery and ceramic techniques, was commissioned

SHAKESPEARE AND HIS TIMES

1558 *Elizabeth I became Queen of England*
1564 *William Shakespeare born at Stratford*
1564 *Birth of Galileo, inventor of the telescope*
1568 *John Shakespeare elected Bailiff of Stratford*
1575 *Queen Elizabeth visited Kenilworth Castle*
1577 *Drake sailed round the world*
1582 *Shakespeare married Anne Hathaway*
1583 *Birth of Shakespeare's daughter, Susanna*
1585 *Birth of Hamnet & Judith, Shakespeare's twins*
1587 *Execution of Mary, Queen of Scots*
1588 *Defeat of the Spanish Armada*
1592 *Shakespeare working in London*
1593 *Publication of Shakespeare's Venus and Adonis*
1594 *Shakespeare joined the Lord Chamberlain's Company*
1595 *Raleigh's expedition to South America*
1596 *Burial of Hamnet Shakespeare*
1596 *Grant of Arms to John Shakespeare*
1597 *Shakespeare purchased New Place*
1599 *Opening of the Globe Theatre, Bankside*
1600 *East India Company founded*
1601 *Death of the poet's father*
1602 *Shakespeare bought land in Old Stratford*
1602 *Bodleian Library at Oxford opened*
1603 *Death of Queen Elizabeth I & accession of King James I*
1605 *The Gunpowder Plot*
1607 *Susanna Shakespeare married Dr John Hall*
1607 *First English settlement in Jamestown, Virginia*
1608 *Birth of Elizabeth Hall, Shakespeare's granddaughter*
1608 *Death of Mary, the poet's mother*
1609 *First edition of Shakespeare's Sonnets published*
1610 *Shakespeare retired to New Place*
1613 *The Globe Theatre destroyed by fire*
1616 *Death of Shakespeare on 23 April*
1618 *Beginning of the Thirty Years War*
1620 *The Pilgrim Fathers landed in New England*
1623 *Publication of the First Folio edition of Shakespeare's comedies, histories & tragedies*

to illustrate 'Shakespeare's Stratford'. She accordingly produced a design which depicted the simple street plan of the town in Shakespeare's time in relation to the River Avon with the mill, the church and the surrounding countryside, and included in it figures suggestive of farming, trading and rural recreations. Stratford was then a small, country market-town, a centre of markets and fairs, and busy with trading activities in its streets. Christina Sheppard set out to portray the essential character of Shakespeare's Stratford, using ceramic tiles of Spanish manufacture to convey her picture. Each of the ninety-one square tiles, eight inches by eight inches in size, used to make up the complete mural was individually designed, coloured, glazed and fired by the artist. The resultant product was a unique artistic mural, pleasing for its overall design and subtle colouring and at the same time notable for the accuracy of its detail. I myself suggested the subject and worked closely with the artist in preparing the design.

It fell to me to supply the historical data, but Miss Sheppard was entirely responsible for the imaginative interpretation and portrayal of the town's layout and buildings, with the skilfully delineated figures suggestive of its busy role as a marketing centre: sheep, cattle and pigs, respectively, as sold in Sheep Street, Rother market and Swine (now Ely) Street; Hornby the blacksmith shoeing a horse in Henley Street; a man and his wife spinning wool; country folk coming and going, with horses and carts; the Avon with its anglers and small river craft; huntsmen chasing deer and sporting with falcons; and many other rural subjects. On the tile occupying the bottom right-hand corner of the scene is a young man in pensive mood, reclining under a tree on the riverbank: I found that this was intended by the artist to be the young Shakespeare himself!

Another feature, entirely different but equally striking, was given pride of place in the Visitors' Centre. A tall, vertical oak screen, the work of the craftsmen of Gordon Russell, Ltd, of Broadway, which covered one of the walls in the central area of the concourse was constructed to display the series

Above and opposite: Shakespeare Commemorative Medallions

of thirty-six bronze medallions depicting scenes and characters from Shakespeare's plays, designed by the eminent sculptor medallist, Paul Vincze. Hungarian by birth but a British subject since 1948, Vincze had an international reputation for his prize-winning medals of famous people and commemorative events. As already mentioned, in 1964 he designed the official medal to commemorate the 400th anniversary of Shakespeare's birth, and in 1969 the official medal struck to mark the 200th anniversary of the first Shakespeare Festival at Stratford-upon-Avon, organized by David Garrick. Largely because of these commissions, he developed his earlier interest in Shakespeare and over a period of ten years or more designed, as a work of love, a medal for each Shakespeare play, portraying his interpretation of a well known episode or character in the play. So far as was known, no individual medallic sculptor had so far undertaken such a project and, when the Trustees were offered the complete set of the large bronzes which originated the medals, they gratefully seized the opportunity to use them to create a unique artistic embellishment. Complementing the national and local background features already described, these medallic studies provide evidence of the extraordinary range of subject matter covered by Shakespeare's plays, as well as giving a visual portrayal of well known scenes or characters from them. Each of the medallions is in itself an artistic study, displaying the individual style and three-dimensional quality characteristic of Paul Vincze's work. By way of record, a self-portrait of the sculptor was incorporated in the display in the bottom right-hand corner.

Perhaps even more eye-catching as visitors pass through the concourse on their way to the Birthplace was the revolving skeletal globe of the world, with its inscription. Bearing in mind that some two-thirds of the visitors who passed through the Visitors' Centre came from abroad, the thought had occurred to me that an exhibit or artistic feature symbolizing the universality of Shakespeare's genius would be appropriate. The first idea was to display a large, traditional globe of the world, but upon discussion with the architect I realized that, because the

The Visitor's Centre

brass letters of the quotation fixed around the equator. The letters were high-lighted in gold leaf and the axle of the model was linked with an electric motor geared to turn the globe slowly to bring into view the quotation from *The Merchant of Venice*: 'From the four corners of the earth they come to kiss this shrine'. In actual fact, this is what happened every day, as visitors passed by the globe to view Shakespeare's Birthplace. Representatives of over a hundred countries come every year.

The Cost

This account of the extension building would not be complete without further reference to its financial implications. Before the decision was made to proceed with the project in 1978, the Trustees asked me to prepare a detailed forecast of the estimated cost of running the new facilities proposed, together with the additional anticipated income expected to be produced. At a time when inflation was constantly changing and without a firm basis of assessment or experience to substantiate many of the items, this was a difficult exercise, rather like making a journey on a very dark night without adequate lighting. However, the estimates I produced were accepted by the Executive Committee as sufficient evidence of a viable proposition. At the same time, the Trustees satisfied themselves that the reserve of funds built up since 1964, as the result of the increased visitor patronage already described, was sufficient to justify investment in a major scheme of this kind. Thus, when the proposal was considered at the Half Annual Meeting in November 1978, the Committee's assurance was accepted by the full governing body that the reserve available, together with estimated additions during the next two years, would be adequate to meet the capital cost and that, once provided, the Trust could afford to maintain the new facilities.

names of countries were constantly changing, this would not be ideal. Discussions accordingly took place with the Stratford firm of Severn-Lamb, Ltd, which specialized in producing individual models for industry, museums and private collectors, and an alternative idea emerged, namely, that a more appropriate exhibit would be an open or skeleton-type of globe which would display the land masses of the world and the expanses of sea without names, and which could be made to revolve and thus display a quotation from Shakespeare symbolizing the universal appreciation of the poet.

Severn-Lamb accordingly designed a novel feature: a six-feet diameter globe constructed in steel with longitudinal lines and the continents cut out and positioned in thin steel. The land masses were flame-cut by hand to the correct radius, as well as the

There was, however, concern that the project should not jeopardize the normal activities of the Trust by consuming all its financial resources and, as already mentioned, the Trustees decided to appeal for assistance from outside sources on a selective basis, setting a target of £250,000. When the Chairman reported on the progress of building operations at the Annual Meeting on 19 May 1979, he referred particularly to the financial situation, asking the Trustees to give their advice and help as to possible sources of support. An initial contribution of £10,000 had already been given by the National Farmers' Union Mutual Insurance Society, Ltd, and the hope was expressed that the appeal would gather momentum when a brochure describing the scheme was available.

The responsibility for organizing the cash flow to take care of payments to the contractors and other agents involved fell to me. Indeed, the Trustees gave me complete authority to manage their investments, using the Money Market Division of the Midland Bank and reporting to the Executive Committee each month. In this way I was able to secure for the Trust the highest possible interest on short-term investments, while ensuring that money was available in appropriate amount to make payments as required. It was an extremely interesting, though responsible, financial exercise, and in the course of it I became quite an expert on money market values and procedures. The fact that interest rates were so high greatly assisted the Trust's need, at a time when borrowing would have been equally expensive.

By the summer of 1979 I had already been alerted to the alarming increase in the cost of labour and materials. Because of unprecedentedly high wages and prices, the provision made in the original contract to take care of escalation during 1979 and 1980 was overtaken well before the end of 1979. At their October meeting that year, members of the Executive Committee were informed by their professional agents that owing to the very considerable increase in inflation, particularly as affecting labour and materials, since the building contract was signed, the anticipated total cost on completion could be £1,730,000, some £100,000 more than when the original calculations were made. The Trustees felt, however, that, in spite of the additional cost, the general standard of the public part of the building should not be lowered, but that modest savings should be made where possible.

This forecast emphasized the urgency of proceeding with the appeal. A brochure detailing and illustrating the project and inviting contributions towards the cost was produced and used from January 1980. Once again I assumed the role of a fund raiser, and each week I set myself the task of writing or making personal approaches to potential donors. The response was slow but encouraging, and by the end of 1980 the total amount raised stood at approximately £25,000. The Nuffield Foundation had again supported the appeal, with a contribution of £1,000; the Cadbury Charitable Trusts had given donations amounting to £5,000, and the Executors of C.A. Rookes £2,500.

But as the building proceeded, costs continued to rise. The Trustees were well served by their professional agents, who monitored the financial aspect of the operation very carefully as it proceeded. By May 1980, due to the level of inflation which could not have been foreseen, the Trustees were informed that the estimated total cost would be £1,185,000. Six months later, on 17 September 1980, I found myself having to inform the Executive Committee that, due to the continuing increase in inflation and the need to provide a few additional items not covered by the contract, the total estimated cost was likely to be £2,000,000, instead of £1,185,000 as previously reported to the Trustees. This unwelcome news was softened by the visible evidence of a fine, new building nearing completion, but it only emphasized the need to pursue the appeal. In reporting the situation to the full governing body at the Half Annual Meeting held the following month, the Chairman again asked for the advice and help of Trustees in making further approaches for possible donations. I am afraid that only a few suggestions were forthcoming, and the burden of furthering the appeal fell again on the Director.

My efforts during 1981 were reasonably successful but, except in a few instances, the amounts given were smaller than was needed to reach the target. A number of the firms with which the Trust had done business over the years responded favourably, as in the case of the publishing firm of Jarrold of

Norwich, which gave a covenanted donation amounting to £6,370 over seven years. The Pilgrim Trust gave £2,500, but my greatest success was with the Wolfson Foundation, which agreed to meet the cost of the lecture room (subsequently called the Wolfson Hall) and its furnishings, amounting to £37,500. My previous experience with the Nuffield Foundation proved extremely useful to me in preparing the submission which led to this welcome decision but, as was invariably the case with fund raising, it was my personal interview with the man at the top, namely the Director of the Foundation, which, I am confident, produced the desired result.

My speciality at that time was to offer what I called gift opportunities: in other words, I encouraged individuals and firms to support the appeal by linking their donations with identifiable parts of the building or items of furnishing which could be labelled with their names. Sir Jack Lyons, a Life Trustee and patron of the arts, who with Lord Harewood had sponsored the 1964 Shakespeare Exhibition, gave £10,000 for a seminar room to be named after him. The Directors of the Coventry Evening Telegraph, with which Lord Iliffe, another Life Trustee, was associated, bore the cost of the publications counter and back fittings in the Visitors' Centre at £5,000, while the C.A. Rookes Trust paid a similar amount for the bar. The Executors of C.A. Rookes also met the cost of providing the fountain, just alongside the path outside the exit from the Visitors' Centre. The Bird family of Stratford gave £3,000 for the ceramic mural of 'Shakespeare's Stratford'. The Friends of Shakespeare's Birthplace paid for the oak screen in the Visitors' Centre to accomodate the display of the collection of bronze Shakespeare medallions donated by Paul Vincze. There were other smaller items, such as a clock, presented by the Shakespeare Club of Stratford-upon-Avon.

As a result of these efforts, the cash flow was maintained and, when the Trustees met at their Half Annual Meeting on 31 October 1981, the Chairman was able to report that the final accounts, which had been agreed, showed that the total cost of the extension project just came within the estimated two million pounds. He was particularly pleased to announce that at no time had it proved necessary to borrow money by reason of this major commitment, and that, although the appeal had not received quite the level of support originally hoped, the Director had succeeded in attracting donations and sponsored contributions amounting to some £130,000. The appeal was closed at the end of 1981.

The Official Opening of the Shakespeare Centre Extension

The Trustees did not find it difficult to decide on arrangements for the official opening of the Shakespeare Centre extension. In June 1974 they had been looking forward to a visit of the Duke and Duchess of Kent, to mark the tenth anniversary of the opening of the Shakespeare Centre. All necessary preparations had been made to receive the royal visitors on Wednesday, 12 June, but a bereavement in the royal family two days before the visit led to its cancellation. An invitation to perform the opening ceremony of the new building was accordingly sent to Her Royal Highness The Duchess of Kent, which she graciously accepted.

Thursday, 25 June 1981, was the date of this important occasion. By that time the Visitors' Centre and the new route of approach to Shakespeare's Birthplace through the garden were already working satisfactorily, while the assembly suite had been 'run in', as it were, by being used for several functions.

Upon arrival at the entrance to the garden of Shakespeare's Birthplace, Her Royal Highness was received by the Chairman of the Shakespeare Birthplace Trust, Mr Dennis Flower, who at that time was also the High Sheriff of Warwickshire. It was a fine, warm morning and Henley Street was lined with interested onlookers, anxious to catch a glimpse of this highly respected member of the royal family. The Duchess looked particularly attractive in a navy blue dress with matching coat, relieved by a white bow, and with a close-fitting hat. Inside the garden Mr Flower presented the Deputy Chairman of the Shakespeare Birthplace Trust (Mr Peter Boddington) and Mrs Boddington, Lady Flower, myself as Director, the Chairman of the Stratford-on-Avon District Council (Councillor Mrs P. Bidwell) and Mr F. Bidwell, and Councillor P.W. Wheeler, representing the Stratford-upon-Avon Town Council, and Mrs Wheeler. Members of the Birthplace Trust's staff stood in a group a little distance away, both to observe the proceedings and to add a further welcome to the Duchess. In company with the Chairman and myself, she passed through the garden, pausing to admire the flowers and to hear briefly about its special associations, and entered Shakespeare's Birthplace through the door at the rear. It then fell to me, as Director, to act as her escort and guide as she made an inspection of the various rooms of the house.

This was her first visit, and she clearly appreciated the opportunity to view the Birthplace away from the gaze of the media and the public. As invariably happened on these occasions, the time allowed in the schedule for this part of the programme was all too short; but I found the Duchess completely relaxed, friendly and most interested in everything I was able to show her. Meanwhile the Stratford-upon-Avon Youth Wind Band, positioned by the mulberry tree in the garden near the Shakespeare Centre, provided music to entertain the crowd waiting in the street.

Her Royal Highness then left the Birthplace by the front door to the cheering welcome of the crowd gathered on the pavement opposite. She walked along Henley Street, past the foundation stone laid by Her Royal Highness Princess Alexandra on 28 June 1962. At the main entrance to the Shakespeare Centre her attention was called to the marble panel recording its official opening in 1964, and she then proceeded up the steps, admiring John Hutton's engraved panels of Shakespeare characters as she entered the building. Inside, Mr Flower presented the Trust's architect, Mr Laurence Williams, who had designed the Centre and its extension, and Mrs Williams, together with the Local Trustees and their ladies: Dr Gareth and Mrs Lloyd Evans, Mr and Mrs T.E. Lowth, Mrs Trevor Matthews, and Mr and Mrs N.S. Pratt.

By this time the Chairman and I had had considerable experience of handling distinguished personages and, within the short time allowed, Her Royal

HRH The Duchess of Kent leaving Shakespeare's Birthplace

HRH The Duchess of Kent performs the opening ceremony

Highness was given a comprehensive introduction to the original Centre and its function. In the reading room a selection of rare books, theatrical material and manuscripts from the Centre's collections were laid out for her inspection, and she chatted freely to members of staff who were introduced. In the basement strong room she examined some of the Trust's rarest items: Richard Quyney's letter to Shakespeare, the First Folio of Shakespeare's plays and the Stratford Parish Register recording Shakespeare's baptism and burial.

After signing the distinguished visitors' book in the entrance hall of the Shakespeare Centre, the Duchess then left by the main entrance and proceeded along the street with the Chairman to the front of the new extension building.

A covered stand erected on the opposite side of Henley Street provided a comfortable viewing position for representative guests, invited by the Trustees. In his address welcoming Her Royal Highness, Mr Flower referred to the feeling of achievement on the part of the Trustees in bringing to completion a project first conceived in the late 1950s. The original Shakespeare Centre, he said, had proved so successful in use, in making possible the development of the Trust's educational and academic work, that the need for the extension building to complete the original project had come much sooner than was originally contemplated. He was confident, he added, that the additional accommodation and facilities now provided would make possible the further development of the Trust's activities and provide for its needs in the next few decades. In particular, he said that the new reception facilities provided by the Visitors' Centre would add greatly to the convenience and pleasure of those coming to Shakespeare's Birthplace. He congratulated the Director, the architect, and all who had contributed, to the creation of what he described as 'a superb building'.

Her Royal Highness was then invited to perform the opening ceremony of the Centre extension. She expressed her pleasure at being associated with such a special occasion and complimented the Trustees on their achievement. She then declared the building open and pulled a cord releasing the Shakespeare flag which covered the inscription, carved on a panel of black marble fixed on the wall under the entrance portico.

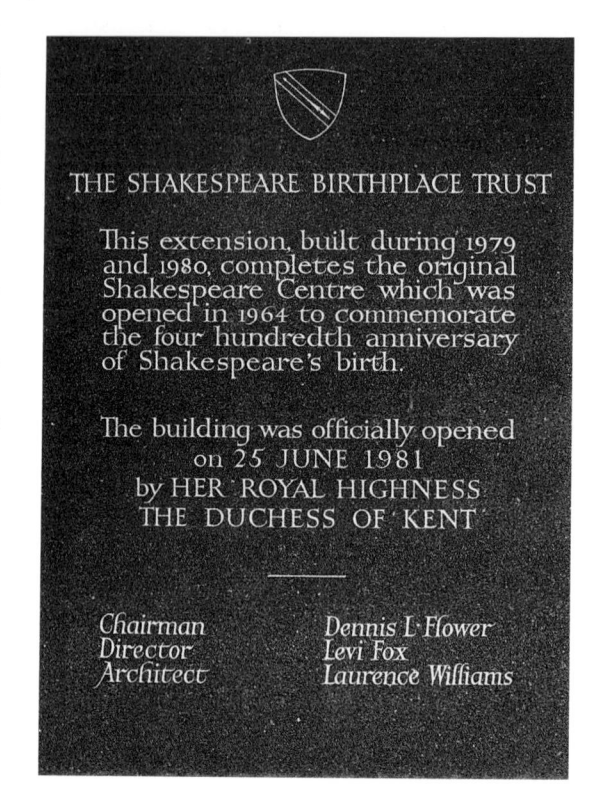

> THE SHAKESPEARE BIRTHPLACE TRUST
>
> This extension, built during 1979 and 1980, completes the original Shakespeare Centre which was opened in 1964 to commemorate the four hundredth anniversary of Shakespeare's birth.
>
> The building was officially opened on 25 JUNE 1981 by HER ROYAL HIGHNESS THE DUCHESS OF KENT
>
> Chairman   Dennis L·Flower
> Director   Levi Fox
> Architect   Laurence Williams

The guests watching the proceedings from the opposite side of the street warmly applauded at this point, and remained in their seats while Her Royal Highness inspected the building, under the guidance of the architect and myself. I had arranged for senior members of staff, as well as the artists and craftsmen who had made contributions to the building, to be stationed at appropriate positions, so that the royal visitor might meet them as she inspected the various rooms. This arrangement worked admirably, the only problem being that the time allowed in the programme proved too short. The Duchess talked in a most friendly, informal manner to everyone who was introduced; and her reaction to the design, furnishings and special features of the building was warmly appreciative.

Leaving from the front entrance of the Visitors' Centre, Her Royal Highness walked across the street to the waiting crowd, the mini 'walk-about' that followed giving great pleasure to the spectators, and especially to the children, to many of whom she spoke and from whom she received posies of flowers. After her departure the invited guests then had an opportunity to view the new building, before returning to the original Shakespeare Centre for a buffet luncheon.

Thus was satisfactorily concluded what the Chairman subsequently described to the Trustees as 'one of the most important dates in the history of the Trust'.

Following the official opening, the Centre's new accommodation and facilities were quickly put to excellent use. The Visitors' Centre, which had already been tried out before the beginning of the season, proved outstandingly successful in providing first class reception facilities for those coming to the Birthplace; the annual Summer School of the Extramural Department of Birmingham University came into residence for six weeks; and during the week of the International Shakespeare Association's Congress in August the Centre served as one of the regular venues for lectures, workshops and seminars. On several occasions the Trust was also able to co-operate with local hotels in offering special arrangements for business conference groups; and a number of local societies began to hold their meetings at the Centre. In other words, the Trust found itself being able to contribute something to the town as well as providing for its own activities.

Years of Fulfilment

The years which remained before my retirement in 1989 could be likened to harvest time, when seeds sown in earlier days came to fruition. The practical and psychological effect of having completed and paid for the Shakespeare Centre extension, and seeing it work so satisfactorily, gave a feeling of confidence and pride of achievement and pointed the way to further developments. In particular, the academic and educational role of the Birthplace Trust, as evidenced by a number of new activities undertaken, became increasingly recognized, and before I retired arrangements for a closer working partnership with the University of Birmingham had been agreed. The short courses for students and graduates, formerly held at Mason Croft, were transferred to the Shakespeare Centre and Dr Robert Smallwood, who had been involved in the running of them as a member of the University's staff, joined the Trust on 1 January 1990 as Deputy Director, with the responsibility of organizing and developing the Trust's educational work. Apart from meeting the Trust's own accommodation needs, the assembly suite came to be used for a variety of activities. The new Records Office proved especially successful and the resources of the library were progressively increased and used for study and research.

The organization continued to grow as the Trust's activities expanded, but it still retained its individual, personal character. Many of the staff had long service records and they worked together happily as a dedicated team. As Director I still concerned myself with, and made decisions about, every aspect of the Trust's work, maintaining a close contact with the heads of the various departments and the staff generally. It was not until 1985, when the Trustees decided to create a new post of administrator, to ease the heavy burden of responsibility I carried, that changes in management arrangements began to occur. Brigadier David Atkinson, who was appointed to fill this position, had spent his life as a professional soldier, latterly working in the Ministry of Defence. Whilst it was recognized that the time had come for me, as Director, to delegate some of my work load, the administrative machinery and procedures evolved over the years were still in excellent working order, and my traditional, personal management role, possibly considered rather paternal by some, remained unchanged. It was only after my successor took over that a new management structure was gradually introduced, involving changes which were not welcomed by a number of the long-serving members of staff.

Meanwhile, the affairs of the Trust continued to be managed according to the established pattern of earlier years. The Executive Committee met at monthly intervals or held special meetings, or made inspections, as necessary. They regularly received the Director's report and financial statement, making decisions on matters arising from them. At the beginning of each year they approved a budget which I prepared, and within its limits I had complete authority to organize the Trust's expenditure. In a similar manner, each autumn the Committee conducted a review of the establishment, dealing in detail with matters affecting staff, remuneration, working conditions and general policy considerations. The Committee's minutes were regularly circulated to all the Trustees, whose formal confirmation was sought at their Annual and Half Annual Meetings.

The Trustees

There were a number of changes in the category of Life Trustees during these years.

Professor Nevill Coghill, who had represented the University of Oxford from 1952 until he was appointed a Life Trustee in 1967, died in 1980. He had been a staunch supporter of the original Shakespeare Centre project and had given valuable advice about its design. The following year saw the death of Mrs T.N. Waldron, a well known public figure and keen Shakespearian, who had been Mayor of Stratford-upon-Avon and a Life Trustee since 1975. Mr Laurence Williams, who had been appointed a Life Trustee in 1981 in recognition of his outstanding service as the Trust's architect for nearly twenty-five years, died in 1985. A memorial plaque, carved by Richard Kindersley, was subsequently installed in the entrance hall of the Shakespeare Centre, to commemorate his work.

My old friend, the American scholar Dr Louis B. Wright, who had taken such an active interest in the affairs of the Trust since he was appointed a Life Trustee in 1964, died in 1984. Dr Wright was immensely proud of his association with Shakespeare's Birthplace and will be remembered for his lively, genial personality. Mr J.B. Priestley, the distinguished novelist and playwright, who lived in retirement at Alveston, also died in 1984, after being a Life Trustee since 1969; his widow, the well known archaeologist, Jacquetta Hawkes, was subsequently appointed a Life Trustee to fill the vacancy caused by the death of her husband. Dame Peggy Ashcroft, the highly acclaimed actress, and Professor Wolfgang Clemen, the eminent German Shakespeare scholar, had been appointed Life Trustees in 1977. They were joined in 1981 by Mr T.E. Lowth, the Stratford solicitor who had been a member of the Executive Committee over a long period of years, and in 1984 by Professor Muriel C. Bradbrook, who had already served as the University of Cambridge's Representative Trustee, and by Professor S. Schoenbaum of the United States.

Sir Frank Francis, a Life Trustee since 1969, died in 1988; his association with the Trust went back to 1961 when he was appointed to represent the British Museum, of which he was the Director. Sir Frank, a man of great experience and wisdom, took a very active interest in the Trust and was always willing to give an informed opinion on any matter, when I consulted him from time to time. Mr Lowth died in 1989, as also Professor Philip Brockbank, who, after serving as the Representative Trustee of the University of Birmingham, had been appointed a Life Trustee the previous year. Mr Peter Boddington, who had been elected a Local Trustee in 1961 and served on the Executive Committee for many years as Deputy Chairman, was appointed a Life Trustee in 1988. He had a great affection for the Trust and was well known to the staff of the properties, which he frequently visited. Incidentally, in 1977 Mr Boddington presented to the Trust its first livestock accession, namely two donkeys, Blossom and Bluebell, for Mary Arden's House. He and Mrs Boddington also gave to the Trust a small plot of spinney adjacent to their home, Timbers, at Welcombe.

The names of these Life Trustees are mentioned to illustrate the good fortune of the Executive Committee and its Director in having people of such eminence associated with the Trust. Similarly, the academic Trustees appointed as representatives by the universities and other institutions, like the British Library and the National Trust, added further prestige and expertise to the governing body. We always looked forward to their attendance at the

Arrival of the donkeys at Mary Arden's house

Trustees' Annual and Half Annual Meetings, and the value of their experience and advice concerning matters of policy and conservation was frequently demonstrated.

In practice, it was the Local Trustees who served on the Executive Committee who managed the detailed affairs of the Trust, and during these years the Trust was fortunate in having local Trustees possessing a wide range of experience and dedicated commitment to the Trust's objects. They included Mr T.E. Lowth, already mentioned; Mrs Trevor Matthews, who had been appointed a Local Trustee in 1966 following the death of her husband and continued until her death in 1983; Dr Gareth Lloyd Evans, Shakespeare author, critic and scholar, who served from 1977 until his death in 1984; Mr N.S. Pratt, the retired Headmaster of King Edward VI School; Miss Myra Tudor, the former Headmistress of the Stratford-upon-Avon Grammar School for Girls, from 1983; Mr A.N. Tarratt, a retired bank manager, from 1982; and from 1985 Mr T.W. Ferrers-Walker, descendant of the old Warwickshire family of Ferrers of Baddesley Clinton, whose knowledge of historic buildings and sense of heritage, together with his experience of business, proved invaluable to the Committee.

Conservation Policy

Quite apart from the detailed attention they gave to the Trust's business, the members of the Executive Committee kept a watchful eye on development proposals in and around Stratford-upon-Avon which they felt might possibly be detrimental to the character of Shakespeare's town and countryside. In 1981, for instance, they objected to a proposed scheme for the construction of a marina, hotel, holiday chalets and leisure centre on a site at Cross o' th' Hill, an attractive rural area just south-west of Stratford. Their concern about the direction of a northern by-pass to relieve traffic conjestion in the town has already been mentioned, and in 1982, at a Public Inquiry, they supported a route skirting Snitterfield which left unspoiled the Welcombe hills, as a safeguard against development. This route was ultimately approved in 1984 and the by-pass subsequently constructed. In the meantime, the Trustees objected at a Public Inquiry against the proposal of the British Broadcasting Corporation to erect a tall and powerful transmitter on high ground at Bearley, which would have been visible from Wilmcote and a considerable distance around, apart from causing serious electrical interference in the area. The proposal was turned down by the Secretary of State for the Environment early in 1985.

It was at this time that members of the Executive Committee were concerned about a number of other development proposals affecting the town, and they spent some time considering and commenting on the Stratford-upon-Avon Local Plan and the County Council's development plan scheme for Warwickshire. They felt it their duty to make known to the Stratford-on-Avon District Council their opposition to proposals for developing the riverside meadows along the Warwick road approach to the town, and informed the Secretary of State for the Environment about their concern for the future preservation of this area. They confirmed their support for the protection of the riverside meadows as open space in 1988, and associated themselves with the 'Shakespeare Heartland' countryside project, whose conservational and educational aims had much in common with those of the Trust.

In 1987 the Trustees supported the planning authority in its refusal to allow residential development on land to the rear of Aston Cantlow Road, Wilmcote. In the same year they made representations concerning the proposal to close Sanctus Road and to remove the bridge. They felt that if this happened the problem of traffic congestion in Old Town would be increased, and inconvenience caused to tour operators and other visitors who used Sanctus Road as their route between Holy Trinity Church and Anne Hathaway's Cottage. The bridge in fact was rebuilt and the road retained.

Perhaps more important was the Trustees' approval of a scheme to render the portion of Henley Street in which the Trust's properties are

The Birthplace, following pedestrianisation, in 1988

situated an area free of traffic. As far back as 1980 they had advocated a pedestrianization scheme of this kind. The police and the Warwickshire County Council were in favour but, because of the opposition of certain shopkeepers in the street, the proposal was deferred. In 1984 the Trustees supported a scheme, which was subsequently implemented, for providing a pedestrian access between Henley Street and the newly constructed shopping precinct called the Minories, off Meer Street. It was not until 1987, however, that a detailed pedestrianization scheme for the section of Henley Street between Meer Street and Windsor Street was prepared by the local authority and submitted for the consideration of the Birthplace Trustees and other interested parties. The Trustees gave their full support, and in the following year the re-paving of the whole area and the necessary traffic re-arrangements were completed. In the opinion of the Trustees, the removal of motor traffic with petrol and diesel fumes from this part of Henley Street represented a considerable improvement to the environment, in addition to conferring safety and convenience on the very large numbers of people coming from all over the world to visit Shakespeare's Birthplace.

Visitor Patronage

For an organization which relied for most of its income on visitor patronage, the 1980s were not an easy period from a business point of view. Following the Silver Jubilee celebrations in 1977, the numbers of visitors to the Shakespearian properties decreased each year, the total number in 1980 being 1,120,545, as compared with 1,486,210 in 1977. The chief reasons for this were the general economic recession and the unfavourable international exchange rate, particularly as affecting the United States. The downward trend continued for the next two years. An improvement in the economic situation and a more favourable exchange rate resulted in a slight increase in 1983, largely due to more Americans and others coming from overseas. The upward trend was continued during 1984 and 1985; it reflected the general improvement in tourist patronage in Britain as a whole and was due almost entirely to the numbers of visitors from overseas, particularly from the United States, a high proportion of whom came to Stratford-upon-Avon by package tour. Visitor statistics for 1985 were as follows:

Shakespeare's Birthplace	606,624
Anne Hathaway's Cottage	449,141
New Place	87,690
Mary Arden's House	115,618
Hall's Croft	79,107
Total	1,338,180

Arrangements for handling the visitors worked smoothly. The new Birthplace coach terminal in Windsor Street and the coach and car parks at Anne Hathaway's Cottage proved especially useful. During 1982 a total of 5,712 coaches used the Birthplace terminal, as compared with 5,531 the previous year. At Shottery the refreshment facilities provided by the recently opened Cottage Tea Garden were much appreciated, and the growing popularity of Mary Arden's House was evidenced by the considerable increase in admissions to that property.

Attendances at the Shakespearian properties during 1986 were disappointing, the total number of visitors, 1,065,953, being the lowest since 1982. This decline was attributable to the fear of further terrorist activity following the Lockerbie air disaster, which resulted in the wholesale cancellation of many of the American package tours brought by agents to the properties. This reluctance to travel on the part of many Americans continued to affect the level of Stratford's tourist patronage during the remainder of my term of office as Director, but there was a welcome increase in the numbers of visitors from Japan and the European countries. In 1987 a total of 7,118 coaches used the Birthplace coach terminal, as compared with 6,062 in 1986. Attendances during 1989 were as follows:

Shakespeare's Birthplace	571,262
Anne Hathaway's Cottage	332,014
New Place	79,017
Mary Arden's House	107,453
Hall's Croft	76,421
Total	1,166,167

The recession in tourist patronage had a direct bearing on the Trust's income from admission fees and sales. Month by month the Executive Committee monitored the situation as I produced the figures, and related these to the budget which had been set for the year. Modest increases in admission charges had to be imposed every year. In 1980 it cost 70p for an adult to visit Shakespeare's Birthplace and 30p for a child; by 1985 the charges had risen to £1.25 for an adult and 40p for a child, with appropriate increases for inclusive tickets and student and school party rates. The upward trend continued, the charge for an admission to Shakespeare's Birthplace in 1989 being £1.80 for an adult and 70p for a child, including the BBC Television Shakespeare Costume Exhibition.

The increased income thus generated offset the decrease in the number of visitors. At the same time, the range of publications and gift items offered for sale was enlarged, with a resultant greater return from this source. By 1988 the surplus earned on sales accounted for £275,098, representing a significant item in the annual budget. Even more important, as enabling a reserve of cash to be built up year by year, was the high rate of interest earned on money not immediately required. With the authority of the Executive Committee, I took advantage of the money market service of the Midland Bank to achieve the highest possible return for fixed, short-term investments. The results were surprisingly good: for example, in 1986 interest earned amounted to £172,726, and in 1988 £165,668. By the end of 1988 the Trust's total cash in hand had grown to £2,215,267. These statistics are given to place on record that, within a decade of building and paying for the Shakespeare Centre extension, the Trust had built up a substantial reserve, sufficient to provide an insurance against recession and at the same time a foundation for the developments in the 1990s which followed my retirement.

International Attraction

The fluctuating level of visitor patronage during these years emphasized the importance of the overseas element, which by this time had come to account for at least two-thirds of the total number of visitors to Shakespeare's Birthplace and the other Shakespearian properties. I often found myself explaining that attendances at the Birthplace were comparable to a barometer which measured the condition of the world's monetary and political circumstances. The Falklands conflict in 1982, for instance, resulted in the immediate loss of the South American ingredient of tourist business, and in 1991 the Gulf War adversely affected visitors from the United States. Yet at all times the Birthplace attracted international attention. Each year an analysis of the addresses of those who came and signed the visitors' book provided evidence that over a hundred nationalities were represented.

The steady stream of distinguished personalities who came similarly emphasized the universal appeal of Shakespeare and a recognition of Stratford-upon-Avon as his birthplace. Every year I welcomed and received on behalf of the Trustees guests of Her Majesty's Government, eminent scholars, actors, public figures and representatives of institutions abroad. In 1980 these included a leading Japanese actor, the Bishop of Dresden and his wife, a group of

Chinese delegates associated with the Peking People's Art Theatre, as well as the members of the Shakespeare Institute's biennial International Shakespeare Conference, for whom the traditional garden party was given at Hall's Croft. The following year visitors from abroad ranged from the Prime Minister of Papua New Guinea to a group of 1981 'Miss Europe' contestants, and also included delegates to the International Shakespeare Association Congress held in Stratford-upon-Avon.

Among those to whom a special welcome was offered during 1984 were the Prime Minister of Mauritius, a party of wives of vice-chancellors of overseas universities, the Nobel Prize winner for literature, Mr Isaac Bashevis Singer, members of the International Shakespeare Conference and Mrs Raisa Gorbacheva, wife of Mikhail Gorbachev, head of the Soviet Union Politburo. I have a particular recollection of this lady's visit, because she was so different from the many Russians I had received in earlier years. She had apparently expressed a wish to visit Shakespeare's Birthplace whilst her husband was engaged in official discussions with the Prime Minister in London. Smartly dressed, she moved with confidence and ease, showing obvious interest in every item she saw, as I escorted her through the Visitors' Centre on the way to the Birthplace. Though having to rely on an interpreter, she was clearly trying very hard to master the use of English. She admired the costumed figures of Shakespeare characters used in the BBC's series of Shakespeare films, which were on display in the reception area; and, whilst trying to read the descriptive captions, she occasionally picked out individual words which she understood and spoke them in English. In the Birthplace itself she appeared to be fascinated by the structure of the building and pointed to one of the solid beams and pronounced it to be 'oak'. I formed the impression that she had a good background knowledge of drama and literature, and her open, friendly manner in asking questions and making comment struck me as typifying the more liberal outlook and policy of her husband. Her enjoyment at coming to Stratford-upon-Avon and Shakespeare's

Traditional garden party given for the International Shakespeare Conference at Hall's Croft

Birthplace was expressed on her face as she stopped to speak to members of staff at various points during her visit. She was without doubt an excellent ambassador for promoting friendship and goodwill.

Mr Richard Luce, Minister for the Arts, visited the Shakespeare Centre in 1986 and was much impressed by the variety and scope of the Trust's library and archive resources for study and research and by the educational and academic activities undertaken by the Trust. This year also brought visits of a number of distinguished guests of Her Majesty's Government from Germany, the Soviet Union and China. Special arrangements were made for the visit of His Excellency Mr V.S. Murakhovsky, the First Deputy Chairman of the Council of Ministers of the Union of Soviet Socialist Republics.

The one I remember very vividly was the visit of Mr Hu Yaobang, General Secretary of the Central

Committee of the Communist Party of China. Advance preparations for his coming were almost as elaborate as those for a royal visit, and when he arrived his accompanying entourage and press almost filled the place. He first made a brief inspection of the Shakespeare Centre, where I had arranged for him to see a selection of Chinese translations of Shakespeare's plays and photographs of Chinese actors and Shakespeare productions, which he instantly recognized. His lively personality became apparent as we chatted, with the help of his interpreter, as we walked through the garden to the Birthplace. There, followed closely by his escorting security and press men, we went through the house room by room. Experience had taught me how to handle the situation: to call attention briefly to particular features of the building and items on exhibition, rather than to attempt a detailed guide commentary. Our distinguished visitor was clearly interested and impressed, and anxious to show his appreciation.

The programme agreed in advance planned that, on leaving Shakespeare's Birthplace, Mr Yaobang was to walk along Henley Street and High Street to the Town Hall, where the Mayor of Stratford-upon-Avon would receive and entertain him to lunch. As he was about to leave the Birthplace, I was invited to act as his escort and guide. Together, side by side and with his escorting staff accompanying, we walked up the middle of Henley Street, and I pointed to various shops as we went. When we got to the top of the street, instead of turning into High Street as arranged, he expressed a wish to continue down Bridge Street, much to the obvious concern of his security staff. However, down the middle of Bridge Street we went, trailed by the press, to the surprise of motorists who were stopped and shoppers on the pavement. He kept up a continuous questioning as we went and was obviously enjoying the experience. The weather was fine and warm. On reaching Waterside he made a beeline for the canal basin, thinking it was the river, and on our way we encountered some young people sitting on the grass having a picnic. Whereupon, to everybody's surprise and without warning, Mr Yaobang sat down in the middle of the group of young ladies, who were naturally bewildered as to what was happening, especially with cameramen taking pictures at the time. However, as Mr Yaobang started to speak and to ask them questions, they realized he must be a special person. At this point his aide, standing nearby, produced some small packages wrapped in colourful paper. He handed one of them to Mr Yaobang, who presented it to one of the girls; he made a similar presentation to a second member of the group and yet again a third time to another girl. The remaining members of the party looked on with expectation, but by this time the supply of gift items had run out. Meanwhile the accompanying photographers recorded this unexpected incident with enthusiasm.

By now the programme was running late and, as soon as Mr Yaobang was on his feet, our objective was to get him to the Town Hall as quickly as possible. I accordingly steered him along the Bancroft, away from the river and past the Theatre, which he asked to see. We then marched up the middle of Sheep Street, with spectators looking on, to the Town Hall, where the Mayor was waiting to receive Mr Yaobang and his party. All was now well and, in the relaxed atmosphere of the ballroom on the first floor, the assembled company enjoyed a pleasant lunch. The Mayor made a speech of welcome to the

Visit of Mr Yaobang

distinguished guest, who concluded his felicitous response by presenting to the Mayor a large ceramic vase of very beautiful pattern and colour. Mr Yaobang then accepted a framed painting of the Stratford Town Hall and, after a round of handshaking, left with his party to keep an appointment in Oxford at the end of the afternoon.

It was with surprise and with a feeling of sadness that, several weeks after his visit, we read reports that Mr Yaobang had been removed from his high office of General Secretary of the Communist Party, presumably because his liberal outlook and policy did not meet with the approval of China's ruling party. The invitation he had promised to send to me to visit China did not materialize.

The International Shakespeare Association

Even more illustrative of the world-wide interest in Shakespeare were the two Congresses of the International Shakespeare Association, held in 1981 and 1986, both of which were organized from the Shakespeare Centre, as the headquarters of the Association, of which I continued to be the Secretary and Deputy Chairman.

Following the success of the first Congress, held in Washington, DC, in 1976, as already described, there was a unanimous wish that the next Congress should take place in Shakespeare's own town, and that the theme should be 'Shakespeare Man of the Theatre'. The second International Shakespeare Congress was accordingly held in Stratford-upon-Avon in the first week of August 1981, under the auspices of the International Shakespeare Association, with assistance from the Shakespeare Association of America, the Shakespeare Birthplace Trust, the Shakespeare Institute of the University of Birmingham and the Royal Shakespeare Theatre.

The planning and preparations for the Congress, involving close liaison with the officers of the Shakespeare Association of America, had taken more than two years. The Congress was attended by some 650 scholars from all over the world and included representatives from countries controlled by the Soviet Union. I recall how difficult it was to get permission for two scholars from East Germany to travel in order to take part in the programme, and how embarrassed they were when they arrived late at the Congress and penniless. They had not been allowed to leave on time as planned, or to bring any currency with them; they accordingly had to rely on the hospitality of the Association. Over the years I encountered several similar situations and I came to realize under what extraordinary restrictions scholars, who were not in the least interested in politics, had to accept as the practical implication of living under communist rule. One of the leading scholars from East Germany, with whom I had a friendly association, once confided to me that the only thing he ever did wrong was to be born 'on the wrong side of the line', namely behind the notorious wall that separated East from West Berlin.

The Congress was based on the Hilton Hotel at Bridgefoot, with the new assembly suite of the Shakespeare Centre providing accommodation and facilities for many of the sessions, together with the Shakespeare Institute at Mason Croft. The programme began with an open-air reception at the Hilton Hotel on Saturday, 1 August. On Sunday there was a special service of Morning Prayer in Holy Trinity Church, based on the Elizabethan Prayer Book of 1559, with an eloquent sermon preached by the Reverend Professor W. Moelwyn Merchant.

The first plenary session, in the afternoon, consisted of a lecture in the Royal Shakespeare Theatre by the playwright and author, John Mortimer, on 'Shakespeare and a Playwright of Today', and this was followed by garden parties at Hall's Croft and the Shakespeare Institute. In the evening a Shakespearian recital, 'William: the Conqueror', devised by Roger Pringle, took place in the Theatre and was presented by John Gielgud, the Association's President, with Barbara Leigh-Hunt, Richard Pasco, and Robert Spencer on the lute. It was a unique experience, hearing Sir John in some of his famous roles, including Richard II, Hamlet, King Lear and Prospero.

For the rest of the week there was a full programme of lectures, papers, and seminars each day, linked with the following themes: Shakespeare and the theatre of his time; Shakespeare and his fellow professionals in the theatre; Shakespeare and the theatre; critical approaches; Shakespeare and the living theatre. Two sessions consisted of forums with theatre directors, and members of the Royal Shakespeare Company conducted workshop sessions. In the evenings, delegates attended performances of *The Winter's Tale* and *A Midsummer Night's Dream* in the main Theatre, and *A Doll's House*, by Henrik Ibsen, at The Other Place. There were also opportunities to see the Coventry Mystery Plays, televised versions of *Macbeth* and *Antony and Cleopatra*, as well as scenes from a film of *Richard III*, made by the Rustaveli Company of Georgia, in the Soviet Union.

A variety of fringe attractions included an exhibition at the Shakespeare Centre, 'All the World's a Stage', comprising books from the collections of the Shakespeare Birthplace Trust relating to Shakespeare and the theatre of his time, and an exhibition on 'The History of Stratford's Grammar School' in the medieval schoolroom of King Edward VI School, in which it is believed Shakespeare received his education.

Back-stage inspections of the Royal Shakespeare Theatre, visits to the Shakespearian properties, tours of Stratford and the Shakespeare countryside, together with receptions and other allied activities, completed the programme; but the most valuable occasions were the informal discussions with colleagues from overseas, hearing about their particular studies and writing projects, and giving them information on what the library collections of the Shakespeare Centre could offer them. By common consent, the Congress was highly successful; it called attention in an unprecedented manner to the role of the Shakespeare Birthplace Trust as the guardian of the Shakespeare heritage and to the Shakespeare Centre as the focal centre of international scholarship. A volume recording the principal papers given at the Congress, entitled *Shakespeare, Man of the Theater*, was published by the University of Delaware Press, in 1983.

The third Congress of the International Shakespeare Association took place five years later, in April 1986 in Berlin, by invitation of the Deutsche Shakespeare-Gesellschaft West. Again, detailed planning and preparations devolved on my assistant, Roger Pringle, but our German hosts, and particularly Professor Werner Habicht and his colleagues, undertook responsibility for the practical arrangements and the city authority of Berlin proved generous in its hospitality. The Congress again attracted some 650 delegates, from 27 countries, including well known scholars, critics and theatre directors.

The overall theme of the Congress, 'Images of Shakespeare', was approached from a multiplicity of perspectives during the main sessions, and in fifteen seminars which had been arranged and assimilated into the Congress proceedings by the Shakespeare Association of America. In spite of the delicacy and practical difficulty of the political situation, there was ready co-operation by the Deutsche Shakespeare-Gesellschaft which ensured the fullest possible movement of playgoers and scholars between East and West Berlin. Altogether, the Congress was extremely successful both as a festive as well as an academic occasion, and there was due recognition of the role played by the Shakespeare Birthplace Trust in organizing this unique international gathering on behalf of the International Shakespeare Association. The proceedings of the Congress were recorded in a volume, *Images of Shakespeare*, published by the University of Delaware Press in 1988.

Maintenance and Improvement of Properties

Special attention was always given to the Shakespearian properties. In 1983 Anne Hathaway's Cottage was rethatched with Warwickshire wheat straw by Mr D.J. Rimell of Alcester, who had dealt with the Trust's thatching requirements for many years. This was quite a major operation involving careful planning, since most of the work had to be done out of season but whilst the property was open to visitors. Finding suitable material for thatching was also quite a problem, since the majority of crops were by now harvested by the combine harvester, which cut the straw into short lengths as part of the reaping process. Wheat straw of sufficient length and quality for thatching had to be specially grown and harvested in the traditional manner, using an old-type reaping machine and setting up the sheaves of corn in stooks in the field to dry, prior to the removal of the corn by the old-fashioned, threshing process, leaving the full lengths of wheat straw to meet the thatcher's requirement. Fortunately Mr Rimell knew a farmer who was able and willing to harvest a field of wheat in this manner, thus being able to supply the straw needed for the roof of Anne Hathaway's Cottage. The thatching process proved to be an additional attraction for visitors, who were much fascinated to see an expert thatcher plying his traditional skills.

Similarly, it was the skill of the tilers that excited interest as they renewed the roof of Shakespeare's Birthplace in 1988. For a few years prior to this I had noticed the gradual deterioration of the handmade clay tiles on the roof – due to severe frost in the winter and excessive heat in the summer – and the need for frequent repairs suggested that the time had come for a complete re-tiling of the building. The work was entrusted to a small Stratford firm of building contractors, Sibbasbridge, Ltd, who had men experienced in tiling in their employment. The job was tackled a section of the roof at a time with necessary repairs to the rafters being undertaken, and completed in a most satisfactory manner. About three quarters of the original tiles were re-used, with the balance made up of suitable, matching second-hand tiles. Opportunity was also taken to re-point the chimney stacks and to repair the gutters; and shortly afterwards the lightning conductor was monitored and serviced by the specialist firm with which the Trust had a long-standing contract for this purpose.

In 1988 a problem affecting the structure of Hall's Croft was successfully resolved. It appeared that the vibration caused by the increased volume of heavy traffic passing the building had resulted in a slight movement of the timber framed front elevation, and steps needed to be taken to stabilize the structure.

Acting on the advice of the Trust's professional structural consultant, an intricate piece of engineering work was carried out to strengthen the front elevation of the house and so remedy the problem of structural weakness and further movement. An operation of this kind, involving the insertion of hidden tie rods, necessitated the lifting of floor boards and caused an element of general disruption. However, the task was successfully completed and the director of the contracting specialist firm that did the work, Anglo-Holt Construction, Ltd, very generously donated his own time and his company's overheads as their contribution to British heritage, charging only for materials and labour. These details are mentioned as evidence of the good relations which invariably existed between the Shakespeare

The White Cottage, Shottery

Brookside, Shottery

Birthplace Trustees and the various firms which supplied goods and services to the Trust over the years.

Each year brought a round of repair and improvement work at the Trust's other properties; much of this was undertaken by the members of the Trust's own maintenance staff, which by 1989 had increased to ten experienced men under the leadership of Leslie Page, who had succeeded Bert Elmore as head of maintenance in 1979. Both these men were experienced working supervisors, extremely versatile and capable of tackling any kind of building work or repairs with the help of their craftsmen team. The variety of tasks undertaken during the year 1982 may be taken as a typical example. The wooden 'tunnel' in the knott garden at New Place was renewed in oak with pegged joints, exactly as it was when originally constructed; the brickwork of this sunken garden was similarly repaired and most of the surrounding balustrade, with its supporting columns and turned finials, was renewed. At Mary Arden's House the open-fronted cowshed, with its uneven, picturesque, tiled roof, received a comprehensive overhaul. All the main timbers were sound, but hand-wrought rafters had to be replaced. Split oak laths were made by the carpenter to carry the old tiles, which had been carefully removed and were then put back and torched underneath to keep them in position. To have been able to complete a restoration project of this kind in traditional style gave a good deal of satisfaction to all involved.

A different kind of roofing operation was undertaken when the Trust's thatcher, Mr D.J. Rimell, completed the rethatching of the roof of the half-timbered, picturesque cottage known as Brookside, situated opposite to St. Andrew's Church in Church Lane, Shottery. This dwelling pre-dated Shakespeare's time, the central portion being a hall, open from floor to roof, with rooms at each end, as was commonly the arrangement in medieval times. The timber framing was treated and the whole structure carefully overhauled. Work on the drainage system at Anne Hathaway's Cottage was also completed in the same year, and improvements were carried out at the Gardener's Cottage at New Place and at 4 New Row, Cottage Lane, Shottery, thus completing the modernization of the row of eight terraced cottages adjacent to Anne Hathaway's Cottage.

From time to time special situations at the properties needed immediate attention. Damage to toilets, blocked drains or broken palings at Anne Hathaway's Cottage were recurring items, as were broken windows at Shakespeare's Birthplace and Hornby Cottage, which were within easy reach of vandals. The safety of John Hutton's engraved panels of Shakespeare characters at the entrance to the Shakespeare Centre was a constant source of concern to me; and, although consideration was given by the Executive Committee as to possible ways of protecting them, it was not until 1989 that a suitable solution was found, when polycarbonate sheets, which are virtually unnoticeable, were installed to give protection to eight of the more vulnerable panels. Notice boards and direction signs were sometimes stolen or vandalized, and intruders who climbed into the Great Garden of New Place during hours of darkness trampled on the flower beds and damaged the topiary hedges by attempting to walk on them. The sundial on the terrace of the Great Garden was vandalized on no fewer than three different occasions.

Burglary at Anne Hathaway's Cottage

More serious was the burglary which took place at Anne Hathaway's Cottage during the night of 4 March 1982. It was a cold, foggy morning when I was called to the scene to view what had happened during the night. Entry had been effected through a window, and the door at the back of the Cottage then opened to make possible the removal of some sixty items of furniture, ornaments and domestic utensils.

It was obviously a carefully planned operation, individual small pieces of furniture and other interesting items being chosen, including the grandfather clock which had been detached from its fastening to the wall. A waiting van in Cottage Lane must have been used to make a 'get away' during the murky weather conditions that prevailed on that particular night.

All the items stolen were marked, and it was possible to hand to the police descriptions and photographs of them. These were immediately circulated in this country and abroad, and a reward of £1,000 was offered by the Trustees for information leading to the recovery of the stolen property. The burglary attracted considerable publicity, and the BBC cooperated by staging a re-construction of the incident in the hope of attracting information useful to the police. I myself received one or two bogus telephone calls and, although the police kept up their efforts to trace the culprits for some considerable time, their enquiries met with no success. To this day, nothing has been heard of the stolen goods. Were agents commissioned to steal these items for a collector because of their association with this historic property, and are they possibly still kept hidden in a secret place? Or did they leave the country within twenty-four hours for a continental destination?

The episode was a matter of serious concern to me personally and to the members of the Executive Committee, who subsequently decided to install more effective alarm systems, on lines recommended by the police, in all the Shakespearian properties and in the original Shakespeare Centre building. Settlement of the Trust's claim, which I negotiated, was made by the General Accident Fire and Life Assurance Corporation. Repairs to the damaged window and doors were carried out immediately, and the gaps in the Cottage's furnishings left by the thieves were filled with suitable substitutes as a matter of urgency.

As had happened years before, when the Cottage was damaged by fire, news of the burglary caused considerable public concern. Within a short time I received offers of pieces of furniture and smaller furnishing items to fill the gaps caused. A few of these proved to be suitable and were accepted. I was particularly moved by the generous gift of Mrs Graham Jacks of Florida, who sent a pair of early brass candlesticks, a rushlight holder and a tinder box, which had been part of the possessions of the Gibbs family, bakers of Stratford-upon-Avon. Before her marriage Mrs Jacks was Jennifer Gibbs, who had been one of my excellent secretaries in the early 1960s, working alongside Shirley Watkins on the Shakespeare Centre project and the 1964 Shakespeare quatercentenary celebrations.

Burnside

When the Trustees took possession of the Burnside properties in Shottery in 1975, a preliminary inspection established that most of them were in need of repair and improvement. As already mentioned, Brookside, in Church Road, had to be rethatched and extensively overhauled. Similarly, the thatched cottages known as Tapestry Cottage and Wild Thyme in Tavern Lane had to be rethatched and repaired and modern amenities installed. The four cottages in the row adjacent to Burnside each needed attention in different ways. The wooden bungalow in Cottage Lane, which had been occupied by the gardener in Mrs Evans's time, had fallen into such a state of disrepair that it was officially deemed unfit for continued use and was accordingly taken down.

The greatest problem was Burnside itself, the former residence of Mrs Evans, which had been leased by her trustees during the lifetime of Mr John Evans, her surviving husband. As already mentioned, the last tenant proved most unsatisfactory and allowed the property to fall into an unbelievable state of neglect and decay, the garden and grounds also having been allowed to run wild. It was only after protracted negotiations that the Trustees were able to obtain possession in 1980.

The Trustees were exercised as to how to tackle the situation. One suggestion was that the house should be demolished, but the Trustees felt that Mrs Evans would have wanted the property to be preserved and used. The advice and help of Laurence Williams, the Trust's architect, was accordingly sought. I remember very clearly the earnest discussions we had about the problem. Several options were considered, but the favoured solution was Laurence Williams's brilliant scheme for converting the house into six self-contained residential units, without changing the appearance of its exterior elevations; in fact by preserving the character of Burnside as it was. As a corollary to this, I suggested that the former garden and grounds should be completely re-allocated, with most of the area, apart from flower beds adjacent to the house, becoming part of the Home Field.

This proposed treatment of Burnside met with the ready agreement of the Executive Committee and was approved by the planning authority. The work of conversion was put in hand forthwith and completed in 1981. The flats were individually named and subsequently rented to members of the Trust's staff and other tenants. Altogether, this was a clever conservation project which fitted well into the Trustees' general policy of preserving unspoilt the immediate area around Anne Hathaway's Cottage.

The Hill

Meanwhile, the question arose as to the future of The Hill, the acquisition of which has already been recorded. Having served as the temporary headquarters of the Shakespeare Summer School of the University of Birmingham while the Shakespeare Centre extension was being built, it was no longer required for this purpose and it was wasteful to continue to use it as a store. A suggestion I put to the Trustees was that the house, with adaptation and extension, would make an ideal Shakespeare guest house or lodging for visiting scholars and students coming to Stratford-upon-Avon. I had in mind the kind of accommodation provided by the Folger Shakespeare Library for the temporary lodging of its visiting scholars. Members of the Executive Committee liked the idea, and tentative plans for the use of The Hill in this way were prepared by the architect. Unfortunately, the Trust did not have funds available at that time to finance a project of this kind and, when enquiries as to possible support from the Universities of Birmingham and Warwick proved negative, the idea had to be abandoned.

The outcome of further discussions was that Laurence Williams was invited to prepare a plan for the conversion of The Hill into self-contained residential units likely to give a satisfactory rental return. Having regard to the Trustees' wish not to alter the exterior appearance of this Victorian house, this was no easy task but, in the event, he produced a masterly plan which, without altering the elevational treatment of the building, provided four attractive homes, each with its own individual features.

The proposal was readily agreed by the Executive Committee, and the work of conversion was carried out by the local building firm of Sibbasbridge, Ltd, and completed in 1982. Improvement grants totalling £11,000 were received from the Stratford-on-Avon District Council towards this conversion project. Major improvements were also made to the Lodge at the bottom of The Hill drive on the Warwick road. All this work, though expensive, was conceived as part of the Trustees' conservation investment policy, which at the same time progressively increased the Trust's rental income from its let properties. For myself, I was delighted that the former residence of the Flower family, which had been so closely associated with Stratford-upon-Avon and Shakespeare, should have been given such a satisfactory new lease of life.

Henley Street Property Acquisition

Another important conservation opportunity occurred in 1986, when the Trustees were able to negotiate the purchase of 38 Henley Street, the

The Hill, Warwick Road

premises formerly occupied by Scott and Company, Ltd, builders' merchants. The property in question consisted of a small retail shop next door to the Centre Bookshop at number 39, which, as already described, had been opened by the Trust some years before, together with a spacious warehouse at the rear used for the storage of builders' merchandise. On the first floor there were rooms that had been used for office purposes and storage. The front part of the building incorporated portions of early timber framing, suggesting it had been originally one of a series of bays of an earlier timbered structure, possibly of sixteenth-century date.

The location of the premises immediately opposite to the Shakespeare Centre was sufficient reason in itself to justify the Trustees' wish to control the use of it; undesirable business or another souvenir shop could possibly have been detrimental to the character of the street. There were other reasons, however, which made the property of special interest to the Trust. The rear part of the building, linked with the back-side area of the adjoining Centre Bookshop, provided a convenient site for erecting an extension block behind the existing street elevation which would meet several practical needs of the Trust.

With the assistance of the Trust's architect, Mr Brian Ellender, a partner in the firm of Wood, Kendrick and Williams who had taken on the Trust's work after Laurence Williams's death in 1983, a plan was produced which linked together 38 and 39 Henley Street and improved the elevational treatment of the former to harmonize with the street scene. The plan made possible an enlargement of the Centre Bookshop, involving the exposure and preservation of the original timber framing referred to above and the construction of a separate entrance from Henley Street, giving access to the new buildings at the rear. On the ground floor these comprised a refurbished warehouse for the storage of publications and stock relating to the Trust's sales activities, a spacious room for an archive conservation workshop, and toilet facilities. A staircase gave access to existing office rooms at first floor level at the front of the building, and these were linked with an entirely new suite of office accommodation erected at the rear. The work of renovation and construction was carried out by the local firm of Sibbasbridge, Ltd, and was completed by the end of 1987.

The Trust's accounts staff, who for some time past had been housed in the rooms at the back of the Shakespeare Centre originally occupied by a resident caretaker, moved across the street, together with the administrator, to take over this new accommodation. The new store room for publications on the ground floor was also equipped and brought into use to supplement the existing stock room at the rear of Hornby Cottage.

It took the best part of 1988 to equip the newly built archive conservation workshop. I enjoyed the task of planning this and was fortunate to have the

Archive conservation workshop

assistance of an experienced conservator, Mrs Clair Walton, whom the Trustees had authorized me to appoint. The West Midlands Area Museum Service also gave their support and made a grant of £4,000 towards the considerable expense involved. For a long time past I had felt the need for the Trust to have its own capability to undertake conservation and repair work on archives, bookbinding and library requirements. Hitherto such conservation work as it had been possible to undertake had been done with assistance from outside. The County Record Office at Warwick had frequently undertaken archive repair work for the Trust, while individual items and books needing special treatment or re-binding had been entrusted to R.H. Maltby, one of the old-established bookbinders of Oxford. On many occasions I found myself transporting valuable items – the First Folio, for instance – to Oxford for Mr Maltby's attention, and I often took advantage of these visits to call on the Printer at the Oxford University Press, to discuss the production of a Dugdale Society publication. By the time I retired, the Trust's own archive conservation workshop was fully equipped and in working order.

Garden Matters

The Trust's responsibilities in connection with gardens and estate grew as each new project was completed, and when I retired in 1989 the head gardener had a staff of fifteen full-time, and one part-time, assistant gardeners, an establishment very different from the time when Frank Jackson, the head gardener when I started, had two assistants to help him and no motor mowers to cut any of the grass. As a matter of record, the Trustees had taken into their employment in 1951 their first and only female gardener, Miss Mary Fearnall, who had served as a landgirl during the Second World War. Within a short time she established herself as a most useful member of the garden team, working mostly at New Place, and continued until she reached retirement age in 1982.

The gardeners' work followed a well established pattern, determined by the seasons of the year, but unusual weather conditions on occasion made extra work. The severe winter weather of 1982, for example, caused some serious problems on the maintenance and garden fronts. The weight of snow damaged or destroyed a number of trees and shrubs; a large branch was torn from the stately, tall cedar tree in the Birthplace garden, and the Judas tree in the garden at Anne Hathaway's Cottage was completely broken down. I personally knew every tree in the Trust's gardens: they were like old friends, and the loss of any one of them made me sad. When the ancient mulberry tree in the Birthplace garden suddenly collapsed overnight in 1988, I arrived early the next morning to find that the gardeners were already busy clearing away the branches and were just about to cut up the prostrate, knarled trunk of the tree into short lengths, to cart it away. I immediately halted the operation and left the trunk lying on the grass. I had noticed that, at the point of breakage near the ground, thin strands of the trunk had not parted company with the root, and from past experience I knew that, left alone, the fallen trunk could well survive and sprout new branches from its horizontal position. This is precisely what happened, and within a year the fallen mulberry tree had blossomed forth and made a most fascinating feature in the garden. The same fate had happened to the ancient quince in 1986, and here again a sprouting from the old root produced a new, young tree before the parent died.

The removal of the 1964 Pavilion from the Birthplace garden in 1982 made possible the reinstatement of the grass and paved area on which it stood. For nearly twenty years this temporary erection had served as a valuable sales outlet, but it was no longer required now that facilities for sales in Hornby Cottage had been extended and improved. When the landscaping of the site of the Pavilion was completed, three large Cotswold stone troughs, which had formerly belonged to Mrs T.N. Waldron, a Life Trustee, and had been given to the Trust after her death in 1981, were placed on the paved area and planted with flowers. This would have pleased Mrs Waldron, who was herself a keen horticulturalist and lover of gardens.

Incidentally, I would like to pay a tribute to Mrs Waldron and to her helper, Mrs Vera Franklin, who continued her work, for arranging the flowers in Shakespeare's Birthplace and the Shakespeare Centre over the years. It all started in 1950, when they arranged a display for the royal visit; and on every subsequent royal, or other special, occasion I was able to leave the arrangement of flowers in the hands of these ladies.

In 1985 the unusually cold spell of wintry weather in the early part of the year, followed by gales in March, was a difficult time for the garden staff. The ancient cedar tree in the Birthplace garden lost another limb during a snow storm. Several trees on Trust property were blown down or subsequently had to be felled, including several of the stately line of poplars at Hall's Croft, which had been a striking feature of the garden.

In 1986 the gravel paths in the Birthplace garden and in the Great Garden of New Place were surfaced, and a considerable programme of fencing was undertaken in Cottage Lane, Shottery. Whenever possible, I always insisted that cleft oak posts, rails and pales were used for fencing, rather than the sawn variety with straight edges. Cleft oak, when weathered, has a character of its own and always harmonizes well with natural hedging. It became increasingly difficult, however, to find a source of supply, because demand had progressively decreased and there were few men left who had the necessary skill to cleave oak logs to produce hewn fencing materials. Nevertheless, a stroke of good fortune came to my assistance when I appointed as a member of the Trust's maintenance team a man who had the experience and expertise to cleave oak in the traditional manner. Before coming to the Trust, Robert Whitehead had worked for a time with the Forestry Commission. I quickly discovered that he was a born craftsman, capable of tackling any kind of carpentry work, conservation or carving; the more intricate and demanding the task, the more did he seem to enjoy it. Following my retirement, Robert assumed particular responsibilities in the field of museum conservation, one of his specialities being the overhaul and repair of some of the larger farm exhibits at Mary Arden's House.

The Hill greenhouse

Details of this kind are mentioned to illustrate the constant round of attention needed to maintain a high standard of condition and appearance. During the summer of 1986 the gardens at New Place were the subject and setting of a very successful television programme, and repeating what had happened for several years in succession, the Trust received awards from the 'Stratford-upon-Avon in Bloom' competition for the excellence of its gardens.

It was also in 1986 that the Royal Shakespeare Theatre gave formal notice to terminate the Trust's use of the plot of ground in the Paddock in Southern Lane, adjoining Hall's Croft, which for over thirty years had served as a reserve garden and as a convenient base for several greenhouses. The Executive Committee readily approved my suggestion that immediate preparations should be made to transfer

Mrs Waldron arranging flowers

the garden headquarters to a new site at The Hill. The necessary work to implement this plan was carried out during 1987.

A new reserve garden was prepared by ploughing up, and bringing back into cultivatable condition, the ground which had originally been the orchard belonging to The Hill residence. The soil proved to be particularly good. Two greenhouses from the Paddock were re-erected as part of a new garden headquarters complex, which involved the building of a new potting shed, a staff room with amenities not previously enjoyed by the garden staff, and a large new greenhouse with a range of frames alongside it, complete with up-to-date heating and ventilating equipment, including a propagating unit. Open-fronted storage sheds were constructed round three sides of a tarmaced parking area, and walls were built to enclose the whole complex, as well as the reserve garden, for the purposes of security. Apart from the large greenhouse, the Trust's own maintenance and garden staff were responsible for all the work, including the buildings, which produced the new garden headquarters. The finished product, achieved in a relatively short period of time, was an outstanding example of team effort.

The Cottage Tea Garden

In 1982 the Trustees achieved a long-standing objective when, after protracted and difficult negotiations, they succeeded in purchasing the property known as 1 Cottage Lane, Shottery, situated on the opposite side of the road to Anne Hathaway's Cottage. It comprised a semi-detached house and spacious garden alongside Shottery Brook, most of which was taken up by a miscellany of untidy sheds and pens which housed a variety of birds, together with a small, wooden kiosk opening on to Cottage Lane, from which refreshments and souvenirs were sold.

In my early years as Director, the owner of this property, a lady named Mrs Norton, used to stand on the pavement just outside the entrance gate to Anne Hathaway's Cottage, and from the basket she carried she offered for sale to visitors as they arrived bunches of lavender, postcards and other souvenir items. Occupying such a preferential pitch, sales were usually very good, as was also the trade in souvenirs at the kiosk. I always felt that this particular activity, and the manner in which it was conducted, gave an unfortunate impression to visitors; the sales kiosk, with its ice-cream signs and other advertisement posters, was quite out of keeping with the natural, unspoilt environment of the Cottage. It was also in direct competition with the Trust's own arrangements for selling postcards and related items inside the Cottage. The situation became even more serious when, following Mrs Norton's death, a so-called 'bird garden' was established in the garden near the sales kiosk, as a means of attracting the attention and patronage of visitors.

The Trustees were as keen as I was to remedy this state of affairs and to prevent further development of the site and its sales potential, but it took many years before changed circumstances led the owner to consider selling the property. Even then, negotiations for purchase by the Trust were difficult. At one stage there was a condition that the Trustees should acquire all the birds except the parrot. Though fond of birds, I had to make it clear that the Trust was not in that kind of business, and eventually terms for the purchase of the property, minus the birds, were agreed.

It gave me considerable pleasure to arrange for the sales kiosk and the bird pens and sheds to be dismantled, and the garden area to be tidied up.

The Cottage Tea Garden

Meanwhile, the Executive Committee considered proposals for the future use of the house and garden, and they readily accepted my recommendation that the property should be adapted to serve as a tea room, to provide a much needed amenity for visitors to Anne Hathaway's Cottage. Laurence Williams, the Trust's architect, produced another masterly plan, which the Trustees approved, though, due to his untimely death in December 1983, he was not able to see it carried into effect. His partner, Brian Ellender, took over at this point and we worked together to get the project completed.

The house itself was converted into two self-contained residential units; a small extension was then built beside it, to provide a kitchen, store and servery, linked with an Edwardian type of conservatory, which was designed for use as a tea room, and with a paved patio area outside, facing the garden. The necessary work was carried out during 1983 and the early months of 1984. With the help of the Trust's head gardener, Michael Johnson, the area of the former 'bird garden' was re-designed and completely cleared and replanted. The bank of Shottery Brook, which ran alongside, had to be strengthened, and new gravel paths were constructed to enclose the middle part of the garden, which was laid with turf. One path followed the line of the watercourse through the spinney, to link the tea garden with Jubilee Walk; another provided access from the roadway, through a new gate opposite the exit used by visitors as they left Anne Hathaway's Cottage. Narrow flower borders were planted in simple, cottage style; a row of roses climbed up rustic poles; and a weeping willow and a variety of shrubs added shape and colour to the scene.

The Cottage Tea Garden was opened early in June 1984, in time for the busy part of the visiting season, and it soon became firmly established as an essential amenity for visitors to the Cottage. The newly planted brookside garden matured surprisingly quickly and has become an attraction in its own right; in addition, the rear of Anne Hathaway's Cottage, previously not easily seen, can now be viewed to advantage from the Tea Garden. The provision of a catering service there was entrusted to Mr Guy Belchambers, the proprietor of the Thatch Restaurant, situated on the opposite side of Cottage Lane alongside the Trust's coach park. This arrangement was one I favoured, because successful catering requires special experience and management skills. The terms of the franchise were also very satisfactory in providing additional income for the Trust.

On one or two occasions in earlier years the Trustees had been given the opportunity to purchase the freehold of the Thatch Restaurant, mentioned above. They appreciated that the property occupied a strategic site within a few yards of Anne Hathaway's Cottage and that there was a risk that it might be developed or exploited in a manner detrimental to the interests of the Trust. Unfortunately, funds had not been available for its purchase, but by the 1980s the situation had changed. When the property came on the market again for sale, the Executive Committee decided that, in the interests of conservation, it was imperative for the Trust to acquire it and so be able to control its future use. The Thatch Restaurant was accordingly added to the Trust's estate in 1988 and arrangements made for its continued use as a restaurant specializing in the provision of meals for parties of visitors to the Cottage.

The Shakespeare Tree Garden

Perhaps even more significant from a long-term point of view was the creation of the Shakespeare Tree Garden, adjacent to Anne Hathaway's Cottage, between 1984 and 1988.

The idea of planting a specimen of every tree mentioned by Shakespeare originated from a general enquiry I received in 1983 from the Tree Council, the national body which exists to encourage the planting of trees. My first discussions with representatives of the Council concerned the possibility of general tree planting by the Trust as part of a national campaign, and it was when I suggested that the Trustees might be willing to make available a special area of ground at Shottery for this purpose that the idea of a Shakespeare Tree Garden emerged, and was enthusiastically received both by the Tree Council and the Executive Committee of Trustees.

For several years previously a small field, situated behind the Thatch Restaurant and the adjoining cottages, and quite close to Anne Hathaway's Cottage and accessible from the Trust's coach park, had lain neglected and unused. It was completely enclosed, and on the far side was separated from Briar Furlong, a large field also owned by the Trust, by a hedgerow, broken here and there by self-set trees. Although one or two offers to rent the field had been received, I always had it in mind that the Trust might be able to use it one day for its own purposes, and for this reason it was left to lie fallow; hence its availability when the Shakespeare Tree Garden idea was proposed.

The Executive Committee agreed to bear the cost of undertaking the clearance and preparation of the field and to maintain the proposed Tree Garden when planted, it being understood that the Tree Council would assume responsibility for designing the layout and providing the trees for the garden. It was on this basis of co-operation that the project was initiated and carried to completion.

Much of the preliminary work was done during the autumn of 1983 and the following spring, by which time a plan for the layout and treatment of the garden, prepared by a member of the Tree Council, Professor Derek Lovejoy, who was a professional landscape architect, had been agreed by the Trustees. The ground was systematically cleared and rotavated, and land-drainage pipes were laid across the area. Paths were constructed and a piped water supply from the main in Cottage Lane was put down at suitable points in readiness for use when planting took place.

On Friday, 19 April 1984, the eve of the Shakespeare birthday celebrations, Her Majesty Queen Elizabeth The Queen Mother visited the Shakespeare Centre extension and, after lunch there, drove to Anne Hathaway's Cottage and subsequently planted a mulberry tree in the orchard, to inaugurate

The Queen Mother at Anne Hathaway's Cottage

The Queen Mother planting the mulberry tree

the Shakespeare Tree Garden. It was a particularly happy and memorable occasion. Before the planting ceremony Her Majesty made an inspection of the Cottage, showing great interest in its architectural features and the furnishings of the various rooms as she went round. Although now in her eighties, she climbed the narrow stairs leading to the upper floor with great agility and apparent ease, clearly enjoying the experience of seeing something she had read about but had never visited.

She then walked to the lower end of the orchard. In the presence of a company of Trustees, representatives of the Tree Council and other guests, she made a short, felicitous speech commending the Shakespeare tree planting project, which she was pleased to inaugurate. With the assistance of the Trust's head gardener, Michael Johnson, she shovelled soil to secure the planting of a young mulberry tree, alongside which a plaque, designed by Richard Kindersley, was subsequently placed to commemorate the occasion.

Her Majesty clearly enjoyed her visit, and the following day instructed her Private Secretary to send the following letter to me:

CLARENCE HOUSE
S.W.I.

22nd April 1985

Dear Mr Fox

Queen Elizabeth The Queen Mother has asked me to tell you how grateful she is to you for all the trouble you went to on Her Majesty's behalf during her time at the Shakespeare Centre.

You made the whole visit wonderfully interesting and rewarding, and it was especially kind of you to put your Flat at Queen Elizabeth's disposal before luncheon.

The Queen Mother's only regret was that time did not allow Her Majesty to enjoy in a more leisurely way the many treasures that you were able to lay before her.

Yours sincerely,
Martin Gilliat

Levi Fox, Esq., O.B.E.,
The Shakespeare Birthplace Trust

The planting of trees and shrubs, most of which were donated with the co-operation and help of the Tree Council, took place during the two following seasons. It fell to me to decide which particular varieties of the chosen species were to be included, and this involved an interesting piece of research to establish which were known to Shakespeare. Rabbit-proof netting was fitted round the entire periphery of the area to protect the newly planted trees. A wooden turnstile type of gate was designed and made, to allow exit only on to Cottage Lane, it having been decided that access into the garden should be from the Trust's coach park beside Anne Hathaway's Cottage. The Tree Garden would thus be freely accessible to everyone during those hours

The newly planted Tree Garden

when the Cottage was open to the public. Spring flowering bulbs were planted alongside the exit path. A small plaque was placed against each tree, bearing the botanical name of the specimen together with a quotation from Shakespeare referring to it. All this work was carried out by the Trust's own garden team, under my supervision, and the major part of the project was completed by the end of 1987.

On Friday, 6 May 1988, His Royal Highness The Duke of Kent, Patron of the Tree Council, came to Stratford-upon-Avon to perform the official opening ceremony of the Tree Garden.

As a preliminary to his visit to Shottery for this purpose, His Royal Highness arrived at the Shakespeare Centre, which he inspected under my guidance. Like other members of the Royal Family before him, he was fascinated by the scope and

HRH Duke of Kent planting the tree

Opening the Shakespeare Tree Garden

variety of the Trust's activities and was impressed by the Shakespeare Centre's facilities for handling visitors and at the same time providing for the Trust's educational and administrative needs.

His Royal Highness then proceeded to Shottery, where the Chairman of the Trust, Mr Dennis Flower, welcomed him and introduced Trustees and representatives of the Tree Council.

A company of invited guests, including donors of trees, shrubs and roses, and of the teak benches sited around the garden, had been asked to witness the ceremony. His Royal Highness made a thorough inspection of the garden. He was clearly very interested and frequently asked Michael Johnson, the Trust's head gardener, and myself about particular trees and their descriptive labels.

At the Chairman's invitation, the Duke of Kent then planted a silver birch tree to mark the formal opening of the Shakespeare Tree Garden, and a small plaque recording the ceremony was placed alongside it. In his speech he referred to the valuable work of the Tree Council and he warmly commended the Trustees for their enterprise in co-operating with the Council to create a garden which, he said, when matured would become unique in its character and attraction. For myself, with my vivid recollection of the original condition of the plot of land which now formed the Tree Garden, I could hardly believe that such a transformation had been accomplished in a period of some three years – another major conservation project to the Trust's credit.

With the careful attention of our gardeners, who had taken such pride in being involved in its preparation and planting, the Tree Garden became established surprisingly quickly and came to be enjoyed by local residents as well as those paying a leisurely visit to Anne Hathaway's Cottage.

A further ceremony took place in the Tree Garden on 1 August 1989 when, in the presence of the Trustees and a few invited guests, including Mr John Kerby, Chairman of the Tree Council, a presentation was made to the Trust on behalf of the Council by Mr Norman Painting, a member of the Tree Council and well known as a radio personality

Unveiling plaque in the Shakespeare Tree Garden

playing a leading role in the BBC's popular programme of rural life, 'The Archers'. This gift was in the form of an illustrated information panel, erected just inside the entrance to the garden, showing the locations of the different trees and recording the names of the donors of trees and seats.

Educational Developments

Following the steady progress of the 1970s, the Trust's educational activities continued to develop in an impressive manner, full advantage being taken of the assembly suite of accommodation provided in the Shakespeare Centre extension. The increased demand for introductory talks offered to school parties and more senior student groups suggested that the Trust should do more to further knowledge and appreciation of Shakespeare with young people. We accordingly set out to encourage, and to assist with modest subsidy from the Trust's Jubilee Educational Fund, projects and courses planned specifically with this in mind.

The existing selection of talks and lectures was gradually enlarged under Roger Pringle's direction. In 1987 the experiment of providing one-day courses for sixth formers, and particularly the first one on *Hamlet*, proved successful and set the pattern for subsequent years. 'Sharing Shakespeare', as the programme came to be called, made it possible for college and senior school groups to enjoy, at a low cost, a carefully prepared programme of talks, discussions, workshops and video presentations, relating to one of Shakespeare's plays and combined with a matinée visit to the Royal Shakespeare Theatre, rounded off, when possible, by an informal session with one of the actors taking part in the current Stratford production. Displays of library, theatrical and archive material were also frequently arranged to meet the requirements of particular groups engaged in study. I recall one such very successful occasion when members of the Cambridge Bibliographical Society visited the Shakespeare Centre, in 1982.

Another experiment which met with a good response was introduced in 1987, in the form of a short series of 'Living Shakespeare' leisure breaks, which were designed to appeal to the interested lay person wishing to spend three or four days in Stratford as a member of an educational group taking part in a programme of talks and discussions, visits to the Shakespearian properties and historic attractions in the surrounding Shakespeare countryside, accompanied by an opportunity to see the performance of a Shakespeare play at the Royal Shakespeare Theatre and other related activities. This unique, complete package, offered at an inclusive price which covered all admission charges to historic properties, accommodation and meals during the stay and a full programme of evening entertainment and theatre visits, was made possible by the co-operation of the Stratford Moat House International hotel, conveniently situated at Bridgefoot, the National Trust and the Royal Shakespeare Theatre.

Illustrative of the wide appeal of 'Living Shakespeare' were the four carefully designed programmes offered in 1988, as follows: 'Shakespeare's Warwickshire World', planned to give an insight into the society in which Shakespeare moved, both when he was growing up and later when he returned from London to Stratford; 'Houses and Gardens of Shakespeare's England', designed for anyone interested in the outstanding architectural and gardening achievements of Shakespeare's age; 'Shakespeare and his Theatre', built around three productions in repertoire by the Royal Shakespeare Company – two plays by Shakespeare and one, at the Swan Theatre, by an Elizabethan or later dramatist, with talks and discussions focussed on the plays in the context of their current staging; and 'Tudor Pleasures and Pursuits', intended to give an enjoyable and informative experience of many aspects of living in 'the golden age' of late Tudor England.

This new idea of reaching out to the lay public, as it were, subsequently became an established part of the Trust's educational role, but it was not done at the expense of other academic activity. The Shakespeare Centre came to be used by the Department of Education and Science for week-end courses for exchange teachers from abroad, and also as the established base for the annual six-week Shakespeare summer school organized by the Extramural Department of the University of Birmingham. This had been held, since its inception in the early 1950s, at the Shakespeare Institute but, when the need to find alternative accommodation for it arose, the Trust was able to offer facilities in the annexe adjoining the Shakespeare Centre. When that building was demolished to make possible the construction of the Centre extension, the summer school was accommodated for two years as a temporary measure at The Hill. When building operations were completed, the Shakespeare Centre became the headquarters of the summer school, an arrangement particularly appropriate because its director, Dr Gareth Lloyd Evans, was a Local Trustee who served as a member of the Executive Committee. He died in 1984 and the first of a series of annual memorial lectures given in his honour was held at the Shakespeare Centre in April 1987.

The Shakespeare summer school was attended by mature students from many countries, who took part in a full programme of lectures and seminars dealing with drama and theatre in the age of Shakespeare. They also attended performances of Shakespeare's plays and other productions at the Stratford theatres and were able to use the Trust's library and archive collections. I myself regularly conducted a seminar on Elizabethan handwriting each year, using the resources of the Trust's record collections as the basis for my instruction. The Trustees offered four studentships from the Jubilee Educational Fund to British students attending the course.

The developing use of the Centre's assembly suite gave me considerable satisfaction. In practice, the accommodation proved most flexible and suitable for a great variety of uses: small conferences; trade displays and exhibitions; musical concerts and poetry readings; fashion shows and receptions; lectures, film shows and meetings of all kinds. It may seem surprising that such functions were encouraged in a building conceived as a study centre. The fact was that, for a number of years, there were periods when the facilities available were not required for the Trust's own activities; letting for use by outside organizations was accordingly a means of earning income towards the cost of staff and overhead expenses. Moreover, the building had been designed for multi-purpose use, so that at all times the work of the library and records office was able to continue without interruption.

Several special occasions spring to mind. In 1985 the BBC used the whole of the assembly suite for its 'Showcase' presentation, to mark the completion of its series of Shakespeare television productions. On that occasion it was disclosed that the complete package of the BBC's Shakespeare films had been bought by more than thirty countries, convincing evidence of the universal appeal of William Shakespeare and his value as a business asset. In June 1987 the counting of votes in the General Election for the Stratford-upon-Avon constituency took place in the Shakespeare Centre, and in the same year accommodation was provided for a meeting of the Section of Psychiatry of the Royal Society of Medicine and a reception arranged by the BBC for the delegates of the European Broadcasting Union Television Programme Committee. In 1989 a two-day meeting of members of the Bureau of the European Parliament, under the presidency of Lord Plumb of Coleshill, occupied the Queen Elizabeth Hall and associated accommodation at the Centre.

Happenings of this kind conferred practical benefit and prestige on the Trust, and indeed on

Stratford-upon-Avon; but most importantly they associated William Shakespeare and his Birthplace with the wider world.

The Trust's Collections

In both the library and records office the 1980s saw considerable development. As the resources of the Centre library and the records office became more widely known, the numbers of readers using their facilities gradually increased, together with enquiries received by post and telephone. By 1982 as many as 1,644 readers used the library during the year, and 1,132 the records office, quite apart from an impressive list of group and project visits. The work of recording and storing accessions, cataloguing and the production of reference aids continued, and a major instalment of book-stack shelving was purchased and erected in 1987, to provide for the re-arrangement of a number of special collections as well as for future growth. The demand for photocopies and photographs for study and publication purposes increased sharply and, to meet the developing use of video recordings, suitable viewing apparatus was provided. In 1984, the first complete year in which these viewing facilities were available for readers, the library's equipment was used over a hundred times and was in considerable demand during the six weeks of the Shakespeare summer school. There was also interest from groups of Ordinary and Advanced Level students who wanted to see a recording of the production of a play of their studies, before taking their examinations.

The staff contributed actively to the talks, lectures and displays already mentioned; they were also responsible for the presentation of the exhibitions which provided a supplementary attraction for visitors to the Shakespeare Centre. Two or three exhibitions were held each year in the entrance hall and the Stratford room and they covered a fascinating range of subject matter. Some were planned with local interest in mind; others, of more general appeal, were on occasion linked with national events or current Shakespeare productions. To give a few examples: in 1980 three exhibitions were arranged: 'Henry Irving and the Lyceum', 'Shakespeare: The Italian Connection', and 'In Praise of Warwickshire'. In 1982 an exhibition entitled 'Roll out the Maps' was arranged by the staff of the records office, and was followed by 'A Kingdom for a Stage', an exhibition illustrating the lives and careers of Elizabethan actors, with particular reference to Shakespeare.

In the following year an exhibition, 'The Home Front', illustrating Stratford-upon-Avon's role during the First World War, attracted considerable local interest, while 'Race Relations in Shakespeare', presented in 1987, had a more general appeal. An exhibition which proved to be very popular was 'Flowers of Stratford: the Family and Brewery, 1831-1968'. It included photographs, records and museum items, together with a video film illustrating the contribution made to the town's economic, social and cultural life by the Flower family. Most of the material for these exhibitions came from the Trust's own collections, though in the case of the Flower exhibition a number of Stratford people whose families had had connections with the brewery came forward and offered the loan or gift of interesting memorabilia.

My final year, 1989, saw three exhibitions: the first commemorated the twenty-fifth anniversary of the opening of the Shakespeare Centre in 1964, and was inaugurated by Lady Flower, widow of Sir Fordham Flower, who had been Chairman of the Trust at the time the Centre was planned and built; another, on 'The Waterway to Stratford', was designed to mark the twenty-fifth anniversary of the re-opening of the Stratford-upon-Avon canal; and later in the year came 'Shakespeare's Fools', with which was mounted a small display on 'Olivier at Stratford', assembled as a tribute to Laurence Olivier following his death in July 1989.

Once the Shakespeare Centre had been paid for, and with additional space now available for future growth, every opportunity was taken to build up the library and archive collections. Each year the Trust received gifts of books, translations, periodicals, pamphlets, festival programmes and tape recordings, together with a regular intake of prompt copies,

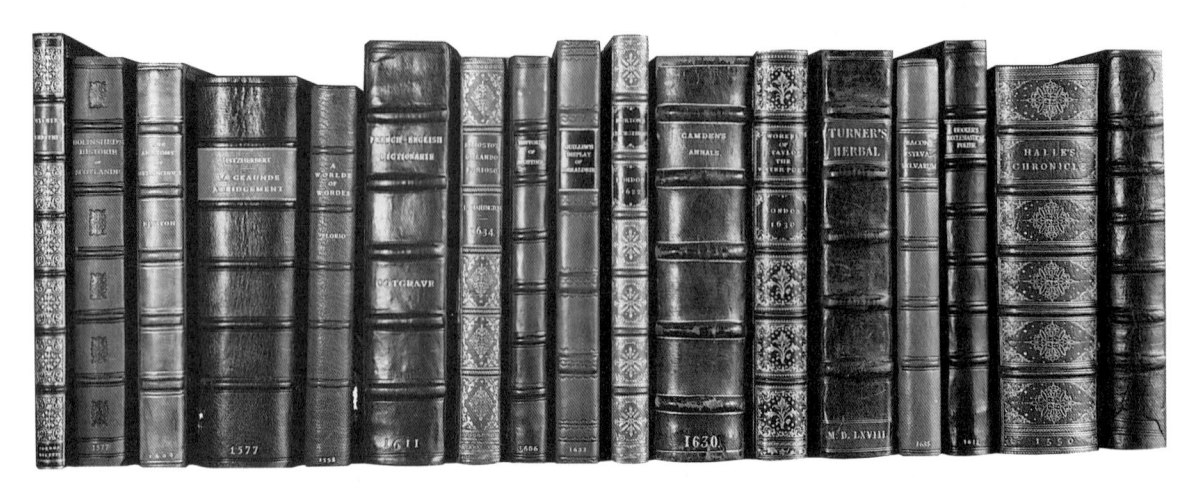

Early printed books

production photographs and theatre material from the Royal Shakespeare Company. Regular purchases were made: they included copies of significant current publications, as well as books to fill gaps in the collection. Early source books purchased in 1982, for instance, included copies of Gasparo Contarini's *The Commonwealth and Government of Venice*, first English edition, 1599, and John Cotgrave's *The English Treasury of Wit and Language*, first edition, 1655. With the help of a contribution of £1,000 from the Purchase Grant Fund administered by the Victoria and Albert Museum, a particularly interesting association copy of North's *Plutarch's Lives of The Noble Grecians and Romans*, 1579, was acquired for the library in 1985, together with a fine copy of Philip Sidney's *The Countesse of Pembroke's Arcadia*, 1613. In the following year the Trustees accepted on deposit a copy of the Second Folio edition of Shakespeare's works, which had belonged to a Warwickshire clergyman during the late eighteenth and early nineteenth centuries. Its current owner was a lady descendant of the family, who was living in the United States and who for some years past had kept this valuable book in a bank safe deposit. I persuaded her that the most appropriate way of safeguarding the future of such an interesting family heirloom was to deposit it with the Shakespeare Centre library; subject to a few simple conditions, this was done.

In 1987 two welcome items were purchased from the funds of the Friends of the Shakespeare Birthplace Trust: a copy of Moffett's *Healths Improvement*, 1655, and a microfilm copy of the *Prompt Books from the Folger Shakespeare Library*. By this time the idea of producing microfilm copies of particular collections had also become fashionable. I accordingly negotiated an agreement with Harvester Press Microform Publications, to reproduce on microfilm the large collection of Halliwell-Phillipps scrapbooks. Subsequently the same publishers completed the copying on microfilm of all the Shakespeare prompt books in the library up to 1975 and produced a printed handbook describing the collection. At the same time, another important publishing project got under way and was completed during 1988 and 1989: Emmett Publishing filmed and published on microfilm, under the title of 'Shakespeare at Stratford-upon-Avon', major sections of the production archive collections of the Royal Shakespeare Theatre housed in the Shakespeare Centre library, together with the complete card catalogue of the Birthplace Trust's book collections. These projects had a dual significance: their sale earned a modest royalty for the Trust; but, even more important, they publicized around the world the scholarly resources of the Shakespeare Centre.

In 1986 a small collection of publications printed at the Shakespeare Head Press in the years when it was operating at 21 Chapel Street, Stratford-upon-Avon, was received as a bequest of Miss Dorothy Withey, who had owned the Chaucer Head Bookshop at the same address. Of similar local interest was the collection of autograph letters of Marie Corelli, purchased in 1987, as well as an important collection of Harley Granville-Barker correspondence concerning the rebuilding of the Shakespeare Memorial Theatre after the fire in 1926.

During 1988 many useful additions were made to the library, archive and museums collections. Early books purchased included Richard Mulcaster's *Positions ... for the Training up of Children ...*, 1581; John Bulwer's *Chirologia, or the Natural Language of the Hand ...*, 1644; Simon Latham's *Falconry, or the Faulcons Lure ...*, 1615-16; and Leonard Mascall's *A Booke of the Arte and Manner how to plant ... All Sorts of Trees*, 1592.

Most years saw the arrival of new translations of Shakespeare's plays. I was particularly interested to receive the first two volumes of an illustrated edition of Shakespeare's plays translated into Georgian, presented by Professor Nico Kiasashvili, with whom I had had a most friendly relationship over the years. Nico was recognized as one of Russia's leading Shakespeare scholars, and on a number of occasions he had been allowed to come to Stratford-upon-Avon to attend the International Shakespeare Conference. Invariably he came to see me, and I was well aware of the frustration and difficulty he had encountered in persuading the State publishing department to publish his magnum opus. Equally impressive were the first translation of Shakespeare's *Complete Works* into Korean and a biography of Shakespeare in Chinese. I was also sent a paperback edition of *Hamlet* with notes in Chinese for Chinese students; I was told that it had quickly become a best seller.

Other special items accessioned are worthy of mention: a handsomely bound, large-size copy of *Hamle*t, illustrated with drawings by Henry Moore, presented by Mrs Joan Sanders Cecchini; and a copy of the first edition of *Shakespeare's Poems*, published in 1640, made possible with the assistance of a grant of £7,500 from the Purchase Grant Fund administered by the Victoria and Albert Museum and a contribution from the funds of the Friends of the Shakespeare Birthplace Trust.

The acquisition of the Thomas Holte theatre photographic collection in 1983 added appreciably to the growing photographic collection of theatre material in the library; it comprised over 1,000 negatives of productions at the Royal Shakespeare Theatre from 1952 to 1981. Most years also saw additions to the topographical photographic collection in the records office. In 1988, for instance, some eight hundred Stratford-upon-Avon photographs collected or taken by Mr Arthur Locke were donated to the Trust, many relating to the Mop Fair and ranging in date from 1900 to 1984.

The development and use of the Trust's archive collections were as impressive as those of the library. During 1985 the new records office was formally appointed by the Lord Chancellor as a place of deposit for public records outside the Public Record Office. Its earlier recognition in 1930 as an approved repository for the safe-keeping of manorial records had already attracted the deposit of most of the extant manorial documents for the whole of Warwickshire, and it was logical that the Trust's new records office at the Centre should attract further deposits and gifts. The following examples illustrate the scope and variety of material received: further instalments of family and estate papers relating to the Leigh family of Stoneleigh, the Ferrers of Baddesley Clinton and the Willoughy de Broke estates; another batch of records of the former Stratford-upon-Avon Borough Council; the business records of several Stratford firms; registers and records belonging to the local non-conformist churches; numerous deeds, property documents and discarded clients' papers from local solicitors' offices; not to mention a number of particularly interesting single items, such as the bundle of papers transferred to the Trust in 1987 by a firm of Cheltenham solicitors which had handled the sale of Shakespeare's Birthplace in 1847.

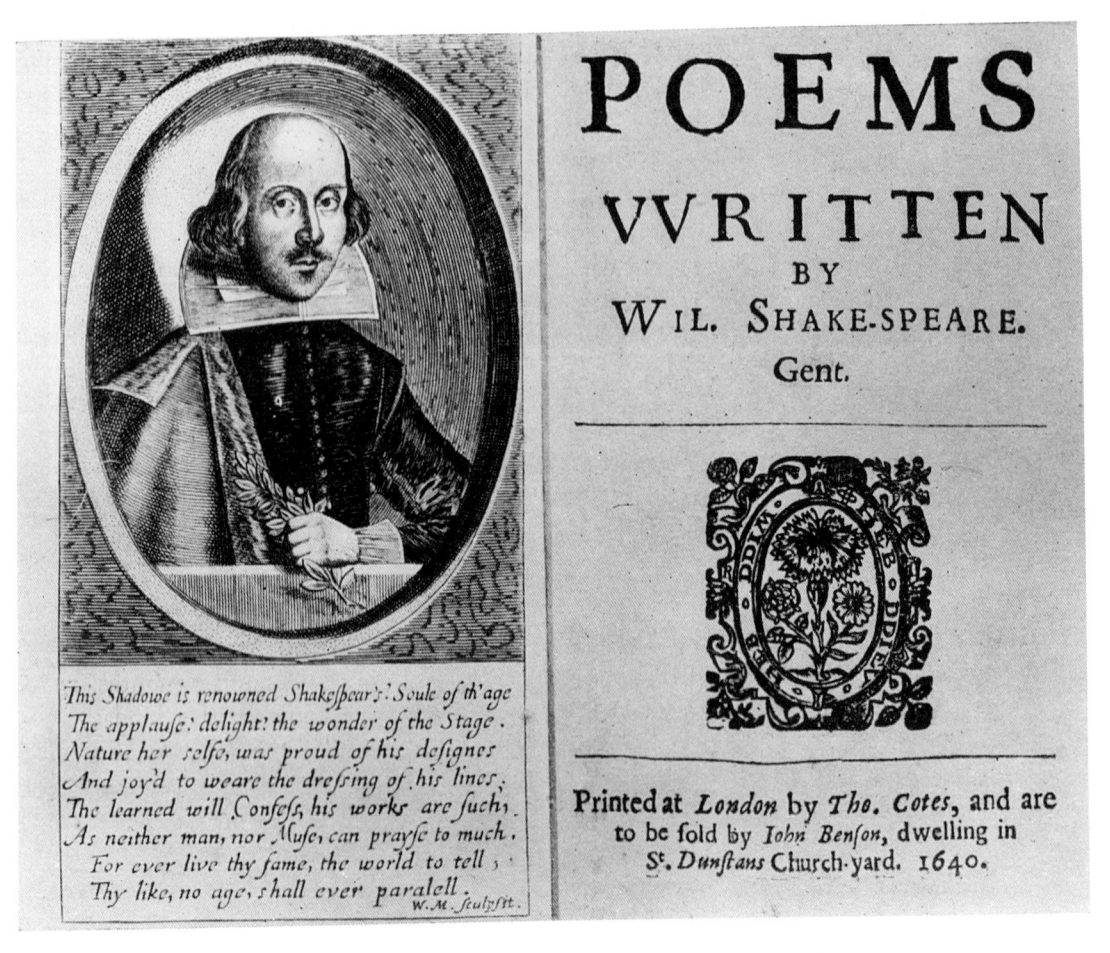

First edition of Shakespeare's Poems

Accessions to the museum collections were infinitely varied. They included items of furniture, farming and craft tools and domestic utensils, acquired to replace those stolen from Anne Hathaway's Cottage and to furnish the Glebe Farmhouse at Wilmcote. A steady stream of old agricultural implements, farm carts and countryside items made useful additions to the Shakespeare countryside museum collection.

Donations of this kind often came about as the result of personal contacts, and I still made time to pay visits to inspect items offered to the Trust. Typical of what occasionally happened was my visit to Claydons Farm, on the Banbury road, in 1989 to view sundry farming items not wanted by the owner, Mr James Rowe, who had sold the farm. I encountered a fantastic medley of farming bygones, heaped together in an out building or lying partially hidden in overgrown grass and nettles outside. There were several items I decided would make useful additions to the Trust's collections, but imagine my delight when I found among them an excellent specimen of a single, horse-drawn plough – last used, I guessed, in the 1920s – which had been made by the Hillson family in their blacksmith's shop at Langley.

It is the local association aspect of the farming collection at Mary Arden's House which gives it special significance. Nearly every exhibit has been collected from within a radius of twenty miles of Wilmcote, the surrounding countryside which

Shakespeare knew and portrayed so vividly in his writing.

In a different category, there were a few noteworthy additions to the Trust's picture collection. In 1984 an unusually fine, large water-colour of Anne Hathaway's Cottage, painted in 1894 by the Stratford artist, W.W. Quatremain, was acquired with the help of funds of the Friends of the Shakespeare Birthplace Trust. Money from the same source also made possible the following year the purchase of a most attractive water-colour of a scene depicting Armado and Jaquenetta from *Love's Labour's Lost*, painted by James Holmes (1777-1860). Another small water-colour of Anne Hathaway's Cottage by W.W. Quatremain was added in 1986, and in 1987 Mr Adam Pollock presented to the Trust a drawing of Hamlet and Ophelia, produced by John Hutton in preparation for his engraved glass panel of this subject, installed in the entrance portico of the Shakespeare Centre. Another benefactor was Mrs Constance Thomson of the Ruskin Gallery in Chapel Street who, shortly before her death, presented two fine pictures by Robert Smirke and Joseph Farington (the backgrounds only being by Farington), illustrating scenes from *The Merry Wives of Windsor* and signed and dated 1796.

Of more immediate local interest was the deposit on loan, by Mr E.B. Nurse, of the Ludford tea-chest, which was carved in mulberry wood in 1760 by Thomas Sharp of Stratford-upon-Avon for presentation to the town's deputy recorder, John Ludford; this fine specimen of Sharp's skill as a carver was accompanied by the original bill, detailing the cost of the mulberry wood and of the carver's labour.

Mention of wood reminds me that in 1982 the Trust received an unsolicited gift from the Connecticut Historical Society: a fragment of wood taken from Shakespeare's Birthplace at the time of its restoration in the 1860s, accompanied by a letter of attestation vouching for its authenticity. I wonder how many other similar pieces of association wood are still hidden away in the United States. I remember Dr Wright telling me that when he was Director of the Folger Shakespeare Library he came across quite a selection of such prized memorabilia, collected by Mr Henry Clay Folger. These included an oak casket, carved by Kendall of Warwick from wood discarded when Shakespeare's Birthplace was restored and accompanied by a certificate of authenticity. It had been bought by Mr Folger for £25 from Mrs Mary Rose, custodian at the Birthplace, through William Jaggard of the Shakespeare Press on 10 March, 1914.

Poetry and Music

Throughout these years the annual Poetry Festival continued to flourish, under the direction of Roger Pringle, who assumed responsibility for devising the programmes and making the detailed arrangements. He was assisted in a number of practical ways by Shirley Watkins, my personal assistant, who took a keen interest in the poetry readings and the musical concerts held during the summer months. The pattern of nine readings on successive Sunday evenings had by this time become an established part of Stratford's cultural calendar, and well known theatrical and literary figures were invited to take part. Mr Pringle himself devised and presented some of the readings, but outside directors were also invited to contribute particular programmes. The range of subject matter covered by the recitals was extremely varied, taking in modern as well as representative verse of earlier periods, centred on particular themes. Sometimes a reading was presented to illustrate the life and writing of an individual poet, and each year living poets were invited to take part in the Festival. They were supported by an enthusiastic audience. When the Queen Elizabeth Hall became available, some of the readings were accommodated there, but others continued to be held in the music room at Mason Croft.

The Arts Council of Great Britain, which had encouraged and subsidised the Poetry Festival since its inauguration some thirty years before, discontinued its financial support as from 1982, from which time the Trustees met its complete cost. In a similar manner, the modest financial support the Trustees had received from the Arts Council towards the cost of its summer programme of music also ceased. However, the Trustees continued to arrange concerts each summer, but by 1985 these were no longer needed. The Stratford-upon-Avon Festival had by this time become firmly established, and it included a number of musical events in its two-week programme. As Director, I served on the Festival Committee in its early stages, and the Trust identified itself closely with this town effort. Several of the Festival events were held at the Shakespeare Centre and, as a specific contribution to the cultural bill of fare, the Trust arranged three public lectures free of charge.

The Shakespeare Birthday Celebrations

Another annually recurring involvement was the organization of the Shakespeare birthday celebrations, which took place on or near to the poet's birthday, St George's Day, 23 April. From small beginnings, when I became the Chairman of the Shakespeare Birthday Celebrations Committee in 1947, the celebrations had grown by the 1980s into a major international event which was unique in its purpose and practical implications.

Throughout the years the Committee had pursued a consistent policy of inviting official representatives of all the countries of the world accredited to the Court of St James to take part in a programme of traditional celebrations, which included the ceremony of unfurling the flags of the nations, the procession to Shakespeare's Birthplace and to lay flowers on Shakespeare's grave in Holy Trinity Church, the birthday luncheon at which toasts to 'The Immortal Memory of William Shakespeare' and 'The Theatre' were proposed, and the performance of a Shakespeare play at the Royal Shakespeare Theatre.

Because of the numbers involved – 621 guests sat down for luncheon in a pavilion marquee erected on the banks of the River Avon, first in the Theatre Garden and later in Avonbank Garden – and considerations of diplomatic precedence, the task of organizing the celebrations involved a major concentrated effort over a period of weeks culminating on the day of the celebrations. I was fortunate in having my personal assistant, Shirley Watkins, as Secretary of the celebrations and Paula Haldenby, who succeeded her, to assist with the detailed work, with the backing of the office staff of the Shakespeare Centre.

Long hours of concentrated, detailed preparations, frequently after office hours, were spent in arranging the order of the flags in the central streets of the town – some 130 in all – and the national representatives and other guests who were to be invited to unfurl them, together with the order of the floral procession, which was determined with reference to the precedence of the ambassadors and high commissioners as set out in the official *London Diplomatic List*, published by the Foreign Office. The preparation of the luncheon seating plan was a nightmare, because seating positions at the tables were always decided with reference to the precedence of the diplomatic representatives present. The difficulty arose because circumstances often necessitated changes in the representatives able to attend, right up to within a few hours before the luncheon; and it was always our policy to make adjustments to the seating plan in conformity with precedence considerations. The cancellation of a senior ambassador, for instance, could necessitate as many as five or six alterations in table places.

There was no shortage of other things to do: briefing and attending on the President and the principal speakers; arranging accommodation for the distinguished guests and also their floral tributes; dealing with the practicalities of flag poles, national flags and shields; organizing stewards to accompany the invited guests, school parties and others taking part in the procession; arranging for the band of the Corps of the Royal Engineers, the military personnel, the police and others concerned with manning the processional route and crowd control; making decisions with the marquee contractors and the caterers who provided the reception and luncheon; liaison with the press, and the production of printed invitations, programmes, luncheon seating plan and the like; co-operating with the management of the

Royal Shakespeare Theatre in connection with reception arrangements and providing guest tickets for the birthday evening performance; and dealing with every conceivable eventuality that might arise, not forgetting the special arrangements for security, which were never made public but provided unobtrusive protection for the distinguished personages taking part.

The one thing I disliked was having to appeal for contributions towards the cost of the celebrations. When I first became involved with arrangements, the Shakespeare Club of Stratford-upon-Avon played a central role and its members and interested local people gave donations towards the cost of hospitality for the invited guests. The Memorial Theatre was also able to offer free seats for the birthday performance. The Celebrations Committee owned the flag poles and their shields, the national flags that had been given for the purpose of being flown in Shakespeare's honour on his birthday, and the tables used for the luncheon, which was held first in the Town Hall and then in the Conference Hall at the Memorial Theatre. It was only when a considerable sum of money was needed to provide and paint new shields, bearing the emblems and names of participating countries, that a new arrangement was agreed.

The Committee's physical assets were handed over to the Stratford-upon-Avon Borough Council, which in return agreed to meet the capital expenditure involved and undertook to offer financial support for the celebrations on the condition that the Birthplace Trust and the Memorial Theatre also made an annual contribution. This tripartite partnership worked very satisfactorily, the cost of the celebrations being met by these three local bodies; and as from local government re-organization in 1974 the Stratford Town and District Councils shared the old Borough Council's responsibility for sponsorship.

However, as the celebrations developed into a whole weekend of festivities and necessitated the erection of a temporary pavilion marquee to accommodate the growing numbers for luncheon, costs increased significantly. As Chairman and organizer, I therefore found myself in the 1980s having to solicit

The Birthday procession along Church Street

Ceremony of unfurling the flags, Bridge Street

supplementary contributions from individuals and firms that I knew. To beg once for such a worthy cause was not difficult, but to repeat the same exercise year after year became embarrassing and distasteful. This was one of the reasons which made me feel that perhaps the time had come for someone else to take on this task.

The Trustees' appointment of Brigadier David Atkinson as Administrator in 1985 provided a suitable opportunity for me to relinquish the chairmanship of the Shakespeare Birthday Celebrations Committee, a position I had held since 1947. The responsibility for organizing the celebrations then passed to Brigadier Atkinson, who succeeded me as Chairman. The celebrations continued in 1986, 1987 and 1988 on traditional lines, but there was evidence of growing opposition because South Africa, where apartheid was a burning issue, was among the countries invited to take part and we found that pressure was actually being brought to bear on ambassadors and high commissioners to shun the celebrations. In 1988 there were demonstrations as the birthday procession approached Holy Trinity Church, and the customary pleasant atmosphere of the occasion was rudely disturbed. In the interest of safety and the wish to keep the celebrations as a dignified corporate observance, the Celebrations Committee decided to dispense with official representation of the nations accredited to the Court of St James, and from 1989, the year of my retirement as Director, the celebrations took on a different character, with emphasis on local, as opposed to international, participation.

Speaking for myself, I was very sad that political pressure, some of it coming openly from certain members of the Royal Shakespeare Company, should have been allowed to disrupt this festive occasion, which had always been held to be above political opinions, and to change the traditional character of the Shakespeare birthday celebrations. To me, the participation of official representatives of all the nations of the world in friendly observance of Shakespeare's genius made the occasion unique. Indeed, it was the only annual occasion outside London to which members of the entire Diplomatic Corps were invited, and it was one which could only be an influence for good in our divided world. In terms of publicity and prestige and the resultant indirect stimulus to local business, there can be no doubt that Stratford-upon-Avon and Shakespeare, and of course the Shakespeare Centre as the headquarters of the celebrations, benefited substantially from this event; and the evident enjoyment of those taking part was sufficient reward for all the effort involved. The history of the Shakespeare birthday celebrations deserves to be recorded in detail.

Public Relations

As the years passed, the publication relations aspect of my position as Director became increasingly important. I came to enjoy an excellent relationship with the press and the media, and somehow I found time to produce articles and publications designed to provide information about Stratford-upon-Avon, Shakespeare and the Trust's properties. On many occasions I gave interviews to foreign correspondents and feature writers, and invariably sent them away with recorded tape descriptions of the role and work of the Birthplace Trust. Frequently, too, I was asked to give advice and assistance to television companies in connection with filming.

In 1982 I wrote the script for a video-cassette of 'Shakespeare's Stratford', the commentary of which was spoken by Anthony Quayle, with whom I had had a friendly association when he was Director of the Shakespeare Memorial Theatre. This video-cassette was made by Video Tracts, Ltd, of Leamington Spa in association with the Trust, and was distributed by Encyclopaedia Britannica Educational in the United States. I was also responsible for two further video tapes intended for the educational market which were made the following year: 'Shakespeare's Country' and 'The Shakespeare Heritage', also narrated by Anthony Quayle. The former was awarded a gold medal at the British Film and Video Festival in 1984.

I was also actively involved with the BBC in the production of a television programme on the work of the Shakespeare Birthplace Trust, introduced by

Norman Painting, the radio personality. This was shown on 21 April 1985, the day of the Shakespeare birthday celebrations in Stratford, and subsequently repeated. That occasion was the first and only time I had to miss taking part in the celebrations, because I had to leave that day for the United States, where I had been invited to take part in the Shakespeare birthday celebrations in Washington, DC, and to give the annual Ramsbottom Lecture at the Folger Shakespeare Library. It was a prestigious occasion. I was the guest of honour at a dinner at the Library attended by distinguished American public figures and Friends of the Library. There followed my lecture in the Folger's playhouse, a replica of the Globe Theatre, which was packed to capacity, the subject on which I had decided to speak, 'My Loving Good Friend and Countryman', attracting an interested capacity audience. The evening's programme was rounded off with an informal party in the exhibition hall. There I met a number of old friends, who were anxious to have news of Stratford and developments at the Shakespeare Centre. During my short stay in Washington I was able to have useful conversations with the Library's Director, Dr Werner Gunnerheimer, and his staff. In particular, I was shown the extension to the Library, recently completed, and inspected the work of bookbinding and conservation being undertaken.

A few other especially interesting involvements spring to mind. In April 1982 filming for the BBC's 'Blue Peter' television programme took place at the Shakespeare Centre, and later in the summer the BBC filmed the Shakespearian properties for the 'Nationwide' television programme. In 1985 I found myself making a recording for the BBC's Arabic programme, and taking part in a filmed television programme for South Korea. The following year a Chinese television unit made a film of the Shakespearian properties in readiness for the visit of Her Majesty The Queen to China, later in the year. In terms of mere advertisement value, exercises like these were worth an incalculable amount, at the same time providing evidence of the world-wide interest in Shakespeare and Stratford-upon-Avon.

Equally important from a public relations point of view were the various publications for which I was responsible during these years. In 1983 an enlarged paperback edition of *In Honour of Shakespeare* brought my original history of the Trust and its collections up to date and provided a useful reference book to the resources and facilities of the Shakespeare Centre. The small, separate, illustrated booklet guides to the Shakespearian properties, which had proved very popular with visitors for many years, were revised and reissued, and *Historic Stratford-upon-Avon*, *Shakespeare's Town* and *Stratford-upon-Avon and the Shakespeare Country* were added, together with illustrated booklets on *Shakespeare's Flowers* and *Shakespeare's Birds*. The series of gift books I had devised also continued to meet with a regular demand: *Shakespeare's Sonnets*, *The Shakespeare Birthday Book*, *A Shakespeare Treasury* and *The Stratford Shakespeare Anthology*. These modest compilations, intended for people who might have little knowledge of Shakespeare, carry the message of Shakespeare and Stratford-upon-Avon round the world and reach a much wider public than the academic books which continued to be published. The *Stratford-upon-Avon Official Town Guide*, for the design and content of which I was also responsible, served a similar purpose.

Apart from my work for the Trust I continued, with the blessing of the Trustees, to be actively involved with several other local organizations. I have already mentioned the Dugdale Society's close association with the Shakespeare Birthplace Trust. After acting as Secretary and General Editor of the Society for many years, I became its Chairman, a position I still retain. In these capacities I was able to help with the planning and production of a whole series of publications of Warwickshire historical records. I also played an active part in founding and developing the Warwickshire Local History Society, of which I served as founder Chairman and later as President.

Because of my interest in education generally, I gave a good deal of time to Stratford's two grammar schools. I first became a governor of King Edward VI

School in 1953, as the representative of the University of Oxford, and subsequently became a foundation governor. In 1974 I succeeded Professor W.V. Thorpe as Chairman of the governing body and subsequently, with the support of my fellow governors, resisted a proposal to include the School in a comprehensive scheme of education for south Warwickshire which would have changed the status of King Edward VI as a selective grammar school. Our efforts succeeded and so Shakespeare's school was preserved.

I was also the Chairman of the Stratford-upon-Avon Grammar School for Girls, having served as a governor from within a short time after its establishment in the 1950s. Prior to that time Shottery Manor had been the residence of Lt.-Colonel Fordham Flower, whom I occasionally visited there. When he moved to The Hill, following the death of his father, Sir Archibald Flower, the property was purchased by the Warwickshire County Council, and a complex of new buildings added on the site to accommodate a grammar school for girls, which came into existence as an offshoot of the Hugh Clopton High School for Girls on the Alcester road. I had always been interested in the education of young people, and frequently offered them advice about further education or career prospects. Over the years I also made a practice of using senior pupils during the summer visiting season as guides and sales assistants in the Shakespearian properties. Incidentally, it was at my suggestion that the Trustees decided to donate an annual prize to both of these schools.

Another of my involvements, as already mentioned, was with the ancient Guild Chapel. As Chairman of the Friends of the Guild Chapel from their foundation in 1954, I helped to plan and organize the programme of restoration of the fabric of the Chapel and the re-furnishing of its interior over the years. Working closely with the Friends' architect, Mr Stephen Dykes Bower, Surveyor of the Fabric of Westminster Abbey, had given me considerable satisfaction, and, in return for its support, the Trust derived recognition from a growing number of people, many of whom became Friends of the Shakespeare Birthplace Trust.

For me personally it was an incredibly busy life, unique in its combination of practical and scholarly responsibilities and at all times shared by my wife and family. Indeed, without their encouragement and support, whatever modest success I may have achieved as Director would not have been possible. The Trust had developed very much as a family concern.

The Shakespeare Countryside Museum

Apart from the various projects and property matters already mentioned, it was the planning and implementation of the Shakespeare Countryside Museum development at Wilmcote that regularly engaged the attention of the Executive Committee during the 1980s.

The circumstances leading to the purchase of the Glebe Farm by the Trust in 1968 have already been described, and it was the acquisition of this property adjoining Mary Arden's House which gave me the idea of linking the two farmsteads together to make possible a Shakespeare Countryside Museum. Though the continued occupation of the premises by the tenant farmer, Mr George Holmes, prevented immediate action, a good deal of thought was given to a possible development on the lines suggested. The Trust's architect, Mr Laurence Williams, was involved with me in these discussions, and at one point *The Sunday Times* showed interest and bore the cost of preparing a feasibility study. It fell to the Trustees, however, to face up to the implications of an extensive restoration programme of the Glebe farmhouse and the complex of farm buildings, as a preliminary to a complete re-presentation of the Trust's farming and folk-life collections in the more ample accommodation available.

As already mentioned, in 1975 the Trustees sought outline planning permission to link the Glebe Farm with Mary Arden's House. This was granted, but it was not until 1979, following the death of the tenant farmer the previous year, that the Trustees gained possession of the premises. On 22 November 1979 members of the Executive Committee and I paid a memorable visit of inspection to the property. The scene we encountered almost defies description. The approach was from Aston Cantlow Road, through the tied-up remains of what was left of the farm entrance gates leading into the farmyard. By this time willow-herbs, grass and weeds covered the area, on which lay heaps of discarded rubbish and unwanted farming equipment. Looking at the range of farm buildings which enclosed the yard, we saw broken doors, where they existed, hung shapelessly from their rusty hinges, giving the impression of utter neglect and decay. This was emphasized by the precarious condition of the roofs of the buildings, with slipped or missing tiles, and especially by the gaping hole over a large part of the great barn where the supporting rafters had collapsed. Inside, the only evidence of former use was a large, concrete block which had supported some kind of corn dryer or farm machinery. The adjoining stable, hardly recognizable as such, had an accumulation nearly three feet deep of trodden-down straw and dung on the floor, and the small sheds which had been used as calf pens were in a filthy, decayed condition and were obviously overrun with vermin.

A walk round the back of these farm buildings did not give any better impression, though most of the blue-grey stonework with which they were constructed was basically sound. In the small, overgrown paddock which separated the Glebe Farm from Mary Arden's House we saw a broken-down pigsty, the remains of hen pens, and a rusty Nissen hut containing discarded farming implements and sundry piles of wood and corrugated iron hardly visible because of the crop of stinging nettles and rank weeds. Similarly, the area at the front of the farmhouse, which had once been a cultivated country garden, had the appearance of a jungle. The enclosing stone wall separating it from the public footpath had collapsed in part, and only a portion of the hand-gate leading to the front door of the farmhouse remained. The stone paths had disintegrated and were partially covered with grass and weeds, while the few trees were overgrown and bushes and flowers had run wild into a tangled maze.

The prize exhibit, however, was the farmhouse itself, approached by the back door from the farmyard. As we entered, the kitchen, now cleared of the fantastic assortment of miscellaneous items I had seen when it was occupied by the farmer tenant, looked bleak and bare, with its brick floor, stone sink, fireplace and copper, and a few insecure shelves on one side of the room. The living room, with its low, raftered ceiling, small leaded-light windows and stone-flagged floor, appeared exceedingly uncomfortable, cold and uninviting. The iron stove in the fireplace was dirty and turning rusty, and the bare ends of electric wiring visible at various places called attention to an antiquated, unsafe installation. There had in fact been a minor fire a year or two before, caused by a defective electric cable. Peeling whitewash, cobwebs and the general neglect of years similarly characterized the adjoining parlour and emphasized the lack of comfort. We found the dairy, with its original low, stone thralls, looking much as it would have been in Shakespeare's time. The former occupants clearly did not understand hygiene, but at least, with its thick outside wall, tiny window and stone floor, the dairy was cold. Upstairs, where the original timber framed structure and wattled panels still remained, conditions were no different: there was evidence of leaks in the roof; floor boards creaked and in places were unsafe; dust and neglect filled the rooms. Finally, in an apartment approached by a separate staircase from the kitchen, we encountered an antique iron bath with large taps and exposed pipes: the only apology for amenity in the house. Altogether, in the half-light of a November afternoon, we felt that the Glebe farmhouse felt lonely, uncared for and almost eerie; looking round it and the farm buildings just described was a unique experience, a kind of historic flashback.

The outcome of this visit was that the Executive Committee decided to ask the Trust's architect to survey and to report on the physical condition of the farmhouse and the farm buildings generally, as a preliminary to a reconsideration of the possibility of linking the Glebe Farm with Mary Arden's House to form a comprehensive Shakespeare Countryside Museum.

At that time we were all busily engaged with matters concerning the Shakespeare Centre extension, so it was not until the spring of 1982 that plans for the restoration of the property and its future use, prepared by Laurence Williams and myself, were ready for submission to the Executive Committee. The plans, illustrating the use to which the component parts of the farm complex could be put and accompanied by suggestions for a phased sequence of restoration work to be undertaken, were approved, and planning permission and listed building consent were subsequently sought and received from the Stratford-on-Avon District Council.

In December 1982 the Executive Committee accepted the tender of the Stratford firm of Sibbasbridge, Ltd, to carry out the first two stages of the restoration scheme, and during the following year work proceeded. The low range of sheds, formerly used to accommodate calves, was overhauled and subsequently converted and equipped for use as a conservation workshop laboratory.

Conservation workshop

I had always been conscious of the need for the Trust to be able to treat and conserve the varied artefacts in its museum collections, and particularly the old farming tools and implements at Mary Arden's House. It therefore seemed appropriate to establish a facility to provide this service as part of the Shakespeare Countryside Museum project. The advice and financial support of the West Midlands

Area Museum Service, with whose director I had a friendly, fruitful association, were especially helpful in planning and meeting the cost of equipping the workshop. It was brought into use when completed in 1984, and Miss Barbara Clayton, an experienced conservation assistant, was appointed to be responsible for this work. Within a short time of the opening of the facility she was busy undertaking a whole range of museum conservation tasks, from the treatment of Roman coins and Anglo-Saxon pottery to artefacts of the medieval and Tudor periods, and almost any kind of farming tool, implement and domestic utensil.

Alongside the conservation workshop, new toilets for male visitors and a staff room above were provided within the space of one of the former cowshed units. The overhaul of the main barn and the reinstatement of its roof proved to be a major item, and was followed by the re-roofing of the stables and smaller loose-box units looking onto the farmyard. It was interesting to find that, within these small, stone-built compartments, some of the framing of an earlier range of timber-built hovels or sheds on the site had survived. By this time we were fortunate to have the advice and approval of the Department of the Environment, and the Trustees warmly appreciated receiving a grant towards the restoration work from that source.

The second phase of restoration work on the farm buildings having been completed, the land lying between them and the small paddock alongside Mary Arden's House was cleared of all the unwanted erections and debris already described. New fencing and repairs to the boundary wall along Station Road were undertaken, and the ground re-seeded and a number of trees planted. A gravel path linking the Glebe Farm to Mary Arden's House was laid through the extended paddock area, for the purpose of encouraging visitors emerging from Mary Arden's House to follow this route into the Glebe farmyard and so to the farmhouse itself.

In the meantime the architect had completed a detailed survey of the farmhouse and, following a discussion with a representative of the Historic Buildings and Monuments Commission, his report was submitted to the Executive Committee in August 1984.

An examination of the structure had substantiated that the earliest part of the Glebe farmhouse dated back to the sixteenth century and that its plan was similar to that of its larger neighbour, Mary Arden's House. Originally it consisted of a single main hall, open from floor to roof, built on a foundation of Wilmcote stone and of a timber framed construction. As happened to the Arden farmhouse, the open hall had been converted at an early date into two storeys by the insertion of a floor, carrying a bedroom above. This explains why the ceiling of the present living room is so low. At the same time, timber framed wings had been built on both sides of the hall to provide additional accommodation.

The report called attention to the considerable alterations and adaptations made to the farmhouse to meet changing needs over the years. The front and side elevations had been largely re-faced in brick, and much of the timber framing at ground floor level had been removed; yet upstairs most of the original timber work, with its wattle and daub, remained intact. Inside, an early twentieth-century iron range had been inserted in the original open hearth, and the chimney-stack above the roof had been renewed in brick. Similarly, the bake-oven had been discarded and bricked up when no longer required. These items are mentioned as being typical of the kind of changes that had taken place.

The report left the Executive Committee in no doubt that a major overhaul and restoration of the farmhouse needed to be undertaken, and there was ready agreement that the programme of work suggested should be put in hand as the next instalment of the museum project. An important decision of principle, however, was made. It was decided that no attempt should be made to reproduce the original sixteenth-century structure and appearance of the building. Traditional materials were to be used to effect all necessary repairs to the house in its present condition, the idea being to preserve it as an example of a farmhouse which had undergone successive

The Glebe Farm, as restored

such as the underpinning of the exterior walls, which, it was found, had only the most shallow of foundations, and the treatment and pointing of the brickwork at the front of the building, which was pitted with holes caused by masonry bees. Re-roofing, drainage and the overhaul of the brick chimney stacks caused no problem. Doors and window frames and their leaded-light glazing had to be renewed throughout. Inside the house, the paved stone floors were taken up and re-laid; exposed timber-work was repaired as necessary, scraped and treated; defective plaster-work and panels were repaired; and a comprehensive cleaning and refurbishing undertaken before final redecoration. Up-to-date concealed electrical wiring, fire detection and security systems were installed. A further grant towards the cost of certain parts of the work just described was received from the Historic Buildings and Monuments Commission.

Whilst this work was proceeding, the remaining farm buildings at the rear of the farmhouse received attention. The granary, approached by a flight of stone steps, was restored and subsequently used as an office for an assistant, whom the Trustees authorized me to recruit to help with the farming collection and the display arrangements of the Shakespeare Countryside Museum which was beginning to take shape. The ground-floor storage shed underneath the granary was converted to provide toilet facilities for female visitors, and the pigsty nearby was reinstated ready for use. The well near the back door, which had provided drinking water for the farmhouse and which had been covered over when no longer required, was opened to view again; it was lined with Wilmcote stone, and a timber well top incorporating a windlass for operating a bucket to draw water from the well was erected over the well shaft. I personally designed this well top, as a replica of one which I remembered as a boy at my grandfather's small holding and which was regularly used to supply all the drinking water.

alterations at various times from the sixteenth century onwards.

Work on the Glebe farmhouse was begun by Sibbasbridge, Ltd, in the early autumn of 1984 and continued throughout the following year. Some tricky, unforeseen problems had to be dealt with,

Meanwhile the plot of ground at the front of the farmhouse, which had once been the garden, was cleared, laid out and planted as a typical country garden. I greatly enjoyed planning this with the help of Michael Johnson, the Trust's head gardener who, being a countryman like myself, had personal knowledge of the items which should be included. Paths of broken stone were put down, and another well, discovered during the process of clearance, had a new circular top of stone built round it so that its Wilmcote stone lining with water at the bottom could be seen. A narrow edging border was prepared around the house and planted with simple, country flowers and climbing roses against the walls. A small patch was left for vegetables at one end of the garden; the middle part was planted with a variety of shrubs, herbaceous flowers and old varieties of roses; the other end was grassed, but broken up by a selection of fruit trees, and gooseberry and currant bushes; and a separate plot of herbs at the end of the house completed the layout. Two beehives were placed nearby.

At Mary Arden's House the building programme envisaged in the Shakespeare Countryside Museum blueprint was continued during 1985 and completed in time for the 1986 season. In addition to the provision of disabled persons' toilet facilities alongside the visitors' toilet block already built, a lecture room adjoining the existing reception building was constructed, together with a kitchen and a room for the service of refreshments.

These new buildings of brick with clay-tiled roofs completed the enclosure of the former rick-yard, and they were designed with a separate entrance from the car park so that they could be used for local functions at times when Mary Arden's House was closed to visitors. Their primary purpose, however, was to make possible the future development of educational activities related to the Shakespeare Countryside Museum. The number of organized school party visits was increasing year by year, and the need for a lecture room where talks and demonstrations could be given was being increasingly felt.

The contract for this part of the work was awarded to John Harris and Sons, Ltd, a highly respected family firm of Stratford builders. The Trustees were fortunate to receive a grant from the English Tourist Board towards the capital cost of these additions. In July 1986 the Chairman of the Board, Mr Duncan Black, unveiled a plaque to mark the completion of the lecture room block.

As building operations reached their final phase, I found myself giving much time and thought to the general presentation of the Shakespeare Countryside Museum and the use to which the new accommodation provided could be put. I was quite certain that, linked together, Mary Arden's House and the adjacent Glebe Farm would make an ideal setting to illustrate the theme of English rural life from Tudor times to the twentieth century, using the considerable collection of farming and folk material built up by the Trust over a period of some fifty years.

Although attractive in many ways, the informal arrangements for the display of the farming collection in the barns at Mary Arden's House needed improving and, in particular, descriptive information about the exhibits was required. It was at this juncture that, acting on the advice of the Area Museums Service, which was prepared to assist with the cost, I sought the assistance of a firm of museum designers, John Kirk, Ltd, who were able to make available the services of an experienced graphic artist. The result was the production of a series of well designed, durable panels, incorporating information and woodcut illustrations. The open-fronted hovel adjoining the reception building was adapted to accommodate a display of these panels, for the purpose of introducing to visitors at the point of entrance the concept and the content of the Countryside Museum. It was in fact a tabloid exhibition, giving basic information about Shakespeare's Warwickshire, the Arden family, Mary Arden's House and a number of facets of rural life in Elizabethan England.

The wagons, carts, farm implements, fire engine and gypsy caravans on display in the open-fronted sheds round the rick-yard were refurbished, and information and interpretative panels were placed in the cider press house, the cow byre and the dovecote. The idea was to provide for the visitors sufficient information and explanation to bring to life the purpose and use of the buildings in question.

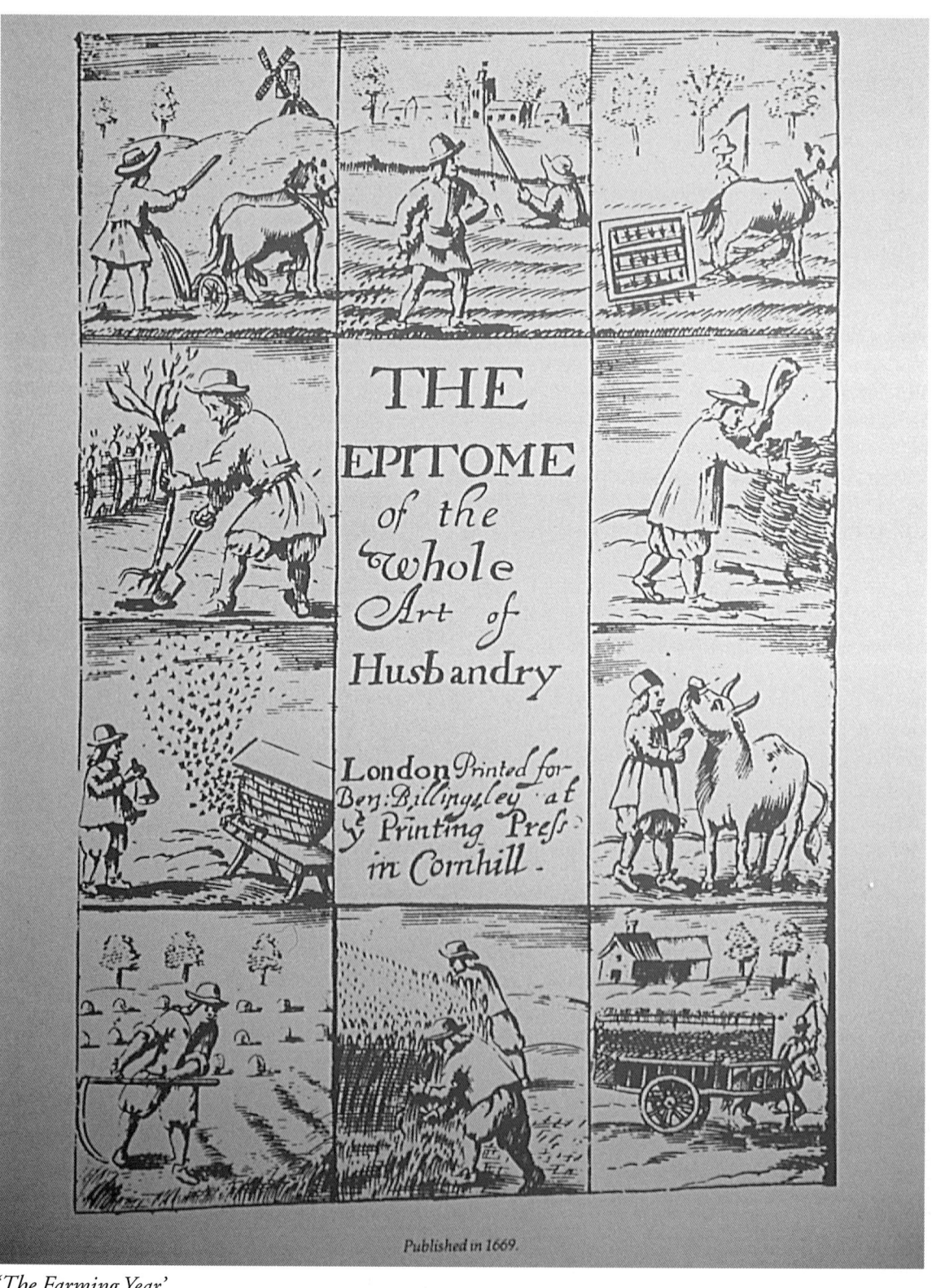

'The Farming Year'

Mary Arden's farmhouse itself, already furnished in characteristic period style, needed little attention, because over the years I had been careful in the arrangement of the furnishings to attempt to recreate the atmosphere of domestic life in Tudor times. Though now presenting a tidy appearance, with polished furniture and cooking utensils, the focal point of interest in the kitchen was the large, open hearth, appropriately equipped, where meat was roasted on the spit and food cooked in a variety of pots and containers. The great hall, which was the principal living room of the Arden family, was furnished with pieces of furniture made by country craftsmen and similar to those which Mary Arden would have recognized. The tall-backed settle, dining table, joint stools and court cupboard, together with a variety of smaller items and utensils, suggested comfortable living quarters, the focus of the family's everyday life; and the dairy, leading from the hall, with its milk pails and cheese and butter making utensils, provided a reminder of the basic role of the farmhouse.

The stable and barns afforded an opportunity for a new presentation. Until the advent of mechanization, the horse had provided the motive power required for all farm operations other than those performed by oxen or manual labour. In the original stable, exhibits illustrating the feeding and grooming of horses and their harness for different functions were displayed, together with the equipment of the horse doctor, frequently the blacksmith, who discharged the duties of the present veterinary office.

The treatment of the great barn presented a challenge. It had hitherto accommodated an extraordinary medley of agricultural implements, farming tools and reminders of rural life in Shakespeare's Warwickshire. I decided that a more selective, meaningful approach would add to the educational and general interest of the collection, and I adopted as its theme 'The Farming Year', as originally described and illustrated in *The Epitome of the Whole Art of Husbandry*, published in 1669. The spacious barn, with its whitewashed walls, provided an ideal setting for a display of implements and tools, accompanied by descriptive panels illustrative of the work of a farmer in winter, spring, summer and autumn. Though many of the farming exhibits used in the display were of later date, they would have been recognizable to a Tudor farmer. The inclusion of contemporary woodcuts and the costumed figure of a ploughman using a breast plough added a feeling of life to these museum groupings.

The path through the small paddock linking Mary Arden's House to the Glebe Farm was directly in line with the large double doors of a building which conveniently provided an entrance to the Glebe farmyard. Inside this building, which had originally served as a storage barn for hay and feeding stuffs, there was space on either side of the central path suitable for display. It occurred to me that at this point visitors would find it interesting to

'The Farming Year' displays inside the great barn

Craftwork displays at the Glebe Farm

encounter exhibits which illustrated the materials and building methods used in the construction of farm and cottage properties in Tudor times.

The space on one side was accordingly used to present a model of a mason, dressed in his working clothes, building a wall of the same blue-grey lias stone which had been used in the construction of Mary Arden's House, the Glebe Farm and many similar buildings in the surrounding countryside. Wilmcote stone, the quarrying of which continued until the early years of the present century, was also widely used for paving slabs and in the production of lime and cement. An enlarged photographic picture of the quarry men at work in the early 1900s provided an appropriate background for this exhibit.

Oak and elm timber from the Forest of Arden, nearby, was the other basic material used in the construction of buildings in the Shakespeare countryside from the fifteenth to the seventeenth century.

Opposite to the Wilmcote stone display, the space was accordingly used to illustrate how timber framed buildings were prepared and constructed. A model of a carpenter, dressed in a style appropriate to his craft, was presented with his tools, working on the timber members of a framed building and against the background of a pair of curved timbers, pegged together and erected as they would have been in a house-building operation. I very much enjoyed planning this particular exhibit, which was constructed by one of the Trust's employees, Robert Whitehead, who was a superb craftsman. We went to untold trouble to get the detail of this display correct, as evidenced by the fact that Robert searched the woods of Ragley Hall, with the permission of the Marquess of Hertford, to find shaped trees suitable for constructing the crucks.

The same care was expended in the treatment of the stable, which was used to illustrate country crafts and particularly those of the carpenter, wheelwright and cooper, who made vital contributions to rural life. Apart from the construction of buildings, the carpenter made farming tools, furniture and domestic items, as well as coffins, and acted as undertaker. Over the years the Trust had built up a considerable collection of different types of old carpentry tools, including a foot-propelled lathe, so with the help of our own Robert the carpenter it was not difficult to re-erect a realistic carpenter's workshop.

The same applied to the craft of the cooper, whose speciality was the making of barrels of different shapes and sizes for the storage of beer, wine, and dry goods such as flour, salted fish, lime and crockery. A complete collection of a cooper's working tools, given to the Trust a few years before, provided the nucleus of an authentic presentation. In a similar way, the wheelwright's display was assembled around the contents of a wheelwright's workshop, including a lathe and parts of wheels in process of being made, which had been presented to the Trust by the family of Parsons of Shawell, a small village in Leicestershire, situated off the Watling Street just over the Warwickshire boundary. This came about as the result of a visit I paid to Mrs Parsons, a widow whose husband's workshop had remained virtually untouched since his death many years ago. The special tools used by the wheelwright to make and repair wagons, carts and various farm implements were exhibited. Seasoned elm, oak and ash were used for the hub, spokes and felloes of a wheel.

It now remained to illustrate the craft of the blacksmith, who was an indispensable member of the rural community. His regular task was to shoe horses (now undertaken by the farrier) and to make all the wrought-iron implements and tools needed for the farm, the house and other craftsmen. To the best of my knowledge the Glebe Farm never had a forge of its own, but I decided that the end portion of the great barn, approached by the double doors from the farmyard, was a suitable place to construct one, as a working example of this important rural craft. In the village where I lived as a boy, I had often watched the blacksmith at work in his smithy and I had a good mental picture of what would be needed. Moreover, the Trust already had in its collection much of the equipment and tools that would be required. An excellent specimen of a blacksmith's bellows, for instance, had for years been included in the display of bygones in the barn at Mary Arden's House; the anvil which was used by Bert Edge, the Stratford blacksmith in Mansell Street who often did repair work for the Trust, had been presented to us after his death; and I had had the good fortune to buy sundry blacksmith's equipment and tools from the disbanded village forge at Pebworth. All this needed to be brought together to form a working smithy.

It was at this juncture that quite fortuitously I received an enquiry from a man seeking employment, Mr R.R. (Bob) Mewis, who had worked as a blacksmith for most of his life. Realizing how useful he could be to the Trust, I offered to take him onto the Trust's maintenance staff. This enabled me to call on his experience in constructing and equipping the forge, which, when completed, proved most satisfactory. Within a short time the blacksmith was able to meet the Trust's own requirements for any type of iron work and also to demonstrate to visitors, as he worked at the forge, the basics of his own craft. This

THE SHAKESPEARE BIRTHPLACE TRUST

element of live activity was an integral ingredient of my Shakespeare Countryside Museum project.

The basic pattern of country life had changed little from Shakespeare's time to the early years of the present century. With this in mind, I felt that the Glebe farmhouse presented an opportunity to portray the way of life of a farming family living in a house which had been altered and improved over the years. Because of safety and security considerations, it was not possible to allow the public to inspect the bedrooms on the first floor; but the ground-floor rooms were readily accessible to visitors from the farmyard. Using material already owned by the Trust and with the addition of exhibits loaned by the Zanussi collection, the farmhouse interior was furnished and equipped with typical domestic items, as it would have been when lived in by a farming family in Victorian or Edwardian times.

The living room was simply furnished with a large working table, chairs and dresser displaying plates and storage jars, and a child's high chair. Life in a farmhouse was always busy, because the family was to a large extent self-supporting. This was suggested by a full-size figure of a farmer's elderly wife, sitting by the table plucking a chicken, and by the various utensils ready for cooking preparations. A traditional cloth-pegged rug on the hearth in front of the iron grate and a variety of ornaments on the fringed mantel piece added a touch of comfort and atmosphere.

The parlour, used for special occasions, was furnished as the best room. It had pictures on the walls, a grandfather clock, comfortable chairs, a table and a chest of drawers. A sewing box, needlework table and hand-operated sewing machine were evidence of useful activity by the lady members of the household; and a parlour, in which occasional visitors were entertained, would not have been complete without a large aspidistra in a colourful jardinière.

The remaining rooms were presented to illustrate the purposes they served. The kitchen, with its iron stove, stone sink and brick-built copper, was a busy place, where daily cooking, washing up and the laundering of clothes took place. It was never a tidy

Inside the Glebe Farm house: the living room, the parlour and the ktichen

room, with buckets and other utensils standing around, and it must have been a nightmare to keep clean as muddy boots from the farmyard came in and out. The kitchen, to my mind, made a perfect setting to portray one of the farmhouse women doing the household laundry in the early 1900s.

The dairy, with its thick walls and small windows, maintained a cool temperature and provided ideal conditions for the making of butter and cheese, which involved the use of a whole range of utensils and equipment; specimens of these were assembled and displayed on the stone slabs and shelves, so as to emphasize the essential role of the dairy in the running of the farmhouse. The sunken store at the back of the building was similarly presented, to illustrate its use as a place where game and perishable goods were kept. Here, as elsewhere in the house, experience of the family's practical needs determined the furnishings and equipment provided.

Most of the work just described was carried out during the years 1986 to 1988. The cost of it represented a major conservation investment, and the Trustees were grateful to receive a further contribution from the Historic Buildings and Monuments Commission towards certain items of builders' work at the farmhouse, and a general grant from the West Midlands Area Museums Service towards the Countryside Museum project.

A capital grant of £8,000 was also received in 1988 towards the cost of a large timber framed shed, built at this time, for the storage and conservation of some of the larger farm exhibits. It was a good example of traditional craftsmanship and was the work of Mr Gordon Lawrence and the Trust's own maintenance men. The shed was sited behind the rick-yard at Mary Arden's House, alongside the extended area of the visitors' car park, which it had been possible to provide as the result of a gift of a small portion of the adjoining field by the trustees of the Simms estate in 1984. A covered loggia adjoining the servery to the lecture room was also constructed at this time.

It is worth recording that at no time did it prove necessary to close the property to the public whilst building operations and the re-presentation of the museum collections were in progress. On the contrary, the appeal of Mary Arden's House continued to grow as the new Shakespeare Countryside Museum development became more widely known. In 1984 the number of visitors exceeded one hundred thousand for the first time. The actual number was 103,162. In 1985 the total admissions rose to 115,618 and, although the next two years showed a small decrease, the total was back to 100,852 in 1988. By this time the potential of the whole concept had become very evident and, with the idea of augmenting income, an arrangement was negotiated for the display and sale of products made by local crafts people in one of the buildings in the Glebe farmyard and for a programme of craft demonstrations during the summer months.

The setting of the combined farmsteads came to be used for special events. Each year the Trustees allowed the residents of Wilmcote to use it for their annual fete, and the village school for its fund raising event. There were also one or two special occasions, such as in May 1988 when, in co-operation with the Warwickshire and West Midlands Rare Breeds Survival Support Group, a display of rare breeds of farm animals was arranged in the paddock. Soon afterwards the Trust acquired two bantam hens and a cockerel, a modest beginning from which followed the more ambitious collection of poultry, sheep and other farm stock after I retired.

By the beginning of 1989 the Shakespeare Countryside Museum was in all its essentials complete, and I suggested to the Executive Committee that the time had come for an official opening. The Trustees readily agreed, and decided to invite Lord Plumb of Coleshill, himself a Warwickshire farmer and President of the European Parliament, to perform the opening ceremony.

The opening ceremony took place on Friday, 1 June 1989. It was a warm, sunny day and, accompanied by the Chairman and members of the Executive Committee and myself, Lord Plumb made a leisurely inspection of the two properties during the second half of the morning. He was particularly complimentary about the general concept of illustrating rural life from Tudor to modern times in the setting of the original buildings of Mary Arden's House and the Glebe Farm; and he obviously enjoyed viewing the individual displays. The company then adjourned to the Billesley Manor Hotel

Lord Plumb of Coleshill at the official opening of the Shakespeare Countryside Museum

for lunch, and by the time we returned a large number of representative guests invited to attend the official opening had assembled.

In introducing the proceedings, the Chairman of the Trust, Mr Dennis Flower, described the Shakespeare Countryside Museum project as a major conservation achievement of a very special kind, which had taken the best part of a decade to complete. He paid tribute to all those who had been involved in the various stages of work, whether the restoration of the buildings or the presentation of the exhibits. In welcoming Lord Plumb, he referred to the valuable service he had given to the cause of English farming and his outstanding record as President of the European Parliament. It was, he said, a great honour for Shakespeare's Warwickshire to have produced a farmer worthy of holding such a position of international importance. In reply, Lord Plumb expressed his pleasure in being associated with a project so near to his heart and he commended the Trustees and the Director on their imaginative portrayal of English social history in such a realistic and meaningful manner. The educational importance of what had been achieved, he observed, could not be over estimated. At the Chairman's invitation he then planted a half-standard plum tree of a variety known as the Warwickshire Drooper and unveiled four panels of Hornton stone surrounding it, with the following inscriptions carved by Richard Kindersley:

MARY ARDEN'S HOUSE
THE HOME OF
SHAKESPEARE'S MOTHER
WAS PURCHASED FOR PRESERVATION
BY THE
SHAKESPEARE BIRTHPLACE TRUST
IN 1930

THE GLEBE FARM
A FARMSTEAD OF SIMILAR DATE
BUT ALTERED OVER THE YEARS
WAS ACQUIRED IN 1968
& SUBSEQUENTLY RESTORED

LINKED TOGETHER
THEY ACCOMMODATE A
SHAKESPEARE COUNTRYSIDE
MUSEUM
OF EXHIBITS ILLUSTRATIVE OF
FARMING AND RURAL LIFE
FROM TUDOR TO MODERN TIMES

THE MUSEUM
WAS OFFICIALLY OPENED
ON 1 JUNE 1989 BY
LORD PLUMB OF COLESHILL
A WARWICKSHIRE FARMER
AND PRESIDENT OF
THE EUROPEAN PARLIAMENT

Ten days later a special week-end event was held in celebration of British Food and Farming 1989, and rare breeds of farm animals and many other farming and rural attractions were to be seen in the paddock between Mary Arden's House and the Glebe Farm. The Shakespeare Countryside Museum had already come into its own!

The Record Ends: My Final Years

It was not easy to relinquish my position as Director of the Trust after so many years of demanding and satisfying work. But it had to be.

Having been blessed with good health and never having given any thought about my age, I still felt able to manage the affairs of the Trust without undue effort and to keep building on the foundations laid over the years. I still had dreams of extending the Trust's influence in various ways. My capacity for work remained undiminished and my relations with the Trustees and staff had never been better, as had been shown by the surprise party arranged by the Trustees and staff to mark the completion of my forty years' service as Director in the autumn of 1985. Meetings of the Executive Committee and the full governing body continued to be enjoyable and my contacts with a wide circle of Shakespeare friends abroad gave me considerable pleasure. Indeed, Shakespeare and the Trust had completely taken over my life.

One or two of the Trustees sometimes joked about my youthful appearance and, when the question of my retirement was raised, they felt that I could continue for a further indefinite period; but there was an understandable anxiety on the part of some of them as to what would happen if I fell ill or had an accident. It was because of this that at the beginning of 1986 the Chairman conferred informally with members of the Executive Committee about possible arrangements to take care of the future Directorship of the Trust. Mr Flower subsequently talked with me and suggested that I should consider the matter and make a proposal about an acceptable date for my retirement.

This was not an easy time for me, but I was sufficiently experienced to appreciate the Trustees' concern to safeguard the future management of the Trust. For the record, I formed the impression that one or two members of the Executive Committee had a possible successor in mind; but, throughout, the Chairman made it clear that the decision when to retire was mine. I was not subjected to pressure and when, after careful thought, I decided to suggest 30 September 1989 as the date for my retirement, this was accepted by the Executive Committee and a report to this effect was submitted to the Half Annual Meeting of Trustees on 24 October 1987.

The Executive Committee was authorized to take all necessary action, and a special meeting was held on 30 November 1987 at which preliminary consideration was given to the question of future arrangements for the Trust and the appointment of a successor from the time of my retirement at the end of September 1989. By invitation of the Committee, I took part in these full and friendly discussions.

The Executive Committee appointed a special committee, representative of all the categories of Trustees on the governing body, to deal with the matter. It was agreed that this Committee should report to the Executive Committee, which in turn would report and submit a recommendation to all the Trustees.

At the beginning of 1988 it was decided to advertise the post in the national press, and I found myself drafting the advertisement and preparing a job description, together with a general statement about the Trust and its activities, for approval by the Committee. There was an excellent response, applications being received from academics, retired service personnel, and administrative and business people, including a few from abroad. These were considered in detail by members of the Special Committee and appropriate enquiries made.

Of the applications received, the one which commended itself most was that of Mr Roger Pringle, Deputy Director of the Trust since October 1985, which I myself strongly supported. I had in fact appointed him nearly twenty years before as the Trust's first educational assistant, and had good reason to know his qualifications and suitability for the position. With such an unusual institution as the Trust, continuity was in my opinion all important and I felt confident that, given a little time, I could impart to Roger Pringle, if appointed, information and expertise about areas of the Trust's work with which he had not as yet been closely involved.

After an interview, the Special Committee reported to the Executive Committee that they recommended Roger Pringle, Master of Arts of Cambridge University, for appointment as my successor. The recommendation was unanimously endorsed by the Executive Committee and subsequently the whole governing body at the Half Annual Meeting of the Trust on 5 November 1988.

I was greatly relieved when the succession was settled, and delighted that of their own accord the Trustees had appointed the candidate of my choice. The remaining months before I handed over to Roger Pringle seemed to pass all too quickly, but I was able to devote time to explain to him the many facets of his responsibilities.

Otherwise, it was business as usual for me. Visitor patronage still continued to be less certain than I would have hoped, but admissions to the Shakespearian properties during 1988 showed a slight increase over the previous year, the numbers for the properties being as follows:

Shakespeare's Birthplace	587,670
Anne Hathaway's Cottage	371,198
New Place	78,927
Mary Arden's House	100,852
Hall's Croft	75,249
Total:	1,213,896

Due to economic recession, the visitors from our own country showed little increase and Americans were still reluctant to travel; but visitors from the European countries and particularly from Japan contributed to make good the numbers.

Indeed, the international regard for Shakespeare and Stratford-upon-Avon became increasingly evident and this was illustrated by the distinguished visitors who came from time to time. During 1988 these included the Minister of Foreign Affairs for the People's Republic of China, the wife of the Minister of Transport for the Hungarian People's Republic, the Deputy Minister of Agriculture, Forestry and Food for the Polish People's Republic, and the Burgomaster and a group from Diever in the Netherlands, where an annual Shakespeare Festival had become established, who presented a five-volume illustrated edition of Shakespeare's *Complete Works* in Dutch for the library.

The usual miscellany of practical matters in connection with the Trust's let properties also received attention and, as already described, the Shakespeare Tree Garden, the Shakespeare Countryside Museum and the archives conservation workshop were all completed. On the academic front the Centre library became increasingly recognized and used as a base for theatre study, while the Trust's educational activities made significant progress. By the time I retired new policy lines for future development in association with the University of Birmingham had already been agreed.

At the Annual Meeting of the Trustees in May 1989 the Chairman, Dennis Flower, referred to my forthcoming departure and spoke in warm, appreciative terms of my unique contribution to the development of the Trust and of the satisfactory state in which I would be handing over the Trust's affairs to the new Director. The Trust's financial basis had never been more secure; a cash reserve in excess of two and a quarter million pounds had been built up, which, in the absence of an endowment fund, provided both an adequate safeguard against possible tourist recession and a firm basis for future development.

The Trustees contributed personally to a presentation for me, but I found it difficult to suggest what form this should take. No immediate, desirable need on the domestic front suggested itself so, with the agreement of my wife and family, I decided to use the money which had been given towards meeting

Dr Levi Fox: commemorative plaque

the cost of producing a sundial, designed by Richard Kindersley, for presentation to the Trust as an adornment to the great barn at Mary Arden's House. I had always felt that a farmstead of the standing of the Arden family's could well have possessed a sundial; and it seemed appropriate that my association with this property should be marked in this way, providing at the same time an additional item of interest for visitors.

During my final week in office I arranged farewell parties at the Shakespeare Centre for friends, colleagues, Trustees and representatives of a few of the firms with which I had built up associations over the years. They were very happy and successful occasions and made me realize the value of personal relations and how fortunate the Trust and its retiring Director had been in enjoying the interest and support of so many different people.

The most moving occasion, however, was on the evening of 26 September 1989 when, in the presence of members of the Executive Committee and their wives, Lady Hersey Flower, widow of the late Sir Fordham, my first Chairman, unveiled a plaque fixed to the brick wall immediately inside the entrance hall of the Shakespeare Centre. The plaque was of a light-coloured Derbyshire stone and incorporated a bronze medallic portrait of myself, executed by my old friend the eminent medallist, Paul Vincze, and an inscription, composed by the Executive Committee and carved by Richard Kindersley.

The company then proceeded to the Welcombe Hotel, where a dinner in my honour had been arranged by the Trustees. There could not have been a more friendly, happy send-off, and I shall always remember the moving tribute paid to me by the Chairman, Mr Dennis Flower. My only personal regret was that my wife, who for many years had been confined to home with rheumatoid arthritis, was not able to share the occasion with me.

There was another memorable party at the Shakespeare Centre on 30 September, which did not involve the Trustees. This was attended by upwards of two hundred present and former members of staff. My successor, Roger Pringle, gave a well researched, illustrated 'This is Your Life' tribute on behalf of the company present, as a preliminary to the presentation of several parting gifts, which included a portrait of myself by the local artist, John Corvin. It was an emotional experience for me, but I shall never forget the warm affection and friendship which permeated the whole proceedings. It was truly a family occasion. In the response I had to make I expressed my appreciation to the Trustees and staff, and spelled out the philosophy of team effort, which had made possible the achievement of my forty-four years.

A few weeks later, on the occasion of the Half Annual Meeting of the Trustees held on 28 October 1989, I received the signal honour of being appointed a Life Trustee of Shakespeare's Birthplace. The proposition, which was unanimously carried, was made by the Deputy Chairman, Mr Peter Boddington, with whom I had established a close friendship going back to 1967, when he was first elected a Local Trustee. He paid tribute to my 'great record of service' and described me as 'possessing a very rare combination of qualities, including both historical learning and extraordinary administrative ability'. I was also invited to plant a young mulberry tree in the Birthplace garden near to the ancient parent tree, which had collapsed during the summer.

A further pleasant surprise followed: at the Annual Meeting held on 19 May 1990, the Trustees unanimously decided to confer on me the honorary title of Director Emeritus, in recognition, so the minute said, of my 'unique service to the organization'.

INDEX

Sources

The documentation on which this history is based is very considerable, because right from the beginning the records of the events leading to the establishment of the Shakespeare Birthplace Trust and its subsequent development over the years have been carefully preserved.

Starting with the minute book of *The Shakespearian Monumental Committee*, there is a complete series of minutes recording the proceedings of the Trustees from the time the decision was made to purchase Shakespeare's Birthplace for preservation as a national memorial right down to the present. The minute books are impressive well-bound volumes of folio size and, throughout, the minutes are handwritten. There are typewritten copies of most of the minutes since 1945.

Printed annual reports contain summary supplementary information concerning the Trustees, the principal events and activities of the year, accessions to the collections, the number of visitors to the properties and a statement of income and expenditure. Until 1945 the format of these reports was a folded sheet of folio size, but from that date separate quarto-sized annual reports and accounts, giving greater detail, were produced. Press reports of the proceedings of Annual Meetings often add further details.

The Trust's book-keeping records have been preserved intact, together with a mass of supporting material in the form of invoices, bank records and day-books kept at the different properties. From the time of my appointment as Director, my annual budgets and financial statements, staff and wages records with confidential establishment review papers, and auditors' reports are available. Taken together, they give a detailed insight into the business side of the Trust's work.

A separate category comprises the Shakespeare Birthplace Trust Acts and the title deeds to the Shakespearian buildings and the other properties acquired by the Trust over the years at different times, together with associated documentation. When alterations and improvements have taken place, the architect's reports and plans have been kept; and for the Shakespeare Centre, both the original building and the extension, a complete archive is available.

With regard to correspondence, prior to my appointment most replies were written by hand by my predecessors, so that it follows that only incoming letters are available up to 1945. As from that date every single letter received and reply sent has been kept, thus providing a complete record illustrating the day-to-day management of the many facets of the Trust's activities. In addition to the general files there are separate categories for special projects, events and activities, particularly for the Stratford-upon-Avon Poetry Festivals, exhibitions and royal visits, the Shakespeare quatercentenary celebrations, the Garrick Jubilee anniversary programme, annual Shakespeare birthday celebrations, accessions to the Trust's collections, the International Shakespeare Association and the Friends of Shakespeare's Birthplace.

My book *In Honour of Shakespeare: The History and Collections of the Shakespeare Birthplace Trust* (1972 and 1982), press reports, photographs, film and tape recordings, together with architects' plans and drawings, provide further material illustrative of special occasions and projects described in the history.

The Trust's collection of prints and photographs is remarkably comprehensive. Over the years photographs and recordings from newspapers, magazines and the media have been presented to the Trust, and a number of these have been used in the book.

The series of albums containing the signatures and addresses of visitors to Shakespeare's Birthplace, dating from the early years of the last century down to the present, constitute a unique source of evidence of the progressive growth of the Birthplace's popularity as a shrine of literary pilgrimage and, particularly, of its international appeal.

Lastly, my personal appointment diaries have been useful for checking dates, and my own recollections have provided information not recorded elsewhere.

Index

Abraham, Harold   232, 236, 241, 269
Accessions   35-39, 72-75, 127, 128, 210-219, 252-256, 319-323
Accessions Reserve   210
Acts of Parliament   144, 346
– Shakespeare Birthplace Trust Act 1891   24, 27, 42, 52, 63, 81, 144, 146
– Shakespeare Birthplace Trust Amendment Act 1930   27, 81, 144, 146
– Shakespeare Birthplace Trust Act 1961   107, 144-148
Adams, Bill (electrician)   283
Adams, John Quincy   139
Adams, Kingsley   212
Admission charges   33, 43, 49, 84, 90, 121, 122, 202, 242, 300
Alamein (house)   136
Albany House   246
Albert, HRH The Prince   5
Aldermen of the Borough   17, 25, 27, 81, 103, 107, 119, 145, 147, 179
Aldwych Theatre   221
Allan, Sir William (painter)   214
Alexandra, Princess of Kent   158-160, 293
Alexandra, Queen   56
Alexandrov, Professor A.D.   131
Allen, T.T. (architect)   20
Allot, Robert, *Englands Parnassus*   72
Alscot Park   140, 211
Alto-relievo Shakespeare statue   32, 33, 56
Alveston   86
Alveston Manor   58
America   173
American Bicentennial celebrations   262-263
American 1964 Shakespeare Committee   173, 174, 191, 193, 195
– 1964 celebrations   173, 191-197, 267
American visit   137-143, 258-259
Amhurst, Lord, of Hackney   39
Amyot, Thomas   5-6

Andrews, Harry   109
Anglia Television   198
Anglo-Holt Construction, Ltd   305
Anglo-Saxon archaeological collection   57-58, 331
Ankara University   131
Anne Hathaway's Cottage   4, 25-26, 29, 39, 40, 41-46, 48-49, 59-62, 68, 81, 84-88, 90-91, 122-124, 127, 135-136, 183, 199-201, 203, 230-236, 240-244, 256, 266, 268-271, 298-299, 304-308, 310, 312-314, 316, 322-323, 342
– Fire   230-236
Anne, Princess   134, 267-270
Ansell, Bob (brewer)   207
Anthony, Alfred, and Mrs   56, 85
Antony and Cleopatra   73
Apothecaries' jars   58-59, 104, 264
Appeal   155-156, 168-172, 278, 291-292
Arbuthnot, Rev. George   43
Archer, J.W.   6
Archer and Coote   170
Archer collection   128
Archive Conservation Workshop   309, 342
Arden family   63, 333
Arden, Robert   63, 65
– Mary   63, 335
Arden's Grafton   67
Arne, Dr Thomas   227
– Oratorio, *Judith*   227
Arnold, Dr, of Rugby School   190
Artistic embellishments   163-167, 285-290
Arts Council   110, 118, 147-148, 171, 183, 186, 209, 257, 323-324
Ascham, Roger *The Schole Maister*   39
Ash, Graham Baron (trustee)   79, 80, 81, 83, 103, 126, 148, 154
Ashcroft, Dame Peggy   134, 226-228, 257, 297
Ashby-de-la-Zouch, Leics.   105
– Grammar School, History of   184

Ashford, Elizabeth Davenport   75
Ashland, Oregon   238
Ashmolean Museum   39
Ashwin, E.   4
Ashwin, Mrs (custodian)   18
Ashwin, M.C.   28
Aston Cantlow   67, 209, 247, 263, 298, 329
As You Like It   134
Athlone, Earl of   105
Atkinson, Brigadier David   296, 326
Atkinson, John   17
Atkinson, Rosalind   109
Audio and visual collection   211
Auction room scene   5-6
Australia   8, 49
Avon, Lord (Sir Anthony Eden)   81, 131, 148, 174, 186
– Lady   131, 174
Avon, River   288

Bacon, Delia   191
Bacon, Francis   175
Baddesley Clinton collection   73, 263, 298, 321
Badger, George   52
Bahrain   131
Baildham, Councillor Eric   92
Baker, Ernest Edward   24-25, 38, 43-44, 47
Baker, Isaac Edwin   31
Baker, Mr of Wellesbourne   32
Baker, Jane   44
Baker, Mrs Mary   41, 43-45, 62, 67, 234, 256
Baker, Oliver   65
Baker, William   43-44, 59, 62
Ball Bros.   66
Balmford, D.M. and Mrs   159
Banbury   13
Bardsley, Rt Rev. Cuthbert, Bishop   139, 148, 221-222, 227

347

Barnum, Phineas T. 238
Barrett, Pat 286, 287
Barrough *Method of physick* 210
Barry, E.M. (architect) 11, 12
Bartlett, Eric (painter) 126
Basson, Percy (bricklayer) 126
Bean, H. 85
Bearman, Dr Robert (archivist) 202
Beattie, Dr William (librarian) 143
Beaumont, Francis 39
Beisley bequest 35-36, 73
Beisley, Harriet 35
Bennett, Frederick 45, 62, 85
Benson, Sir Francis Robert 47
Bermuda 171
Berry and Sons of Huddersfield 29
Berry, Jim 217-219
Beveridge, Lord 196
Bidford-on-Avon 57, 67, 98, 230, 263
Bidwell, Councillor Mrs 293
– Bidwell, F. 293
Billingsley, Ben *Epitome of the Whole Art of Husbandry* 334-335
Binyon, Laurence (poet) 168
Bird family of Stratford-upon-Avon 292
Birmingham 69
Birmingham City Museum and Art Gallery 80-81, 83, 125
Birmingham Fire Brigade 29
Birmingham Guild 126
Birmingham Post and Mail IX
Birmingham University 27, 81, 92, 103, 119-120, 127, 147-148, 181, 201, 209, 221, 224, 250, 262, 296-297, 303, 308, 318, 342
Birthplace *Catalogue* 39
Birthplace Coach Terminal 276, 281-282, 299
Birthplace collections 14, 18, 23, 38, 40, 54, 63, 71, 75, 128, 140, 151-176, 201, 209, 254, 319
Birthplace Library 13, 17-18, 21-22, 34-39, 48-72, 79, 84, 102-104, 160, 162, 201-202, 319, 342
Birthplace Museum 13, 17-22, 28, 34, 49, 96, 100-101, 109-110
Bishop of Coventry Diocese 147-148
Bishop, George *A catalogue of the bishops of England* 127

Black, Duncan 333
Black, Hon. Eugene, R. 173-175, 177-178, 191, 193, 196
Bland, Rev. Thomas 148, 177, 211
Blight (artist) 9, 14, 63, 140
Bloom, J. Harvey 29, 72
Blunden, Edmund (trustee) 81
Boase, Dr T.S.R. (trustee) 129, 148, 152-154, 227
Boddington, Peter, and Mrs 148, 246, 260, 264, 268, 293, 297, 344
Boddingtons Farm, Luddington 216
Bodleian Library 40, 182
Bolshoi Theatre Ballet Company 130, 201
Bomford and Evershed 219
Borges, Jorge Luis 261
Borough Council of Stratford-upon-Avon 4, 17, 25, 47, 81-82, 107, 119, 122, 131, 148, 209, 221, 224, 237, 254, 272-273, 321, 325
– *See also* Corporation of Stratford-upon-Avon
Borough of Stratford-upon-Avon 30, 82
Borough records of Stratford-upon-Avon 13-14, 23, 28, 68, 70-71, 98, 103, 119-120, 254, 279, 321
Borough Town of Stratford-upon-Avon 103, 120
Borseler, Peter (painter) 212
Boshier, G.E. (architect) 52, 69
Bower, S.E. Dykes (architect) 129, 328
Boydell Gallery 32
Bracebridge, Charles Holte 5, 13, 17, 32
Bradbrook, Professor Muriel C. 297
Braden, Bernard 183
Briar Furlong 123
BBC 211-212, 219, 230, 232, 254, 279, 285, 298, 301, 307, 317-318, 326-327
– Shakespeare Costume Exhibition 300-301
Brewery Club 249, 279
British Airways 251
British Association for the Advancement of Science 30
British Council 84, 92, 103, 118-119, 127, 130, 186, 200, 209, 225, 256
British Food and Farming, 1989 340
British Library 297

British Medical Association 30
British Museum 23, 28, 36, 60, 140, 147-148, 168, 227
British Philatelic Society 186
British Transport Hotels, Ltd 247
British Travel Association IX, 219
Brockbank, Professor Philip 119, 297
Brooklands 91, 111, 249, 270-271
Brookside, cottage 136, 305-307
Brown, Miss Patricia 128
Brown, Stephen, QC 207, 274
Browning, Robert 95
Budapest, Museum of Literature 201
Bulmer, Bower 31
Bunbury, Henry William 255
Buckingham Palace 173, 197
Bucknall family 61
Burbage, Richard 39
Burbridge, Ernest 103, 119
Burgess, Anthony 261
Burglary at Anne Hathaway's Cottage 306-307
Burman, William 60
Burnside 135-136, 207, 249, 307-308
Burnside bequest 106, 207
Burton, Robert *Anatomy of Melancholy* 72
Burton, Will 113
Busby, Mrs Joan 128
Butcher, John (nurseryman) 12, 20-21, 23, 29-30, 32
Byng, Hon. John 3, 75

Cadbury Charitable Trust 291
Calcutta Arts Society 190, 191
California 8
Callaway, Maria Charlotte 18
Calloway, George (builder) 13
Cambridge Bibliographical Society 317
Cambridge House 112
Cambridge University 27, 81, 93, 105, 129-130, 147, 148, 154, 297, 341
– University Press 119
Canada 8, 49
Canal, Stratford-upon-Avon 178, 180
Canterbury 28
Capron, Frederick (Fire Chief) 231
Carew, Sir George of Clopton 39, 75

348

INDEX

Carlyle, Thomas   95
Carnegie, Andrew   34, 151
Carroll, John   183, 209, 226, 257
Cash, J. and J. Ltd   186
Cecchini, Mrs Joan Sanders   321
Celebrating Shakespeare   184
Centenary celebrations   92-93
Centre (Shakespeare) Bookshop   205, 309
Centre Coffee House   248
Centre Craft Yard   249
Challen, Lt-Col. J.B. and Mrs   159
Chamberlains' accounts   14, 70, 182
Chambers, Sir Edmund Kerchever   27
Chandos portrait   212
Chapel Lane   33, 56, 126, 223
Charlecote Park   6, 184, 209, 257
Charles I, King   182
Charles, Prince, Duke of Cornwall   108, 133
Charnel house at Holy Trinity Church   75
Charter celebrations   119, 120
Chattaway, Miss (custodian)   23, 31
Chaucer Head Bookshop   321
Chesterfield, Earl of   193
– Portrait of Shakespeare   193, 212
Chettle, Henry *Englandes Mourning Garment*   75
Chicago Exhibition   30
Chichibu, Princess   266, 267
china   8, 189, 301, 303, 327, 342
Chmiel, K. and Partners   277
Cholmondeley, Reginald   36
Chubb security   162, 283
Civil War   158
Clarendon, Earl of (trustee)   81
Clark, Sir Kenneth   196
Clarke, W.R. (signwriter)   235
Claydon's Farm   322
Clayton, Ashley (trustee)   82-83, 103, 108, 129
Clayton, Miss Barbara   331
Clemen, Professor Wolfgang   297
Cleverdon, Douglas   209, 226
Clifford Manor   234
Clopton Bridge   178
Clopton, Frances   75
– Sir Hugh   33, 35
– Sir John   35

Clopton House   75
Coach and Horses Inn   186, 205, 248, 249
Cobden, Richard   190
Coghill, Professor Nevill   130, 148, 151, 297
Coins   38, 331
Cokain, Sir Aston, *Small Poems*   72
Collier, John Payne   6, 11, 17
Collins, Mrs Grace   236
Collins, Wilkie   191
Commemorative items   184-187
Complete Peerage   128
Compton Verney   69, 192
Congregational chapel, Wilmcote   247
Connecticut Historical Society   323
Conservation policy   298
Conservation Workshop   330
Cooke, Alistair   261
Coombe, John   73
Coombe, William   72
Cooper, Councillor B.S.   107
Copenhagen, Royal Porcelain Factory   171, 180
Coppedge, Dr Walter R.   258
Corelli, Miss Marie   104, 119, 321
Coriolanus   73
Coronation of Queen Elizabeth II   121
Corporation of Stratford-upon-Avon   14, 17-18, 20, 24, 26, 38, 50, 57, 67, 68, 71, 92, 226-227
– *See also* Borough Council
Corvin, John (artist)   344
Cotgrave's *Dictionarie*   127
Cottage Lane   61, 200, 203-204, 230, 249, 268-270, 306-307, 311-312, 315
Cottage Tea Garden   299, 312-313
Coughton Court   69
Council of Industrial Design   187
Court, Elisha (builder)   20
Court of Chancery   6
Court of Equity   11
Court, Thomas   9
Court, Widow   4
Courtauld Institute of Art   129
Covell, William *Polimanteia*   252
Covent Garden   6, 238
Coventry   72, 79, 81, 129
– Cathedral   79, 139, 164, 221, 227
– City Archivist   79-80

– *Coventry Evening Telegraph*   IX, 292
– *Coventry's Heritage*   103
– Herbert Art Gallery   80
Coyne, J.S.   5
Creed, Oswald   63, 64
Cupboard of Boxes   50
Cust, Lionel   47
Cross o' th' Hill   298
Cunningham, Peter   6

Daily Telegraph   43
Daniels, Ernest (photographer)   98
Darvill, Mrs M. (librarian)   202
Davies, Gwen Ffrancon   109
Davies, John, *Scourge of Folly*   72
Davies, Malcolm (photographer)   IX
Davies, S.B., Mrs (neé Baker)   104
Davis, Percy (carpenter)   126
Dawber, Guy (architect)   45, 63
Day, Richard Digby   228
Death-watch beetle   246
De Grey, Thomas *The Compleat Horseman*   268
Delaware University Press   262, 304
Dench, Jeffrey   226
Dench, Dame Judi   183, 227, 257
Denmark   171
Dent, Alan   254
Department of Education and Science   318
Deputy Record Keeper of the Borough records   13, 68, 119
Deutsche Shakespeare-Gesellschaft West   304
Devonshire, Duke of   182, 226
Dictionary of National Biography   46, 73, 74
Dickens, Charles   4, 6, 190
Dingley, Leigh (Alderman) and Mrs   148, 157, 159, 244
– *See also* Phillips, Councillor Gwendoline
Dixon, N.W., Ltd   283
Dobb, Dr C. (librarian)   202
Dobson, William (artist)   75
Donkeys   297
Drake   4
Drayton, Michael   39
Dubai   131

349

Dugdale, Sir William (trustee)   81, 129, 148
– *Antiquities of Warwickshire*   129, 211
– *Monasticon Anglicanum*   128
Dugdale Society   79-80, 103, 129, 140, 211, 310, 327
Dulwich College   39, 182
Duncan, E.   6
Dunn, Dr S.G.   93
Durham College of Science   31
Dyer, D.J. (builder)   93, 126, 203
Dyke, W.H.   132, 241
Dyson, Bell and Company   145

East Indies   8
Easton, Miss Jane   128
Edge, Bert (blacksmith)   337
Edmonds, A. and Co. Ltd   100, 235, 284
– Edmonds, Ewart   100, 125
Educational activities   209, 296, 317, 318
Education and Science, Dept of   251
Edward, Prince   173
Egypt   8
Eisenhower, General Dwight D. and Mrs   191-192
Eldridge (artist)   9
Elizabeth, Princess   109
Elizabeth I, Queen   4, 10, 151, 261
– Elizabeth, Queen (later the Queen Mother)   106, 107-109, 178-180, 314-315
– Elizabeth II, Queen   120, 131-134, 137, 159, 172, 173, 186, 197, 251, 263-266, 270-271, 327
Ellender, Brian (architect)   309
Ellis, John   88, 202
Elmore, Bert   306
Elridge, Hugh (artist)   75
Ely Palace portrait   16, 101
Embassy Club   285
– *See* Brewery Club
Emmett Publishing   320
Emms Court, Sheep Street   26, 33
Encyclopaedia Britannica Educational   326
English Historical Scholarship in the Sixteenth and Seventeenth Centuries   129
English Speaking Union   135
English Tourist Board   333
Environment, Dept of   272, 274, 275, 298, 331

Erdington   31
Estienne, Henri *A Mervaylous Discourse*   252-253
– *Maison Rustique*   254
Ettington   13
European Parliament   318
Evans, Rev. Charles   25
Evans, Dr Gareth Lloyd and Mrs   268, 293, 298, 318
Evans, Sir Ifor   148, 196
Evans, Mrs J.L.T. (Emily)   135-136, 249, 307
– John   135-136, 307
Every, J.H.   65
Exhall   67
Exhibitions   181-183, 209, 225, 251, 254, 257, 284, 304, 319, 346

Fairholt, F.W.   6
Fane, Sir Francis   75
Faucit, Helen   36
Fearnall, Miss Mary (gardener)   310
Ferrers, C.R.   75
Ferrers-Walker, T.W.   298
Festival of Britain   106, 110, 112, 115, 118, 121
Field, Nathan   39
Field, Richard (printer)   73
Fieldhouse, W.J.   58
Fielding, Fenella   183
First Folio   36-37, 101, 130, 133, 140, 173, 179, 208, 268, 294, 310
First World War   46-48, 54, 59, 69, 85
Fitzroy-Newdegate, Capt F.H.M.   268
Fleming, Thomas of Gaydon   216
Fleshood, Dr Arnold   258
Flood at Shottery   45, 61
Florio, John *World of Wordes*   39
Flower and Sons, Ltd   186, 210, 221, 234
Flower, Caroline   93, 108
Flower, Charles   93, 108
Flower, Charles Edward   19, 20, 24-26, 82, 221
Flower, Dennis L.   148, 206, 220, 223-224, 228, 237, 260, 264-266, 268-269, 271, 282-283, 291-295, 316, 339, 340-341, 344
Flower, Edgar   25, 34

Flower, Edward   133-134
Flower, Edward Fordham   17, 82
Flower, Elizabeth   133-134
Flower, Lt-Col. (later Sir Fordham)   81-83, 86-88, 91-92, 103, 108, 110, 121, 123, 132-133, 147-148, 151-152, 154, 159-160, 174-181, 191-192, 195-197, 203, 206, 220-223, 259-260, 319, 328, 344
– Hersey (Mrs, later Lady)   108, 132, 159, 174-175, 179, 191-192, 196, 206, 221, 259, 293, 319, 344
Flower, Mrs Spenser   264
Flower, Sir Archibald   46, 58, 62, 82, 86, 88, 93, 96, 109, 221, 247, 328
Flowers Brewery   47, 202, 205, 210, 221, 223, 248, 249, 319
Foakes, Professor Reg.   252
Folger, Henry Clay   31, 131, 139, 190, 237, 323
– Shakespeare Library   14, 31, 63, 130, 137-143, 178, 190, 192-193, 195, 201, 211, 237, 259, 274, 291, 320, 323, 327
Foundation stone ceremony   159, 160
Forbes, Michael (architect)   175
Foreign Office   200
Forest of Arden   336
Forestry Commission   123, 203
Fowler, Mrs Elaine   263
Fox, Elizabeth   IX, 132, 159
Fox, Mrs Jane   86, 108, 132, 159, 174-175, 179, 181, 197
Fox, Levi   174-175, 179, 196-197, 201, 264-265, 269-270, 293-294, 314-315, 341-344
Fox, Patricia   132, 159
Fox, Roger   189, 311
France   8, 189
Francis, Sir Frank   148
Franklin, Mrs Vera   310-311
French National Theatre   131
Friends of Shakespeare's Birthplace   214, 252, 255, 292, 320, 323, 346
Fripp, Rev. Edgar   73-74
– Publications   74
Frost, Robert (poet)   196
Fuller, Roy   183

Gadsby, W.G.   85
Garland, Patrick   183, 209

INDEX

Garrick Bicentenary celebrations 224-229, 240
Garrick Bicentenary medal 228-229
Garrick Celebrations Committee 224
Garrick Club 224, 225-227
Garrick, David 22, 36, 54, 74-75, 214, 224-229, 289
– Engraved portrait 216
– Medallions 214, 216
– Mrs Garrick 190, 214, 216, 225
Garrick, George 75, 224
Garrick Jubilee 3, 75, 116, 140, 214, 224-229, 289, 346
Gascoigne, George *The Whole woorkes* 128
Gastrell, Francis 36
General Accident etc. Corporation 235-236, 307
George III, King 95
George IV, King 254
George V, King 56
George VI, King 106, 107-109, 121, 265
Genealogists' Magazine 69
Gentleman, David 188
George Washington University 191-192, 197
Germany, Federal Republic 122, 171, 189, 254, 260, 281, 301
– East 303
Gibberd, Frederick (architect) 153
Gibbs, Edward (architect) 7, 10, 11, 13, 14
Gibbs, Jennifer 189, 309
Gibbs, Thompson and Colbourne (builders) 11, 14
Gielgud, Sir John 109, 262, 303
Gift books by Levi Fox 327
Gilbert, Cass 56
Gillan, Miss Elizabeth 128
Girtin, Thomas 75
Glebe Farm 207-209, 219, 246-247, 322, 329-333, 335-340
Globe, revolving model 289
Globe theatre 49, 193
Glover, Julian 226
Godden, Professor 172
Goethe 171
Golf course 247-248
Goodyear, Harold 112, 128, 242, 265
Gorbacheva, Mikhail and Raisa 301

Gordon Russell, Ltd 162, 167, 171, 235, 283-284, 288
Grace, Colonel Richard 252
Grace, Princess, of Monaco 257
Grainger-Brown 98, 205
Grand Union Canal 178
Granville-Barker, Harley 321
Graves, Henry of Pall Mall 16, 25
Gray, Nicolete 167, 168
Great Garden of New Place 19-21, 32, 54-56, 121, 250
Great Western Railway Company 89
Green, Harold 170
Greene, Rev. Joseph 128, 140, 211
– Correspondence 140, 211
Greene, Richard 9, 51, 128, 140, 211
Gregory-Hood, Col. Alexander 129
– Major Charles 69, 79, 81, 85, 128-129
– Collection 128-129, 210
Grete Herbal, The 36
Greville, Fulke *Certaine … workes* 210
Gucht, B. Van de (painter) 75, 216
Guidebook publications by Levi Fox 184, 327
Guild Chapel 120-121, 124, 129, 139, 235, 254, 265, 269, 328
– Friends of the Guild Chapel 120-121, 328
Guildhall in Church Street 13, 182
Guild Street (Guild Pits) 10, 12, 52, 91, 179, 204-205, 249, 273, 279-280
Gunnerheimer, Dr Werner 327
Gunpowder Plot 23, 75, 287
Gypsy caravans 216-219, 333

Habicht, Professor Werner 304
Hailsham, Lord 261
Haines, Frederick 24, 25, 41
Haldenby, Miss Paula IX, 242, 324
Hall, Martin 284
Hall, Peter 221
Halliwell, J.O. (Halliwell-Phillipps) 6, 13-14, 16-17, 19-20, 22-24, 35, 53, 63, 68
– collection 14, 35, 140, 300
Hall, Dr John 38, 58-59, 109-111, 115-116, 251, 264
– *Select Observations* 116
– Susanna 109-110, 115-116, 252-253, 264

Hall's Croft 106-119, 121-122, 124-125, 127, 151, 160, 175, 181, 183, 199, 201, 203, 205-206, 209, 225, 240, 244, 249-251, 256-257, 263-266, 299, 301, 305, 311, 342
– Festival Club 106, 110, 112, 115-119, 127, 203, 209, 256-257
Hamlet 38, 182, 186, 210, 321
Hampton Court 55-56
Hanbury 28
Hanworth, Lord 46, 69, 71
Hardison Jr, Dr O.B. 259
Hardwick, Paul 183
Harewood, Earl of 225, 292
Harness, Rev. William 41
Harris, John and Sons Ltd 333
Hart family 4, 10
Harting, Professor Pieter 93
Harvard House 104-105, 138, 246
– Harvard Club 138
– Harvard, John 104
– Harvard University 104
Harvester Press Microform Publications 320
Hassall, Christopher 257
Hathaway, Anne 41, 123
Hathaway, Bartholomew 123
Hathaway family 41, 232
Hathaway Hamlet 122, 234
Hawkes, Jacquetta 297
– *See also* Priestley, J.B.
Hawthorne, Nathaniel 191
Henley-in-Arden manor 36
Henley Street 3-4, 12, 26, 49-52, 80-81, 84, 86, 91, 96-98, 104, 127, 132, 134, 151-154, 157-159, 163, 167, 174, 179, 199, 204-205, 241, 248-249, 268, 272, 274-282, 284, 288, 292-294, 298-299, 300-309
Henniker-Major, Sir John 225
Henrietta, Maria, Queen 252
Henry IV 5-6, 182
Henry V 180, 205
Henry VIII, King 97, 99
Henslowe, Philip, *Diary* 182
Heritage Theatre 267-268
Hermeticall Banquet 36
Herne's oak 97
Hertford, Marquess 337
Hewlands 60, 204, 230, 241

351

Hester, James M.   196
Higgs and Hill, Ltd   156-157, 159
Highfill, Professor Philip Henry   192
High Sheriff of Warwickshire   159, 174, 292
High Steward   4-5, 17, 25, 46, 81, 93, 145, 147-148, 159, 174-175
High Street   57, 83, 96, 109, 134, 157, 268
Hill, The house and estate   82, 124, 206, 221, 247, 250, 308, 312, 318, 328
– Garden headquarters   311-312
Hill, Ronald   157, 159, 160, 175
Hillson family of Langley   322
Historic Buildings Commission   331-332, 339
Historical Manuscripts Commission   23
Hobbes, Robert Hione   17, 20
Hobbes, Robert W.   13, 15, 75
Hodges family   255
Hodgson, Sir Arthur   24-25
Holinshed, *Chronicles*   35, 127
Holmes, George (farmer)   207, 209, 329
Holte, Thomas, photographic collection   321
Holtom, William (builder)   10, 11, 34
Holy Trinity Church   4, 31, 75, 83-84, 97, 107, 109, 131, 134, 140-141, 147-148, 178, 180, 190, 194, 206, 209, 211, 214, 222, 225, 227, 257, 264, 298, 303, 324, 326
Hope, W.H. St John   39, 50, 53
Hopkins, Mrs   62
Hopper, Charles   18
Hopton, *Concordancy of Yeares*   210
Horn, Miss Marian (librarian)   252
Horn book   60
Hornby, blacksmith   34, 288
Hornby Cottage   11, 26, 29, 34-35, 49, 68-69, 71, 83, 92, 93, 127, 151-152, 157, 237, 256, 279, 285, 306, 309-310
Hornby, Mrs Mary   3, 190
Hornton Quarries, Ltd   158, 160
Howard, Alderman W.S.   148
How Group   281, 283
Hudson, Thomas (artist)   75
Hugh Clopton High School   328
Hughes, John (antiquary)   211
Hugo, Victor   191
Hungary   8

Hunt collection   14, 16, 68
Hunt, Thomas   36
Hunt, William Oakes   12-14, 17, 19-20
Hutchings and Deer   62
Hutchings, Geoffrey   226
Hutchins, Rev. Charles   256
Hutton, John   164-166, 172, 175, 306
– engraved glass   164-165, 179, 295, 306
Huxley, Sir Julian   196
Huxley, W.H. (Mayor)   159

Ibstock Building Products, Ltd   281
Illiffe, Lord   109, 178, 292
– Langton   177-178
Illustrated London News   6
Ingleby, C.M.   23
India   93, 171, 189, 191
In Honour of Shakespeare   184, 239, 327, 346
Inland Waterways Association   178
International Shakespeare Association   189, 254, 260-262, 303-304, 346
International Shakespeare Conference   92, 173, 181, 201, 262, 267, 301, 321
International Shakespeare Congress   260-262, 295, 303-304
International Theatre Institute   186
Ireland, Samuel   9, 41
Ironside, Robin and Christopher   188
Irving, Henry   25
Irving, Washington   3, 10, 238
Isles of South Pacific   8
Izod, Mrs   4

Jackman, Charles (librarian)   19, 22
Jacks, Mrs Graham (neé Jennifer Gibbs)   307
Jackson, Sir Barry   102, 154, 221
Jackson, Frank (head gardener)   56, 85-86, 108, 112, 310
Jackson, Stops and Staff   110
Jacques, Alan Charles   233, 234
Jaggard, William   323
Jamaica   171
James I, King   4
Jamestown Foundation   259, 287
Japan   8, 47, 189, 260, 267, 300, 342
Jarratt, Mrs   7

Jarrold & Sons Ltd   184, 291
Jeaffreson, J.C.   14, 23
Jefford, Barbara   226
Jerusalem, Deputy Governor   131
Johnson, Michael (head gardener)   313, 315-316, 333
Johnson, Philip M.   51
Johnson, President, Lyndon B. and Mrs   195-196, 266-267
Joinery Products Ltd   162
Jones, George   5
Jonson, Ben   4
– *Pleasure reconcild*   182
Jordan, John   63
Jubilee Educational Fund   270, 318
Jubilee Walk   241, 269-271, 313
Julius Caesar   73
Justices of the Peace   17, 25, 27, 81

Keen, Edmund   95, 190
Keene, Arthur   264
Kelly, Barbara   183
Kemp, C.G., Councillor and Mrs   174
Kendall of Warwick (carver)   325
Kennedy, Jacqueline Bouvier   173, 196
Kennedy, John F., President   173
Kent, Duchess of   292-295
– Duke of   315-316
Kerby, John   316
Kew Gardens   56
Keymer Brick and Tile Co. Ltd   281
Kiasashvili, Professor Nico   321
Kibler Morgan (estate agent)   63
Kindersley, Richard (carver)   286-287, 297, 315, 344
Kineton   107, 210
King Edward VI School   16, 18, 80, 100, 128, 135, 140, 254, 269, 304, 327-328
– Headmaster   17, 25, 81, 83, 103, 147-148, 154, 211, 268, 298, 327-328
King Henry VIII   107, 109
King Lear   39
King's Players   227
Kirk, John, Ltd   333
Kirstein, Lincoln   193, 212
Kite, Thomas (parish clerk)   190
Knight, Rev. A.C.   79-80, 83, 88
Knight, Charles   4, 6, 238

INDEX

Knolles, Richard *The generall historie of the Turkes* 104
Knott garden at New Place 54-55, 85, 306
Knottesford-Fortescue, Rev. J.M. 58
Knowles, Sheridan 6

Lambard, *Eirenarcha* 210
Lanchester, Waldo and Muriel 205
Langner, Lawrence 193
Lascelles, Sir Alan 108, 209
Law, Ernest 47, 56
Lawrence, Gordon (carpenter) 339
Lea, Alderman George (trustee) and Mrs 83, 148, 159
Lea, Margerie IX
Leaver, John Shapcote 10, 18, 28
Lecture tour 258-260
Lee, Sir Sidney 34, 38-39, 46, 52, 53, 56, 68, 73-74
Leicester Forest 103
Leigh-Hunt, Barbara 303
Leigh, Lord, of Stoneleigh 72, 182, 210, 321
Leigh, Ray 284
Leningrad, Gorki Theatre 204
Leningrad State Kirov Ballet Company 201
Leningrad University 131
Library of Congress 138, 141, 192
Lichfield Museum 140, 211
Liddell, M.A. 145
Linton, W.J. 6
Liverpool, Roman Catholic Cathedral 153
Liverpool, Theatre Royal 5
Liverpool, University 260
Locke, Arthur 321
Loggin, C.F. 13
London 3-7, 16, 23, 28, 46, 51, 55, 62, 73, 75, 98, 145-167, 170-172, 196, 199, 214, 221, 266, 301, 317
– University 27, 81, 130, 147-148, 226
London and North Western Railway Company 30
London Gazette 146
London Star 43
Longfellow, H.W. 190
Lord Lieutenant of Warwickshire 17, 25, 107, 121, 147-148, 159, 179, 264, 271

Lovejoy, Professor Derek 314
Love's Labour's Lost 55, 103, 182
Lovett, Ted 111
Lowell, J.R. 191
Lowin, John 39
Lowson, Sir Denys and Lady 159, 174, 175
Lowth, T.E. and Mrs 107, 145, 153, 260, 264, 268, 293, 297, 298
Loxley 31, 85, 129
Lucas, Councillor R.A.C. 283
Luce, Richard 301
Ludford tea-chest 323
Lyly, John, *Euphues and his England* 36
Lyon, Robert 212
Lyons, Sir Jack 292

Macbeth 263
Machiavelli *The Arte of Warre* 254
Mack, Professor Maynard 262
Maddocks, W.M. and Mrs 174
Malayan Teachers College 189
Malenkov, Mr 130
Maltby, R.H. 310
Manchester 6
– University 80
Mann, Miss Phyllis 119
Manor Fruit Farm 207
Manorial records 69
Mansbridge, Albert (trustee) 47, 81
Manwood, John *Lawes of the Forrest* 128
Margaret, Princess 107, 108, 109
Mansell, Les (plumber) 126
Market cross 14, 38, 96
Marquand, Richard 183
Marshall, John (carver) 19
Marshall, Mrs S. 244
Martin, Helen Faucit 191
Martin, Sir Theodore 24-25, 36, 43
– Lady Theodore 36
Mary Arden's House 61, 63-68, 81, 84-87, 90, 122, 126, 149, 199, 201, 203, 207, 216-219, 240, 243, 245-248, 250, 252, 271, 297, 299, 306, 311, 322, 329-331, 333, 335, 337, 339, 340, 342, 344
Mary, Queen 56
Mason Croft 92, 104, 118-119, 173, 201, 257, 262, 296, 303, 323
Master of the Rolls 46, 69, 71

Matthews, L.T.R., Alderman 79, 83, 103, 110, 118, 148, 154, 159, 260
– Mrs Helen 159, 260, 264, 268, 293, 298
May, Thomas 58
Mayor of Stratford-upon-Avon 17, 25, 81, 82, 92, 93, 97, 107, 121, 145, 147-148, 154-155, 157-158, 174, 178, 180, 191, 221, 225-226, 302
May's *Illustrated Guide* 41
McCowen, Alec 183
McMurran, Hon. Lewis 259
Meadows, George 67-68, 85-87
Measure for Measure 254
Medals 75, 181, 184-185, 196, 225, 262, 267, 283, 292
Meer Street 277, 279
Merchant of Venice 38-39, 290
Merchant, Rev. Professor W. Moelwyn 303
Meriton *A Guide for Constables* 210
Merry Wives of Windsor 97, 268-269
Mewis, R.R. (blacksmith) 337
Midland Bank (Old Bank) 111, 169, 291, 300
Midland Electricity Board 250
Mie, University, Tokyo 267
Miller Buckley Construction Ltd 277-278
Ministry of Works 112
Mishima, Yukio, Japanese novelist 201
Mitchell, John 62
Montagu, Lady Elizabeth 110
Montaigne, Michel de, *Essays* 39
Montgomery (house) 136
Moore, Henry 321
Mop Fair 321
Morpath, Lord 5
Morris, Edward, of Chicago 104
Morris, Richard 252
Moryson, Fynes, *Itinerary* 128
Moscow Arts Theatre 131
Motorways Plant, Ltd 287
Mount Vernon 195
Much Ado About Nothing 192-193
Muir, Professor Kenneth 260
Mulberry tree/wood 13, 31-33, 36, 38, 54, 75, 114, 216, 225, 228, 265, 293, 310, 314, 323, 344

353

Murray, Dr Donald Sutherland 104
Music 158, 184, 209, 217, 225-228, 254, 257, 323-324
Myers, Dr, M.S.A. Cultural Attaché 172

Nash, Elizabeth 19, 32
Nash, Thomas 19, 32
Nash's House 19-20, 27, 32, 50, 52-59, 68, 87, 124-126, 244-245
Nason. George (carpenter) 126
Natick Shakespeare Club 267
Nation, Sarah 286
National Farmers' Union Mutual Insurance Society 83, 291
National Gallery of Scotland 214
National Geographic Society 259, 262-263
National Portrait Gallery 39, 212, 226
National Shakespeare Fund 19
National Trust 147-148, 178, 204, 209, 257, 297, 317
Neighbour, William 63
Nelder and Southam 114, 235
Nepal, King and Queen 131, 201
Nesbett, Professor Marion 258
New Place 14, 19-22, 27-33, 35-36, 38-40, 46, 48, 50, 52-59, 68, 81, 84-87, 90, 106, 120, 122, 124-126, 199, 203-204, 216, 222-223, 228, 240, 244-245, 249-250, 252, 254, 256, 266-267, 299, 306, 310-311, 342
New Place, Foot of Fine recording its purchase 182
New Place Museum 19, 20, 27, 32-33, 36, 50, 52-54, 56, 57-58, 216, 244-245
New Row cottages 61, 63, 91, 203, 249, 306
Newstead, J.H. 98
New Testament, Queen Elizabeth I's polyglot copy 182
New York 137-138, 193, 238
New York State Historical Association 131, 201
New York University medal 196-197
Nicoll, Professor Allardyce 119, 148, 152
Nikholayeva-Tereshkova, Valentina 201
'Noate of corne and malt' 182
North, Sir Thomas, translation of *Plutarch's Lives* 73

Norton, Mrs 312
Norwich, Dean of 56
Nuffield Foundation 169, 291-292
Nuffield Library 169, 179
Nuffield, Lord 169

Okada, Akira, Professor 201
Old Bank (Stourbridge and Kidderminster Banking Company) 12, 18, 47
– See also Midland Bank
Old Stratford/Town 73, 110, 205-206, 264, 298
Othello 140, 227, 254
Ovid, *Metamorphoses* 35, 128
Oxford 98, 129, 152, 259, 303, 310
– *Oxford History of Art* 129
– University 27, 74, 80-81, 130, 147-148, 297, 328
– University Press 129, 154, 184, 256, 310

Packwood House 80, 83, 103
Page, Leslie 242, 306
Painting, Norman 316, 327
Pakistan, Parliament 131
Papua New Guinea 301
Parish Register of Holy Trinity Church 4, 109, 180, 211, 294
Pasco, Richard 257, 303
Parsons family of Shawell 337
Parsons, Mrs Winifred 264
Pavilion, The 1964 155-157, 159, 310
Payton, John (Alderman) 97
Pearce and Cutler, Ltd 281
Pears, Peter 257
Pearson's Fire Alarm system 29
Pebworth 337
Pedestrianization scheme 299
Peek, J. Whitmore 59
Pemberton, Guy (architect) · 51-53, 56, 60
Penang 189
Penny, Christine (librarian) 202
Perkins, Mr 12
Persia, (now Iran) 172
Pharmaceutical Society 30
Philatelic Traders Society 186
Philip, Prince, Duke of Edinburgh 131-134, 137, 173-176, 180
Philippines 201

Phillips family 83
Phillips, Councillor Gwendoline 121
– See also Dingley, Leigh, Mrs
Phillipps Library 252
Pickin, Robert 230
Pilgrim Trust 292
Piper, David 212
Place, Thomas 69
Plumb, Lord, of Coleshill 318, 339-340
Plutarch, *Lives* 210
Plymouth, Earl of 128
Poetry Festival 106, 127, 181, 183, 209, 225-226, 256-257, 323-324, 346
Polish Popular Theatre 201
Pollock, Sir Frederick 68
Pooley, Sir Ernest (trustee) 27, 81, 109, 130, 148
Portland, Duke of 39
Poulenc, Francis (composer) 196
Pound Ground 123, 203
Postmaster General 186-187
– Post Office 186, 187-188, 225
– Stratford-upon-Avon postmark 225
Pragnell, George 170, 226
Pratt, N.S. and Mrs Pratt 260, 264, 268, 293, 298
Prentice, Rev. Canon Noel (trustee) 83, 103, 109, 134, 154
Price Bros. (builders) 54, 64-66, 69
Priestley, J.B. and Mrs Priestley 245, 251, 257, 297
– See also Hawkes, Jacquetta
Prince of Wales 56
Prince Regent 190
Pringle, Mrs Marian (librarian) 268
Pringle, Roger x, 202, 252, 257, 260, 303-304, 317, 323, 341-342, 344
Priory, from Warwick 258
Profumo, John, MP 186
Public Inquiry 207, 246, 274-275, 298
Public Library 104, 180
Public Record Office 46, 138, 182, 279, 321
Public Relations 326-328
Puckering family 258
Puddephat, Wilfred 254
Pugh, Mrs Joyce 255
Puppet Centre 205
Purland, T. 6

INDEX

Quatercentenary celebrations   144, 154-155, 157, 159, 169, 181-198, 220, 223
Quaritch, Bernard   39
Quarto editions   38-39, 97, 103, 140
Quatremain, W.W. (artist)   323
Quayle, Anthony   109, 221-222, 326
Quayle, Rosanna   109
Queen Elizabeth Hall   285, 318, 323
Queen's Own Warwickshire and Worcestershire Yeomanry   175
Quyney, Richard   15-16, 74
– Quyney's letter   15, 133, 182, 194

Racing at Stratford   226
Radcliffe, Lord (Viscount)   145, 148, 186, 274
Ragley Hall   18, 337
Ramsbottom Lecture   327
Ramsbottom, Sir Peter   261
Randall, Geoffrey   242
Rape of Lucrece   252
Rare Breeds   339
Ray, E.P. (Alderman)   103
Ray, Malcolm (Councillor)   226
Record Office   68-72, 109, 249, 255, 319-322
Reed, Joseph Verner   193
Reich, Tibor   162, 180, 185-186, 225
Reynolds, Edwin F. (architect)   52, 84, 90-91, 93
Rich, John F. and Company   155, 169
Richmond, Virginia   258-259
Rigg, Diana   183
Rimell, David J. (thatcher)   235, 304, 306
Riviere, Messrs (bookbinders)   39
Robbins, Ronald (mason)   160
Roberts, Sir Sydney C.   130, 148, 154
Robins, Edmund (auctioneer)   6
Robins, George   6
Robinson, Miss Eileen (librarian)   202, 252
Rogers, Katherine   104
Romanchuk, Ellena   188
Romano-British settlement   57-58
Romeo and Juliet   168, 182, 263
Rooke, George   268
Rookes, C.A.   284, 286, 291-292
Rookwood, Ambrose   74

Rose, Alfred   31
Rose, Mary   31, 323
Rosser, S.C. (Councillor)   148
Routh. C.R.N.   148
Rowe, James   322
Rowe, Nicholas   182
Rowley Regis stone   10
Royal Air Force   158, 159
Royal College of Art   163
Royal Commission on Public Records   68
Royal Doulton   186
Royal Engineers   158, 170, 174, 324
Royal Fine Art Commission   153
Royal Pioneer Corps   158
Royal Shakespearean Club   4, 7
Royal Shakespeare Theatre   140, 148, 158, 173, 178-179, 181, 183, 188, 195, 197, 209, 215, 220, 222, 224-226, 251-252, 254, 257, 263, 265, 269, 279, 302-304, 311, 317, 320-321, 324, 325-326
– Centenary Garden   244, 265
– Theatre collections   264-265, 320
– *See also* Shakespeare Memorial Theatre
Royal Society of St George   186
Royal visits   30, 74, 106-109, 131-134, 175-176, 178-180, 252, 263-270, 310, 314-315, 346
Ruggle *Ignoramus*   210
Ruskin Gallery   323
Russell, Sir Gordon   162, 284
Russia   8

Sackville, Thomas   39
Sale catalogue   4
Sale poster   2-3
Salmon, T.W. (custodian)   31
Sanctus Road   298
Sankey Sheldon, Ltd   163
Sapcote, William   113, 114
Sapcote, William and Sons, Ltd   112, 124, 126, 233-234, 247
Sarpi, *Historie of the Council of Trent*   210
Saunders, Capt. James   16, 68
Saunders, T. (engraver)   216
Savage, Richard   IX, 26, 28-39, 45, 52, 73-74
Saville Tractors, Ltd   170
Schoenbaum, Professor S.   256, 297

Scott and Co., Ltd   52, 309
Scott, Sir Walter   95, 190, 214-215
Scriven, Mrs   48, 49
Scriven, Miss M.G.M.   210
Second Folio   36, 320
– King Charles I's copy   182
Second World War   46, 54, 67, 71, 79, 103
Selincourt, Professor Ernest de   27
Severn-Lamb, Ltd   284, 290
Severn-Trent Water Authority   45, 270
Shakespeare Anniversary Book The 1964   184
Shakespeare Anniversary Council   155, 172, 178, 181-182, 184, 186-187
Shakespeare Anniversary Festival   181
Shakespeare Association of America   261, 303-304
Shakespeare Birthday celebrations   131, 135, 170-171, 198, 211, 225, 254, 314, 324-326
Shakespeare Centre   36, 102, 107, 129, 140, 149, 151-180, 187, 193, 197-199, 201-202, 205, 208, 211-212, 218, 220, 223-225, 237, 240, 249-252, 254, 256, 260, 262, 266-268, 272, 274, 279-282, 284-285, 293-299, 301-304, 306-307, 309-310, 315, 317, 319-320, 324, 326-327, 344
Shakespeare Centre Extension   35, 52, 71, 205, 241, 269, 272-295, 300, 308, 314, 317-318, 320
Shakespeare Club   170, 226, 292, 325
Shakespeare coat of arms   164, 170-171
Shakespeare commemorative items   184-186
Shakespeare Countryside Museum   67, 207, 219, 246, 322, 329-340, 342
Shakespeare Exhibition   172, 176, 180-181, 183, 292
Shakespeare Films   212, 259, 262-263, 318
Shakespeare Head Press   210, 321
Shakespeare garden in Paris   121
Shakespeare Institute   119, 209, 224, 254, 262, 301, 303
Shakespeare, John (glover and wool dealer)   9, 97, 99, 108
– Mary   97, 98
Shakespeare, John of Worthington Fields, Leics.   10, 12

355

Shakespeare, Mary   97-98
Shakespeare medals   176, 189, 229, 262, 288-289, 292
Shakespeare Memorial Theatre   47, 49, 75, 80-83, 87-88, 92, 102-103, 107, 109-110, 115, 119, 124, 127, 129, 131, 134-135, 147, 154, 321, 325-326
– Memorial Library   22, 68, 102, 127, 160, 176, 202, 252
– Theatre garden   102, 128
– *See also* Royal Shakespeare Theatre
Shakespeare Monumental Committee   4, 346
Shakespeare Morris Men   226
Shakespeare Pictorial   103
Shakespeare portraits   4, 14, 16, 22, 97, 101, 193, 212-213
Shakespeare postage stamps   186-187
Shakespeare Rarities and Artistic Miscellanies   140
Shakespeare Staffordshire figure   98
Shakespeare statue   116-117, 166-167, 179
Shakespeare Summer School   250, 252, 267, 295, 308, 318-319
Shakespeare Survey   92, 119
Shakespeare translations   75, 183, 320
Shakespeare Tree Garden   313-316, 342
Shakespeare, William   3, 14-16, 25, 41, 68, 103-104, 144, 146, 168-169, 171, 180, 182, 188, 201, 211, 267
Shakespeare's Birthplace   2-17, 24-31, 47-52, 75, 81, 83-84, 87, 89, 91-101, 106-109, 121-122, 124, 127, 131-134, 140, 183, 190, 192, 199-200, 204, 225, 243-244, 299, 300, 342
Shakespeare's desk   100
Shakespeare's marriage bond   282
Shakespeare's monument   4, 97
Shakespeare's *Poems*   321-322
Shakespeare's tomb   4, 131, 190, 214, 324
Shanks, Rosalind   226
Sharjah, the Ruler   131
Sharman, Gobal (writer)   201
Sharp Parsons and Co.   47, 89
Sharp, Thomas   97, 323
Shaw, Glen Byam   221
Sheppard, Christina   287, 288
Sheppard, Dorothea   85

Shaw, Julius   210
Shirley, Evelyn P.   13
Shottery   6, 47, 60, 102, 124, 135-136, 203, 207, 232-233, 249, 270, 299, 305, 312-313
Shottery Brook   45, 61, 91
Shottery Lodge   61, 84, 90-91, 203, 230, 249
Shottery Manor   221, 328
Siam, King of   75
Sibbasbridge, Ltd   305, 308, 330, 332
Silk and Frazier   277
Silver Jubilee of Queen Elizabeth II   240, 241, 251, 270, 271
Silver Jubilee Educational Fund   271
Silvesters of Solihull   98
Simms estate   339
Sinden, Donald   227
Singer, Isaac Bashevis (Nobel Prize winner)   301
Skelton, John (sculptor)   164, 223, 285
Skidmore of Coventry   20
Skipsey, Joseph   31
Slater, John (actor)   110
Slevin, Peter (thatcher)   123
Sly, William   39
Smallwood, Dr Robert   296
Smart, Philip (Borough Engineer)   122
Smith, G.   63
Smith, John (Alderman)   58
Smith, R.M., Alderman (trustee)   79, 83, 103
Smith-Ryland, Charles   264, 271
Smith, S.C. Kaines   79, 80-81, 83, 103
Smith and Unitt (builders)   91
Snitterfield School   31
Society for the Protection of Ancient Buildings   64
Soest, Gerard   212-213
– Shakespeare portrait   212, 213
Sole, Mr, of Banbury   13
Sotheby's   252
Sources   346
Southampton, Earl of   39
South Warwickshire College   255
South Warwickshire Sports Trust   206
Soviet Union   170-171, 188, 201, 266, 301, 303

Spencer, Herbert   191
Spencer, Robert   303
Spencer, Professor Terence   119, 148
Spenser, Edmund, *Colin Clouts*   72
Sports Centre inquiry   206-207
Spreadbury, H. Vernon   125, 235
Squire, William   226
St. Andrew's Church   135-136, 306
St George's Day   159, 172, 225
Stationers' Company   182
Stephen, King   254
Stock, Fred and Mrs   170
Stone, Sir Benjamin   44
Stoneleigh Abbey   103, 128, 210, 321
Stow *Annales*   72
Strange, Miss Margaret   82
Stratford Board of Studies   103
Stratford Chamber of Trade   186, 225
Stratford-on-Avon District Council   241, 246, 273-278, 282-283, 293, 298, 308, 325, 330
Stratford Race Course   107
Stratford-upon-Avon Electricity Company   52
Stratford-upon-Avon Festival   324
Stratford Festival Theatre, Connecticut   138, 173, 192-193, 195, 212, 238
Stratford Fire Brigade   29
Stratford, Ontario   238
Stratford, Past and Present   256
Stratford-upon-Avon, Grammar School for Girls   328
Stratford-upon-Avon Guild   52
Stratford-upon-Avon Herald   IX, 146
Stratford-upon-Avon Local Plan   298
Stratford-upon-Avon, Town Council   241, 282, 293
Stratford-upon-Avon Youth Wind Band   285, 293
Strickson, John   227, 257
Strong, Sir Roy   225
Sundial   244, 344
Swan and Maidenhead   4, 9-13, 95-96
Swan Theatre   317
Swift, Clive   183
Swinburne, *A briefe treatise*   127
Switzerland   171
S.W.S. Electric Power Co.   67

INDEX

Tagore, Rabindranath   191
Talbot, William   54
Tamagawa University, Tokyo   201
Taming of the Shrew   72, 160, 182
Tapestry Cottage   135-136, 249, 250, 307
Tarratt, A. Neville   298
Tavern Lane   135-136, 207, 249-250, 307
Taylor, John, the water poet *All the Workes*   128
Tercentenary celebrations   16, 48
Thatch Restaurant   313-314
The Times   3, 60
Thomas, Sir Alfred Brumwell   105
Thomas, Rochelle   38
Thompson, Francis Ladbury   47
Thompson, William (Alderman)   43
Thomson, Mrs Constance   323
Thomson, Thomas, Dr   4-6, 11, 17
Thorpe, Professor W.V.   328
Throckmorton of Coughton Court   210
Throckmorton, Sir Robert   69
Tibbits, George   71
Tiddington Road   57
Timmins, Samuel   25
Tomlins, E.G.   6
Tompkins, Frederick William   31, 85
Tompkins, Sylvia (librarian)   252
Topping out ceremony   161
Toronto, Shakespeare Festival   121
Tottil, Richard *A Profitable booke*   72
Town Hall   13, 29, 36, 56, 107, 110, 127, 131, 179, 183, 207, 209, 224, 225-228, 257, 269, 302-303, 325
Town Clerk   17, 25, 28, 81, 107, 119, 145, 147, 153, 159, 260
Translations   75, 101, 183, 210, 252, 254, 321, 342
Tree Council   313, 315-316
Trevelyan family   82
– Robert   69
Trinity College   104
Trueman, Charles   86
Tucker, Richard, QC   275
Tudor, Miss Myra   298
Turberville, George *Booke of Falconrie* and *Noble Art of Venerie*   268
Turner, Dr William, his *Herbal*   36
Turkey   8

Turton, Thomas, Bishop of Ely   16
Twelfth Night   5
Tyndall, Bruce (librarian)   22-23, 28

Ukraine   131, 188, 201
Ulanova, Madame   130
United States   3, 8, 30-31, 49, 105, 122, 137, 143-144, 169, 172-173, 189, 191-197, 230, 237-238, 241, 251, 258-259, 260-261, 267, 297, 299, 300, 320, 323, 326-327

Valentinus, *Enchiridion Medicum*   254
Vatican Librarian   201
Vautrollier, Thomas (printer)   73
Venables, Henry, Ltd, of Stafford   162, 284
Venesta (Veneers), Ltd   162
Venus and Adonis   79
Vicar of Stratford-upon-Avon   17, 25, 41, 81, 83, 103, 109, 134, 147-148, 154, 177, 211
Victoria and Albert Museum   60, 115, 138, 224, 252, 321
Victoria, Queen   38, 160
Video Tracts, Ltd   326
Vincze, Paul (medallist)   175-176, 196, 225-226, 228-229, 251, 259, 262, 267, 283, 289, 292, 344
Virginia   115, 137, 141-143, 258-259, 287
– Commonwealth University   258
Visitors' books   8, 49, 140, 175, 190, 199, 346
Visitors' Centre   92, 179, 281, 283-284, 288-290, 292, 294-295, 301

Wade, Robin   219
Wain-Hobson, Douglas, (sculptor)   163, 166-167, 179
Walker Barnard and Son   62
Walker, Sir Edward   74
Waldron, T.N. Mrs   148, 191, 195, 297, 310-311
Walpole   3
Walton, Mrs Clair   309
Walton, Isaak   95
Ward, Rev. John   140
Warner, Sir George   23, 28
Warwick   52, 71-72, 91, 129
Warwick Castle   30
– Earl and Countess of Warwick   30

Warwick County Record Office   309
Warwick Fire Brigade   29
Warwick, St Mary's church   125
Warwick University   120, 145, 147, 308
Warwickshire Agricultural Society   67
Warwickshire County Council   147-148, 221, 247, 272-273, 298-299, 328
Warwickshire County Planning Authority   206, 207, 208, 233, 272
Warwickshire Drooper   340
Warwickshire Local History Society   327
Warwickshire and Worcestershire Magazine   219
Washington, DC   138-141, 143, 178, 190-197, 256, 259, 261-263, 303, 327
Waterhouse, J.J. (trustee)   81
Watkins, Leslie (trustee) and Mrs   83, 108, 132, 148, 154, 159, 260
Watkins, Shirley   IX, 128, 189, 202, 307, 323-324
Watson, Gary   226
Watts, Isaac   95
Webb's English Crystal glasses   185-186
Wedgwood commemorative gifts   185-186, 268
Wedgwood, Dame Veronica   226
Wehrle, Paul (sculptor)   285
Weir, William (architect)   64-65
Welcombe estate   61-64, 75, 82-84, 102, 127, 182, 203, 206, 247-248, 250, 287
– Golf course   247-248
– Hotel   62, 83, 178, 206, 247, 287
Wellington, Duke of   190
Wells, Professor Stanley   VII, 119, 224
Wellstood, Constance, Mrs (neé Langley)   76, 79, 128
Wellstood, Frederick, Christian   IX, 40, 45-46, 57-59, 79, 80, 86, 103
West, Hon. James, of Alscot Park   140, 211
Westbrook, John   257
West Midlands Area Museum Service   309, 331, 333, 339
Westall, Richard (artist)   160
Westminster Abbey   110, 129
Westwood, Dr R.V. (librarian)   104
Wheeler, P.W. (Councillor) and Mrs   179, 293
Wheler, Ann   16

357

Wheler, Robert Bell   4, 7, 10, 16, 68, 211
Whitbread Flowers, Ltd   221, 248
Whitehead, C.H.   216
Whitehead, Robert   311, 337
White Cottage, Shottery   207, 250, 305
White House, Washington DC   195-197
White Lion Inn   10, 12, 19, 35, 52, 158, 204, 276, 285
White, Mary (librarian)   252
Wickhamford   67
Wild Thyme cottage   135-136, 249, 250, 307
William IV, King   190
William Shakespeare: A Documentary Life   256
Williams, Very Rev. H.G.N (Provost)   221
Williams, Laurence (architect) and Mrs   151-155, 159-163, 168, 174-176, 179, 189, 191, 219, 232, 245, 248, 264, 272, 274-275, 281, 293-294, 297, 307-308, 313, 329-330
Williams, Sir William Emrys   148
Williamsburg   115, 137, 141-143, 259
Willoughby de Broke, Lord, and Lady   69, 107, 121, 148, 159, 179, 210, 321

Wilmcote   63, 66, 87, 89, 124, 158, 201, 218, 224, 246, 298, 322, 329, 331-332, 336-337, 339
Wilmcote stone   55, 94, 124, 158
Whincop, Mr of Birmingham   44
Wilson, Professor John Dover (trustee)   27, 81, 93, 129, 148, 212, 222, 252
Wilson, Thomas, *Arte of Rhetorike*   36
Willmott, E. Ann   60
Windley, R.A.   235
Windsor Street   273, 275-277, 280-282, 299
– coach terminal   275-276, 281-282, 299
– multi-storey car park   275-276, 281-283
Wint, Peter de (artist)   198
Winter, Alderman F.   71
Winter's Tale   171
Withal, *Dictionarie in English and Latine for Children*   254
Wither, George, *A collection of emblemes*   128
Withey, Miss Dorothy   321
Wolfson Foundation   292
Wolfson Hall   284, 292
Wood and Kendrick and Williams   151-152, 309

Wood, T. Spencer (architect)   91, 93, 110-113, 126, 148, 151
Wolsey, S.W   115, 125, 235
Woodman, D.E. (Councillor)   148
Worcester   28-29
Worcestershire Record Office   182
World of William Shakespeare series of films   263
Worlidge, *Systema agriculturae*   127
Worth, Councillor P.R.   132
Wright, Bill (caravan builder)   218
Wright, Dr Louis B. (trustee) and Mrs   130, 137, 139-140, 177-178, 190, 192, 195, 237-239, 259, 262-263, 297, 323
Wright, Rt Hon. Lord   71
Wymark, Patrick   183
Wyon, Allen   26, 75

Yaobang, Hu   301-302
York museum   217
Yorktown battlefield   259
Young Farmers' Club   271
Youth Hostels Association   61
Yuxon, Dr Amado M. (poet laureate)   201

Zanussi collection   338